D1644836

5 092 517 2

MONUMENTAL BRASSES

MONUMENTAL BRASSES

The Memorials

MALCOLM NORRIS

I

Phillips & Page
London

ISBN 0 9503942 1 1 the set

Phillips & Page, 50 Kensington Church St., London W8 4DA

Filmset by Spectrum Typesetting Ltd, London
Illustrations and Printing by Biddles Ltd, Guildford
Design by John A. Goodall, in consultation with
The Whittington Press

Contents

I

II

Preface

The Memorials is the second and longer part of the book, *Monumental Brasses,* written as a single work but published as two interrelated books for reasons of economy. The first part, *The Craft,* published by Faber and Faber, consists of an overall study of important aspects of monumental brasses, relating to origins, manufacture, geographical and social distribution, motive and interpretation, engravers, patrons and designers. Acquaintance with this part is assumed, and reference is made in the text of *The Memorials* to the illustrations in *The Craft.*

The Memorials is a chronological examination of brasses, discussing them according to engraving centres. While costume and other aspects are described as important attributes of the subject, they are subordinate to the main focus, which is on the brasses as monuments associated with particular workshops. Stylistic characteristics and links are accordingly considered in some detail. The pattern series of the London workshops are treated broadly, with particular attention to armed figures, though comparative civilian, ecclesiastic and other examples are cited, and series are identified in the Notes on the Figures. Research in this aspect of English brasses is making significant progress, and a comprehensive treatment is appropriate to specialist studies by the scholars concerned.

Despite its length, *The Memorials* makes no claim to be a definitive work. Intensive current research is bound to require many revisions. It is hoped on the other hand that the book will provide a badly needed framework for study, and stimulate interest both in the monuments themselves and present and future lines of research.

The actual presentation of the book has involved slight but insignificant compromises in the presentation of mediaeval texts and Polish place names. Quite extensive redating of brasses occurs in certain chapters.

Acknowledgements

The author acknowledges a great debt to many friends and scholars for help in the completion of this book, and to clergy and museum authorities throughout Europe, who have given every facility for studying the treasures in their charge.

Particular thanks is recorded to the following:

To H. J. B. Allen, M.A., K. O. Butterfield, M. A., the Rev. J. N. Coe, Dr. H. T. Norris, I. T.W. Shearman, and my late father, E. de la Mare Norris, for companionship and aid over many years in making rubbings of brasses in England and on the Continent. To F. A. Greenhill, F.S.A., F. S. A. Scot, for reading and checking the entire manuscript, and making many contributions and suggestions; to J. R. Greenwood, for information on English brasses of provincial origin, and challenging discussion of the entire topic; to J. A. Goodall, F.S.A., not only for his role in the production of the work, but also for much valued advice, corrections and notice of unpublished original references; to J. C. Page-Phillips, M.A., for invaluable support in the publication of *The Memorials,* and information on various aspects of English brasses, most particularly palimpsests, and to the late Major H. F. Owen Evans, M.B.E., F.S.A., for guidance in the conception of this work.

To A. Baird, C. Blair, M.A., F.S.A., W. J. Blair, J. Bromley, F.S.A., J. Coales, F.S.A., A. C. Cole, O.St.J., B.C.L., M.A., F.S.A., R. C. Emmerson, Dr. W. N. Hargreaves-Mawdsley, F.S.A., L. E. James, N. H. MacMichael, F.S.A., and Dr. S. Perry, for help in varous aspects of the study.

To Dr. H. K. Cameron, F.R.I.C., F.S.A., President of the Monumental Brass Society, for advice and information over many years on brasses in Belgium and Germany.

To Dr. H. Nowé and Dr. A. de Schryver for information on brasses in Belgium. To Dr. H. Eichler, Dr. M. Hasse, Dr. J. Mundhenk, Dr. M. Tennenhaus, and most expecially Dr. H. P. Hilger, for information on brasses in Germany; also to the Gesellschaft für Kulturelle Verbindungen mit dem Ausland for generous help in studying examples in the East German Republic. To Magister J. Chróscicki, Magister R. Kaletyn, Dr. H. and Dr. S. Kozakiewicz, Dr. P. Skubiszewski, and Magister K. Wróblewska for information on brasses in Poland. The author is especially grateful to these Polish scholars, whose unstinted help and kindness during his journey in Poland in 1959, and subsequent answers to queries, have made available a wealth of information on European brasses. The remnant of the Polish series still contains several of the finest examples in existence.

Acknowledgement for the use of rubbings is made below, but particular thanks are due to H. W. Jones, F.C.A., whose superb collection has greatly enriched the illustrations, including examples made at the author's request. The author is also most grateful to the Monumental Brass Society for use of Portfolio plates and other illustrations, and to the Society of Antiquaries of London for use of their collection of rubbings.

The interest shown and journeys undertaken by K & S Commercial Photographs Ltd of Leicester, and E. & A. Wright of Stansted Mountfitchet, are greatly appreciated. Acknowledgements for particular pictures are due to the following: National Monuments Record 243; the Victoria & Albert Museum, 53, 150; the Bodleian Library, University of Oxford 1-4, 51, 57, 129-32, 258, 297; the Bibliothèque nationale, Paris 127, 128, 259; Landeskonservator Rheinland 145-6, 148; Muzeum Mazurskie 141; Institut Sztuki, Warszawa 34; Institut royal de patrimonie artistique A.C.L., Bruxelles 47, 52, 124, 255-6; the Society of Antiquaries, London 28, 69-70, 85, 89, 90, 112, 160, 177, 187, 217, 222, 225, 245, 263, 269, 273; M.B.S. repair laboratory, Cambridge 12; K. & S. Commercial Photographs Ltd, 5, 6, 14-20, 22, 26, 27, 38, 67, 73-5, 80, 88, 92, 93, 96, 106, 115, 154, 162, 174, 178, 188, 194, 195, 197, 199, 204-11, 215, 223, 226, 232, 237, 238, 241, 242, 246, 247, 249, 250, 261, 262, 266, 274-7, 279, 280, 289, 291, 293, 294, 306, 307, 309; E. & A. Wright 37, 171, 295; Camera craft 300, C. S. Bailey, Bromsgrove 183; K. Hubbard 103; Hutchins, Oxford 302-3; Deutsche Fotothek 139; A. Baird 149; J. A. Goodall 121, 292; M. Tenenhaus and A. Hills 138; Dean of Susa 50; H. W. Jones 23, 76, 84, 95, 102, 113, 153, 167, 179, 180, 184, 203, 213, 219, 233, 240, 244, 270, 288; I. T. W. Shearman 107; H. F. Owen Evans 36, 79, 125, 126, 234, 235, 305; H. J. B. Allen 137, 281; Rector of East Sutton 278; H. T. Norris 202, J. R. Greenwood 186, 189; Waller 161; Stephenson 168, 231, 304; Connor 100, 272, 287; Creeny 7, 8, 35, 56, 58, 60, 119, 134-6, 144, 257, 298; OPMB 24, 72, Belcher 29, Beloe 31, 296; Gaillard 44; MBS 13, 21, 43, 45, 46, 48, 55, 63, 71, 117, 118, 122, 133, 159, 220, 252, 254, 265, 271, 282; Luchs 9-10; and Künstdenkmäler Brandenburg 66.

In conclusion the author records his thanks to J. H. Hopkins, M.A., Librarian, and the Assistant Librarians of the Society of Antiquaries, for much assistance in research, to W. E. Rupprecht for translation and correspondence to Germany, and to my wife Laurie for typing the original manuscript.

Corrigenda

p. 58 line 18: read 'Roland'
p. 85 line 5 from bottom: Exeter is 'B' series as in caption
p. 117 list line 6: read 'Szamotulski'
p. 121 line 20: for 'major' read 'mayor'
p. 130 lines 9 from top and 11 from bottom: read 'Wielgomlyny'
p. 131 line 4 from bottom: 'Figures or subsidiary'
p. 162 lines 5 and 13: read 'Bushe'
p. 166 line 9 from bottom: read 'Taylard'
p. 172 line 25: for 'final' read 'finial'
p. 195 line 3 from bottom: for 'insertion' read 'inscription'
p. 196 list line 2: read 'Peper-Harow'
p. 208 lines 7: read 'husband lost' and 9: read 'engr.'
p. 212 line 5: read 'Fig. 247'
p. 215 list line 5: read 'Varendorp'
p. 218 line 4 from bottom: read 'Fig. 245'
p. 233 line 2 from bottom: read 'that can'
p. 235 list line 8: read 'c. 1620'
p. 246 line 22: read 'Weston Colville'
p. 256 line 8 from bottom: read 'Gawthorp'
p. 266 line 10: read 'Szamotuly' and 'Szamotulski'
p. 302 n. 27: read 'Scorbrough'
p. 308 n. 22: read '*Arch.*, 74 . . .'
p. 548 line 13 from bottom: read 'Roland'

1. French, German and Silesian brasses, 1180-1365

The very earliest engraved monumental brasses were credited in *The Craft*, Chapter One, to workshops in France and Germany. The earliest brass still existing is in Germany, and it is first appropriate to describe Continental examples, so viewing the far more numerous English brasses in perspective.

The Low Countries

The oldest brasses of which there is any evidence in the Low Countries were to Bishops Hugh de Pierepont d.1229, and his successor Jean d'Aps d. 1238, at Liège.[1] These are only recorded and no example of the thirteenth century is known to exist other than an inscription of 1294 to Peter Outcoren at the Museum de Bijloke, Gent. Flemish brasses of the first half of the fourteenth century are of such outstanding interest that they are treated separately in Chapter Four. It is sufficient to note that brasses were made in Tournai during the late thirteenth century, and perhaps in other centres of Flanders or the Meuse country though only the highly developed products of the fourteenth century are available for study.

French brasses

The almost total loss of French brasses in France similarly limits knowledge of these memorials in the thirteenth century. Fortunately, the drawings of François-Roger de Gaignières give a very good impression of the types of brass that survived till the close of the eighteenth century. The majority were probably made in Paris though in some cases their origin is doubtful, and a few, especially those of separate inlay, may have been made in Tournai or its vicinity. The majority of early French brasses represented ecclesiastics. The figures were shown recumbent, with their feet resting on dragons or wyverns. Practically all these brasses were engraved on sheets, together forming a single quadrangular plate. Many of the oldest tapered considerably towards the base in the manner of a coffin. The canopies of these brasses had straight gabled pediments with large cusps. Figures of angels were placed above the pediment, swinging censers or casting flowers. The backgrounds of the plates were plain or boldly decorated with fleurs-de-lys or some other device. During the first half of the fourteenth century the pediments became more elaborate, deeper in form and filled with tracery. The figures as drawn by Gaignières resembled English rather than Flemish types.

The wealth of brasses to be described precludes a detailed summary of this lost series. The brasses of Archbishop Pierre de Corbeil and of the two Princes Phillippe and Jean, sons of King Louis VIII, have been mentioned in *The Craft*, (Fig. 4). Another commemorated Jean, 1247, son of St Louis (Fig. 1). A group at Sens represented five archbishops of the Cornut family, the earliest commemorating Archbishop Gautier Cornut, 1241 (Fig. 2). No attempt was made, unless perhaps with colour inlay, to impart an impression of depth to the designs; the figures lay clear of the canopy and the background was left plain. The canopies consisted of narrow cusped gables. Only that of Gautier supported a light roof and two mitres resting on architectural supports. The slightly later brass of Archbishop Henri Cornut noticeably tapered to the base. The semi-profile figures of Bishop Philippe de Cahors of Evreux, 1281, signed by Guillaume de Plalli at Evreux (*The Craft,* Fig. 106), and Bishop Pierre de Nemours, 1270, at Notre Dame, Paris, were more elaborate. Their canopies had a substantial pediment, and Philippe's background was decorated with fleurs-de-lys and two seated monks. Bishop Jacques de Guérande 1268, at Nantes cathedral, was a particularly good figure, set against a background of ermine spots. The arrangement of the canopy and figure with the censing angels above gave a strong impression of recession by emphasizing the different planes of the design.[2] Bishop Nicolas Geslent 1290, at the cathedral of Angers (Fig. 3) was richer still, with attendent angels supporting his head, and a background of shields and devices cunningly arranged to set the figure forward.

A most sumptuous brass commemorated Queen Marguerite de Provence 1295, wife of St Louis, at the abbey of St Denis (*The Craft*, Fig. 21). The structural form of the canopy was fully worked out, and the queen's dignified figure was in fine contrast to the background. Two notable female figures were at the Abbey of Ourscamp to Marie de Maucicourt, 1318?, and Agnès de Forceville, c.1325, the former having an unusual canopy and border.[3]

Three military brasses recorded the transition in France from mail to plate armour. The earliest at the Abbey of Longpont commemorated Hervil de Cérizy, Lord of Muret, c.1320?, in coif and skull cap, surcoat and hawberk. with ailettes engraved in front of his shoulders (*The Craft*, Fig. 107). Bouchard VI, Count of Vendôme, 1343, at St George's church, Vendôme, was a remarkable figure, apparently wearing a bascinet under the mail coif (*The Craft*, Fig. 108). The remains of his canopy were elaborate, and the brass was an example of French separate inlay work. The rectangular brass of Messire Philippe de Clere, 1351, and Jehanne, at the church of the Jacobins, Rouen, was valuable as an early illustration of plate armour and distinctively French female dress (Fig. 4). The canopies had deep pediments filled with tracery of a type which was retained throughout the fourteenth and fifteenth centuries.

An important discovery was the finding in 1976 of an incised slab of Tournai marble with substantial brass inlays, only the inscription fillet being almost wholly lost, in the sacristy of Noyon cathedral. It had been placed there after being found under a floor during the repairs after World War I but had never been fully published. Made c.1325-50 it depicts an archdeacon, canon deacon or subdeacon, vested in dalmatic etc. and holding a closed book with the Blessed Virgin on the cover. A full publication by the finders W. J. Blair, R. Emmerson and P. Lankester is being prepared.

Several early English brasses have been ascribed to French workmanship without sufficient justification. On the other hand, two important palimpsest survivals and two figures are most probably French. A large fragment of canopy work on the reverse of Robert Fowler and wife, 1540, St Mary, Islington, shows part of a canopy pediment, and a censing angel in French style of the fourteenth century. More substantial are the reverses of Sir Anthony Fitzherbert and family, 1538, Norbury. Most of the fragments fit to form the greater part of a canopied brass, c.1320, which has been attributed to one of the wives of Sir Theobald Verdun, being loot from Croxden Abbey. The serious but graceful figure of a lady with a lion at her feet is almost complete. Much of the canopy remains including parts of the side shafts with a monk, and a representation of Christ in the pediment. The arrangement and detail bears very great resemblances to the incised slab of a Michel, '(Bur)gensis' of Neauphle-le-Château, at the Abbey of Vaux-de-Cernay. The canopy in particular is unlike English work of the period.[4]

The most famous of these English examples are the two figures at Minster in

Sheppey, to members of the Northwood family. One, a military figure, may be ascribed with confidence to Sir John de Northwood, 1319 (Fig. 5); the other, a female figure, is probably that of Elizabeth, second wife of Roger de Northwood, d.1335 (Fig.6).[5] Both these figures are peculiar in treatment and arrangement, and though cut in separate inlay, contrast with their English contemporaries. The knight is armed in mixed mail and plate, though his forearms are protected by a form of scale armour. His shield hangs on his left hip, a Continental, not an English, arrangement. A large cushion supports his head, which is protected by a bulbous but shallow bascinet, secured by a guard-chain to a breast plate. The pose of the figure is confused by the crossed legs which are a later English restoration. The original figure probably had straight legs as is indicated by the position of the poleyns. The female figure is of similar workmanship. her costume is distinctively French, similar to three effigies illustrated in Montfaucon (1729, in particular Marguerite de Beaujeu 1336, 2, pl. cviii), and the drawing by Gaignières of the brass to Jehanne de Clere (Fig. 4). Her wimple is very deep and held out from her face. Her loose gown has slits for the arms and a substantial hood. This hood could be buttoned up the front to protect the face, but hangs open on the brass, exposing the lining of fur. There are no other brasses of this style in England, though a comparable palimpsest fragment has been discovered at Little Walsingham.[6] The figures are unlike known Flemish examples and are presumably French, precious survivals of a style created in a Paris or Normandy workshop.

German Brasses

Germany and Silesia possess the only existing Continental figure brasses earlier in date than 1325.

First in order is the remarkable plate of St Ulrich (engr. 1187), now buried in the church of St Ulrich and St Afra, Augsburg (*The Craft,* Fig. 7). This memorial of a tenth-century bishop has already been considered in *The Craft* as a brass by circumstance rather than intention, being the product of metal workers who did not subsequently develop this particular application of their skill. It is an engraved copper coffin plate, apparently the work of a goldsmith, but in all respects of its treatment comparable with the floor brasses that follow. The date of execution can be defined accurately, falling between a fire in the church and the reinterrment in 1187, which was celebrated with great pomp, the Emperor himself participating.[7] The Saint is depicted recumbent in death, his eyes being closed, his right hand resting on his crozier and his left loosely grasping a book. Notwithstanding this representation and the shallowness of the engraving, the design has a sensitive flow of line devoid of stiffness. Detail is restrained, though the beard and hair are executed in numerous lines, concentrating attention on the face. St Ulrich is vested for Mass, wearing an early form of the mitre and the pallium as a mark of honour. From the viewpoint of the antiquary it is regrettable that this plate has been returned to total obscurity.

A small but neatly cut inscription in Lombardics at St Emmeram, Regensburg, records the consecration of an altar in 1189, and is probably contemporary with the event.[8]

The figure brass to Bishop Yso von Wölpe (spelt Wilpe on his inscription), 1231, in the Andreaskirche, Verden (*The Craft,* Fig. 8), is a simple but vigorous engraving. The bishop holds aloft representations of the Church of St Andrew and the city which he fortified, and his crozier rests against his right side. His Mass vestments are depicted with little elaboration, omitting the tunicle, and with a low mitre. Like St Ulrich, and even more prominently, he wears the pallium, the distinctive vestment of an archbishop.

The representation is nevertheless correct, and the figure has been arranged to give it prominence. It appears that Bishop Yso applied to Pope Innocent III for the pallium between 1205 and 1208, was granted it, and was invested by Philipp von Schwaben.[9] Yso took an active part in a crusade against the Latvians, and it was most probably for this reason that he was specially honoured. The severity of the design is accentuated by the plain background, a lack of fine detail, and the small and unattractive lettering of the border inscription. The figure is engraved on a single plate of most unusual length.

The brass of Bishop Otto von Brunswic, 1279, in the cloister of Hildesheim cathedral, is a more competent though less dynamic design (*The Craft*, Fig. 112). The bishop holds his crozier and a large representation of the castle of Wolgenbergh. His vestments, while plain, are well expressed, and the border inscription is strongly cut. All these brasses may be compared with the bronze cast effigy of Archbishop Wichman, d.1192, Magdeburg cathedral, and the incised slab of Bishop Rudolph, 1262, Schwerin cathedral. None of these three brasses takes advantage of the highly decorative possibilities of the medium. The engravers were satisfied with a simple effect.

Another engraved plate of a different character is preserved in the treasury of the cathedral of Halberstadt, and commemorates grants of indulgences (*The Craft*, Fig. 111). The inscription is in rather crude Lombardics and the border incorporates four different patterns. The greater part of the brass is filled with a freely drawn and lively representation of the Blessed Virgin and Christ Child, seated upon a throne and set against a background of dots. The brass is dated c. 1285 and has slight affinities in style to the Hildesheim bishop.

The separate inlay figure of Bishop Bernard von Lippe, 1340, Paderborn cathedral, is a more formal work (Fig. 7). The detail of the chasuble, worked with lions, eagles and fleurs-de-lys arranged in a cross is elaborate. The pose of the figure is animated, and in keeping with contemporary tomb sculptures at Bamberg and Mainz. It is probable that all these monuments were engraved in different workshops as they have little apparent connection with one another.

Two brasses on the Baltic seaboard prove the participation of engravers within this region. One forms the base plate to the fine cast figure of Bishop Heinrich Bocholt, 1341, from Lübeck cathedral, and is engraved with the border inscription, arms, helms with double fan crests of the arms, and canopy with angels. The monument is attributed to the famous Lübeck caster Johann Apengeter.[10*] The second is an attractive bronze plate to Ramborg Fran Wiik, 1327, at Väster Aker (Fig. 8). The simple representation of the lady is set within a slight canopy. Two censing angels stand beside the pediment. The background is decorated with a geometric pattern and the border inscription is in bold Lombardic capitals. This plate may have been engraved by a craftsman in Sweden, but was more probably brought from Lübeck.

Two shields for Heinrich Goldast, 1354, one being edged with an inscription, are preserved in the castle museum at Frauenfeld. Both display gold branches, alluding to the name of the deceased. The execution is coarse, and the work is presumably local.

Silesian brasses

In contrast to these scattered German examples the Silesian brasses form a closely associated group. The city of Wroclaw, the capital of the province of Silesia, has been described as an important centre of brass engraving. The province itself is rich in all the raw materials required in the casting of latten plate, most of which were being used by the twelfth century. These include coal, iron, copper, zinc and lead. Silver was also obtained from the lead, while marble was quarried in considerable quantity.

By the fourteenth century the city was noted for a wide variety of metal work, stained glass and a flourishing weaving industry. After the death of Henryk VI in 1335, both the city and the province came by purchase under King Ján of Bohemia, thereby strengthening the already strong ties between Wroclaw and Praha. Much of the city's craft was developed by Germans who were invited to settle when Silesia became a duchy independent of Poland in 1163. The proportion of these settlers greatly increased following the Mongol invasion and depredation of 1241. Wroclaw was accordingly most favourably placed in the development of brass casting and engraving, both by its resources and its connections. Its industries had the same beneficial influence upon each other as their greater counterparts in Flanders. A sufficient number of Silesian brasses exist to illustrate their development from the thirteenth century into the sixteenth century. Their peculiar style and relationship to other Silesian works of art leaves little doubt of their local provenance, while documentary evidence of the fifteenth century gives conclusive proof of the engravers' activity in Wroclaw.

The earliest brasses of Silesian origin are a group of four in the monastery of Lubiaz some twenty five miles from Wroclaw. Dating at the latest from the earliest years of the fourteenth century, they form a collection unique in Europe. Some of the group underwent minor restoration in the sixteenth century, and all were considerably damaged in the Second World War. They are, nevertheless, still the most elaborate of their period. The brasses represent three dukes and a knight:

Boleslaus 'the tall', d. 1201, Duke of Silesia (*The Craft*, Fig. 114)
Premislaus (Przemko) Skinawski, d. 1289, Duke of Steinau (*Ibid.*, Fig. 113)
Conrad, d. 1304, Duke of Sagan (*Ibid.*, Fig. 115)
Martin Buswoyz, c. 1300, knight (*Ibid.*, Fig. 116).

The first three lay before the high altar, while the fourth was set into the wall of the north ambulatory in 1885. The date of the engraving of these brasses cannot be entirely related to the date of decease of the persons commemorated. The first two are similar in style and scale. The third differs in its scale, being considerably smaller. The fourth differs from the other three in its detail, scale and construction, but is similar to the second in design. If the brass of Duke Boleslaus had been engraved about 1201, it would be all but the earliest figure brass extant. This date cannot be accepted (see *The Craft*). Boleslaus was regarded as the founder of the Lubiaz monastery by his grants to the Cistercians in 1175. It is accordingly appropriate that a monument should have been erected to his memory in retrospect, once the foundation had become well established. His brass is too similar to that of Duke Premislaus to allow an age difference of nearly a century between them. Duke Premislaus and Conrad were brothers, sons of Conrad III of Glogau, and dukes of petty principalities which developed in the twelfth century from the fragmentation of the duchy of Silesia. A third brother Henryk was also buried at Lubiaz, and is believed to have been once represented by a brass, though no trace remains. Premislaus died as a young man in battle, fighting the Lithuanians at Siewierz, and his memorial was clearly laid posthumously. Conrad, who led a more peaceful life and was made provost of the church of St John, Wroclaw in 1287, was possibly responsible for the preparation of all three monuments. The details of the armour and costume represented, the style of the engraving, the inscriptions in Lombardic letters and the form of the heraldic shields are all consistent with the date of c. 1305.

The similarity between the brasses of Premislaus and Boleslaus, and the tombs of Duke Bolko I, d. 1301 at Krzeszów, and Henryk IV, d. 1290, at Wroclaw, is a further important indication of the date of engraving. The brass of Premislaus and effigy of Bolko seem to have been based on the same design. The suggestion of Dr Luchs that the brasses were prepared under the supervision of 'Frater Fredericus, magister operis monasterii Lubensis', who supervised the reconstruction of the monastery until 1307, is an interesting but unsubstantiated proposition. The evidence generally supports the conclusion that these brasses were engraved between the years 1290 and 1310. They are associated with other Silesian monuments of the period, and were almost certainly engraved in Wroclaw. The badly mutilated brass of Bu̇swoyz, which is similar to Premislaus and Bolko in design, appears to be slightly earlier in date than the other three.

The brass of Premislaus is the most impressive (Fig. 11). He lies under a light canopy holding his sword across his right shoulder and his shield over his left thigh. The border inscription in fine Lombardic capitals frames the whole. The entire design is presented in separate inlay in a matrix of local sandstone. Premislaus was surrounded by fourteen small shields all bearing the arms of the Silesian duchy: Argent an eagle displayed Sable on the breast and wings a crescent enclosing a cross Argent. The canopy is of simple but unusual form. Narrow shafts form a frame within which springs a cusped arch with open tracery in the spandrels. The border inscription is in separate inlaid capitals. The representation of Premislaus himself is remarkably youthful and virile. His proportions are not naturalistic, the figure being excessively broad, and the overall effect produced is one of great human strength. His large cross-hilted sword within its scabbard is held across his right shoulder, cutting across the canopy frame. His is armed in mail hauberk, stockings and hood defined in the banded convention. The hood is thrown back behind his neck, exposing an aketon. The surcoat is worn over the mail, and a belt decorated with fleurs-de-lys originally supported a heavy dagger on the right side. A finely executed shield is held over his left knee, also bearing the arms of the duchy. His feet have no support and lie wide apart with the toes pointing towards the base. Premislaus's head is particularly well conceived. His youthful face is framed by long rolling curls, his eyes are alert and a slight smile plays on his lips. A jewelled ducal bonnet covers the crown of his head. The figure, including the tassel of the bonnet, was constructed of sixteen different pieces. The joining of the plates and the continuation of the lines from plate to plate is by no means exact. The position of the sword is unusual for brasses, though apparently not in Silesia, as Martin Buswoyz is similarly posed. No English examples are known, and among Flemish brasses only that to King Eric Menved. The Flemish designers of brasses and slabs often represented the sword as held vertically upwards parallel to the body, and the brass in Gent to Willem Wenemaer is an instance (*The Craft*, Fig. 142).[11] The representation of the feet, extended without support, is also peculiar, though probably fairly common on the Continent at the close of the thirteenth century. The placing of the shield at the thigh was widely adopted on Continental brasses and slabs but is alien to English usage.

Although surpassed in quality by a few English examples, the brass of Premislaus can undoubtedly claim to be the most elaborate in conception of all early separate inlay brasses, and its value is enhanced by its relationship to the other Lubiaz monuments.

The brass of Duke Boleslaus was apparently made by the same craftsmen (Fig. 9). It is now seriously damaged and it is very probable that the original was restored in the seventeenth century. The single architectural canopy is similar in form and tracery to that of Premislaus, though two important differences are the elaborate cusps and the cornice of open trefoils, which is an important feature as it occurs in various forms in later Silesian brasses. Eight small shields bearing the arms of the Silesian duchy surrounded the figure. Boleslaus himself is armed similarly to Premislaus, but he is represented holding a spear, with his shield held over the left shoulder. His sword, dagger and belt create a somewhat confusing effect at his waist. The spear extends to the base of the canopy beneath his feet. The junction of the main plates is again poorly completed. The original figure was constructed of fifteen plates of which eleven now remain.

By far the most serious loss is the head. This was fortunately illustrated in a drawing by Dr Luchs and showed Boleslaus as bearded, wearing a princely bonnet surmounted by a cross. The top of his spear consisted of a blade of glaive form. There is reason to question the date of this head. The features of Boleslaus's face bore little resemblance to those of Premislaus. His curls had little shape, his eyes and mouth were less vigorously drawn, while his moustaches had a decidedly seventeenth-century appearance. The bonnet had no jewel enrichment and the cross at the top was inconsistent with early fourteenth-century design. The spear head as shown did not coincide with the sharp point evident in the indent. Most significant of all, the form of the mail hood had been confused. The outline of the indent indicates that the heads of Premislaus and Boleslaus were very similar, but this impression was contradicted by the actual engraving. There are sufficient inconsistencies in the recorded head to regard it as a seventeenth-century restoration. In its original setting this brass was protected by a wooden platform, on which was painted an inscription. This had been destroyed in 1625.

The memorial to Duke Conrad is also stylistically associated with Premislaus (Fig. 10). The canopy form, the inscription and the two small shields set by his head are of the same pattern. The scale is a little smaller. Conrad is represented in his capacity as Provost. His face is finely engraved with short wavy hair and his hands are presented as outstretched in a gesture of adoration. His vestments appear to consist of a large surplice, over which is a hooded cloak with an opening down the front. His feet protrude into the inscription, reproducing the effect of a sculptured effigy as viewed from above. The engraving of the drapery is bold, but the junction of the plates had been very carelessly completed and many drapery lines end abruptly. The centre plate on his left side is lost but has now been replaced by engraved wood.

The last of the group, Martin Buswoyz, was already severely mutilated when it was moved from its slab in the nineteenth century. At the time of this alteration the remaining fragments of the brass were badly muddled, and the inscription was rearranged in a meaningless jumble. A crescent from a shield is set most curiously to the side of the figure. Much of the headless effigy was lost in the Second World War and only two plates of it survive (*The Craft*, Fig. 116). Martin was armed in mail, with his sword across his right shoulder. Some of the remaining detail is excellent, especially a small shield and a lady's figure decorating his belt. Much of the pediment of the canopy is left, consisting of an arch supporting an embattled structure of masonry pierced by tracery. The workmanship of this brass is of better quality than the other three, and the metal on which it is engraved is twice the thickness.

While these memorials form a closely connected group, the individuality of Buswoyz's brass is pronounced. Furthermore, though the designs of these brasses have counterparts in Silesian sculpture, they have some peculiarities of treatment akin to those of Tournai slabs of the period, in particular the presentation of the mouth and lips. Such similarities may be coincidental, but monks from the Low Countries played an important role in establishing the Silesian and Polish Cistercian houses. It is possible foreign influence through this contact introduced monumental brass engraving to Silesia, and that Buswoyz's brass was a model for those that followed. This is no more than a conjecture but sufficiently possible to justify statement.

All four of these brasses, having been for many years preserved in fragments and widely dispersed, are now preserved in the Muzeum Slaskie, Wroclaw. The illustrations in *The Craft* are from rubbings in which all surviving parts are assembled. Particular attention has been given to their description as they form a unique group, which has until very recently been overlooked in English studies of brasses.

Relics of three episcopal brasses and another of an Abbess record the style of the Silesian engravers to the mid-fourteenth century. The Bishops' memorials are little more than indents and only survive on account of a layer of sand and tiles which were laid over the choir of Wroclaw Cathedral in 1677 by Cardinal Friedrich von Hesse. The brasses of Bishops Heinrich I von Würben, 1319, Nanka 1341, and Stephan of Lubiaz, 1345, were separate inlay compositions. They all lay before the high altar in the Wroclaw Cathedral and were moved to the choir of the church of the Holy Cross after their recovery in 1836. No trace could be found by the author of fragments of Heinrich or Nanka, though the indent of the latter is very well preserved. Jungnitz records that a few finely engraved Lombardic capitals of Heinrich's inscription were found loose in 1886, while his illustration of Nanka shows an extremely worn figure and a few pieces of the canopy shafts. Eighty-eight Lombardic letters of Stephan's inscription remain in situ, while the figure is preserved in the Archdiocesan Museum, Wroclaw. Fortunately most of Stephan's indent is still clear. These three derelict brasses form an important group, relatable though inferior to the Lubiaz monuments. The delicate use of the separate inlay technique is repeated, though the canopies of these later brasses were even more fragile in construction. The size of the main figures is much reduced in proportion to the canopies, which is a development observable in English brasses of the same period.

Anna, fifth Abbess of St Clare's Convent in Wroclaw, who died in 1343, was commemorated by a brass in her own church. This memorial is now stripped of most of its inlays. It was a canopied composition, representing the deceased probably with the patron saint of her house. The border inscription retains seventy-nine of its brass letters, several of which have floral decorations.

The only figure from this group available for study is that of Bishop Stephan (*The Craft*, Fig. 117). He lies vested for mass, gripping a crozier in his left hand and raising his right in benediction. His hair is long, a small beard covers his chin and his lower lip is obtrusive and engraved in recessed-relief. The manner in which he grasps the crozier with his forefinger grotesquely extending is a local peculiarity. The actual construction of the figure is interesting in that the junction of the two main body plates follows the drapery fold of the chasuble. This was also apparently a feature of Nanka, whose figure was very similar.

The canopies were particularly interesting. That of Nanka consisted of a single pediment with elaborate cusps and a broad finial. A parapet of quatrefoils was set behind, supported on a row of narrow shafts. The main canopy shafts were broad and linked to the border by flying buttresses. Part of this shafting is shown extant in Jungnitz's illustration. All this architectural detail was separately inlaid, requiring great care by the engraver and the cutter of the indent. Slanting shields were set at shoulder level. In conception the canopy is an adaptation of that of Duke Boleslaus at Lubiaz, retaining the parapet but extending the canopy proper. Bishop Stephan's canopy elaborated the design. The parapet consisted of a double course of open tracery. The pediment was more richly cusped, and flying buttresses connected independent side shafts. The handsome design of the canopy is in contrast to the rather graceless figure. Abbess Anna's canopy had a double pediment, with parapet similarly supported on shafts. Above her were subsidiary figures, two pairs of censing angels with a representation of Christ above, which are the sole examples of such details on these early Silesian brasses.

2. English brasses, 1200-1325

In England, as in the rest of Western Europe except France, there is scant evidence of brasses until the close of the thirteenth century. Various historical references indicate that brasses were used to commemorate founders or the higher clergy in the first half of that century, though the brasses themselves are gone and their character and origin are for the most part unknown. By repute the earliest brass was recorded by Leland, who noted the existence of an inscription set before the high altar of St Pauls, Bedford, to Sir Simon de Beauchamp d. 1208. This read 'De Bello Campo jacet hic sub marmore Simon Fundator de Newenham'. There is now little trace of this monument, and the date of its actual preparation is very doubtful.[1*] Founders' tombs were often laid long after death. According to Leland and other authorities there was a figure brass at Wells, representing Jocelin, Bishop of Bath d. 1242.[2] This brass was apparently sold in 1550. Weever recorded second hand an inscription at Old St Pauls, London, to Bishop Fulk Bassett d. 1259.[3] Other authorities record brasses at Westminster Abbey to Richard de Berkyng, d 1246, and more doubtfully at Lincoln cathedral to the great Bishop Grosseteste d. 1253.[4] An existing brass which purports to date from this period is an inscription at Ashbourne, recording the consecration of the church in 1241 (Fig. 13). It is rather rudely engraved on a small rectangular plate. Whether the brass is contemporary with the event or later is difficult to decide. It is very possibly the oldest surviving English brass.

Certain evidence from the second half of the century is provided by work in Westminster Abbey. Several separately inlaid Lombardic letters of latten remain of the inscriptions laid in the pavement before the high altar. This work was ordered by Abbot Richard de la Ware, and carried out under the supervision of Odoric of the Roman Cosmati school in 1268. Further remains consist of Lombardic capitals and small fragments of the stems of crosses to Margaret and John, the children of William de Valence, who died 1276 and 1277 respectively. The brass attributed to Margaret has already been noted in connection with its mosaic inlay (*The Craft*, Fig. 68). These details were fortunately protected by a step at the east end of the Confessor chapel. Their importance lies not only in their quality and early date, but in their probable association with work carried out under court patronage.

The use of brasses as acceptable memorials seems to have developed rapidly at the close of the century. Sculptured effigies from this period are found in considerable numbers. King Edward I may be claimed to have stimulated this development by setting up cast latten effigies of King Henry III and Queen Eleanor at Westminster, and of the latter at Lincoln, all executed by William Torel, citizen and goldsmith of London.

Men in armour

Reputedly the earliest English figure brasses are six examples in armour. Four are life size and rank among the very finest in the country. They are alleged to be:

Sir John Dabernoun, d. 1277, Stoke d'Abernon (*The Craft,* Figs. 118-9)
Sir Roger de Trumpington, d. 1289, Trumpington (Fig. 15)
Sir Robert de Bures, usually cited as 1302, Acton (Fig. 14)
Sir Robert de Setvans, d. 1306, Chartham (*The Craft,* Figs. 120-1).

Two smaller scale half figures represent:

Sir Richard de Boselyngthorpe, c. 1300, Buslingthorpe (Fig. 16)

Unknown in armour, c. 1300, Croft (Fig. 17).

The traditional dating of these brasses is highly questionable. There is very little either in the equipment of the figures or their presentation to establish their age precisely within the period 1270-1330. All are armed in mail hauberk, coif and mufflers for the hands. All wear the surcoat, which in the case of Sir Robert de Setvans is emblazoned with his arms of winnowing fans. The full-length figures wear mail stockings, single spike or 'prick' spurs, hold shields on the left arm and bear crosshilted swords hung from rich sword belts. Ailettes, heraldic shoulder wings made of leather either painted or covered with textile, are shown at Trumpington, Chartham and Buslingthorpe. The Trumpington, Acton and Chartham figures are cross-legged. None of these features is inconsistent with the accepted dates of these monuments. Nevertheless, documentary evidence shows that these traditional, nineteenth century, dates are not correct.

Dr J. C. Ward in a penetrating article has shown conclusively that the Acton brass represents Sir Robert de Bures who died in 1331. Sir Robert was the first of his family to acquire an interest in Acton, which he did by marriage in 1310.[5] The brass can hardly be earlier than c. 1320, though its treatment and scale make a later date highly unlikely. The absence of plate armour other than the poleyns protecting the knees, and the very size of the figure are features in marked contrast to those of known brasses of the period c. 1325-1335. The date, 1302, is certainly no longer tenable. Sir Robert de Setvans, if the brass is indeed his, is probably no earlier. The indent of his inscription is very badly decayed, and all that has been established is that the figure represented is a "son of Sir Robert de Setvans", a description equally applicable to Sir Robert who died in 1306 and to his son Sir William, who died in 1323. Goodall, revising Waller's description, prefers the latter attribution. Another dimension to this problem has been exposed by Greenhill who has shown that a brass of similar size and overall design existed at Canterbury cathedral and attributed it to Sir William or his father, as several members of the family were later buried there.[6] This brass, though lost, was for a while fixed to the exterior of the undercroft of King Henry IV's chantry, and the silhouette can still be seen on the plaster. The outline is clear, showing the figure with shield, aillettes, crossed legs and apparently flaring hair — the most striking feature of the Chartham brass.

The date and ascription of the Trumpington figure are no less controversial. The brass is set in a slab upon an elaborate high tomb with a canopy of c. 1330. Although the general appearance of the brass is consistent with the late thirteenth century, the indent of a marginal inscription engraved on a fillet is indicative of a date no earlier than c. 1320. Similarly the use of a helm as a pillow is a fourteenth century monumental convention. There can be no doubt that the figure is a member of the Trumpington family, but the label on the arms emblazoned on the ailettes and scabbard is wrong for either Sir Roger I who died in 1289 or his son, Sir Giles I, who died between 1327 and 1332, but would be proper for the latter's son, Sir Roger II, who predeceased his father in 1326. There can be little doubt that the person represented is Sir Roger II. The issue is however complicated by the nature of the label, which has apparently been subsequently added, and the appearance of the main shield, which has only part of the field cut away. The figure was evidently intended for someone else but subsequently appropriated. It has been suggested that the brass was indeed laid for Roger I but was then altered and placed in its present situation. This flagrant disregard for the memorial of a distinguished ancestor in the lifetime of his immediate descendants is unacceptable. The wholly consistent explanation for these peculiarities, presented by Spittle, is that Sir Giles prepared a brass for his father or for himself during his own lifetime, and altered its purpose on the early death of his eldest son. We may conclude that the work was in hand in 1326 and that the long accepted date of 1289 is hardly credible.[7]

The date of the brass of Sir John Dabernoun has only once been seriously questioned, namely by C. H. Hunter Blair,[8] but in a context and manner that deprived the doubts of influence. The certain grounds for revising the dates of the Trumpington and Acton figures now compel a reappraisal, especially as the Stoke D'Abernon and Acton brasses have for long been considered as the work of one engraver. P. M. Johnston, referring to Sir Robert de Bures in his article on the Stoke D'Abernon brasses, describes it as "a brass which in many details bears so close a resemblance to the one we are considering that it can hardly be doubted they are by the same hand, despite nearly thirty years' difference in the dates assigned to the two".[9] So strongly was Johnston convinced of this that he presumed the Acton brass had been engraved many years before Sir Robert's death, then believed to have been 1302. The similarity between these brasses is self-evident. Not only is there a general resemblance in overall treatment, in the execution of the mail, the position of the lion's head, and especially the presentation of the faces, but this extends to the use of the same or almost identical details in the decoration of the guige, sword pommel, sword belt and other small but revealing features. Sir John is the simpler and probably slightly earlier. Now however it is certain that Sir Robert was not engraved before 1310 at the earliest, it would seem illogical to accept the date of 1277 for the other.

Apart from this comparative argument there are other grounds for suspecting the dates of the early Stoke D'Abernon brasses. There were three successive Sir John Dabernouns. The first died by 1277, the second in 1327, and the third died before 1350 but was alive in 1335.[10] In addition to the two important figure brasses at Stoke D'Abernon, there is an indent, bearing traces of an inscription in separately inlaid Lombardics and four shields. One of the shields survived until 1919, engraved with the Dabernoun arms and a label of four points. The third Sir John bore a label on his arms at the battle of Boroughbridge, and for this reason the slab has been associated with him. This battle was fought in his father's lifetime, and therefore the label would have been set aside after succeeding his father and the only reason for it to have been displayed on a memorial would be if the deceased died before his father. The indent may well be that of a minor who died in the lifetime of the last Sir John. Hunter Blair argued in effect that the earlier existing figure commemorated the second Sir John and should be dated 1327. It is known that he was very sick for at least three years before he died, and it is possible that he laid his own brass in his lifetime. If in spite of these problems it is accepted that the mailed figure with lance is Sir John who died in 1277, the view maintained by C. A. Raleigh Radford,[11] it is reasonable to presume that his brass was laid in retrospect by his son.

Suffice it to say that the identity of these brasses, let alone their dates, is not as certain as has been presumed. Furthermore it can hardly be doubted that if the date of death of the first Sir John had been unknown, no date of engraving earlier than c. 1320 could have been seriously suggested for it in the light of comparable examples. The date of death is at best an uncertain indicator, notably so in these early years of the craft. The writer is convinced that c. 1320 is correct for the earliest of the Stoke D'Abernon figures.

The two Lincolnshire half figures have been dated between 1290 and 1310 by various writers. Buslingthorpe is in a coffin slab and both have inscriptions in separately inlaid Lombardics. The oblong slab at Croft is much mutilated, but its form is clear, bearing the indents of two inverted shields. Both these brasses appear to be early, that at Croft being of coarse workmanship. It seems certain however that they are later than has been believed. W. J. Blair has established that Sir Richard de Boselyngthorpe was alive in 1330, and surprisingly as late as 1344,[12*] while his father Sir John, mentioned in his inscription, died c. 1345. Even if the brass had been prepared in Sir Richard's lifetime, and its design suggests this, it can hardly be earlier than c. 1335. Such a revision, strictly applied, places this brass outside the period of direct concern, though it is convenient to describe the memorial in this context on account of its associations. The Croft brass remains an uncertain case, and may be tentatively dated c. 1325, being a date which reduces the potential margin of error. In view of the doubts surrounding all the examples, Sir John Dabernoun will no doubt retain his place as primus inter pares.

Controversies over the date in no way diminish the splendour of these brasses. The figure at Trumpington is boldly engraved. The mail is represented as a series of alternating crescent incisions; drapery lines are irregular, and the field of his shield is unfinished. Yet the overall effect is vigorous and distinguished. The arms: Azure crusily two trumpets in pile or, appear on his shield and, with the label added, on his aillettes and scabbard. A great helm, secured to a pair of plates under the surcoat by a guard-chain, lies beneath his head. The brass is on a high tomb with a carved canopy above.

In contrast, Sir John Dabernoun and Sir Robert de Bures are most richly and finely finished. Every detail is expressed with care, especially the interlocking links of mail, the buckles, stitching and decoration of belts and straps. Sir John's lance is unique in England. Sir Robert's brass is superior in the presentation of the drapery, the inherent strength of the figure, and the lavish decoration worked into carefully chosen details (fig. 14). The hairy lion beneath his feet is most effective. Sir John in comparison appears top heavy and static. The figure is nevertheless of the highest quality, and the colour combination of dark copper-rich brass, blue enamel and the grey purbeck marble setting is most effective.

Sir William or Sir Robert de Setvans is an impressive figure (*The Craft* Figs. 120 and 121), similar in design to the effigy of William Lord de Ros d. 1317, in the Temple Church, London.[13] He is shown with bare head and hands, his coif fallen behind his head and mail mufflers hanging down at his wrists. There are several French examples of this arrangement on slabs and effigies and many authorities have attributed this brass to French workmanship. But similar designs were being used in English tomb sculpture, and the cross-legged pose almost certainly denotes an English origin. The lines of the figure, especially in the drapery, are freely represented, and some details such as the scabbard are very decorative. In contrast the mail is unfinished except for a small section by the instep of the right leg, and the lines of the central plate join do not match. This economy and carelessness is particularly incongruous in so accomplished a brass, and can only be explained in terms of hasty completion. The border inscription was originally inlaid in separate letters.

In addition to these existing figures there remain clear indents at Hawton, 1308; St Mary's Abbey, York and Norton Disney c. 1310; Aston Rowant 1314; Stoke-by-Nayland 1318; Emneth and Letheringham c. 1320. Furthermore, Sir William Dugdale's drawings record the crossed-legged brass at Peterborough Cathedral to Sir Gascelin de Marham (*The Craft,* Fig. 123), and an indent formerly at Drayton Bassett of an armed figure with shield, spear and banner. The value of these indents and drawings lies in their evidence of details which supplement the surviving examples. The figure at York appears to have worn a flat-topped helmet.[14] The Letheringham indent shows the legs crossed in the manner of the effigy c. 1260 ascribed to Sir Geoffrey de Mandeville (d. 1166) at the Temple Church, London, with both feet placed in the same direction.[15*] Indeed the full range of poses used on sculptured effigies seems to have been copied by the engravers. Lawrence Stone's assertion that: "It is highly significant, however, that the sword-drawing pose of knightly effigies of the late thirteenth century was never adopted on brasses" is apparently refuted by the Peterborough figure which is depicted in this very posture.[16]

Three palimpsest fragments at Pettaugh, Clifton Campville, and Cople give interesting details. The first is very small showing part of a hauberk. The second is a large section showing a portion of a cross-legged figure with hanging mufflers as at Chartham. The third figure is similar to the second, showing the hanging mufflers, belt, sword and sufficient of the legs to show their crossed position. A bold rose pattern decorates the exposed poleyn, and it is probable that this figure was engraved c. 1320.

Two knights are perhaps of this period, but are later than the examples described. Both are smaller in scale though they originally lay within canopies. They represent:

Sir William Fitzralph, c. 1325-35, Pebmarsh (*The Craft* Fig. 122)[17]*

A knight of the Bacon family, c. 1325, Gorleston (Fig. 18).

Sir William Fitzralph is akin to the earlier knights, though somewhat cruder in execution. His mail armour is defined in series of links of irregular size, and is reinforced with plate. His shield, which is nearly all lost, is shown turned to the side, while at Gorleston the shield is presented full view. Sir William is a further example of the crossed-legged pose, and is little inferior to the earlier figures. The memorial must have been arresting when complete with canopy, shields and fillet border. The Gorleston figure is worn and much mutilated, having lost the greater part of the legs below the knees. The knight is armed in mail, shown in the banded convention, though reinforced with plates. Early forms of besagews, couters, rerebraces and vambraces protect the arms; poleyns and greaves protect the legs. The mail coif and mufflers are of the earlier style, and ailettes bear the cross of St George. The knight was cross-legged and rested his feet upon a boar. The treatment of the figure is very stiff, and lacks the quality of the earlier plates.

Females

Male civilians of this period are unrepresented. There are four examples of female dress:

Margarete de Camoys, c. 1315, Trotton (*The Craft* Fig. 124)

Dame Jone de Kobeham, engr. c. 1320, Cobham (*The Craft* Fig. 125)

A lady, c. 1320, Pitstone[18]

A kneeling lady, c. 1320, Sedgefield (fig. 12).

The first two are excellent brasses, and the scale and treatment would associate them with the best of the early knights. Both are dressed in a short-sleeved surcoat, worn over the tighter fitting kirtle with buttoned sleeves. Their headdress consists of a kerchief falling to the shoulders, and a wimple covers both chin and throat. The overall simplicity of the dress, treated in the graceful and restrained manner of the period, confers dignity to the figures. A decorative feature at Trotton was nine small shields set into the surcoat. These were most probably of enamelled copper.

The Pitstone and Sedgefield figures are very small. The first is similar to Margarete de Camoys, but measures 31 cm only, and may have been associated with a cross brass. Two pocket-like slits are shown on her surcoat. The second wears a mantle over all and is a curious little figure. The almost complete face of a woman, c. 1320 has been discovered on the reverse of the heart and scrolls plate of the Bacon brass, 1437 at All Hallows-by-the-Tower, London. A very fine indent c. 1307 at Weekley contained a brass to Dame Anneys le Vavasour who seems to have been shown in semi-profile, accompanied by censing angels.

Ecclesiastics

Only four ecclesiastical figures survive:

Archbishop William de Grenefeld, 1315, York Minster (Fig. 23)
Head of a priest in a cross, c. 1320, Chinnor (Fig. 24)
Head of a priest, c. 1320, Ashford
Richard de Hakebourne, half eff., 1322, Merton College, Oxford[19*]
(*The Craft.* Fig. 126)

Grenefeld's brass is a fragment of a large canopied memorial, consisting of two thirds of the figure. The archbishop is vested in pontificals with pallium and cross staff. His face has large staring eyes and protruding ears, and thick curly hair below his mitre. The feet of the figure originally rested upon two dogs.[20] The demi-figure of Hakebourne is fine. The amice and apparels of his mass vestments are decorated with varieties of fylfot and other geometric patterns. His face is similar to that of the Pebmarsh knight, but his ears are very prominent, his hair curly and his chin dotted with stubble. The Chinnor priest shows only the head and hands. At Ashford little more than the head remains, and the quality of the work is poor. The figure of Adam de Bacon c. 1320, Oulton, was stolen in 1857. This was a life-size representation similar to Hakebourne but showing the priest full length. His chasuble was edged with a band of quatrefoils, which were repeated on apparels, amice, stole and maniple. The form of the stole and maniple was noteworthy, as the ends widened with an intervening section to a broad rectangular panel with pendant fringes, a form found on brasses only for a short time. His feet rested on a crouching lion with upraised tail.[21] A large palimpsest fragment at St John Maddermarket, Norwich (obverse Rugge, 1558), preserves about half the figure of an abbot or bishop holding a large clasped book in the left hand, which may be dated c. 1320.

Arrangement and composition

All the existing figure brasses of this period have been described, but these are only indicative of the types fairly widely laid during the first quarter of the fourteenth century. As has been noted, the metal of these plates is thick, the brasses are not riveted, and many must have proved easy and attractive plunder. Indents, small fragments and records give a clearer picture of the distribution of brasses at this time which were laid as far west as Llanfaes and as far north as Durham. A considerable number of Lombardic capital letters have been found, not only in churches as at Dean[22] and Hornchurch, but on abbey sites such as Dale, Glastonbury, Bardney and Basingwerk. A fine enamelled shield c. 1300 from Leez Priory, is another fragment of a brass destroyed in the dissolution of the English religious houses. It may be deduced that the use of brasses was widespread by 1320.

Architectural and background ornament during this period can only be appreciated from a study of indents. The canopy of Dame Jone de Kobeham remains, its missing parts restored, and follows closely that of Queen Eleanor (*The Craft,* Fig. 125). A graceful pediment is supported by slender columns. The pediment itself consists of a lower arch with large cusps, and an upper straight sided gable decorated with crockets terminating in a large foliated finial. Similar canopies framed the figures at Trotton, Gorleston and Pebmarsh. A well preserved indent at Bottisham, records the canopied figure of the judge Elyas de Bekingham c. 1310. On the indent at Emneth a large tabernacle replaces the finial. The indent of Bishop Walter de Haselshaw, 1308, Wells Cathedral, records a most ambitious design.[23] The brass measured 4.52m. by 1.88m., and the figure alone, 2.74m. The feet of the bishop rested on a lion, supported by a bracket of tree form possibly intended for a hazel. The pediment of the canopy was supported by broad shafts containing compartments and subsidiary figures. Large representations of religious subjects lay beside the pediment. The indent of Bishop Ketton, 1316, Ely Cathedral, is almost as large. A remarkable indent at Tewkesbury is attributed to Maud de Burgh, d. 1315. Four banners and angels were arranged on and around a canopy with tabernacle and subsidiary figures. The powdering of slabs with shields and devices was a further decorative arrangement. Lady Camoys at Trotton was surrounded with shields, stars and perhaps flowers. The indent of William Archer, rector, 1310, Saltwood, displays a powdering of small lions. One detail survives of the background inlays to the indent of Bishop Thomas Cantilupe at Hereford cathedral, the seated figure of the martyred King Ethelbert of East Anglia d. 794 holding his head against his breast.[24] This young king was killed by Offa, King of Mercia, and a shrine was subsequently raised to his honour in Hereford.

Plain Latin crosses or quatrefoil open headed crosses containing figures have been noted as important early designs, and their indents are quite numerous. Wells cathedral contains the indents of three slender Latin crosses of early date. Crosses with half effigies above have several examples, notably William de St John, c. 1325, Ramsbury; unknown, Great Hale and Sir Boniface de Hart c. 1320, two half effigies, Hornchurch. Richard de Hakebourne, Merton College, Oxford, is represented as imposed upon an open cross head which is almost totally destroyed. The Chinnor priest appears within the head which has large foliated terminals. The stems of both these crosses are lost. Excellent indents of this type are at the cathedrals of Salisbury, and St Alban's. An unusual form of the cross is shown on the indent of Richard de Wotton c. 1320, Wotton-under-Edge, the priest kneeling in prayer below a cross head containing a representation of the Blessed Virgin. The lettering of his prayer swept up in place of a formal stem. A few cross brasses were enriched with canopies. The double cross slab to Sir Thomas and Eleanor de Luda, at present divided at Askerswell and Whitchurch Canonicorum, is a remarkable example.[25]

Inscriptions

In contrast with this elaborate ornament, inscriptions of the period are simple in expression. The use of separate inlay Lombardic letters of good rounded form was general, and though the letters are gone, indents are often legible. W. J. Blair has shown that these letters are of standard sizes, which are occasionally mixed on inscriptions, and it must be presumed they were cast in quantity, and probably not by engravers. A cross normally marked the beginning and the words were separated by stops. The inscriptions of priests were usually in Latin, and those of other persons in Norman French. A very brief Latin text: "HIC IACET W DE ALWALTONA', exists on a slab at Peterborough cathedral. The inscriptions to Sir John Dabernoun is more typical, concluding with a prayer for the soul:

> '†SIRE : JOHANN : DABERNOUN : CHIVALER : GIST : ICI : DEU : DE : SA ALME : EYT : MERCY.'

The Latin inscriptions of Bishop Haselshaw and Hakebourne conclude with the phrase 'CUIUS : ANIME : PROPICIETUR : DEUS : AMEN.', which became extremely common in the later fourteenth and fifteenth centuries. The inscription of Lady Jone de Kobeham is of greater interest as it contains a clause promising pardon to those who pray for the deceased:

> '†DAME : JONE : DE : KOBEHAM : GIST : ISI :
> DEUS : DE : SA : ALME : EIT : MERCI :
> KIKE : PUR : LE : ALME : PRIERA :
> QUARAUNTE : IOURS : DE : PARDOUN : AVERA'

A similar promise was made in the inscription of Sir Robert de Bures, and one hundred days pardon was recorded on that of Sir William Fitzralph:

[†VOUS : ET:] VOUS : QE: PAR : ISSI :PASSEREZ :
POUR : LALME : LE : DIT : WILLIEM : [PRIEZ :
POUR : UN : PATER : NOSTER : ET : UNE : AVE :
CENT:] IOURS : DE : PARDON : [ENT : AVAREZ:]

Only a small fragment of this inscription survives, engraved in Lombardics on a border fillet.[26] As described in *The Craft,* such rewards were an incentive for securing devotions on behalf of the deceased.

The year 1325 is an arbitrary date with which to close the subject of this chapter. It is nevertheless appropriate. During the years 1320-1340 important changes were made in armour, costume and the design of brasses, giving the memorials at the close a very different aspect. The latest brasses described in this chapter are transitional but their affinity with earlier work is strong.

The engravers of these first English brasses are unknown. Most of the plates may be ascribed to London marblers, though the Lincolnshire half effigies may well have been engraved in the north east.[27*] The little Sedgefield lady is most probably northern work. Whatever the engravers' identity, their skill is clear. The brasses are in no sense 'primitives'. They reflect the application of an excellent craftsmanship to a fresh use. They are fine monuments, well and boldly executed, having a grandeur which was rarely to be surpassed.

3. English brasses, 1325-60

Artistic achievement between the years 1310 and 1350 has aptly attracted to this period the description "the age of the decorator". The use of architectural forms for purely decorative purposes, the application of figure work decoratively, the ornamental arrangement of heraldry and the exploitation of the grace of the ogive arch in tracery, were important aspects of the decorative style. Patronage from the court and the church provided masons and metalworkers with abundant scope for their skills. The construction and enrichment of the main upper chapel of St Stephen's, Westminster, begun in 1327, was a masterpiece of the age, intended to rival the finest French achievements. In accordance with an insatiable desire for ornament, tombs and major church fittings were enriched with tabernacles, niches and façades of tracery. Tabernacle work filled stained glass windows at York. The Lady chapel in Ely, begun in 1321, epitomised the style. The walls were lined with sedilia supporting brackets, and scenes from the life of the Virgin formed a frieze. Space was treated as a challenge to the carver, and surface decoration of paint, gesso and stained glass was freely applied to the work. French influence was particularly strong in London, and is especially reflected in the activities of the craftsmen employed by the court at Westminster.

Men in armour

The Fitzralph brass at Pebmarsh may be regarded as the last characteristic representation of the first period of English brass engraving. From 1325-1360 new and rapidly changing forms of presentation appear, many being clearly influenced by French or Flemish patterns. The novelty of design was further enhanced by remarkable experiments in the structure of armour. The knightly class and church dignitaries were the main purchasers of brasses, though of the latter only one brass of the first rank survives. A widening social distribution is nevertheless evident, and a rich London fishmonger is among the male civilians represented.

Well executed figures in armour supposedly represent Sir John Dabernoun d. 1327 and Sir John de Creke with wife c. 1330. The mixture of mail and plate is accurately represented, especially noteworthy being the ridged iron bascinet to which the mail aventail is laced. The surcoat is shortened in the front, a fashion of brief duration, revealing the coat of plates, layers of mail and quilted body defences. Vambraces of plate completely protect the forearms. Spurs are of wheel or rowel form in contrast to the prick spurs of earlier figures. The knights are slim and decidedly less than lifesize. Sir John de Creke who died after 1324, with his wife Alyne afford the earliest existing full length example in England of the married pair (Fig. 19). Both these brasses were canopied. It should nevertheless be noted, with respect to the issues raised in the last chapter, that the dates of these brasses depend on the accuracy of the attribution at Stoke D'Abernon. If Sir John is in fact the third of that name his brass may well date c. 1340, and would still remain consistent with the style of such monumental effigies as that of John of Eltham, Earl of Cornwall d. 1337 at Westminster Abbey. This possibility exists, and any certain revision would apply equally to the making of the brass at Westley Waterless. Both brases should at present be dated no earlier than c. 1335.

Referring to the facts presented above it would appear that Sir Richard de

Boselyngthorpe, Buslingthorpe is contemporary with these brasses. His simple, almost archaic, appearance in comparison with them strengthens the impression that his brass is a provincial engraving.

The next military figure is perhaps separated from these by an interval of twelve years. The brass of Sir Hugh Hastyngs, 1347, Elsing, is claimed by many to be the most remarkable of all English brasses. The monument is now seriously mutilated but several of the missing portions were recorded in rubbings made in 1781 and 1782 by John Carter and the Rev. Sir John Cullum together with Craven Ord.[1] Furthermore a late seventeenth-century transcript of the proceedings of the court of Chivalry between Reginald Lord Grey of Ruthin and Sir Edward Hastings in 1408 has most fortunately preserved a record of the complete memorial. Sir Edward Hastings presented the brass of Sir Hugh, his grandfather, as evidence of his claim. The court adjourned to the church to inspect it and a very detailed description was written down.[2]

The brass when complete showed Sir Hugh armed, his feet resting on a lion and his head on a cushion supported by two angels. A most elaborate canopy surrounded him. The oculus or circular centre of the pediment was filled with a representation of St George slaying the dragon, and between the centre cusps below the soffit the soul was shown borne heavenwards by angels. A crested helm rested upon the finial, and springing from the pediment were two large brackets bearing tabernacles, which contained a representation of the Coronation of the Virgin. Beside them were placed two angels holding censers. The canopy shafts were widened to contain niches. Within these were armed figures of relatives and friends of the deceased, his companions at Calais on his last campaign. On the dexter side were King Edward III, Thomas de Beauchamp, Earl of Warwick, Edward le Despenser and Sir John Grey of Ruthin. On the sinister side were Henry Plantagenet Earl of Lancaster, Laurence Hastings, Ralph Lord Stafford and Almeric Lord St Amand. The tops of the shafts were surmounted by narrower tabernacles. Four shields of arms were laid around the pediment, two of Hastings and two of Foliot. The whole design was framed by a border inscription, having the same shields at the corners, and four medallions of the Evangelists' symbols unexpectedly in the centre of each side. The brass plates were gilded and the heraldry inlaid in proper tinctures. Open tracery within the canopy was inlaid with coloured glass. The brass was fixed with rivets to a slab of purbeck marble, and the four shields around the pediment were apparently made of composition inlaid with glass and cemented to the stone.

The greater part of this elaborate composition still exists (fig. 21). The canopy shafts have lost the figures of Despenser and Hastings, and their topmost tabernacles. The pediment is broken, and the border and shields of arms are lost. All the figure below the knees is gone. Nevertheless, in 1905 the panel with Grey of Ruthin was recovered, and one of the supporting angels was discovered in London as recently as 1964, so further recoveries are possible.

The execution of the brass is of the highest quality. Sir Hugh, though armed in mixed mail and plate, displays many differences from earlier figures. His surcoat is shortened at both front and back and emblazoned with the arms of Hastyngs. His helmet, a rounded bascinet with visor and aventail, is unusual, especially the additional defence of a plate bevor to cover the throat. His thighs are protected by some form of brigandine defence (plates riveted to a base of canvas), the round studs of which protrude through a covering of material. The leg defences were entirely of mail, which is represented in interlocking pairs of half circles.

The weepers are similarly armed with additional greaves of plate to protect the legs. The visors of the Earl of Warwick and Lord Stafford are drawn in a distorted profile. Almeric, Lord St Amand, is represented in an iron kettle hat with comb and deep brim, and is the sole example of this type of helmet on an English brass (Fig. 22). King

Edward carries a sword, the Earls of Lancaster and Warwick hold lances, Lord Grey rests on a pole axe, and Lord St Amand holds "une grande baston", a short stout staff with a point at one end. All the weepers are in heraldic surcoats, the King's being emblazoned with France Ancient and England quarterly, and Lancaster's with England with a label of France. St George is appropriately armed, the visor of his bascinet being raised. His shield is heart-shaped in the French or Flemish fashion.

The origin of this brass, which can only be deduced from the design, has been the subject of dispute. Hartshorne, concluding a most detailed study of the brass, decided that it was "foreign, possibly Flemish, but more likely French work".[3] The features quoted in support of this view are the six-tasselled cushion, the unusual representation of the mail, the early bevor, and the heart-shaped shield of St George. This opinion has received considerable support. The author, however, upholds the contrary view of Gawthorp and Stone that the brass is English. The "foreign" influence is confined to detail and is no more significant than in much undoubted English art of the period. There is no record of a similar French brass. The distinctive representation of mail is repeated on a contemporary brass at Wimbish which was undoubtedly the work of the same designers. The Wimbish figure with his wife is set within an octofoil crosshead, an English brass pattern of which no French or Flemish counterpart is known. The very setting of the Elsing brass in Purbeck marble is inconsistent with French or Flemish work, unless the craftsmen were practicing in England. Especially in favour of English origin are the similarities of this brass to the Westminster tomb of the Earl of Pembroke d. 1324, which was inlaid "after the mosaic manner with stained glass", and the painted glass of the Ely chapter house, obtained from William Pyroun and Simon of Lynn.[4] These comparisons have been made in *The Craft,* Chapter Nine (Figs. 102-3). Stone has drawn attention to the deep perspective of the Elsing tabernacles and that shown on recorded paintings from St Stephen's chapel, Westminster.[5] There are therefore good grounds to ascribe the Elsing brass to London engravers, working to the design of court artists employed in the decoration of St Stephen's chapel. The similarity of some detail to East Anglian glass painting is not surprising, when it is considered that several of the Ely craftsmen were employed at Westminster, and a Royal Master mason of the time, John atte Grene, was himself from Norfolk.

Five other figures in armour are important though not in the same class as the Elsing brass. These are:

Sir John de Wautone with wife, formerly in cross, 1347, Wimbish (Fig. 20)
Sir John Gifford, 1348, Bowers Gifford
John Wardiewe, c. 1350, Bodiam
Sir John de Cobham, canopy, 1354, Cobham (Fig. 29)
William de Aldeburgh, d. 1388, engr? c. 1360, Aldborough (Fig. 28).

The Wimbish brass has many peculiarities in common with Elsing and was undoubtedly designed by the same master. The unusual treatment of the mail, the form of the faces, and other details are very significant points of similarity. This is the earliest surviving English military brass depicted without a shield. Sir John Gifford is headless, and plate forms a very small part of his armour. His finest feature is the shield, skilfully engraved with fleurs-de-lys on a diapered ground (*The Craft,* Fig. 131). John Wardiewe has lost both head and legs but is nevertheless interesting. His gauntlets are folded so that the back of one is completely seen and the other almost entirely concealed. This is a typically Flemish feature and in other respects the figure reflects continental influence.[6] His shortened surcoat takes the form of a jupon emblazoned with his arms. This tight-fitting garment was worn over the body armour consistently until c. 1410. Sir John de Cobham is the earliest of the famous series of Cobham knights, and is recognisably the first of an important group of figures which can be traced into the early fifteenth century. His arms and legs are completely protected by plate and brigandine, and his armour illustrates the end of a period of transition.

William de Aldeburgh is a figure of unusual design, carrying a shield and resting his feet on an inscribed corbel. A heart is held between his gauntlets. While his armour is of a style on the whole appropriate for the close of the period and William died in 1388, it is clear that he is wearing open greaves, and this, together with the shield itself, might indicate a date rather closer to c. 1350. It would however be pointless to lay overmuch emphasis on such details, as this is probably northern rather than London work, York being the likely place of origin. As is emphasised in Chapter Seven there was much Flemish influence in York monumental and glass design in the fourteenth century, which is reflected in this example in the execution of the major lines, especially of the legs. These wide lines required definition by two engraved outlines, the surface between being chiselled or scored away. This is not a London technique. It is unfortunate for purposes of research that the stone of the monument is gone, and the brass is at present "skied" preventing easy inspection.

Male civilians

Civilian brasses are few, and female costume is best represented on the wives of the military figures at Westley Waterless and Wimbish. The following list is complete:

John de Bladigdone and wife Maud, half effs., in cross, c. 1325, East Wickham
Nichole de Aumberdene, in cross c. 1350, Taplow
Civilian and wife, half effs., c. 1355, Upchurch (Fig. 25)
Richard and Margaret Torryngton, canopy lost, 1356, Great Berkhamsted.

Only the Taplow and Great Berkhamsted figures are full-length effigies, and Bladigdone and Aumberdene, being shown in cross heads, are very small. Nevertheless the group illustrates male costume adequately. This consisted of a tight undertunic, a loose overtunic, a combined shoulder piece and hood, hose and pointed shoes. An interesting detail of the East Wickham and Taplow figures is the long pendant tippets falling from the short sleeves of the overtunic, a fashion used also on female dress. All have full beards, John de Bladigdone's being forked. All the figures appear to sway at the waist imparting an illusion of movement. This tendency is noticeable also on the military figures described. Richard and Margaret Torryngton are large and were originally set within canopies which are almost entirely lost. They clasp hands, and are the earliest English figures so represented. The Upchurch figures, though small, are very well executed.

Females

The female figures shown with their husbands display a greater variety in dress. The kirtle and surcoat are worn by all. Alyne de Creke, whose slim and haughty figure is especially well engraved, wears an early form of the sideless surcoat, with slits extending to the waist. A mantle is held very close to the body. Maud de Bladigdone wears pendant tippets from the sleeves of her surcoat, a feature also well illustrated by Margaret Torryngton. A change in hair arrangement is shown by Margaret, who wears the reticulated or nebulé headdress, an arrangement of frills described in Chapter Four. This extravagant fashion is in marked contrast to the veils and wimples worn by the others.

Ecclesiastics

It may be doubted if the military and civil brasses of this period are a truly representative fragment of those originally laid. It is certain that ecclesiastical brasses in no way represent the period adequately. The great religious houses held many brasses of the most elaborate type as is proved by indents at Durham, Ely, Lincoln, St Albans and at York. The indent of Bishop Lewis de Beaumont, 1333, Durham cathedral, records a brass that must have been larger and more complex than any now extant in Europe.[7] Not a single example remains representing a bishop, abbot or prior. The majority of the clergy commemorated were parish priests and their figures are mostly small.

134)

Nichol de Gore, in cross, d. 1333, Woodchurch (*The Craft,* Fig. 134)
Laurence de St Maur. canopy, 1337, Higham Ferrers (Fig. 26)
John de Grofhurst, canopy, c. 1340, Horsmonden (Fig. 27)
Richard de Beltoun, Half eff., c. 1340, Corringham *(The Craft,* Fig. 133)
Unknown priest, half eff., on bracket, c. 1340, Great Brington
Thomas de Hop, half eff., 1347, Kemsing
William de Herleston, formerly in cross, 1353, Sparsholt
A priest, perhaps Roger de Inkepenne d. 1361, formerly in cross, c. 1355, Stoke-in-Teignhead.

All the figures, with the exception of Robert de Tring, are represented in mass vestments. Laurence de St Maur is by far the finest.[8*] His chasuble is shown as of light material, falling in deep artistic folds and has the prayer "Fili dei miserere mei" incised above his hands. Two dogs fight for a bone beneath his feet. The tall and graceful figure has considerable affinities in treatment to the Crekes at Westley Waterless. John de Grofhurst is in complete contrast. His vestments are remarkably bulky and stiff. The orphrey of the chasuble falls vertically in disregard of engraved fold lines. The stole, maniple and amice are large and boldly decorated with fylfot and geometric patterns. A great scroll lies across his breast recording his grants in 1338 to the abbot and convent of Bayham, to the church of Horsmonden and the chapel of Leveshothe. His face is peculiar, having a small mouth and very deep chin covered with stubble. A lion with upraised tail lies beneath his feet. A comparison between these two priest brasses is of considerable interest as they seem to present designs influenced by different motives. Laurence de St Maur is large but restrained and graceful. John de Grofhurst is peculiar but highly decorative. Both these compositions were clearly special designs. They are nonetheless precursors of two divergent series of London patterns for all types of figure, which can be traced throughout the fourteenth century.

The smaller figures require little comment. Nicol de Gore is simply engraved. The Kemsing half effigy is good, appearing to be earlier than the known date of death, but probably not so as this priest became rector in 1341. The Corringham figure is akin to Horsmonden. The Great Brington priest wears a pileus indicating academic status. Warden Tring at Merton College is interesting as his dress is possibly academic. The warden is tonsured but also bearded and quite similar to the Taplow fishmonger. The last two priests are well engraved, adopting the slightly swaying posture noted on other figures of this period. The importance of the smaller priest brasses is enhanced by their cross or bracket settings.

Arrangement and composition

The most significant development in the architectural ornament of this period is the use of the ogive arch. Part of the ogival pediment exists at Stoke D'Abernon, and a double canopy is now lost from Westley Waterless.[9] The Elsing pediment is only slightly ogival in form, and the pediments of the canopies of the side shafts are straight sided. Yet the cusps below the soffit are of very pronounced ogival form. Similarly the saint filled shafts at Higham Ferrers are straight sided whereas the narrow inscribed pediment is ogival. An important feature of this canopy is the embattled tabernacle above connected to the shafts by flying buttresses. This contains representations of Christ receiving the soul, two angels. SS. Peter, Paul, Andrew and Thomas. The canopy of John de Grofhurst is both clumsy and ornamental, in keeping with the figure. The canopy of Sir John de Cobham is slighter and has an open oculus. Indents record some unusual designs. The canopy of John de Gurney, 1332, Harpley, was no more than two strips forming a gable with two cusps beneath. At Westleton a priest, c. 1325 or possibly earlier, was shown with a canopy curving back behind his head like an auriol. Most elaborate of all is the Durham indent of Bishop Beaumont, showing a triple ogival pediment flanked by double side shafts, containing apostles and "ancestors in their coat armour", and supporting above a wide tabernacle with representations as at Higham Ferrers. A fairly detailed description of this superb brass was made in the sixteenth century and recorded in *The Rites of Durham.*[10]

Several of the small figures recorded were enclosed within cross heads. These include Wimbish, East Wickham, Taplow, Woodchurch, Merton College, Sparsholt and Stoke-in-Teignhead. No fragment of the last named cross exists and only the Taplow and Woodchurch crosses are in a fairly complete state. All these crosses, with the exception of Woodchurch, had octofoil heads enclosing the figures. At Woodchurch the attractive cross head is formed by a circle inscribed in Lombardic letters (*The Craft,* Fig. 134). Four internal cusps form a quatrefoil and four fleurs-de-lys spring from the outer circumference. The stem is gone. A small fragment at Wimbish is decorated with circles and is the earliest example of this conventional ornament. The stem of the East Wickham cross is inscribed and rises from a base of three steps. The Wimbish cross sprung from the back of an elephant. The Sparsholt cross sprung from a shield, and the Taplow cross appropriately rises from the back of a dolphin, alluding to the trade of the deceased.

Indents are a valuable supplement to this evidence. Especially noteworthy are a figureless cross with a catherine wheel head at Toftrees to Thomas de Melham, c. 1330; a floriated quatrefoil cross springing from a lion at Watlington to Robert de Montalt; a cross to Adam de Brome c. 1325, St. Mary-the-Virgin, Oxford, having the Blessed Virgin and Child in the head and the deceased kneeling at the base; and a remarkably elongated cross to Prior Crauden 1341, Ely cathedral, which rose from the kneeling figure of the Prior. A most interesting indent is at Tormarton to Sir John de la Rivière c. 1350. The armed figure of Sir John lay within an octofoil cross, the upper part of which was apparently obscured by a large representation of a church with tower and spire. The stem was interlaced and was broken by two compartments.

The half effigy at Great Brington rests upon a small bracket, which presumably once had a stem. It is the earliest existing example of this arrangement, which retained its popularity into the sixteenth century, long after the fashion for figured crosses had declined. The inscribed corbel at Aldborough is little more than an architectural foot support and is of lesser significance.

Brasses of unusual form were made during this period of which a few may still be traced on indents or from other records. At Haveringland the indent of Sir Roger Bylney reveals that he was depicted in semi-profile with prominent visor and bevor. The brass of Abbot John de Sutton, 1349, Dorchester, consisted of an extended arm grasping a crozier.[11*] At Langdon Hills a brass apparently consisted of two heads only, unconnected with any incised design on the stone. An interesting drawing by Francis Thynne, Lancaster Herald in 1604, purports to represent a brass at Burton

Agnes to Roger de Somerville, 1336.[12] The figure is shown in plate armour, cross legged with a most peculiar canopy inscribed in Lombardics, attendant angels supporting a shield, and a background of stars. Even allowing for considerable inaccuracy, the design must have been highly original.

Inscriptions

The form of inscriptions underwent gradual change during this period. Lombardic letters, separately inlaid or engraved on a fillet, were in general use until 1340, the circular inscription on the Woodchurch cross being an example. Indents of separately inlaid inscriptions are found until the end of the period.[13] After 1340 black letter script in short and broad characters became usual with Lombardics for the capital letters. This combination occurs on the border fillet to William and Margaret Bateman c. 1340, from Heigham now in the Norwich Museums. Inscriptions recorded in lines on rectangular plates serve as complete monuments. Examples are at Fawley 1347; Holme Hale and Barton-in-the-Clay 1349; Ludham 1351 and Greystoke 1359. The second commemorates Sir Esmon de Ileye and his family, all of whom probably perished in the Black Death.

Most inscriptions contains little more than the name status and a prayer for the soul. The Ludham inscription reads:

> Hic iacet d*omi*nus Thomas de Honyngg quo*nda*m rector eccl*es*ie de Heyham cui*us* anime pr*o*picietur de*us*.

Even inscriptions on very elaborate compositions such as Higham Ferrers maintain simplicity. It is merely written of Laurence de St Maur:

> Hic iacet Laure*n*cius de S*anct*o Mauro quo*n*dam rector isti*us* eccl*es*ie cuius anime propicietur deus.

Occasionally an inscription is in verse. The indent to Abbot Godfrey de Croyland 1329, Peterborough cathedral, reads:

DE : CROILAND : NATUS :
JACET : HIC : GODFRIDUS : HUMATUS :
BURGI : PRELATUS :
CUI : SOLVAS : CHRISTE : REATUS : AMEN :

An inscription in French, relating to the laying of the foundation stone of Bisham Abbey by Edward III at the request of Sir William de Montagu and following the successful siege of Berwick in 1333, is preserved as a palimpsest reverse at Denchworth. This presumably became spoil at the suppression of the Abbey. Although French continued to be used for inscriptions, as for Sir John de Cobham, Latin was chosen for other than ecclesiastics and gradually became more usual. The lost inscription for Sir Hugh Hastyngs was, for example, in Latin.

Notwithstanding the limited number of figures surviving, the years 1325-1360 were an important period in the development of English brasses. Brasses were increasingly adopted as memorials by bishops and knights and in addition the engraving of small half figures and inscription plates made this type of memorial available to a wider segment of society. This growing interest is reflected in the remarkable increase in the number of English brasses during the latter half of the fourteenth century. The engravers of these monuments are not known. The mark at the feet of Alyne de Creke has been described (*The Craft*) and its association with a Walter "le masun" is highly improbable. It may nevertheless be assumed that the London marblers were actively engaged in this work. This conclusion is not only supported by later developments, and the undoubted association of the Elsing brass with work of craftsmen under court partonage, but also by the setting of brasses in Purbeck marble slabs. The participation of craftsmen in the North, suggested in the previous chapter, is indicated strongly by the unusual knight at Aldborough.

The growing importance of brasses as a monumental form in England is both revealed by the increased demand for English plates and the excellence of many of those made. It is also reflected in the purchase of brasses from the Continent by wealthy merchants and eminent ecclesiastics. The main suppliers of these imported monuments were the engravers of Tournai and West Flanders, whose contribution to this craft in the fourteenth century was of unique distinction.

4. Brasses made in Tournai and West Flanders, 1280-1365

Pre-eminence in monumental brass engraving throughout the fourteenth century must be accorded to the craftsmen of Tournai, Gent, and probably of Bruges. While the metalworkers of the Meuse, at Dinant, Bouvignes, Huy and Namur surpassed those of West Flanders in many aspects of their skill, they failed to equal them in the craft of engraved memorials. The incised slab and engraved brass were specialities of the Western Communes. This claim for the supremacy of the craftsmen of Tournai and Western Flanders is not based on an artistic appraisal of their work, which must by its nature be subjective. It is founded on mediaeval choice. There is certain evidence that many of the wealthiest purchasers of these memorials throughout Northern Europe chose to import Flemish brasses in preference to those of local manufacture. The assertion that these brasses of international fame were engraved in Western Flanders and Hainaut is justified in the course of this chapter.

The excellence, quantity and reputation of Flemish brasses are reflections of the commercial prosperity, flourishing craftsmanship and specialisation of labour within the region. Gent and Bruges were towns of outstanding importance in European trade, the centres of famous industries in textiles and metalwork, and meeting places for merchants of the Hansa league, English woolmen, Venetian traders and Italian financiers. Tournai, a thriving centre enjoying close contacts with Paris and the Flemish towns, was in a peculiarly favourable position. Her industries rivalled those of Bruges. Her large population, enhanced by an influx of immigrants, stimulated the development of specialised skills. Raw materials — stone and copper — were available in abundance either locally or through trade. The river Scheldt afforded an easy route for transport. Latten founding was well established in the town by the close of the thirteenth century.[1]

Tournai workshops

The archives of Tournai preserved until 1940 a particularly valuable record of brass engravers. Several contracts of the late thirteenth and fourteenth centuries have been published, to which some reference has already been made.[2] On the 29th March 1296, Jehan Li Poingnières agreed to make an incised slab to commemorate Beatrice de Clermont, Châtelaine de Lille. The size was to be eleven feet by five and a half feet, and the price 23 Parisian pounds. Although the main design was to be incised in stone, the border inscription, the canopy work, 12 shields, two little dogs and the lady's mantle, "semenchié d'Escuçons des Armes", were to be inlaid in brass. The slab was to be sent to the Abbey of Beaulieu near Nesle. In February, 1330, Jehan d'Escamaing, Jean de la Croix and Lotars Hanette undertook to prepare a rectangular sheet of brass with canopy and shields of arms ten feet long and four and a half feet wide. The design was to be based on the monument of Jehan Leroy at the church of Notre Dame at Tournai. The complete brass was to be set in Tournai stone, the whole costing 60 Parisian pounds. The destination of the memorial was Arras but the commemoration is not stated. Hannette (his name is spelt Lothaire Hanaitte) was involved in another contract of 1345, to engrave a brass to two canons, Jean and Simon du Portail. This monument was to be of the quality of the brass of Jakemon de

Corbri. Lotars seems to have died in 1378, and desired to be commemorated by "une lame".

On the 7th of July 1335, Jacques de Baissi and Catherine du Tiel agreed to sell to Huart Platecorne a monument having "II Images de Laiton" as good as that of Watier Gargate. The brass was to be laid at St Quentin, and the price agreed was twenty six Parisian pounds. Jean Alous, presumably the purchaser of slabs in 1314 (see *The Craft*), contracted on 21st July 1341 to make a brass in memory of Andrieu de Monchi and his wife, with canopies and figures separately inlaid. The design was to be based on the brass of Jehan le Borgne at the church of St Nicolas, Arras, and it was to be laid at the Abbey of St Vaast at Arras, the total cost being thirty six Parisian pounds. The most detailed and important of the contracts, that made in 1301 or 1311 with Jacques Couvès, has been quoted in *The Craft,* chapter eight. All these contracts concern tombs supplied within the vicinity of Tournai. Other references prove a wider distribution of these and other Flemish monuments.

The French court, in 1255, ordered from Tournai a cast effigy of Blanche of Castile, mother of St Louis, a remarkable proof of the prestige of the latten founders. From Lübeck come two important wills of fourteenth century councillors. Wedekin Warendorp in his will of 1350 requested "Item volo quod lapis bonus in Flandria factus ponatur in sepulcrum meum'.[3] Hermann Gallin, who died in 1365, desired to be buried in the Marienkirche, Lübeck, "et poni facient super meum supulcrum unum flamingicum auricalcium figurationibus bene factum lapidem funebralem".[4] Both these wills refer to Flemish brasses in a general way, and the place of purchase is not specified. However, the statement of Archbiship Jastrzambiecz at the Gnieznó chapter of 1426 disclosed Bruges as the source of his memorial, engraved in the manner of a fourteenth century example (see *The Craft*), and it is probable that Bruges and Gent as much as Tournai would benefit from such distant orders.

Tournai no longer possesses a single example of her own fourteenth century production of brasses. Gent has four fourteenth century brasses and Bruges has nothing earlier than 1370, and that a palimpsest reverse. This void is a result of plunder and neglect. Even until the nineteenth century there were many examples in Tournai. A canon, Gregory of Florence, d. 1350, lay at the cathedral. The churches of St Jacques and the Béguinage had several of the late fourteenth century. The convent of the Récollets possessed a brass of 1350 to Pierre de Wattripont and wife. The church of St Marie-Madeleine had three to the family of Clermés, dated 1312, 1323 and 1343. Most fortunately drawings of the last two, Rogier de Clermés and his two wives and Guillaume de Clermés and his daughter, are preserved in the church archives.[5] The pictures are not very detailed, but show the figures recumbent within elaborate canopies supporting tabernacles and shields. The borders are broken by medallions filled with heraldry. The heads of the figures rest on cushions, and the feet of Rogier are placed on two figures, one being bearded and holding a large club. These brasses are all lost, along with those referred to in the contracts, but their main features are evident. They were of great size and richly decorated, with elaborate canopies and backgrounds. Some were large rectangular plates, and others were of separate inlay type. On one, alabaster was inlaid; in another the brass provided the finish to an incised slab.

The connection between the brass and slab engravers in Tournai is particularly important, as many slabs complement the designs in use. Especially fine are those at Tournai itself of an ecclesiastic c. 1290, found on the site of the quarry at Chercq, and Isabeau de Cambrai, 1342, at St Jacques.[6] Their similarity to the brasses described in the contracts and to those of this type which still exist is close, the former illustrating an early stage in the development of these models. Even more exact comparisons can be made with the illustrated slab — as existing in 1939 — of a civilian c. 1350 from the Musée de l'École Saint-Luc (Fig. 30). The face and hands were originally inlaid, but in all other respects the detail is as identical to the brasses as the medium allowed. The distribution of such slabs is very wide. A fine but worn series pave the nave of Boston while others are found in Essex, Leicestershire, Lincolnshire, Norfolk, Suffolk and other English counties. A particularly well preserved Boston example is to Wessel called Smalenburgh, citizen and merchant of Munster d. 1340. The connection, furthermore, is not only deduced from design. It is proved by the contract of 1296, by the use of the local 'marble' for both sorts of monument, and other documentary evidence. In 1350 Jean d'Escamaing was given the work of re-engraving the slab of the ancestors of the Camphin family.[7] Jean can hardly be other than the craftsman who was working with Lotars Hanette in 1330, or his son. This family apparently worked on slabs and brasses as a business for some generations. In 1391 Jacques d'Escamaing finished a slab to Gilles Wellequin at the Church of St Brice.

Gent workshops

Documentary evidence of the Gent marblers is as conclusive as that of Tournai, though primarily relating to the fifteenth century. Jan van Meyere, a celebrated marbler and the founder of a flourishing business in brass and stone engraving, died in 1382. One of his contracts of 1378 is described in Chapter 5.[8] It is noteworthy that his son Jan, many of whose contracts survive, engraved not only brasses but in 1424 incised a slab of Tournai marble inlaid with white stone.[9]

In the absence of personal and makers' marks on the brasses, there is no way of establishing which of the great Flemish brasses of the fourteenth century were engraved in Tournai, Bruges or Gent, though it is probable that two separate inlay figures at Gent are of local origin. All three centres may take credit for these superb memorials, though the craftsmen of Tournai and its vicinity most probably held a dominant part until c. 1350.

Flemish brasses — royalty

The earliest and finest of these brasses are found in Denmark, England and Germany. Their quality compensates for their limited numbers. The earliest dated brass, at Ringsted, is that of King Eric Menved of Denmark and his wife, Ingeborg, both of whom died in 1319 (*The Craft,* Fig. 135). It is a great rectangular sheet, measuring 2.84m. by 1.68m., composed of smaller plates. The entire surface is engraved, and the design reveals all the main characteristics of Tournai work. Macklin considered that the brass was made not earlier than 1350 but gave no reasons for his view. The style of the work is consistent with the earlier date. The King and Queen are represented within a double canopy frame and border inscription. The figures are monumental in conception and stylised in treatment. Both faces were inlaid in alabaster. The King's face was restored in 1883 but the Queen's is the original. Her eyes are very wide open, imparting a staring expression. Her nose is large and broad and her lips boldly defined. The robes of both figures are simply but gracefully arranged, the drapery folds being expressed by very broad lines. The King is crowned; holds both sword and sceptre, and wears a mantle over a form of surcoat embroidered with the lions and hearts of the Arms of Denmark. His feet, richly shod, rest on two crouching lions. The Queen holds a sceptre and a closed book. Her kirtle appears clearly beneath a sideless surcoat, and an ample mantle, secured by a chain, is slightly gathered under both arms. Two small dogs play by her feet. The gloves of both figures, the under sides of their garments, and the King's hose, are all carefully hatched to receive colour inlay.

The architectural framework is elaborate. The canopy proper is formed of two narrow arches, with large cusps, crockets and broad finials. Resting on these are tabernacles, joined to the shafts by flying buttresses. They are formed of a series of five connected compartments, three of which support canopies with lofty pediments. The compartment covers appear behind as small tiled roofs. The surfaces of the tabernacles are intricately decorated with tracery and geometric patterns, the whole having the complexity of a goldsmith's masterpiece. Small figures of angels bear the naked souls of the deceased in sheets, while others swing censers and offer heavenly crowns in place of those of earth as trumpeters sound a welcome above. The canopy shafts are formed of a series of compartments, finely canopied, and containing representations of prophets, apostles and the evangelists. The prophets face the apostles, the former distinguished by their hats and sandals and the latter by their haloes, bare feet and personal emblems. The base of the canopy is in the form of a plinth, decorated with small medallions and scenes from the hunt and forest. While in certain respects this architectural arrangement bears comparison with the most remarkable façades of northern brick Gothic, its model lies in the miniature architecture of caskets and reliquaries. The metalsmith, unhampered by structural considerations, used architectural forms for pure ornament. The engraver did the same. The background against which the design is set is equally rich, forming a surface of geometric patterns filled with flowers, birds and monsters appearing behind the figures and the canopy work.

A frame is provided by the border inscription and an outer fillet of flowers and stops. The inscription is in Latin, engraved in bold Lombardics, its course broken at intervals by shields in medallions.

This great brass, as well executed as any existing, sets the scale and pattern of the other Flemish memorials which are here grouped according to their military, civilian and ecclesiastical representations.

Men in armour

The only military figure of this period and group, excluding a somewhat peculiar example at Gent, is at Oslo. Fragments of the brass were discovered on the site of the church of St Mary-the-Virgin, which was destroyed in 1533, and are now preserved in the museum of the University. The knight has rolling curls, a stubbled chin and jowl, staring eyes, bushy eyebrows, broad nose and thick lips. A small portion of mail is clear. An angel supports a cushion behind his head against a background of howling monsters. Fragments of the canopy show the soffit, cusps and finial, and the naked soul borne heavenwards by angels in the tabernacle above.

Civilians

Civilian brasses form a most important group. The six persons represented in the list below were citizens of standing in the government of their towns as well as wealthy merchants and landowners. They were men of influence and power, and their memorials reflect their prestige as well as their prosperity.

Adam de Walsokne and wife, 1349, St Margaret's, Kings' Lynn (Fig. 31)
Johann Clingenberg, 1356, Petrikirche, Lübeck (*The Craft,* Fig. 97)
Albrecht Hövener, 1357, Nikolaikirche, Stralsund (*Ibid.,* Fig. 58)
Johann von Zoest and wife, 1361, St John's Church, Torún (Figs. 33-4)
Alan Fleming, 1361, Newark (Fig. 32)
Robert Braunche and wives, 1364, St Margaret's, Kings' Lynn (*The Craft,* Fig. 139).

The first of these is very badly worn, especially in the upper half, where the design is almost obliterated. The brass of Clingenberg was wrecked in the destruction of the Petrikirche in 1941. Portions of the canopy are preserved in the St Annen Museum, Lübeck.

With this list should also be considered a brass, lost in the nineteenth century, to Jan Cortscoef 1368, his wife 1361, and son Colaert 13 . . . , at the cathedral, Bruges,[10] and a number of palimpsest fragments in England. Outstanding among these is a large piece of a merchant and wife c. 1350 on the reverse of the brass of Thomas de Topclyffe, 1391, at Topcliffe.

These civilian brasses have a particular grandeur in the contrast between the elaborate background and canopy and the boldness of the figures. The heads and hands of the dead are defined in the manner described, with large recessed lips and stubbled chins. Their garments are simple. Male civil dress of the period consisted of an undertunic with tight sleeves, usually covered by an overtunic or cote. This generally had short sleeves, from which often hung streamers or tippets. The lower arm of the undertunic was exposed. Hose and buckled shoes covered the legs and feet. A shoulder-piece with a hood which covered the shoulders, could be drawn over the head if desired. Very few of these garments were embroidered or otherwise decorated, and on the brasses large surface areas are only broken by major drapery lines.

Walsokne, Clingenberg, Fleming and Braunche wear the dress described. The sleeves of Walsokne's overtunic hang slightly below the elbow and Fleming's overtunic has additional side pockets. Johann von Zoest wears a rich undertunic, a shorter overtunic with an elaborate belt, and a full mantle over all, buttoned on the right shoulder. Albrecht Hövener is by far the most elaborate. His tunic is largely covered by a loose robe, split up the sides and cut square in front. His shoulders are covered with a cape of stiff material, decorated with ornamental bands. The sleeves of his undertunic are also embroidered with a leaf pattern. An unusual feature of Jan Cortscoef's figure was a large bag worn at his hip, through which a small sword was suspended.

The ladies' dress likewise gave scope for bold engraving with sufficient decoration to avoid severity. Kirtles are beautifully worked with vine and other foliage patterns and even birds. The wives of Walsokne and Braunche wear mantles and surcoats of the sideless variety, exposing large areas of the kirtles. The wife of von Zoest has her hair arranged in the nebulé fashion (Fig. 33), while the others wear a simple veil headdress and wimple.

Canopies, backgrounds and borders are similar to the Ringsted brass in design with certain differences in treatment and detail. At Toruń the blessed souls are borne towards a higher compartment within the tabernacle, in which God the Father is represented. At Stralsund and Kings Lynn 1364 God the Father, holding the soul, is attended by angels with censers and musical instruments. The structure of the background decoration is more regular, but in all cases the pattern is filled with rows of howling and leering monsters, many with human heads.

Latin is the language of the inscriptions on all though a palimpsest fragment at Fivehead with the Spanish words 'QUE.FINO.VIERNES' illustrates the use of a vernacular, and Spanish again occurs on a brass of 1333 at Sevilla. The border of the brass of Johann Clingenberg was remarkable. The outer fillet was expanded, and the usual pattern of flowers and stops replaced by a tree of Jesse. The head of the Virgin Mary at the top was linked to the sleeping figure of Jesse at the bottom by two courses of vine pattern containing crowned heads.

The foot supports and base compartments are full of interest. Their subjects are either whimsical or worldly, alien to the solemnity of the figures and the sacred representation of the canopies. The contrast appears both deliberate and symbolic, emphasizing the passing from earth to heaven. Small belled dogs play in the folds at the ladies' feet. A squirrel is shown at Toruń. The men's feet rest on wodehouses or wodewoses — hairy wild men — who do battle with adversaries (Fig. 34). The battle is fought with a lion beneath Walsokne and Fleming. A griffin is attacking beneath Braunche, while at Stralsund a curious monster bites a woodwose who blows a horn. The most remarkable feature of the Topcliffe palimpsest are the masts, rigging and pennon of a ship placed at the feet, an appropriate emblem for a merchant.[11] A hunt scene, the subject of the Ringsted panel, is repeated at Stralsund and Newark and formerly decorated the Lübeck brass. Scenes of country life, sport and harvesting are at King's Lynn 1349, and Toruń. The King's Lynn panels are particularly good, depicting a Post Mill and an idiot carrying his donkey on his shoulders. The base of the Cortscoef brass showed similar scenes, with a group playing at bowls. Woodwoses appear in number at Toruń carousing in a woodland feast. Most of these scenes are depicted against a background of highly stylized fruit bearing trees and plants, which are found in Flemish tapestry design.[12] By far the most elaborate is the panel of the Braunche brass (*The Craft,* Fig. 140), where the entire width of the base is devoted to one scene. This represents a Peacock feast. Lords and ladies dine at a long table, while peacocks are brought in to a fanfare and the music of attendant minstrels. The peacock was reserved for the most sumptuous feasts and served in the most exotic fashion — feathered with gold leaf or with a camphor fireball in its mouth.[13] It was regarded as the "Food of Love and Courage", over which vows were taken and services pledged. This particular representation has been associated with a feast given to King Edward III at King's Lynn in 1344, but no documentary evidence for this link is known and it may equally well refer to one of the fabled feasts of the romances. The prominence of the subject suggests a precise order.

Dr Hans Eichler, in his important study of these brasses, traces the origin of the grotesques, introduced into backgrounds and orphreys, to stained glass designs in Normandy. He compares them especially with glass in the cathedral of Evreux and the church of St Ouen at Rouen. Carvings of similar creatures adorn the portal of the Booksellers at Rouen Cathedral.[14] There are nevertheless equally close parallels from Limoges enamel tombs and German textiles, and a variety of sources should be presumed. The Flemish designers apparently applied these decorations in their own style to a new medium.

Important changes in design and arrangement are reflected in the latest brasses of this group. At Ringsted, there is little to indicate depth or differences of plane within the composition. The background pattern is not varied. The figures are confined within the canopies, and the canopies within the border. Only the King's sword passes under one of the canopy cusps, and his feet slightly pass the top edge of the base compartment. The brasses of Zoest, Fleming and Braunche are very different. In the first the feet of both figures encroach upon the base. A small figure is carefully represented standing on the foot rest and on Johann's left foot, butting against the canopy shaft in the process (Fig. 34). The canopy itself has a deep grained vault, studded with stars. The pinnacles of the canopy break in the border. The background of monsters is under the canopy and the surface above is left plain. In the second example these features are further exaggerated and a curious attempt at perspective is indicated by the forms of the canopy shafts. The third is slightly more conservative but shows the vault and a varied background. All these features were clearly planned to emphasize depth, to impart an illusion of a third dimension. The Newark brass is the most surprising, and may have been engraved as late as 1370, the inscription being the earliest in black letter script. Nevertheless, the figure is entirely consistent with the date of decease.

The Toruń brass displays a further peculiarity in the representation of the hands

(Fig. 33) which are folded one over another, giving a full view of the back of the right hand. This presentation became general after 1365 on Flemish brasses and slabs and occurs in sculpture.[15]

A badly mutilated canopied brass is that of the wife of Francisco Fernandes (1333), now in the Museo Arqueologico at Sevilla.[16] The lady in veil headdress, wimple, kirtle and mantle is finely executed. Her kirtle is caught up slightly under her left arm revealing an embroidered underdress. A long-haired dog sits at her feet. The brass is lost above the level of the lady's mouth. The background decoration is in geometric sections and is consistent with the date recorded on the inscription. The early character of this treatment is demonstrated in Dr H. K. Cameron's detailed artistic analysis of these brasses.[17]

Ecclesiastics

Rich clergy employed the Flemish engravers. The wealth of the priest concerned, rather than his ecclesiastical rank, apparently dictated the quality of his monument. Three great rectangular sheet compositions represent four bishops and an abbot. Two smaller but good separate inlay brasses represent parish priests. It is likely that the early composite memorial to a deacon at Noyon cathedral (noted in Chapter One) is yet another of the series, though attribution should await forthcoming publication. The established examples are as follows:

Bishops Ludolf and Heinrich von Bülow, 1347, Schwerin, (Fig. 35)
Bishops Burchard von Serken and Johann von Mul, 1350, Lübeck cathedral (*The Craft,* Fig. 136)
Unknown priest with chalice, c. 1350, St Severin, Köln[18]
Abbot Thomas Delamare, engr. c. 1360, St Albans cathedral (Fig. 37)[19*]
William de Kestevene, 1361, North Mimms (*The Craft,* Fig. 141).

The Lübeck brass was somewhat torn and dented by an air-raid in 1941, and was moved to the St Annen Museum. The rectangular plates are of a remarkably large size, that at Lübeck measuring 3.61m. by 1.88m. In arrangement they are similar to the mercantile brasses though the detail is somewhat less frivolous. The base panels of the Schwerin and St Albans brasses are facades of tracery. Those at Lübeck contain scenes from the lives of St Nicholas and St Eligius (*The Craft,* Figs. 137-8). Among a selection of incidents depicted are the raising of the children from the butcher's tub by St Nicholas, and the feat of St Eligius in pinching the devil's nose with tongs. The canopy work is of similar description and design. At Lübeck the tabernacles form two distinct tiers of unusual size. At St Albans two large compartments in the canopy shafts contain the figures of King Oswin or Offa, King of Mercia, founder of the church, and St Alban the Martyr. The Schwerin background is similar to Ringsted. The writhing monster pattern is repeated on the others. The most unusual feature of background detail is the four achievements of arms placed on either side of the tabernacles on the Schwerin brass. In order to accommodate these the tabernacle work has been very much reduced, and the canopy shafts narrow into a series of pinnacles.

The engravers found ample opportunity for decorative schemes in the presentation of the vestments and enrichment of the figures. The amices, orphreys, apparels, stoles and maniples are beautifully worked, the mitres heavily jewelled and embroidered. Gloves and albs are carefully hatched, probably for a white inlay. Human heads, grotesque beasts, flowers, heraldry, prophets and saints are lavished on the vestments. Representations of the Agnus Dei fill the volutes of the croziers (*The Craft,* Fig. 136).

The faces of the dead are treated in the Flemish stylized manner. Abbot Delamere at St Albans lies in the relaxed pose of death, his hands crossed downward and his eyes partly closed. The bishops at Lübeck raise the right hand in benediction.

A fragment preserved in the British Museum, London, consists of the mitred head of a bishop or abbot under a canopy, the centre portions of which is complete. The engraving is excellent and probably dates from c. 1365 (Fig. 36). This plate was in the possession of Pugin and was said to have come from a Belgian church.

The Köln priest is large, but mutilated by the loss of nearly a third of the figure. William de Kestevene is smaller and slightly inferior in treatment, though the design of the whole composition is ambitious (*The Craft,* Fig. 141). His hands are placed stiffly together in prayer, and his feet rest on a stag. A chalice is placed below the hands. A canopy with tabernacles and saint-filled side shafts rises on a bracket formed of two seated lions and a shield of arms for Kestevene. Both figure and architectural details are in separate inlay.

The North Mimms brass is indicative of the variety of designs employed, and the readiness of the engravers to work on a small scale. It is even possible that the reverse of the Topcliffe brass contains a fragment of a Flemish cross emblem brass. The double line of inscription, reading in opposite directions, could have formed part of an inscribed stem.[20*]

Gent brasses

The brasses described are unquestionably associated with each other. The influence of patterns and copy books, and the following of precendents is apparent in their similarity of detail and design. They do not, however, completely represent the style of engraving in West Flanders. Two figures at Gent, formerly in the chapel of the Hospice Wenemaer, are of rather different appearance and were probably made in Gent itself. The figures, now preserved in the Museum de Bijloke, represent Willem Wenemaer 1325, and his wife, Margrete s'Brunnen d. 1352. Their disparity in size and contrast in pose indicate independent commemoration.

The lady is of usual design, but very plainly and stiffly engraved. Her drapery lines have little flow, and the pose of the figure is rigid. The male figure appears as a peculiar contrast (*The Craft,* Fig. 142). His position and expression are alert. His head, with a shock of curls and striking eyes, is turned in a half profile. His left hand grasps the top of a heart-shaped shield, his right a drawn sword, held upwards. His feet have no support, though one may have been engraved on the original slab. The armour is typical of the period, showing the hawberk, surcoat, padded aketon and guard chains connected to sword and dagger. Poleyns and greaves of plate protect his legs. The engraving of his figure is in most respects consistent with Flemish skill and method. The design is exceptional, though the position of the sword, which gives much vitality to the pose, has several counterparts in sculptured and incised figures in the vicinity of Gent. Minor restorations were made to this brass in 1589, which no doubt accounts for the short scabbard. Other military brasses, separately inlaid in Tournai stone, representing knights of 1326, 1331 and 1366, lay in the chapel of the Dominicans, Gent. It is appropriate in connection with this style of work to mention a fragment preserved in the Wallace Collection, London. This consists of two legs c. 1325 entirely protected by mail, with rowel spurs. The feet were turned very stiffly downwards in the manner of Wenemaer and several incised Flemish slabs, such as that of Birger Petersson and wife 1328, Uppsala cathedral.

It is very difficult from the few remaining brasses to appreciate the quantity of such memorials produced by the Flemish engravers, or the facility with which alabaster and other inlays were combined with brass. It is clear that Flemish brasses became fashionable in certain towns and among certain classes. One brass encouraged the order of another. In no place is this clearer than Toruń, where the floor at the east end of the nave of St John's church is covered with indents in Tournai stone, mostly of separate inlay figures and canopies. These represented members of the local merchant families of Zoest, Allen, Loa, Wale and Werle.[21] Johann von Zoest was only one of a large collection. The incised slabs in Boston reflect a similar popularity. Many churches must have been practically paved with such brasses and incised slabs.

Certain Scottish indents at St John's, Perth; Whithorn Priory and Dundrennan Abbey reveal the use of separate inlay more strikingly than the brasses. An early fourteenth-century example from Dundrennan, depicting a knight (in surcoat) and his wife under canopies, is remarkably detailed. The faces and hands of both figures were inserted in alabaster, marble, or some other material requiring a specially deep indent.[22] These were certainly made in or around Tournai.

It is clear that Flemish brasses were not produced in this period by a single workshop. Documentary evidence and the proof of extensive production reveal the participation of a number of independent engravers. Some of these worked in brass or stone as customers required. Some worked individually, some in association, but most observed certain conventions and used similar patterns in their designs. Our consequent inability to discriminate between the products of particular centres, let alone workshops, justifies the convenient if over-simplified concept of the 'Flemish school'. Further research may enable more precise descriptions to be made. Yet in the meantime the origins of this superb metalwork should not be obscured. The marblers of the French borderland centered on Tournai, benefiting from French precendents and experiments, drawing on the decorative arts of both France and Germany and exploiting the raw material at their disposal, worked their slabs and brass inlays to a remarkable richness and technical perfection. In the first period (c. 1270-1330) separate inlay brass compositions were a major part of their product, as was appropriate to decorators of incised slabs. Nevertheless the immigration of craftsmen, aided by the close trading links between Tournai and the cities of West Flanders, together with the incentives to copy successful models, ensured that the business spread, first to Gent and Bruges and ultimately by the fifteenth century into Brabant. Moreover, as the prestige of these memorials increased so greater emphasis was given to the engraved metal. The rectangular plate superceded the separate inlay presentation in demand, though not so far as to exclude it. The precedents set and the conventions established in the early years were not forgotten, and continued to influence the craft to the close of the Middle Ages.

The North German controversy

It is fitting to conclude this chapter with a brief reference to a long-standing controversy to which a convincing answer has been made by Dr Cameron.[23] Macklin (1907, Chapter Five) doubted that these monuments came from Flanders, described them as "North German", and proposed Lübeck as their source. This view has been followed by modern writers.[24] Macklin, unaware of much of the evidence now available, believed them to be "unlike any brasses now existing in the Low Countries", and that both their distribution and those commemorated had North German rather than Flemish connections. None of these points have any substance and the brasses are dissimilar from North German brass and incised slab designs.[25]

The Mosan controversy

More recently it has been suggested by Trivick (1969, pp. 30-4) that the great reputation of the Mosan metalworkers points to that area rather than West Flanders as the source of the brasses. Unfortunately for his thesis there are neither relevant examples in the area of production nor any known contracts for brasses to be made there. It also implies that there were no skilled metalworkers elsewhere in Flanders, and he discounts the known trade in Tournai and Gent incised slabs by suggesting a dichotomy between the two crafts.[26]

While it is clear that marblers were active in Liège, producing incised slabs such as those at Gothem (1296 to 1358), Fooz (1407), and Hognoul (1457),[27] the last with brass inlays, a feature also found on a fine slab at Thys (1349). These slabs can be distinguished from the Tournai slabs by the inclusion of mica, the canopies are simpler and the figures less impressive, but they do possess a freedom of line and the faces are bolder and more natural than the Tournai and Gent figures. Any Mosan brasses would presumably share these characteristics.

A Mosan workshop would seem to be confirmed by the founder's grave slab of Godescalc de Morialmé at St Barthélmi, Liège. This consists of a high slab of dark stone, inlaid with blue and white tiles and an engraved latten inscription with the Evangelists symbols at the corners. The tiles seem to be part of the eleventh century memorial but the inscription records its removal to the choir in 1334 and was added then. The lettering is in bold Lombardics indistinguishable from those used on the brasses in dispute but the border is plain, there is no initial cross, and the worn symbols are different in treatment. In particular St Matthew is depicted as a bearded man with book and spear. If this is to be ascribed to a local, Mosan workshop, then the presumption must be against such an origin for the Flemish brasses.

Although no contracts have been found for these early brasses, the claim of the Tournai craftsmen is strong as their reputation even attracted orders from the French kings and the general character of their work is known from contracts for lost brasses. One of 1301 or 1311 describes in detail several of the peculiarities of these brasses: their canopies with tabernacles and brick work and inlays of alabaster. The stone used for the setting came from the quarries at Antoing or Chercq, a dark marble also used for the incised slabs.[28]

We may conclude that the splendid brasses known for over a century as Flemish were made in Tournai, almost certainly at Gent and perhaps Bruges as well, and that their origin is no longer a matter for speculation.

5. French and Flemish brasses, 1365-1460

In the course of the century, from 1360-1460, brasses in England became a much used form of monument. Similarly, on the Continent the number of centres active in this craft increased, and brasses are found in greater quantity and more widely dispersed. This and the following chapter describe Continental developments and achievements during the same period, against which English brasses may be compared.

Late fourteenth-century Flemish brasses

The remarkable compositions described in the previous chapter set the pattern of Flemish brasses until the close of the fourteenth century, and their influence did not entirely disappear until the sixteenth century. The figures of Roger Thornton and wife, dated 1411, at St Nicholas formerly at All Saints, Newcastle-upon-Tyne, are of the same conventional type already described (*The Craft,* Fig. 143). On most brasses hands are expressed in the "flattened" fashion at Toruń, and faces and drapery retain their well established strong and formal presentation.

Men in armour

There are only two military brasses from the period 1365 to 1420 which in the author's opinion should be certainly attributed to the Flemish workshops, though one English palimpsest is sufficiently large to be considered as a third.

Bonifacio Rotario, 1368, Susa Cathedral (Fig. 50)
Ralph de Knevynton, 1370, Aveley (Fig. 38)
Palimsest fragments of an armed man, c. 1375, Constantine, (obv. 1574) and South Weald (obv. 1567).

The Susa brass is a unique composition, being in the form of a triptych, with a central panel and two hinged side panels all of latten. The central panel depicts the Blessed Virgin and Christ Child seated beneath a canopy. On the panel to her right, St George, armed and riding on a horse partially protected with horse armour, strikes down the dragon. Bonifacio is engraved kneeling on the left hand panel, presented presumably by St Boniface. He is armed but bareheaded, his helmet above and shield set beside him. The design and technique of execution is entirely consistent with Flemish treatment. This is the sole brass now existing taking this triptych form, and it continues to serve its original purpose though removed from a chapel in the Rocca Melone. It is accordingly inaccessible to close examination, but a cast has been made which is in the possession of the cathedral authorities.

The Aveley brass is small, the rectangular plate containing the figure and canopy measuring only 51cm by 23cm. The detail of the engraving is good but the proportions of the figure poor. The knight wears a breastplate and skirt of hoops or lames covered with material, as revealed by the numerous studs, and long guard-chains from the breast are attached to his sword and dagger. The canopy is well finished but contains no subsidiary figures. The inscription is recorded on a rectangular plate extending well beyond the width of the main design, and reads:

Hic iacet Radulphus de Kneuynton' obitus idem die Jouis ante festum s*ancti* Nicholai Episcopi (5 December) an*no* do*mini* mill*esi*mo. CCC.LXX. L*ite*ra do*mini*cal*i* f.

Not only is the exactness of the date unusual in that the Sunday letter of the Gregorian calendar is recorded, but the whole inscription in its style of engraving and arrangement appears to be an English addition. The indents of two separate inlay shields remain above, which is highly unusual for a Flemish rectangular brass. It is suggested that a Flemish figure plate was combined with English accessories.[1]

The Constantine fragment, which shows the upper half of a man in armour, with an embroidered cushion and attendant angels, is similar but of superior workmanship. The Essex fragments show parts of the belt and legs.[2] All three of these military figures are depicted bare-headed.

An outstandingly interesting military figure was that of Michiel van Assenede c. 1400, commemorated with his two wives at St Walburge, Bruges (Fig. 44). The detailed drawing illustrated by Gaillard fortunately preserves a good record of this destroyed monument, though it is not clear whether the brass or the drawing was left unfinished. The small shield on the aventail and the full sleeved coat were very unusual features.

An important brass engraved c. 1395, formerly at Heere near St Trond, is now in the Musées Royaux d'Art et d'Histoire at Bruxelles. It commemorates Sir Jan d. 1332, and Sir Gerard van Heere d. 1398, both of whom are depicted in armour, bare-headed, and lying within elaborate canopies filled with subsidiary figures (Fig. 56). Both wear embroidered jupons and have shields placed at the hip. The detail of the work is well executed but the design of the brass is stiff and heavy, indeed rather clumsy. The faces of the two knights lack conventional Flemish treatment, and neither the background nor canopy entirely accord with examples so far examined. Though this brass is perhaps an uncharacteristic example of Flemish design, some Belgian authorities are of the opinion that it is a product of Mosan craftsmen.[3] The figures bear considerable similarity to sculptured knights at Hal, and to the incised slab of Gerard de Gothem 1358, at Gothem. There is sufficient probability in this Mosan attribution to set this brass apart from others of its period.

Civilians

Brasses to civilians vary greatly in detail and scale. None is the size of the earlier mercantile brasses, but all are of good quality. The following is a complete list:

A civilian, c.1365 under canopy, very small, Gt Bowden (On rev. of inscr. 1403)

A civilian and a priest, 1368, under canopies, small, Museum de Bijloke, Gent (rev. of inscr. 1604)

Gillis van Namain, c.1370 under canopy. St Jacques, Bruges (rev. of Pedro de Valencia and family 1615). About two thirds of the earlier brass can be assembled from the reverses[4]

Bruno von Warendorp, 1369, Marienkirche, Lübeck. Large separate inlay figure

Martin Ferrades de las Continas, 1373, under canopy. Museo Arqueológico Nacional, Madrid (from Castro Urdiales) (Fig. 46)

Thomas de Topclyffe and wife, 1391, under canopies, Topcliffe

Pedro Zatrylla, c.1400, The Louvre, Paris (from Solzona, Spain) (Fig. 43)

Roger Thornton and wife, 1411, under canopies, St Nicholas, Newcastle-upon-Tyne

Lysbet van den Dylis 1391, and son 1418, under canopies, small, Museum de Bijloke, Gent (on reverse of inscription 15th century) (Fig.39)

All the male figures are dressed in tunic and undertunic, hose and shoes. Those at Gent, Bruges, Madrid and Topcliffe wear a mantle and also a hood. The short sword is well illustrated on the Topcliffe brass. The Great Bowden figure is very attractive, though slightly out of proportion in the manner of the armed figure at Aveley. Long tippets hang from the short sleeves of his overtunic and the shoulder-piece of his hood has a dagged fringe. The finest of these figures is undoubtedly that at Madrid, whose flowing mantle and long beard are in the best fourteenth-century Flemish style; furthermore, the whole brass is in superb condition.

Three lost brasses from England of which rubbings or an adequate record remain are those of Simon Walshe and wife c.1370, St Alkmund's, Shrewsbury; Robert Attelath and wife 1376, St Margaret's, King's Lynn; and Ellen Freville 1380, Little Shelford.[5] The first and last were small rectangular plates with figures and canopies; Ellen Freville's brass was of doubtful origin, and may have been French or English work, influenced by a foreign model. The second was a very large quadrangular composition. Craven Ord in 1870 made a reversed impression of Robert Attelath himself, but of his wife he noted 'as her dress did not differ from those in the Quire, I did not take her'.

Ecclesiastics

Apart from the priest in mass vestments with the Gent civilian, there are only three brasses to ecclesiastics or religious illustrating the extremes of Flemish grandeur and modest beauty. The memorial of Bishops Gottfried and Friedrich von Bülow, in Schwerin cathedral, is the largest and most elaborate of all brasses extant. It was engraved about the time of Bishop Friedrich's death in 1375, and was probably inspired by the brass of two earlier bishops of Schwerin of the same family. Its immense size, 3.84m. by 1.93m. facilitated the execution of a most ambitious design. The two recumbent figures, their eyes half closed in death and their hands crossed downwards, are robed in gorgeous vestments. The orphreys of the chasubles are decorated with shields of arms, human figures and heads, the maniples with angels playing musical instruments, and the orphreys of the albs with grotesque beasts and prophets. The howling monster motif, commonly found in earlier background designs, appears as the base pattern of a chasuble, and wyverns writhe beneath the bishops' feet (Fig. 40). In the base panels wodehowses carouse in a feast (Fig. 41), and seize a lady for their hairy king, while a mounted knight follows in hot pursuit. The canopy shafts filled with apostles and prophets rise on either side of this profane base. In the centre shaft between the figures is a representation of the martyrdom of St Sebastian. Angels, supporting the cushions behind the bishops' heads, lead the eye to the tabernacles above with their angelic choirs and the Deity receiving the souls. The whole design is surrounded by a border inscription forming, by its curves, the branches of a Jesse tree. The symbols of the Evangelists appropriately occupy the corners of the plate. This fantastic monument is the last of the great series of which the royal brass at Ringsted is the first. A slightly later brass of similar splendour was that of Bishop Wicbold von Kulm 1398, formerly at Altenberg near Köln. The delightful base panels of this brass represented wodehowses fighting a lion and a bear and catching a stag, and the triumphant return of the hunters carrying the bear and riding the stag towards the welcoming arms of a hairy female. This monument was destroyed in the nineteenth century, but a rubbing is preserved in the Rheinisches Landesmuseum.[6]

The nearly lifesize separate inlay figure of the Yorkshire priest Simon de Wenslagh (d.1395, engr. c.1375) is another example of the most expert Flemish craftsmanship (Fig. 42). The brass is laid in a large slab of Tournai marble, from which the border inscription and medallions have been lost. The priest lies in the repose of death, his hands folded downwards and a chalice placed on his breast. The orphreys of the chasuble, the amice, stole, maniple and apparel of the alb are all engraved with foliage patterns and grotesques, and the surface of the alb has been hatched for inlay. Two angels support a cushion behind his head. His face is a purely conventional representation, the stubble carefully patterned and lips large and recessed. Simon died in 1395, and the ornate and stiff treatment of features and folds indicate a date no earlier than the last quarter of the century, though the brass was probably made in his lifetime.

In complete contrast the brass of the Béguine Griele van Ruwescuere 1410, in the Béguinage, Bruges, measures only 0.43m. by 0.27m. She is simply dressed in her habit, veil, wimple and mantle with a reticule hung on her arm (*The Craft,* Fig. 27). Her canopy is of delicate but simple architectural form, the border inscription bold in style but irregular in width.[7]

The last major brass of this group is the sombre but dignified shrouded figure of Wouter Copman (1387), at the cathedral, Bruges (Fig. 47). The shroud completely covers the deceased apart from the lower part of the face. Four angels bear scrolls, two above and two below.[8]

Arrangement and composition

While the costume of the Newcastle figures indicates a changing fashion, it is in the backgrounds and arrangement of canopy work that transition is most clear. In most of the canopied brasses background decoration is confined within the canopy itself; outside the limits of the shafts or tabernacles the plate is plain. Likewise the turrets of the tabernacles cut into the border inscriptions, giving the semblance of a third dimension. Perspective effects are attempted, not only in the deep canopy vaults but in the shafts, as on the brass of Gillis van Namain, where saints appear in profile from the sides of the shafts. One saint displays the curious feature of a halo as viewed from the back, which being solid conceals the head behind the disc. More significant are the brasses of Pedro Zatrylla and Wouter Copman. In both of these the figure rests against a diaper background, upon which attendant angels are similarly imposed. The figures lie clearly away from their setting. Transition from the fourteenth century decorative pattern towards the formal curtain design of the late fifteenth century may be recognised. The merry base panels end with the Schwerin and lost Altenberg scenes. At Newcastle-upon-Tyne the canopy base is formed by a row of canopied niches, within which are set the figures of Roger Thornton's children.

A lozenge with a circular inscription, surrounding an angel set against a background of stars, commemorates Machtelt Roela(n)ts (1396). The symbols of the Evangelists are engraved in the corners. This attractive though rather worn Flemish composition has only recently come to public notice, and is in private possession in Aachen, though originally laid at the great Béguinage in Louvain.[9]

Other Flemish brasses and fragments of the period include three unusual and controversial examples. The heraldic plate with helm, cock crest and shield of arms to Diederic Brant van Campen 1368, in the Universitets Historiskas Museet at Lund appears too plain a composition for such an origin (Fig. 45). Yet the inscription lettering bears a semblance to that normally adopted, the hatching of the crest and shield is very carefully done unlike other Baltic examples, and the inscription is recorded in Flemish. It would seem correct to include this as Flemish, though being of a type of which there are no other comparable subjects.

The engraved latten panels, fixed to the sides of the tomb or shrine of St Henry of Finland d.1158, at Nousisainen, are of greater importance, and have confused the judgement of scholars.[10] The memorial or cenotaph consists of a high tomb, erected in honour of the Saint by Bishop Johannes Petri shortly before his death in 1370. The top is inlaid with a large brass, prepared in the fifteenth century by order of Bishop Magnus Olsson Tavast of Abo (now Turku); and representing the Saint with the kneeling figure of the donor. The sides of the tomb are also inlaid with plates depicting scenes from the life of St Henry, and recording his posthumous miracles. The invasion of Finland by the Christian King of Sweden (*The Craft*, Fig. 145), the life and murder of the saint, his burial (*The Craft*, Fig. 144) and miracles, are all fully recorded. The battle scenes between the Swedes and Finns show warships, a medieval cannon, and an array of glaives, axes and other staff weapons very rarely illustrated on brasses.

In spite of the apparent fourteenth century style of these panels, it has become established to date the brasses to the fifteenth century, in order to explain the character of the top plate. Dr Cameron has shown however that this is not necessary, and is most probably erroneous.[11] Bishop Johannes is recorded as having "decorated" as well as constructed the tomb, and metallurgical analysis has shown marked differences between the consistency of the side and top plates. The panels should accordingly be regarded as part of the initial work, the top plate being a later attempt by Bishop Tavast to improve the memorial, and include himself upon it. The style of the work is consistent with Flemish treatment, as is also the scheme of decoration.[12]

Yet another brass, and one of remarkable interest, should in the author's opinion be attributed to Flemish craftsmen. This is the fine and curious inscription to the memory of Brother Estavao Vasques Pimental, at Leça do Balio (Fig.48) dated 1374. The plate is engraved with an inscription in relief lettering, bordered at the sides with saints under canopies, at the base with shields, grotesques and symbols of the Evangelists, and at the top with representations of the Holy Trinity, the Annunciation and the heads of Christ and the twelve Apostles. The form of the lettering is unusual, but the decoration is entirely consistent with Flemish models. This brass has been attributed to French craftsmen, which, while possible, is unlikely in view of the other Flemish brasses in Spain and Portugal.[13] There can be little doubt that the design was influenced by the decoration of illuminated manuscripts, as is indicated by a Matins page in a late fourteenth-century Book of Hours, (Fig. 49).

Three fragments from the close of the fourteenth century deserve mention. The first is a medallion with the seated figure of a prophet at Borgloon. The second at Tolleshunt Darcy is a very pleasing fragment of a border inscription decorated with representations of apostles and the Blessed Virgin Mary and inscribed with clauses from the creed. This is a palimpsest with similar work on the reverse. The third is an armed foot and part of a lion from a large separate inlay brass formerly in the cathedral of Iona, traditionally ascribed to Macleod of Macleod.[14]

Early fifteenth-century Flemish brasses

The first half of the fifteenth century, during which a large number of brasses must have been engraved, is now numerically poorly represented. In addition to the Thornton brass at Newcastle-upon-Tyne, and the small van den Dylis brass at Gent, there are three important rectangular plates at Bruges, and four smaller votive compositions at Basel, Nivelles, Tournai and in the Louvre, Paris. At Nousisainen, Finland, is the elaborate cenotaph of St Henry having a top plate from this period.

The three brasses at Bruges are:

Joris de Munter and wife, in shrouds, 1439, the cathedral (*The Craft*, Fig. 147)
Sir Maertin van der Capelle, 1452, the cathedral (*Ibid.*, Fig 148)
Kateline D'Aut, with her brother and 'her good angel', 1460, St Jacques (Fig. 54)

Joris de Munter's brass was evidently influenced by that of Wouter Copman, the two deceased being enveloped in their shrouds and lying with attendant angels against a background of medallions filled with flowers, birds and birds' legs with ostrich feathers. The broadly chiselled drapery lines, common to most early Flemish brasses, are used with excellent effect. Sir Maertin van der Capelle is engraved in a rather less stylised fashion, and his face could have some resemblance to the deceased. He is shown bareheaded and in armour, which is partly concealed by a heraldic coat with close fitting sleeves. His feet rest on a lion and a great achievement of arms lies behind and above his head. A pavement in exaggerated perspective forms a base while the background is worked with small dogs and motto 'MOY'. The border inscription is surrounded by a secondary border of horse bits (perhaps the Capelle badge).

The brass of Kateline D'Aut is a beautiful and touching design, the young girl standing with her brother and the angel. She is in bridal costume with flowing hair and coronet, he in civilian tunic with a dagger. The background is finely diapered and the transport of souls by angels is depicted above.

Though smaller in scale, the votive compositions are of equal richness and interest. Votive panels of incised stone, carved stone relief or engraved brass, were made in large numbers at Tournai, and many such stone memorials are still to be found on the walls of the cathedral and churches there.[15] It is likely from their general stylistic resemblance that these surviving brasses were made in Tournai workshops. They commemorate the following:

Foundations of Duchess Isabella of Portugal, wife of Duke Philip of Burgundy, c.1450, Historisches Museum, Basel (*The Craft,* Fig. 149).

Jean Moüen, wife and family, 1453, The Louvre, Paris (*Ibid.*, Fig. 152)

Jehans de Dours with wife and family c.1454, St Brice, Tournai (Fig. 52).

Foundation of Abbess Marguerite de Scornay, c.1460, Nivelles (*Ibid.,* Fig. 151).

The first is an outstanding example of Flemish work, and a brass of unusual importance. A large part of the plate consists of a record of foundations in raised letters, and states the foundations to have been made in 1433, though the money involved was in fact paid in instalments until 1438 and many of the liturgical objects granted were not handed over until 1446. The upper half of the brass consists of a pictorial panel. The centre is occupied by a Pieta, the Duke and Duchess (showing a rare side view of the horned headdress) kneeling on either side with their patron saints and family grouped behind them. Charles kneels behind his father, both wearing armour, tabards, and the collar of the Order of the Golden Fleece of which the Duke was the founder. The representation of deceased children with crosses in their hands is a typically Flemish treatment. The tapestry-like background is partially filled with shields of arms and an achievement. The latter includes the shield of arms of Duke Philip, encircled by the collar of the Order of the Golden Fleece, and has above the Duke's motto 'Aultre naray'. The arms of the Duchess are set within an enclosure of palings, which, together with the motto 'tant que je vive', signifies fidelity. The centre of the plate has suffered damage but the overall condition of the brass is good. Traces of blue, red, black and white inlays still exist in the lines. The carved frame of the brass is original, having been discovered in 1929. The stone has been identified as Tournai marble.

This commemoration has been described in detail by Pierre Quarré, Conservator of the Dijon museums. He cites conclusive evidence that this brass is but one of an original six laid at various Carthusian houses, which benefitted from the Duchess's piety. All were apparently of the same design, and this was certainly the case with those at Champmol-les-Dijon and Mont-Renaud near Noyon.[16] On the fair assumption that all were made together these brasses were not engraved earlier than 1448, the date of the foundation at Mont-Renaud. In all probability the model for the designs was a panel painting, which still survives in a seventeenth-century copy at the château of Montmirey.[17*] This painting shows the group exactly as at Basel, the only differences being the stylistic modifications of the later artist, the position of the head of Christ, and the heraldic mantle of the Duchesss (*The Craft*, Fig. 150).

There can be little doubt that the painting, evidently a portrait group, was made before the brasses. Duke Charles is shown as of twelve or thirteen years of age, and the faces on the Basel brass are far too stylised to provide the basis of a real likeness. The identity of the artist can only be guessed in the absence of the original work. It is nevertheless probable that no less a person than Roger Van der Weyden was responsible. This great artist was Duke Philip's most favoured painter in Bruxelles, portrait painter of several of the outstanding members of the Order of the Golden Fleece, and was employed between 1455 and 1459 on monumental design and decoration at the Duke's direction.[18] It is accordingly suggested that Roger used the drawings from one of his own approved works when these plates were required. This proposition is further supported by the brass, which gives every indication of a Tournai provenance. Roger was born in Tournai and retained his contact with the leading masters of that place. Perhaps in this excellent work the skills of Roger Van der Weyden and the engraver Alard Gènois are happily combined.

The brass of Jean Moüen and wife is smaller and of less expert workmanship (*The Craft*, Fig. 152), though the composition is full and decorative. The plate is in perfect condition and was formerly in the Onghena collection, Gent. The overall arrangement recalls the pen drawing by the painter known as the Master of Flèmalle, depicting a family group kneeling before the Blessed Virgin.[19] The Tournai brass is of similar workmanship, though having the Holy Trinity in the centre and Saints Catherine and John the Baptist in attendance[20] (Fig. 52).

The fourth brass is an exquisite plate, possibly by the same hand as that at Basel (*The Craft*, Fig. 151). The Abbess in her habit and mantle and carrying her crozier kneels before the Blessed Virgin and Child, supported by St Margaret wearing a large hat and attended by her dragon. The background is exceptionally rich, the Evangelists' symbols are set at the corners, but the enamel was destroyed in 1940. The date of the brass is not certain. The foundation commemorated was made in 1461, but the brass may have been made in anticipation. Even though it is more probable that the execution is very slightly later than the period in question, the affinities with that at Basel justify its inclusion at this point.

The remaining example with figures to be mentioned, that of St Henry of Finland at Nousisainen, is a most interesting brass, whether judged on its own merits, or its place in the development of Flemish engraving. The memorial or cenotaph as described consists of a high tomb, its top inlaid with the main plate, depicting St Henry with his feet placed on his murderer Lalli, and kneeling beside him the figure of Bishop Magnus Olsson Tavast of Abo (Fig. 55). The sides are also inlaid with plates depicting scenes from the life of the Saint. The origin and date of the top plate is open to question. St Henry is engraved in distinctly fourteenth-century Flemish style. His canopy likewise, its shafts filled with saints, four of whom are female, follows well established Flemish conventions, as does also the decorative border to the inscription. There is nevertheless a stiffness in the treatment of the tabernacle, niches and tracery, which is closer to the Newcastle-upon-Tyne brass and later compositions than earlier examples. A revealing detail is the figure of Christ, standing within the tabernacle. The two censing angels beside him are derived from a fourteenth-century pattern, but he himself is evidently of considerably later design. There are moreover errors in execution, without precedent in earlier Flemish work. Bishop Tavast administered the bishopric from 1412-1450. He resigned in the last year and died two years later. It would seem a reasonable presumption from its appearance that this elaboration of the existing cenotaph was undertaken as a devotional act towards the close of his period of office, and may be dated c.1440.

There can be little doubt on the question of origin that this is Flemish work. As has been shown in *The Craft*, Chapter Nine, the fourteenth-century conventions were carried on in the Flemish workshops into the last quarter of the fifteenth century, and the execution of the brass is comparable to that of several fragments from Flemish churches, now on the reverse of brasses in England. It is not impossible that this is a skilfull German copy, but there is no reason to prefer such an origin.

A few well-engraved inscriptions survive in Belgium, being records of pious foundations. Three at Notre Dame, Hal, are dated c.1423, 1448 and 1458; another of c.1430 is at St Sauveur, Jollain Merlin and another of 1449 at Warcoing. An interesting inscription with two shields of arms is that of Sir Alexander de Irvyn of Drum d.1457, and his wife, St Nicholas, East Church, Aberdeen. The relief lettering and ornamental band dividing the plate strongly indicate Flemish origin, or at least Continental as against English workmanship. The dates are left blank and the brass was presumably made c.1450.

Gent and Tournai engravers

None of the brasses mentioned is marked or signed and the makers are unknown. It is, however, to this period that the Polish record for a Flemish brass from Bruges applies. Evidence of the activity of Gent engravers is substantial.[21] In 1378 Messire van Sevenberghe contracted with a marbler Jan van Meyere to make a slab with a border of latten for the church of the Jacobins at Antwerpen. Jan died in 1382 and was followed by his son, another Jan, who owned a house in the Saystrate in 1414. Jan agreed in 1418 with Simon de Formelis to provide a large stone and brass for Madam de Lovendeghem, to be placed in the choir of Saint-Michel, Gent. The tomb was to follow a design already provided, and was to be similar to that of Jan Daens in the same church. The agreed price was fourteen pounds. In 1423 Jan prepared figures for Loonis van der Moure and wife, modelled on those of Willem van Ravenscot and Daniel van den Holle, and a border of latten, like that on the tomb of Bloc van Steelant. This was to be placed in the church of St John, Gent. After 1430 a third Jan of the family apparently carried on the craft. Five of his contracts have been recorded. One of these, of 1435, was for Jan van der Zype, requiring a separate inlay figure in mass vestments with two angels holding shields of arms and a border inscription with the Evangelists' symbols at the corners. Another of 1446 ordered a border inscription with arms and medallions in latten to be inlaid in Antoing stone for Monfrant Alarts.

Hugo Goethals, an apprentice of the van Meyere's, can be identified as an independent craftsman between 1426 and 1458. He was required, in 1429, to make a figure brass for Sir Jan van Rokeghem on a stone nine and three quarter feet by five and three quarter feet, and various inscription plates in the years 1433 and 1437. It was Hugo who in 1442 made the brass of Sir Wouter van Mullem described in *The Craft,* similar to the tomb of Simon Clocman. In 1444 he contracted to make a large figure brass for Sir Jan van Vaernewyc.[22]

Towards the close of this period Tournai evidence records the fame and achievements of Alard Génois, who was made a burgher of Tournai in 1451.[23] He engraved several brasses between the years 1457 and 1464 for the Abbot of Saint-Aubert de Cambrai and canons of Cambrai cathedral. The description of an elaborate composition is given in *The Craft,* Chapter Eight, Appendix III. It is interesting to note that Roger van de Weyden completed an altarpiece for the same abbot in 1459,[24] and it is possible that the 'patron en papier' of the votive group brass of the abbot's parents was drawn in his workshop. Alard may be presumed to have had a prosperous market in Tournai itself.

It is impossible at present to ascribe most of the existing brasses of this period to any one of these great centres. The peculiarities of the workshops, if any, cannot be identified. Antoing marble was apparently used in both Tournai and Gent and very possibly in Bruges. It must be hoped that documentary evidence relating to some of them will be traced. The brass of the Heere brothers is perhaps a lone example of brass engraving from the Meuse towns.

French brasses

The achievement of the workshops of Normandy and Paris remains a serious void, with the drawings of Gaignières as the only substantial guide. A detail of a soul wearing a mitre, held in the arms of Abraham, is probably French, and is now in the Victoria and Albert Museum, London.[25] More revealing of French treatment is the brass in three plates to Philippe de Mézières, Chancellor of Cyprus d. 1405, who retired to the monastry of the Célestins in Paris in 1380 (*The Craft*, Fig. 153-4). This brass is of unusual interest, and of undoubted French work, showing the deceased kneeling to an enthroned Madonna accompanied by St Philip. Philippe's face is portrayed with notable naturalism. The inscription in relief lettering is on another plate, and on a third is a remarkable representation of the crucifixion. The most striking element is the crucifix itself, which appears to be a twelfth-century reliquary, inlaid with jewels, and altogether out of keeping in style with the beginning of the fifteenth century. The groups around the cross are portrayed with feeling, and the iconography of the sun and the moon is curious. This valuable monument, most probably from the church of the Célestins in Paris, destroyed in 1847, is in the Mayer van den Bergh Museum, Antwerpen. A small undated plate of c. 1456, showing the figure of Bishop John Avantage kneeling before the Blessed Virgin and Christchild and introduced by his patron saint St John, is in Amiens cathedral (Fig. 53). The Bishop is vested in a cope, and his mitre is placed on the ground beside him. This brass is reputedly French, but is very similar in workmanship to presumed Flemish plates such as that at Nivelles to Abbess de Scornay. It would nonetheless be rash to assert a clear distinction between Flemish and French art in this region. Dr Cameron *(1970)* refers to a small figured plate at Dargnies to canon Guillaume Faulcqueur (1433), depicting the deceased in cassock, kneeling at a desk, and a small dedication plate of 1446, formerly at Tours, is preserved in the collection of the Society of Antiquaries, London.

These surviving brasses appear unimportant in comparison to a series of large quadrangular compositions to ecclesiastics and noblemen, copied by Gaignières. The features of four will suffice to record their styles. Abbot Jean de la Bernichière 1375, from the Abbey of St Aubin at Angers, was represented in rich pontifical mass vestments though bareheaded, and with his feet trampling on a dragon. His canopy, supported by figured shafts, had a straight gabled pediment. Apart from two shields the background behind the figure was entirely plain.[26] The highly elaborate design for Abbot Paschal Huguenot 1399, from the Abbey de la Couture at Le Mans (Fig. 51), was more comparable with Flemish examples. The Abbot, mitred and in mass vestments with a scroll issuing from his hands, lay against a background of floral patterns. His canopy, supported by broad shafts containing tiers of double niches, consisted of a rising cluster of tabernacles, enshrining Christ holding the soul and attendant saints and angels. Bishop Jean d'Arsonval 1416, formerly at the Cistercian church, Paris, was significantly different in style, though retaining the canopy supported by saint-filled shafts. The figure in pontifical mass vestments was traditional though apparently more natural in treatment. The canopy itself was represented in careful perspective, especially the groined vault above the head, and the subsidiary figures were set upon rather than within the shafts.[27]

An especially notable French brass of the period, also treated in a three-dimensional manner, was that at the church of the Célestins at Marcoussy. It commemorated Rémon Raguier, a member of the Royal Council who died in 1421

(Fig. 57). He was represented in armour with a tabard slit up at the sides, and resting his feet on a large muzzled dog or bear. The canopy with its vault, sacred figures and weepers was designed to impart the impression of depth. The illustration indicates the grandeur of these destroyed French memorials.[28]

6. German and Silesian brasses, 1365-1460

Monumental brass engraving became more strongly established east of the Rhine during the early fifteenth century, and by the end of this period the main workshop centres in the Rhineland, in Central Germany, on the Baltic and in Silesia can be identified with greater certainty

Central German brasses

A considerable collection of brasses is at Nordhausen, a group of fourteenth-century plates only surpassed in number for their period by the Cobham series in England. They are at present displayed in the Meyenburg Museum, though laid in the first instance in the Martinikirche. There are altogether eight brasses, all but two of which are of quite small size. With one exception they represent members of the von Urbach and von Werther families, though in the following list the names have been recorded with regard to the spelling of the inscription:

Henrich von Urbech, 1394, kneeling in civil dress with scroll
Jacob von Immenhausen, 1395, kneeling priest with chalice (*The Craft,* Fig. 156)
Hermann von Werther, 1395, kneeling in civil dress (Fig. 58)
Katerina Verter, 1397, kneeling in widow's dress (*The Craft,* Fig. 157)
Hinrich Urbech, 1397, kneeling in civil dress
Heinrich von Werther, 1397, in civil dress with scroll, mutilated (*The Craft,* Fig. 158)
Lower half of civilian (a von Werther), c. 1400, kneeling in civil dress
Johann and Symo Segemund, c. 1410, kneeling in civil dress.

All these brasses appear to be the products of one workshop, probably sited in Thuringen, and their design has affinities to that of some incised and low relief slabs at Erfurt.[1*] The figures are set against hatched backgrounds, and under canopies of unusual form, which probably had their origin in painted glass. Crested helms are introduced with shields either separately or as achievements. The engraving of all is competent. A remarkable feature is the extravagant forms of the male civilian dress, displaying long pointed shoes, immense cuffs with dagged edges, rich belts and a hat with a large feather. In many respects the most interesting figure is that of Heinrich von Werther. The lower part is gone but the remainder shows the deceased in prayer under a canopy, with the Dextera Dei extended in blessing from a trefoil below the soffit perhaps symbolising the Holy Trinity. Heinrich wears an ornament of pendant bells from his girdle, and an elaborate hornfessel similarly decorated with bells. This was in origin the leather strap worn over the shoulder to carry a hunting horn, but during the latter part of the fourteenth century it was adopted in parts of Germany as an article of dress. In this case the leather was presumably cut into two bands of antler form, held together at intervals with crowns of brass or silver. Hermann von Werther has bells decorating his belt and a broad upstanding collar. This unusual display of pretentious civilian clothing is perhaps explained on two grounds. In general the passing of the plagues of the mid-fourteenth century led to widespread expressions of relief and vanity, as in the words of the Chronicle of Limburg: 'After the pestilence the world started again to live and be merry, and they made new garments'. Furthermore, the von Werthers secured their prosperity through trading in oriental fabrics, and were prominent in the local guild of Merchant Tailors. As well as munificent benefactors to the hospital at Nordhausen they were probably fashion setters in the town, a distinction recorded in their memorials.

The latest of these brasses is by far the largest and has some peculiarities of treatment. The two figures appear to be swaying towards each other and above their heads two happy looking angels swing large censers. The faces of the brothers have character and their hair is profusely curled. The border inscription with large Evangelists' symbols at the corners is engraved on separate plates, the words being divided by a wealth of extraordinary dragons. The priest, Jacob von Immenhausen, is depicted in the act of celebrating mass, and is the only main figure on brasses so to be shown (*The Craft,* Fig. 156).[2]

An important brass, having some but no close resemblance to this group, is that of Bishop Rupprecht von Ravensberg, 1394, at Paderborn cathedral (Fig. 59). Rupprecht's brass has several distinctive features. The figure lies vested in a surplice with an almuce lying folded over his shoulders. Two angels support a mitre over his head indicating the fact that he was never consecrated, though he administered the diocese for four years. Beneath his richly shod feet lie two knights, one wearing a visored bascinet, the other wearing a broad-rimmed war hat with aventail. A small triple canopy contains figures of angels with musical instruments, and six more like angels occupy the side shafts. A very light appearance is imparted to the canopy as a patterned background continues behind the whole composition. An earlier bishop, Heinrich Spiegel von Dessenberg 1380, is commemorated at Paderborn by a large separate inlay figure in pontifical mass vestments. The treatment of the figure is bold and the engraving deep. His head rests on a large cushion, and he holds a crozier and a clasped book. A knight and a lion are under his feet.[3]

Another bishop, Lambert von Brun 1399, at Bamberg (Fig. 60), is represented in an animated separate inlay design. He rises in half effigy above a large shield, wearing the pallium and with a cross as well as the crozier, the insignia of an archbishop, a privilege granted to the see of Bamberg. A much mutilated figure of a priest with a chalice c. 1390 is at Erfurt cathedral, (Fig. 61). Parts of the figure have apparently been recut, and the lower third is lost. A triple canopy is set against a background of fleurs-de-lys. The most important feature of this brass is that the figure is placed in semi-profile, and is the earliest noted German example of this arrangement, which became very popular in the fifteenth century.

Three brasses to ecclesiastics of the early fifteenth century are:

Canon Eckhart von Hanensee, 1405, Hildesheim cathedral
Herman Schindeleyb, 1427, Erfurt cathedral
Bishop Johannes II of Naumburg, c. 1434, Zeitz (Fig. 64)

All three figures are represented under canopies in semi-profile, the first two having slanting shields placed at their feet. Canon Hanensee bears a Gospel book with a representation of the Lord in majesty on a rainbow on the binding. He wears a dalmatic over his amice and alb, and an academic cap on his rather comical head.[4] Schindeleyb is in mass vestments. In the tabernacle of his canopy appears a figure of Christ holding His Sacred Heart. The brass is now badly corroded having been moved to an open cloister. The third brass is more important. Bishop Johannes is well engraved in pontifical mass vestments holding a crozier and book. His vestments show several interesting and unusual details, in particular the amice inscribed 'AVE MARIA', and the infulae of the mitre which are clearly defined. It is, however, the background setting which is most significant. The Bishop stands under a canopy of simple gothic form, though the shafts are rounded columns, entwined by a decorative spiral. The vault of the canopy and the tiled floor below are represented in deep perspective. Behind the figure falls an embroidered curtain with a fringe. The monument conveys the impression of a room within which the Bishop stands, and presents the earliest known example of what may be termed the standard type of German brass, later brilliantly executed by the Vischers of Nürnberg. It is a design which in a simpler form can be recognized in the two Erfurt brasses but is almost fully developed in this monument. Memorial brass engravers in central Germany were at the close of this period on the threshold of remarkable achievements.

Brasses from Baltic workshops

The trading cities of the Baltic offered excellent markets for the sale of Flemish monuments. They also offered a profitable business to local engravers of brasses and slabs. None of these engravers has so far been identified, but it is clear that Lübeck was the main craft centre, though other cities such as Gdańsk were probably involved. North German brasses during this period are distinguished by the grandiose scale of their compositions combined with a very uneven standard of execution. Casting of the plate itself seems to have been poorly carried out, as most of the larger brasses are constructed of numerous irregular shaped pieces, many of very small size. The majority of these brasses are of separate inlay type, and in two cases the canopies are incised upon the slab. A peculiarity of northern design is the large scale of shields and Evangelists' symbols, and the relative unimportance of canopy work.

The only known military brass is at Nowemiasto Lubawskie near Borodnica, and is by far the most interesting monument of this group (*The Craft*, Fig. 160). It commemorates Sir Kuno von Liebensteyn, Bailiff of Brattian 1391. The origin of this brass has been discussed in *The Craft*, and its attribution by K. Wróblewska to Master Peter of the Marienburg, Court Painter of the Teutonic Order.

Sir Kuno was a highly regarded knight and adviser to the Grand Master Winrich von Kniprode. He is depicted in all the panoply of his rank. The Order's crusading cross is emblazoned on his jupon, on a large pavise-shaped shield, and on the left shoulder of his mantle, which is worn over his armour. Nine angels fly around him bearing four achievements of arms and the scroll 'Her Kune de Libensteen'. Kuno is represented as bareheaded and his aged, full-bearded face is almost certainly appropriate to him if not an attempted portrait. The long-tailed lion and dogs at his feet are an unusual combination, while some of the conventional flowers on the grassy mound are of familiar Flemish pattern. The design of a recumbent figure with flying attendant angels set against a background without a canopy, had Flemish precedents at this period. Wouter Copman at Bruges is an example. It is very possible that the artist concerned obtained ideas from an imported monument, though such a reference did not influence the treatment of the design which is essentially Prussian. The variety of plates forming this fine memorial are typical of brasses from the Baltic region. The smallest plate measures 6 by 8cm.

It is appropriate to mention in connection with this brass an engraved silver gilt reliquary, made at Elblag in 1388 for the Grand Master Thielo Dagister von Lorich. The reliquary was captured by the Poles at Grünewald and is now preserved in the military museum at Warszawa. The covers of the small reliquary are engraved with a representation of Christ surrounded by the emblems of His Passion, and a representation of the Grand Master, wearing the mantle of the Order, kneeling before the Blessed Virgin and Child and aided by St Barbara. The scene is framed by a small canopy from which hangs a shield of arms. The arrangement is similar to that of a votive brass composition. It is a valuable source of comparison with the Nowemiasto brass, both being of similar origin and period, and representing members of the same order.[5]

Two other figure brasses of the fourteenth century represent ecclesiastics:

Bishop Bertram Cremen, d.1377, Lübeck cathedral

A canon, c.1390, Poznań cathedral (Fig. 62)

Size is the only distinction of the first of these, a singularly coarse brass. The bishop's figure is constructed in ten plates. He is represented in semi-profile, blessing and holding a crozier. The left hand, extending beyond the outline of the figure, is engraved on a rectangular plate. The lines of the drapery and physical features are both badly drawn and unsurely cut. Some of the decorative detail of the episcopal mass vestments is carefully executed, but the overall effect is of incompetence. Two large slanting shields are placed by his feet. The border inscription, of superior workmanship, confined with tiers of canopied saints, is joined at the corners by exceedingly large representations of the Evangelists, who appear both as figures and emblems. There has been a definite attempt to imitate Flemish motifs in the decoration. The date of the brass is difficult to establish and it is likely that it is rather later than the date of decease. The second brass is much better, though simpler. The border inscription and large Evangelist figures are lost. The canopy with a rounded arch and masonry above, together with a cushion behind the priest's head, is incised on the slab. The figure is vested in almuce and mass vestments, a common combination on Lübeck incised slabs, and wears a cap, most probably that of an academic. He is depicted blessing a chalice held in the left hand with the Host above it. The quality of the engraving is considerably superior to that of Cremen's brass. The orphrey of his chasuble has many Flemish precedents. A particularly fine detail is the shield at his feet engraved with an angel bearing a motto 'Utinam'. This is the only brass at Poznań to have escaped destruction in the second world war.

Two heraldic plates of Lübeck or other Baltic origin purport to date from the fourteenth century. A shield is at the Historiska Museet at Lund. The second, a shield with merchant's marks and small inscription to Gottfried Sak 1361, though perhaps engraved later, is at the Museum of Antiquities, Bergen University (Fig. 63).

The quality of early fifteenth-century northern brasses is yet lower than the worst described. Queen (?)Agnes of Sweden 1432, Gadebusch, is of outstandingly poor quality. The figure is uninteresting, gross and feebly designed. The large slanting shields and Evangelists' symbols are more attractive, though of similarly bad workmanship. Hermann Schomekers 1406, Bardowick cathedral, is no better. Like the Poznań canon he is vested in mass vestments and almuce, though in this example the almuce is worn over the head, a common feature on Continental monuments. The canopy is incised in the slab; the figure, two shields and the border inscription being in separate inlay.[6]

A large shield composed of four plates commemorates Bernard Maltzan (1462) at the Nicolaikirche, Stralsund. Another shield emblazoned with fishes for der Wittich is preserved in the Hamburg Museum für Kunst und Gewerbe.

A peculiar but more complicated memorial is the thin copper plate engraving of Ludeke Lameshoved and wife d.1410. This was formerly in the Petrikirche but is now in the St Annen Museum, Lübeck. Ludeke, in civil dress, kneels with his wife before a representation of the Crucifixion with Mary and John beside. On either side, resembling the open doors of a triptych, are arranged four female saints holding emblems. The design is quaint and the engraving shallow. The background to all the figures is worked in series of fine incisions. Lübeck authorities are of the opinion that the plate is somewhat later than the recorded date.

Before the high altar of St Mary, Gdańsk, is a large indent indicating a double canopy with broad side shafts and two figures with very prominent shoes lying with slanting shields below. This brass was probably of Baltic origin, deriving some inspiration from Flemish models, but presented in a local and distinctive style.

The brasses of the Baltic seaboard are easily distinguished. It is possible that surviving examples are misleading and that memorials of a better quality were often made. Yet such an interpretation is unlikely as Bishop Cremen and the Queen were distinguished persons. These brasses, with the exception of those at Nowemiasto and Poznań, give the impression of being experimental works. The engravers, or at least the designers, perhaps normally employed on incised slabs, were unused to the metal medium. Their engravings were in consequence large, rough and uncertain. It is not surprising that Flemish imports were popular, when the locally made monuments were of such inferior quality.

An interesting brass, of North German design, though different in treatment to those described, is that of Johann von Rintelen 1376, at the Petrikirche, Braunschweig. This priest is represented in mass vestments, holding and blessing the chalice. He is set within a canopy against a hatched background. A marginal inscription in bold lettering is separately inlaid. It is perhaps improper to describe this monument as an engraved brass, as much of the form is achieved by recessed relief and around the head some details are in very low relief. A rubbing, such as that illustrated by R. H. Edlestone in *The Sixtieth Annual Report of the Peterborough Natural History, Scientific and Archaeological Society*, 1930-31, pl. 11, can hardly do justice to the quality of the work. Braunschweig was an important German city, and this brass was presumably prepared there.

Rhenish brasses

Evidence of another series of brasses, produced in the Rhenish cities of Köln and Aachen, appears in the second quarter of the fifteenth century. Considerable numbers of craftsmen emigrated from the Meuse towns to those cities where there already existed fine craftsmanship in metalwork. Köln has been noted as a major source of latten plate. The small worn quadrangular plate brass of Heinrich von Imbermonte 1433, Aachen cathedral, shows an angel with outspread wings holding a shield. The design is apparently not Flemish, and may be regarded as the earliest of the Rhenish brasses.

Silesian brasses

The workshops of Wroclaw, the most easterly centre of the craft so far noted, enhanced their prestige. Reference has been made in *The Craft* to Jodok Tawchen of Wroclaw, who received orders from the Chapter of Gnieznó to engrave archiepisopal monuments including that of Archbishop Nicholas Trabá in 1422. Tawchen is known to have been born in Legnica (Liegnitz) and seems to have lived from c. 1395 to 1470, acquiring a good reputation early in his career. Several monuments and larger church furnishings have been attributed to him in Wroclaw, more out of conjecture than certainty.[7] Only three figure brasses of this period remain for study, all representing bishops, and all quadrangular compositions:

Heinrich, Duke of Liegnitz and Bishop of Wroclaw, d.1398, Wroclaw cathedral (Fig. 65)
Johann Deher, 1455, Fürstenwalde (Fig. 66)
Peter Novak, 1456, Wroclaw cathedral (*The Craft*, Fig. 42).

The first, which may be later than the recorded date, is an inferior monument to the earlier Silesian brasses described. It is an unusually wide plate in which much of the space available is wasted in a graceless canopy executed with journeyman shoddiness. The flying buttresses, gracefully shown on the Holy Cross brasses, have here degenerated into a curious series of buttresses which rise in stages, framing crude tracery. The canopy itself forms a hexagonal recess, revealing two Romanesque windows drawn in an exaggerated perspective. The background to both figure and canopy is formed by carelessly drawn brick work. The figure in pontifical mass vestments is undistinguished, though the large lion at his feet is in a crouch commonly depicted in Silesian mediaeval art. The Bishop's face is in recessed relief.

Bishops Deher and Novak are similar brasses, and the symbolism of their curious design has already been described in *The Craft*, Chapter Six. The execution of both is rough, but the overall effect is quite impressive. The faces of both bishops are in low relief, whereas various details are in recessed relief. Novak's brass was seriously damaged in the Second World War, but is not beyond expert restoration. Bishop Deher wears a pectoral cross and stands on a great dragon. Two dogs sport at the base of the canopy shafts, snakes and birds are placed between the pediments, perhaps alluding to evil snaring souls. A small figure with a book supports his mitre. Chief interest in both brasses lies in the members of the episcopal household represented in the canopy shafts, including a butcher, huntsman, porter and a Silesian miner with pick and sack. It is tempting to ascribe these memorials to Tawchen but there is no proof.

Two large border inscriptions require mention. The first in relief black letter with four medallions containing arms surrounds the sculptured figure of Bishop Preczlaw von Pogarell 1376, in the cathedral of Wroclaw. The effigy itself has been attributed to the famous Prague sculptor, Peter Aler or Parler, and the inscription may have been engraved in Bohemia. The second inscription of Ditwin Dumelos, 1405, is certainly Silesian. It lies in St Elizabeth's church, Wroclaw, and frames the indent of a rectangular plate. The inscription, now incomplete, is inlaid in separate Lombardic letters of a very narrow form. This is a late usage of such a script on brasses, especially to be separately inlaid.

Conclusion

Existing brasses throughout the Continent are presumably only a sample from the workshops represented. It is possible that whole series have disappeared completely without trace. On the basis of available evidence the supremacy of Flemish engraving until 1460 can hardly be disputed. French brasses were apparently as fine though less numerous. The engravers of Saxony, Lübeck, the Rhineland and Silesia were not in the same class, though this great difference in quality rapidly altered after 1460.

It is against this background that the achievement of English engravers is remarkable. English brasses from 1360 to 1460 do not equal the Flemish in intricacy, splendour or expertise. They do, however, present a series of fine and consistent quality, and of a grace and dignity, which may be compared with those of Flanders without disadvantage. The superiority of Flemish over English design and product is largely a matter of subjective preference, though it may certainly be claimed that the rich medieval buyer patronised Flanders. The worst English examples are poorer than any known Flemish brass, but English numbers are much greater. The best English work rivals the Flemish, an impressive measure of its excellence.

7. English brasses, 1360-1410

Writing of the second half of the fourteenth century in England, J. H. Harvey concludes "The Reign of Edward III, in spite of its overshadowed close, had been among the greatest in English History", and "Richard II's personal government was, artistically speaking, one of the most brilliant periods in English History".[1] Despite the ravages of the Black Death in the middle of the fourteenth century, the years 1360-1399 were, with brief interludes, a period of intensive building under court and ecclesiastical patronage, giving expression to the designs of notable architects, among whom Henry Yevele, William Wynford, John Clyve and John Lewyn were the most outstanding. The construction and enrichment of cathedrals and churches created unusual opportunities for other craftsmen. The demand for memorials within the buildings, for monumental effigies, slabs and brasses, was immense, and royalty favoured the metal workers.

King Edward III himself is commemorated by a gilt latten effigy at Westminster, the side niches of the tomb containing statuettes of his children in the same material. The tomb, begun in 1377, was designed by Yevele, the superb wooden tester being made by Hugh Herland, and the metal work almost certainly cast and engraved by John Orchard "latoner", and Richard Rook.[2] Edward's eldest son, Edward the "Black Prince" d. 1376, is represented in Canterbury cathedral by an effigy of similar workmanship though of less vital conception, which Professor W. R. Lethaby presumes on good and obvious grounds to be another achievement of Yevele and Orchard. The King's youngest son, Thomas of Woodstock, Duke of Gloucester, murdered in 1397 at the instigation of King Richard II, was represented at Westminster on an engraved brass of unusual design (*The Craft,* Fig. 20), the indent of which still lies on the floor of the Confessor's Chapel. Thomas's widow, Eleanor, dying in 1399, is depicted on another large brass in the Abbey (*The Craft,* Fig. 173). King Richard II ordered the preparation of his own and his wife's memorial during his lifetime, a work begun in 1395 and finished about two years later. Henry Yevele and Stephen Lote, marblers, and Nicholas Broker and Godfrey Prest, copper smiths, were responsible for the task.[3] Again the effigies are of gilt latten, lying on an engraved sheet of latten plate and surrounded by a canopy.

These memorials are of supreme importance, but it is the prevalance of engraved brasses of merit which is most indicative of the activity of the latteners and marblers in this medium. Generalisations need no longer be based on isolated examples as numerous figures survive, and series of patterns can be precisely identified. While representation of the knightly class and clergy is prominent, brasses to property-owning farmers and merchants become increasingly common. Small figure brasses, half effigies and inscription plates, form a significant proportion of these. Equally evident is the adoption of brasses by certain families as their chosen type of monument. Most prominent are the Cobhams and their connections, nine of whom are represented at Cobham by brasses of the period covered by this chapter, with another of 1380 at Chrishall. The Stapletons in Norfolk and the Wingfields in Suffolk similarly laid numerous brasses at Ingham and Letheringham respectively.

Engraving throughout the period was of good quality. Lines are deeply and freely cut. Ornament is rich but not overdone. Compositions are often large and elaborate, but maintain a happy balance between the figures and canopy surround. Separate inlay is normally used and several discernible series of patterns were developed by the craftsmen, styles peculiar to particular workshops or groups of engravers. Most numerous are a series of well-conceived and formal figures, executed with economy of line and consistent competence. The style of the canopies reflect the influence of the court craftsmen and masons. The canopy of Archbishop Robert de Waldeby 1397, at Westminster abbey, has a bold and open oculus with quatrefoil cusping having marked similarity to Herland's tester canopies above King Edward's tomb. Similarly the unusual heavily buttressed canopy shafts with double pediments on the brass of Bishop John de Waltham, 1395, were probably modelled on those upon the marble tomb of Queen Philippa d. 1369, a work on royal commission by Hennequin of Liège. In contrast are groups of brasses on which ornament enriches figures of a more vital if in some cases poorer design, presenting memorials of a higher decorative quality. Occasionally as at Bottesford (*The Craft,* Fig. 170), the canopies of such brasses use ornament in ways that were eschewed at this time by the court craftsmen in their sculpture. A comparison was made in Chapter 3 between the important brasses of priests at Higham Ferrers, and Horsmonden. The differences noted are marked throughout London work of the period, suggestive of a rivalry between court and independent designers.

It is not yet possible to identify engravers, though the known craftsmen of the royal tombs afford a basis for conjecture. Henry Yevele, Stephen Lote and at least some of the marblers who worked with them were presumably skilled in engraving and Yevele bequeathed engraving tools. The effigy of Richard II and his Queen have a regal repose and dignity, qualities shared by the formal series of brasses. Furthermore the fine detail pounced onto the figures and flat back sheet has close similarities to that applied to the brass of Thomas de Beauchamp at Warwick, the most accomplished of the formal series. The effigy of King Edward III is in contrast less relaxed. As Harvey describes the tomb "the figures are conceived in a spirited style; considering the circumstances, the little statues of the royal children might even be called jaunty".[4] While Lawrence Stone does not entirely agree with this opinion, contrasting the static pose of the children to the vitality of the weepers on earlier monuments such as that of John of Eltham, he emphasises the naturalism of the representation, and the similarity of the King's face to that of his death mask.[5] Ornamental details, such as the floral device in the oculi of the horizontal canopy or gablet, have counterparts in the more decorative brasses. It is nonetheless a most uncertain and potentially misleading exercise to relate three dimensional effects to those in two dimensions. The engraved marginal inscriptions of the royal tombs do however permit more precise comparisons.

Examination of these inscriptions has not led the author to definite conclusions, but certain details strongly support the suggestion that Edward III's tomb and that of his son are connected with the more decorative series, whereas that of King Richard has affinities with the other. Comparisons are complicated, in part by the excellence of the craftsmanship, but also by the fact that the letters are engraved into relief, a treatment which was not commonly used on brasses in the fourteenth century. Nevertheless there are characteristic letters of the decorative series such as the slanting W and notched G, which are illustrated both by the Tonge inscription 1389, at All Hallows-by-the-Tower, London (Fig. 68) and details from Prince Edward's tomb at Canterbury (Figs. 69-70).[6*]

While these similarities are indicative rather than conclusive, there can be no doubt that John Orchard, 'Latoner', emerges as the central figure in a major workshop, working in the very media with which this study is concerned. Not only is it all but certain that he undertook the major works of Edward III's tomb and most probably that of Prince Edward, but he was also paid for six copper angels for Queen Philippa's tomb,[7] and a further twenty shillings for his part in procuring the miniature alabaster tombs of William and Blanche, children of Edward III.[8] He was living in 1395, as he sold property in Old Jewry in that year, but he was not favoured with the contract for Richard's tomb. In all probability he was a major engraver of brasses of the more vital style. Likewise it may be presumed that Broker and Prest were brass engravers, and it is possible that London marblers such as Henry Lakenham (d. 1387)[9] and John Mapilton (d. 1407) were others. The relationship of these craftsmen to Henry Yevele could have a strong bearing on the problem posed by the contrasting patterns of English brasses in the latter half of ths fourteenth century. We are possibly faced with the work of the Court school marblers and their associates, who were inevitably deeply influenced by major monumental design, complemented by the rich, varied and uneven work of the London latteners. With such an interpretation in view, it is appropriate to examine the brasses in detail, starting with the most revealing group — the men in armour.

Men in armour

Military equipment had, by 1360, developed into a form which is shown with few variations on monuments until the early fifteenth century. Most of the body was protected by plate, though the neck was covered by the mail aventail laced to the iron bascinet. All brasses depict the arms as completely guarded by vambraces, couters and rerebraces, the last terminating at the shoulders in two or three overlapping plates called spaudlers. Gauntlets protect the hands. The breastplate or coat of plates and mail shirt are practically concealed by the tight fitting jupon, usually finished with a scalloped border. Leg armour consisted of cuisses, poleyns and greaves, and plate sabatons covered the feet. The cross-hilted sword and dagger were suspended from a narrow belt or the heavy belt worn round the hips and fastened by a rich clasp. The shirt and stockings of mail still worn under the plate are all but concealed on monuments, though glimpses often appear at the armpits and above the sabatons.

Military brasses illustrate this equipment well, though the visor, commonly attached to the bascinet, is only shown once (and inaccurately). Several figures, especially in the first ten years of the period, exhibit extensive brigandine defences for the legs. Heavy studding of the cuisses is common, and on the brass of Thomas Cheyne, 1368, Drayton Beauchamp, the greaves appear to be of the same construction. Similar studs appeared on the body of the lost figure of Sir Miles de Stapleton 1364, Ingham, indicating a brigandine (Fig. 296). At the very close of the period examples occur in which the bevor (a throat and chin defence) and other plate defences almost completely obscure the mail, marking the transition to the complete plate or 'white armour' of the fifteenth century.

The remarkable diversity of engravers' patterns is admirably illustrated by the figures of Thomas and William Cheyne, 1368 and 1375 (Figs. 71-2), both lying on the chancel floor at Drayton Beauchamp. Thomas is a large but quaint figure with a heavy drooping moustache and surprised expression. He appears to lean slightly to the left, possibly in an unsuccessful attempt to copy the subtle sway of some earlier designs, and is clearly related to the brass of Sir John de Cobham 1354. These shortcomings are in part offset by lavish detail — the studding of his leg armour, the rich belt, the bold handle-like reinforcement to the poleyns and a remarkable decoration of pendant balls or bells hanging below the knee. The straight edge to the bascinet above his eyes and the bands separating the rows of mail lines in the aventail are typical features of this pattern. The lion under his feet is a wide-eyed apprehensive creature with a flowing mane. William Cheyne is a far more dignified and powerful figure, engraved with great competence and economy of line. His eyes are long and narrow, his nose broad, and his moustache turns sharply down at the corners of his mouth. He is, notwithstanding, of less intrinsic interest than Thomas or other figures of his type. The only unusual detail is that his sabatons are of scale armour, of which there is only one other example, at Methwold.

Figures in the style of Thomas Cheyne, described in Dr Kent's study as series 'A', include:

Sir John de Cobham, under canopy, d. 1408, engraved c. 1365, Cobham, *(The Craft,* Fig. 38)
A Compton, c. 1365, Freshwater
Sir John de Mereworth, canopy, 1366, Mereworth

Sir John de Cobham is notable as he holds before his breast a representation of Cobham college. The Compton at Freshwater wears a jupon with a small shield of his arms thereon. Sir John de Mereworth, though large, is mutilated by the loss of his legs.

The brasses engraved in the more formal manner of William Cheyne, are listed by Kent as series 'B', and include:

William de Audeley, canopy lost, 1365, Horseheath (Fig. 73)
Sir Adam de Clyfton, canopy, 1367, Methwold
Thomas Stapel, sergeant at arms, canopy lost, 1371, Sutton
Sir John de Foxle with two wives, on bracket, canopy lost, 1378, Bray, *(The Craft,* Fig. 174)
A Dallingridge with wife, canopy, c. 1380, Fletching
Sir John de la Pole with wife, canopy, 1380, Chrishall
Sir John Harsick with wife, 1384, Southacre (*The Craft,* Fig. 161)
Sir Reginald de Malyns with two wives, 1358, Chinnor
Thomas Lord Berkeley with wife, 1392, Wotton-under-Edge
Sir Robert Bardolf, canopy, 1395, Mapledurham

Most of this series are large and of considerable merit, and are canopied or once had canopies. Two of those without, at Southacre and Wotton-under-Edge, have almost life-size figures. There are considerable variations among these brasses, as would be expected over a period of thirty-five years. The earliest are slim and slightly more ornate partly on account of the studding of cuisses and gauntlets. On some the sword belt is represented as tightly clasped, on others it is ample with a long pendent end falling from the buckle. The jupons of the Methwold, Bray, Fletching and Southacre knights display the arms of the wearer. Mention has been made of the scale sabatons at Methwold and Drayton Beauchamp. The Sutton figure, formerly at Shopland, probably bore a mace on his right hip, signifying his office as Sergeant-at-arms.

Three brasses of this fine collection are of outstanding quality and deserve particular mention. Sir John Harsick and wife are severe figures represented holding hands, the knight grasping his belt in his left and his wife toying with her mantle cord with her left (*The Craft,* Fig. 161). Above them is set a great helm and shield. The simplicity of the monument is impressive and reveals the restraint of this series at its most effective. Thomas Lord Berkeley and wife are similarly dignified, but certain details have been chosen for intricate decoration. Lord Thomas's gauntlets and belt, which latter was originally inlaid in some kind of stone or composition, and Lady Berkeley's hair and cushion are especially ornamental in their treatment. Sir Robert Bardolf at Mapledurham is less well known but similar to Lord Berkeley and of equally fine workmanship.

A series of armed figures related in detail to the ornate and peculiar brasses of the 'A' series first described arise after 1380, and are probably the products of the same engravers or their successors. Richard Charlis 1378, Addington, and an armed figure of the Pecok family c. 1380, St Michael, St Albans, may be regarded as transitional examples. Sir John de Wyngefeld 1389, Letheringham, is typical of the series.

Especially noteworthy is the slimness of the figure, emphasized by the length of leg and the steep turn downwards of the feet. The aventail is represented with great care, approaching the separate link treatment of the early fourteenth century. Plate joins are decorated. The hip belt hangs slightly loose. The gauntlets do not completely touch. His features are asymmetrically represented, the eyes being particularly uneven. This pattern with various modifications is traceable down to 1410 and the following are among the chief examples:

Sir Richard Attelese with wife, canopy, 1394, Sheldwich
Sir Reginald Cobham, 1403, Lingfield
Thomas Seintleger, Esq., 1408, Otterden, (Fig. 67)
John Hauley with two wives, canopy, 1408, St Saviour, Dartmouth
Thomas de Frevile with wife, 1410, Little Shelford (*The Craft,* Fig. 162)
Robert de Frevile with wife, c. 1410, Little Shelford
John Wylcotes with wife, canopy, c. 1410, Great Tew

Sir Reginald Cobham and the later figures do not wear the jupon, and show the breastplate and the fauld of lames protecting the pelvis. Small oval besagews cover the armpits of Robert de Frevile, and the armour of John Wylcotes reveals the almost complete transition to full plate armour. A bevor of plate covers his throat and the aventail appears as a deep fringe beneath.

This group of figures is highly distinctive and can be readily related to civil and ecclesiastical figures of the series. On some of these brasses from c. 1390-c. 1405, Wanlip being a good example, an oak leaf device appears in the initial capital letter of the inscription and a dragon appears near the opening or termination of marginal inscriptions. The presentation of the initial would appear to associate the group with the marginal inscription on the tomb of Sir Bernard Brocas (1400), at Westminster Abbey.

A few military figures are similar in conception and much detail but different in treatment. Five assorted examples, grouped by Dr Kent in a series 'C' are:

John Bettesthorne, 1398, Mere
Sir George Felbrigg, canopy lost, 1400, Playford
Unknown (appropriated by the Dalyson Family), canopy, c. 1400, Laughton.
Sir Nicholas Dagworth, 1401, Blickling, (Fig. 74)
Sir William Bagot with wife, 1407, Baginton.

These figures, with the exception of that at Laughton, are ungainly and remarkably lean and stiff. Their feet are long, and their expressions hostile and sour. Armour decoration is rich. Sword scabbards are embellished with small canopies, gauntlets are ornamented, and the links of mail intricately cut. The fringe of Sir Nicholas Dagworth's jupon has a bottom edge of leaf pattern.

Three less closely associated figures, classified by Kent in a series 'D' and probably a development of series 'A', are:

Sir William Tendring, 1408, Stoke-by-Nayland.
(?) John Wynter, c. 1410, Barningham Winter.
William Loveney, c. 1410, Wendens Ambo, (Fig. 75).

The large figure of Sir William Tendring is celebrated on account of his long double-forked beard.[10] John Wynter is less well known but of considerable interest as an example of full plate armour. His bevor and circular besagews are early of their type. His jupon, in contrast, is a very late example, and the only one worn with complete 'white armour.'

Lastly there are three figures which are difficult to ascribe to any particular series and have little relationship with each other. Their common feature is the arrangement of the sword sloping behind the legs.

Sir Nicholas Burnell, canopy, 1382, Acton Burnell.

John Cray, 1392, Chinnor.

Sir John Russell, canopy, d. 1405, Strensham.

John Cray is the most conventional of these and is a good illustration of contemporary armour.[11] The others are decidedly unconventional, though probably of London workmanship. The date of the last is controversial, as some authorities regard it as a copy of an earlier pattern.[12*]

Among later examples of the 'B' series are:

Sir William de Bryene, 1395, Seal

Sir (?) William Moyne with wife, 1404, Sawtry All Saints (Fig. 76).

(?) Thomas Massingberd with wife (later appropriated), canopy, c. 1406, Gunby St Peter

Thomas de Beauchamp, Earl of Warwick, with wife, canopy lost, 1406, St Mary, Warwick (*The Craft,* Figs. 163-5)

Sir William de Burgate with wife, canopy, 1409, Burgate (*The Craft,* Fig. 36)

Thomas de Braunstone, canopy lost, d. 1401, engr. c. 1410, Wisbech[13*]

Sir Nicholas Hawberk, canopy, d. 1407, engr. c. 1410, Cobham (*The Craft,* Fig. 57)

Sir Thomas Burton with wife, c. 1410 or later, Little Casterton.[14*]

The brasses are all of good quality, showing the armour both simply and accurately. The figures are rather thicker set than their predecessors. Small alterations in detail are evident, especially the covering of the lacing to the aventail by a plain or decorated band. The latest examples, with the exception of Sir Thomas Burton, no longer show the jupon.

By far the most interesting of the group is the Earl of Warwick, a superb brass robbed of its canopies, and now placed at a great height above the entrance to the Beauchamp chapel. The pattern used for the Earl and his wife is not remarkable but the application of detail is unique. The Earl's heraldic jupon, his armour and weapons, and the mantle and kirtle of his wife are delicately pounced with a rich diaper (*The Craft,* Fig. 164). The ragged staff badge is similarly repeated on the Earl's scabbard, bascinet and couters. The finish of the engraving is altogether exceptional. Close comparisons can be made between the application of this detail and the pointillé work on the effigies of King Richard II and his queen[15]. Nicholas Broker and Godfrey Prest, coppersmiths, were engaged to make the royal effigies in 1394, a time when the Earl was largely rebuilding the collegiate church of St Mary, and he may well have ordered his own memorial from them. It is probable that the royal craftsmen were responsible for this brass.

The Wisbech and Exeter brasses are unusually large but suffer from very serious wear. The figure of Sir Peter Courtenay K.G. at the latter is mostly obliterated, but he was apparently not represented wearing the Garter. Sir Ingram Bruyn at South Ockendon is seriously mutilated but is now unique in having a two-line inscription set on his jupon.[16*]

Collars

An interesting detail, and one not confined to any particular series, is the introduction of ornamental and livery collars. Lord Berkeley wears over the aventail a collar of mermaids, a badge of the Berkeleys (Fig. 78). The famous collar of SS is found at Baginton (Fig 77), Gunby St Peter and Little Casterton. The letters were made of gold or silver and set upon a blue band. The origin and significance of this collar has not been finally established. It is unquestionably associated with the House of Lancaster, and a reference to such a collar occurs in John of Gaunt's register as early as 1383. The two most probable interpretations for the S are 'Senescallus', an office which John of

Gaunt held, or 'Souverayne', a motto adopted by Henry IV when Earl of Derby, and retained by him after seizing the throne. (This motto is painted upon the tester of the king's tomb at Canterbury.) The reference in John of Gaunt's register would seem to support the former rather than the latter interpretation. Some documentary evidence has been traced to support the interpretation of 'Souvenez de Moi'. The detail of this controversy is, however, outside the scope of the present book.[17] An unusual collar of doubtful significance was attached to the aventail of a knight (now lost) at Mildenhall. This consisted of a collar which had been cut away for colour inlay, with a large pendent crown. Within the crown was a small animal, which was possibly intended to be collared. The Duke of Brittany is known to have granted collars with pendent ermine and crowns, and this may have been the engraver's intention.[18*]

Before leaving the subject of armed figures it is appropriate to note Richard Shawell, the champion on the brass of Bishop Wyvil 1375, at Salisbury cathedral (Fig. 79). This is the sole representation on a brass of the equipment used at a trial by combat, namely a leather jack, a shield with a large boss and a heavy military pick.

The various patterns used for these figures have been described in detail as they constitute the known range used by London engravers during this period. Civilian and ecclesiastical figures can generally be ascribed with confidence to the appropriate series, each of which has its own peculiarities. The wide distribution of these brasses and their overall concentration in the Home Counties leave no doubt that London was their source.

Male civilians

Male civilians display a uniformity of dress throughout the period which by its simplicity allowed for little individuality or decorative interest. The tunic with hood, or tunic with hood and shoulder-piece, are invariably worn, together with hose and pointed shoes. Buttoned mittens often cover the hands. A mantle is also shown on large figures, open at the right side and held up and back by the left arm. A short sword is commonly included. Hair is worn loose and long to the close of the fourteenth century, but a close-cropped fashion becomes usual after 1400. Most examples show beards, generally taking the form of a double fork. The large civilian c. 1370, at Shottesbrooke, is an excellent example of both costume and the simple and strong 'B' series patterns in use by the most prolific workshop or group of engravers. He has been described appropriately as a frankelein, a freeholder of substantial property though not of gentle rank. The priest beside him was probably his brother. An exceptional figure of the same series, and part of a most sumptuous composition, is Walter Pescod 1398, Boston (*The Craft,* Fig. 171). The brass is unfortunately both worn and damaged, but the embroidery of his tunic is still clear, covering his left side only, with a pattern of his rebus, peascods and the letter W. Two important figures are examples of different series. John Curteys with his wife 1391, Wymington, was a wool merchant and mayor of the Staple of Calais. His decorative canopied brass is of the freer 'A' series. John Corp with a younger relative 1391, Stoke Fleming, is of the 'C' series with a deep frown, staring eyes and long wide-splayed feet. He wears no mantle but his sword is suspended by a small thong passing over a long and ornamental belt slung from his right shoulder. The peculiarities of Corp's canopy indicate that it was a specially ordered design, and Chaucer's description of the shipman suits him well:

> 'A dagger hangyng on a laas hadde he
> Aboute his nekke under his arm adoun.'

Other full-length male civilian figures are as follows:

Unknown, c. 1360, Hampsthwaite
John Pecok with wife, c. 1370, St Michael, St Albans

Symond de Felbrigg with wife etc., c. 1380, Felbrigg
Two civilians, c. 1380, King's Sombourne
Unknown with wife, canopy, c. 1390, Northampton Architectural Soc.
John Scott with wife, canopy (worn), 1392, Musée Lapidaire, Bordeaux
Unknown, 1394, cross lost, Hereford cathedral
Woolmerchant with wife, c. 1395, Northleach (Fig. 80)
John Mulsho, Esq., with wife, on bracket, 1400, Geddington (*The Craft,* Fig. 60)
Vintner with wife, canopy, c. 1400, Cirencester
Unknown with wife, c. 1400, Tilbrook[19]
William Grevel with wife, canopy, 1401, Chipping Campden
Richard Martyn with wife, canopy, 1402, Dartford
Herry Notingham with wife, c. 1405, Holme-next-the-Sea
Robert Parys with wife, cross, 1408, Hildersham (Fig. 92).
Robert de Haitfeld with wife, 1409, Owston
Roger Keston, 1409, Astwood (*The Craft*, Fig. 167).

Three brasses — Sir John Cassy, Chief Baron of the Exchequer and wife 1400. Deerhurst; John Rede, Sergeant-at-Law 1404, Checkendon; and Nichol Rolond, Sergeant-at-Law and wife c. 1410, Cople, respectively examples of the 'A', 'C' and 'D' series — represent members of the legal profession. The first and second are canopied and are among the more important brasses of the period. Cassy shows the artistry and uneven quality of the 'A' series to a marked degree, the treatment of his figure being highly stylised, yet his face perceptively portrayed, projecting shrewdness and understanding. Rede has the tense expression, typical of his series, and prominently placed feet. The peculiarities of legal costume are describe in the next chapter.

The Hampsthwaite figure, small and later reused, is represented in the swaying posture of the previous period and may well belong to it. The Chipping Campden brass is particularly large and fine, showing the austerity of 'B' series design at its most effective. Grevel was an outstanding woolman and rebuilder of Chipping Campden church. Brasses to wool merchants and other traders are examined in more detail in the following chapter. The King's Sombourne pair illustrate two 'B' variations, the one bearded and the other clean shaven. The largest examples of the 'A' series are at Cirencester, Dartford and Northampton, though the first is worn and mutilated. The figures at Northleach and Tilbrook are impressive, the former resting his feet on a woolsack. Even the smaller 'A' figures, as at Holme-next-the-Sea, Owston and St Albans, have a decorative quality far more attractive than their 'B' counterparts. Roger Keston at Astwood is a recently discovered figure, with several unusual features, in particular the high decorative collar to his tunic and the check pattern base below his feet. The Hereford civilian is an interesting, though mutilated, example of 'C' design. The Geddington and Hildersham figures kneel at the base of crosses, affording a profile view of the costume.

The brass of John Pecok and wife is interesting as an example of conservative design in the 'A' series, which makes dating on typological grounds rather difficult.[20*] The costume is plain, but the drapery and facial features are engraved with a direct simplicity, consistent with work of the earlier half of the century. The inscription in French, though an excellent example of relief lettering, is no clear indicator of age. The details which support the date offered are the unsureness of the drapery lines, the graceless presentation of the hands, and the slight turn of John's head. The problems are not confined to this brass, the priest Walter Frilende at Ockham appearing to be no later than c. 1350, though dying in 1376. It would seem that the range of patterns in the 'A' series lacked the systematic development of those from 'B', probably through the participation of a variety of pattern makers.

Half effigies are found as follows: c. 1360 Graveney, Nuffield; c. 1370 Deddington; c. 1390 East Horsley; c. 1400 with wife Letchworth; and 1406 with wife Lambourne. A bust at Blickling (*The Craft*, Fig. 43), probably commemorates James de Holveston 1378. Despite their partial representation, these figures reflect the differences in the pattern series very clearly. The simply drawn 'B' figures at Nuffield and Deddington, may be contrasted with those of 'A' at Graveney and East Horsley, and of 'C' at Letchworth and Lambourne. Notwithstanding its worn condition, the Letchworth brass remains an unusually detailed presentation, with long chevrons decorating the man's tunic.

Females

Female effigies are numerous. In addition to those on brasses already mentioned there are several to women alone, some of which are canopied and of the best quality. The following list is a representative selection.

Isabel Beaufo, c. 1360, Waterperry[21*]
Dame Elizabeth Cornewaylle, lower part restored, c. 1370, Burford
Margaret Briggs, canopy lost, 1374, Great Berkhamsted
Dame Maude de Cobeham, canopy, 1380, Cobham
Unknown, c. 1390, Holme Pierrepont
Dame Margaret de Cobeham, canopy, 1395, Cobham
Eleanor de Bohun, Duchess of Gloucester, canopy, 1399, Westminster Abbey (*The Craft,* Fig. 173)
Margaret Pennebrygg, 1401, Shottesbrooke.

The simplicity of female dress throughout the period, with the exception of headdresses, which are often elaborate, admirably suited a bold treatment. The pattern varieties noted among military and civilian brasses are discernible in the female figures though with less clarity, especially between the 'A' and 'C' series. Details of faces and hands are the most easily differentiated. The small figure of Isabel Beaufo, whose gently swaying pose is consistent with an earlier period, is clearly of a kind with Sir Thomas Cheyne. Dame Margaret de Cobeham 1395, is an example of the most competent and conventional 'B' series work. The Holme Pierrepont lady and Margaret Pennebrygg belong respectively to the more decorative 'A' and 'C' pattern series. The gradual transition over the period from deeply cut and even chiselled lines to an equally graceful but finer delineation is very marked.

All women are shown wearing the kirtle which fits the figure closely. The sleeves usually cover part of the hand in the form of a mitten, and are profusely decorated with buttons. At Southacre and Warwick the kirtle is emblazoned with arms. Dame Maude de Cobeham 1380, wears a kirtle cut away for inlay near the feet, presumably to represent fur or other rich edging. The surcoat is commonly worn over the kirtle. Dame Elizabeth de Cornewaylle is a large and excellent example of the plain surcoat, the only feature of which are two hand slits or pocket holes. The Winterbourne brass shows the same arrangement. Some surcoats are of sideless form, and are deeply edged with fur at Lingfield, Spilsby and Stoke-by-Nayland. At Ashford and Cobham 1375, the surcoat is shorter than the kirtle and slit up the sides almost reaching the hip. In other examples the short-sleeved surcoat is represented with long tippets hanging almost to the ankle. The Necton 1372, Chrishall and Bray figures (*The Craft,* Fig. 174) are good illustrations. At Bray the surcoats of both wives are emblazoned with arms. Buttons are a prominent feature on many surcoats and kirtles, especially on the more ornate patterns as at Holme Pierrepont, Sheldwich and Dartmouth. Clarice, wife of Robert de Frevile, Little Shelford wears a loose gown over the kirtle. This has a high collar and loose surplice-like sleeves, and is tightly belted at the waist. The fur lining is clearly shown. It is probable that this is a form of the houppelande, of which there are many examples in French manuscripts, though this garment usually appears open down the front and is a form of coat rather than a gown as shown in this case.

A less ostentatious form of gown, similar to the male tunic but extended in length, is worn at the close of the period. Margaret Briggs at Great Berkhamsted is the earliest noted case and the wool merchant's wife at Northleach is an example illustrated (Fig. 80). Others are at Chipping Campden, Tilbrook, Holme-by-the-sea, Wrentham, Shottesbrooke and Great Tew. A mantle is commonly shown fastened across the breast by a tasselled cord, and is usually worn over the kirtle alone. The Gedney brass is a good example, in which the engraver has relieved the plainness of the garments by the fine detail of the mitten edges.

The headdress affords the most decorative feature on female figures. The graceful and simple veil headdress is shown on several brasses, as at Burford, Winterbourne, Graveney, Hellesdon, Rusper, Felbrigg, Northleach and Hildersham. More common is the elaborate nebulé headdress, in which the face is framed by veils starched into wavy flounces, and smaller flounces at the bottom of the veil are arranged on the shoulders. The form of this arrangement is well displayed on the sculptured effigy of Lady Maud Harcourt c. 1370, Stanton Harcourt. By 1390 these frills are mainly shown framing the forehead only, and not falling below eye-level. Ladies at Ashford, Bray, Cobham 1375, Felbrigg, Fletching and Chinnor 1385, are good examples of the fuller style, and ladies at Broughton, Cobham 1395, Dyrham and Warwick of the smaller kind. An apparently similar arrangement has been described as the zig-zag headdress, from the manner of its representation, the undulations being expressed in a less contracted form to give a zig-zag outline. Examples of this treatment are at Waterperry, Necton, Lingfield and Chinnor, 1385. Another form of headdress, identical in shape but decorated with jewelled network, is usually described as the 'reticulated'. Examples are at Wanlip, Sheldwich, Deerhurst and Goring. On a few brasses the hair is exposed, plaited at the sides of the face and bound by a jewelled band. The Southacre (*The Craft,* Fig. 161) and Dartmouth figures are excellent examples, as was the lost effigy of Joan de Stapleton 1364, at Ingham. Lady Burton at Little Casterton has braided hair richly netted and surmounted by a narrow tiara. The crespine headdress, from which the horned headdress of the fifteenth century developed, appears both in transitional and complete form. Here the hair was netted above the head and bunched over the ears, and a veil was pinned over the front, falling behind and to the sides. Margaret Briggs at Great Berkhamsted is the earliest instance, the network being very heavily defined. Others are at Wotton-under-Edge, Wrentham and Shottesbrooke. Good examples of the crespine proper are at Rougham, Gunby St Peter, Wymington and Burgate, and an especially fine representation is that of Mary Moyne at Sawtry All Saints.

Widows

Widows are represented in dignified but plain dress, its most distinctive feature being the plaited barbe covering throat and chin. The head is covered with a veil, and a plain mantle is worn over the kirtle. This costume is indistinguishable from that of nuns. The most important brass of a widow is that of the Duchess of Gloucester at Westminster, excellent in both conception and execution. Her canopy is among the finest of the period. Eleanor retired to Barking Abbey in Essex after the death of her husband in 1397, and may well have taken religious vows before her death. Other good figures are at Norbury and Necton, and are shown with their husbands at Wymington, Draycot Cerne and Little Shelford. (*The Craft,* Fig. 162).

Ecclesiastics

The secular clergy are well represented. Among surviving memorials are those of an Archbishop and at least three bishops. The majority of figures represent parish priests, though a small but important group commemorate eminent ecclesiastics below episcopal rank. All clerics are shown clean shaven and generally with a grave expression, often accentuated by wrinkles and sunken cheeks. Hair is shown rather long and wavy until the close of the fourteenth century, but is treated in a shorter and stiffer manner by the close of the period. Stippling of the chin to indicate stubble is common until c. 1380. The clergy were regarded as serious, learned and mature men, and their memorials were designed to this effect.

Archbishops and bishops

The archiepiscopal and episcopal brasses are of importance both on account of the eminence of those commemorated and the quality of the work. Robert de Waldeby, 1397, Archbishop of York, was a friend of Richard II, to whom he had acted as tutor. His 'B' series canopied brass in Westminster Abbey is large but simple in treatment depicting the archbishop in full pontificals with pall and cross. John Trilleck 1360, Bishop of Hereford, at his cathedral, is another dignified figure, set within a canopy (Fig. 81). He wears pontificals and holds a crozier. His right hand, like that of Waldeby, is raised in blessing. Robert Wyvil 1375, Bishop of Salisbury, whose unique 'A' series brass in his cathedral has been described in *The Craft,* is depicted in pontificals standing at prayer in the window of the castle (*Ibid,* Fig. 62). The headless figure of a ? 'A' series bishop or abbot c. 1390 at Adderley represents an ecclesiastic in Mass vestments with dalmatic holding a crozier and book. The identity has not been established. The 'B' series brass of John de Waltham 1395, Bishop of Salisbury, is now a wreck and concealed beneath the floor covering of the Confessor's chapel at Westminster Abbey. Waltham was appointed Lord High Treasurer of England by Richard II, who ordered the bishop's burial at Westminster in spite of opposition. Much of the lower part of the figure is gone and practically all the elaborate canopy. An unusual feature of the effigy is the chasuble decorated with crosses and the Blessed Virgin and Child, the latter an allusion the the arms of the See of Salisbury.[22]

Canons and wardens

The adoption of brasses as memorials by lesser church dignitaries – canons, prebendaries, wardens and Masters of Colleges – was significant, not only in increasing the market for expensive and elaborate monuments but also in promoting a type of brass of special richness and interest. Some of those commemorated had influence outside their ecclesiastical duties – John Sleford at Balsham was Master of the Wardrobe to Edward III – and all were persons of prestige or wealth. The scale of the brasses was generally appropriate to their rank. Furthermore, it was customary to represent such persons in processional rather than mass vestments, which in certain respects increased the scope for decoration. Processional vestments worn over the cassock usually consisted of the surplice, almuce (also called amess), and the cope. The surplice with its loose hanging sleeves almost obscures the cassock on brasses. The almuce, which strictly speaking was a habit and not a vestment, was a form of hooded fur cape which varied in quality and colour according to the rank of the wearer. Its lower edge was decorated with tails and two long fur pendants hanging down in front. In brass representations its surface is commonly cut away for lead or colour inlay. The cope was a semi-circular cloak, worn over the shoulders and held across the breast by a band of cloth or a clasp called a morse. Copes were of two main types. The choir cope was worn at ordinary services, or as part of the choir dress in certain Orders, and was made of plain material with a hood attached. The festal cope, in contrast, was made of costly materials and often richly embroidered. This was worn at solemn services other than the Mass and varied in colour according to the feast or time of the year. Originally made with a hood this soon became a mere ornamental flap falling behind the shoulders. Some copes were embroidered over the whole surface but most, including those shown on brasses, only have finely decorated orphreys. Even so this gave considerable scope for the engravers to depict the textile patterns and the tiers of canopied saints on the orphrey on the more elaborate brasses.

The earliest example of a priest in processional vestments, William de Rothewelle 1361, Archdeacon of Essex, at Rothwell is a very unusual figure showing strong foreign — probably French — influence (Fig. 84). His cope, apparently of light material, is so plain that its exact character is doubtful. The choir cope is worn by:

(?) John Brigenhall, engr. c. 1380, Watton-at-Stone (Fig. 82)
Nicholas de Luda, prebendary of Salisbury, canopy, 1383, Cottingham.

The festal cope is worn by:

John de Campeden, Canon of Southwell, 1382, St Cross, Winchester
William de Fulburne, Canon of St Paul's, canopy, 1391, Fulbourne
John Sleford, Canon of Ripon and Wells, canopy, 1401, Balsham (Fig. 88)
William Ermyn, 1401, Castle Ashby
Richard Malford, warden, 1403, New College, Oxford (Fig. 83)
Henry de Codyngtoun, Prebendary of Southwell, canopy, 1404, Bottesford
John Prophete, Dean of Hereford and York, canopy, d. 1416, eng. c.1405, Ringwood[23*]
Thomas de Busshbury, Canon of Hereford, 1409, Ashbury.

All these figures may be classified in the 'A' or 'B' series of patterns. The heavy face of Henry de Codyngtoun, with its wrinkles, curly hair and stubble marked chin, and those of the associated 'A' series brasses at Ashbury, Ringwood and Shillington, makes a striking contrast with the refined features of Richard Malford. A special interest lies in the ornament of the orphreys and morses of copes. Small canopied saints form the orphreys at Balsham, Castle Ashby, Bottesford and Ringwood. On others the orphreys are divided into sections by lozenges or circles interspersed with a floral pattern, the centres of the sections being filled with roses, fleurs-de-lys or four-petalled flowers. Personal initials are introduced in the embroidery at Fulbourne and New College, and leopards' heads at St Cross. The morse has no standard decoration. The Holy Trinity is represented upon it at Bottesford, and the Sacred face of Christ or Vernicle at Ringwood. Personal arms appear at Fulbourne and Castle Ashby, and the initials J. S. at Balsham. Others are decorated with a variety of geometric or floral patterns. The arresting quality of these details is increased by the simple vertical lines of the cope folds and the surplice and the contrasting surface of the almuce, which in turn emphasizes both head and hands.

An interesting though headless half figure at North Stoke represents Roger Parkers c. 1363, Canon of St George's Chapel, Windsor. The canons of St George's were, and still are, privileged to wear a choir cope of purple with the arms of the Order on the left shoulder, Argent a cross Gules for the patron St George. The cope is fastened by cords, and these, together with the badge, are clearly shown.

Parish priests

Brasses of parish priests vary greatly in scale and quality. The wealth and standing of a priest were closely related to his family connections. Two examples of priests commemorated by Flemish brasses have been noted, and others have large memorials. The majority of their brasses, however, rarely exceed 76 cm in length, and half effigies form a substantial proportion. Most are vested for mass in the manner already described, and differ from earlier figures of their type mainly in details of ornament and variations in facial treatment and expressions found in the series of patterns. The fylfot, other geometric ornament and bold floral decoration gradually give place after 1380 to more delicate and repetitive patterns of four-petalled flowers within lozenges. The stole and maniple alter form over the period, the panel above the fringe becoming first square in shape and then generally disappearing altogether. The apparel at the wrists ceases to encircle the cuff. Chasubles are shown entirely plain after 1380, without orphreys or a decorative edge.

Full-length figures include:

Unknown, with frankelein, canopy, c. 1370, Shottesbrooke
Peter de Lacy, part of canopy now in British Museum, 1375, Northfleet
John Seys, bracket lost, 1376, West Hanney
Nicholas Kaerwent, canopy lost, 1381, Crondall
John de Swynstede, 1395, Edlesborough (fig. 87)
Thomas and Richard Gomfrey, 1399, Dronfield
John Vynter, 1404, Clothall
John Balsam, 1410, Blisland (*The Craft,* Fig. 30).

These figures at West Hanney, Shottesbrooke, Northfleet, Crondall and Edlesborough are large and finely engraved, especially the last. Others are of uneven quality, and the Dronfield and Blisland figures, though apparently of the 'A' pattern series, are noticeably peculiar. On both of these the stole is omitted, a defect found also on the Clothall brass. It is unlikely that this was entirely deliberate.

Two remarkable and large half figures are those of Chinnor and Stanford-in-the-Vale. The former, to Alexander Chelseye 1388, is very freely engraved. The latter, to Roger Campedene 1398, though evidently of the 'C' series, is elaborate, peculiar and individualistic.

Only two examples remain of priests represented in their garment of everyday use — the cassock. This is not surprising as this attire is not immediately distinctive of their status, and may easily be confused with civil dress. William Groby 1398, High Halstow, is in half effigy. More interesting is Thomas Awmarle c. 1400, Cardynham, a small figure of the 'A' series. He wears, in addition to his belted cassock, a hood and sword. His inscription bears the distinctive oak leaf device in the initial capital.

Regular clergy and women in Religious Orders

No brass to the regular clergy exists, and only the head of a nun c. 1360 is preserved at St Mary, Kilburn (Fig. 85). The subject is accordingly examined in the following chapter.

Academics

Three figures are presumed to commemorate academics, but only one is of value for the illustration of dress. Two are kneeling figures at Upper Hardres, 1405, and Aspley Guise c. 1410. On these the cassock is worn with a large hood and shoulder piece. John Strete at Upper Hardres wears on his head the rounded pileus, indicative of his status as Master in Theology. The large and excellent half effigy of John Hotham, Master in Theology and Provost of the Queen's College, Oxford 1361, at Chinnor, is far more distinctive, showing him in a pointed pileus, fur-lined hood and cappa clausa with two slits for the arms, a garment normally reserved for Doctors but allowed also to Masters in Theology, this being the highest degree in that faculty.

Children

Children are seldom represented on fourteenth-century brasses. The half effigies of Raulin and Margaret Brocas c. 1360, Sherborne St John (*The Craft,* Fig. 168), and Joan Plessi c. 1360, Quainton, are the only independent brasses known. The latter's status is doubtful but her hair, like that of Margaret Brocas, is shown loose and long, and the figure is very small. An important group of four sons of Sir John Salesbury 1388, kneeling below a representation of the Resurrection, was formerly at Great Marlow, but was lost in 1832. Rubbings exist in the Craven Ord collection and the Society of Antiquaries.

Eleanor Corp 1391, is depicted with her relative at Stoke Fleming raised on a bracket by his side. The veil of her headdress blows out freely from her recumbent head.[24] Smaller children on inscribed pedestals appear at the feet of Sir Reginald Braybrok and Sir Nicholas Hawberk (both engr. c. 1410) Cobham. These figures, which bear no natural relationship in scale to their fathers, were early precedents for the diminutive figures, which were later set in groups below the parents.

Provincial workshops

The varieties of figure brasses which may be presumed to have been engraved in London have now been listed and described. There are nevertheless others of equal interest which were evidently the work of provincial engravers in York or at some centre in Lincolnshire. Harvey has shown that Robert Patrington fl. 1353-73, master mason of York Minster, made marble tombs for six archbishops, expensive monuments now lost.[25]

The military figures and their wives are the most important and consist of the following:

Sir John de St Quintin and wife, 1397, Brandsburton (Fig. 91)
Sir John Mauleverere and wife, 1400, Allerton Mauleverer
William, Baron Willoughby d'Eresby K.G., and wife, canopy, engr. c.1405, Spilsby
Man in armour, worn, c. 1405, Brancepeth
Unknown, canopy lost, c. 1410, Holbeach
Richard Hansard and wife, c. 1410, South Kelsey (*The Craft,* Fig. 166).

Knowles has proved the influence of fourteenth-century Flemish designs on York stained glass,[26] and Crossley likewise has illustrated similar influences on Yorkshire stone memorials.[27] It is accordingly of interest that the Brandsburton figures show strong Flemish influence, not only in their form but also in their execution. The figures are very large and engraved with much detail, and the loss of the knight's head is particularly regrettable. The treatment of the gauntlets and leg armour bears a close similarity to known Flemish examples, as does the hound at the Knight's feet. The cutting of the lines is in keeping with Flemish rather than English methods. The figure of Lora de St Quintin is more consistent with English workmanship, though unlike any known London pattern. The treatment of the inscription is most unusual.[28*] The Allerton Mauleverer brass is curious, presenting the two figures on a small quadrangular plate. The knight is lean with his feet pointing sharply downwards. His jupon is emblazoned with his arms, three greyhounds (levriers) courant. His head is turned in semi-profile to facilitate the representation of a raised visor on his bascinet (Fig. 86). The engraving is of only moderate quality, and the hatching between the figures very rough. The Spilsby, Brancepeth and Holbeach figures are more clearly related to the London 'C' pattern but have features which are alien to it. Kent was cautious in classifying these figures, but ascribed them to the London workshop as in the absence of any direct evidence there seems to be nothing distinctly provincial in their style'.[29] The peculiarities of Lady Willoughby d'Eresby however strengthen the contrary conclusion, that these particular brasses are provincial adaptations of London patterns. The Spilsby lord is richly armed with two belts, elaborate gauntlets, a bevor over the aventail and a jewelled orle round his bascinet. In contrast to this, Richard Hansard lacks small ornament, but is a bold example of early complete plate armour. His design has affinities to the later patterns of the York engravers.[30*]

Only the feet remain at Boston of a civilian, standing on a bracket with two wives, who fortunately survive. These figures are undoubtedly provincial work.

Female figures add substantially to the impression that these brasses have entirely different origins from the numerous London examples. Lora de St Quintin is easy in posture; her gown is of unusual form with a high collar, and strings of pearls are arranged at the sides of her headdress. Lucy Willoughby d'Eresby at Spilsby, holds her hands apart palms forwards in the orans manner, a pose similarly taken by the wives of the Boston civilian. Her hair is held in a form of crespine headdress with a coronet, and her gown is very full with immense sleeves. Joan Hansard at South Kelsey is graceless but boldly cut, and rests her head on a large pillow (*The Craft,* Fig. 166). Another rather similar female figure c. 1410 is at South Ormsby. A worn half effigy c. 1380, St Mary Barton-on-Humber, imitates the Flemish presentation of the hands, one folded over the other.

The headless half effigy of a priest, William Darell 1364, set on a bracket, Brandsburton, is possibly of northern provincial work. A large priest in choir cope c. 1380, Auckland St Andrew, is undoubtedly provincial, and probably by the same engraver as the St Quintins at Brandsburton (Fig. 90). His hands are folded in the manner of Lora, and his feet jut out from beneath his cassock without any grass or other support.

A very uncertain case is the large but worn figure of a priest in cope, perhaps John Stransgill 1408, at Boston. It appears in most respects to be of the 'C' series, but the shock of curled hair and the wide spread bottom of the cope are unexpected features. It may be a provincial copy of a London model, but the existing evidence is inconclusive.(Fig. 89).

The participation of northern engravers at this period is beyond serious doubt. In addition to the documentary evidence cited by Harvey, the brasses described are not of established London types, are found only in Yorkshire, Lincolnshire and Durham, and exhibit peculiarities, some of which can be related to the conventions of York designs in other media.

There is no evidence of substance to prove the activity of engravers in other areas, though Sir Nicholas Burnell, at Acton Burnell, invites speculation.

Arrangement and Composition: Figure arrangement

Throughout this period, on both London and northern brasses, the great majority of figures are represented as recumbent with their hands placed together in prayer. Their attitude is confirmed by supports for the feet and quite frequently for the head also. Most military figures rest their feet on lions, though several of the 'A' series place them upon hounds which stare upwards. Many women rest their feet upon single or pairs of lop-eared dogs, or small dogs with belled collars sit among the folds of their dresses. The foot rest is in most cases presented in a pleasing style, indicative of pets or beasts of benevolent disposition. The lion at Southacre 1384, is one of a very few in which ferocity is a visible quality. The remarkable named dog, 'Terri', below the feet of Lady Cassy at Deerhurst 1400, is undoubtedly intended to be a pet, and this name was presumably included by specific request. The ecclesiastics at Watton-at-Stone and Shillington have lion and dog supports respectively. The Earl of Warwick rests his feet on a bear, a badge of the Beauchamps. John Curteys at Wymington, 1391, rests on a dog, though most civilians and priests have grassy plots beneath their feet and even military figures at Ticehurst and Draycot Cerne have such rests. The (?) cushion at Rothwell, the bedesmen at St Stephen's, Norwich and the tiles base at Astwood, Bucks., are unusual arrangements. The wool merchant at Northleach, who rests his feet upon a woolsack, and the vintner at Cirencester who rests upon a wine cask, are early examples of the use of trade emblems in this context.

Several of the military figures rest their heads upon crested helms, even though all but one of their number wear the bascinet. Examples are at Bray, Seal, Blickling, Lingfield, Sawtrey All Saints, Cobham, c. 1410; Stoke-by-Nayland and Exeter cathedral. The crests make interesting details and include at Bray a fox's head, at Seal a hunting horn and at Sawtry All Saints a monk with a scourge (Fig. 76). The Saracen's head at Lingfield and the fish at Cobham are both restorations. Several ladies rest their head upon pillows. Some are embroidered, as those at Burford and Hemel Hempstead. Most have knobs or tassels at the corners. The pillows behind the head of Eleanor de Bohun, Duchess of Gloucester 1399, at Westminster Abbey, are especially elaborate, the upper one engraved to indicate its convex shape. Pillows support the heads of ecclesiastics at Rothwell and Ringwood.

Angels are depicted supporting the cushion on one brass — that of Archdeacon William de Rothwelle, and this is notably influenced by Continental designs. One of a pair of small angels issuing from clouds, who once supported a helmet set above the head, still exists at Horseheath.

Figure arrangements of some vitality appear where man and wife clasp hands, a semi-profile view of the head is given, or where figures are kneeling. Examples of clasped hands are found at Southacre, Crishall, Draycot Cerne, Dartmouth, Little Shelford (both brasses) and Owston. Semi-profile is shown on four brasses. The head of John Pecok at St Michael, St Albans, is subtley turned towards his wife. At Allerton Mauleverer the knight is slightly turned to show the form of the raised visor. At St Saviour's Dartmouth the wives of John Hauley are turned towards the central figure. Thomas de Frevile and his widow at Little Shelford, Cambs., are deliberately turned, and have an unusual ease of posture for the period. Kneeling figures are or were associated with brackets or figure crosses. The half figure of Rauf de Cobham 1402, Cobham, is a unique design, showing him holding his inscription plate as if presenting it to the reader.

A few examples illustrate symbols of office or other emblems held in the hands: for example the representation of Cobham College held by Sir John de Cobham, a chalice held by the priest at Stanford-on-Soar and a chalice with inscribed Host by Alexander Chelseye at Chinnor. The latter are early examples of a feature which became fashionable in the latter part of the fifteenth century. Hearts are held by the Redford knight and his wife at Broughton.

Canopies

Canopies of graceful ogival form commonly surround the figures and examples have been noted in the text. They are more numerous than at any later period in proportion to the number of figure brasses surviving. This may be an indication of the very clear relationship between brass and other monumental design at this time and of an appreciation of architectural ornament for its own sake. Most canopies consist of an ogival pediment, with a soffit cusped on its under side. Courses of foliage breaking out into equally spaced crockets decorate the outer edges, and combine at the apex to form a finial. The soffit is decorated with small quatrefoils. Canopy shafts are usually slim and of three stages, the first plain, the second faced with a narrow canopied recess and the third rising to its pinnacle top almost parallel to the finial of the pediment. The pediment is filled with tracery, commonly taking the form of an ornamental circle or oculus and three spandrels. Occasionally, as in the Dallingridge brass c. 1380, Fletching, the oculus is dispensed with and the spandrels form an elongated trefoil. This treatment occurs in the sculpture of the court craftsmen, as for example on the canopies of the tomb chest of Sir Simon Burley, K.G., formerly at Old St Pauls. More commonly, as in the canopy of Dame Margaret de Cobham, Cobham, the upper spandrel is combined with the oculus, forming an elegant and assymetrical centre. The pediments of the Rahere tomb at St Bartholomew the Great, London, are of a similar design. This tomb is attributed by Harvey to Henry Yevele.[31] Though lions' heads and other corbels commonly jut from pinnacles, there is a marked absence of figure decoration within the pediments, a restraint, in contrast to French fashion, found in all work of the Westminster court sculptors and architects of the period. Only two exceptions are known to the author and these occur in canopies connected with the figures of the decorative 'A' patterns. The upper spandrels of the canopies of the Curteys brass at Wymington are filled with winged dragons. The upper spandrel and oculus of the Codyngtoun brass at Bottesford enclose a figure of the Blessed Virgin and Child (*The Craft,* Fig. 170). The pediments in canopies of the 'A' patterns are richer in general decorative detail than those of the 'B' series. The oculus is sometimes surrounded by a circle enriched with flowers or quatrefoils as at Sheldwich, 1394, and spandrels are filled with freely drawn foliage. At Dartmouth, 1408, the oculi are enriched with elaborate variations of tracery. In general the oculus in all patterns is usually left plain or decorated with a rosette or similar floral centre. The use of an oculus to contain a shield of arms as at Dyrham, or a trade mark on a shield as at Chipping Campden, 1401; personal initials as at Norbury 1360; a motto on scroll held by a hand as at Great Tew, c. 1410; and the chained swan badge and lion's head on the brass of Eleanor de Bohun 1399, Westminster Abbey, is exceptional.

The most common canopy arrangement is for a single pediment to cover one figure, double pediments occurring when man and wife are represented together. There are, however, considerable variations. Triple pediments are used to cover a single figure as at Laughton, c. 1400, and Spilsby, c. 1405, or to cover two figures as at Chrishall, c. 1380. A canopy may have a double soffit but only one pediment, an arrangement shown on the Waldegrave indent 1410, Bures. The form of the canopy itself may be individualistic. The slightly curved and embattled canopies with distinctive lanterns at Stoke Fleming 1391, and an almost identical indent at Dittisham were no doubt specified in the order. The curved embattled canopy of the Countess of Athol c. 1375, Ashford, is highly curious in that banner staves formed the canopy shafts.[32] Other variations are found in the form of the architectural shafts. At Playford 1400, the shafts are duplicated and the pairs connected by flying buttresses. A central shaft separates the figures of William and Marion Grevel 1401, Chipping Campden. Canopy designs were further enriched in a variety of ways. An embattled parapet or super canopy is found at Hereford cathedral 1360, and Fletching, c. 1380, supported by the side shafts and carried over above the finials of the pediments. This arrangement was adopted more widely in the fifteenth century. A tabernacle or cluster of tabernacles is set upon the pediment in a few choice examples. The canopy of Sir Reginald Braybrok at Cobham supports a single tabernacle enclosing a representation of the Holy Trinity. God the Father, shown as an aged bearded man, is seated with the crucified Christ before him. The dove, symbol of the Holy Ghost, rests upon the Cross. The canopy of Sir Nicholas Hawberk, also at Cobham, has a similar tabernacle and representation but also adjoining niches enclosing figures of the Blessed Virgin and Christ Child and a spirited St George on foot slaying the dragon (*The Craft,* Fig. 57). The tabernacle above the central pediment of the triple canopy of John Sleford at Balsham is elevated by two slim shafts and breaks through the border inscription. A representation of the Trinity fills the tabernacle, and two angels below bear up the soul of the deceased in a winding sheet (*The Craft,* Fig. 56). Seraphim with folded wings rise upon the finials of the side pediments. Sacred representations were not necessarily contained within an architectural framework. A figure of the Blessed Virgin and Christ Child is supported directly by the canopy finial on the brass of Dame Margaret de Cobham. A similar figure is lost from the canopy of Sir John de Cobham. A representation of the Coronation of the Virgin was supported by a bracket rising from the central shaft of a canopied brass at Worcester cathedral, the indent of which lies in the crypt.

The most elaborate canopies of all were those in which the architectural structure served as a framework of tabernacles and niches for figures of Apostles and Saints and the Glorious Company of Heaven. The canopy of Walter Pescod and his wife 1398, Boston, is the sole survivor of these magnificent compositions. Indents at the cathedrals of Ely and Lincoln preserve some record of others, as do the drawings by Dugdale and Hollar of brasses in St Paul's cathedral prior to the fire of 1666. The canopy of Thomas de Eure 1400, containing a large representation of the Annunciation, was of a type now totally lost.[33] The Pescod canopy is both worn and mutilated, but retains the side shafts and triple pediments over each figure, and a considerable part of the upper tabernacles. Peascods, alluding to the name, are worked as decorative ornament into the canopy (*The Craft,* Fig. 171). The canopy for Baron Willoughby d'Eresby and wife, Spilsby, was equally ornate, but only the pediments and architectural base remain.

Excellence is not necessarily measured in scale or intricacy, and no canopy survives from this period that is better conceived or executed than that of Eleanor de Bohun 1399, at Westminster Abbey (*The Craft,* Fig. 173). The triple pediment is graceful and delicate and strongly buttressed with wide shafts. Shields of arms hang upon the shafts and are a specially good feature of the design. The architectural base, with blank shields in quatrefoils, is reminiscent of the façade of a tomb chest and the whole is an admirable surround to the severe but graceful figure of the Duchess, whose head is made the centre of attention by the ornate cushions behind. It is an example of English brass engraving at its very best. In this and most other canopy work little attempt is made to suggest moulding or depth. Only on the canopies at Acton Burnell, Cirencester, Laughton, and both Woburn and Haddenham (from which the entire figures of John Morton 1394, and William Noion 1405, are lost) is the groined vault within the pediments brought into view. But these five brasses, none of which are of the 'B' series, are clumsy in their effect and prove the wisdom of the designers in eschewing such detail.

Crosses and Brackets

The open-headed cross and the bracket brass were alternative forms of architectural frame for the presentation of figures or subsidiary subjects. Though the destruction of these types of brass was widespread, and generalisations based on their numbers are speculative, it would appear that the crosses were losing favour by the close of the fourteenth century, and brackets were gradually taking their place. Though causes for such a change of taste are obscure, the change appears to be real. Only four examples of figured crosses survive at Hereford cathedral 1386, St Michael's, St Albans, c. 1400; Buxted, and Stone, 1408. The Hereford and St Albans crosses are of octofoil form and comparable to the earlier cross at Taplow both in their shape, finials and circular decoration. Another cross at Hereford, surrounding the figure of a civilian 1394, was similar but is now completely lost. The only remarkable detail among these is the stem at St Albans which is elaborately decorated with diamond-shaped ornament and flowers. The Buxted and Stone crosses are more interesting. The first is in commemoration of the priest Britell Avenel. The cross is quatrefoil in shape, rising on a long narrow stem from a base of steps. The priest lies almost three quarter length in the centre against a background of simple geometric pattern. John Lumbarde's at Stone is of octofoil shape and very handsome. The stem, bursting with small foliate branches, bears the inscription which continues onto the steps. The arms of the cross are inscribed with an abbreviated form of the text from Job 19: 25-27. This was used in the mediaeval Office of the Dead, and occurs on brasses in a variety of contexts. (*The Craft,* Fig. 169).

Brackets, which were of little significance before the mid fourteenth century, survive in greater numbers than figured crosses and in a variety of forms. The most elaborate consisted of a bracket, set upon a shaft with stepped or animal base, supporting a figure or figures with a canopy of single, double or triple pediments. Brackets are found, though mostly in a very damaged state, at Clifton Campville, c. 1360, Brandsburton, 1364; Harrow, c. 1370; Bray, 1378; Boston, Ore, c. 1400; and Cobham, 1402. Only the last is almost perfect, and missing fragments have been restored. The bracket has an inscribed stem and supports a canopy with triple pediments. At Harrow, Boston and Ore only the canopies remain. At Clifton Campville and Bray the canopies are lost. The Brandsburton bracket was of simple form without canopy. The Foxle brass at Bray is the most unusual (*The Craft,* Fig. 174). The three figures are set upon a base of quatrefoil supported by a broad bracket on a short stem, rising from the back of a fox. John Seys 1376, West Hanney, originally had a bracket support. An excellent bracket indent probably dating from this period is at Woodbridge.

Crosses continued to be used as a framework for votive compositions, and brackets too began to serve this purpose. The two crosses of this type and the one bracket are all brasses of outstanding interest. John Mulsho, Esq., and wife 1400, Geddington, kneel at the foot of a rather plain quatrefoil cross (*The Craft,* Fig. 60). Short prayer scrolls are addressed towards a figure of St Faith, standing in the cross-head and holding a sword and gridiron. Robert Parys and wife 1408, Hildersham, (Fig. 92) kneel halfway up the stem of an octofoil cross of usual design, the head of which is filled with a large representation of the Holy Trinity. The bracket brass to John Strete 1405, Upper Hardres, has been justifiably much illustrated (*The Craft,* Fig. 175). The priest kneels at the foot of a lofty bracket, his long prayer scroll twisting up the stem to figures of Saints Peter and Paul above. This brass shows clearly the advantage of such an architectural feature to bind the composition.

The figureless cross was probably a fairly common type of memorial which has been almost completely destroyed. Two valuable examples survive at Grainthorpe, c. 1380, and Higham Ferrers, 1400. These are described in detail in relation to other emblem brasses in Chapter Fourteen.

Additional Representations and Ornament

Other accessories require comment. The Evangelists' symbols are found towards the end of the period, framed in medallions and occupying corner positions within the border inscription. Good examples are at Addington 1378; St Cross, Winchester, 1382; Wanlip, 1393; Seal, 1395; Balsham, 1401; and Strensham, 1405. Unusually prominent sets are engraved on shields around the figure of Roger Campedene 1398, Stanford-in-the-Vale, and on the terminals of the arms of the Higham Ferrers cross. They are not, at this period, a common feature, and are noticeably absent at Cobham. Two interesting emblematic shields are incorporated on the brass of John de Campedene, 1382, at St Cross, Winchester, the dexter being an example of the verbal device of the Holy Trinity, in which three circles inscribed with the contracted words 'PATER', 'FILIUS' and 'SPIRITUS SANCTUS' are separated from each other by the words 'NON EST' and linked to a central circle inscribed 'DEUS' with the word 'EST'. The sinister shield contains emblems of the Passion — the cross, the crown of thorns, a spear, the reed and sponge, a scourge, a whipping post, nails and a hammer. Such details increased in popularity during the course of the fifteenth century and are examined more fully in Chapter Fifteen. Background decoration in the form of a powdering of devices was rarely applied. The indent at Chichester cathedral to Bishop(?) Rede c. 1380, recording an inlay of stars and crescents, is exceptional.

Heraldry

Shields of arms when appropriate to the deceased are usually inlaid around the figures or canopy work. Seven of an original eight are placed around Margery de Wylughby 1391, Spilsby. In some cases a shield and rectangular inscription form a complete memorial, as for John Govys c. 1360, Long Crichel; Sir John de Rokesle 1361, Lullingstone; Alice Tyrell c. 1380, Downham; John de Cobham 1399, Hever; and Richard Roos 1406, West Drayton. The shield of William Tonge 1389, All Hallows-by-the-Tower, London, is set within a circular inscription. Four shields are laid with the inscription of Henry Frowyk 1386, South Mimms. Achievements of arms were apparently rare, but an excellent example, laid horizontally above the heads of Sir John Harsick and his wife 1384, Southacre, is very similar to the gilt latten Garter plate of Sir Ralph Bassett (1368-90) at St George's chapel, Windsor.[34] The vintner's brass, c. 1400, at Cirencester is the earliest to display civic arms (Bristol). The banners above the Countess of Athol at Ashford have been mentioned.

While shields of arms are generally correct and well executed, certain artistic liberties were taken by the engravers. A swan badge, now lost, appeared on a shield at the base of the canopy of Eleanor de Bohun. Other shields were used as background to non-heraldic accessories, such as the Evangelists' symbols at Stanford-in-the-Vale, and the prayers 'JESUS MERCY' and 'LADY HELP' on the vintner's brass at Cirencester. Particularly fine features of the worn Courtenay brass at Exeter cathedral, are two badges set at the upper corners in quadrilobe medallions representing falcons attacking a duck and a(?) heron. The history of this falcon badge and the curious sequel to its adoption is described at length by Haines.[35]

Inscriptions

Inscriptions throughout the period are engraved on rectangular plates or narrow border fillets, and on several of the larger compositions both types are used. The circular inscription of William Tonge is a unique survival. Occasionally, as at Etchingham, 1388, part of the inscription is engraved on a semicircular plate above the head, or as at Stone, 1408, is engraved upon the cross shaft. Black letter script in short and well spaced letters is used on all, though often with Lombardics for capitals. The lettering is usually engraved into the plate, though there are several examples in which the ground has been chiselled away leaving the letters in relief; the border inscriptions in latten on the Royal tombs are treated in this manner. French and Latin are the languages mainly used. French declined in popularity by the end of the period. The inscription at Rothwell to William de Rothwelle 1361, has sections in both. The first inscriptions in English begin to appear, at this time.

The majority of inscriptions retain the simplicity of content of earlier periods. A few, such as that of Alban de Fen c. 1372, Much Hadham, are engraved in one line on a narrow strip. The following examples to two priests are typical of brief French and Latin texts. The first, to Walter de Annefordhe 1361, Binfield, reads:

Water de Annefordhe gist icy
dieu de sa alme eit mercy.

The second, to John Verieu 1370, Saltwood reads:

Hic jacet d*omi*nus Johannes Verieu quonda*m* rector eccl*es*ie de
Sandherst cuius a*nim*e *pro*picietur omnium rector d*eus*.

Many inscriptions record the date of death, and particulars of rank and parentage run to some length, but few diverge far from these simple statements. There are variations of opening and conclusion. At Cobham, c. 1365 and 1367, Mereworth 1366, and Etchingham, 1388, the line 'De terre fu fet & fourme et en terre fu retourne', with variations, precedes the main text. The inscription of Reginald de Asshe c. 1375, Ash-next-Wrotham, is flanked by representations of ash trees (on separate plates) and begins with the words 'Ih*esu*s Nazaren*us* rex iudeor*um*'. The inscription of Thomas de Cobham 1367, Cobham, concludes with a prayer, 'le haut Trinitie luy soyt defender denfern abysme'. The inscription of Sir William Fienlez 1402, Hurstmonceux, includes a promise of one hundred and twenty days pardon for those saying a Pater and Ave for the soul of the deceased. At the close of the fourteenth century lines are included to command the attention of the reader to the transience of life. The inscription of John Bettesthorne 1398, Mere, concludes:

Tu qui transieris videas sta, perlege, plora,
Es quod eram, et eris quod sum, pro me precor ora.

The foot inscription at Fulbourne to William de Fulberne 1391, reads:

Vermibus hic donor, et sic ostendere conor,
Quod sicut hic ponor, ponit omnis honor.

These particular lines are engraved on several fifteenth- and sixteenth-century brasses. In contrast to this morbid emphasis on corruption the text from Job 19: 25-27, used in the mediaeval Office of the Dead, is confident and forward looking in its conviction. The use of this text has already been noted on the Flemish brass at Newark and in part on the cross at Stone. It is recorded in full on the border inscription of John de Campeden 1382, St Cross, Winchester:

Credo q*uo*d redemptor meus vivit, & in novissimo die de terra surrecturus sum, & rursum circumdabor pelle mea et in carne mea videbo deum salvator*em* me*um* Quem visurus sum ego ip*se* & oculi mei conspecturi sunt & non alius reposita est hec spes mea in sinu meo.

The short foot inscription reads:

Hic jacet Johannes de Campeden' qu*on*dam custos istius hospitalis cuius a*nim*e *pro*piciet*ur* deus.

A very curious Latin inscription is found below the figure of John Flambard c. 1390, Harrow:

Ion medo [*sic,* for modo?] marmore Numinis ordine flam tumulat*ur*
Bard q*uia* verbere stigis E fun*ere* hic tueatur.

The reading is obscure, it may be that there are mistakes in the text, but it may be translated: 'John Flambard even now entombed in marble by God's ordinance, Because of (His) stripes is here preserved from Stygian burial.' The reference to the Styx is an early allusion to classical mythology. Four inscriptions in English are from this period though one is not monumental. The earliest, to John the Smith c. 1370, Brightwell Baldwin, is of great interest. It has been translated with notes by Professor W. W. Skeat, who describes it as being in a West Midlands dialect.[36] Major H. F.

Owen Evans, when refixing this brass, discovered that the rivetting was of very inferior quality, and the inscription may be an early example of provincial work. It reads:

> Man come and se how schal alle dede be: wen *th*ow comes bad and bare no'th hab ven we away fare: All ys ozermen*s* *th*(a)t ve for care: Bot *th*(a)t ve do for godysluf ve have nothyng *th*are: Hundyr *Th*is grave lys John *the* Smyth god Yif his soule heven grit.

Professor Skeat's translation reads:

'Man! come and see how all (the) dead shall be
When to you comes evil and bareness (so as)
To have naught when we travel away.
All that we care for is other men's.
Except that which we do for God's love
We have nothing there (i.e. in the grave)
Under this grave lies John the Smith,
God give his soul Heaven's peace.'

The second inscription is of copper c. 1382, on the wall of Cooling castle, and commemorates the construction:

'Knouwyth that beth and schul be
That I am mad in help of the cuntre
In knowing of whyche thyng
Thys is chartre and wytnessyng.'

The third, to Sir Thomas Walsh and wife 1393, Wanlip, partly concerns the good works of Katherine who 'made the kirke of anlep and halud the kirkerd first in wurchip of god and oure lady and seynt Nicholas'. The English is far more intelligible than that on the Smith inscription, and occurring on the memorial of a knight is indicative of its increasing respectability. The fourth inscription in rhyming verse c. 1405, Holme-next-the-sea, is recorded in *The Craft.* A selection of rectangular inscription plates without figures or shield of arms may be cited from Hertingfordbury, Malpas, Erith c. 1360; Cholsey, Stansted Mountfitchet, 1361; Manton, 1364; Goring, Oxon. 1375; Ockham, c. 1380; North Walsham, 1397; Chinnor c. 1400; Waltham c. 1400; Morley (fine relief lettering), and Great Bowden, 1403.

Conclusion

The fourteenth century was a period of great achievement for the English engravers and at the close of that century their work was of a consistently good design and execution. Brasses were sought by the highest dignitaries and yet were available to such humble members of society as John the Smith. English brasses achieved their quality through grace and simplicity of line, and an avoidance of decorative detail for its own sake. Canopies were often elaborate and selected features highly ornamental, but richness was rarely allowed to confuse form or detract from the essentials of the design. The uncompromisingly lineal treatment of figures and their architectural surrounds, and the neutral background of the Purbeck slab, were an effective combination. The English engravers, in contrast to their Continental counterparts, entirely accepted the limitations of their medium, and worked within them. Their genius lay in this discipline.

8. English brasses, 1410-1460

It was during the first half of the fifteenth century that brasses became common memorials for merchants, civic dignitaries and petty landowners, and were proportionately less sought after by the nobility and eminent ecclesiastics. The great increase in the production of effigies in alabaster and freestone did not reduce the market for brasses or incised slabs, though it did attract away a certain class of wealthy buyer, and the engraver's business seems to have turned towards the making of numerous medium-sized or small compositions. The change was very gradual, however, and by no means complete. Many of the finest English brasses date from this period. Yet the most noticeable development lies in the great increase in quantity rather than quality. Moreover, reduction in scale may have been influenced by other factors than choice and status. As Lawrence Stone suggests[1], a decline in the value of rents and a dissipation of wealth to obtain security may have reduced the capacity of the English gentry to emulate their ancestors.

The satisfaction of numerous modest purchasers brought predictable consequences. Patterns, though revised and modified, became more repetitive. The creation of small figures favoured conventional treatment. The standard of engraving remained good, and the widening class of those commemorated is reflected in interesting details of costume and accessories. But the difference in quality between the best and inferior brasses is very significant. There are, in addition, signs of change in artistic taste. The simplicity of fourteenth-century line was abandoned in favour of a more laboured treatment. Lines were duplicated for better decorative effect, and were in consequence less deeply and broadly cut. The flow of the lines is noticeably less free by the end of the period, and the resultant figures stiffer and more angular. Simulated shadow in the form of cross hatching was applied, at first carefully, but later tended to confuse through extravagant use. The period is one of outstanding but unequal achievement, in which even masterpieces at the close do not conceal the coarsening of design and execution. English engraving attained during this period a supreme refinement in complex but controlled compositions such as Thomas Nelond, 1433, Cowfold (*The Craft,* Fig. 188). Yet accomplished, ornate but poorly balanced canopied brasses, like that of Robert Staunton, 1458, at Castle Donnington (*Ibid,* Fig. 189), indicate a fundamental change in the standards of beauty demanded.

Dr Kent identifies, through military figures, three main series of brass patterns of apparently London origin, which were used extensively throughout the period. He ascribes them to three independent workshops, a conclusion on which this author is more guarded. His analysis is meticulous, and these three distinctive series may be traced with consistency in figures of all types. The first is a continuation of the restrained designs, classified as series 'B', on which many of the best fourteenth-century English brasses were based. The early fifteenth-century examples are equally impressive, but though their economy of line is not compromised, a stiffening of line becomes increasingly apparent after 1425. This tendency is particularly noticeable on female dress, where drapery lines have their greatest potential freedom. The second series, classified as 'D', has already been noted as probably having its origins in the fourteenth century ornate 'A' series. But, whereas the 'A' figures tended to be decorative and ungainly, those of the 'D' series are often laboured in detail but well drawn. Their representation of armour and costume is perceptive and accurate. These also tend to become static in appearance as the century progresses, and to lose their freedom and grace of pose. The third series, classified as 'E', is of an original type, experimental in arrangement and detail, and engraved with a marked inconsistency of skill. It is a less integrated series than the others, but can be traced from c.1415-1450, and is related to series 'D' rather than 'B'. These patterns do not necessarily cover the entire range of brasses made in London during the period, but the great majority of figures can be related to them.

Only a few of the engravers' names are known, but most may be presumed to have been London marblers and latteners. The names of four notable craftsmen are recorded in connexion with the preparation of the gilt latten tomb at Warwick to Richard Beauchamp, Earl of Warwick, d. 1439, for which contracts were made in 1453. The craftsmen were John Essex, marbler, William Austen, founder, Thomas Stevyns, 'Copper smyth', and Bartholomew Lambespring, 'Dutchman and goldsmith of London'. Austin is described as of London, and all were probably from that city, Essex having a workshop in St Paul's yard. Parts of the tomb are of flat engraved latten sheet, and it may be concluded that some if not all these metalworkers were engravers of monumental brasses. Furthermore research by Emmerson has shown that the marginal inscription is engraved exclusively in lettering associated with 'B' series brasses. William West, who figures prominently on the brass of his parents at Sudborough, is described on the inscription as a marbler. Emmerson has also established that on stylistic grounds the Sudborough brass was probably engraved nearer to 1440 than 1415, the date of Joan West's death. It is accordingly probable that this brass of the 'B' series was engraved in William's workshop.[2*] Richard Stephen and Richard Ronge or Rouge, shown in chapter seven of *The Craft* to have been active marblers in 1445, were possibly involved. The names of other London marblers are known, but they were not necessarily engaged in engraving.[3*]

The different types of effigies, their appearance and their costume, have greater variety than those of the preceding period. The legal profession, academics and the regular clergy are represented in sufficient numbers to provide a useful record of their respective dress. Children gradually became a customary part of family memorials. The intricacies of full plate armour add to the interest of military figures. Civil and female dress reflect a greater range of fashions and some extravagances. The effigies are most usefully described according to type, though keeping in view the peculiarities in treatment of the various patterns used. A separate description, as in Chapter Seven, is given of brasses of northern origin which are of a distinctly provincial style.

Men in armour

All military figures of the period are represented in full plate armour. It is doubtful if in practice such fashionable and expensive equipment was so common, but the earlier mixed mail and plate was unacceptable for monumental design. The only example of the aventail and jupon in all the London series is that of Sir Robert Swynborne d. 1391, shown with his son 1412, at Little Horkesley and deliberately portrayed in the style of armour still in vogue at the time of his death though following a pattern of c. 1405. (*The Craft,* Fig. 177).

The main pieces of armour worn with variations of shape and style were as follows. A bascinet was worn on the head and the throat was protected by a plate bevor, which first covered and then replaced the aventail. The body was protected by a breast-plate with backplate, and the thighs by a series of narrow overlapping plates known as the skirt of lames or fauld. This body armour was sometimes worn over the hawberk of mail, the lower extremity of which occasionally appears on brasses as a fringe below the fauld. Vambraces and rerebraces of plate inclusive of couters and spaudlers were worn on the arms. Fingered gauntlets were worn on the hands. Besagews of plate protected the vulnerable points at the armpits. Leg armour consisted of cuisses, poleyns and greaves, with pointed sabatons covering the feet. This equipment is admirably illustrated on effigies of the 'B' series, with minor variations until the year 1445. The following are among the chief examples, and are canopied or have large figures.

Thomas de Cruwe with wife, canopy, 1411, Wixford
Sir Robert and Sir Thomas Swynborne, canopy, 1412, Little Horkesley *(The Craft,* Figs. 176-7)
Robert, Lord Ferrers of Chartley, with wife, 1413, Merevale
John Peryent with wife, 1415, Digswell
Walter Cookesey, and Sir John Phelip with wife, canopy, 1415, Kidderminster
Sir Symon Felbrygge, K.G., with wife, canopy, 1416, Felbrigg *(The Craft,* Fig. 24)
Bartholomew, Lord Bourchier, with two wives, d. 1409 engr. c. 1420, Halstead
Sir John Harpeden, 1438, Westminster Abbey.

From amongst this well engraved group the Wixford, Little Horkesley, Digswell and Felbrigg brasses are outstanding. Their bascinets are quite high and pointed. Fringes of mail appear below the fauld, and below the gorget in the case of Sir Thomas Swynborne. At Digswell the belt is of late fourteenth-century style, worn low on the hips, but the others wear a narrower sword belt, set high on the right hip and sloping down to the left side. Most belts are plain or decorated with a regular course of quatrefoil or flowers, though Sir John Phelip at Kidderminster wears an unusual belt inscribed with his initials and adorned with a row of hanging tassels. A variety of minor changes are noted after 1430. Bascinets become more globular, gauntlets are formed of large articulated plates in place of the fingered type, elongated besagews are almost invariably shown, and the small plate below the poleyn is sharply pointed. Sir John Harpeden 1438, is a good example of these details. A more important innovation is the addition of two tassets to the bottom edge of the fauld, well illustrated on the large and austere figure of John Leventhorpe 1437, at Sawbridgeworth, and on the small brass of John Poyle d. 1424 but possibly engraved later,[4*] at Hampton Poyle.

About 1440 these patterns were more drastically altered. The significant change was initially in the presentation of the person rather than the armour. The helmet was omitted altogether, revealing the bare head. Whereas it had been the custom to portray the deceased as a serious, mature man, generally with drooping moustache, now faces appeared of a more youthful aspect. This was partly ensured by the clean shaven fashion of the time, and the treatment of the hair, which was cut into a bobbed fringe well above the ears. This circumstantial explanation does not seem completely adequate and a change in taste was probably also involved. The main figures of this type include:

Sir Hugh Halsham and wife, canopy, 1441, West Grinstead
(?) John St Leger, 1442, Ulcombe (*The Craft,* Fig. 85)
Sir William Echyngham with wife and son, canopy, 1444, Etchingham
William Fynderne, Esq., with wife, canopy, 1444, Childrey
Thomas Reynes, Esq., with wife, 1451, Marston Mortaine (*The Craft,* Fig. 88)
John Digges, Esq., with wife, c. 1456, Barham (*The Craft,* Fig. 86)
Thomas Shernbourne, esq., with wife, 1458, Shernbourne.

The West Grinstead, Etchingham and Childrey brasses are the most impressive. William Fynderne is especially interesting as his body armour is covered by a very full tabard with wide sleeves, offering ample space for the embroidering of his family arms. Variations in the representation of armour are best shown on the later figures. The spaudlers protecting the shoulders were replaced by large single plates called pauldrons, worn at this period in conjunction with reinforcements. All the examples from 1447 to 1456 show this feature well, and in addition represent the fauld as ridged. Thomas Reynes is a typical figure of this type. The 'great bascinet' behind his head is a fair representation of this large war helm with ridged sight and rounded visor. The Barham figure is transitional. The significant changes are the omission of gauntlets and the positioning of the sword across the front of the body. The weapon is shorter and broader than before, especially in the grip. The impression created indicates a growing uncertainty on the part of the designer as to how the armour should be represented. There is no confusion of line, but the pattern lacks conviction. A comparison between this figure and its counterparts of c. 1420 reveals a loss both of freedom and understanding.

A particularly valuable brass is that of John Stathum and wife, 1454, at Morley (*The Craft,* Fig. 89). The kneeling pose of the figure exposes both front and back plates, and the broad surfaces of the pauldrons and the fauld. It is, furthermore, a remarkable link with an earlier pattern of this series, that at Standon, Herts., to John Ruggewyn 1412 (*The Craft,* Fig. 90). A comparison reveals just how small many adaptations were, and how strong was the fundamental conservatism of the pattern makers. The arrangement of the legs, the arms, and the helmet placed under the knee on the grass mound, are identical.

Another series of almost equal importance, already noted as series 'D', is of a more delicate treatment than those described. Much of the armour detail is expressed in double lines and a border of fine trefoils is for a period worked freely onto helmets, gauntlets and besagews. Couters have large fan type side-wings, and the gauntlets are distinctive. The following are among the most important examples:

Unknown, c. 1415, Barsham
(?) Sir John Drayton, mutilated, canopy and wife lost, 1417, Dorchester
John Knyvet, Esq., 1417, Mendlesham (*The Craft,* Fig. 41)
Sir William Calthorp, canopy, 1420, Burnham Thorpe
Thomas Baron Camoys, K.G. with wife, canopy, 1421, Trotton
(*The Craft,* Fig. 178)[5*]
Sir William Molyns with wife, 1425, Stoke Poges
Peter Halle with wife, c. 1430, Herne (Fig. 93)
Sir John Lysle, canopy, d. 1407 engr. c. 1430, Thruxton
Sir Giles Daubeney with wife, canopy, d.1445 engr. c.1430, South Petherton
William Harwedon with wife, bracket, canopy lost, 1433, Great Harrowden
Roger Elmebrygge, Esq., 1437, Beddington.

The brass of Baron Camoys 1421, Trotton, is a superb monument and might well be chosen as the finest English brass of the fifteenth century. The baron is armed exactly as described above with very large decorative round besagews. His pose fully displays the left gauntlet. It is a remarkable feature of this series as a whole, that even upon small figures, and those at Dodford c. 1420 and Dinton 1424, are very small, the utmost care has been taken over the representation of armour and ornament. The modest figure of Sir William Molyns 1425, Stoke Poges, is an example. His gauntlets have articulated cuffs, clearly riveted. His besagews are long with jewelled studs. His dagger is ornamented with circles and a rose, and the pommel of his sword engraved with a shield bearing a cross for St George (?). A variety of unusual details occur, such as the decoration of a belt with leaves at Dorchester, Oxon., and most particularly the use of initials as ornament on sword scabbards. J.S. is inscribed at Dorchester, R.S. at Barsham, and J.K. on the chape of the scabbard at Mendlesham. These initials have given cause for considerable speculation, as the identity of the Dorchester and Barsham figures is uncertain. The Mendlesham example is a conclusive indication that at least one forms the initials of the persons represented. The other two, however, are improbable.[6*] Roger Elmebrygge 1437, Beddington, is a fanciful figure, transitional in style, wearing two tassets strapped to the fauld. John Knyvet is unusual for his large beard falls freely over his bevor. The very worn and headless figure of Nicholas Maudyt, canopy lost 1420, Wandsworth, is unusual but probably of that group. He was Sergeant at Arms of King Henry V (described in his inscription as 'servens (sic) Regis Henrici quinti post conquestum ad arma') and wears his official mace of military type at his hip.

About 1435 the armour represented on these patterns was substantially revised, representing the Milanese armours, which were imported by those who could afford them. These armours were fashionable and expensive, and their forms altered the conventional symmetry of the figures. The most distinctive variations were the heavy reinforcement of armour on the left shoulder and elbow, a lengthening and pointing of the gauntlet cuffs, the shortening of the fauld and the consistent use of tassets. The following figures are excellent examples of some or all of these changes.

Richard Delamare with wife, canopy, 1435, Hereford cathedral
Richard Dixton, canopy, 1438, Cirencester
Sir William Wadham with mother, canopy, c. 1440, Ilminster (Fig. 94)
Sir John Bernard with wife, canopy, 1451, Isleham.

The Hereford and Cirencester figures are the largest, but most of the smaller examples are as rich in detail. Studs, buckles, straps and arming points are meticulously represented, and the forms of the plates are competently defined. The Newland 1443, and Isleham figures are bareheaded. The former has a remarkably full bushy beard and rests his head on a great bascinet with raised visor.

Two brasses at the close of the period may be described as transitional, though their most notable features belong to new fashions. These are:

Robert Staunton with wife, canopy, 1458, Castle Donnington
(The Craft, Fig. 189)
William Stapilton with wife (?) added c. 1470, 1458, Edenhall (Fig. 95).

Both wear the sallet, a light visored helmet, shaped to protect the back of the neck. This was usually worn with a bevor which is not shown in these examples. Robert Staunton's couters are of enormous size, and exaggerated beyond credibility. His pauldrons are also massive.

The military figures of a third pattern series (Kent's 'E' series) are less interesting as illustrations of armour but distinctive as designs. The pattern is comparatively regular but the examples differ considerably in quality of execution. Armour is rather clumsily presented, and on some figures the sword is hung slanting steeply outwards. Spurs are usually shown long and crossing each other. An interesting peculiarity of treatment is seen in the faces. Noses are rather long, mouths strongly defined, and in most cases the eyeball is shown as a complete circle, imparting a staring aspect. The following are examples:

John Wantele, 1424, Amberley
Thomas Salle, 1422, Stevington (*The Craft,* Fig. 51)
Sir John de Brewys, 1426, Wiston
Thomas Beckingham 1431, Northleigh
Thomas Widville of Grafton with two wives, canopy, 1435 (appropriated 1535), Bromham, Beds. (Fig. 96).

Two small and rather poorly-engraved figures, both probably of this pattern and engraved c.1415 are at Stokenchurch. Half effigies, the earlier with wife, are at Debenham c. 1425, and Battle 1435. The dates of engraving of several of these brasses may well vary by ten years from those recorded in the inscriptions, or alternatively the engraver adhered stubbornly to his patterns. The Faringdon, 1443, figures in particular appear to be earlier than indicated.

The Wiston, Northleigh and Bromham brasses are the finest and Sir John de

Brewys the most remarkable. He is both large and carefully engraved, and set against a background of six shields and thirty small scrolls forming a rich composition. John Wantele at Amberley is small but interesting. His hands and head are bare, revealing his close-cropped hair and protruding ears. He wears a form of tabard, the earliest depicted on a brass, emblazoned with the arms: Vert three lion's faces Argent langued Gules. In contrast to the tabard of 1444 at Childrey, which is almost of the conventional herald's style, that at Amberley appears as a shirt with short open sleeves. This form was presumably a transition from the heraldic jupon.

Collars and the Garter

The collar of SS associated with the House of Lancaster is commonly shown at this period on military brasses of all types. It is generally held in place over the bevor by a trifoliate clasp with two buckles. The groundwork of the collar is cut away for colour inlay, leaving the letters in relief. In a few examples the ground has been completely chiselled out, as at Digswell 1415, and Blakesley 1416, and the nature of the collar may only be surmised. An undoubted representation is Little Horkesley 1412 (*The Craft,* Fig. 176); Sir Thomas Brook, 1437, in civilian dress at Thorncombe, wears a long collar of this kind as do wives at Digswell, Trotton and Thorncombe. A knight of the Warren family, perhaps John Waryne c. 1430, St Michael Lewes, bears on the besagew the badge of a swan, used by Henry IV in right of his first wife Mary, heiress of the Bohun Earls of Hereford descended from the 'Swan Knight' Charles of Lorraine, d. 994. A similar badge is worn by Joan Peryent at Digswell who was chief lady in waiting to Joan of Navarre, Henry IV's second wife.[7]

The famous Garter worn by knights of that 'Most Noble Order' is depicted below the left knee of Sir Symon Felbrygg, K.G., Felbrigg, and of Baron Camoys, K.G., Trotton. The arms of Camoys are also encircled with the Order's device of a buckled Garter inscribed 'hony soit qy mal y pense.'

Male civilians

Civilian effigies are numerous and vary greatly in scale and quality. The majority are less than 76 cm in length and several are half figures. Nevertheless there are a considerable number providing excellent representations of civil dress. These important brasses were laid by select members of society. Foremost were wool-merchants, who were a very influential and well organized body of traders. Wool was the most important element in English commerce, and control of the wool trade by means of approved organizations and locations became a major interest of the Crown. The woolmen were not flock owners but middlemen financiers, who bought wool from all sources and resold it. John Lyndewode, whose fine brass is at Linwood, left among his legacies the item 'I bequeath to the thirty churches in whose parishes I was wont to buy wool that they pray for my soul and for the souls of those to whom I am beholden, £10, leaving it to the discretion of my executors to choose the villages.'[8] It is especially in the rich wool areas of the Cotswolds and the Lincolnshire wolds that these brasses are found. The woolmerchants' preference for brasses is most probably explained by the matter of 'degree'. While many could have afforded effigies, their station did not qualify them. Other merchants, in particular the clothiers and vintners, laid similar memorials. Civic dignitaries, mayors and aldermen, themselves usually being merchants, are represented by brasses of good but not outstanding quality. A few well connected and influential families have members represented by very elaborate civilian brasses, those of William Chichele and wife 1425, Higham Ferrers, and Nicholas Carrew and wife 1432, Beddington, being especially noteworthy.

Occasionally a knight was represented in civil dress as Sir Thomas Brook, 1437, Thorncombe. Other distinguished persons whose effigies may be most appropriately described as civilian were the judges and lawyers.

Civilian figures may be grouped within the pattern series 'B', 'D' and 'E', which have been described, though their dress gives less scope for variety and in consequence for contrast as compared with the armed figures. Changes in fashion were not dramatic, and the brasses may be described conveniently within two periods.

Between the years 1410 and 1418 there is little change in costume from that of the first ten years of the century. Civilians are shown in a long belted tunic, generally with a hood, and wearing hose and shoes. The sleeves of the tunic were usually narrow. Mantles and short swords are worn by a few. Typical examples are at Ashby St Legers 1416, and Pakefield 1417, with half effigies at St Helen's Abingdon and Wanborough.

The only unusual figure of this period is Hugh de Gondeby 1411, Tattershall, whose sword is hung centrally from a long shoulder strap. Most are of the competent 'B' series, though three at Bristol, Trinity Almshouse Chapel; St Albans cathedral, & Tattershall all 1411, appear to belong to the 'A' series.

Around the year 1418 there were changes in the dress represented which acquired an almost standard pattern by 1425. The cut of the tunic becomes shorter, and much fuller in the sleeves, which are of bag form, though narrow at the wrists. Fur linings or edgings were usually shown at the cuffs and along the bottom edges of tunics, and are exposed by slits cut in the tunics to facilitate movement. A central slit is that most commonly shown, though John Olyver 1446, Naseby, reveals a slit to the side. The tight fitting undertunic appears at the wrists. The hood is rarely shown, and then in conjunction with the mantle, which ceases to be common and is usually worn by persons of civic standing only. On many brasses the hose and shoes are undifferentiated, though in others the form and lacing of the shoes are shown in detail. The rare instances of swords are for the most part very well engraved. The following are among the most important examples of full-length figures:

John Lyndewode, Woolman with wife, canopy, 1419, Linwood
John Lyndewode woolman, canopy, 1421, same
Nicholas Carew with wife, canopy, 1432, Beddington
Simon Seman vintner, 1433, St Mary, Barton-on-Humber (*The Craft,* Fig. 179)
Robert Skern with wife, 1437, Kingston-on-Thames
John Bacon woolman, with wife, 1437, All Hallows-by-the-Tower, London
John Spycer with wife, kneeling, bracket, 1437, Burford, Oxon.
Sir Thomas Brook with wife, 1437, Thorncombe
Robert Pagge woolman, with wife, canopy, 1440, Cirencester
John Browne woolman, with wife, engr. c. 1442 and inscription added c. 1460, All Saints, Stamford (Fig. 102)
Reginald Spycer with four wives, 1442, Cirencester (*The Craft,* Fig. 33)
William Scors tailor, Thomas Forty, woolman, with their wife, canopy, 1447, Northleach (*The Craft,* Fig. 180)
Richard Manfeld with sister and brother in shroud, 1455, Taplow (Fig. 97)
John Fortey woolman, canopy, 1458, Northleach.

These brasses are good representations of costume and notable examples of the pattern series to which they belong. Beddington, Thorncombe, Stamford and Northleach are of the prolific 'B' series. Nicholas Carrew is large, and his strong and handsome face hardly reflects the description of age in the inscription 'Senex et plenus dierum'. Sir Thomas Brook wears a long and ostentatious overtunic, high in the collar and with deep sleeves. John Browne wears the mantle and hood, by that date unfashionable and most probably a token of civic status. The ample purse or gypcière hung from his belt is an especially fine detail. His face, in contrast to the others, is of an ageing man. The smaller but good figure of Richard Manfeld, and a civilian c.1455 at Sundridge, show the changes in costume taking place at the close of the period. The overtunic is narrower, with sleeves shorter in length and padded at the shoulder. Nevertheless, a comparison of treatment of facial features and hands on these brasses reveals little change. The very pleasing kneeling figure at Burford offers a valuable profile view of the hood with its long pendent liripipe. The woolmerchants at Linwood, All Hallows-by-the-Tower and Cirencester, together with Skern at Kingston-on-Thames and a fine small figure at Swainswick 1439, are admirable 'D' figures, all wearing shoes covering the ankle which are a normal detail of this series. Lacing, fur lining and other small features are carefully finished. The representation of the hands is peculiar to this pattern, in which the slim fingers curve gracefully together in contrast to the stiff lines of the 'B' series. The treatment of hair is also interesting, in some cases slightly curled above the ears, on others, such as Pagge, severely cropped. Short swords are best depicted in the 'D' series. John Langston 1435, at Caversfield and Edward Courtenay c. 1450, at Christchurch Oxford are both notable in that respect. Their scabbards have a slight curve at the base, and support sheathed hunting knives. At Baldock is a 'B' series huntsman with horn c.1420.

'E' pattern figures have some common features with those of 'D' but are, on the whole, both clumsier in design and coarser in treatment. By far the best executed example is that at Northleach to Agnes Fortey and her two husbands William Scors, tailor, and Thomas Fortey, woolman, the latter being recorded as a repairer of churches and roads. Both men lie with their feet set rather wide apart, shod in high laced shoes. Their hands are slightly rounded in treatment and are not completely closed together. These hands and the deep chin and round staring eyes of Scors may be compared with those of the wives of Thomas Widville of Grafton 1435, at Bromham, a brass already identified in the 'E' series. The other figures of this series are small but most wear a sword and some form of well-defined shoe. John Quek 1449, with the figure of his son at Birchington is typical.

Lawyers

A small but important body of civilians were the lawyers, and their memorials deserve special notice. The legal profession in England by the early fifteenth century consisted of two main strata. The upper was occupied by the Serjeants-at-Law, whose rank was a degree, and the judges, who were office holders appointed by the Crown from among the serjeants. Both judges and sergeants were described as brothers of the coif, which headdress they wore in common. The lower stratum which may be described as the junior Bar, consisted of the Apprentices-at-Law who aided the serjeants in court. The apprentices included among their number many accomplished lawyers and this description is open to misinterpretation. Several brasses of this period represent judges and serjeants, and together with the few examples mentioned in the previous chapter, provide a valuable record of legal dress.

The official dress of a judge consisted of a long gown with sleeves—the supertunica, a hood and deep shoulder-piece lined with miniver, a mantle — the 'armelausa' — buttoned on the right shoulder and open down the right side, and the coif. Green was at this time the preferred colour for these robes, except for the coif which was white. The coif, the most distinctive feature of this dress, was made of white linen or silk and tied under the chin. It was a headdress of dignity widely used at court, and was not in origin or use peculiar to the serjeants or judges, though it became especially associated with them. Judges, on account of their office, were regarded as having the standing of Doctors of Law and in this capacity commonly wore a black skull cap or pileus over the coif.[10] This dress, excluding the skull cap, is admirably illustrated on the brass of

Sir John Cassy, chief Baron of the Exchequer 1400, Deerhurst.

The following brasses of London origin of this period represent judges:

Sir Hugh de Holes, Justice of the King's Bench, 1415, Watford

William de Lodyngton, Justice of the Common Pleas, canopy, 1419, Grunby St Peter

John Staverton, Baron of the Exchequer with wife, c. 1430, Eyke

John Martyn, Justice of the Common Pleas, with wife, canopy, 1436, Graveney (Fig. 103)

John Cottusmore, Chief Justice of the Common Pleas, with wife, canopy, 1439, Brightwell Baldwin

The same shown kneeling, c. 1445, Brightwell Baldwin

Sir John Juyn, Chief Justice of the King's Bench, 1439, St Mary Redcliffe, Bristol.

All these figures are apparently of the 'B' pattern series with the exception of that at Gunby St Peter which is undoubtedly 'D'. The Graveney, large Brightwell Baldwin and Bristol figures are very similar and clearly drawn from the same pattern. The Graveney brass is outstandingly fine and the small representation of Judge Cottusmore, laid down after his wife's death, is valuable in showing the dress in profile. Sir Hugh de Holes is broken and John Staverton now headless.

The headdress worn by these figures gives rise to controversy. The earliest Deerhurst brass undoubtedly shows the coif, stitched down the centre. The remainder show a similar type of headdress, though cut away, apparently for a lead or composition inlay. Dr. Hargreaves-Mawdsley describes this not as the coif but as the skull cap or pileus worn by judges over the coif. The grounds for this conclusion are not given. The author doubts the accuracy of this interpretation. There would seem to be no substantial difference between the coif worn by Serjeant Rolond at Cople and the headdress worn by these judges. Although the judges were entitled to the pileus, nevertheless their distinctive head wear was the coif, and this would accordingly attract the brass designers.[11]* On the evidence of the remnants remaining, the inlays were white, appropriate to the coif. It is, nevertheless, impossible to be certain about these conventional and full frontal representations.

The dress of Serjeants-at-Law consisted of a long supertunica which was often covered in part by a sleeveless tabard, similar in cut to that in academic use. Over these were worn a hood and shoulder-piece lined with lambswool. Serjeants wore the coif but not the mantle. The most distinctive aspect of their dress lay in the colour rather than the form. Supertunicas and tabards were parti-coloured and often striped as vividly represented on the excellent illuminations of a Law Treatise of c. 1460, originally preserved at Whaddon Hall and now in the possession of the Inner Temple.[12] Existing brasses do not attempt to indicate these contrasts.

Another notable feature of serjeants' dress were labels — two pendent tongues of material falling on the shoulder-piece from under the hood. Labels were a token of authority and were used by academics as well as lawyers. Hargreaves-Mawdsley argues convincingly that labels were in fact appendages of the hood, used to keep it in place when in use. They were pulled round from underneath when the hood was thrown back, and set to the front.

The two brasses of serjeants, previously noted in the last chapter, are only of moderate interest as illustrations of costume. John Rede 1404, Checkendon, is dressed in a long supertunica with tight sleeves and hood, and would pass as an ordinary civilian. He has the sour expression of the 'C' series figures, and lies within a good triple canopy. Nicol Rolond c.1410, Cople, is very plain but shows the supertunica, hood with shoulder-piece and coif. Serjeants' dress, allowing for the absence of colour, is fortunately better illustrated by the figure of Thomas Rolf 1440, Gosfield (Fig. 98). A graceful example of the 'D' pattern, Rolf shows the dress fully, including the tabard and labels. The inscription states of this serjeant, 'inter iuristas quasi flos enituit iste'. There are no illustrations of costume from the 'Junior Bar'. Robert Skern 1437, Kingston-on-Thames, as 'Lege peritus', is shown in fashionable civilian dress.

Females

There are many female figures and the majority of the best examples are found as companions to their husbands on the military and civilian brasses. In addition, there are a considerable number of figures, some quite small, recording attractive costume details. The pattern series to which these figures belong can usually be judged from the shape of the hands, details of the faces, and the ornament of the dress, which is almost invariably more extravagant in the 'D' and 'E' series than in the 'B'.

The headdress, as in previous periods, remains the most subject to changes in fashion. The crespine headdress as already described is shown on brasses as late as c. 1420. Good examples are an unknown lady c. 1410, Hillmorton; Julian, wife of Thomas de Cruwe 1411, Wixford; and Joan Urban, Southfleet, both on her single effigy brass of 1414 and with her husband c. 1420. A square arrangement of the netted hair is shown by Margaret, wife of Sir Simon Felbrygge, K.G., Felbrigg, and by the fine single figure of Dame Philippe Byschoppesdon 1414, Broughton. By 1415 the nets were apparently being expanded to an artificial fullness, standing far out from the face, and spreading the veil widely. Two superb examples are the large figures of Dame Millicent Meryng 1419, East Markham, and Elizabeth, wife of Baron Camoys 1421, Trotton. These arrangements were designed for display, and are accordingly best shown on the 'D' series patterns. Their dimensions far exceed those of the crespine headdress, the most distinctive of the period. A few alternative arrangements are also illustrated. A veil set to fall gracefully about the face is the only apparent headdress of Ellen, wife of Thomas Stokes 1416, Ashby St Legers, or of the wives at Wanborough, Wilts. 1418, and Debenham, Suff. c. 1425. A young woman, almost certainly of the Clopton family c. 1420, Long Melford, wears a wide but shallow cap, decorated with small flowers, beneath which her hair falls outwards in short curls. Most spectacular and curious is the headdress of Joan Peryent 1415, Digswell, its precise nature is uncertain. Haines describes it as 'an interlaced caul, forming, together with the face, an inverted triangle; a veil lies loosely gathered on the top'. Whether the whole setting is artificial, or a cunning setting of the hair in supported nets, is not revealed. The figure is engraved with great care, including unusual details having personal reference to the lady, and the effect must be presumed to be precise (*The Craft,* Fig. 184).

The horned headdress is most common after 1420. The hair was set in cauls of a lofty sweeping form. The veil rested on the peaks of the cauls, from where it fell down in folds behind the head or over the shoulders. An early example of this headdress appears on the brass of Margaret Cheyne 1419, Hever (*The Craft,* Fig. 55). Her cauls are plain, a common feature of 'B' patterns throughout the period. Others of the series (e.g. Joan, wife of Sir William Echyngham 1444, Etchingham) show the cauls bound in broad open network. Far more elaborate are many of the cauls of the 'D' and 'E' series, decorated with floral patterns and edged with jewelled bands. Agnes Salmon 1430, Arundel, and the wives of Thomas Widville, Bromham, are especially notable. Occasionally the cauls are shown exceedingly high as at Minehead c. 1440. The veil headdress was used as an occasional alternative to the horned, and is especially associated with the dress of widows. It was not, however, peculiar to them. Margaret, wife of Robert Pagge c. 1440, Cirencester, wears a veil, apparently over a cap or stiff covrechef and other similar examples are at Melton c. 1430; Sudborough c. 1440; and Cirencester (*The Craft,* Fig. 33). A unique and valuable survival from the close of the period is the figure of Jane Keriell 1455, Ash-next-Sandwich (Fig. 104).

Her horseshoe-shaped headdress, decorated with large spots, has often been illustrated, and misinterpreted as an extreme type of the horned headdress. Druitt was correct in recognizing the horseshoe as being other than a veil. The headdress is undoubtedly intended to be a bourroulet, an extravagant fashion popular at the French court. It was, in effect, a heavily padded ornamental cap, resting on the head above the hair nets or cauls. A sculptured representation revealing the form more clearly, is on the effigy of Jeanne de Montejean c. 1425, at the church of Bueil, France.[13]

The representation of long hair without any cover other than a narrow band, is usually an indication of youth and an unmarried state. This, however, is not always the case and two examples to the contrary can be cited. The palimpsest fragments at Okeover show Elizabeth St John, second wife of William Lord Zouch 1447, with streaming hair. Cicely Boleyn 1458, Blickling, though portrayed as a girl, is recorded as having 'decessed in her maydenhode of the age of L yeeres'.

Other female garments show few major changes from the early years of the century. The tight-fitting kirtle is commonly shown, worn with a loose mantle which is held by a cord across the breast. The clasps are in some instances formed by intricate brooches or even shields of arms as at Luppitt c. 1440. The sideless surcoat is occasionally worn over the kirtle as at Trotton 1421, and Herne c. 1430. The high collared gown with full sleeves is worn by Joan Urban c. 1420, Southfleet. Far more common is a somewhat similar gown with looser baggy sleeves, identical with those on the male tunic, and a low-cut open collar. This is shown belted above the hips. Joan, wife of John Bacon 1437, All-Hallows-by-the-Tower, London, is a good example. A richer treatment of this dress is at Bromham 1435, where one of the wives wears, in addition, a fur lined mantle. A handsome style of gown, possibly a form of houppelande, is worn by a few ladies of importance. Its most distinctive features are a deep turned-down collar and immense surplice-like sleeves which in some cases almost drag the ground. The finest examples are those of Joan Peryent 1415, Digswell; Millicent Meryng 1419, East Markham; Margery Arundell 1420, East Anthony; a lady c. 1420, Horley and Agnes Salmon 1430, Arundel. The last of these figures is outstandingly fine with a wealth of detail and ornament including a long S.S. collar. Only a central fragment of her husband remains, but a rich double canopy with super-canopy is in quite good preservation (*The Craft,* Fig. 181).

Two brasses illustrate heraldic dress. The kirtle of Alice Shelton 1424, Great Snoring, is inlaid with lead and charged with her arms: 'Argent, a cross moline Gules'. The figure of Elizabeth, wife of William Fynderne 1444, Childrey, is almost entirely inlaid except for the face and hands, bearing on her kirtle the arms of Fynderne, and on her mantle those of her first husband, Sir John Kyngeston, and her paternal coat. The mantle of Elizabeth Dencourt 1455, Upminster, Essex, is chiselled for inlay, but probably for decorative colour only.

Widows

The costume of widows remained the same as in previous periods though its presentation was influenced by the use of finer lines. The kirtle, usually covered by a plain gown, is worn with a mantle. The head is covered with a covrechef and veil, and the plaited barbe covers the chin and throat. Many good figures of widows so dressed occur on their husbands memorials. Examples of 1419 at Linwood; c.1425 Stoke Poges; 1436 Ewelme; and 1445 Fladbury may be cited as typical. Single figures include:

Alice Bryan, canopy, 1435, Acton

Maud Clitherow, 1455, husband lost, canopy, Ash-next-Sandwich.

Alice Bryan is the outstanding brass of this type, a large, tall figure of the 'D' series set within a fine triple canopy. The mutilated figure of Maud Clitherow is interesting in that her veil has the humped contour of the horned headdress.

On a few brasses the costume associated with widows is worn without the barbe. Three examples are at Higham Ferrers 1425, Cobham 1435, and Sawbridgeworth 1437. The intended status of these women is not clear. Joan, Lady Cobham, who in contrast to the others is a single adult figure, certainly did not die a widow. Her inscription, however, records her as being wife of Sir Reginald Braybrok, who was in fact the second of her five husbands, and the heraldry shows that the monument was designed to illustrate the descent of the title to her son-in-law. In so far as she was left a widow, the representation may be justified. It is, however, possible that this plain but dignified costume was chosen to signify a mature matron, the barbe of widowhood being deliberately omitted.

Ecclesiastics

Ecclesiastical brasses of the period include among their considerable number selections of the regular clergy and academics in addition to the secular. The grave demeanour, portrayed with consistency in earlier periods, is generally maintained. Ornamental detail is less bold, and most orphreys, amices, stoles and apparels are decorated with series of lozenges or circles enclosing flowers or quatrefoils. The fylfot is rarely used, though it is found on a cope at Chartham as late as 1454. The average size of the brasses is small — there are many half effigies — and even some figures in processional vestments are diminutive.

Archbishops and bishops

Archiepiscopal and episcopal brasses have been all but entirely destroyed. Indents survive in the cathedrals at Canterbury, Lincoln and Winchester, and in churches such as Hawkesbury and Maidstone, which once contained splendid brasses of such dignitaries. There are only two examples now remaining, one of which is in Germany. The earlier is to Bishop Robert Hallum, who died in 1416 attending the Council of Konstanz. His admirable canopied brass is in almost perfect condition on the choir floor of Konstanz cathedral (Fig. 105). It is of undoubted English workmanship, most probably of the 'D' series, and may well have been prepared shortly before his death. It was unexpectedly exported to the bishop's resting place. Hallum's figure is austere in treatment with some similarities to the brass of John Vynter 1404, parish priest at Clothall. He wears pontifical mass vetsments without stole or tunicle, and his chasuble is without orphreys. His amice is inscribed with his initials, but his mitre is the only rich detail, an example of the jewelled 'mitra pretiosa'. His right hand is raised in benediction, and a crozier is held in the left. The second brass, also canopied, commemorates Thomas Cranley, Archbishop of Dublin 1417, and is in the chapel of New College, Oxford (*The Craft,* Fig. 22). It is a large and excellent example of the 'B' series, and a perfect example of the vestments of a metropolitan. The fringed edges of the dalmatic and tunicle, and the ends of the stole and maniple are both freely and finely executed. The mitre, gloves and sandals are jewelled. The pallium is carefully engraved with its ornament of crosses patée fitchée and lead weighted end. The cross staff, though mutilated, is similarly well finished with a crucifix. Both these brasses come from the early and best engraving years of the period, combining grace with refinement of line.

Canons and wardens

Few brasses to church dignitaries, represented in processional vestments, match in scale or quality earlier examples of their type. Numerous large memorials have been destroyed, in particular at Lincoln and Old St. Pauls, London, but it is nevertheless notable that many of the surviving brasses are modest and even diminutive. Robert London 1416, Chartham, and Simon Marcheford 1442, Harrow, are exceptionally small. This development may be explained by humility or economy, and the fact that such representations were adopted by some relatively insignificant clergy. Simon Marcheford was nonetheless canon of both Sarum and Windsor.

The choir cope has but one illustration, a worn effigy c. 1420 at Haddenham, among the finest examples of the festal cope are:

William Langeton, canon of Exeter, kneeling, 1413, Exeter cathedral (Fig. 108)
Thomas Aileward, rector, 1413, Havant
Simon Bache, canon of St Paul's London, 1414, Knebworth
Thomas Clerke (mutilated), d.1411,[14] engr. c.1418, Horsham
Thomas Pattesle (mutilated), canopy, 1418, Great Shelford
Robert Wyntryngham, canon of Lincoln, canopy and bracket, 1420, Cotterstock *(The Craft,* Fig. 63)
John Mapilton, Chancellor to Queen Joan of Navarre, canopy, 1432, Broadwater (Fig. 106)
Henry Martyn, rector, 1435, Upwell (Fig. 109)
William Prestwyk, Dean of St Mary's College, Hastings, canopy, 1436, Warbleton.

The only one of these brasses to illustrate a cope adorned with orphreys enriched with figures is at Knebworth. This handsome brass, which is the earliest to depict an Italian brocade or cut velvet cope, and also shows a morse engraved with the Vernicle, appears to be a late use of an 'A' pattern, comparable to those at Bottesford and Ringwood, but with a less stylised face. At Exeter, Havant, Great Shelford, Tredington 1427, Broadwater, Fladbury 1458, and Winchester College 1450, orphreys and morses are decorated with personal initials or devices. The orphreys of William Langeton include in their ornament the Stafford knot. William being a kinsman of Edward Stafford, Bishop of Exeter. His figure is represented kneeling, and is a good representation of the form of the cope. At Havant, the heraldic device of a wheatsheaf is interspersed with fleurs-de-lys and leopards' heads and the morse is inscribed with the wearer's initials T.A. Maple leaves at Broadwater allude to the surname Mapilton. The entire name Thomas Patesle is exhibited in separate letters at Great Shelford. At Warbleton the orphreys are inscribed with the quotation from Job 19 and the word 'Credo' is set within a cusped circle on the morse. A few brasses illustrate other combinations of vestments. At Canterbury 1438, and Theydon Gernon 1458, the almuce is omitted, and the neck of the surplice clearly shown. On the Horsham and Upwell 1435 figurs the cope is worn revealing the crossing of the stole over the alb.[15] A restored half effigy of similar design is that of John Wyllynghale 1432, Winchester College. A small and badly mutilated figure c.1420, Bennington, is peculiar. He appears to be vested in a festal cope but wears on the left shoulder a badge, which seems to be an incised rose. The priest's identity is unfortunately unknown, and the conjecture that he is intended to be a canon of Windsor with the Garter badge has neither been confirmed nor refuted. The majority of these coped figures are identifiable as of the 'B' or 'D' series of patterns, the brasses as Broadwater, Exeter and Warbleton being important examples of the latter. Exceptions are the 'A' figure at Knebworth, a large 'E' figure ?1428 at Upwell, and the restored figure at Winchester College which has some peculiarities associated with Norwich work, and is further considered in Chapter Thirteen.

Some minor dignitaries are represented in choir dress showing the almuce with its pendent tails and the surplice far more fully:

John Morys, Warden, 1413 facsimile 1882, Winchester College
William Tannere, Master of Cobham College, half effigy 1418, Cobham
William Whyte, Master of the College 1419, Arundel (Fig. 110)
John Huntington, warden, canopy restored, 1458, Manchester cathedral.

These brasses, with the exception of one at Bampton c.1420, represent the almuce by chiselling down the surface and inlaying the recess with lead or other whitish composition.

Parish priests

The great majority of ecclesiastical brasses represent parish priests in mass vestments. Most are small and many are half effigies. The only existing large examples are at Hoo St Werburgh and Great Bromley, the former hardly belonging to the period and the latter made sizeable by its canopy. Decorative detail is generally of a very regular geometric type, a small quatrefoil being the most common. Most chasubles are plain without orphreys or embroidered edges. The stiffening of line and increasing use of shading as the period closes is especially evident in the chasuble. The following are a selection of the best examples:

Walter Seller, 1427, Iden
William Byschopton, canopy, 1432, Great Bromley
Robert Clere, c.1445, Battle
Richard Goldon, 1446, Willian (Fig. 107)
John Baker, 1455, Arundel
Roger Gery, c.1455, Whitchurch
?John Spycer, 1460, Monkton in Thanet.

Among such figures are a variety of examples from the 'B', 'D' and 'E' patterns series. The majority, especially of the half effigies, are of the 'B' types. The good figures at Great Bromley and Iden are both 'D', displaying some refinement of detail. The 'E' figures are among the most interesting, including those at Battle and Arundel. The apparels of the amice of Dean Clere lie well out from the neck, revealing the inner folds of the vestment, a detail reflected at Addington, 1446. The chasuble of John Baker has a rich central orphrey inscribed with his personal initials. The introduction of such ornament on a chasuble is unique on English brasses but was undoubtedly a mediaeval practice. Although half effigies command less attention than full figures, those at Addington and Wilshamstead c.1450, are particularly noteworthy, the first for its distinctive 'E' series presentation, and the latter for excellent 'B' series execution. The custom of representing the priest holding the chalice and sacramental wafer became fairly common by the middle of the century.

Two representations of priests wearing cassock and hood are John Whytton c.1420, on his combined memorial with John Bloxham, Merton College, Oxford and John Lewys 1422, Quainton, the last small and kneeling.

Regular clergy and Women in Religious Orders

Brasses commemorating regular clergy were almost totally destroyed at the dissolution of the English monasteries, and the subsequent iconoclasm of the seventeenth century in churches which had been turned from monastic to public use. There can be no doubt they were once numerous. Several Benedictine foundations, such as St Albans, still retain considerable numbers of indents of brasses to members of their communities, and there were nearly three hundred Benedictine houses in England at the beginning of the sixteenth century. The Benedictine rule was hard but not austere, and much of the energy of its followers was devoted to learning and the cultivation of the arts. The Benedictine houses were very rich, and memorials to abbots and monks were common. The monastic orders based upon the Benedictine rule, such as the Cluniac and Cistercian, though placing a greater emphasis on contemplation and worship, were not opposed to the expensive commemoration of their distinguished members, as is shown in the sumptuous brass of Prior Nelond of Lewes at Cowfold, and the indents of Abbots at the Yorkshire Abbeys of Byland and Fountains. Some of the Canons Regular were sent to serve parishes, the livings of which had been appropriated to their abbey or priory; and could be buried in their parish church with a memorial like any parish priest. The wealth and influence of the religous orders in England was immense, and a small group of brasses from this period provides only a slight record of their members.

A distinctive feature of brasses to regular clergy is the form of the tonsure. The hair was shaved over the crown and from the neck to the ears, leaving a narrow band of hair only. This detail readily distinguishes them from secular clergy, whose hair invariably falls around and behind the ears. On most examples, monastic dress is shown, further clarifying their status. The dress or habit of the Benedictines consisted of the scapular, the tunic and the frock. The frock (also known as the cowl) was a long loose garment with deep surplice-like sleeves, which all but obscured the undergarments. A large hood was attached to the frock, and is shown on brasses resting in deep folds around the shoulders. A good representation is given on the figure of Geoffrey Langeley 1437, Prior of the Benedictine monastery of St Faith at Horsham near Norwich (Fig. 111). At the dissolution his brass was fortunately brought to the church of St Laurence within the city, but the inscription, which describes him as 'Prior istius loci', leaves no doubt of the original situation. The brass has recently been refixed in the parish church of Horsham St Faith. Part of the bracket supporting the figure remains but a plate of St Faith above, rubbed and illustrated by Cotman, no longer exists.

Two other monks in the same habit represent Reginald Bernewelt 1443, and Robert Beauner or Beauver c.1455; and are both at St Albans cathedral. The latter is a very lean figure, holding a bleeding heart. According to his long inscription, he served the abbey for forty-six years in a variety of posts in the kitchen, refectory, infirmary, sub-refectory and spicery and was made third prior. Another representation of the same dress as worn by a Cluniac is afforded by the superb brass of Prior Thomas Nelond 1433, Cowfold (*The Craft,* Fig. 188). He was head of the priory of St Pancras at Lewes, and a figure of the saint is appropriately set on a bracket within the canopy. It is an immense memorial, including a life-size figure and one of the most elaborate of all English canopies. The grace and dignity of the figure is made possible by the simplicity of the habit, and the brass is among the most impressive of all the 'B' designs. Portions of smaller but similar figures are on palimpsest reverses at Norbury, Derbs. (obv. 1538), and Twyford (obv. 1550).

Three small brasses of friars exist, two of which are on the reverse of later brasses but almost complete, and a fourth has been recently stolen. The last, an unknown friar at Great Amwell c.1440 (Fig. 299), is shown in a long gown girdled with a knotted cord, which hangs down in front but is covered at the waist by the folds of the gown. He wears in addition a hood with deep shoulderpiece, and his feet are only covered with open sandals. A similar figure, though now footless, is at Denham to John Pyke, on the reverse of a brass of 1545. In addition to the inscription is a shield bearing a staff and birch in saltire between the letters I.P.M.S. Mill Stephenson suggests the possible interpretation of 'Johannes Pyke magister scholae', the device being a professional emblem. A well executed bust with hood and shoulderpiece, for 'Frater Willms Jernemu(t)', is at Halvergate, on the reverse of a brass of 1540.

Mention has been made of the two representations of Martin Forester in half effigy (c.1460) on the lectern at Yeovil (*The Craft,* Fig. 37). He is dressed like the Great Amwell friar and shows the cord. The head has been deliberately defaced in both cases. The upper part of another brass to a regular has come into the possession of the Kent County Record Office, and was most probably from Bayham Abbey, a house of Premonstratensian Canons. The figure is of the 'E' series and dated c.1445. He is represented in mass vestments, but his tonsure shows conclusively that he is of the regular and not the secular clergy.[16]

Some substantial palimpsest fragments on the reverses of brasses at Ellesborough 1544, Harlington 1545, and Lambourne, Essex 1546, all form part of a large figure c.1440, in gown and mantle, with feet resting on a finely engraved dog. The detail of chief interest on these pieces is a cross forming part of an elaborate pendant of cords and tassels. This pendant is highly unusual in form, and can only be that worn by members of the Religious Order of St John of Jerusalem — the Hospitallers. This crusading Order, first centred upon the Latin hospice of St John at Jerusalem, was after the year 1310 settled at Rhodes. Judging from both its scale and quality the brass must have commemorated an important member of the English Priory.[17] Another palimpsest fragment of comparable style and date has been recently discovered at Ashby St Legers.

Two women in Religious Orders are commemorated. Dame Mary Gore, 1436, was Prioress of Amesbury, and lies at Nether Wallop. Her dress is identical to that of widows, and she bears no insignia of her office. Dame Joan, widow of Sir William Clopton c.1430, Quinton, died a vowess, thereby renouncing remarriage. She is also dressed as a widow and is a better figure, set within a single canopy.

Academics

In contrast to the brasses of regular clergy which have suffered extraordinary loss, the memorials of academics have survived remarkably well. Many brasses of this class were laid in the college chapels of Oxford and Cambridge, and substantial series remain at Oxford, in the chapels of New College and Magdalen. Academic dress has been seriously misinterpreted in the past, and these errors are repeated in most books on brasses. An exception is the admirable guide to the Magdalen College brasses by F.E. Brightman and R.T. Günther. The subject as a whole has lately been re-examined by W.N. Hargreaves-Mawdsley, and the following description of examples is made in the light of his study. Brasses are of moderate value only as a guide to mediaeval academic dress. Their record is limited in range. They lack colour and the form and significance of the garments represented are occasionally doubtful. The figures are nonetheless a distinctive collection, including several examples of unusual interest.

The origin of academical dress is not entirely clear. The discipline of universities and the establishment during the thirteenth century of a system of degrees made desirable the adoption of appropriate and identifiable garments by academics. Mediaeval universities were associated with the church and most academics were ecclesiastics. Academic costume has accordingly been related to ecclesiastical and monastic dress. It has, however, been shown that several of the most prominent garments were essentially civil in origin, and that their formal adoption by clerics scarcely preceded their use in universitites. The distinguishing dress of most doctors was common civil attire in the thirteenth century. Their headdress — the pileus — was adopted by the church for clerical use as late as 1311, at the Synod of Bergamo and admittedly 'after the manner of laymen'. Changes in styles of dress often confer a certain dignity and gravity on superseded fashions, making out-dated costume attractive for ceremonial purposes. Such apparently was the origin of academic dress, and once so adopted it changed to the peculiar circumstances of its use.

Academic dress in the fifteenth century at the Universitites of Oxford and Cambridge consisted of four main items. Two long garments were worn together. These were the tunica and supertunica, the first and lower of which may be described as a cassock. Over these were worn distinguishing habits of various cut, colour and length, together with a hood and shoulder-piece attached. A special headdress was permitted to doctors. It was the habit which most particularly signified the degree, though its shape and colour varied from time to time, and alternative dress was in most cases allowed. The highest degrees conferred were those of Doctor or Professor in Divinity, Canon Law, Civil Law and Medicine — representatives of all but the last are commemorated by brasses.

Doctors in Divinity at both Oxford and Cambridge were required to wear on formal occasions the cappa clausa and were allowed the pileus as a headdress. The cappa clausa, similar in shape to the civilian cape or pluvial, was a long sleeveless robe enveloping the body. Passage for the hands was usually made through one central slit, though a form of this cappa with two slits was also used and eventually superseded the other at Oxford though not at Cambridge.[18] The hood and shoulder-piece were permitted to be lined with miniver. The pileus was a cap commonly fitted with a tassel or stalk to facilitate removal. This dress is well illustrated by the kneeling figure of Richard Billingford, D.D. 1442, at St Benedict, Cambridge, whose posture fully reveals the hood with its pendent liripipe (Fig. 101). Only the lower half exists of a large recumbent figure of John Holbrook 1436, Chancellor of Cambridge University and chaplain to King Henry VI, at St Mary-the-Less, Cambridge, but the central slit of the cappa clausa is clear. Doctors in Canon Law at Oxford and Cambridge were also required to wear the cappa clausa and pileus and were allowed the use of a large hood. This dress is illustrated on the brass of William Hautryve 1441, New College, Oxford, a good figure of the 'E' series. In the fourteenth century doctors in Civil Law at Oxford were required to wear the pileus and the cappa manicata, a long-sleeved habit. In the fifteenth century they commonly wore a form of the cappa clausa with two slits for the arms. Two interesting examples of this dress are John Lowthe, D.C.L. 1427, New College, Oxford and a half effigy at West Monkton attributed to Henry Abyndon 1438. Both have the characteristics of the 'E' series. Lowthe's cappa is decorated with two long pendants, falling from the back of each shoulder to the ground. This arrangement appears to have had no academic significance, and was later regarded as ostentatious and unsuitable (Fig. 99). The West Monkton figure is the only example on a brass of the academic use of labels, indicative of authority (Fig. 100). The pendent tongues below the hood may be compared with those of the warden of New College, Oxford, depicted in the valuable Chaundler drawing c.1463, of the assembled college members.[19] Doctors in Laws at Cambridge were similarly required to wear the cappa manicata and the pileus. They were also allowed the pallium, a plain, closed and sleeveless garment, as an alternative dress. However, the large but headless figue of Eudo de la Zouche, LL.D. 1414, at St John's College chapel, Cambridge shows him wearing a sleeved tabard, shoulder-piece and hood over the supertunica.[20] This brass, the most elaborate of the academic brasses surviving, has been wretchedly treated. In the nineteenth century the mutilated figure and canopy fragments were fixed behind the organ in the chapel, but the indent, which showed the outline of the pileus, was left to the elements in the churchyard of All Saints, Cambridge. Eudo was brother of Lord Zouche and Chancellor of the University.

Brasses to Masters and Bachelors during this period are less useful to the student of academic dress. It appears that for the majority of representations a standard pattern was used which left the exact form of the habit in doubt. Unless the degree is stated it is generally difficult to establish whether the short loose sleeves shown belong to the habit itself or to the supertunica, having been thrust through a sleeveless habit. This ambiguity has understandably confused writers on brasses, and the degrees of some anonymous figures cannot be identified.

Masters in Arts at both Oxford and Cambridge were forbidden the use of the pileus. Their dress of dignity, in conjunction with the hood worn over the supertunica, was at Oxford the cappa nigra and at Cambridge the cappa manicata. The cappa nigra was a title given to a short form of the cappa clausa with two slits. The earliest example of its representation on a brass is alleged to be on the half effigy of John Kyllyngworth, M.A. 1445, Merton College, Oxford. However, it became increasingly common for Masters to discard the habit altogether, wearing the supertunica with the hood and shoulder-piece as an outer garment in its own right. The gradual discarding of the habits in favour of the supertunica or roba, which became an outer gown, was an important transition in mediaeval academic dress. An early instance is the half effigy of Walter Wake, S.T.S. 1451, New College, Oxford. The Masters on the Chaundler drawing are similarly dressed.

There are no known brasses to Cambridge Bachelors. Bachelors of Divinity at Oxford wore the cappa clausa with two slits and the hood on formal occasions. John Bloxham d.1387, on his combined memorial engr. c.1420 with John Whytton at Merton College, Oxford, and John Darley 1446, Herne, Kent, are excellent illustrations. Bachelors in Civil Law at first wore the sleeveless tabard or pallium as a habit, but by this period they wore a sleeved tabard. John Mottesfont, B.C.L. 1420, Lydd, Kent, is a good example. Bachelors in Arts similarly were allowed the sleeved tabard by the fifteenth century, which is shown at New College, Oxford, on the brass of Geoffrey Hargreve, S.T.S. 1447. It is, however, necessary, to repeat that the representation of these tabards and the cappa nigra is in effect identical on brasses at this time, and it is doubtful whether the engravers were always conversant with academic fashions. Druitt described Kyllyngworth as wearing the sleeved tabard, and his similarity to Hargreve is undeniable. There are no known fifteenth-century representations of undergraduates.

Children

Brasses commemorating children are rare, though groups of children arranged below the figures of their parents are fairly common by the close of the period. Children are for the most part dressed as adults, though the headdresses of girls show some peculiarities. The daughter of John Waltham 1420, Waltham has her hair bound with a narrow circlet, and plaited above the ears. More often, the hair is encircled by a roll or orle which is slightly raised over the plaited hair, as on the daughters of Joan Lady Cobham 1433, Cobham. Possibly such an orle or flat cap is worn by the sisters of Philipe Carreu 1414, Beddington (*The Craft,* Fig. 187). Isabel Manfeld 1455, with her brothers at Taplow, wears her hair loose as a token of virginity. Two small but attractive figures of girls c.1450 at Kimpton and Lingfield wear their hair long and free, but with a jewelled garland round the brows. A larger but less artistic figure to Denis Finch alias Harbord 1450, is at Brabourne. The most remarkable brass laid to commemorate children is that of Philipe Carreu 1414, Beddington, together with her seven brothers and six sisters. Philipe is shown full length but her brothers and sisters are represented by a tightly wedged row of busts, each with the appropriate christian name recorded below. The arrangement is unique. A small figure in a long, plain tunic at Headbourne Worthy represents John Kent, a scholar of Winchester College, who died in 1434.

A very curious circular brass in the British Museum collection, engraved on the reverse with a mathematical instrument in the seventeenth century, represents a priest and presumably four of his students (*The Craft,* Fig. 185). The inscription refers to John Mevyn, Thomas Jaraw and Walter Marner. Only the heads of the figures are depicted, two of which are badly defaced. The circumstances giving rise to such a memorial are difficult to explain, unless this small plate was a subsidiary brass, set up as a mark of respect by the students who are included on it, or as a memorial to dead students laid by a college.

The four sons and twelve daughters of Thomas Stokes 1416, Ashby St Legers, are the earliest massed groups of children placed below the parent figures. All are kneeling, but in many later groups the children stand. In two brasses certain children are singled out for special treatment. Below the feet of John Lyndewode and wife 1419, Linwood, the children are set out under a row of simple canopies. One son, William, became Bishop of St David's and is represented in academic dress. More interesting are the children of William West engr. c.1440, Sudborough, who are arranged in a combined group with their own inscription (*The Craft,* Fig. 186). William, who is described as a marbler, is the dominant figure, in civil dress, and his brother John, a chaplain, is vested in alb and crossed stole only. This is the clearest representation of these vestments on any brass. A few children are engraved upon or around adult figures. Especially noteworthy are the excellently engraved miniature representations of Sir Richard Camoys at Trotton (*The Craft,* Fig. 178), and the tiered family groups of Robert Staunton and wife 1458, Castle Donnington (*The Craft,* Fig. 189).

Provincial workshops

The large and varied selection of figure brasses of London origin and inspiration form the major part of the English work. There remain, however, a few brasses of provincial origin, which unlike earlier examples show some consistency in style and treatment. Two small and unusual military figures in Lincolnshire are apparently the work of some Yorkshire or Lincolnshire engraver, and are influenced by London patterns. The earlier, John Skypwyth 1415, Covenham St Bartholomew (Fig. 113). shows the attachment of the dagger to the fauld by a small cord. Robert Hayton, 1424, Theddlethorpe All Saints, is a copy of an outmoded London 'C' pattern, showing the bascinet and aventail. The more important brasses were almost certainly made in York, and have affinities with the clumsily but strongly designed figures at South Kelsey, Lincs. The following brasses depict men in armour:

George Salveine and wife, 1417, Lowthorpe
Sir Thomas de St Quintin and wife, canopy, 1418, Harpham
Thomas de St Quintin, Esq., 1445, Harpham (Fig. 112)
Robert Hoton and wife, worn, 1447, Wilberfosse
Robert Constable, Esq., mutilated, 1454, Bossall

The Harpham brasses are of greatest interest. Sir Thomas de St Quintin is armed in a simply defined suit of plate. A great feathered orle encircles his bascinet. He wears two besagews, one of which is oblong and curved, and a curiously ornamented belt. George Salveine at Lowthrope is smaller but very similar. Thomas de St Quintin is armed in the Milanese fashion with asymmetrical couters, and his brass appears to have been strongly influenced by contemporary London 'D' patterns. Yet the rather crude simplicity of the engraving and curving of line is unusual and effective. The remains of Robert Constable are comparable but his heavily studded sabatons are peculiar. Agnes de St Quintin wears a deep-sleeved gown with open collar and immense cuffs, and a crespine headdress. The head of Elizabeth Salveine, her sole remaining fragment, is almost identical. Isabel Barnardston c.1420, Great Coates, evidently of provincial origin, bears closer comparison with the earlier South Kelsey lady, especially in the proportions of the great dog at her feet.

Two priests in mass vestments are apparently of York work. Robert Thresk 1419, Thirsk, is a half effigy accompanied by two angels. Roger Godeale 1429, Bainton, is a poorly proportioned figure holding a chalice.

Richard Norton, Chief Justice of the King's Bench 1420, with his wife at Wath, may be another York engraving, but the lines are far too effaced for certainty.

In addition to the unusual treatment of these brasses, the inscriptions connected with them are in a slightly different and broader script than those of London workshops. Other similar inscriptions are found in the City churches of York of 1412 at St Saviour, and 1413 at St Crux. The similarity of script used is shown by S. Badham [21] to support the view that such apparently heterogeneous figures as those of Allerton Mauleverer, Covenham St Bartholomew, Harpham 1418, and Bainton, are part of a York series of c.1390-1440, though the Harpham brass of 1445 belongs to a later series described in Chapter Thirteen. Chalice brasses, described separately in Chapter Fourteen, are found at Ripley 1429, and Bishop Burton 1460, and are without parallel at this time near London. There can be no doubt that the York engravers responsible for these monuments were served by local designers. Their patterns have a distinctly provincial quality, though revealing, as did those of the previous period, the influence of London models. These comments do not apply to York alone. Towards the close of the period there is sufficient stylistic evidence to prove the activity of engravers in East Anglia, who appear as prolific makers of brasses during the latter part of the fifteenth century. The peculiarities of their early designs are most usefully related to later examples of their work, and are accordingly described in detail in Chapter Thirteen. The year 1460 effectively closes the period in which the London marblers were undisputed masters in this craft in England.

Arrangement and composition: Figure arrangements

The general arrangement of brasses followed very closely the designs of the earlier period, and changing ideas and interpretations are discernible in details rather than in the major elements of compositions. The recumbent pose is most usually depicted, as is proved by the continued use of foot supports and rests for the head. Hands are most commonly shown set together in prayer, though a few examples, as at Trotton 1421 (*The Craft,* Fig. 178), and Herne c.1430, present husband and wife clasping hands. There are no main recumbent figures engraved in semi-profile. In certain respects, however, there is evidence of an increasing inconsistency in presentation which indicates a change in ideas. The children groups arranged below the recumbent figures are usually animated and quite evidently standing. On the brass of Robert Staunton and wife 1458, Castle Donnington, they are arranged by the feet of the parents in a manner only consistent with a standing group, although Robert himself rests his feet on a hound. The designer was clearly unconcerned by this contradiction and welcomed this lively effect. The foot support was too well established to be abandoned.

Foot supports convey little spiritual meaning. Lions, dogs and flowered plots of earth are most commonly used. Each pattern series has its own peculiar types of animal. The shaggy dog of the 'D' series as at Cirencester 1438, and the wild lions of the 'E' series are particularly noteworthy. Dogs placed at ladies' feet are absurdly small pets. A named dog 'Jakke', apparently a type of poodle, was shown on the lost figure of Sir Brian de Stapilton 1438, at Ingham (*The Craft,* Fig. 44). Another 'poodle' rises at the feet of John Darley 1446, Herne. A hound at the feet of the huntsman at Baldock was leashed to his master's belt. Other animals are of purely heraldic significance. Thomas Chaucer, Esq. 1436, at Ewelme rests his feet on a unicorn, a beast derived from the crest of his mother's father (Fig. 114).[22] At his wife's feet is a double tailed lion taken from her family arms of Burghersh. Most interesting are the supports of the merchants, many of which are emblems of their trade. At Northleach John Fortey 1458, rests his feet on a sheep and a woolpack (Fig. 115). Thomas Fortey 1447, also has a pack, and William Scors, tailor, on the same brass, a pair of scissors. Woolpacks bearing personal trademarks are placed at the feet of John Lyndewode 1421, Linwood and Robert Pagge 1440, Cirencester. Plain woolpacks, singly or in pairs, are at Linwood 1419; All Hallows-by-the-Tower, London 1437, Chipping Norton 1451; Lechlade 1458; and on the brasses at All Saints, Stamford, to John Browne 1442 and William Browne engr. c.1460. The vintner Simon Seman 1433, St Mary Barton-on-Humber has two wine tuns as a support. A palimpsest fragment of c.1445, at Lambourne shows the feet of a merchant resting on a bale of cloth. Headrests are almost confined to the helms of some military effigies; crested helms at Mendlesham 1417 (*The Craft,* Fig. 41), and Sheldwich, are notable. Margaret Cheyne 1419, Hever (*The Craft,* Fig. 55) and the priest John Lovelle 1438, at Canterbury are the sole examples to show a cushion headrest. The omission of headrests is matched by the absence of attendant angels, which are only found at Hever and Thirsk, both of the early fifteenth century. These details had never been a common attribute of English brasses but their almost complete disappearance left the recumbent attitude of figure representation more doubtful.

Representations of symbols of office or heart emblems held in the hands are rare. The chalice is held by priests at Addington, Kent 1446, and Whitchurch, Oxon. c.1455, the latter showing the Sacred Host above. Hearts are held by figures at Sheldwich 1431; Graveney 1436; Willian 1446; and St Albans Cathedral c.1455. The last, in the hands of Robert Beauner, is covered with drops of blood.

Canopies

Canopy design follows closely that of the previous period in the consistent use of the single, double or triple pediment and pinacled shafts. There is, however, a noticeable decline in the enrichment of canopies with subordinate figures, compensated by ambitious experiments in purely architectural forms. Common styles of canopy may be conveniently classified into two main types, according to whether they are associated with the 'B' pattern figures or other series. Canopies of the 'B' type are most usually light in structure with slender shafts and graceful ogival pediments. Their oculi are cusped and have as a centre a four-petalled rose with four barbs. There are few exceptions to this form of decoration, the most important being that of William Browne at Stamford where the one remaining oculus frames a stork sitting on a nest, and the motto '+ me spede', the bird being a rebus, for Margaret Browne was the daughter of John Stokke. The canopies of Sir Symon Felbrygge, Felbrigg, and Sir William Etchyngham, Etchingham, are admirable examples of their type, enhancing the dignity of the figures without distraction. A very elaborate development of the pattern is revealed in the canopies of the Swynbornes at Little Horkesley consisting of double triple pediments, with side shafts hung with shields and a central shaft (*The Craft,* Fig. 177). In contrast, the canopies of the 'D' and 'E' patterns are heavier in form and highly decorated. Oculi and spandrels are filled with elaborate tracery. The moulding of the soffit is in several instances carried down the inside of the shafts. Groining is occasionally introduced, as at Bobbing 1420, Northleach 1447, Isleham 1451, and Castle Donington 1458. On the first, of Sir Arnald Savage, the groining is semy of escallops, the device being derived from the arms of Scales, his wife's family. The last in its excessive elaboration and bulk sacrifices good design for ornament, and dominates the figures (*The Craft,* Fig. 189). Crockets on the later canopies of the series are usually bulbous and of realistic leaf formation terminating in large finials. The finial at Warbleton supports a representation of the pelican in her piety. Undoubtedly the finest of these canopies is that of Baron Camoys at Trotton 1421, combining good form with detail. Three fine examples, though the figures within them are entirely lost are:

?Sir John Howard and wife, 1426, Stoke-by-Nayland
Sir Brian de Stapilton and wife, 1438, Ingham
Nicholas Dixon, 1448, Cheshunt

The embattled parapet, an addition to a few fourteenth-century canopies, is similarly set above the pediments at Konstanz, 1416; New College, Oxford 1417; Trotton 1421; Burnham Thorpe 1420; Upwell ?1428; Hereford cathedral 1435, and Ilminster c.1440. A different treatment of this ornament is introduced in the canopies of Dame Eleanor Cobham 1420, Lingfield, and Nicholas Carrew 1432, Beddington, where there are no pediments, but the canopy shafts are directly integrated with the parapet. The effect of a crenellated building is enhanced at Lingfield by the inclusion of a banner (now restored) flying from the battlements. The brass of Bishop Hallum at Konstanz is the only existing example in English work of the period of a canopy supported by shafts, containing subsidiary figures. These consist entirely of seraphim with crossed wings and rayed haloes. Indents of similar compositions exist, that to John Wotton, first Master of the College at All Saints, Maidstone, still retains one shaft concealed by the stonework of the sedilia. There appears, nevertheless, to have been a decline in the use of such designs. The finest canopies of the period are distinguished by the merit of their architectural form rather than wealth of figure detail. Most outstanding is the canopy of Thomas Nelond at Cowfold. An elegant tabernacle rises above the central pediments. The representation of the Blessed Virgin contained within is flanked by figures of Saints Pancras and Thomas of Canterbury, raised upon the outer pediments. The entire canopy is supported by double shafts connected by flying buttresses. The lightness and form of the design focuses the attention around the head of the figure, the point of chief importance. A comparable canopy was that of Abbot John Stoke 1451, St Albans cathedral of which substantial portions remain (Fig. 295). Indents of similar brasses are at Hawkesbury and Winchester cathedral. The precedents for these compositions may be traced to the canopies of Sir Reginald Braybrok and Sir Nicholas Hawberk at Cobham and to the mutilated fragments of Seman Tong 1414, Faversham. The Cowfold canopy is entirely English in its conception and treatment, and the brass of Nelond as a whole represents the most admirable qualities of the English craft.

Crosses and brackets

Figured crosses, in so far as existing examples are a reasonable guide, were almost completely superseded by bracket compositions. The foot, stem and one finial of the cross brass to John Gerye 1447, Cobham are the only remains of this type of memorial. The inscriptions of Robert Walsshe, 1427, Langridge, and of William Beaufitz 1433, Gillingham, were formerly associated with figured crosses, and there are probably similar indents relating to the period. In contrast to this meagre evidence there are eight bracket brasses in good or fair condition. In two cases, those of Joan Urban 1414, Southfleet, and Quartermayn c.1420, Thame, the brackets are short-stemmed and without canopies. Five others show the bracket with a canopy and the figures:

John Bloxham and John Whytton, c.1420, Merton College, Oxford.

Robert Wyntryngham, 1420, Cotterstock (*The Craft,* Fig. 63)
William Harwedon, with wife, 1433, Great Harrowden
Prior Geoffrey Langeley, 1437, Horsham St Faith
Thomas Roose with wife, 1441, Sall

The first two are in good condition, that at Merton College being especially interesting. The tall stem of the bracket rises from a small tabernacle containing a representation of the Agnus Dei, and the main tabernacle has deeply groined pediments. The canopies of the others are almost completely lost. The Great Harrowden brass when complete was very large. The composition at Horsham St Faith is difficult to reconstruct. Part of the side shafts exist, but old rubbings show that a large representation of St Faith was set above the prior's head, which is not easy to relate to the other fragments. The Sall brass is further described as Norwich work in Chapter Thirteen.

Though mutilated by the loss of the tabernacle and the figure of the Blessed Virgin within, the brass of John Spycer and wife 1437, Burford, Oxon., is a good example of another use of the bracket. As with the crosses at Hildersham and Geddington, the architectural feature integrates a votive composition. The commemorated kneel at the foot and long prayer scrolls rise beside the stem towards the tabernacle.

Four figureless crosses are described in Chapter Fourteen together with the heart and chalice brasses which are first found towards the close of this period.

Additional representations and ornament

Ornament or representations additional to the main composition remain unusual. Evangelist symbols are frequently found at the corners of border inscriptions and inlaid separately around the figures of Richard Byll and wife 1451, Hull. A shield bearing the verbal presentation of the Holy Trinity is on the Nelond brass at Cowfold 1433. Above the figure of John Oudeby 1414, Flamstead, is a small tabernacle which contained a representation of the Blessed Virgin and Christ Child. This is an interesting detail in that the figure of devotion is unconnected with any canopy structure, bracket or cross. A further development of such arrangements is seen in the small isolated figure of St Christopher above John Stathum and wife 1454, Morley (*The Craft,* Fig. 89). These are early examples of a style of design common in the early sixteenth century. Powdering of slabs with scrolls or heraldic devices was a form of decoration rarely used. The only surviving example in remarkably good preservation is the brass of Sir John de Brewys 1426, Wiston. The slab was inlaid with six shields and thirty one small scrolls inscribed 'Jesus' and 'Mercy'. All but one of the scrolls remain. A similar decoration surrounded the lost cross fleury at St Mary, Reading, to William Baron 1416. The indents of a powdering of sickles, a badge of the Hungerfords, surrounds the indent of Walter Lord Hungerford and wife 1449, Salisbury cathedral.

Heraldry

Heraldic shields remained an important element in brasses to persons of status. These are commonly set slightly above the figures and below the inscription plates, or, in the case of canopied brasses, around the pediments. Occasionally shields are set upon the shafts, as at Little Horkesley 1412; Felbrigg 1416; and Etchingham 1444. Shields are encircled by the inscribed Garter at Konstanz 1416, and Trotton 1421. Achievements of arms were uncommon. Two have been lost from the brass of Sir Symon Felbrygge, K.G., and four from that of Elizabeth Pole 1423, Sawston. Three crested helms with mantling exist. The finest is a fragment of the brass to John Iwardeby and wife 1436, Great Missenden. The second is a complete memorial with inscription to William

Hoton 1445, Sedgefield, and is probably of northern work. The third is at Newland set above the figures of Robert Greyndour and wife 1443. The crest is remarkable, consisting of a miner of the Forest of Dean with pick, hod and candle. (Fig. 116). Heraldic badges are found on three brasses. The badge of a foot is repeated eight times on and around the canopy of Thomas de Cruwe and wife 1411, Wixford, and as stops between every word of the long border inscription. The Fetterlock badge is twice charged upon shields at Felbrigg 1416, and the Hart badge of King Richard II set upon a corbel at the junction of the two canopy pediments (*The Craft,* Fig. 24), appropriate to Sir Symon Felbrygge's service. An enamelled badge, depicting a horse galloping under an oak tree, is the only surviving fragment of a brass consisting of arms and badges to John Fitzalan 1421, Arundel. The Royal Arms are emblazoned on a shield with inscription to Richard Burton, chief cook to the King 1443, Twickenham. They appear again with those of the Duchy of Lancaster above John Leventhorpe and wife 1437, Sawbridgeworth. Examples of shields and inscriptions constituting complete brasses are at Felbrigg 1411; Catterick 1412 and Orpington 1439. The first of these, to George Felbrygge, is in fact lost but its unusual diapered quatrefoil setting remains.

Heraldic banners are shown on a few brasses. One of an original group of three is attached to the canopy of Sir Hugh Halsham and wife 1441, West Grinstead. Another, but restored, example has been noted at Lingfield 1420. A banner has been lost above the figure of Bartholomew, Lord Bourchier c.1420, Halstead, and there is evidence of four on an indent at Dennington.

Merchants' marks

An interesting aspect of the merchant brasses of the period is the personal or trade marks, most commonly represented on shield-shaped plates. The subject of these marks has received valuable analysis by F. A. Girling. The origin of these marks is obscure, though it is held with some reason that many were derived from Runic House Marks, of German or Scandinavian origin. The Hansa League was undoubtedly influential in spreading their use over northern Europe. Distinctive appearance and quick execution were essential qualities of trade marks which were stamped or painted on the merchants' goods. They consist in most cases of the 'four' symbol. The base is usually formed by an inverted 'V' or 'W' or double 'X', or occasionally an orb. Certain marks, which Girling describes as of southern influence, incorporate a heart device. Marks usually appear upon shields, of which the heralds strongly disapproved, though in a few examples they are appropriately engraved on woolsacks.

Two early and well executed examples have already been noted in the oculi of the canopy of William Grevel 1401, Chipping Campden. A very large mark in part engraved on a shield and in part on a second plate, is that of John Barstaple 1411, Trinity Almshouse Chapel, Bristol. It consists of an upright, crossed at top and bottom, with a central circle and three pennons. A somewhat similar device, but flanked with the initials 'R.S.' is on the brass of Reginald Spycer 1442, at Cirencester (*The Craft,* Fig. 33) The finely executed marks of Robert Pagge 1440, Cirencester, incorporate the letter 'P' within a lozenge at the base of the upright. This mark is engraved on shield plates and also upon the woolpack at Robert's feet. Another mark, very similar in form to that of Pagge but including a shield on part of the device itself, is that of John Stokes 1450, Chipping Norton. The initials 'J.S.' are set within the shield. John Fortey's mark at Northleach is flanked by his initials and represented within a wreath of ivy. This handsome feature is set six times within the border inscription. A simpler device for the Huddleston family c.1450, Stocking Pelham, has an upright with two pennons rising from a heart, and forming part of the initial 'h'.

Other marks of particular interest are that of John Lyndewode 1421, Linwood, which is engraved on a woolpack, and John Browne, All Saints, Stamford, incorporating a heart device. The brass of William Browne at Stamford bears two representations of storks standing on woolsacks, combining the merchant's trade emblem with his wife's rebus. Marks are also found at St Laurence, Norwich 1425 and 1436, Barton-on-Humber 1433, East Hendred 1439, Dunstable 1450, and Holy Trinity, Hull 1451.

Inscriptions

Towards the close of the period inscriptions, both in their content and treatment, differ from earlier examples described. French rapidly fell out of use as a language for these memorials. A late French inscription is that of John Hunger: 'escuyer jadis maistre queux (cook) de la royne Katheryne' 1435, All Saints, Hertford. Another of 1453 to Joan Clay, Cheshunt, is now lost. A unique plate c.1412 at Aldershot, on the reverse of an inscription to Mary White 1583, bears an inscription in French, Latin and English to Richard Spage and his wives:

'Prie pur lame de Ricard Spage que gist Ici —
Et pur les almes, de Emeline & Alice ces f*e*mmes auxi,
Deprofundis clamavi, cum pater nost*er* & Ave mari,
Jhesu Mercy, Lady helpe, Jhesu Mercy, Amen:'[23*]

English inscriptions remain uncommon. The two following have long and unusual texts. The brass of Richard Adane and his wife 1435, Kelshall, moralises in verse:

Her lyth the bones of Rychard Adane & maryon hys wyff:
God *gra*unt her soules ev*er*lastying lyff
The which Rychard dyed (Blank)
In the yer of our lord M°CCCC° (Blank)
The which Rychard Adane as y now say:
leid here *th*ys ston' be hys lyff day,
The yer of our lord was *th*an truly M°CCCC° fyve & thrytty.
Man behoveth ofte to have in mynde:
That *th*ou gevest w*ith* *th*yn hand *th*at shalt *th*ou fynde —
For wommen ben slowful & chyldren be*th* *unkynde:*
Executors bi*th* coveytous & kepe all *tha*t they fynde,
for our bo*the* soules unto *the* tr*i*nyte, seyeth a pat*er* nost*er* for charite.

The sad record of the children of Robard Manfeld 1455 Taplow reads:

Here lythe' Rychard *the* sone and *the* Eyre —
Of Robard Manfeld Squyer, & kateryne his wyfe,
Wyth' Isabelle hys Suster bothe yonge & feyre —
That at xix yere of age he lefte hys lyfe
Wyth Yong John' his brother be the seconde wyfe —
The yeer' full complete of crisitis incarnacyon
Rychard dyde. the . vj. daye . of Aprill A. M.ccc.l. & v —
God rewarde her' soulys wyt eternall salvacyon'

An unexpected use of a vernacular is the inscription of the Chronicler Adam of Usk c.1430 at Usk, entirely in Welsh. The lettering is unusual, and provincial workmanship may be presumed.

Latin was most commonly used for the inscriptions of all types of person, and contractions of well established phrases are usual. A typical short text is that of Richard Ruggenale c.1420, Hornsey:

'Hic iacent Ric*ard*us Ruggenale et Isabella ac
Alicia Uxores eius quor*um* *A*n*i*mab*us* p*ro*ciet*ur* deus Amen.'

Many longer inscriptions are in verse, either Elegiac or corrupt rhyming Leonine verses. A good example of the former is on the footplate of Justice Martyn 1436, Graveney:

'Inclines ocul(u)m; me conspice marmore pressum
O vir sum speculum mortis imago tuum

Nunc flens prospicito; stans ora sepe memento
Magnificam vitam; mors inopina rapit.
Ante fui iudex; iam iudicis ante tribunal
Respondens paveo; iudicor ipse modo.
Transit lux ubi lex; ubi laus meu fama silescunt
Ymmo vix nomen; vox semiviva sonat
Non sum qui fueram; viduata caro spelitur
Ac prius acta male; mens renovanda luit
Nam post carne mea; dotatus luce superna
Cernere spero deum; te salutare meum.

Another elegant epitaph is that for Thomas Frowyk, Esq. 1448, at South Mimms, obviously the work of an accomplished Latinist, and possibly by Abbot John of Wheathampstead, who is said to have been his friend:

Qui iacet hic stratus Thomas ffrowyk vocitatus,
Moribus et natu gestu victu moderatu,
Vir generosus erat generosa q*ue* gesta colebat,
Nam quod amare sole*nt* generosi plus q*ue* frequentant,
Aucupiu*m* volucru*m* venaticium q*ue* ferarum,
Multum dilexit. vulpes foveis spoliavit,
Ac taxos caveis breviter quecum*que* propinquis,
Intulerant dampna pro posse fugaverat ipsa,
Inter eos eciam si litis cerneret umq*u*am,
Accendi faculas medians extinxerat ipsas,
ffecerat et pacem. cur nu*nc* pacis sibi pausam,
Det deus et requiem que semp*er* permanet Amen.

Long Leonine verses are set with John Asger 1436, St Laurence, Norwich, and Thomas Rolf 1440, Gosfield. The short inscription below John Fortey 1458, Northleach, is sufficient to record the style:

'Respice quid prodest pr*e*sentis temporis evum
Omne quod est, nichil est, preter amare deum.'

In some cases, in order to force the rhyme, dates and other particulars are divided in a confusing fashion, as in the border inscription of Bishop Hallum at Konstanz:

'Anno Milleno tricent' octuageno
Sex cu*m* deno cum *Christ*o ameno.'

The majority of inscriptions contain few personal details of the deceased, though there are exceptions. The standing and service of the husbands of Lady Phelip 1415, are set out in rhyming inscription at Kidderminster:

'Miles honorificus; Johannes Phelip subiacet intus —
Henricus Quintus; dilexerat hunc at amicus —
Consepelitur ei; sua sponsa Matildis amata —
Waltero Cooksey: prius Armigero sociata —
Audax & fortis; apud Harffleu Joh*annes* bene gessit —
Et Baro vim mortis: paciens migrare recessit —
M. C. quater X.V.; Octobris luce secunda —
Sit finis alme Jesu; tibi spiritus hostia munda —'

Lastly the long inscription of the mural brass to John Cottusmore d. 1439 and wife, Brightwell Baldwin, deserves complete record in translation, both for its description and its eulogistic character. The actual plate is cut in strips of two line couplets. It reads:

'Stand, read, learn in noble verse how a man worthy of praise has been put into this tomb by sad fate. For John Cottusmore is being dissolved into ashes. Formerly Chief Justice of the Common Pleas (in common secular matters). He practised justice, he was fair in all things. He cherished the rights of Holy Church above all. Judging civil suits with wondrous power, he was not swayed by love, money, fear or hatred nor by the prayers of the great; therefore he will possess the bright kingdom of Heaven. O! with how many tears with how much weeping, does England commemorate his death! The lofty sky rings with lamentations. Now the King, now the Lords, now the Common People deplore the sad fate that has taken so just a judge from the world. Now also the Church bewails the death of her friend! But still more does his sorrowing bereaved wife Amice left with eight (octo) children deplore his passing, she whom death has now taken at last and now joins him in the tomb. That their marriage was blessed by Heaven who can doubt? From which flowed a most beautiful offspring the eighteen (octodecim) fair children whom they beget. In the year 1439, the third day before the Kalends of September he was taken. Therefore Paul embrace the aforesaid John, and with the aid of your prayer, may he live gloriously for ever in Heaven'.

The inconsistency in the number of children is resolved by the floor brass to the family in the same church where eighteen children are depicted. Presumably only eight were alive when their father died.

All the inscriptions of the period are engraved in black letter script. The letters are usually tall and narrow, and often difficult to differentiate. Several of the best inscription plates, especially those connected with 'D' series figures, have the letters engraved in relief and the ground was presumably coloured. Decorative details are occasionally worked into letters, as the grotesque faces at Cowfold 1433, and Worstead 1440. A few border fillets are ornamented with animals and devices. Especially noteworthy is that of Dame Joan Clopton c.1430, Quinton, in which pears between the words allude to Pearsford, her father's alias. More extravagant is that at Northleach to Agnes Fortey and her two husbands 1447. Here the words are interspersed with a cock, a boar, a hedgehog, two dogs fighting, a castle, a dragon, a goose, fighting cocks, a snail and a slug. This fanciful decoration is an appropriate conclusion to this chapter. As the century advanced so the engravers became more interested in detail and less apparently concerned with the dignity of their composition. The greatest period of English brass engraving was undoubtedly past. Fresh ideas and objectives were required to revitalise the art. These were, however, delayed for a century. It was predictably the Continental engravers who were to make the break with established conventions.

9. Flemish and French brasses, 1460-1560

The development of monumental brass engraving in Flanders during the fifteenth and early sixteenth centuries offers many striking contrasts. The changes in artistic aims and influences were great. Between mid-fourteenth and mid-fifteenth century brasses there are evident similarities and lines of derivation. Whereas many of the conventions of the mid-fifteenth century were retained into the sixteenth with little modification, types of composition appear which represent fundamental changes in outlook and design. The period includes the careful copies of fourteenth-century models, as at Bruges, Bremen and Poznań, the late gothic successors of Sir Maertin van der Capelle, the natural and intimate family groups reflecting the realism of art in the Low Countries, and lastly Italianate compositions of Renaissance inspiration.

The excellence of Flemish engraving of itself was in no respect compromised, and many brasses were made on the grandest scale. It may nevertheless be concluded that the designers over-reached themselves in efforts to demonstrate their skill. The search for relief effects, evident in the fourteenth century, was largely satisfied by the sixteenth. The use of perspective and simulated shading simplified the definition of different planes. The engraver could successfully emulate the painter. But the overall effect was too often confused. The gaze of the spectator ranges in admiring bewilderment over the ornate surface. It is accordingly the smaller brasses which are the most successful.

Flemish workshops

The location of the main Flemish workshops can be identified with some confidence. The celebrated Tournai engraver Alard Génois bought a house on the Quai Taillepierre in 1457, and presumably worked into the latter part of the fifteenth century. A later Tournai engraver, Jean Bidet, is recorded as having made brasses in 1506; and others, Jacquemart de Rosteleu and Jean Maleurée worked during the same period.[1] The Dedelinc family carried on the craft in Gent from 1464 to c.1540. The Gent archives refer to Jan, two Willems and Philip Dedelinc, and there are existing contracts with references to seventeen of their brasses between 1482 and 1523.[2] According to the Halyburton ledger a brass for William Scheves, Archbishop of St Andrews, who died in 1497, was despatched from Bruges to St Andrews via Veere.[3] This brass was possibly made in Bruges, though such evidence is inconclusive. In addition to these three centres it would appear beyond reasonable doubt that Antwerpen and its environs became a fourth. Antwerpen was a communal centre of outstanding importance by the close of the fifteenth century, developing in particular at the expense of Bruges. In 1503, for example, the King of Portugal transferred his principal consular and commercial representation from Bruges to this city. In addition to its rapid commercial development, Antwerpen attracted skilled metal workers from the Ardennes towns, especially following the sack of Dinant by Charles the Bold in 1466. The exports from this port of copper, bells, latten lecterns, crosses, censers and other 'objects of piety', reflect the activity of craftsmen in the city, and also at Mechelen nearby. A signed brass of the early seventeenth century from Mechelen affords confirmation of these conclusions. In the absence of signatures it is impossible to ascribe brasses to a particular centre as there is a distressing lack of correlation between the contracts and existing brasses. The arguments of Dr Op de Beeck are very persuasive in favour of an Antwerpen origin for brasses exported to Portugal. The numerous brasses in the vicinity of Bruges may have come from any of the four centres.

Late fifteenth-century Flemish brasses

Flemish brasses of the latter half of the fifteenth century form a small and varied group. First for consideration are four plates, which, like St Henry at Nousisainen, repeat the design and conventions of the previous century. The brass of Jacob Bave and wife 1464, at St Jacques, Bruges, is a worn and badly battered memorial. It represents the deceased in shrouds, in the manner of Joris de Munter and wife though less artistically represented, and set within canopies of fourteenth-century pattern. The tabernacle work is graceless but the Apostles and Prophets are accurate copies of earlier models. This example, situated in West Flanders, is valuable in proving this conservatism within the Flemish centres. Another brass of similar workmanship, but to a priest, Nicolas Lancbaerd 1471, formerly at St Walburge, Bruges, is now destroyed. Attention is drawn to the palimpsest fragments, described in Chapter Nine of *The Craft*, which came from comparable memorials to this, looted from churches in the Low Countries.

Two other brasses would also appear to be of the same type, though the finer was removed from Poznań Cathedral during the Nazi occupation, and has not since been traced. The great figure of Johann Rode 1477, at the Bremen Cathedral, has many of the peculiarities of St Henry, and is designed on a fourteenth century Flemish model (Fig. 117). It is a splendid, but rather stiff and excessively ornate design. The entire surface of the chasuble is engraved, and some of the detail is unusual, in particular the stubble on the tonsure. In the absence of the original slab, which would be most valuable, it must be questioned whether this is indeed Flemish, or a Lübeck imitation of which there are good precedents (see next chapter). In support of this second alternative are the two wild looking lions at the feet, and the absence of the recessed lips, which are so characteristic of earlier Flemish work. On the other hand some modifications of the earlier patterns is to be expected within the Flemish workshops. The figures of saints on the orphreys, and the execution of the plate as a whole, are entirely consistent with English palimpsest evidence at Brundish and Marsworth. The author views the Flemish origin as the more probable from the evidence available, while admitting uncertainties.[4*]

The other brass, that of Bishop Andrzej Bninski (*The Craft,* Fig. 81) was in most respects a companion to the cover plate of St Henry. All its detail was of undoubted Flemish derivation, in particular the Annunciation on the Bishop's mitre, the Vernicle on his chasuble, and the figures on the orphreys, which are comparable to those presented on the marginal Lansaem inscription 1489, at Ypres. There would seem to be less need for reservations about the Flemish origin of this brass, which has no inconsistencies, and has no direct connection with the Vischer foundry, to which it was attributed in the nineteenth century.

The date of Bishop Andrzej's brass is a nice problem, and is likely so to remain. This prelate has been shown from the Chapter records (referred to in *The Craft*) to have pondered upon his death many years before the event, and to have taken steps to secure his commemoration. The record confirms that he ordered the preparation of a brass twenty years in advance, a memorial which was in fact on his tomb when he was buried. In addition he ordered the erection of a crypt under the chapel of St Andrew his patron saint, which may well have been the work accounted for in 1455 by a mason Piotr of Ostrowko. It is in doubt, however, whether the magnificent brass described was that referred to in the Chapter record. According to Thomas Treter, in his *Vitae Episcoporum Posnaniensium* of 1604, there were two inscriptions on the Bishop's tomb, the one on the known brass and another long since destroyed. The wording of this second plate recorded by Treter is most interesting in that no date of death was stated on it, neither were titles of dignity given. It reads as the type of statement a pious cleric could properly set down during his lifetime.[5*] Although in Poland it has been long believed that this brass was engraved c.1460 on account of the Chapter record, it now appears far more likely that it was made soon after 1479. There is no indication on the inscription of a later completion, and so highly derivative a work is as consistent with the later as the earlier date. Furthermore, the later date is entirely in keeping with the subsequent influence of this memorial on the Górka brasses at Poznań. Bishop Uriel would understandably have been impressed with this great brass, so recently laid in his cathedral, and the very patterns were probably still to hand and available for his subsequent orders to Peter Vischer the Elder.

Two conventionally arranged brasses, though by no means copies, are the excellent memorial at Evora to Branca de Vilhana c. 1490, and the less important group with long inscription of Peter Escheric and wife kneeling before the Blessed Virgin c. 1470, at Dendermonde. Branca is shown recumbent, her head resting on a large cushion (Fig. 118). She is dressed in a very ample gown, lifted on her left side to reveal the kirtle and a small dog by her left foot. Her head is covered by a plain veil and wimple. The simplicity of the dress is partly offset by the shade lines lavished upon the surface. Around her is a canopy of late gothic style, but modelled upon earlier patterns. God the Father with attendant angels and two monastic figures is set within the tabernacle above. The wide side shafts are filled with weepers. The background is framed by a rich curtain worked in a pomegranate design with a deep fringe at the base. A tiled floor in the background helps to throw the figure into greater prominence. The design is framed by a marginal inscription with the Evangelists' symbols in quadrilobe medallions at the corners. The work is highly accomplished but loses clarity by over-ornamentation. In the words of Dr Op de Beeck, 'the quest of relief has visibly damaged the balance of the composition'.

The brass of Jakob Schelewaerts 1483, at the cathedral, Bruges, is entirely different in character (Fig 119). Jakob was a Doctor in Theology of the University of Paris, and is depicted in the midst of an academic session. He is seated, dressed in a cappa and hood, and discourses from an open book. Beside him stands a beadle holding a rod. The persons seated around him are, however, not students in the usual sense, but graduates wearing the dress of their degrees, gathered respectfully to hear the learned doctor. The setting, with gothic windows and vault and a low curtain background, is cleverly represented. The choice of such a scene on a floor monument is not unique. Gaignières illustrated several French incised slabs in Paris of such a kind, and an excellent example is preserved in the Musée Bossuet at Meaux. (*Greenhill 1976,* pl. 38)

The only other figure brass to show the deceased is at Soignies, 1490, consisting now of a few fragments. These include the worm-infested legs of a large cadaver and the lower part of a marginal inscription with the symbols of St Mark and St Luke. These pieces were protected by a platform of masonry covering them at the time the rest of the monument was reaved.

An important plate at Zevenaar, originally laid at Emmerich, commemorates Henrick van Elverick d.1456, and wife (Fig. 124). It takes the form of an altarpiece, depicting the Crucifixion with Mary and St John and attendant figures of St Catherine and St Anthony, the latter accompanied by his belled pig. The engraving is of good quality and the design has many affinities with the painted altarpieces of the Low Countries. The execution of the inscription is similar to that of

Jean Moüen (*The Craft*, Fig. 152). Nevertheless, the rather shallower lines, the heavy shading and late gothic arches, which provide a framework, suggest a date of completion later than the middle of the century. A date of c.1480 is to be preferred to those given on the inscription. Fragments of the kneeling figures and a Resurrection in memory of Gilles de Hertogue and wife 1499, are in the Town Museum at Dixmunde, formerly in St Nicolas.

Two brasses in separate inlay consist of angels bearing arms, a fairly common subject for the Flemish engravers. A beautiful figure, apparently descending from heaven, is at Nieuport. This has been attributed to a memorial to Thomas Lambaert, 1466. The angel's wings are strong and well finished and his long curly hair is bound with a fillet bearing a jewel and an upright cross. A much larger angel of good but less vital treatment commemorates the Wielant family c.1490, at St Jacques, Bruges. The arms of Wielant are suspended below a crested helm held in the angel's hand.

The remaining brasses are inscriptions of exceptionally fine quality, incorporating heraldry or other decoration. Two inscriptions recording the foundations of Pieter Lansaem and Lyssebette Pauwelijns in the Hôpital Notre-Dame, Ypres, are notable. One, a marginal inscription with Evangelists' symbols 1489 undulates between representations of the seven ages of man, where infancy, youth, courtship, marriage, maturity and death are ingeniously portrayed.[6*] The other (1467) is rectangular and of great length, consisting of thirty-six crowded lines of small black letter script relieved only by two shields and a small device. Another such inscription with small shields in quadrilobe medallions commemorates Jan Vasque and Marguerite van Ackere 1466, at the cathedral, Bruges. The rectangular plate of Ruy de Sousa 1497, Evora, is unique, consisting of a double marginal inscription enclosing a rich pattern of intertwined foliage, resembling a magnificent bronze grille. The graceful lettering of this inscription, with ends twisting at intervals across the border, is flawlessly executed.

Early sixteenth-century Flemish brasses: Traditional compositions

Between the years 1500 and 1540 examples are in greater concentration, and the range of Flemish work can be better appreciated. Fourteenth-century patterns no longer exert an evident influence. The only exception is the large and remarkable brass of Hermann Wessel 1507, at Emden (fig. 120 and cf 121). In this the small figure of the commemorated, carrying his almuce over his right arm, prays from the canopy shaft to a representation of Christ, whose figure in a loose and simple robe, dominates the composition in a manner reminiscent of St Henry at Nousisainen.[7*] The canopy is fanciful in character, bearing among its turrets representations of the Church Fathers. The bold curtain, embroidered with pomegranates, forms an effective background to the rather severe central figure. The overall treatment and especially the lettering of the border leave little doubt that it is Flemish work, a probability enhanced by Tournai marble indents still remaining in the church.

Other large compositions can be related to the design of Sir Maertin van der Capelle at the Bruges cathedral. Recumbent figures are pictured in a setting of indeterminate character. A tiled floor recedes to a curtain background, the upper part of which is obscured by achievements or angels holding arms. Twisted columns form a partial architectural framework. Where two persons are depicted, the figures are shown as slightly turned towards each other, if not in body, then in the placing of the hands. The following important quadrangular plate brasses are of this arrangement.

Lodewijc Cortewille, Esq., with wife, 1504, (from Watou, Belgium) Victoria and Albert Museum (*The Craft,* Fig. 190)

Bishop Alfonso de Madrigal (d.1455 engr. c.1505), Avila cathedral (Fig. 122)
Jehan de Likerke with wife, 1518, St Sauveur cathedral, Bruges
Florentine Wielant, 1524, Vichte.

The destroyed brass of Tydeman Berck and wife, 1521, from the Marienkirche, Lübeck, was certainly of this type,[8] as is a large palimpsest fragment c.1520 at Hadleigh.

The figures of Lodewijc Cortewille and Jehan de Likerke are in armour, being careful representations of early sixteenth-century equipment. A short fauld with long tassets partly covers a mail skirt with invecked edge. There is some pointed ridging of plates, but the armour on the whole is rounded in form. The ladies are simply but richly dressed. The trains of their ample fur-lined gowns are caught up under the left arms, and their kirtles are slightly exposed. A veil or hood covers the head leaving the face free. Cushions support the heads of all. Hounds are placed at the feet of the knights and small dogs at those of the ladies. The Avila Bishop is in full pontificals, shown in semi-profile, with his episcopal hat, ensigning his arms, placed over his mitred head. This brass is inlaid in the side of a raised tomb and protected by bars, so preserving the coloured inlay.

Other known brasses of varying scale shared or share many of the characteristics of these plates. The pleasing circular brass of Matheus de Codt and wife 1506, from Nieuport was presumably destroyed in 1914, but has fortunately been illustrated. Matheus faced his wife in semi-profile, apparently standing on a tiled floor (though their heads rested on cushions), with their children kneeling in front of them. A rich curtain formed a background and two shields bearing merchant's marks hung by straps from the edge of the inscription border. Matheus was dressed in a loose wide-sleeved gown with fur facings. Substantial fragments of large figures of this type are on the reverse of palimpsests at St Giles, Edinburgh (obverse 1570), and at St Jacques, Bruges. The latter obverse is a latten tabernacle, installed in 1593. The reverse consists of a major part of the brass of a Spanish merchant with wife, displaying the Royal arms of Spain and a merchant's mark. Other palimpsest reverses of comparable workmanship are those at St Peter Mancroft, Norwich (obv. 1568), showing a civilian in gown and cap under a heavy canopy c.1510, and at St Janskerk, Gouda (obv. 1568), showing two ladies (also c.1510) under a canopy of double pediment, with an embroidered curtain serving as a background. The brass of Antonine Willebaert 1522, St Jacques, Bruges, is another of the same group, though of inferior treatment (Fig. 123). The central figure of the lady and the kneeling children are inartistic, and the design is compromised by the peculiar shape of the plate. Portions of the kneeling composition at St Nicolas, Dixmude, of Augustine Ghiselen and wife 1519, with representations of the Crucifixion, St Augustine, St Margaret and a recumbent cadaver, survived the destruction of the First World War.

All the sixteenth-century Flemish brasses so far noted have certain common characteristics. The figures are conventional. Their faces are without personality and their hands lack well observed structure. Form and depth in dress is imparted more by shading effects than by the true shape of the garments. The figure settings are a clash of ideas combining painters' background arrangements with recumbent representations of the deceased and sepulchral heraldry. Relief is indicated by all available devices, shadow, receding pavements, and the intrusion of one plane upon another. The elbows of Jehan de Likerke and his wife are placed ostentatiously across the medallions of the border. But in all this the engravers added little to the effects of the late fourteenth century beyond a wealth of hatching and variety of ornament. These memorials are in their essentials traditional. It is the smaller realistic compositions that constitute a significant change.

Realistic compositions

An important group of Flemish brasses dating from 1525 to 1540 have a character entirely different from that described. The arrangement of the figures is intimate and confined within a carefully defined space. Most of the figures are undoubtedly standing, and their features and garments are represented perceptively and accurately. The faces of the adults have character and may in some cases be portraits. All these designs convey the impression of paintings interpreted in engraved brass. It is hardly coincidence that the painter Jan Mandijns of Antwerpen was employed to carry out the painting for the brass of the Scottish bishop George Crichton, or that one of the surviving brasses is to Margaret, wife of the Fleming Gerard Hornebolt, Court painter to Henry VIII. Whereas it is probable that earlier artists and draughtsmen of many sorts co-operated with the mediaeval engraver to produce a brass, they did not seek to transform the nature of the memorial.

The following is a complete list of these brasses:

Thomas Pownder with wife, 1525, Christchurch Mansion Museum, Ipswich (*The Craft*, Fig. 65)
Margaret Hornebolt, 1529, Fulham
Ruy Paeez with wife, c.1530, Evora
Andrew Evyngar with wife, 1533, All Hallows-by-the-Tower (Fig. 126)
Bernardin van den Hove, d.1517, engr. c.1533, Bruges cathedral
João Correia, 1537, Penafiel

Thomas Pownder and his wife Emme are a finely delineated pair, the man wearing a partlet, doublet and gown with false sleeves, and the woman wearing a kirtle, full sleeved gown and delicately pointed pedimental headdress (*The Craft*, Fig. 65). Eight children are grouped before them, the two sons being carefully defined, the daughters, other than the eldest, set in a formal row. The draughtsmanship of the group is of a quality entirely different from earlier sixteenth-century examples. The shading, though heavy, is purposeful and not decorative; the expressions on the faces gentle and relaxed. The setting takes the form of a recess flanked by cumbrous ornamental pillars supporting an arch exotic of design, from which are suspended the Arms of Ipswich and of the Merchants Adventurers Company, with Thomas's merchant's mark as a centre piece. The inscription border is of late gothic pattern.

Margaret Hornebolt is a simpler memorial, showing a shrouded bust set in a lozenge with a shield of arms and angels supporting the inscription. The figure is represented as in death with closed eyes. The treatment is realistic and severe, in keeping with the formal arrangement of the plate.

The brasses of Ruy Paeez and Andrew Evyngar are comparable with that of Pownder. The former shows a rather more animated pair. Ruy's deeply lined face, hooked nose and lean neck, if not a portrait, at least conveys the aspect of an individual. His wife is slightly overwhelmed in drapery. Her head is covered with a veil, and her neck by a stand-up wimple. The train of her gown is caught up under the left arm. The setting is both imaginative and clever. The figures are set within a portico, against a curtain background of pomegranate pattern. The pillars of the arch are, however, almost concealed and the arch itself entwined with leafless vine. The ground is strewn with finely pictured flowers. The effect, as Dr Op de Beeck has noted, is to convey the illusion of a pleasure garden, which is only dispelled by the hanging fringe of curtain. Evyngar's brass is more gothic in arrangement, and the engravers may have been required to conform with contemporary English style. The adults are half turned, with prayer scrolls issuing to a representation of Our Lady in Pity. The children are grouped between and behind their parents. The figures are well and sensitively drawn, and Andrew's large and chubby face is in its way as striking as the intense and drawn aspect of Ruy Paeez. The setting is clearly three-dimensional, consisting of two gothic arches, meeting at a large corbel, on which the Pieta rests. A tiled floor recedes to reach the curtain background. The arms of the Merchant Adventurers, the Salters's Company (wrongly drawn) and a merchant's mark are imposed rather as an afterthought upon the scene.

The plate commemorating Bernardin van den Hove is only part of a very large and excessively ornate composition to the memory of several founders of foundations connected with St Sauveur, the latest of whom died in 1533. Whether the entire brass dates from this year, or was laid earlier and subsequently completed, is uncertain. A wide marginal border, engraved with two undulating and intertwined inscriptions, is set at the corners with medallions and arms. Framed by the border are two plates, one being a lozenge bearing four shields and an inscription for Jan van Coudenberghe, his wife Margaret and their kinsfolk. The upper plate is that of Bernadin who died in 1517. An inscription is arranged over a lozenge, within which the deceased stands. He was a notary in the court of the bishop of Tournai, and is appropriately shown with a pen behind his ear, and an ink holder hanging at his waist.[9*] He wears a doublet and gown with false sleeves, and stands within an arch, the columns of which are faced with antique ornament. A chequered pavement in good perspective meets the fringe of a background curtain, while a wealth of surrounding flowers, branches and foliage give the impression of a bower. The detail of the figure is suggestive of a rather earlier date though the setting is more consistent with c.1530.

The last of the group, João Correia, combines traditional and Renaissance motifs. Though placed in semi-profile, João has his eyes almost closed and a cushion is placed behind his head, despite which he is standing in a scalloped recess, hung with garlands and supported by columns with extravagant foliage decoration. Cherubs fill the spandrels formed by the arch. Whereas the earlier examples are expressions of Flemish realism, Italian influence is now evident.

Before considering figure brasses of Renaissance character it is appropriate to mention two ecclesiastical memorials. The delightful small medallion plate to Jean de la Fontaine 1531, Damme presents a realistic figure in a late gothic setting (Fig. 125). The pavement and curtain background are inconsistent with the recumbent figure who lies with a chalice resting on his breast. Beside him are a beautiful rebus and a merchant's mark. Jan van den Couteren engr. c.1535, Melsele, is a similar figure, though engraved in the separate inlay manner, and set within an incised canopy.[10]

Renaissance compositions

Renaissance influence found expression through monumental brass design in four main respects. Interest in the antique, especially the art and architecture of Roman Italy, stimulated experiment with classical forms. These affected the setting of the figures, the ornament of the setting and background and the nature and lettering of the inscription. Realism and character, already advanced in some figure representation, was taken yet further. Attention to the true aspect of forms became minute, especially in relation to perspective. The early sixteenth-century realist designers used perspective as an aid to three-dimensional effects. Their successors pursued it with a pedantic devotion. The Roman architectural writer Vitruvius was widely regarded as the authority on classical architecture. His writings were studied by artists as much as builders, and classical porticoes were gradually introduced as canopies to the figure. Late gothic canopies and massed heraldic display gave place to the architrave, frieze and cornice with triangular pediment above, supported on classical columns. Decoration took the form of medallions, trophies, bucrania, swags, urns and garlands, and naked boys with or without wings were used as supporters or subsidiary figures. Black letter script gave place to Roman capitals, occasionally engraved on inscription plates shaped as antique tablets.

Renaissance decoration has been noted on the brass of João Correia. It is equally evident, especially in detail ornament, on the large but broken and worn brass of the judge Gregoris Bertolff 1528, now in the Friesch Museum, Leeuwarden. It is nevertheless, at Thielen, in the brass of Sir Lodowijk van Leefdael and wife 1538, that the full force of Italian influence is revealed (Fig. 133). In this plate the portico and base inscription are essentially Roman, and even the figures, especially the man, have a certain antique quality. Lodowijk is in armour, but his thighs are covered by a rich pleated skirt and his equipment seems more appropriate to a parade, tourney or masque than a battle. The foreshortening of his sabatons make an interesting contrast with the treatment of the feet on the Cortewille brass. The large and confused brass of Sir Ricald van Rivieren and wife engr. 1554, now in the Musées Royaux d'Art et d'Histoire, Bruxelles, is another example of a classical setting burdened with decoration. The figures are difficult to discern in the mass of lines, shading and motifs. Ricald himself, in armour, has slight links with earlier work, especially in the placing of a shield at his hip. But this accompaniment in its flamboyant twists and curves is no more than an ornament.

Two other brasses of comparable inspiration but superior conception and execution are those of the Dean Willem van Gaellen 1539, in Breda cathedral, and the shrouded Pieter Claessoen Palinck and his wife Josina 1546, at Alkmaar, and quite possibly the work of the same master. Willem van Gaellen is represented in the repose of death, set within a scalloped niche (*The Craft*, Fig. 191). Two naked angels support shields of arms, and large medallions are affixed to the bottom stage of the niche. The draughtsmanship of the figure and architecture is admirable, whatever doubts may be entertained as to the appropriateness of such a treatment, and the brass itself is of superb quality. The Palincks are in no way inferior. The deceased appear to stand within a domed recess. Their eyes are open and their expressions alert. But their hands are folded downwards, and behind them the texture of a matting pallet subtly takes the place of a curtain or other background. The shrouds hang loosely and unobtrusively, in Pieter's case rather like an ample toga. Long scrolls sweep around the figures and angels above support a shield backed by crossed palm fronds. It is a design of grace and dignity, expressing the sombre nature of the subject without harshness or morbidity.

Two further brasses are almost certainly of Flemish origin. The earlier, a pair of separate inlay figures to João Esmeraldo and wife c.1550, is found in geographical isolation in the cathedral of Funchal, Madeira, a Portuguese possession. The brass was probably engraved in Antwerpen. It is a very detailed, heavily shaded memorial. The man's head is well expressed with broad short beard and thick hair, and his wife's dress is unusual, showing a mantle worn with the hood raised. The other brass is a quadrangular plate commemorating Joost van Aemstel van Mijnden with his wife and son 1554. It is now in private possession at Schloss Welschenbeck, Westfalen, but was originally in the castle chapel at Loenersloot near Utrecht. The style is unusual, and not of the best Flemish quality. It bears some similarity in treatment to contemporary Rhenish plates, but not sufficient to justify a German ascription, and may well be Mechelen work. The knight, who wears a tabard over his armour, kneels with his wife and son before a representation of the Holy Trinity in which Christ is seated by God the Father and holds the cross. The inscription below is in rather poor lettering and the background is cut away in close hatching.

Miscellaneous examples

Other brasses of the first half of the sixteenth century are of lesser significance. A fine angel 1505, bearing two shields is in the Rijksmuseum, Amsterdam. The design, incorporating a chalice and separate symbols of the Evangelists, commemorates Gijsbert Willemszoen de Raet.[11] Its indent lies in the Stade-Museum, Gouda. Part of an angel holding two shields from the brass of Willem van den Kerchove and wife 1541, Nieuport is now is private possession. Later angels in Renaissance style commemorate Adrien Roeland 1550, Breda, and Marie van den Berghe 1559, St Jacques, Bruges, the latter portraying two angels, one supporting a lozenge of arms and the other a lozenge beside an achievement. Note has already been taken in *The Craft*, Chapter Six of the curious punning design to Abel Porcket (1509) in the Gruuthuse Museum, Bruges (*Ibid.*, Fig. 53).

There are large heraldic compositions at Bruges and Bruxelles. At St Jacques, Bruges, is a superb marginal inscription with Evangelists' symbols and shields of arms, framing a large lozenge containing an achievement with rabbit crest for Jehan de Tongues 1512, and wife. A helm with eagle crest and shield, shields and an inscription, commemorate Catherine van Messems and her daughter Barbe Roelandts, 1515. There is a cartouche of arms at Bruges cathedral, for Pieter Snouckaert 1543. Other shields at the cathedral are of the Bave and Halewyn families. A large quadrangular plate with numerous coloured shields, achievement, angel and Evangelists' symbols, now at the Musées Royaux d'Art et d'Histoire, Bruxelles, is the memorial of Guillaume de Goux and wife 1552. Another fine plate to Jerosine Dennetières and wife 1535, probably of Flemish origin though with an inscription in French, is in the Musée de Cluny, Paris. This represents an angel holding a lozenge and an achievement of arms with supporters, the two designs being divided by a palm branch. At Beveren-Waas near Antwerpen is a smaller brass commemorating the heart burial of Adolf de Bourgogne 1540, a Knight of the Order of the Golden Fleece. Most of the composition consists of an achievement of arms and the collar of the Order, though the heart is also represented. Alexander de Bosquiel and wife 1512, are commemorated by an elaborate marginal inscription at Notre Dame, Bruges. Inscription plates of special note with small shields, figures of saints or other devices are at the Hôpital St Jean, Bruges 1510 and 1543, and Gouda 1525.

French brasses

In contrast to the substantial number of Flemish brasses only four figure brasses of undoubted French workmanship are known to survive. This evidence can fortunately be amplified by the drawings of Gaignières, and the selection is impressive. Yet brasses appear to have been rare in comparison with the incised slabs, and to have been used mainly for clergy or other persons of high rank, and their quality was excellent. Moreover the divergence between Flemish and French patterns would seem to have been sufficiently distinct to ascribe French origin with some assurance.

Mediaeval patterns persisted in use well into the sixteenth century with only slight modification. Gaignières illustrates a number of large rectangular compositions, the canopies of which are of typical fourteenth-century type. Subsidiary figures fill the side shafts and upper tabernacles. In a few cases, such as Archbishop Denis du Moulin 1470, and Jacques Robertet 1519, both formerly lying in the choir of Notre Dame, Paris, the very soffit of the pediment was engraved with a course of canopied figures. Even more conservative was the brass of Abbot Helins 1535, at the Abbey of St Aubin at Angers. The straight-sided canopy pediment, with representations of the deceased, borne up in a sheet, was of thirteenth-century inspiration. The figures were shown in very rich vestments, with large cushions supporting their mitred heads. Many backgrounds were left plain, in part compensating for the wealth of ornament.

Among the few lay persons commemorated two were of unusual interest, and were fortunately carefully drawn by Gaignières. The brass of Guillaume Juvenal des Ursins 1472, formerly at Notre Dame, Paris, must have been among the most remarkable brasses of the fifteenth century in Europe (*The Craft*. Fig. 192). Guillaume des Ursins, Chancellor of France, was dressed in a square cut open-sided gown with horizontal bars of (?) gold braid on the shoulders. His full sleeved tunic beneath was completely embroidered and a large falchion hung from his belt. By his head lay a symbolic treasury chest and a rigid cylindrical headdress — the mortier — to be worn by nobles and court presidents. A figure beside him was armed, wearing a tabard, with large bears (alluding to the name) clinging to his legs. The second brass, to Marie de Graville with her son 1503, was in the church of the Célestins, Marcoussy (Fig. 127). Marie wore a heraldic sideless surcoat, and an ostentatious bourrelet headdress. Her small son clung touchingly to the side of her dress.

The earliest brass by inscription date to show strong Renaissance influence was at the church of the Cordeliers, Dijon, to Jean d'Amboise 1498, Bishop of Langres. Antique ornament covers the classical columns of the portico (Fig.128). A comparable brass, but even more decorative, was that of Bishop Louis de Villiers de l'Isle-Adam 1520, at Beauvais cathedral. This plate was signed by 'Mathieu le Moine tumbier à P(ar)is'. Other rich classical canopies in the form of escalloped niches were at Notre Dame, Nantes 1524; St Aubin, 1525, and St Maurice, Angers 1535. In the latest of these crossed fasces were among the motifs on the facings of the columns. Small figures of saints were apparently brought into the frieze. The representations of the deceased within these settings appear to have differed little from earlier types. Archbishop Thomas le Roy at Nantes was an essentially gothic figure, and 'Moderator' Johannes at the Abbey of St Aubin was austerely shown in monastic habit.

An exception, and in all respects an extraordinary plate, was the brass of Charles d'Amboise, Sire de Chaumont d.1511, and his son Georges, killed at the battle of Pavia in 1525 (*The Craft,* Fig. 193). Both figures seem set to stride out of their Renaissance canopies. Charles wore an anchor badge as Admiral of France and held an immense arrow. This curiousity was in the church of the Cordeliers at Amboise.

Conservatism in figure representation and experiment in the canopy, is reflected in the sole surviving French brass of this scale and form. The plate of Abbot Marcial Formier 1513, at St Junien is disappointing compared with the memorials that are gone. It is, nevertheless, a valuable remnant showing the abbot in pontificals under a late gothic canopy with groined vault but represented with pronounced perspective effects. The surface is rather worn, but is well enough preserved to retain important detail.

French brasses were not entirely confined to large canopied figure representations. Smaller kneeling compositions were placed, especially to record the foundation of masses or other acts of piety. These were intended to be mural plaques and were occasionally set in carved or painted frames. A curious octagonal brass of this type is preserved in the Musée de Cluny, Paris. The plate records the foundations in 1461 of masses in the chapel of the Jacobins at Beauvais by Guillaume de Hellande, Bishop of Beauvais. Two thirds of the surface is lightly engraved with the kneeling figure of the bishop praying to the Blessed Virgin and Child, and aided by Saints Barbara and Agnes. The bishop's arms are placed above his head. The quality of the work is poor and parts of the design are ridiculous. The bishop's hands are represented in profile, emerging from one side of the chasuble of which a frontal view is given.

A later and superior brass, intended by its delicate engraving for mural display, is that of Nicholas le Brun, bailiff of Jeumont 1547, now in the collection of the British Museum (*The Craft*, Fig. 194). The main section of the design shows a Crucifixion with the Blessed Virgin and Saints John the Evangelist, John the Baptist and Mary Magdalen. The emaciated cadaver of Nicholas lies below on a rolled mattress. Dr Cameron lists a brass at Nouans to Michel Hérel, priest 1517, kneeling before a representation of the Crucifixion. Another small plate commemorates François Senocq and wife 1552, now at the Musée de la Princerie, Verdun. This has been noted in *The Craft*, Chapter Two, in connection with its painted surface. Both figures kneel towards a crucifix (*Ibid.*, Fig. 19).

Gaignières illustrates several of these mural brasses. Bishop Louis de Poitiers 1468, at the church of the Cordeliers, Amboise, was depicted standing in a small room. Bishop Thibaut de Luce 1454, but probably engraved later, at St Martin's Church, Tours, knelt before a representation of St Martin dividing his cloak with a beggar (Fig. 130). At the Abbey of St George at Angers the brass of Anthoine de Brye c.1520, showed two ecclesiastics in separate compartments, one kneeling at prayer, the other lying in state on a tomb or dais. The Abbess Jaquete de Rothais 1525, was shown at the Abbey of Beaumont completely concealed in a shroud and lying between a canopy and an Italianate representation of the Blessed Virgin and Christ child (Fig. 131). The brass of David Patry and family in the Abbey of Beaulieu near Le Mans was a rare example of a brass to a 'bourgeois' (Fig. 129). The figures aided by St John the Evangelist and St Mary Magdalene, knelt before a Pieta. The church of St Maurice at Angers had four mural plates, two with crucifixion scenes, set against a background of blood drops. Both were obviously sixteenth-century, though one was dated 1374. Gilles Comers (1522) knelt before a curious representation of Christ in Pity. Christ stood as an almost nude figure with two angels holding a cloth or shroud behind him. Lastly, Jacques Maschac and his nephew Pierre 1537, knelt with their patron saints before the scene of the Ascension (Fig. 133). Christ's feet were shown disappearing into clouds above the heads of the assembly. These brasses are unusual counterparts of contemporary English and Flemish votive compositions.

Spanish brasses

Brasses in Spain and Portugal can, for the most part, be satisfactorily attributed to Flemish workshops. Examples have nevertheless been noted from this period which reflect neither Flemish treatment nor quality, and may well be products of Spanish craftsmen. The once important examples to Archbishop Gonsalvo Fernández de Hereida 1511, Tarragona Cathedral, and to Don García Ortiz de Luyando and wife 1503, Santa Maria, Vitoria, are now badly worn — the former nearly effaced. The first is constructed of sixteen horizontal pieces, and showed the archbishop fully vested with pallium, lying within a canopy bearing subsidiary figures. The second is a kneeling composition with Renaissance setting. The large rectangular plate with marginal inscription, shield of arms and episcopal hat, to Bishop Innicus Manrique le Lara 1476, at Córdoba, is far too coarse for Flemish craftsmanship.[12] Similarly, the plate with heraldry and inscription at St Miguel, Segovia, to Jacob Ferdinand a Lacuna engr. 1557, is, perhaps, another brass of Spanish workmanship. It is impossible from such meagre evidence to draw conclusions of Spanish skill or interest.

Conclusion

There can be little dispute that by the sixteenth century Flemish brasses were far superior to English in conception and execution, and advanced in their response to the artistic influences of the age. French brasses, had they survived, would be similarly regarded. There is no evidence of stagnation, even though the courses adopted led by stages to the decay of the craft. It is, however, evident that the Flemish supremacy, reflected in continental trade, had passed by the close of the fifteenth century. This was not the effect of failing skill, but the competition of other workshops further east. Flemish engravers no longer enjoyed an unrivalled prestige. The wealthy of Germany and Poland turned to Nürnberg for their memorials.

10. German Silesian and Polish brasses, 1460-1560

Central German brasses

Nürnberg of the late fifteenth century was a free Imperial city of European fame, situated favourably on the land routes from Italy to the North and East. Among its distinguished community were the artist Dürer, the sculptor Adam Krafft and for a period the remarkable painter and wood carver, Veit Stoss. Notable humanists such as Schedel, Schrier and Pirkheimer were their companions. Alongside these men of genius were large numbers of highly skilled craftsmen, whose powerful and well organised guilds played a major role in the civic administration. Their activity produced a minor renaissance in German art. Its inspiration was essentially German, and owed little to alien influence. The family of Vischer, bronze founders and casters, flourished in this stimulating environment, and their fame added to the lustre of the city. Engraving was only one aspect of their metalwork, but their 'brasses' are among the finest of the late Middle Ages.

The Vischer Atelier

More is known of the Vischers than of any other mediaeval brass engravers. Hermann the Elder, who established the family foundry, bought his citizenship in 1453. He died in 1488, but in the meantime had acquired a good reputation for the casting of large church fittings. The bronze font at Wittenberg, dated 1457, bears his name and mark. His preference to work on a large scale was crucial to the future of his children. Hermann's son Peter, better known as Peter Vischer the Elder, was made a Master in the guild of Copperfounders in 1489, and by 1493 was the sole owner of the family foundry. In 1488 he submitted a design for the proposed shrine for the relics of St Sebald, which after many vicissitudes he completed in 1519 with the aid of his sons. Peter made his great reputation in the casting of bronze effigies in the round and in relief, and between 1493 and 1496 was away from Nürnberg completing the great cast effigy and tomb of Archbishop Ernst at Magdeburg. Peter moved his foundry within the city in 1506. He died in 1529 nearly seventy years of age, having outlived the ablest of his sons. The most celebrated of all his works are the Sebald shrine at St Sebald, Nürnberg; Archbishop Ernst's tomb at Magdeburg; and two of the great statues surrounding the tomb of the Emperor Maximilian at Augsburg.

Peter's eldest son Hermann became an effective partner to his father by 1500, and it appears that for a period the greater part of the monumental work of the family came under his direction and influence. Among the most notable of the works ascribed to him are the exquisite relief cast of Philip Callimach, Royal Secretary d.1496, in the church of the Dominicans, Kraków, and the sarcophagus with relief effigies of Count Hermann VIII von Henneberg and wife 1507, in the church of Römhild. Hermann, far more than his father, was attracted to the new ideas of the age and travelled to Italy in 1515, but it was a tragedy that he died in a sledge accident at Nürnberg before he could effectively apply his new knowledge. Hermann's brother, Peter Vischer the Younger, succeeded as an important influence in the family. He studied in Padova and Venezia and was profoundly influenced by humanism. He was the creator of several distinguished monuments, that to Duke Friedrich of Saxony at Wittenberg being his official masterpiece. He also died young in 1528. Peter Vischer the Elder's third son Hans inherited the foundry from his father but his work was handicapped by poor assistants, and in 1549 he left for Eichstätt, renouncing his craft. For nearly a century German tomb casting was dominated by the prestige and industry of this one foundry. Engraved plates, the main concern of this study, were but a subordinate part of the production. The variety and excellence of the most ambitious Vischer works and the life of the family may be studied in Meller's scholarly and fully illustrated text.

Few mediaeval engravers have been identified, and it is tempting to credit the exceptions with works they might have carried out. A curious variety of engraved plates have been attributed to the Vischers. The nineteenth century German authority Bergau held them responsible not only for the Flemish brass at Poznań to Bishop Andrzej, which is understandable, but also for the Silesian brasses at Wroclaw and the probably Silesian brass at Gnieznó. These, combined with genuine Vischer memorials, form a collection of unacceptable range in skill and style. Dr Kramer in his analysis of the Vischer brasses was more systematic and cautious, but he also ascribed to the foundry a small series of plates from 1460 to 1481 which Meller disregards. The author concurs with Meller's view. By 1450 a particular arrangement of figure and canopy had evolved and was used widely by German founders, and engravers of stone as well as metal. This pattern creates a genuine but superficial similarity between certain Vischer brasses and others of the period. It is accordingly necessary to examine the examples critically, especially between the years 1460 and 1480.

Early Vischer Brasses and other Workshops

A conventional pattern for German memorial plates has already been noted in Chapter Six, in connection with the brass at Zeitz to Bishop Johannes II. This general pattern was not invariably used, but was the most common for canons and other church dignitaries below the status of Bishop. These churchmen were the greatest users of low relief and engraved plates. There are nearly fifty, all but three in relief, in Bamberg cathedral alone.

It is fortunate that one brass can be attributed with certainty to the Vischer family during the lifetime of Hermann the Elder. Canon Georg von Lewenstein 1464, in Bamberg cathedral, is commemorated by a brass of the type described.[1*] He wears a cap and is vested in processional vestments without the cope, his almuce falling very amply around his shoulders. He holds a closed book and rises above a large achievement of arms. His canopy is little more than a narrow arch, serving to frame the figure. On the lower edge of the border is engraved a fish and the pennon mark peculiar to the Vischer family (*The Craft*, Fig. 71). The origin of the brass is certain, and there is no reason to doubt that it dates from the time of the canon's death. A second Bamberg canon, Johann von Limburg 1475, is of similar design, though smaller and somewhat inferior. Judging by these two brasses, no others earlier than 1475 may be ascribed on stylistic grounds to the Vischer family.

Five figure brasses and an incised slab with brass inlays form an inter-related group mostly dating from the third quarter of the fifteenth century. It is tempting to regard these brasses as of Vischer workmanship, which was the view taken by Dr Kramer. There is, however, no evidence to support the conclusion, and one example unknown to Kramer appears as proof to the contrary. The brasses, all in Germany, are as follows, though the first must be regarded as an uncertain member of the group:

Canon Eghard von Hanensee, 1460, Hildesheim cathedral
Bishop Schönberg, 1463, Meissen cathedral

Friedrich 'the Good', Duke of Saxony, 1464, Meissen cathedral, (Fig. 134)
A canon of the Bocksdorf family, c.1465, Zeitz, (Fig. 137)
Bishop Dietrich von Buckenstorf, 1466, Naumburg cathedral
Canon Heinrich Gassman (head, chalice and shield inlays only), 1481, Erfurt cathedral.

These brasses are connected by common and obvious characteristics. All the figures have fattish faces, heavily lidded eyes, prominent lips and profusely curled hair. Drapery is stiff, and strongly shaded. Canopies, when introduced as at Hildesheim, Zeitz and Naumburg, show a depressed late gothic arch with windows above and a groined vault within. Pavements are decorative and intricate. A noteworthy feature of all of these brasses is the use of small crescents or circles for decorative purposes, applied freely on vestments, curtains, floor tiles or surrounds.

The brass of Duke Friedrich is the most important, and is the first of a series to the Dukes of Saxony, who seem to have had a predilection for engraved memorials. He wears a long gown with a deep fur cape and a tall hat edged with fur. He holds a drawn sword, which rests across his right shoulder. Bishop Dietrich von Buckenstorf is the finest in design, and is deeply and vigorously engraved. He is vested, as is Bishop Schönberg, in mitre, alb, dalmatic and cope, a combination which is common on German episcopal memorials. Canon Hanensee, wearing a tall cap and holding a clasped book over his heart, is the least typical. The canon at Zeitz is in many respects the most interesting. His brass presents all the peculiarities of the group; the figure is unusual, the cap remarkably tall, and the choir cope sufficiently open to reveal the full length of the stole worn over the alb. A particularly valuable detail is a mark engraved beside the column on the right-hand side. It takes the form of a Z with a dividing stroke and has not been connected with the marks of the leading Nürnberg foundries.[2] It is unlikely that this is merely a designer's mark. It is probable that this group of brasses was cast and engraved in Erfurt or another Thuringian centre of importance, and has no connection with Nürnberg.

Three other figure brasses are of more uncertain provenance. Another plate at Zeitz to Bishop Peter von Schleinitz c.1463, is highly unconventional. The bishop stands in semi-profile. All his features are cleverly portrayed, as also an open book in his left hand. Both the amice and the infulae of the mitre are worked with words. The figure stands beneath a canopy of mixed gothic and classical or romanesque structure with a background of quatrefoil lattice work. Canon Hunold von Plettenburg 1475, Erfurt cathedral, is a very large figure vested in a rich and ample cope. He stands on a bracket, and holds a scroll which falls downwards. The composition is in separate inlay, and has suffered badly from wear and weathering. This may be a Vischer work, but there is unsufficient evidence to substantiate the claim.[3] The rather clumsy flat relief plate of Duchess Elisabeth of Saxony 1484, formerly at the Paulinerkirche, Leipzig, has the arrangement of a Vischer memorial, but is coarse in execution.[4]

Brasses of Peter Vischer the Elder

The masterly plates of Peter Vischer the Elder form a coherent and impressive corpus between the years 1485 and 1505. Peter's responsibility for this work is for the most part certain. One brass is proved by documentary evidence to have come from his foundry. Two have details which were derived from Peter's own drawing of the Sebald shrine. Another commemorates a friend and admirer of the Vischers. All may be closely compared with Peter Vischer's cast relief plates. The following list includes the established examples which existed in 1939.

Margaretha, Duchess of Saxony, 1486, Schlosskirche, Altenburg
Feliks Padniewski (presumed destroyed), 1488, Dominican church, Poznań

Ernst, Duke of Saxony, c.1486, Meissen cathedral

Lukasz of Górka (presumed destroyed), d.1475, engr. c.1490, Poznań cathedral *(The Craft,* Chapter Nine and Fig. 80)

Bishop Uriel of Górka (presumed destroyed), 1498, Poznań cathedral, (Fig. 298)

Ameleie, Duchess of Bavaria, 1502, Meissen cathedral (Fig. 139)

Duchess Sophie of Saxony, 1504, Torgau (Fig. 138)

Elisabeth Countess of Stolberg, 1505, Stolberg

Canon Johann von Heringen, 1505, Erfurt cathedral (Fig. 142)

Canon Eberard von Rabenstain, 1505, Bamberg cathedral

Canon Rudolf von Bünau, 1505, Naumburg cathedral (Fig. 136)

? Mikolaj Salamon, 1509, Church of the Blessed Virgin, Kraków (Fig. 143).

Though widely differing in scale and subject these brasses have many common characteristics. The figures in all dominate the composition even when, as with the Górka brasses at Poznań, a canopy based on a Flemish model was introduced. Their features are finely expressed, the later examples showing a definite affinity with the art of Dürer. The faces are, as Meller has described them, idealistic in quality. They are typecast, and lack the peculiarities of a personal likeness. In the cases of Duchesses Ameleie and Sophie the faces are almost obscured by the wimple, showing no interest in portraiture as such. Drapery folds are very boldly defined, and the powerful shading lines serve to emphasize the form of the garments. Whether the figures lie or stand is in some cases doubtful, and the engraver was apparently not overmuch concerned. The outlines of the figures, and many of the drapery and feature lines, are cut in very deep angular section, helping to effect an impression of relief.

The background is invariably a curtain or arras, with pomegranates, hanging on runners from hooks. The floors are composed of tiles. Canopies are varied. The great majority take the form of intertwined branches, curving above slender decorative columns. Woodwoses climb in these branches at Altenburg.[5] Feliks Padniewski was shown under a canopy of late gothic architectural form with interlaced tracery and gargoyles. Lukasz of Górka's canopy was a copy, whereas that of Uriel was in part derivative and in part an innovation with its brick domes. Marginal inscriptions are a far stronger feature than the canopies, being cut in bold black letter script, and forming a broad framework often with a decorative fillet. Corner medallions are frequently omitted. Heraldry is introduced on several in the form of a large shield placed under the feet of the deceased. This arrangement is particularly common on the cast reliefs.

The brass of Duke Ernst is unusual and greatly influenced by that of Duke Friedrich, though the detailed presentation is very different. The tall cap, the placing of the sword, and the lion support at the feet reflect the earlier plate, though the figure is altogether younger and more vital. The engraving is shallow, in contrast to all other Vischer works of this kind, and the brass may not have been fully completed. There is doubt about the date of execution. Ernst died in 1486, but there is some documentary evidence to suggest the brass was made in 1495.[6]

The three military figures were of varied style. Lukasz of Górka was in armour of 'gothic' type shown with sallet and raised visor, and with large circular besagews at the armpits. Much of the detail of this plate was in recessed relief, especially the facial features. The great lion may be compared with that below the feet in the cast to Bishop Georg I of Bamberg by Peter's father. Feliks Padniewski was in contrast bare-headed with a youthful face and tossing curls, and wore over his armour a mantle which was full of movement. The hands were weakly drawn, but the figure on the whole was far less monumental in quality than Lukasz. (?) Mikolaj Salamon is a comparatively small but beautiful figure with long streaming hair and peaceful expression. He stands full face in armour of simpler and more rounded shape, holding within the bend of his arm a lance with floating banner.

The ladies are plainer, all being dressed in a long-sleeved gown, with mantle, veil headdress and wimple. All hold rosaries. Duchess Margaretha is shown full face, in a rather lifeless manner. The later duchesses are engraved with greater vitality and feeling. Ameleie is represented at her devotions and Sophie, though clearly living, lies in an impressive recumbent pose.

The three ecclesiastics further emphasize the change which came over Peter Vischer's work at the turn of the sixteenth century. Uriel of Górka was a magnificent figure, vested in a very rich mitre and chasuble and holding a clasped book and crozier. His mature and alert appearance contrasted with the idol-like expressions of Hermann Vischer's cast bishops, such as Georg I at Bamberg and Thilo von Trotha at Merseburg. There is, nonetheless, an easily discernible development in the Erfurt and Bamberg canons, whose easy pose and lifelike presentation have no association with death. Both are vested in a heavy furred almuce and grasp a chalice, with the fingers of the right hand splayed on either side of the knot of the stem. Johann von Heringen's plate is an inlay within an incised slab, the lower part of the figure being badly worn. It is a splendid engraving, revealing the perceptive and powerful draughtsmanship of Peter Vischer. The strength of such memorials compares most favourably with the undisciplined ornateness of some contemporary Flemish work.

The finely engraved but macabre representation at Naumburg, showing an emaciated, disembowelled cadaver, has for long been attributed to Bishop Johann von Schönberg 1516. The arrangement of the composition, with its curtain background and canopy of branches, is nonetheless far more consistent with Vischer work of the previous decade. Skeleton and shroud brasses were frequently laid during the lifetime of the commemorated, though in this case recent research suggests that details relating to the Bishop have been wrongly associated with the brass, the figure being that of Canon Rudolf von Bünau.[7]

Brasses of Hermann Vischer the Younger

Small but significant changes in monumental products of the foundry become discernible during the time that Peter Vischer himself was absent at Magdeburg. The changes became increasingly noticeable after 1505. Meller presents a convincing case that Hermann, Peter's eldest son, was responsible for casting and engraving in his father's absence, and through his ability retained his influence. His arguments are based on artistic evidence and have not as yet been supported by documentary proof. Peter Vischer's monumental style developed from a disciplining of late gothic forms to a German classicism which owed nothing to Italian inspiration. Peter was not a copyist. His monumental representation was, as has been stated, idealistic rather than realistic. But many monuments from the foundry from 1500 onwards were clearly conceived by an artist with a different aim and resources. Their ornament is classical in origin incorporating antique motifs. Their design often closely follows the woodcuts and paintings of Albrecht Dürer, and one reflects the influence of Viet Stoss. The figures themselves reveal a naturalism alien to Peter Vischer's representations. The occurrence of these figures, moreover, coincides with the period of Hermann's active participation in the work of the foundry.

Dürer paintings which profoundly influenced relief and engraved plates by the Vischers, were the side panels to the Paumgärtner altarpiece, now at München. A panel depicting St Eustace, being in fact a portrait of Felix Paumgärtner, shows a partly-armed figure standing in semi-profile.[8] He holds a banner in his right hand and places his legs in a distinctive and natural pose, the right leg bending at the knee whereas the left is shown frontally, pointed towards the viewer. The elements of the pose are to some extent noticeable in the brass of Duke Albrecht of Saxony 1500, at Meissen cathedral,[9*] yet the copy of St Eustace is more clear in the relief plate of Piotr Kmitas 1506, in the Wawel cathedral, Kraków. Duke Albrecht is undoubtedly a Vischer work, though not necessarily by Hermann. It is an admirable representation of late gothic armour and heraldry, but is an unusually confused composition for these masters (*The Craft*, Fig. 195). The canopy combined both an arch and branches and parts of the figure do not stand out clearly against the curtain background. More in keeping with Hermann's presumed style is the large but battered and worn brass of Emeram Salamon, Prefect of Drolbycz 1504, at the Church of the Blessed Virgin at Kraków. Emeram stands in the manner of St Eustace but without a banner. His armour is of rounded transitional form with a good lance rest, and he wears on his head a large high-brimmed hat. A similar hat is worn by Emeram's brother Piotr d.1516, whose relief cast is in the same church. The background consists of the usual curtain on runners, with distant windows appearing from behind. The canopy above is complex. Two entirely different structures are interwoven — a flattened semi-circular arch and a complex arrangement of gothic canopies. Small figures are inserted in the side shafts and above are two-winged cherubs of Italian type. Emeram's head, though worn, reveals features alien to Peter Vischer's style. His nose is large and hooked. His face is heavily drawn and could be accepted as a likeness.[10]

Similar qualities, naturalism, classical ornament and a close connection with Dürer's art may be discerned in the following engraved plates, which should on Meller's analysis be ascribed to Hermann.

Zedena (Sidonia), Duchess of Saxony, 1510, Meissen cathedral (*The Craft,* Fig. 196)

Cardinal Fryderyk Jagiello, son of King Casimir, engr. 1510, Kraków cathedral (Fig. 140)

Friedrich, Duke of Saxony, 1510, Meissen cathedral, (*The Craft,* Fig. 23)

Andrzej Szamoutulski, Palatine of Poznań, 1511 (presumed destroyed), Szamotuly, (*The Craft,* Fig. 197)

A Canon, half only left,? c.1515. Kraków cathedral.

In the author's opinion the first four rank among the very finest engraved brasses of the early sixteenth century in Europe. Zedena is shown as a pensive and gentle person, her eyes cast downwards towards the beads held in her praying hands. Her dress consists of a gown, mantle and long scarf and is dignified but not ornate. Her headdress of a tightly-bound veil and wimple is plain, and the effect is arresting against the curtain background and skilfully arranged windows. The canopy is little more than a circular arch with two cherubs flying above. The design is thought to be the work of Albrecht Dürer (see *The Craft,* Chapter Nine).

The memorial of Fryderyk, son of King Casimir the Great, Cardinal Deacon of Sta Lucia, is the largest and most magnificent. The main plate, composed of eight pieces, is set in its original position on a platform before the High Altar of Kraków cathedral. The steps up to the altar pass on either side, and the front of the platform and the sides exposed to the stairway are covered with relief casts. On the frontal plate, the Cardinal kneels before the Blessed Virgin and Christ Child. An inscription records that the monument was erected by order of King Sigismund in 1510 to his brother's memory. Cherubs decorate the side panels. The engraved design was probably influenced by that of Uriel of Górka at Poznań, and so indirectly by an earlier Flemish model. This return to the traditional is nevertheless superficial, and no more than befitted a great ecclesiastic. The triple canopy with its upper lanterns is a fanciful frame of gothic ornament rather than structure, serving as a setting to the achievements of arms and to the large subsidiary figures of Saints Stanislaus and

Albert. The immense figure of the cardinal dominates the composition. The upward sweep of the drapery of the alb, the narrowed front of the chasuble, and the tall mitre add to the impression of height. He is portrayed as recumbent, but such is the nature of the immediate background and the calm strength of his figure that he appears to step out from an ornate recess. The overall treatment of the design is in the manner of Dürer. The saints, as shown in *The Craft,* Chapter Nine, are slightly altered copies of the Saints Nicholas, Ulrich and Erasmus woodcut. The relief figure of the Virgin is another close copy of a Dürer woodcut of this subject of 1510. The derivative character of these details supports the view that Hermann Vischer as an admirer of Dürer, rather than the great Nürnberg artist himself, was responsible for the pattern. The marginal inscription is in Roman capitals, a small but clear indication of growing Renaissance influence.

Duke Friedrich is in some respects a comparable work with interesting variations of arrangement. He is a vital and smiling figure holding beads in his raised right hand. He is fully armed, but wears over all the mantle of the Teutonic Order, of which he was Grand Master. His whole appearance, especially in the detail of the armour and the shock of curly hair, bears a strong resemblance to Dürer's St Florianus among the Austrian Saints, cut in 1516.[11] The canopy and background are in keeping with that of Duchess Zedena, though cherubs are brought into the design. An important change in the decoration is found in the ornamental border to the marginal inscription. This border, which in fifteenth-century plates was no more than a narrow fillet of running foliage, vine leaves, or flowers with stops in the early Flemish manner, was widened during this period. This is noticeable in Duchess Ameleie's brass but far more so in this case where the lateral borders are as wide as the inscription. They form a substantial margin of classical motifs. Such arrangements replaced the border inscription entirely by 1535.

The fourth major brass of the group, to Andrzej Szamotulski, was removed from Szamotuly church during the Nazi occupation and can only be presumed to have been subsequently destroyed. It is a particularly grievous loss on account of the exceptional merit of the engraving. Andrzej was represented in armour, standing in the act of prayer on a low platform. His face was defined with character, his mouth bearing a slight smile and his eyes having a watchful gaze. A hat with upturned brim partly covered the long curls which flowed onto his shoulders. His armour was well presented. The breastplate was globose and ridged, the pauldrons heavy with prominent haut-pieces and the sabatons bulbous. Mail breeches were distinctly visible beneath the cuisses. The strap work and detail of joints were carefully finished. The sword, an extremely heavy weapon, was placed independently to his left. A banner stood to his right, and an armet with plumes of ostrich feathers was placed at his feet. The canopy was formed by a three-centred arch springing from narrow columns, the soffit being decorated with winged infants inspired by an antique model, and the form of the arch possibly suggested by the Romanesque blind arcade in Bamberg cathedral, where Hermann Vischer made many drawing studies. Classical influence is also evident in the inscription, where the Palatine was described as one regarded as a 'delphic oracle' among the people.

The ecclesiastic at Kraków, probably a canon, is only a fragment of a large design. The figure is vested in surplice and almuce, and wears a cap. His setting is a classical recess which resembles in its form and decoration the relief cast of Canon Kress 1513, at the Laurenzkirche, Nürnberg, a work attributed to Peter Vischer the Younger. The date of this brass is doubtful. Meller favours Hermann as the maker on the strength of the treatment, the use of wyverns in the upper corners of the canopy, and the Kraków connection. The work is nevertheless inferior to the others described. It is probable that in the complete brass the almuce cut across the line of the pillars supporting the arch, a feature common in monuments of this kind by 1530. It is possibly the work of Peter Vischer the Younger or even Hans.[12]

Other brasses associated with the Vischers

Other brasses may be attributed to this famous foundry with qualification. Two brasses of Abbots from the region of lake Konstanz are of a quality and treatment consistent with work of the Vischer atelier. The earlier, at Mittelzell on the island of Reichenau, commemorates Abbot Georg Fischer 1519. His figure is in separate inlay, vested for mass with mitre, book and crozier.[13] His inscription is lost and a surviving shield is in low relief. This brass is undoubtedly from the foundry, but appears to have been made after Hermann's death, either by the younger Peter or Hans. The second is the large and well-engraved brass to David von Winkelsheim 1526, last Abbot of St Georg, Stein-am-Rhein, at Radolfzell.[14] The design is competent and derived from Dürer's St Ulrich figure. The marginal inscription is in gothic lettering but its border shows Renaissance influence. Much of the detail is well-finished, such as the slits in the glove covering the right hand to accommodate the large ring beneath. One of the shields at the Abbot's feet shows the upper part of an armed St George holding a banner. Nürnberg origin, though very strongly indicated, is less certain in this case. Brass engraving and casting were practiced in Southern Germany, as is shown by the early Augsburg coffin plate of St Ulrich, the wealth of relief casts at Ulm, and the finely engraved back plate to the cast of Jörg Truchsess von Waldburg at Waldsee. It is likely that the well-engraved inscription and achievement of arms to Cristan and Andres Kornfail 1496, formerly in the Carthusian monastery at Ittingen and now in the Thurgau museum, Frauenfeld, came from a South German workshop.

A highly-questionable attribution is the brass of Margaretha, Duchess of Braunschweig 1528, at Weimar. She is depicted in widow's dress with a high wimple, set against a classical recess. The design might pass as a Vischer plate, but the engraving lacks contrast. Overall it has more affinity with the later brasses at Freiberg than with those at Meissen, and may be an early work of Martin Hilliger.

There can be no doubt that many of the numerous inscriptions, some set with shields in relief, in the St Johannisfriedhof and St Rochusfriedhof in Nürnberg were made in the Vischer foundry.

Four canons in almuce under canopies at Halberstadt are now defaced with wear, but were clearly much inferior to the brasses described. The latest, to Johann von Marnholt 1538, retains some good detail, especially in the Evangelists' symbols. An important episcopal brass at Braniewó, considered by some authorities to be Peter Vischer's work, is in the author's opinion not so, and is discussed later in this chapter. On the other hand, a heraldic plate in the Albrechtsburg at Meissen, to Albrecht, Duke of Saxony 1513, depicting the Arms of the Duchy of Saxony surrounded by the Collar of the Golden Fleece, is of likely Nürnberg origin.

It would seem that after the death of the great master and his sons, Hermann and Peter, the chief centre for engraved brasses shifted from Nürnberg to Freiberg in Saxony. The Meissen series to the Ducal House of Saxony are an indication of this. Seventeen years separates the plate of Barbara, Duchess of Saxony 1534, from Duke Friedrich, and the latter is of entirely different inspiration. Attention accordingly turns from the Vischers to the Hilligers of Freiberg, their successors in the patronage of the Saxon Dukes.

The Hilligers of Freiberg

The family of Hilliger, bell and cannon founders, had a long and distinguished residence in Freiberg.[15] Hans Hilliger is known to have lived there in 1412. Nicol

Hilliger occupied a foundry in the town in 1460. He died in 1482 and was succeeded by Oswald. Martin Hilliger, who succeeded Oswald in 1517, greatly enhanced the reputation of the family, especially as cannon founder to Duke Heinrich the Pious between 1505 and 1539. Several of the cannons were of elaborate design, and while the casting was undertaken by Martin, the drawings for figures and ornamental reliefs were made by the painter Lukas Cranach. It is the combination of Martin Hilliger's work with this famous artist and other painters of the court that supports the view that Martin made the three later Meissen plates and the brass of Duke Heinrich himself at Freiberg. The Dukes of Saxony, for want of further space at Meissen, adopted the choir of Freiberg cathedral as a mausoleum. The three Meissen brasses represent Barbara, Duchess of Saxony 1534, Johann, Duke of Saxony 1537 (Fig. 135), and Friedrich, Duke of Saxony 1539. They differ from the earlier plates in several important respects. The background is entirely plain. There is no trace of a canopy, but the ornamental border, filled with shields, arms, cherubs, birds, arabesques and other decoration, forms a wide and elaborate framework. The inscription is on a rectangular plate at the feet of the figure. The figures themselves are engraved with much detail, but lack the strength of the Vischer representations. The lines are deeply but evenly cut. The heads of both the Dukes protrude into the border and become slightly confused with the detail. The Dukes are richly armed in fluted suits of the so-called Maximilian style. Both hold hand-and-a-half swords. Duchess Barbara stands in semi-profile in an embroidered gown, with her face mostly covered by a wimple. Her hands are folded at her waist.

Similar in treatment to these, but far more interesting and impressive is the earliest of the Freiberg series, Duke Heinrich 'the Pious' 1541, (*The Craft*, Fig. 105). The figure of the Duke, shown in the dress of a landsknecht with the hood of mail, sometimes called a 'bishop's mantle', striped hose and double-handed sword, is demonstrably a copy of Cranach's portrait (*The Craft*, Fig. 104), and may be directly attributed to this artist, who was in the Duke's employment. The background, which has no connection with the painting, shows a room with a barrel vault and circular lights, and tall recesses apparently faced with classical reliefs. The late gothic curtain gives place to the Renaissance set. Martin Hilliger died in 1544 and was succeeded by Wolf. Wolf is known to have engraved at least eight of the Freiberg brasses before his death in 1576, and these are treated collectively in Chapter Seventeen.

Turning from the activities of these great craftsmen it is appropriate to conclude with a work of a lesser man. Eckhart Kucher was a Thuringian bellfounder, and left his initials, E.K. on a large plate to Eobanus Zcigeler 1560, in Erfurt cathedral.[16] This is an ugly work, parts being in recessed relief, showing the priest in mass vestments and cap. His fat left hand grasps a chalice, and his heavy face recalls that of Martin Luther. The background is mostly plain with a crude classical canopy arch rising above. It is not a fine brass, but even in its naïveté it captures the spirit of the time.

Brasses from Baltic workshops

Brass engraving in the Baltic centres has been assessed in earlier chapters as of minor importance and of uneven quality. Throughout this period also there are few examples, but these are of exceptional interest and merit. The three most important are in Lübeck. No engravers of this city are known but six notable casters are recorded, Hinrich Gerwiges, Lorenz Grove, Clawes Grude, Tile Bruith and Arndt Musmann from the fifteenth century and the bellfounder Peter Wulff from the sixteenth century. Dr Paatz is of the opinion that such brasses as were made were probably cast by these craftsmen and engraved with the aid of city goldsmiths and the designs of local artists.[17] This hypothesis fits happily with the appearance of the existing memorials.

The most outstanding of them is that of Johann Luneborch (engr. c.1470), at the Katherinenkirche, which has been described in *The Craft,* Chapter Nine, Fig. 96. It is an astonishing engraving, copied in part from the fourteenth-century Clingenberg brass formerly in the Petrikirche, enriched with a medley of Flemish motifs, but undoubtedly German in its canopy, bold border inscription, and much of the detail. The figure of Johann in a richly embroidered and furred gown is an admirable representation of the period. His face is stern and full of character, though treated in a stylised manner. The circular patterns of dots indicating stubble are yet another adoption of Flemish technique. It is in part the treatment of this face, in part the arrangement of the rich garments with little regard for the structure of the figure beneath, that have led both Dr Eichler and Dr Paatz to attribute the design to Hermen Rode, an important North German artist whose work is found as far east as Tallinn.[18] They support the attribution by comparison with the St Luke altarpiece at the St Annen-Museum, Lübeck, a certain Rode work completed c.1483, and with other paintings, probably the work of this artist, completed in 1468 in the church of St Nicholas, Stockholm.

The date of the Lunerborch brass is commonly stated as 1474, though this is rather misleading. The marginal inscription commemorates two persons — Johann d.1461, who was major and whose figure is depicted, and a councillor Johann of the same family, who died in 1474. There are marked differences in the lettering of the inscriptions to these notables, indicating that the brass was made after the mayor's death and only completed at the death of his kinsman.

Another brass, less known but of unusual interest, is that of Hermann Hutterock and wife 1505, depicted in shrouds at the Marienkirche in Lübeck (*The Craft*, Fig. 198). It is a highly individualistic memorial engraved in great detail, and elaborately coloured. The canopy is in ornate late gothic style, with two large branches, hung with shields, meeting within the tracery. Figures of St John the Evangelist and St Catherine stand within the shafts. Hermann and wife are portrayed as dead, their eyes closed and their hands folded across the body. The drapery of their shrouds is complex, falling into jagged branch-like forms, but drawn to reveal the limbs beneath. It is a rich and strange memorial which Dr Paatz ascribes with little reserve as a late work of the Baltic artist Bernt Notke.[19] Bernt Notke is best known for his large statuary — the St George of Stockholm, Sweden, and the great rood from the cathedral at Lübeck. He also painted several important pictures of which the Totentanz and the Mass of St Gregory at the Marienkirche were destroyed in the Second World War. He also worked in precious metal, and a statuette of St George in silver by him is still preserved. He was a very versatile artist, who would be readily approached to design in this medium.

The brass of Bartolomäus Heisegger 1517, formerly at the Marienkirche but now in the St Annen-Museum, Lübeck, is a work of much smaller scale (*The Craft*, Fig. 200). It was mounted in a wooden frame and set vertically, and was clearly not intended to suffer heavy wear. It is engraved with much delicate detail showing Bartolomäus kneeling to the Blessed Virgin and Christ Child and aided by St Bartholomew, his patron saint. An original detail is the large clock which the Christ child reaches towards and strikes. A macabre aspect of this otherwise beautiful composition is the dead shrouded figure of the commemorated lying on a mat in the foreground. The whole group is set beneath a late gothic canopy with deep shaded vault, supporting a merchant's mark. Reference has been made in *The Craft*, Chapter Nine to Paatz's view that the designer of this plate was Jacob van Utrecht, a painter who was resident in Lübeck at this time. The mark on St Bartholomew's knife gives some support to his arguments based on style, though the case made does not appear conclusive.[20]

A large roundel at the St Annen Museum, Lübeck, is engraved with the winged lion of St Mark and its peculiarities are entirely consistent with Lübeck work. This may be dated c.1500. Other Lübeck brasses have been lost without detailed record. Three of these to the Bere family were of the fifteenth century and lay in the Burgkloster. In addition to the brasses in Lübeck, a small mural plate of less expert workmanship is preserved at Kloster Isenhagen, and commemorates Abbess Barbara Antoni 1510.[21] It represents the Abbess kneeling before the Blessed Virgin and Child, though this composition fills less than half the plate. The remainder consists of an inscription in relief lettering. Main interest lies in the figure of the Abbess, who kneels in front of a tree, her crozier resting against her, and her hands covered by extended sleeves. Her veil is encircled by a narrow fillet bearing crosses. This is evidently North German work and probably from a Lübeck source.

A further brass of importance, though attributed by several authorities to Peter Vischer the Elder, is in the author's opinion of Baltic origin.[22*] This is a large separate inlay figure with border inscription and arms, commemorating Paulus Legendorf, Bishop of Warmia d.1467. According to the inscription the brass was laid by the Bishop's successor, Lukasz Waczenrode, in 1494. The monument lay on the choir floor of the great church of Braniewo, but though broken, is now preserved complete at the Muzeum Mazurskie, Olsztyn (Fig. 141).

Bishop Legendorf is vested in mitre, cope and alb. He holds an open book and a crozier rests against his right side. His head is supported by a large pillow. Slanting from the bottom folds of his alb is a shield bearing his arms — a branch with six buds. The border inscription is broad and engraved in curious lettering, a cross between Lombardic and Roman capitals. Four shields bearing the arms of Waczenrode — a gryllus with an eagle's head and armed legs — cover the angles. The field of the shields, the edge of the border and vacant spaces between the words are filled with entwined foliage.

There are some resemblances to Vischer work, but the overall design of the figure is deliberately heavy. Trivial shading is introduced to emphasize lines. The drapery folds are realistically if gracelessly expressed and in marked contrast to Peter Vischer's woodcut of St Sebald, where a similar problem of drapery is resolved clearly and simply. There are apparent errors in detail. The infulae of the mitre, for example, appear from beneath the Bishop's hair and behind his ears in a curious manner. In contrast to the rather ugly design, the treatment of detail is precise. The jewellery of the mitre, the life-like face of the Bishop, the half figure of Christ holding a birch and scourge in the volute of the crozier, two spotted dragons in the border, and the twining foliage background to the shields and inscription, are unusual features. Neither the defects nor the merits of this brass have counterparts in known Vischer examples. It would seem more satisfactory to regard the memorial as of a local origin. Braniewo is on the Baltic, and of easy access by sea from Gdańsk or Lübeck. The majority of brasses from this region are of separate inlay. A Nürnberg connexion is neither convincing nor necessary.

Arriving independently to this conclusion, the author is convinced by Wróblewska's study that this brass is the work of Hans Brandt of Gdańsk, assisted by the bell-founder Andreas Grottkau.[23] Brandt was responsible for a wide range of sculptured work in Gnieznó, Torún, Poznań and Gdańsk, including the sculpture of St Adalbert at the first. The effigy on this tomb has affinities with the Legendorf brass, both in its treatment and deliberate ugliness. Grottkau, Brandt's associate, cast candlesticks and chandeliers for the Warmian Chapter at Braniewo and Frombork, between the years 1490 and 1495.

Yet another large brass of unusual style may be attributed to Baltic engravers. This is the memorial at Lidzbark to Hilderbrand Ferber 1531. The deceased is depicted as clean shaven, wearing a heavy furred coat and large round-toed shoes. The figure is not well-drawn and confused with shade lines. The design is curious. Hilderbrand rests his head on a pillow, and a skull, bone, and strange little lion are set at his feet, yet he is flanked by two classical columns and angels. The marginal inscription with shields at the corners is more conventional. There do not appear to be any other brasses with which this may be usefully compared, and a local origin should be presumed.

Rhenish brasses

A significant number of brasses in Western Germany bear witness to the activity in this period of at least one and possibly several workshops in the Köln region. Köln, situated strategically on the Rhine, was a large mediaeval city, and an emporium of Northern European trade. It was, furthermore, a major market for the copper of Upper Saxony, and was noted for its latten plate. Documentary evidence affords conclusive proof of engravers in this city. Aachen cathedral has four figure brasses, and the important brass of Cardinal de Cusa at Kues on the Moselle, was, according to its inscription, made at the expense of a Dean of Aachen. Considerable quantities of calamine ore were mined near Aachen and metalwork flourished in the town before the tenth century. Both Köln and Aachen welcomed immigrant metalworkers from the Low Countries during the fifteenth century, and it is likely that both were centres of monumental engraving. There is proof of monumental casting in Köln from the thirteenth and fourteenth centuries, but no evidence of engraved brasses at this earlier period.

There are, in addition, sufficient brasses west of the Rhine to support the hypothesis of a Rhenish 'school' of engravers. It must be immediately admitted that the term 'school' is used in a very general sense. Few of the examples have much evident connection with each other. They are, nevertheless, easily distinguished from brasses of the Flemish series, or those from North or Central Germany. The term "Rhenish' may be loosely used to embrace work some of which may have been executed in Mosan centres as well as Germany. Such was the migration of craftsmen and the close trading connections of this extensive region that the term is in fact more appropriate than might appear. The majority of the brasses are undoubtedly German, but some may be included of uncertain origin.

There are no common memorial patterns which may be identified as typically Rhenish, but there are peculiarities of treatment which are distinctive. Many Rhenish brasses were influenced by contemporary Flemish designs, but their execution is less confident and effective. Some are exceedingly intricate and engraved with an excess of cross-hatching and confusing decoration. Others are simpler in design, but lack contrast in their preparation, all lines being of apparently equal importance. Large late gothic canopies with interlaced tracery occasionally unbalance the composition. In contrast to Flemish derivations, the marginal inscriptions are usually in a script of heavy German type, strong but less graceful than Flemish scripts. The presentation of heraldry is consistent with German rather than Flemish memorials. Subsidiary figures such as angels, and the beasts placed at the feet, appear more akin to central German than Flemish examples. Rhenish brass designs are a fusion of models and ideas from both sides of the Rhine, but sufficiently complex to possess a character of their own.

The representation of an angel holding a shield for Heinrich von Imbermonte 1433, at Aachen cathedral, has been mentioned in Chapter Six as perhaps of Rhenish origin. Far more distinctive are three military brasses of the third quarter of the fifteenth century. One destroyed in the Second World War to Count Gerhard von Marck 1461, at the Agneskirche, Hamm, was a very large memorial. The count was armed in a surprisingly simple suit of armour, but wore a tall cap and the collar of the Kleve's Knightly Order of St Anthony — a gold chain with pendant, a tau cross with a small bell suspended from it. His feet were protected by leather shoes, and a long but light two-handed sword was placed at his left side. His canopy, deeply groined and of depressed form, was topped by an elaborate cornice. The sides of the plate were filled with achievements of arms and the Evangelists' symbols, and below his feet two swans supported a shield of Kleve impaling Marck. In no respect can this brass be related to contemporary western Flemish work, whether in conception, execution or detail.

A smaller but comparable plate to the Count is that at Linnich to Werner van Pallant 1474, shown in armour but without weapons (Fig. 149). The background is formed by achievements of arms and coarse cross-hatching. The marginal inscription is in large black letter with symbols of the Evangelists at the angles.

A very large brass, but of inferior design to that formerly at Hamm, is that at Altenberg, near Köln, to Gerart, Duke of Jülich 1475 (Fig. 144). The Duke's figure is rather crudely engraved but is interesting both for his sallet and bevor, and especially for the collar of knots and bugle horns round his neck. A horn with a similar knot hangs from a large shoulder-belt. The collar is the chain of the Order of St Hubertus, founded by this Duke in 1444, which became through inheritance the oldest and highest ranking Bavarian order.[24] It occurs again at Altenberg on the tomb of Duke Wilhelm von Jülich-Berg 1511. The gothic canopy is inartistic, as is the background of coarse foliage, and the overall detail is poor for a work of this pretentious scale. All these brasses are probably of Rhenish origin, and very possibly from Köln.

The important brass of 1488 to Cardinal Nikolaus Krebs, called de Cusa d.1464, lies on the floor of the chapel at Kues on the Moselle, where the Cardinal was born and where his heart was ultimately buried (*The Craft,* Fig. 94). As has been noted in *The Craft*, Chapter Nine, the design is a German variation on the Italian pattern for the Cardinal's incised slab at Rome. The figure lies as in death with his hands folded upon an inscription plate, which covers most of the lower part of his body. This arrangement was most probably derived from an early monumental design in which a pall covers the lower part of the body exposing the feet below. The inscription was intended to have a hatched background, which was never carried out. The draughtsmanship of the figure, compared to that on the slab, is graceless. The ascetic face at Rome is at Kues both fat and insensitive, and the Kues chasuble of a heavier and stiffer texture than the one at Rome. This brass is of unusual interest both on account of its alien inspiration and the personality of the man concerned. Cardinal de Cusa, rising from humble origins, was renowned both as a scholar and a zealous reformer within the Church. It is likely that this brass was made at Aachen where Erklans, who ordered it, was Dean.

Willem Loeman of Köln

The Rhenish origin of these memorials is conjectural; that of two important brasses, at Nijmegen and Kleve, is fortunately certain. In 1512 Elsken, 'Meister Willem Loemanss huysfrouw van Coeln', received the sum of sixty guilders, which she receipted with her mark, 'soe ick nyet schryven en kan'.[25] The money was part of the price paid for the sepulchre of Catherine de Bourbon, ordered by her son Karel, Duke of Egmont. Willem Loeman was evidently a master craftsman of distinction. It is known that he was born at Urdingen, and lived in the Copper Alley (Kupfergasse) in Köln. In his will of 27 February, 1512, the completion of his unfinished work was placed in the hands of the goldsmith Lambert, at St Laurentius, Köln. Other evidence connected Willem with the brass of Duke Johann II of Kleve and his wife at the Marienkirche in Kleve. This was a draft of the tomb with brasses, together with a disposition, which was preserved until the Second World War in the Staatsarchiv in Düsseldorf.[26*] Stylistic similarities and other circumstantial evidence leave no doubt that the brasses of Duke Johann I and wife d.1483, at Kleve, and of (?) Katharina, Duchess of Geldern d.1496, at Geldern, are also works of this master.

The brass of Catherine de Bourbon d.1469, is a splendid monument consisting of a high tomb inlaid with a cover plate of engraved latten and twelve side panels depicting the Apostles. Catherine is shown as a young lady, heavily but still gracefully robed, and wearing a truncated form of the 'steeple' headdress (*The Craft*, Fig. 201). Around her shoulders hangs a chain and pendant, apparently part of the Livery of Our Lady of the Swan. Two fierce lions glare from the bottom folds of her gown and two fine and elaborate achievements take the place of a canopy above her head. The curtain background has some of the richness of the best contemporary Flemish examples. It is difficult to establish when the monument was made. The nobility were habitually dilatory in settling accounts with artists and craftsmen, but it would seem likely in view of the sixteenth-century payments that the work was commenced some years after the date of death, and c.1480 is suggested.

Duke Johann I of Kleve d.1481, and his wife d.1483, are commemorated by a monument of similar grandeur (Figs. 145-6). Again the plate with figures is set on a high tomb, its sides inlaid with further panels engraved with achievements of arms. The Duke and Duchess are both well represented, the former having his eyes closed. Both rest their heads on cushions; the Duke rests his feet on a swan, a badge of Kleve, and the Duchess hers on two lop-eared dogs. The armour is well conceived with buckles, rivets and arming points properly shown. The Duchess appears to wear an early form of the pedimental headdress, a loose surcoat, embroidered under garment, and over all a mantle. Like Catherine de Bourbon she wears also an elaborate collar and pendant. The background and setting is exceedingly rich and confused. A fine but low embroidered curtain is set before a wall of ornamented bricks. Above are canopies of interlaced forms, in which shafts and pinnacles are entwined with the pediments. The pavement base is in a distorted perspective, made more curious by the tiles beneath the wife being of a different pattern, shape and direction than those below the Duke. Dr H.P. Hilger regards both the figures and the ornament of the plate as based on designs of the late Köln masters of 'The Holy Kinsfolk' and 'St Severin'.[27] The side panels are equally well engraved, and are splendid heraldic representations, made finer by the coloured inlay still remaining. The arms of Kleve and Kleve Mark are surmounted by grotesque helms, in keeping with their horn crests; the crest in the first shows evident signs of alteration. There has been dispute as to whether this brass represents Duke Johann I or is a second memorial to Duke Johann II. The first attribution is undoubtedly correct, and is proved by the arms of Burgundy and Etampes, the Duchess being a daughter of Jean I of Burgundy, Count of Etampes.[28*] The execution of the memorial was probably protracted, and the date c.1490 more appropriate than the date of death.

The Duchess at Geldern d.1496, is in most respects nearly identical to the Duchess at Kleve, and was clearly based on the same pattern. Even such details as the feet, the arrangement of the girdle with its long hanging end, and the drapery of the undergown are exactly repeated. The dogs at the feet are similarly reproduced. The face and headdresses are rather different; the Kleve Duchess is slightly more ornamental, and the pendant to the collar at Geldern appears to depict a male half figure with scroll. The Geldern brass is unfortunately mutilated; a veil or angel above the head is almost completely lost together with the canopy and base including the dogs' legs. The figure is now surrounded by a late nineteenth-century incised inscription in gothic style. The Duchess rests her head against a cushion, but the background is different from that at Kleve. A curtain decorated with flowers in circles hangs behind, and the pavement base follows an eccentric pattern. Hilger has noted that the Duchess was succeeded by the Duke of Egmont, who ordered his mother's memorial from Loeman, so adding support to the existing stylistic connection.[29]

A further important brass is that of Duke Johann II of Kleve d.1521, and his Duchess Mechthild of Hesse d.1505 (*The Craft,* Fig. 202). This depicts the Duke in armour kneeling with his wife beneath a representation of Our Lady in Pity, supported by St John the Evangelist, and St Elizabeth, patron saint of Hesse. Achievements of arms are set on either side of the Pieta and a gothic arch, framing the composition, is enriched with sixteen applied shields. This is superimposed upon a canopy of interlaced tracery. The base below the kneeling figures is formed of a tiled floor in curious perspective. Underneath is an inscription of eleven lines in black letter. Both Drs. Scholten and Hilger ascribe the brass to Loeman, having been begun after the Duchess's death, but left incomplete at the engraver's death.

The pattern, formerly at Düsseldorf, was decisive evidence concerning this brass, and, in spite of its loss, the description by Scholten preserves much of its record. The interpretation of this scholar is demonstrably faulty, as he believed that both the Kleve brasses commemorated Duke Johann II, a view refuted by the heraldry. There is, however, no reason to doubt the accuracy of his statement insofar as it relates to the drawing. He writes, 'The Staatsarchiv in Düsseldorf preserves this sketch of Meister Loeman for the Clevian sepulchre and also a disposition. According to this, the tomb was originally designed to rest on eight copper lions with enamelled shields showing the arms of the Ducal couple. The lions may have been lost when the tomb was moved. On the plates between the supports Loeman, as at Nijmegen, wanted to place the twelve apostles. The plate, which is now mounted on the wall, was originally surrounded by a stone frame and set at the feet of the memorial on a column of the apse. Loeman left a will on the twenty seventh of February 1512 at Coln in the Kupfergasse. After his death it appears that the goldsmith Lambert at St Laurentius, Coln, completed the memorial. It was valued by goldsmiths, engravers and sculptors to be worth 400 guilders. Difficulties in obtaining payment for it were encountered in Cleve also.'[30]

This description raises many problems. It is nevertheless clear that the brass of Duke Johann II was started by Loeman, and was intended for a vertical setting. The pictorial panel is presumably the work of Loeman, and the inscription with its statement of the Duke's death in 1521 a later completion by the goldsmith. It is noteworthy that a small portion of the border decoration was never completed, together with one shield and perhaps the scrolls below the shields. The other information is puzzling. The valuation seems far too high for this plate complete, let alone in an unfinished state. Furthermore it is not clear why sculptors were involved, unless the stone frame was elaborate. The most probable explanation is that two memorials were at first envisaged, the larger based on that of Duke Johann I but with significant differences of detail. This great work was presumably only partially finished at the master's death, and would most probably have been beyond the skill and means of Lambert to complete. Under these circumstances the project could have been abandoned, and the difficulty in securing payment is readily explained. Whatever the facts there can be little doubt of the origin of the mural plate.

No other brasses can be confidently ascribed to Willem Loeman, though four large heraldic compositions, surrounded by border inscriptions at the St Elisabethkirche at Marburg are consistent with this master's style and skill. The earliest, to Anna von Wiershausen 1481, is original in design and especially well cut (Fig. 147). The central panel takes the form of an octofoil cross engraved with two achievements and a small seated hooded figure. The inscription is in large black letter script. The other three, to Anna von Katzenelnbogen 1494, Luckel von Hoitzveld 1497, and an unknown person c.1495, are all finished in a shallower manner, with an excessive quantity of shading and decorative hatching. Another more doubtful case is a quadrangular heraldic plate at Schloss Monrepos, commemorating Count Wilhelm von Wied and wife 1472. This consists of an inscription and an angel holding two shields, well executed but only possibly by Loeman.[31]

Later Rhenish brasses

Three other brasses of the late fifteenth century, all commemorating ecclesiastics, were most probably engraved in Rhenish workshops. The rectangular plate to Abbot Heribert von Lülsdorf 1481, at Kornelimünster, near Aachen, depicts the figure as in death. The Abbot's hands are placed palms inwards on his breast, his eyes are closed and his mouth shown partly open with the teeth exposed. He is vested in a cope and two hovering angels support the mitre on his head. Only the upper half of the figure is shown. A canopy is formed by a series of interlaced arches, and a shield of arms of von Lülsdorf with angel supporters is imposed on a panel beneath. A border inscription with the Evangelists' symbols and angels bearing arms in medallions is now completely lost. Abbot Adam Hertzogenrade 1483, at Brauweiler, is a full-length but plainer figure, shown in amice, alb, dalmatic and chasuble and wearing an almuce upon the head. His crozier is very large and lies slantwise across the body. Two lions are set below his feet. A canopy of a single pediment with interlaced cusps supports a façade of gothic tracery. The treatment of the brass is simple, all the background being recessed by fine hatching. The third brass, to Canon Arnold von Meroide 1487, in Aachen cathedral, shows the deceased kneeling before the Blessed Virgin with his patron saint and guardian angel. It is an inferior version of the Flemish type of votive composition, varied slightly by the inclusion of banners.

Further sixteenth-century brasses, apparently of Rhenish origin, are of very uneven quality. The largest, the ungainly figure of Sibert van Ryswick 1540, in Xanten cathedral, is a further example of craftsmanship which falls far below the standards of western Flemish or the Nürnberg workshops. The priest, who wears a pileus and carries an almuce, is ugly in appearance and formless in his capacious robes. The surface of the plate is heavily and carelessly shaded, which further confuses the inadequate draughtsmanship. Two shields at his feet are of better execution. Four votive compositions are more competent. Heinrich von Berchem 1508, in surplice with almuce, shown kneeling before the Blessed Virgin and aided by St John the Evangelist, is depicted on a small panel within a long rectangular inscription at St Maria-im-Capitol, Köln (Fig. 148). A chalice is represented in another smaller panel. The composition is framed by a border of flowers in lozenges, very similar to that on the plate of Duke Johann II of Kleve. This is possibly a work of the goldsmith Lambert, or even Willem Loemann.

More interesting is the devotional group with Canon Johann Pollart 1534, at Aachen cathedral, who kneels before the Blessed Virgin and the Christ Child. He is vested in a surplice and carries his almuce over the left arm. With him stand St John the Baptist and St Christopher, the latter standing in a stream. The plate is painted heavily in a variety of colours almost without doubt original. Above the group are two hovering angels and an interlaced canopy, and below, achievements of arms flank a lengthy inscription. A somewhat similar though poorer composition at Aachen commemorates Johann Pael 1560, also a canon, who kneels before the Blessed Virgin, who is herself attended by St John the Baptist and St Mary Magdalen.

Greatly superior to any of these in execution is the plate of Canon Heinrich Oskens 1535, said to have been formerly at Nippes near Köln and now in the Victoria and Albert Museum (Fig. 150). This is a fine brass by any standards and its origin is uncertain. The canon kneels in cassock with his almuce over his arm. In the centre is elevated the Blessed Virgin with her feet on her attribute of a crescent moon. St Peter and St Henry are in attendance. Within the canopy above is a small representation of the Annunciation. The inscription is engraved in good lettering of a distinctly Flemish character. Much of the surface is still inlaid with colour, of which details have been given in *The Craft,* Chapter Two. It is defensible to ascribe this brass to Flemish engravers, though the figures are not entirely consistent with such an origin. It is accordingly more satisfactory to regard it as a memorial made in Köln, reflecting the very considerable influence that Flemish brasses had at that time.

The kneeling figure of Hermann Blanfort 1554, formerly at St Columba, Köln, was an ugly representation of an academic, part of which was worked in recessed relief. An emaciated corpse with inscription at Aachen commemorates Johann and Lambert Munten 1559, a brass which has been described in *The Craft* for its painted reverse. An attractive medallion of good execution c.1510, depicting two angels supporting a chalice and shield, is preserved in the Diözesan-Museum, Köln.

It is surprising, that, judged on existing material, Rhenish brasses were neither numerous, nor of the consistent quality that could be expected from a well developed craft. This conclusion is difficult to explain in a region of great achievement in other forms of metalwork, and especially in one which was renowned for its export of latten plate. Among the best examples those at Nijmegen, Kleve and Geldern are undoubtedly impressive. The plate of Canon Oskens from Nippes is excellent if it be of Köln work. But the majority, regardless of their scale, bear unfavourable comparison with most other contemporary Continental brasses. It is possible that the destruction of these memorials has been great in the course of repeated wars, yet there is little obvious indent evidence to indicate widespread loss. It may be tentatively concluded that such was the activity of Rhenish monumental sculptors, as exhibited in the cathedrals of Mainz and Köln, that monumental engraving did not become a serious speciality. The brasses that exist may be treated, as those in Lübeck, as occasional works, which would account for their modest numbers and inconsistency in treatment. Such a situation, if true, is unexpected, and it may be hoped that German scholars will publish more evidence to support or refute this interpretation.

Silesian brasses

East of the Oder there were at least two centres of memorial brass engraving by the late fifteenth century. Wroclaw was well established. Kraków is noted in this connection for the first time. Surviving examples of Silesian work are with one exception confined to the city of Wroclaw itself, and consist in the main of inscription plates. The brass of Archbishop Jakub Szienienski 1480, at the Gnieznó cathedral (*The Craft*, Fig. 93), a very large memorial based on Flemish patterns, has already been partly described in *The Craft*, Chapter Nine. The Archbishop is vested in rich pontificals, holding both his crozier and cross staff. His mitre is jewelled and his chasuble has a pattern of pomegranates. The canopy is very pretentious, bearing tabernacles above the pediments filled with representations of God the Father receiving the soul of the deceased, and supported by broad shafts forming niches for apostles. The background is worked in a lattice pattern filled with flowers. A marginal inscription frames the whole with fine Evangelists' symbols in medallions at the corners. The engraver's mark is set in a small shield at the upper right-hand side of the plate. The peculiarities of this great brass have been discussed and the author is convinced that it is from a Wroclaw workshop, though greatly influenced by earlier and imported models. Gdańsk is an alternative source, on account of the Archbishop's relations with the sculptor Hans Brandt.[32]

Two other figure brasses, both being quadrangular compositions, have suffered severely during the Second World War. The earlier is in Wroclaw cathedral, commemorating Bishop Rudolf von Rudesheim 1482. It was badly twisted and cracked but is otherwise complete. This brass closely follows Silesian precedents. The Bishop is rather crudely represented in pontificals with his right hand raised in blessing, and holding his crozier in the left. A large lion crouches at the feet, and directly below are three shields of arms. A canopy pediment of debased gothic type is supported by shafts containing the figures of four saints. The border inscription is in black letter and provides a continuous frame. The background to the figure and canopy is created by deep hatching. Much of the detail is executed in recessed relief with a considerable degree of moulding in the subsidiary figures. The arms and parts of the drapery are treated in the same way. The Bishop's face is embossed in thin metal and riveted to the plate below, a very unusual way of creating low relief. It is a large and curious memorial, barely earning the description of an engraved brass.[33] The other brass commemorated Duke Wenczeslaus 1488. This is now preserved in worn fragments at the Muzeum Slaskie. The original design showed the Duke in gown and bonnet, holding a sword point downwards. A large achievement of arms was set at his feet, and the figure lay against a curtain background, with a canopy of late gothic style. Small figures of SS. Peter and Paul were placed in the side shafts. The lower third of the composition was lost by the nineteenth century, and the central plate containing the body and lower part of the head was destroyed in the Second World War.[34] The surviving portion of the head is partially worked in recessed relief. The brass is presumably of Wroclaw workmanship, though the design is influenced by Nürnberg models.

The best of the minor plates are two heraldic achievements within marginal inscriptions to Hans Krappe 1497, and Martha Krappe 1508, set on the wall of the Krappe chapel in St Elizabeth's church. Both are quite small quadrangular plates of competent execution. The inscription of 'Magister Erasmus' 1502, engraved with a hatched background, incorporates a trade mark with initials. The other inscriptions, all of the early sixteenth century, are in relief lettering. Most are of the common German type though that of Elizabeth Cristof 1508, has short and sharply angled letters. Even allowing for the possibility of substantial losses, it would appear that the craft of monumental brass engraving was declining in Wroclaw by the close of the fifteenth century, and had been all but abandoned half a century later. A curious brass in memory of two Hospitallers, Mikulas Puchner and Erasmus, is set in the crypt of the church of St Francis at Praha. This is possibly Silesian work but more probably made in the city. It includes two inscriptions dated 1454 and 1490 of very different quality, forming a composite memorial. The most interesting elements, probably contemporary with the later inscription, are a large six pointed star and a plain cross.

Kraków workshops

The city of Kraków was a centre of the arts which equalled Wroclaw, yet there is no evidence that brass engraving became as well established there. Distance from the necessary raw materials placed craftsmen at a disadvantage, and the connections of the Kraków merchants and nobility encouraged the import of monuments from celebrated foundries. No local enterprise could easily prosper against such competition. The great monumental wealth of the Wawel cathedral, the church of the Blessed Virgin and the numerous lesser churches in and around the city gives little cause to suspect that large numbers of engraved brasses have been destroyed, especially as imported brasses and casts have survived in considerable numbers. Incised slabs of local design are also very numerous and were available to patrons unable to afford the expense of a commemorative cast. Fortunately a documentary record proves that monumental brass engraving was carried out in Kraków in the sixteenth century. This is the order in 1525 by Jan Karnkowski for the casting of a brass to Dieslaw Zaliwski. The order was made to a local caster and engraver, Hanusz, instructing him to represent the deceased in armour with the appropriate heraldry and an inscription in Roman capitals.[35*] This brass no longer exists but three others seem to have a genuine connection with the city.

The earliest of the monuments is the elaborate memorial to Jan Koniekpolski and his two sons Przedbor and Jan (*The Craft*, Fig. 203). The brass is fixed to the north wall of the chancel of the remote village church of Weilgomlyny, in the vicinity of Radomsko. It is a rectangular composition, constructed of eighteen plates. Jan the Elder was chancellor to the Polish crown and prefect of Sieradz. He died in 1455. His sons inherited the prefecture, Przedbor dying in 1475, and Jan in 1471. A third son, Jakub, canon of Kraków and Gnieznó, died later, and it is likely that shortly after 1475 he promoted the erection of this monument to the memory of his father and brothers.

The overall arrangement of the brass follows a pattern normal for the period. The three armed figures stand on a tiled floor against an elaborate curtain. A triple canopy rises above, while large achievements of arms are placed below. The border inscription in black letter surrounds the whole. In contrast the treatment of the monument is unusual and can only be associated with Silesian work or incised slabs in the vicinity of Kraków. The canopy work is carelessly finished, and the junction of the plates reveals inaccurate engraving between the parts. The cornice of quatrefoils and tracery below indicates an influence from Silesian brasses of the fourteenth century, while the details of the heraldry and the flowers on the curtain have similarities with the design of the heraldic plates of the Krappe family at Wroclaw. A Silesian origin for this plate is possible. The great individuality of the design of the figures of the deceased is, however, against such an attribution. All three stand in a gangling stance, their feet pointing almost vertically downwards. Their faces are strongly engraved in recessed relief, with large lips and noses, while their hair streams down behind their shoulders. The elder Jan is bearded. Important features of the armour are the wide fauld and deep standard of mail, the besagew on the left hand figure, and the broad jewelled belts worn round the hips. The swords depicted are of great size. Only the father wears spurs, as also a long fur-lined cloak to emphasize his seniority. A particularly revealing detail is the representation of the hands which touch at the fingertips while the thumbs are placed well back (Fig. 151). Many of these peculiarities are found on incised slabs in Kraków and its immediate vicinity. The destroyed slab of Jan Kovilensky d.1471, formerly at the Augustinian church, Kraków, was an especially clear example showing the same pose, armour, long face and placing of the hands. Other details, such as the jewelled belt and wildly streaming hair, occur on the slab to Jan Sprowa 1460, at the Cistercian church of Mogila. These similarities leave little doubt that all these monuments were designed by craftsmen whose centre was Kraków. The geographical position of Weilgomlyny and the status of Jakub Koniekpolski in the city are also circumstantial factors in support of a Kraków origin.

The second example is to Mikolaj Tomicki, ensign of Poznań (Fig. 152). This brass is now fixed against the chancel wall of the small church of Tomice near Steszew. He was a gentleman of local importance in Poznań, and was first commemorated c.1490 by a modest stone monument at Tomice, where he is shown in armour, his left hand on his hip and his right outstretched, a large two-handed sword placed by his left elbow. The portrayal is clumsy, and the lettering of the border inscription poorly executed. Mikolaj's distinguished son, Piotr, Bishop of Kraków, was clearly dissatisfied with his father's monument, and ordered a finer memorial, which, according to the record of its inscription, was made in 1524. This second representation is superb. Mikolaj stands bare-headed and clean-shaven, his hands placed as in prayer, with a great lance and banner resting in the crook of his left arm. The armour has the elaboration and extravagance of a parade suit. The breast plate is ridged and cusped, and the pauldrons are slashed, with extravagant haute-pieces. The deceased is portrayed as a proud man, with a large dominating nose. The architectural setting behind the figure is intricate, revealing a floor set with floral tiles below an open colonnade and barrel vault. The architecture reflects Italian influence, especially in the pillars and capitals. A narrow border surrounds three sides of the whole, engraved with urns, floral and fruit decorations, and trophies. The inscription is in fine Roman capitals. A slightly fanciful shield set slantwise bears an ancient boat device.

The origin of this memorial is uncertain. The stance of the figure and its superficial affinities to the Vischer plates at Meissen would suggest Nürnberg craftsmanship. Yet the detail of the figure is very different from those at Meissen, the Italianate background and foot inscription are early of their kind, and the decorative border bears a very close similarity in its ornament to the grille of the Sigismund chapel in the Kraków cathedral. This grille was made in Kraków at this time by German and Italian craftsmen employed for the purpose. It is accordingly most likely that the Tomice brass was made in Kraków, and its excellent quality was achieved through the participation of these visiting masters. The donor of the brass, through his influence in the cathedral and the city, was well placed to obtain their services. It is also possible that the local engraver Hanusz was involved, as the general specifications for the Zaliwski plate would be equally applicable to that of Mikolaj.

The third brass is less important and commemorates Lukasz Noskowski, doctor of medicine and philosophy, and rector of the Jagielonski University at Kraków, who died in 1532. It consists of a rectangular inscription and four shields of arms. The treatment of the inscription is curious and the shields of arms are presented boldly but artlessly. Its rough execution is consistent with the work of a local metal worker unaccustomed to such orders.

The brasses ascribed to Kraków are of considerable significance for the period. Not only does their provenance indicate the widespread European character of engraved brasses by the early years of the the sixteenth century, but the quality of the Tomice brass proves the skill of the craftsmen involved. It is this quality which is the great development in the craft east of the Rhine. German and Polish figure brasses were evidently not numerous, in the sense that Flemish brasses were numerous. They did, however, interest the finest engravers and metalworkers. Furthermore, the established German conventions in brass and slab design aided the engravers' skill. The emphasis on figure and border, with a minor interest in background, canopies, subsidiary figures of surrounding ornament, was a valuable advantage. Flemish design was increasingly compromised by realistic detail, excessive decoration and changing ideals. The German model was in these respects less vulnerable. Many of the surviving memorials are accordingly of European distinction.

11. English brasses: the London workshops, 1460-1500

Turning from the brilliance and innovation of the best Flemish and German craftsmen, it is a contrast to view the conservatism of English brass engraving. Patterns, which had served with various modifications for a century, continued in use with relatively little alteration. The only change which may be interpreted as a concession to realism lay in an increasing use of semi-profile poses, which imparted a certain ease and vitality. Whether these were chosen for artistic reasons or because they suited the display of particular fashions in dress is a matter for conjecture. More significant is the fact that the largest and most elaborate compositions adhere most closely to traditional arrangements.

There were serious defects in the craft. Whether judged on grounds of execution or conception English figure brasses in general deteriorated in quality throughout the latter years of the fifteenth century. One reason for the decline was undoubtedly social. By the close of the century brasses as a class of memorial had lost status. Production of brasses was prolific and most of those commemorated were esquires, royal officers, small landowners, petty traders and parish priests. Brasses to more notable persons exist, and a few of the most influential administrators of the period are so commemorated, but in the majority of cases they form only part of the monument, which consists of a high tomb of elaborate construction. A great many brasses of the period are of small size, and a few, such as John Yerde c.1480, Cheam, which is only 16.5 cm in length, are diminutive. In treatment, the stiff and angular delineation, which has already been noted in work of the mid-fifteenth century, became more pronounced. Drapery lost grace and even perceptible form. Standards of accuracy in the presentation of forms were not maintained. The interpretation of armour, for instance, is often imaginative or ignorant, and brasses cease in this respect to be reliable sources of evidence. Pretentious fashions in dress, unsuited to a simple linear treatment, add to the clumsier appearance of both male and female figures. Canopy work, in late gothic style, is burdened with coarse tracery and enrichments.

In order to vary conventional arrangements the engravers experimented with ornament, resorting to elaborate inlaid backgrounds, extraordinary foot-rests and the liberal enrichment of border inscriptions. Brasses are particularly varied in their decoration, and the period is accordingly rewarding for the student of details. The chief merit of most brasses of this period lies in their intrinsic interest. This quality was greatly enhanced by the participation of provincial engravers working from patterns very different in inspiration from those of London. Their work is sufficiently important to require separate description, which is made in chapter Thirteen. Furthermore, within the limitations described engraving of a fine quality is found both from London and the provincial centres and some ambitious compositions were successfully carried out. Macklin's judgement that 'there are very few of the three hundred and fifty brasses [1453-85] which can in any sense be described as "fine", is over severe. The more important late fifteenth-century brasses are intricate but exciting compositions, and must have been striking with their varied inlays and occasional gilding. Representation has a certain rich heraldic quality, stiff, formal and erring on the trivial, but is certainly arresting.

The majority of English brasses were evidently made in London, though by this time the craftsmen in the capital faced significant provincial competition from workshops in the North and East Anglia. Few of the engravers are known, though the situation is becoming clearer.[1] The eminent marbler John Essex and the coppersmith Thomas Stevens (Stevyns), who were employed in the major Beauchamp contract (see Chapter Eight), maintained their association until the former's death in 1465. Stevens was certainly supplying Essex with stone in 1460.[2] Richard Stevens, marbler and glazier, has been noted as acquiring a business in 1445, may well have been a close relative of Thomas, and was an executor to the will of Sir Peter Arderne in 1467.[3] This role may be unconnected with his craft, but it seems probable that with such a relationship the brass of Sir Peter would have been placed in his hands. This memorial fortunately exists, and is a good example of 'D' series design. There are further connections. Sir Peter Arderne was First Baron of the Exchequer, and a close friend in his profession of Sir Brian Roucliffe,[4] the remains of whose brass is at Cowthorpe. Roucliffe required in his will that the marbler James Reames (*The Craft,* Chapter Seven) should lay an epitaph for him in the Temple, and it may be suggested by this unusual nomination that he was also responsible for the Cowthorpe brass, prepared during the judge's lifetime. It is a special design, but reflects strong 'D' pattern influence, especially in the canopy. It may accordingly be proposed that the Stevens family were prominent in the production of the major 'D' series brasses, while Reames was associated with them. Reames was of St Paul's Yard. John Lorymer of the Blackfriars, who died in 1499, has been noted (*The Craft,* Chapter eight) as a marbler and engraver, and his brother Henry was paid in 1488-9 for work on the Earl of Oxford's tomb at Earl's Colne. Another marbler, John Manning of St Andrew Undershaft, died in 1487, but his connection with this work is not clear. The identity of the "no klenly portrayer" of St Brides in 1482 (see *The Craft*) is unknown, though he may have been a descendant of John Howell, marbler of that Parish in 1413. These facts are no more than an initial step towards the truth, but they support the interpretation of multiple workshops in London

Pattern series of the period are confusing, and may be interpreted as consisting of two or three basic series with many variations, or a number of different but closely inter-related designs. Within a distinctive pattern variations of quality and execution are considerable. The numerous 'D' series, which is traceable into the 1490's, exhibits a marked diversity of accomplishment. The rich figures of the Earl and Countess of Essex 1483, Little Easton, which are clearly the work of a master, have several simpler counterparts, some pleasing and well engraved, but others dull repetitions of an established design.

Men in armour

Prevailing styles in London can be most conveniently identified in military figures. Armour represented on later fifteenth-century brasses retained many of the characteristics already described in Chapter Eight. Considerable changes in appearance were, however, introduced by the highly pointed and cusped forms associated with 'gothic' armour, and especially with the suits of such distinguished German armourers as the Helmschmieds of Augsburg. The fauld is shortened and tassets elongated. Cuisses are often represented as constructed of a number of overlapping plates of an acute chevron shape. The breastplate is usually composed of two parts, the lower, called a plackart, rising to a point in the centre. Sabatons are long and articulated. Most armoured figures on brasses are shown bareheaded, with the neck protected by a bevor or more commonly by a collar or 'standard' of mail. There are, nevertheless, several good illustrations of the sallet, both front and side view. The ridged and pointed outlines of this armour, genuine enough in inspiration, are often distorted in their interpretation. Couters and pauldrons are displayed of an immense size, and certain pieces of armour shown would have been quite unwearable. Henry Parice, 1466, Hildersham, is a well-known example (*The Craft*, Fig. 87). His poleyns are made to curve behind the back of the joint, so preventing the knee from bending. Exaggeration gives place to definite misrepresentation.

The accurate and restrained 'B' series of patterns are represented by a fairly small number of examples, which come to an end about 1470. Henry Parice is a good illustration and one easily related to earlier figures described, such as Thomas Shernborne 1458, Shernbourne. The position of the sword, which is hung across the body, is typical and certain details are of interest, namely the arming points on the couters and the lance rest riveted to his breastplate. The padded garment worn under the fauld is unusual, and the profile representation of the legs but not the feet is curious. Other important examples are as follows:

John Ansty, Esq., wife lost, 1460, Stow-cum-Quy
Sir Robert del Bothe with wife, canopy, worn, 1460, Wilmslow
Sir Thomas Grene with wife, 1462, Green's Norton
Thomas Colte, Esq., with wife, 1471, Roydon (Fig. 174).

The increasing use of semi-profile representation is revealed by these figures. John Ansty and Sir Robert del Bothe are both so shown, as also Joan Colte. The military figures are bareheaded, except for the mutilated brasses at Cambridge (Museum of Archaeology) and Wappenham, the former undoubtedly being part of the figure of George Langham 1462, from Little Chesterford. He wears a rounded bascinet with bevor, in the earlier tradition. The Wappenham figure c.1465 wears a remarkably deep and pointed sallet. Sir Thomas Grene is in several respects unorthodox, especially in the arrangement of a long dagger hanging centrally between the legs. This awkward arrangement is repeated in some later examples with a full-length sword, and was widely used by the East Anglian engravers.

A small group of figures has certain similarities to these but affords many contrasts also. The earliest, (?) Sir John Barre and wife 1474, Clehonger, is a handsome but unconventional brass, on which the armour is treated in a decorative manner. The lower part of the knight's feet is protected by mail only. His wife's figure is peculiar and is described later in this chapter. A well engraved small figure of a Yeoman of the Crown c.1475, with the crown superimposed on his left pauldron, is preserved at the Society of Antiquaries, and has several corresponding features. Two other military figures, wearing the sallet and facing in towards their wives, representing John Chudderle and wife c.1475, Hinton St George,[5*] and (?)Henry Barley and wife c.1475, Albury are undoubtedly associated with the Society of Antiquaries figure, as is a less vigorous representative at Aldington 1475. It is possible that the large and unusual brass of John Boville 1467 and wife, Stockerston, has connections with these, though its peculiarities are described later in the context of provincial work.

Two excellent associated brasses are:

Simon Norwiche, wife lost, 1476, Brampton Ash (Fig. 155)
John Feld with his father, 1477, Standon (Fig. 158).

An examination of these figures provides a valuable link between those just described and an important group which Dr. Kent has identified as series 'F'. Both Norwiche and the younger Feld stand in a distinctive semi-profile manner, one leg to the front with the foot pointed downwards, the other turned sideways. The former shows the sword hanging directly to the front, and gauntlets hung from the hip. The Feld brass deserves special note. John is turning towards his father, a stocky figure in the attire of an Alderman of the City of London. John wears a tabard inlaid with lead (*The Craft*, Fig. 18) and has an immense sword passing diagonally across his left thigh. The flowered plots at the feet of both figures are supported on a crenellated band, and below on individual plates are the other children of John Feld the father. The form of the girls indicates beyond all doubt that this is of the 'F' series, or of a pattern most closely related to it.[6*]

We now return to the main stream of designs from the London workshops. The accomplished and ornamental 'D' series, which has been followed through the first half of the fifteenth century, passes through a bewildering number of variations during the remainder of the century, encompassing both the dullest and the most remarkable of the period. A group of memorials, dating from c.1460-1470, illustrates a gradual transition from the mid-century treatment to the so-called 'Yorkist' brasses. Hair shown above the brow deepens, especially above the ears, and falls to the neck behind. The lines of the jaw are harsh, noses long and straight, while the eyes have an elongated 'mongoloid' quality. Hands lose their smooth artificial line. The brasses have many features closer to the earlier than to the later style. They include Adderbury c.1460, Cirencester 1462, Thame and Harpsden engr. c.1465, Arundel 1465 (with staff of office), Richard Wylloughby, Esq., with wife, engr. 1467, Wollaton (Figs. 243-4),[7*] Sawley and Tong, 1467, Haccombe 1469, Addington 1470 and Swinbrook, c.1470. Other examples include a squire with two wives at Knodishall 1460, and good single figures at Warkworth d.1454, engr. c.1460; Holton 1461; and Sawbridgeworth c.1465. Emmerson, through a detailed examination of scripts and figures of this period, has identified a group of brasses which do not fall satisfactorily into either the 'B' or 'D' series, drawing on the conventions of both. The affinities of the figures are close to 'D', but 'B' influence predominates in the scripts used. He suggests that this confusion of style was produced by the movement of craftsmen with the decline of the workshop using the 'B' patterns. Certainly most of the examples occur in the late 1460's and early 70's. The group has been designated 'Sub-B' to differentiate it from the others described and armed examples are:

Robert Eyr with wife, d.1463, Hathersage (Fig. 153)
Henry Grene with wife, 1467, Lowick
John Bartelot, d.1453, engr. c.1470, Stopham.

Richard Quatremayns at Thame was a Councillor to Richard, Duke of York, and to King Edward IV, and Sir William Vernon at Tong, Constable of England. These, together with the brasses at Hathersage, Lowick, Wollaton and Sawley are set on high tombs. Only at Adderbury are the figures large, but several of the compositions as a whole are substantial, that at Tong containing twelve children, flying scrolls and eight shields. Robert Eyr is an admirable illustration of the distortion of armour, with his immense pauldrons and couters. The left couter at both Thame and Wollaton is excessively enlarged. The sallet is reasonably represented at Holton, Cirencester, Arundel and Addington. Henry Grene wears a tabard. Sir William Vernon's armour illustrates the somewhat top heavy but balanced style of suit, shown with consistency over the following twenty years.

Among the military brasses connected with this series between the years 1470 and 1485, three are outstanding and may be related to other remarkable brasses to civilians and ecclesiastics. All three in their treatment and construction appear to have come from the same source. They are:

Sir John Say, Speaker of the Commons with wife, 1473, Broxbourne
Ralph Baron Cromwell, Lord High Treasurer, with wife (now lost), canopy, engr. c.1475, Tattershall
Henry Bourchier, K.G., Earl of Essex with his countess, 1483, Little Easton (Fig. 154).

It is possible that the last was engraved some years before the date of death. Sir John Say wears a tabard, still enamelled, and his figure is made up of several pieces to facilitate firing. In spite of this the important details of his equipment are clear, in particular the massive mitten style articulated gauntlets, and the tasselled sword. The points and cusping of his leg armour, and his long spurs are in the best 'gothic' style. His head is unfortunately gone; despite this loss it is a particularly fine brass. Baron

Cromwells' brass is now a wreck. Originally it consisted of figures of the baron and his wife set within a canopy of doubly triple pediments, with saint filled side shafts and embattled super-canopy. A drawing of the whole is fortunately preserved at Revesby Abbey,[8]* but all that now remains is the headless male figure and large portions of the canopy and inscription. The armour is very similar to that at Broxbourne, but with a mantle worn over the shoulders and no tabard. The figures of Henry Bourchier and his countess are still in good condition, constructed of multiple pieces, and elaborately coloured. The Earl wears the mantle of the Order of the Garter with the badge on the left shoulder, and the Garter below his left knee. His armour is almost identical with that of Sir John Say. His face is rather more rounded in shape than was conventional.

The contract for the Say chapel with Robert Stowell, Master mason at Westminster, makes it clear that the tomb was to be made 'as can be thought good by thadvyce of a marbler.'[9] Its design is in the court tradition, established by Yevele, and can be related to a series of such high tombs in Hertfordshire and Essex. It is however likely that the brasses were made under sub-contract, and it would be rash to attribute them to Stowell's personal workshop. The tombs of Abbot Estney at Westminster and of John Feld at Standon would also appear to have come from the same source, and their brasses belong to other series.

Brasses of a similar but usually simpler type are found as late as c.1490, easily recognized by their facial treatment, broad rounded pauldrons and the particular shape of their couters and gauntlets. Sir Anthony Grey 1480, St Albans cathedral, is a well-known example possessing some of the refinements of the Broxbourne figure.

Others are:

Sir Thomas Stathum with two wives, 1470, Morley (*The Craft*, Fig. 72)
Ralph St Leger with wife, 1470, Ulcombe
Robert Ingylton with three wives, canopy, 1472, Thornton
Robert Bothe with wife, 1478, Sawley
Thomas Playters with wife, 1479, Sotterley
Peter Frechwell (mutilated) d.1503, engr. c.1480, Staveley
Edmund Molyneux with wife, canopy (worn), 1484, Chenies
Roger Dynham canopy (mutilated), 1490, Waddesdon (*The Craft*, Fig. 206).

The family groups at Morley and Thornton are important, the latter brass being set on a high tomb with elaborately carved sides.[10] Peter Frechwell and Roger Dynham both wear tabards. Dynham's memorial originally lay in the chapel of Eythrope, Bucks., and was discovered on the site. Its mutiliations, though considerable, do not affect the essential features of the handsome composition.[11] Edmund Molyneux wears the sallet. Thomas Playters turns slightly towards his wife, possibly a reflection of the influence of a somewhat earlier 'B' figure, such as that at Stow-cum-Quy, Cambs.

Two brasses of an unusual character, though most probably connected with those just described, are an unknown figure c.1470 at Howden, and Thomas Peyton and two wives 1484, Isleham. The latter is an ambitious design with a large triple canopy and female figures which are outstanding examples of costume. The confusing aspect of the brass is that Thomas himself was undoubtedly designed on a pattern of fifteen years earlier. The ladies are also unusual in arrangement having slight East Anglian affinities. It is possible that the pattern was specified by the deceased or executors, or that the entire brass is imitative of London patterns but engraved by provincial craftsmen. The first alternative seems by far the more probable as similarities to work of the Norwich engravers are essentially superficial.

The remaining London-type brasses of the period may be broadly classified into two main pattern series, one being a direct continuation of the 'D' series and the other the 'F' series already mentioned. The chief examples of both types are easily recognized, but there is some difficulty with minor and poorly engraved figures. Both series provide examples of full face, semi-profile and kneeling presentations, and in a few cases details from one series have been introduced into the other. Standards in quality vary considerably, as, for example, in the 'F' series between the finely executed and designed civilian figure of Geoffrey Kidwelly 1483, Little Wittenham, and the competent workmanship and peculiar arrangement of Henry Stathum and his three wives 1481, Morley.

The late fifteenth-century armed figures of the 'D' series reflect the transition to the rounded forms of plate armour adopted in the early sixteenth century. The draughtsmanship behind the engraving was evidently careless, and many of the plate lines have no clear significance. Certain changes are, however, indicated with some consistency. Leg armour is simplified in its detail, and sabatons are broad and rounded at the toe. The heavy gauntlets are retained almost to the end of the century. The couters are very much less pointed in shape, being usually shown as formless, and pieces offering no scope for the bend of the arm. All figures are bare-headed. Their faces become increasingly more rounded, in overall shape and in particular features such as the eyes. Hair is worn long, and by 1500 usually falls behind the neck. Nicholas Kniveton at Muggington is a good example of the style. He also illustrates well the problems in the past of dating accurately brasses of this period. This brass has been consistently dated 1475, though, as Dr Kent has noted, the collar of SS with its pendant portcullis badge is a Tudor decoration — pointing unquestionably to a date of engraving after 1485, and probably nearer 1495 when Nicholas died. The following list of other examples contains a few suggested revisions of recorded dates:

William Harper with wife, c.1490, Latton
Unknown, c.1490, Hereford cathedral
Unknown in armour, c.1490, Heacham
Sir Robert Clyfton, d.1478, engr. c.1491, Clifton[12*]
Roger Salusbury and two wives, 1491, Horton (Fig. 167)
John Southill with wife, 1493, Stockerston
John Conquest with son and wife, 1493, Houghton Conquest
Richard Sydenham, 1499, Chedzoy.

The variation in the armour shown is considerable. At Horton there is little change from the earlier style except in the rounded sabatons, while at Chedzoy 'Tudor' forms are nearly complete. The examples require little comment. They are on the whole larger in size than those of the 1470s, those at Chedzoy and Stockerston being about 1.22m in length. Some of the details of the equipment are noteworthy, as, for instance, the crosses and other devices engraved at the chape of the sword sheaths or on the pommels. In the later brasses the fauld is rather wide and a skirt of mail shows prominently beneath. At Chedzoy the tassets hang curiously beneath this mail, and not from the fauld.

Five kneeling figures belong to this series. John Brocas 1492, Sherborne St John, Richard Chamburleyn with wife 1496, Shirburn, and a Compton with wife c.1500, Surrey Archaeological Society, Guildford (*The Craft*, Fig. 205), conform in general treatment to the recumbent figures, though the first is slightly peculiar, holding up his hands in the orans manner, and kneeling at a faldstool on a tiled floor. The last is remarkable for its background treatment described later. Nicholas Gaynesford with wife engr. c.1490, Carshalton, and Robert Whyte d.1512, South Warnborough, are more peculiar. Both kneel on the right knee only, upon deep, grassy, flower strewn mounds, with gauntlets and sword laid down. Both are in armour which is ridged and articulated in a somewhat modified form of earlier gothic fashion. Robert Whyte is the more remarkable as his features also bear the characteristics of the 1470's. These brasses are certainly of the 'D' pattern series, but their dating poses problems. The South Warnborough figure, in accordance with Mill Stephenson's description, may well be a sixteenth-century copy of a late fifteenth-century pattern, and some of the extravagances of the armour might indicate this. Serious arguments have been raised in favour of an earlier date of preparation in the deceased's lifetime, and the brass is certainly comparable with Nicholas Gaynesford's.[13]

Five additional armed figures from the close of the century reflect innovations in style, being either adaptations of the 'D' pattern or the introduction of a related but new series. These commemorate: —

Richard Curzon with wife, d.1496, Kedleston
John Trenowyth 1497, St Michael Penkivel
Thomas Huntingdon with wife, 1498, Hempstead
Sir William Pecche, d.1487, engr. c.1500 Lullingstone (Fig. 156)
Sir Hugh Johnys and wife, engr. c.1500, Swansea.[14*]

The Kedleston and Hempstead brasses are presented in semi-profile and may be stylistically related to a number of brasses from the first ten years of the sixteenth century, tentatively classified in the following chapter as series 'G'. The crucial examples are those shown full face. Unfortunately the very decorative brass of William Pecche is difficult to date satisfactorily,[15*] and the ornament of his scabbard indicates the use of a specially ordered detail. The overall arrangement of his figure is consistent with 'D', but the bended fingers, rather baggy eyes and the execution of detail are new features. Some aspects of the armour are also noteworthy, especially the looped end of the sword belt. John Trenowyth has some similarities with Pecche, though his hands are differently placed, and his sword is set on his left side. Sir Hugh Johnys appears in many respects to be a simplified version of the Pecche figure, though his sword is shown at the side. His relationship with the 'G' figures that follow are apparent. It may be argued that these are transitional examples, extending the 'D' series into the sixteenth century. The author at present interprets them as new designs, though strongly influenced by others still current.

The excellence of the workmanship of the Feld brass at Standon has already been emphasized, and it is within the group of brasses of the 'F' patterns that several of the best military figures are to be found. The series falls into two main classes of recumbent full-face and semi-profile figures, and the connection between the two is not immediately apparent. The relationship is, however, made clear by comparison between the two Standon figures and other related civilian brasses. In overall arrangement the full-face figures differ but slightly from those of the 'D' patterns. The sword is most commonly hung transversely in front of the body and the presentation of the armour has few peculiarities. There is, nonetheless, a significant difference in the definition of detail. The component parts of the armour are carefully shaped. A decoration of circles is generally found on the arm defences. The skirt of mail below the fauld is more prominent than with the 'D' figures. The faces are well defined and rather more severe in expression. Hair is worn thick and long and frames the face. The following are the main examples:

John Estbury d.1508, engr. c.1485, Lambourne
Thomas Halle 1485, Thanington
Edward Peytoo, wife lost, 1488, Fladbury
Henry Covert, 1488, North Mimms
Thomas Caple 1490, Ledbury
Unknown, c.1490, Stanstead Abbots.

John Estbury wears a tabard in which much of the colour inlay still remains.

Two other figures shown full face, while belonging to the pattern series, are more closely related to the semi-profile figures in the style of their armour, especially in the detail of their leg defences. These are John Welbeck 1476, Putney (stolen as at 1975), and Henry Stathum with his three wives 1481, Morley. An interesting aspect of the

Morley brass is that the legs are shown in a position similar to the semi-profile representations, though the upper part of the figure is in frontal view.

The figures in semi-profile are a particularly distinctive group, falling into two classes, approximately according to date. The earlier are of graceful proportions, lying with the right foot pointing downwards towards the viewer and the left set forward and shown from the side. The sword hangs transversely behind the legs. The armour is more 'gothic' in form than that of most contemporary 'D' figures. The tassets and plates of the fauld are sharply ridged and the plackart is very prominent. Slim haute pieces — a form of neck protection — rise from the pauldrons. A mail shirt or mail-reinforced arming doublet is revealed under the breast-plate at the armpit. The armour is carefully though not entirely accurately defined. The side-wings on the poleyns are, for instance, displayed to pictorial advantage, being fully shown at both knees. The following are examples:

Thomas Wayte 1482, Stoke Charity (Fig. 239)
Sir William Skypwyth with wife, canopy, 1482, South Ormsby
Thomas Hampton with wife, 1483, Stoke Charity
John Weston with wife, 1483, Ockham
Paul Dayrell with wife, 1491, Lillingstone Dayrell (*The Craft*, Fig. 92)
A Northwood in tabard with wife, c.1495, Milton-next-Sittingbourne.

Paul Dayrell is the most intricate and shows a variety of interesting details, including a swivelled lance-rest on the breastplate. His gauntlets hang from his sword grip. Thomas Wayte is the only figure depicted wearing gauntlets, which are of heavy and simple design. The Milton-next-Sittingbourne brass is an almost complete transition to rounded Tudor conventions.

The later class is closely connected with the brasses shown full-face. Their armour is more rounded in form, especially in the toes of the sabatons. The sword hangs straight down on the left-hand side. The fauld is reduced in depth, exposing the under-skirt of mail. The contrast in the placing of the feet is much reduced. The chief examples are: Wraysbury 1488, Goudhurst d.1480, engr. c.1490, High Laver c.1495, Hutton 1496, and Floore 1498.

The only surviving kneeling military figure of the 'F' series, Bernard Brocas 1488, Sherborne St John, may be compared with these five brasses (*The Craft*, Fig. 240).

A complete analysis of the 'F' series gives cause to relate a few other brasses to it, though appearing to be of a separate origin. The link lies in such very boldly-cut civilian figures as William Crofton 1483, Trottescliffe, and is confirmed by certain details in common such as the floral decoration on grassy foot-rests, and peculiarities of lettering. The most important military figure is the striking Sir Walter Mauntell and wife d.1487, probably engr. c.1495, Nether Heyford (*The Craft*, Fig. 204). The design is confident, with an economical but strong use of line. The representation of the fauld as constructed of rectangular sections is peculiar. A smaller but similar figure, shown full face, is John Newdegate 1498, Merstham. Another comparable armed figure with wife c.1495, though more curious and now anonymous, is at Goring. William Burgh 1492, and wife, at Catterick appears from its design to be another associated example, though the execution is indifferent for series 'F'. It is likely that the ornamental though now mutilated figure of Sir Thomas Vaughan at Westminster Abbey is an early example of this variant, his facial features being distinctive. Vaughan was executed in 1483, and his brass was presumably laid in its honourable situation after 1485. These figures have civilian and other counterparts but do not form a numerous group.

A London figure of uncertain connections but great interest is John Teringham 1484, Tyringham, shown in semi-profile wearing a tabard and sallet. The latter is the best representation of this helmet on a brass, showing the chin strap and other fittings.[16] His foot defences, which have no plate lines, were presumably intended to be of leather.

A greater curiosity is the small quadrangular gilt plate in St George's Chapel, Windsor, to Sir Thomas Sellynger and wife Anne d.1475, engr. c.1495, Duchess of Exeter and sister to King Edward IV. Sir Thomas kneels, wearing armour and a tabard, Anne is in heraldic dress and a representation of the Holy Trinity is set above them. The treatment of the figures is unusual and the engraving exceptionally shallow for the period. Some of the drawing is very poor, especially the helmet. There would seem, nevertheless, to be inadequate reason to doubt the antiquity of the brass. The work is consistent with that of a goldsmith (*The Craft*, Fig. 66). A further votive composition, engraved on a rectangular plate of 1475, is at St Mary Redcliffe, Bristol. This is probably London work, but its design is sufficiently unusual to justify consideration as provincial work in Chapter Thirteen.

Collars

Livery collars are worn by armed figures of both the 'D' and 'F' series and also by civilians. Two collars were current during this period. The collar of SS, worn by adherents of the Lancastrian monarchs, was assumed also by Henry VII as a token of legitimate continuity. Some servants and supporters of the Tudors were anxious to display this collar on their memorials, as is revealed by the will of Thomas Fetherston of 1489 requiring 'a picture after my persone in Laton to be gravid and fast sett in the said stone with a coler of esses of King Henry is livery a bought my nekk.'[17] The Adderbury figure wears a collar of uncertain character and its inlaid colour is now gone. The Tudor collar with pendant portcullis badge of the Beauforts is worn on brasses c.1490 at Little Bentley, Mugginton, and 1496 Hutton. The collar of suns and white roses set upon a red ground was worn as a token of favour or allegiance by the followers of Edward IV. It was based on the Yorkist badge of the rose and sun in splendour which Edward is said to have adopted after the battle of Mortimer's Cross in 1461. Examples of the collar are found at Roydon (wife, Fig. 174), Rougham 1472, Sawley 1478, St Albans Cathedral 1480, and Raveningham 1483 (*The Craft,* Fig. 50), and the white lion of March is worn as a pendant to this collar at Little Easton. A few civilians wear the collar, as at Lillingstone Lovell d.1471, but in some cases the surface has been recessed for inlay and the character of the collar is uncertain. Surprisingly the finest brass representation of the collar of suns and roses is at Bruges and was set in the slab of Joos de Bul 1488, at the Hôpital St Josse. It is now in the Musée des Hospices Civils.[18*]

Male civilians

Civilian figures survive in plenty, especially those of moderate or small size. Few persons without title presumed to set up extravagant memorials, and even brasses to woolmen, clothiers and civic dignitaries are rarely canopied or impressive in scale. An exception is that of John Jay, who was Sheriff of Bristol in 1472, and who lies under a restored double canopy with his wife and family at St Mary Redcliffe, Bristol. John Beryf 1496, Brightlingsea, was a ship owner and church benefactor but his brass is of modest size. Henry Myllet with his two wives 1500, at Perivale is a mere 18cm long and in proportion to the groups of diminutive children. There are no existing equivalents in London work of the great woolmen brasses of the early fifteenth century, though a few memorials of that scale are known to have been destroyed.[19*]

Male civilian dress is adequately illustrated with little notable variation. In most cases a belted overtunic with long sleeves almost obscures the undertunic with its tight-fitting sleeves and stiff upstanding collar. The form of the sleeves of the overtunic varies noticeably. The baggy sleeves of the 1460's became narrower and of uniform width throughout by 1470, only to return to ample proportions but with wide cuffs at the close of the century. Shoes are pointed in the toe until 1480, after which they become rounded. A headdress, typical of the period, is often shown lying on the shoulder. This round padded cap with pendant hanging folds, known as a chaperon, is attached to a broad band of stuff, which hangs to the front and was used to wind round the face or cap to form a variable headdress. Many civilians in the last quarter of the century wear large purses and heavy rosaries from their belts, and occasionally a knife or sword. All are clean shaven. Their hair, like that of the military figures is shown longer towards the end of the century. The following is a list of the more important civilian brasses to be attributed to the London workshops:

Richard Bertlot with wife, 1462, Stopham (Fig. 159)
Unknown, c.1465, Abington Pigotts
John Lethenard with wife, 1467, Chipping Campden
John Croke with wife, 1475, All Hallows-by-the-Tower, London (Fig. 170)[20]
John Feld with son in armour, 1477, Standon, Herts. (Fig. 158)
Thomas Rowley with wife, 1478, St John, Bristol
John Jay with wife, canopy, c.1480, St Mary Redcliffe, Bristol
Geoffrey Kidwelly 1483, Little Wittenham
Thomas Kyllegrew and wife, c.1485, St Gluvias
Woolman with wife,c.1485, Northleach
William Maynwarying, d.1497, engr. c.1485, Ightfield[21*]
John Lambard with wife, 1487, Hinxworth[22*]
Nicholas Deen with wife, d.1479, probably engr. c.1490. Barrowby (*The Craft,* Fig. 91)
Richard Amondesham with wife, kneeling, c.1490, Ealing
John Taylour with wife, c.1490, Northleach
John Camber, 1497, Sevenhampton (Fig. 157)
John Rusche, 1498, All Hallows-by-the-Tower, London.

All of these civilian brasses may be separated into the 'D' and 'F' series. Richard Bertlot 1462, with his wand of office at Stopham is a good 'D' figure. The fur of his overtunic is well expressed, and his face has character if also a sour expression. The brasses of John Lethenard and the unknown at Abington Pigotts are very similar. Especially good in the middle period are the London aldermen, Croke and Lambard, and the Bristol Sheriffs Rowley and Jay[23*]. All except Jay are shown wearing the aldermanic gown. Lambard is outstanding and his brass is among the best of the 'D' series at this time. Croke's brass is mutilated by the loss of the head, but is finely engraved on thin plate. The Alderman kneels at a faldstool opposite his widow, their children crowded behind them. The later 'D' figures are coarse in treatment. The two Northleach woolmen are important, though Taylour, standing in semi-profile, is plain and graceless. Both these brasses are enhanced by details relating to their trade. Thomas Kyllegrew at St Gluvias is unattractive, but displays the chaperon clearly. The kneeling figures of Richard Amondesham and wife are well executed, though marred by the clumsy design prevailing. John Rusche is larger than average, his size magnified by a minute dog between his feet.

The 'F' figures, as might be expected from earlier comparisons, are on the whole superior. The Standon and Little Wittenham brasses are of very high quality, John Feld being shown in the aldermanic mantle, inlaid with engraved lead. Geoffrey Kidwelly is an admirable example of dress including the chaperon and scarf, purse and beads. His hair is neatly shaped to curve round behind his neck, a characteristic of this pattern repeated at Church Oakley 1487, the British Museum c.1485, Harrow 1488 and Trottescliffe d.1483. Earlier examples of the series, dating from c.1475-1479, are at Mereworth, Odiham, Steventon and Ware, and comparable in treatment to the

Yeoman of the Crown at the Society of Antiquaries, London. The representations of Nicholas Deen, Edmund Grene c.1480, Hunstanton, and Thomas Williams 1495, St Helen's Bishopsgate, London, are similarly allied to the semi-profile designs of men in armour. John Camber, and civilians with wives at Basildon and Harlow c.1497, are examples of the bold 'F' series variant noted in connection with the Nether Heyford knight.

John Frankeleyn and wife 1462, at Chearsley, are typical of the latter 'B' series products. The peculiar 'Sub B' examples at Flamstead, and Stopham engr. c.1470, and All Saints Stamford 1475, register a decline both in skill and competent design. Early 'G' series patterns are simply but well illustrated by the brasses at Hawkhurst 1499 and Seend. A regrettable loss from St Mary Magdalen, Canterbury, which was destroyed in 1871, was the brass of John Elcock 1492. This 'D' figure had false sleeves to his overtunic, which hung down slightly below the elbow. The brass had fortunately been rubbed and is illustrated by Belcher.

Lawyers

Brasses to lawyers are of less distinction than those of the first half of the fifteenth century. They cover, however, a valuable range, including seven judges and good representations of the junior bar and a notary. Among the former are:

Sir Peter Arderne, Chief Baron of the Exchequer and Justice of the Common Pleas with wife, 1467, Latton (Fig. 162)

Sir William Yelverton, Justice of the King's Bench with wife, 1472, Rougham

Sir William Laken, Justice of the King's Bench, wife lost, 1475, Bray.

Five Judges are depicted wearing the coif, mantle and hood, though at Bray the shoulder-piece is omitted or concealed. The exceptions are Sir Thomas Urswyk 1479, Dagenham, and Sir Brian Roucliffe who wear only the mantle with the supertunica. None of these figures is large, though the mutilated memorial of Sir Thomas Billyng 1479, Wappenham, was extensive by reason of its inlaid arms and scrolls, and that of Sir Brian Roucliffe d.1494, Cowthorpe, is a wreck of an ambitious composition. The Latton brass, a work attributed to Richard Stevens, is in most respects the best preserved on account of its high tomb setting. Sir William Laken is an early 'F' series figure, displaying a sword and rosary hung from a loosely fixed belt. Sir William Yelverton is of the 'D' series, and is sufficiently peculiar to have acquired a provincial attribution. He is depicted wearing armour under the armelausa, and his head, wearing the coif, is disproportionate and turned towards his wife. The whole brass is of rather poor workmanship, and the metal itself is thin, but such faults are as possible in a London as in a Norwich workshop. The pattern is unmistakeably of London style. Another judge of the period is considered in Chapter Thirteen, being of midland origin.

Two brasses commemorate barristers. John Edward 1461, Rodmarton is described in his inscription as 'ffamosus apprenticus in lege peritus', indicative of a grade lower than that of serjeant. His dress is that of an ordinary civilian except for his hat which is extraordinarily tall (Fig. 160). A similar and even taller hat, probably of velvet and edged with fur, is worn by an unknown civilian c.1460, canopy lost, at St Peter, Chester. The identity of this very worn figure is unknown, but he may be presumed to be a barrister. However, there was nothing exclusive to lawyers about such a headdress, which seems to have been a fashion of Italian origin. It possibly became associated with them for a period, at least in the eyes of brass designers.

Notaries kept legal records and drew up, witnessed and sealed legal documents. They do not seem to have enjoyed any special dress, but there was a convention among brass engravers to show them with the penner (pen-case) and ink-horn, which were symbols of their profession, and are featured to this day in the arms of the Scriveners' Company to which City of London notaries belong. A large and excellent 'D' series brass of a notary c.1475, though now deprived of its canopy and other details, is at St Mary Tower, Ipswich (Fig. 161). It is a fine illustration of civil dress, especially the chaperon. A simpler figure with penner and ink-horn is at Great Chart c.1470.

Females

Extravagance in female dress and ornament, confined hitherto to the headdress, is expressed more freely in brass design. The most distinctive headdress of the period, known as 'the butterfly', was extensive and ostentatious. Heavy necklaces and elaborate girdles are often shown, the latter hanging loosely round the hips. Skirts drag the ground in their ample folds and many gowns or mantles are enriched with fur or embroidery.

The dress most commonly shown on brasses until 1475 is worn by Elizabeth and Thomasine, wives of Sir Thomas Stathum 1470, Morley, and Joan Eyre 1463, Hathersage. This consists of a kirtle, surcoat and horned headdress, but of a different shape and cut from those of the 1450's. The cauls of the headdress are brought far closer together, and the horns are accordingly higher, deserving the description sometimes given of the 'mitre' headdress. The neck of the kirtle is cut to a deep point. The surcoat is cut extremely low, and its deep fur edging rests on the shoulders and falls nearly to the waist. The sleeves of the surcoat are fairly close-fitting, with large fur cuffs at the wrist. There are many variations of this fashion. The late form of the horned headdress is well depicted on the unusual figure of Dame Elizabeth Burton c.1465, Bigbury, worn with a kirtle and sideless surcoat (Fig. 164). A finer example is on the remarkable brass of Dame Christine Phelip 1470, Herne (Fig. 165). This brass is unusually well engraved, and may well be a goldsmith's work. Dame Christine's husband was Matthew Phelip, Mayor of London in 1464, and a Goldsmith. Her mantle is richly lined and of great size, falling in a deep fold at her feet. The rosary is a carefully executed detail.

A variation of the horned headdress, surmounted by a coronet, is shown on the brass of Joyce, Lady Tiptoft, d.1446 but engraved c.1475, Enfield (Fig. 166). This memorial of unmistakable 'D' style is one of the most outstanding brasses of its period, and its costume is comparable to that of the Countess of Essex 1483, at Little Easton. Both Lady Tiptoft and the countess wear the kirtle and the sideless surcoat, the latter being deeply edged with ermine. Both wear mantles secured by a long tasselled cord though Lady Tiptoft's is charged with the arms of Charlton impaling Holland. The countess wears a mantle coloured as that of the Order of the Garter. A wide necklace of jewels with pendant enriches the neck of Lady Tiptoft, and the collar of Suns and Roses is worn by the other. Both these figures are top heavy in proportion but otherwise reveal the high standard still achieved by the London engravers.

Margaret John 1466, Ingrave, wears a good and early example of the butterfly headdress, which rapidly became the fashion most characteristic of the period. The hair was gathered into cauls which were rectangular in shape and set behind the head. These provided a base for a framework of wires supporting great veils of gauze or other light material, which formed the wings. The exposed brow was shielded by a veil, which was very often itself of semi-transparent material. The shape of this remarkable headdress demanded a near profile representation. There are several notable examples, in particular worn by the wives on the 'D' type brasses at Broxbourne 1473; Isleham 1484; and Carshalton c.1490. Some of the 'F' series renderings are very large as at Barrowby, engr. c.1490 (*The Craft*, Fig. 91), and on the single figures probably of Margery Clopton d.1425, and Alice Harleston at Long Melford, both engraved c.1480 (*The Craft*, Fig. 207). Other good instances on unaccompanied figures are: c.1468 at West Peckham; c.1480 Hatley Cockayne, Saffron Waldon (two), Museum of Archaeology and Ethnology, Cambridge; 1480 West Tytherley; 1485 Combe Florey kneeling; c.1485 Micheldean (two); c.1490 Coggeshall (two); 1493 St Laurence, Thanet.

Towards the close of the fifteenth century the size of the wings is, in many cases, reduced, leaving the headdress with a displeasing sagging aspect. A mutilated figure c.1490, Newington-next-Hythe, and the wives of Walter Duredent 1494, Denham, are examples.

A variety of dresses are worn in conjunction with this headdress. The sideless surcoat, kirtle and mantle are found in a few cases, Joan Colte 1471, Roydon, and Elizabeth Say 1473, Broxbourne, being particularly good examples. Lady Saye's mantle is emblazoned with arms, and she wears in addition one of the richest necklaces shown on brasses. The low-necked surcoat and kirtle are more commonly worn. The sleeves of the surcoat have large cuffs, sometimes turned back but often left to form a loose mitten, covering all but the fingers of the hand. The latter fashion is seen on Ann Playters 1479, Sotterley; Amy Lambard, Hinxworth, and on several other brasses. Occasionally the surcoat is not lined with fur but with some diapered material as at Clehonger. By far the most elaborate example of this dress is the figure of Margaret Peyton I 1484, Isleham. Her kirtle is almost entirely covered by the surcoat which is apparently of a rich Italian brocade or cut velvet (Fig. 163). Even the caul of her headdress is decorated with the words 'Lady Help Ihesu Mercy', though only partly visible. Her poise has the elegance characteristic of the best brasses of the period. The two ladies c.1480 at Long Melford are noteworthy for their heraldic display, emblazoned on their kirtles and mantles (*The Craft*, Fig. 207).

About 1490 many brasses illustrate a change in the headdress. The veils of the butterfly headdress are much reduced in size or altogether omitted. The caul covering the hair takes the form of a slightly pointed cap, and the veil covering the brow is of thicker and opaque material such as velvet. This fashion may be described loosely as the 'cornet' headdress, but is in fact hardly a distinctive type. It is very much a transition from the butterfly to the pedimental or kennel headdress most commonly shown on early Tudor brasses and in early Tudor portraits. Emme and Anne, the wives of Roger Salusbury, Horton, are examples of this transition, showing also the mitten-like extension of the sleeves and the long girdles which are usual. A peculiar feature is the deep section of fur, forming the lower part of their surcoats (Fig. 167). Elizabeth Mauntell engr. c.1495, Nether Heyford, is another admirable illustration (*The Craft,* Fig. 204). In addition to wives with military and civilian figures, there are single figures of particular note as at Checkendon 1490, and Tidmarsh 1499.

By c.1500, the headdress had reached the form it was to maintain for nearly forty years. The veil headdress is rarely worn other than by widows, though Anne Oxenbrigg 1493, Brede, is an example.

Long streaming hair has been noted as an indication of youth, and usually of an unmarried state. Examples are at Bletchingley c.1470; Etchingham 1480; Low Leyton 1493 and Bobbing, Kent 1496. Of these the Etchingham brass deserves comment. It is a composition of the 'F' series, showing the young Elizabeth Echyngham with long hair, tied only by a narrow band, facing the rather older and larger Agnes Oxenbrigg, whose hair is held up in plaits. This convention of the hair is not without exceptions. Married women, Douce del Bothe 1460, Wilmslow, and Joan Kniveton, c.1490, Muggington, wear the hair long, the latter having it bound by a circlet of rosettes.

The well designed figure of Helyn Hardy 1486, Lyddington may well be another London work, but its origin is questionable. Greenwood suspects that this may be a copy of a London pattern by an engraver working in the vicinity of Stamford (see Chapter Thirteen).

Widows

The widow's dress remained unchanged. Several are shown with their husbands and others are alone, as are:

Dame Anne Norbury, 1464, Stoke D'Abernon
Lady Maud Willoughby, canopy, d.1497, engr. c.1475, Tattershall
Isabel Cheddar, c.1475, Cheddar
Joan Brokes, kneeling, 1487, Peper-Harow
(?) A Rotherham, canopy, c.1490, Luton
Joan Swan, canopy lost, 1497, Stretham.

Of these the brasses at Tattershall and Luton are the most important. Lady Maud Willoughby is a very large figure of 'D' pattern within an elaborate canopy with triple pediment, parapet and side shafts filled with saints. The lady of Rotherham family is a well engraved 'F' figure in semi-profile, showing a long knotted cord binding her mantle. A similar cord is engraved front view on the figure of Joan Swan, a brass of the same series. The small brass of Dame Anne Norbury is notable on account of the eight children grouped on the folds of her dress and framed by her falling mantle.

Ecclesiastics

Ecclesiastical brasses are for the most part of small size and lacking in special interest. There are a few distinguished exceptions and many others undoubtedly existed in cathedrals and abbey churches. Nevertheless, the great majority of figures remaining are of parish priests, which are consistently small and show a disappointing variety of detail. Judging from surviving examples, the 'F' series workshop received little business from the clergy.

Bishops

There are two episcopal brasses. The earlier of 1478 to John Bowthe, Bishop of Exeter, East Horsley, is especially valuable for its unusual pose (Fig. 168). The Bishop kneels in complete profile, offering a view of the back of the chasuble, with its central orphrey. The infulae of the mitre are also brought into prominence. This memorial, though of 'F' design and well executed, is of very modest scale for a prelate of this rank. Richard Bell, Bishop of Carlisle 1496, Carlisle cathedral, is, in contrast, commemorated by a large and splendid brass, unfortunately damaged by wear. The Bishop, engraved in the 'D' conventions but obviously influenced by earlier figures, is vested in full pontificals. His chasuble is of Italian material, and he holds a large open book over his breast (*The Craft*, Fig. 208). His rich but heavy canopy, and decorative border inscription are described later.

Canons and wardens

There is a fair selection of church dignitaries wearing processional vestments and the following examples span the period:

Unknown, c.1460, St Mary Redcliffe, Bristol[23]
John Blodwell, Dean of St Asaph, canopy, 1462, Balsham
John Byrkhed, rector (headless), canopy, 1468, Harrow
Henry Sever, warden, canopy, 1471, Merton College, Oxford

Thomas Key, Canon of Lincoln, 1476, Charlton-on-Otmoor
Richard Rudhale, Archdeacon of Hereford, canopy, 1476, Hereford cathedral
Richard Bole, Archdeacon of Ely, canopy, 1477, Wilburton
William Tibarde, President, 1480, Magdalen College, Oxford
Walter Hyll, Warden, 1494, New College, Oxford.

Of these brasses, those at Balsham, Harrow, Merton College and Hereford are the most important. John Blodwell's memorial is a late example of the 'B' series, and by far the finest at the series' close. The surface of his cope is worked with leopards or lions and the orphreys are decorated with canopied saints. St John the Baptist and St John the Evangelist occupy the upper positions, and others, such as St Asaph, were undoubtedly chosen with regard to the Dean's appointments. The side shafts of the canopy are similarly filled with saints, and the inscription at his feet is engraved in both incised and relief lettering, forming a dialogue between the deceased and his guardian angel. John Byrkhed and Henry Sever both wear copes having orphreys embroidered with canopied saints. The former, identified by Emmerson as 'Sub B', is fine but badly mutilated. Sever's is an excellent example of the 'D' series, though somewhat marred by the stiff and heavy aspect of the cope.[24] The representation is probably accurate but its effect is poor. Richard Rudhale's brass is mutilated but is still impressive. His cope is richly adorned and he wears, as does Blodwell, the Doctors' pileus.

Some of the other coped figures are good though not large, as those at Faversham 1480, Stevenage c.1485, New College 1494 and Hitchin 1498, the last being of distinctive 'F' design. The Wilburton brass, though canopied, has been extensively restored and inlaid to its disadvantage. A few, such as that at Little Hadham c.1470, are very small. The ornament on the orphreys on all but the finest brasses described, consists of a diaper of lozenges, large sections of foliage, or, as at Quainton, a jewel pattern. Walter Hyll is unusual in that his personal initials are worked into the design as in several earlier brasses, including that of Warden Malford 1403, in the same chapel. Thomas Key has been the subject of serious speculation, as the style of much of his figure appears too early for this period. Torr argued that the figure was an appropriation or discarded plate of c.1420. While a case can be made to support this interpretation, the engraving lacks the confidence of early fifteenth century work, and confusion around the surplice sleeves is more consistent with a derivative design.

The plain choir cope is worn by the priests at All Souls College 1461, Shillington 1485 and Bampton 1500. The first, though now mutilated beyond recognition, was probably shown in conjunction with an academic hood.

Choir dress is shown, displaying the fur almuce with its pendant tails, at Byfleet c.1480; Billingham c.1485; Eton College 1489; St Cross, Winchester 1493; and Great Haseley 1494. The last two are clear-cut representations of the 'F' series, and at Great Haseley the engraved lead inlay of the almuce is intact.

Parish Priests

Parish priests in mass vestments form a considerable but undistinguished group. Most are very small, and even the largest, at Laindon c.1470, and Childrey c.1480, are less than 90cm. in length. Chasubles are plain, and orphreys embroidered with lozenges or a leaf pattern. The 'D' pattern face with its lined cheeks and straight short hair appears with monotonous regularity. Geoffrey Bysschop, Fulbourne 1477, is exceptional in that his hands are placed downwards crossing at the wrist. The figure of William Neele, Blockley, though dated 1510, can hardly have been engraved later than c.1490. This brass is unusual in that the priest is shown kneeling with his alb covering his heels and displaying the orphrey at the back. Chalices held in the hands are a common detail. It is regrettable that the finest example of the period, Robert Lond 1461, St Peter's, Bristol, must be presumed to have been destroyed in the bombing of that church during the Second World War.

On one brass c.1480 at Cirencester a priest is depicted wearing the cassock only.

Regular Clergy

The remnant of brasses to regular clergy is even smaller than that of the preceding period. One large memorial surviving, that of Abbot John Estney 1498, Westminster Abbey, is an admirable example of 'F' type design. his long face with wide eyes and large mouth with full lips are typical of these patterns in the last years of the century. The abbot is vested in pontifical mass vestments, wearing an extravagantly jewelled mitra pretiosa, and chasuble, with vine pattern orphrey and jewel pattern border. He holds the crozier with vexillum in his left hand and raises the right in blessing. The figure is set within a canopy of three tall pediments. Palimpsest fragments presumably of an abbot, have been discovered at Somerton (obv. 1552); the main body of the figure is largely complete and shows a unique treatment of the chasuble orphrey, which has branches extending to the bottom border. A substantial fragment at St Albans cathedral, showing the bottom third of an abbot, is probably correctly dated c.1460, and may commemorate William Albon, d.1476; current research by Goodall indicates that a surviving Evangelist symbol is later than 1450, and other details support this view.

The only brass to a monk is a small half effigy at St Albans cathedral c.1470, in frock and hood.

There are no brasses to female religious, though two nuns are well represented among the groups of children at Dagenham 1479, (Fig. 173) and Hornby 1489. An almost perfect palimpsest reverse at Lambourne (obv.1546), shows the figure of a nun or vowess with her delicate hands spread as an orans. This may be dated c.1465.

Academics

There are about twenty figures apparently in academic dress though few are of special interest. Most show the hood and shoulder-piece, worn with a supertunica or sleeved tabard. Thomas Hylle 1468, New College, Oxford, is the most important wearing the cappa clausa, hood and pileus of a Doctor in Divinity (Fig. 169). He holds in his hands a small cross bearing the sacred wounds. The brass of William Town, D.D. 1496, at King's College, Cambridge, depicts a similar habit, but is in other respects peculiar, both in general treatment and the arrangement of a scroll sweeping down on both sides from his hands. Richard Wyard, Bachelor in law 1478, New College, Oxford, is a boldly engraved figure of the attractive 'F' series holding a small tau cross. He wears the hood, shoulder-piece and a sleeved tabard, well represented. The sleeved tabard is also shown on John Palmer, B.A. 1479, at New College. The large 'F' series half effigy of Ralph Vawdrey, M.A. 1478, Magdalen College, Oxford, presents the hood and shoulder-piece worn with a supertunica. Thomas Sondes, S.T.S. 1478, in the same chapel, is a larger than average figure of a 'D' pattern. Thomas Mareys 1472, at Stourmouth is a late usage of an essentially 'B' series pattern.

Children

Representations of children, rarely as single figures but commonly in groups below the main figures, are especially deserving of study.[25] The engravers, unlike their early sixteenth-century successors, often chose to contrast the children's dress with that of the parents to display new fashions. Whereas Amy Lambard 1487, Hinxworth is shown wearing the butterfly headdress, her eldest daughter below (known as Jane Shore, mistress of Edward IV) is in the early pedimental or cornet headdress and her younger daughter has long flowing hair. The eldest son was a priest and is shown in almuce and surplice. His younger brothers are in belted tunics. John Lambard himself wears an alderman's mantle. All the children's figures are in separate inlay.

Apart from the Echyngham/Oxenbrigg brass at Etchingham, which has been described, the only independent memorial to a child is that of John Davers 1478, Aldbury, a small figure in belted tunic, with very pointed shoes, and almost identical to the younger Lambard sons. The subordinate groups, however, are important. The most valuable is undoubtedly the daughters of Sir Thomas Urswyk 1479, Dagenham, the eldest of whom is shown as a nun in mantle, veil and wimple (Fig. 173). Behind her two sisters wear butterfly headdresses. Further behind, in two rows, are six younger sisters with streaming hair wearing a form of the steeple headdress. This headdress, shown in a number of manuscript illustrations, is represented only on this one brass but survives on at least two incised slabs.[26] The eleven sons of Roger Kyngdon 1471, Quethioc, are of comparable interest (Fig. 172). The eldest is shown in almuce and surplice. The second, who has a shock of curly hair, was a Yeoman of the Crown and wears the badge on his shoulder; the others are of standard pattern. The twelve sons of John Ansty 1460, Stow-cum-Quy, a decorative group, all kneel in very ample tabards (Fig. 171). The four kneeling daughters are also of note and may be intended to wear the bourrelet. The brass to the children of Thomas Mountford 1489, Hornby, contain three armoured figures, an academic and a nun. Diminutive armoured figures occur at Muggington c.1490, and Carshalton c.1490, whereas the son of Richard Quatremayns c.1465 at Thame is comparable in scale to his parents. Sons in academicals are found at Harrow 1488, and Carshalton, c.1490. A particularly regrettable loss since 1945 is the small figure of John (eldest son of William and Katherine Lucas c.1460 now at Elmdon) Abbot of Waltham, shown in pontificals holding his crozier, in company with his three brothers.

Several little girls show unusual variations of headdress, such as the circular caps at Stoke Charity 1483. The large and varied groups at Thornton 1472, and Stapleford, Leics. 1492, and the separate inlay figures at Tong 1467, are also interesting, though conventional in dress. Children's figures though small were engraved with resourcefulness as well as skill.

Arrangement and composition: Figure arrangements

The arrangement of brasses was for the most part based on established conventions. The recumbent effigy is generally intended, even though in many cases the figures are turned in semi-profile. It is, nevertheless, clear that the designers were little concerned with considerations of consistency. Groups of children are almost invariably standing though their parents are recumbent: at Stow-cum-Quy and Lillingstone Lovell they kneel below the main figures. At Clehonger (?) Sir John Barre is represented full face in the traditional manner, while his wife appears in a most naturalistic profile view, completely obscuring her right arm. There is but one example of certain London work showing the 'clasped hand' pose (*The Craft*, Fig. 204), though the ecstatic stance of the orante is not infrequently found among kneeling figures as at Ealing and Kingston-on-Thames and occasionally as at Herne and Isleham in standing figures. The growing popularity of kneeling compositions is indeed the chief development. Entire families are grouped together, and in several cases a precise setting is created by the inclusion of tiled floors and faldstools. The latter are represented in perspective with books and rosaries on them at All Hallows-by-the-Tower, London, Peper-Harow and Carshalton, or with books set in the sides, as at Sherborne St John. These designs may be viewed as a rational development of the mural brass, and there may be no need to seek inspiration beyond stained glass patterns. It is nevertheless tempting to detect a certain Flemish influence, introduced not by Flemish mural brasses but by the importation of paintings and painted panels. The rectangular brass, in the possession of the Surrey Archaeological Society, Guildford, with its rich background of mottoes and devices gives support to this view, though its detailed treatment is uncompromisingly of London style (*The Craft,* Fig. 205). It is noteworthy that brasses precede sculptured tombs in these arrangements.

The traditional supports of the recumbent figure — the foot and head rests — were made the excuse for lavish ornament. The most common foot support for all figures is the grassy mound, but this is sown in many of the best brasses of the 'D' series with exotic plants and ferns. Warden Sever 1471, Merton College, Oxford, is an outstanding example. A simpler and common treatment with thick grass and a single clover leaf in the centre is shown on Sir Thomas Stathum's brass. The beautiful plots of the 'F' series at Standon 1477, are strewn with primulas. Hounds, stiffly drawn in profile with long pointed faces and broad collars, are found under the feet of military figures of the 'D' series throughout the period. Lions are rarely used in the series, though there are good examples as at Rougham 1472; Dagenham 1479; and Clifton, Notts. 1491. Lions are also occasionally introduced in the 'F' series, their heads being shown front view with snarling jaws and long protruding tongues, and their tails ending in a triple fork of hair (*The Craft*, Fig. 92). Alternatively, a small lop-eared dog with a curled tail is introduced, as at High Laver c.1495, and Hutton 1496.

These common supports are quite often replaced by unusual animals or devices, which have some special connection with the deceased. Great eagles lie beneath the feet of the Earl and Countess of Essex at Little Easton. Two wodehowses with clubs crawl beneath Baron Cromwell at Tattershall. Other unusual features of heraldic significance, deriving from the arms or being the badges of the owners, are the boars at Sawley, the heifer at Sandon, Herts., the bear at Lowick, the horse at Ledbury, the martlets at Lillingstone Lovell, the stag at Waddesdon and the whelk shell at Wollaton, Notts.

Other outlandish supports, such as the fanciful elephant at Tong and the griffin at Sawley, were perhaps intended as dragons since both are at the feet of ladies named Margaret and could allude to St Margaret's triumph over a dragon. The tun under the feet of John Stockton, mayor, 1480 at Hereford cathedral, alludes to the latter part of the surname. There is an excellent example of the trade emblem support, taking the form of a sheep and woolpack with mark below the feet, on the brass of a civilian and wife c.1485 at Northleach.[27]

Head supports rarely occur except for figures in armour. The countess of Essex at Little Easton rests her head upon a pillow held by small angels. Other ladies with pillow rests are at Bigbury, Lowick, and Tattershall.

Helmets behind the heads of armed figures are common and many of these have rich mantling and bear striking crests. The Earl of Essex has lost a Saracen's head crest since Waller's drawing was made. The crest at Muggington illustrates the legend of the tiger deceived by the hunter's mirror. At Ulcombe there is a griffin; at Morley large spoonbills; at Tong a boar's head and at Wollaton a small owl.

Canopies

Canopy work is for the most part an adaptation of earlier patterns. The coarseness of detail, especially in the size and shape of crockets, the vaulting within the pediments, and the width of shafts and pinnacles, deprive most of any claim to elegance. The canopy of Lady Tiptoft at Enfield with its triple pediment and shields is undoubtedly one of the finest of the 'D' pattern series. It has far better proportions than that at Isleham to Thomas Peyton 1484, and lacks the oppressive weight of the canopy of Robert Ingylton and wives 1472, Thornton, of which the quadruple pediment is in almost perfect condition. Groined vaulting is introduced below soffits and oculi are inscribed. Several of the 'D' pattern canopies, such as those at Merton College, Oxford, and Waddesdon have squat pediments which give a stunted impression to the architectural design. Other canopies of the series are at Hildersham, Harrow, Carlisle cathedral, Wilburton, Chenies and Carshalton.

The few remaining canopies of the 'F' series are of a loftier and more intricate character. The triple canopy of Abbot Estney at Westminster is especially good. Each oculus is engraved with different tracery and the pediments sweep up to an impressive height. The canopy of the Luton widow is similar though plainer. Those above the ladies in heraldic dress at Long Melford are of a heavier character. The pediment rises from a very broad vault enriched with an angel boss. Other canopies of this series are at South Ormsby, Goudhurst and Wraysbury. An unusual canopy of exaggerated ogival form is among the mutilated remains of the brass of John Hacche and wife c.1485, Nayland. All that survives of the figures is the upper part of the lady with a book under her arm.

The composition of the brass of Sir Brian Roucliffe d.1494, and wife at Cowthorpe was unique, and though sadly mutilated still retains its most curious features. It was probably the work of James Reames of London, and made or at least designed c.1480. The excellent drawing by Waller reveals the design before the theft in 1855 of the wife, canopies and inscriptions. Brian rebuilt the church and was depicted holding it with his wife. Between the figures was a subsidiary memorial to John Burgh consisting of a bier covered with a pall bearing an escutcheon of his arms. The canopies were fine, with shields in the pediments and scrolls imposed upon the soffits. The figure of the judge, the church and the bier still remain though in a worn condition.[28*]

None of these canopies has subordinate figure work other than sacred representations, as one supported on shafts at Carshalton or imposed upon the pediment as at Carlisle. the saint-filled canopies at Balsham, Tattershall and Hereford cathedral are still more important. John Blodwell's canopy, formed by a semi-circular arch with embattled cornice, is happily combined with rich side shafts. Only fragments remain of Baron Cromwell's memorial, which formerly consisted of a double-triple pediment and super-canopy. Two armed saints in sallets, Maurice and Candidus, are all that exist of the original shaft figures. Lady Maud Willoughby's canopy is of the same scale and better preserved, with all eight saints in tabernacles intact. A third canopied brass at Tattershall is described under Norwich work. Richard Rudhale's canopy is much broken and worn, though the main shafts are almost complete. These contain among their figures the local saints, Thomas of Hereford and Ethelbert. Such great compositions, all that now survive of a once much larger group, are essentially based on fourteenth- and early fifteenth-century models.

Crosses and brackets

Conservatism in canopy design did not extend to other forms of architectural arrangement. Figured cross designs were apparently abandoned and brackets were a feature of provincial rather than London work. the matrix of a large slender bracket at Burford to (?) William Leggare and wife c.1490, was probably of London origin, but the existence of other earlier bracket brasses in this church may well have influenced the pattern.

Additional ornament

Sacred representations and forms of inlaid ornament have a greater prominence. This was, in part, due to the increase of kneeling compositions, and to a current delight in the display of badges, mottoes and other devices. The representations are sufficiently numerous and interesting to require special description in chapter Fifteen. Not all were religious subjects, and at Wormley, between the figures of John Cok and wife c.1490, is a curious quadrangular plate depicting dogs chasing a hare. Evangelists' symbols are rare, as the majority of border inscriptions are set on the chamfered edges of slabs, but there is an excellent group, surrounded with conventional clouds, at Lowick 1467. The powdering of slabs with devices was unusual, but more common than in the preceding century. Several small precatory scrolls remain at Bigbury c.1465, and Wappenham 1479. At Lambourne their indents surround the figure of John Estbury. At Lowick the scrolls of Henry Greene bear the motto 'Da gloriam deo'. The motto 'A dew en Blayne' is on a scroll at Sawston. The indent of Sir William Chamberlain, K.G., and wife 1463, East Harling, shows the matrices of inlaid banners, a panier and arrow sheaf, and the indent of Robert Lord Hungerford 1463, at Salisbury, is powdered with the family's badge of sickles.[29] The shields and badges of Sir Humphrey Bourgchier 1471, at Westminster Abbey, still exist though the figure is gone. These badges have been described as elbow pieces, but their form is similar to that of a Saracenic shield; each is engraved on the top with the Bourgchier knot. Whelk shells surround Richard Wylloughby and wife 1467, at Wollaton. Sir Robert Strelley and wife 1487, Strelley, had an inlay of stars in circles of which one remains. Crescents are among the other background inlays for the brass of John Rudyng 1481, Biggleswade. The quadrangular plate of the Compton family c.1500, in the museum of the Surrey Archaeological Society, Guildford, is powdered with roses, pomegranates and fire-beacons and the motto 'So have I cause'. Apart from the Knight's head, the sole surviving fragment of the once handsome brass of Sir John Fogge 1499, Ashford, is an angel with spread wings holding an inscription within a wreath of roses.

Heraldry

Shields of arms are arranged above and below the figures wherever appropriate. Sir William Vernon and wife 1467, Tong, have a display of eight bearing different arms. Shields are hung on the canopy shafts at Enfield and Waddesdon. Shields borne by angels are set into the sides of the Kniveton tomb at Muggington. On two brasses — Stoke Poges 1476, and Rainham c.1480 — the arms are emblazoned on tilting shields shaped to accommodate a lance.

Complete achievements are rare, though there is a good example above Sir John and Lady Say 1473, Broxbourne, and others at Strelley and Denham. The lattener's skill in engraving and colouring these is best studied in the Garter stall plates at St. George's Chapel, Windsor.[30]

Arms of the London Guilds are found on three brasses, precursors of numerous examples in the sixteenth century.[31] The Mercers' Company of London were incorporated by Letters Patent in 1394 and was one of the more important of the City companies including Merchants of the Staple and Merchant Adventurers among the members. Their business was primarily concerned with luxury fabrics, the damasks and velvets, imported from Italy and the Near East. The arms depict the Blessed Virgin, the patron saint of their company. They appear on the brasses of John Lambard at Hinxworth, and Thomas Hoore at Digswell. The faces are inlaid in lead without lines and may have been painted.

The Company of Skinners was incorporated on 1 March 1327, and its members were concerned in preparation and sale of furs. The arms of the the Company are shown on the brass of William Shosmyth, citizen and skinner of London 1479, at Mereworth.

Merchants' marks

Merchants' marks and trade emblems on shields are adequately represented, especially among the Gloucestershire woolmen and merchants. An unknown woolman at Northleach with wife c.1485 have a mark placed on the woolpack at their feet. This takes the form of an inverted 'W' with a cross and streamer. John Taylour c.1490, also at Northleach, has a remarkable device, showing a sheep standing on a woolpack which bears a mark of two crossed shepherds' crooks (*The Craft*, Fig. 210). Other marks, some incorporating initials, are at Standon 1477; St John's 1478 and St Mary Redcliffe, Bristol c.1480; Brightlingsea 1496; Cirencester 1497; and Hawkhurst 1499. John Jay at St Mary Redcliffe has in addition to his mark two shields bearing wool carding combs. A shield at All Saints, Maldon c.1480, is charged with a butcher's block brush,[32] an early example of 'butcher's broom', which in 1540 was granted as part of the Butchers' Company's arms. The shield bearing shears on the restored brass at Norton Bavant to John Bennett and wife c.1470 is probably original.

Occasionally a shield is treated as a setting for prayers or a rebus. Two inscribed 'Ih*es*u mercy' and 'Lady helpe' are set above Roger Hunt and wife 1473, Great Linford. A shield bearing the canting device of a roe is placed above Thomas Rowley 1478, St John's, Bristol.

Inscriptions

Inscriptions differ in a few respects from those of the mid-fifteenth century. Letters are in general slightly shorter and broader, and capital letters more ornate. The effect is to make individual letters distinct and the inscription easier to read, though the impression is less elegant. The groundwork of inscriptions is frequently recessed leaving the letters in relief. This technique is most commonly found on plates placed vertically, as at Lavenham or Carshalton. The content of the inscriptions changed little, the majority consisting of the name, status, date of death and a plea for prayers on the deceased's behalf. There is no significant increase in the number of inscriptions in English. The last point is surprising especially having regard to the evident popularity of the vernacular after 1500.

Three inscriptions of the period are appropriately recorded in full on account of their length and unusual interest. Sir Hugh Johnys at Swansea was a much travelled and adventurous knight, and his inscription engr. c. 1500 describes his career.

> Pray for the sowle of sir Hugh Johnys knight and dame Mawde his wife which s*i*r Hugh was Made knight at the holy sepulcre of oure lord ih*es*u crist in the city of Jerusalem the xiiij day of August the yere of oure lord gode M[l] CCCC xij And the said sir Hugh had co*n*tynnuyd in the wrrris ther long tyme byfore by the space of fyve yer*es* that is to sey Ageynst the Turkis and sarsyns in the p*ar*tis of troy grecie and turky under John *tha*t tyme Emprowre [sic] of Constantynenople and aftir that was knight marchall of ffrawnnce under John' duke of som*er*set by the space of ffyve yere And in likewise aftyr that was knight Mar chall of Ingland under the good John' duke of Norfolke which John' gyave vnto hym the manor of Lanymore [Landimore, in Gower] to hym & to his heyr*es* for ev*er* more appon whose soulis ih*es*u have mercy.

The woolman and wife at Northleach c.1485, are surrounded by a border inscription in English verse. These lines are recorded by Weever as being in several churches in and around London, and were apparently a standard prepared text:

'+ a ffarewell' my frendes the tyde abideth no man
I am departed from hense and so shall ye
But in this passage the last songe that I can
Is requiam eternam now Ihu graunte it me
When I have ended ' all myn adversitie
Graunte me in paradise to have a mansion
That shed thy blode ffor my redempcion. '

In contrast, the foot inscription of the Judge Nicholas Assheton 1465, Callington, is in Latin verse, and a typical example of the confusing lines and extensive word contractions used. The inscription records the judge's professional excellence and his pious work in restoring the ruined chapel at Callington:

Assheton' *cum* tumulo Nichol*aus* *conditur* isto —
Condit*ur* et secu*m* Judiciale dec*us*
Vulg*us* eu*m* sensit mit*em* iustu*m* miseratu*m*;
Na*m* cu*m* lex stricta Seviit hic deluit
Hic qui*n*quagenis missis interffuit a*n*nis;
Nulla dies fueras leta qu' audierat
Hanc q*ue* ruinosa*m* in q*ua* iac*et* ip*se* capellam:
Sustulit ex propriis su*m*ptib*us* ac op*er*ibus
Pavit vicinos & egnenos as p*er*egrinos:
No*n* solu*m* dapib*us* immo suis op*er*ib*us*
Qui regis & leges & leg*(um)* arte p*er*itos —
ffac sibi iudiciu*m* sit Rogo mite tuu*m*.

The dull factual content of several marginal inscriptions is enlivened by the decorative stops, which were frequently used towards the close of this period. Joyce, Lady Tiptoft, at Enfield has an especially curious selection including heads, a moon with a human face, and various animals. The details extracted from the inscription of John Ceysyll 1493, Tormarton are the most noteable feature of this memorial (Fig. 175); the violin and bellows being particularly unusual. The words of the inscription of Brian Roucliffe 1494, at Cowthorpe were separated by chess rooks and standing dishes alluding to his and his wife's names. The marginal inscription at Kedleston to Richard Curzon and wife d.1496, is punctuated with the popinjay of Curzon, the owl of Willoughby and the water bouget of Bugge. Other rich selections of animals and devices are at Swarkeston 1473; Lambourne c.1485; and Carlisle cathedral 1496. The fragments at Muggington preserve the engraving of a fish. A tool included at the end of the inscription to John Taylour c.1490, Northleach, is thought to be a cutting instrument, used for chopping sheep's tails.[33] Perhaps most curious of all the inscription of the lost brass to Walter Coney 1479, at St Margaret's, King's Lynn, was decorated with animals including a beaver, depicted in the act of avoiding pursuit by biting off his testicles, which according to tradition were highly prized! This fine and unusual monument was illustrated by Gough (II.iii, Pl. 99), rubbed in part by Craven Ord, and still survives as a superb indent.

Conclusion

The London engravers, though becoming more careless and coarser in their technique, succeeded until the close of the fifteenth century in maintaining variety and individuality in their designs. Patterns were repeated consistently, but not slavishly, and the brasses of this period deserve more credit than they have received. It was, above all, the witless repetition of poor models that so debased the London craft in the following generation.

12. English brasses: the London workshops, 1500-1560

The manufacture of engraved brasses, rapidly expanding in the late fifteenth century, became a veritable industry by the turn of the sixteenth century. Many hundreds of small figure brasses, mainly commemorating persons of little distinction, were laid in the churches of southern England. Large memorials were still prepared, but these formed a small minority in what appears from its quantity, monotony and carelessness to have approached mass production. More brasses survive from this period than from the whole of the fifteenth century, the great majority coming from the first thirty-five years. It was a prolific finale to the mediaeval craft.

There seems little doubt that the widespread demand for brasses in London, far from stimulating new ideas, encouraged hack work on a large scale. Tudor recumbent effigies are coarse adaptations of slightly earlier models. There was little conscious approach to realism, let alone naturalism. Lines are usually deeply and broadly cut. Shading, though frequently applied, has often no artistic significance, and serves only to decorate an otherwise plain surface. Human faces and hands are usually oddly drawn, and are often grotesque. Canopies are of traditional style, but treated in a particularly cumbrous fashion. The standards of different pattern series vary, and isolated examples are of considerable merit, but judged en masse Tudor brasses from c.1510 to 1545 show a further marked decline from the deteriorating standards of the late fifteenth century. Criticism is not levelled at the conservatism of their design, which was in many respects well suited to the medium; they were simply poorly conceived and crudely executed. Two brasses, which are among the largest and most elaborate of the period, may be cited in support of this statement. The rich Devon merchant, John Greenway and wife 1529, are commemorated by almost life-size figures at Tiverton. Far from exploiting the scale of this memorial, the engraver reproduced a proportionately larger version of the most uninteresting type of civilian model. Little additional detail was attempted, and apart from its size the brass has no particular merit. Henry Hatche 1533, baron of the Cinque Ports and a great benefactor to Faversham church, is commemorated with his wife by a large canopied brass. The canopies are ugly in design, and the pediments entirely filled with great roses of startling prominence. The figures, too small for this massive surround, are portrayed in a stiff and rather comical fashion. Neither brass can be described as good, though both are grandiose in scale. Many of the small figures appear ridiculous to a modern judgement.

Notwithstanding these general defects, one type of Tudor brass has a consistent attractiveness that is a distinction to the period. This is the kneeling votive group, usually set against the wall or the back of a raised tomb. Many of these figures in these groups are shown in heraldic dress. Large shields are set above and below, and in the centre is usually placed the subject of their devotion. These are highly decorative memorials, notable for their heraldry, packed groups of children, faldstools and other details, and admirably displayed in their carved settings.

In the midst of mediocrity, remarkable skill now and then asserts itself. the brass of Sir Thomas Bullen, K.G., at Hever, is an engraving by an expert (*The Craft*, Fig. 212). The group of brasses at the close of the period known as the Fermour series are works of careful craftsmanship (*Ibid.* Fig. 213). The great figures of Roger Gyfford and wife 1542, at Middle Claydon, are massive but unquestionably fine.

The engravers and designers of early Tudor brasses are anonymous. It is known that a Nicholas Ewen, coppersmith and gilder and Humphrey Walker, founder, were initially intended to prepare the cast and gilt effigy of King Henry VII, and it is possible that the first if not both these craftsmen had an interest in engraving. It may be presumed that the craftsmen mainly responsible were members of the Guild of Marblers such as Henry Lorymer, and their patterns can to some extent be traced as a continuous development from those of the preceding period. It is, however, noteworthy that the peculiarities in detail of many Tudor brasses, especially in the faces, are repeated in contemporary woodcuts. The assembly of clergy and notables shown at the coronation of King Henry VIII in a woodcut from Stephen Hawes, *A joyful medytacyon to all Englonde of the coronacyon of our most naturall souerayne lorde kynge Henry the eyght*, 1509, have precisely the same grinning visages that appear on brasses.[1]

Early sixteenth-century pattern series pose confusing problems, which will only be satisfactorily resolved by an exhaustive and *independent* analysis of figures as well as inscriptions. Independent analysis is essential, as it is the author's view that figures of apparently different series occur on single monuments, indicating a merging of workshops, use of purchased stock, or an indiscriminate copying of patterns. Particular characteristics of series continue to be most easily perceived in armed figure representations, though even with these the poor quality of many examples leaves their association doubtful. At the present stage of research it is not possible to offer a conclusive classification, and it is accordingly preferable to group examples of clear association, accepting that many of the surviving memorials are not adequately described.

Men in armour

Armour of the first half of the sixteenth century is represented with consistency even at the cost of accuracy, leading to the inevitable comment that 'Brasses are of little or no value as evidence of armour for some years after 1500.[2] In most cases a globose breast-plate is worn with a short fauld from which tassets are suspended, and a deep skirt of mail is a prominent feature. Arm and leg armour is of simple construction and rounded form, though often poorly drawn. Sabatons are broad and rounded at the toe. Occasionally a lance rest is shown on the right side of the breastplate. In some cases, of which Sir Thomas Brooke 1529, Cobham, is especially notable, obsolete fashions are reproduced, including a double plackart on the breastplate. All military figures, presumably from London workshops, are shown bareheaded, though one at Ashford (now lost) wore a helmet without visor.[3*] Tabards of arms are frequently shown and almost completely conceal the body armour.

Some attractive semi-profile figures of the 'F' series are easily recognized in the first ten years of the century. The Worcestershire brasses of John Blount with wife at Mamble c.1500 (Fig. 176), and Philip Chatwyn, gentleman usher to King Henry VIII 1524, at Alvechurch, (Fig. 183), are typical illustrations; the latter is a late example with an unusually prominent dagger. The fine flowing hair, the arrangement of the hands and placing of the feet are consistent peculiarities of the series. An example in superb condition is that of John Tame with wife 1500, Fairford, which lies on a high tomb with carved screen above (*The Craft*, Figs. 209, 211). Robert Baynard with wife 1501, Lacock, is a good figure wearing the tabard. Others of note are at Blisworth 1503; Ardingly, with canopy, 1504; Terling c.1505; Ashover 1507; Iver 1508; Wybunbury 1513; and Tilty 1520.

Examples of the 'F' series kneeling in tabards are the groups of Robert Eyre with wife c.1500, Hathersage; Morys Denys and son, 1505, Olveston; (?)George Catesby 1506, Ashby St Legers; Sir Robert Clyfford with wife, 1508, Aspenden, and Henry Pudsey with wife, d.1520 engr. c.1510, Bolton-by-Bowland, all of which are designs intended for a vertical setting.

It is among the recumbent full-face figures that the distinction of types becomes very confused. Two certain 'F' figures are William Poyntz with wife, 1502, North Ockendon, and the handsome, nearly lifesize figure of a Scarisbrick c.1500, Ormskirk. The latter is an unusually fine brass for this period, showing the man with long rolling curls and pillowed head. Almost certainly of this series are the armed figures of John Toke with two wives 1513, Great Chart, and Sir Edward Grey with two wives d.1528, Kinver; as also others in tabards of Anthony Fetyplace 1510, Swinbrook; Thomas Knightley 1516, Fawsley; and Henry Leynham 1517, Tidmarsh.

In addition to a common treatment of faces and armour details, there is a consistency in the use of three and four petalled flowers in the grass plots, though such decoration is also found on disassociated brasses. The rather grotesque face of the Fawsley squire presages the debasement of the series. The well-known figures in heraldic dress of John Shelley with wife, d.1526, Clapham, have considerable similarities to the Kinver brass, but its peculiarities are not entirely consistent with this series and it is likely that the brass was put in hand after Elizabeth Shelley's death in 1513. The unusual group of late fifteenth-century figures related to the 'F' series, of which Sir Walter Mauntell d.1487, at Nether Heyford is the best, is reflected in the small but neat figure of Richard, Lord Grey, dated 1521 but the figure probably c.1500, 'on of the heyr*es* apparant to Richard erll of Kentt', in Eton College Chapel.

About 1520 the 'F' series underwent most evident changes in treatment, to such an extent that s clearer to redesignate the brasses 'debased F'. There is a direct connection between the 'F' and 'debased F' series, as is shown in civilian groups such as John Awodde and wife 1525, Sanderstead, where the man is of 'F' type and the wife of 'debased F', yet the appearance of 'debased F' brasses is so distinctive that they deserve their own sub classification. Sir Richard Fitzlewes with his four wives 1528, Ingrave, is typical of the best products of the type (Fig. 178). His face, with large nose, astonished eyes and deep chin is framed by long finely engraved hair. His small hands touch at the fingertips. His armour is constructed of a number of curious pieces, with occasional studs, and his tabard is apparently of very stiff material. The representation has the gay caricature quality of a playing card, though from the number of remaining examples of this series the style was well regarded.

Military figures of the 'debased F' series are fairly numerous and shown in full face, semi-profile and kneeling presentations. Almost all are ugly, clumsily cut, and often carelessly finished. The first group are full-face 'recumbent' representations in the manner of the Fitzlewes brass, though except on the last the wives are shown in semi-profile.

John Colt in tabard with two wives in heraldic dress, 1521, Roydon
Sir Peter Legh with wife, 1527, Winwick (Fig. 177)
Sir Edmund Tame with two wives in heraldic dress (one added later),
d. 1534, Fairford.

Sir Peter Legh is an extraordinary figure, superior to his wife, different in character from others in the series, and based on a special design.[4*] He was ordained after the death of his wife and is shown in armour, with a chasuble worn over it, and his shield in front between his hands. This unique brass is now unfortunately worn. It is very likely that Sir Edmund Tame and one wife were executed c.1526, as the second wife is of a different style and consistent with 1534. Sir Edmund is curious in that his upper half is shown full face, whereas his legs are viewed from the side. Semi-profile figures in tabards include Blewbury and Finchingfield 1523, Childwall 1524, Wrotham 1525 and Chesterfield 1529. The following are kneeling figures, those at Kenton and Puddletown being on quadrangular plates:

John Garneys, Esq., in tabard with wife in heraldic dress, 1524 Kenton, (*The Craft,* Fig. 98)

Christopher Martyn, Esq., in tabard, 1524, Puddletown

John Sacheverell, Esq., with wife, d.1485, engr. c.1525, Morley.

Evidence has been presented in the previous chapter of the emergence of a new pattern series, designated 'G', which, nevertheless appears to have had close affinities with the designs of 'D'. This termination of, or drastic alterations in, the 'D' series partly accounts for the stylistic confusion at this period. Certain brasses, such as that of John Leventhorp, Esq., 1510, St Helen's, Bishopsgate, London (Fig. 181) appear to be successors of late fifteenth century 'D' brasses, and the dog at the feet is an obvious adaptation of that as shown at Horton. There are several such figures until 1520, those in semi-profile being closely related to 'F' designs but stiffer in treatment than those listed. In some cases, as at Denchworth 1516, and Heythrop 1521, an obviously 'F' male is faced by an incongruous wife, the latter being of 'G' pattern.[5*] The most striking detail in this otherwise rather dull miscellany is the crested helm occasionally supporting the head. These figures may be interpreted as modifications of 'F', though some have residual 'D' characteristics: 1505, Westminster Abbey; 1508, Yealmpton; 1510, Hitcham, Ardingly; c.1510, Over, Nettlestead; 1511, Shottesbrooke; 1513, Writtle, Luton; 1514, Watton-at-Stone; 1515, Blewbury; 1516, Denchworth; 1517, Upton; d.1545, effigy engr. c.1520, Flitton; 1521, Heythrop.

The figures of the 'G' series are not easily confused with those described. The characteristics of early transitional examples are discernible in the unusual figure at Lullingstone of Sir William Pecche (Fig. 156), specially in the pliant rendering of the hands and the deeply lidded eyes. Successors to this plate appear to be Sir John Guise 1501, Aspley Guise, and Oliver St John with wife 1503, Stoke Rochford.

Although widely differing in form and in much of their detail, four of the greatest brasses of the early Tudor period would seem to have some common origins in 'G' design, though all have the quality of specially prepared patterns. The most notable is the carefully engraved figure of William, Viscount Beaumont 1507, Wivenhoe (Fig. 182). The draughtsmanship is of moderate quality, but much of the detail is well and thoughtfully expressed. The treatment of the fauld, tassets and sword belt is unusually good for the period, as is also the handling of the feet and the splendid elephant and castle device below. The peculiar rendering of the grass is a detail of some importance in occasional use through the series until 1540. The canopy, which is described later, is now much mutilated. Another brass is that of John, Lord le Strange with wife and daughter, laid in 1509, Hillingdon. This is a canopied memorial, well engraved, and a convincing representation of armour, though the centrally hung tasset is peculiar. The noble's head is youthful and framed by long and delicately engraved hair. Very different from these, though identifiable with the earliest 'G' patterns are the canopied brasses of Peers Gerard d.1492, Winwick, and William Catisby d.1485, Ashby St. Legers. The latter was engraved c.1506, though some slightly earlier canopy work was apparently incorporated (Fig. 180).[6*] The former would appear to date from about the same period and may be compared with John Burgoyn 1505, Impington. Gerard, now much worn, is shown full face wearing a very ample tabard. His poleyns and sabatons are elaborate but clumsily engraved. The lion at his feet is a degenerate version of a late fifteenth-century model. Below are large heads of flowers, set among the irregular grass blades which also appear at Lullingstone. William Catisby has some similar features but is turned in semi-profile. His sombre face with baggy-lidded eyes and feeble looking hands are striking characteristics.

The normal workshop products of 'G' series fall into two main groups, the earlier consisting of a number of figures of uneven quality. Their armour is usually badly represented and fancifully constructed. Most are shown in semi-profile, though there are frontal representations, as on the poor brass of Richard Conquest and wife 1500, Houghton Conquest, and the better figure of William Roberts with two wives 1508, Little Braxted.

Typical recumbent figures are: c.1500, Purse Caundle, Writtle; 1502, Otterden, Strensham; 1503, Slaugham; 1505, East Grinstead, Impington; 1507, Merstham; c.1510, British Museum, London; 1514, Dauntsey and Little Wenham (*The Craft*, Fig. 216). The kneeling family groups of John Samwell c.1500, Cottisford, and Hugh Wylloughbye 1513, Wilne, are good examples of the series (Fig. 179). In the latter group the squire kneels with his only son, both wearing tabards.

Later figures of the series, from c.1510-1530, are on the whole badly proportioned, and poor representations of armour. Many have a hunched appearance, created in part by their short necks and partly by the high haute-pieces on the pauldrons. Several wear long faulds with absurd tassets. A common distortion in presentation is the excessive length of the legs from the knee to ankle, which is exaggerated by the pose. The legs are either slim or shown in semi-profile. Examples are: c.1515, Middleton, Darlton; 1516, Bromham; 1518, Ewelme, Sundridge; 1520, Burton; 1522, Grade, (d.1505) Wootton Wawen; 1523, Longdon, Roxby Chapel; 1524, Cossington, Brabourne; Richard Covert with three wives, kneeling, d.1547, engr. c.1525, Slaugham (*The Craft*, Fig. 35); 1525, Crewkerne; 1528, Moulsoe and Wrotham.

Sir Thomas Brooke 1529, Cobham, is a much illustrated brass exhibiting many of the worst features of the group in an ostentatious fashion. The long slender legs with their fanciful poleyns, the curious fauld, the fluted double plackart, outsize arm defences and small hands, give a most ungainly impression. Much shading is worked on the armour joints. The face of the knight is fattish, and his small mouth has prominent lips. These characteristics are easily recognized, and may be related to those of the only considerable series of brasses of the mid sixteenth century. Evidently by c.1530 most of the London marblers were working in close association, so close in fact that the majority of brasses appear to come from a single workshop, the interrelationship of fragments on the reverses of many of these memorials demonstrating the common source of the plate. The brasses of this period have been examined in detail by Page-Phillips 1958 who traces the examples of the 'G' series into a succession of recognizable models. Roger Gyfford at Middle Claydon is an outstanding example of the 'G' series, as is also Richard Fermer 1552 at Easton Neston (*The Craft*, Fig. 213) though the latter is markedly different in detail. In the absence of several concurrent contrasting series, designations related to typical examples are necessary to complement the letters so far adopted, and clarify the transition of patterns more effectively after 1545. Brasses in the 'G' series will accordingly be described as 'Gyfford', 'Fermour', 'Lytkott' or 'post-Lytkott' figures depending on their appearance and peculiarities.

Attention has been drawn in *The Craft* to Page-Phillips's conclusions, following a close examination, that the later 'G' style figures, referred to from now on as 'Gyfford' figures, have several variations, and their inscriptions are engraved in several different scripts, but the overall integrity of this considerable series cannot be doubted. The hunched, long-legged knights, with their thick lips, wide eyes and over-shaded armour, are found with numerous comparable civilian and ecclesiastical examples until the early 1550's. After 1545, however, their proportions are improved and the overall execution is more refined. The following are the best. The first group are shown full face, semi-profile or kneeling but do not wear the tabard: Dolwyddelan d.1525; John Horsey with wife, 1531, Yetminster; 1532, Camberwell, Ampthill; William Brocas, kneeling, d.1506 engr. c.1535, Sherborne St John; 1537, Erith; 1537

Harefield, and another (d.1514) c.1537; 1539, Atherington; c.1540, St Mary, Islington; 1540, Edlesborough, Taplow, Marcham, Clovelly, Addington; Roger Gyfford, Esq., with wife, 1542, Middle Claydon; 1543, Rufford; 1544, Ellesborough; 1545, St Mary Lambeth, Nettleden[7]*, Harlington, Narborough; 1546, All Hallows-by-the-Tower, London, St Mary, Islington; 1548, Blatherwyck.

By far the finest of this group is the great memorial of Roger Gyfford, which is among the most notable brasses of the century (Fig. 184). The figures are surprisingly large, and well engraved within the limitations of contemporary design. The detail of the armour is carefully finished, and the massive sword slanting behind the knees typical of the semi-profile figures. The wearing of gauntlets is unusual. The Yetminster figures are above average in size, and John Horsey has the rare feature of a breastplate entirely engraved with scrollwork. William Brocas is small, but his features and equipment are well cut and shown in almost complete profile, revealing the join of his breast and back plates.

Tabards of arms, often bearing complex quarterings, are an attractive aspect of the following; the wives, except at Blewbury, wear heraldic mantles: 1534, Fairford; 1539, Thame; Sir William Gascoigne with two wives, 1540, Cardington (Fig. 189); 1547, Aldbury, Faringdon and 1548, Blewbury.

Sir Ralph Verney at Aldbury is the most pleasing and Sir William Gascoigne the most arresting. The well proportioned and neat appearance of the former contrasts with the stiff and lank figure of the latter.

Kneeling figures of the 'Gyfford' series are invariably set in the backs of canopied tombs, or on specially prepared mural slabs. A few of the recumbent figures are or were on the tops of high tombs. Many of these brasses are engraved on reused metal from dissolved monastic houses, or have slabs appropriated from earlier memorials.

From about 1548, notably illustrated at Blewbury, changes in the 'G' patterns are clearly discernible, leading into two series, one of brief duration, the other continuing well after the close of the period. The so-called 'Fermour' type brasses have become well known in recent years, primarily because almost all have proved to be palimpsest, but also for the intrinsic merits of the brasses themselves. 'Fermour' figures differ from their 'Gyfford' predecessors mainly in points of detail and finish, but in most respects they are marginally superior. Faces, though still wide-eyed, are more natural, hinges and other armour fittings are perceptively portrayed, hands are well drawn, and the figures have a better balance. Those commemorated appear youthful, unless seniority is deliberately intended. Then beards are introduced after an absence from English brasses of nearly a century. The following are armed 'recumbent' figures of the Fermour group:

Thomas Seintaubyn with wife, mutilated, c.1550, Crowan
Thomas Giffard, 1550, Twyford
Thomas Grenewey, 1538 with wife, engr. 1551, Dinton
Richard Grenewey with wife, 1551, Dinton
Peter Coryton with wife, 1551, St Mellion
Reynold Peckham with wife, 1551, Ossington
Richard Fermer with wife, 1552, Easton Neston (*The Craft,* Fig. 213)
William Fermoure with wife, 1552, Somerton
John Hutton with wife, 1553, Dry Drayton
Sir John Hampden with two wives, 1553, Great Hampden
Sir Richard Catesby in tabard, 1553, Ashby St. Legers
William Foxe with wife, 1554, Ludford

Three kneeling groups commemorate Sir Humfrey Style with two wives 1552, Beckenham, Sir Thomas Henneage with two wives 1553, Hainton, and Nicholas Saunder 1553, Charlwood. Both knights wear tabards and their ladies heraldic mantles. The upper part of the Sir Thomas Henneage brass is a respectable modern restoration.

The Twyford and Ashby St Legers figures are both large and shown full face. The latter was covered by pews for about three hundred years and the surface is in fine preservation. The Easton Neston brass is also in excellent condition. Richard Fermer rests his head on a crested helm, as does also Sir Richard Catesby, in contrast to the small close helmets introduced but almost obscured on many of the 'Gyfford' and most of the 'Fermour' figures. Peter Coryton is shown with a long beard and hair receding with age, and Thomas Grenewey is also bearded. John Hutton is rather curious with unusually large head, short thick hair and a puzzled expression.

One of the characteristics of the 'Fermour' brasses is their blatantly appropriated origin. Almost all are composed of miscellaneous reused pieces, often joined in unexpected places, and some are set in the matrices of earlier brasses. The Catesby slab still retains the buffed down rivets of the destroyed plate. Richard Fermer's wife is laid on the indent of a lady with butterfly headdress, and much older carving is integrated with the Henneage tomb.

Other brasses, a few apparently contemporary with, but most successors to the 'Fermour' group, form a long series diverging significantly from the 'Fermour' model but clearly based upon it. A very good example is Christopher Lytkott 1554, who is shown with his wife at Swallowfield, (Fig. 186). His face appears older and is more lined. His fauld is deeper than those of the Fermour group, but is arched at the centre (? to make room for a codpiece) and the curve downwards follows the inner line of the tassets; these are of fan-like shape and the skirt of mail has an invecked edge. The leg armour is more rounded in shape and the sabatons have rounded toes, in contrast to the flattened ones of 'Fermour' and later 'Gyfford' figures. Shading is applied heavily. Christopher Lytkott's head is protected by an armet with visor raised, a rare detail competently executed. The majority of figures of this series are closely comparable to this, except for the helmet, though many have long beards and some are less carefully drawn. The following are other examples within this period:

John Shelley with wife, kneeling, d.1550, Clapham
Humphrey Cheynie, 1557, West Hanney
Sir William Drury with two wives, 1557, Hawstead
Sir John Porte in tabard, with two wives in heraldic mantles, kneeling, 1557, Etwall (*The Craft,* Fig. 214)
Sir Edward Greville in tabard, 1559, Weston-upon-Avon
Erasmus Forde with wife, kneeling, 1559, Thames Ditton
Thomas Fyndorne and John Lord Marnay in tabards with wife in heraldic mantle, d.1549 engr. c.1560, Little Horkesley.

Unlike the 'Fermour' group, which Page-Phillips established as having a common script, the inscriptions of these brasses are in three somewhat different scripts. Presumably several craftsmen were involved in their manufacture, and their quality varies.

Sir William Drury is shown with his eyes closed in death, which is most unusual. The Clapham kneeling figures are well engraved. The combined memorial at Little Horkesley is of great interest, though now sadly broken through war damage. The brass commemorates Lady Marnay d.1549, who is shown in a heraldic mantle. Her first husband, John Lord Marnay, is depicted in armour and tabard similar to her second husband, Thomas Fyndorne. The latter, however, has the short hair and beard fashionable c.1560, whereas the former's face is clean shaven with long hair, and was apparently derived from the earlier 'Gyfford' pattern. A lion is placed at Lord Marnay's feet in contrast to the grass beneath those of Thomas Fyndorne, and his figure is carefully cut out, whereas the other is engraved on a partly rectangular plate. The difference in treatment is deliberate and effective.[8*]

The brasses so far described form the major series carried out by the London workshops. There are in addition a small number of brasses of inferior design which seem to have a different origin, though almost certainly engraved in London as their distribution is concentrated in the South East. The best executed example of a man in armour is that of George Stonnard with wife 1558, at Loughton (Fig. 187). It is a decorative rectangular plate, and the representation of George is spirited, even though the armour is poorly defined. The position of his legs and hands is typical of the group. Guy Wade 1557, Standon, is another example though different in detail. He is clean-shaven and wears a helmet with raised visor. His inscriptions are complete, and allow comparisons with other contemporary London scripts. An unknown man in armour c.1555, Cobham, is another such figure but with a long beard. His armour includes a codpiece set much too high. Three other figures, similarly executed and rather imaginatively armed, are Edward Shurley with wife 1558, Isfield, John Parker 1558, Willingdon, and a headless man c.1560, at Upper Hardres. An unknown man in armour with wife c.1555, at Margaretting, appears to be another example, the lady and children groups being unusually animated representations. All the figures are shown in semi-profile, and in no case has the spare metal been cut out between the legs. There are other comparable civilian figures in this series, which may appropriately be designated 'H'.

Collars, pendants and insignia

Collars and pendants are occasionally found during the first thirty years of the sixteenth century. The SS collar is well shown at Aspley Guise 1501, and is also worn by Robert Rochester 1514, Sergeant of the Pantry to Henry VIII, at St Helen's Bishopsgate, London. More frequently a chain is shown round the neck with a pendent cross or tau cross. Sir Thomas Brooke 1529, at Cobham, wears a pendent cross bearing the Five Wounds. Examples of the tau cross are at Tilty 1520, Ingrave 1528, and Hillingdon 1528.

Before leaving the subject of military figures it is appropriate to describe the brass of Sir Thomas Bullen, K.G., Earl of Wiltshire and Ormond 1538 (*The Craft,* Fig. 212). This is set upon a high tomb at Hever and is by far the best executed English brass of the first half of the sixteenth century. The Earl is shown recumbent, his head resting against a large crested helmet, and his feet upon the Ormond beast, a male griffin. He wears armour and apparently a heraldic coat, but much is concealed by the insignia of the Order of the Garter, including the mantle with badge, the collar of roses and garters and a chaperon with scarf. The detail is beautifully finished. The drawing of the design has been done by a very competent artist with a good understanding of perspective. It has been suggested in *The Craft* that the court painter Lucas Hornebolt may have been employed for the purpose. The figure has no similarity to other contemporary work in this medium, a difference further emphasized by the inscription in Roman capitals with its antique form. The unique representation of insignia on this brass has diverted attention from its artistic merits.

Male civilians

Civilian brasses of the period fall fairly satisfactorily into the series described, though the poor quality of many defies accurate classification at this stage of research. Civilian costume lacks variety and the presentation is unenterprising. The dress usually consists of an undergarment, a doublet, tight fitting hose and a large wide-sleeved gown, lined or faced with fur. Unfortunately the gown is usually shown closed and belted, which all but obscures the undergarments. The brass of Robert Southwell 1514, with wife, Barham, is exceptional (Fig. 185). He was a member of the Junior Bar, described as 'apprenticius ad leges', but wears normal civilian dress. His gown is shown open, and his doublet and hose are well exposed. They are, moreover, hatched or incised for inlay, and show up well against the fur lining. His shoes are of broad round-toed form, typical of the period. The Barham brass is of the 'F' series. Another example with open gown, but of the curious 'debased F' pattern, is the large figure of William Beriff, 'mariner', with his wife 1525, Brightlingsea. The undergarments are not so decorative, but the furred gown is very rich. Another interesting 'F' pattern figure is William Eyre 1509, Great Cressingham. His gown is closed, but the undergarment is partly exposed, embroidered with the monogram 'Ihc'. The 'F' pattern is recognizable from the fine flowing hair and handsome faces of the men, the 'debased F' pattern from its grotesque faces, curious hands and poor proportions.

A peculiarity of the 'F' series is the occasional rendering of fur in large pounced dots in contrast to the short parallel lines usually adopted; a civilian c.1510 at Lechlade is an example.

The 'G' pattern figures are generally simpler and plainer in treatment. Typical examples of early 'G' figures are Thomas Goodriche with wife 1500, Aspenden, and William Croke with wife 1506, Great Gaddesden. A good figure is that of John Reed with wife 1503, Wrangle (*The Craft*, Fig. 32), the sleeves of his gown having a slit near the elbow allowing the arms to emerge.

Many civilians are depicted with purses and rosaries hanging from their belts, though these are uncommon after 1530. An especially large purse is carried by John Colman 1506, Little Waldingfield. Henry Elyot with wife, 1503, Wonersh, is interesting, as he has a purse and knife attached to his belt and a well displayed example of the chaperon on his right shoulder. There is no illustration of the early Tudor male headdress.

Among the very large numbers of civilian brasses dating from 1500 to 1530, most of which are small and of mediocre quality, a few examples are either unusually well engraved, interesting or large figures of their type and include:

Richard Wakehurst d.1454 with wife, canopy, engr. c.1500, Ardingly
John Avenyng with wife, kneeling, 1501, Cirencester
William Wyddowsoun with wife, kneeling, 1513, Mickleham
James Tornay with two wives, 1519, Slapton (Fig. 190)
John Smalwode (alias Wynchcom) with wife, 1519, Newbury
Walter Hichman with wife, 1521, Kempsford
John Haryson with two wives, kneeling, 1525, St Mary, Hull
Thomas Busche, woolman with wife, canopy, 1526. Northleach (*The Craft,* Fig. 215)
John Greenway with wife, 1529, Tiverton
William Bloor, gent., 1529, Rainham.

The Ardingly brass is of 'F' style. The kneeling compositions at Cirencester and Mickleham are both carefully engraved, the former 'G' the latter 'F'. The Hull brass is engraved on a quadrangular plate, from which a representation of the Holy Trinity has been not altogether successfully erased. This is of early 'Gyfford' type. The Kempsford brass and Thomas Busche at Northleach are examples of the inartistic 'debased F' series on a grand scale. John Greenway, as has been mentioned, is outstandingly large. William Bloor is very unusual; his gown is short, his doublet embroidered and his shoes bowed and flattened at the toe. The engraving of the plate, though recognizably of London 'G' style, is nonetheless curious. James Tornay, though badly drawn, is interesting as an early example of the gown worn with glove sleeves, and showing the badge of a Yeoman of the Crown on the shoulder. The substantial but wretchedly designed brass of John Smalwode at Newbury illustrates the low standard of work which was by that time acceptable. John, known as 'Jack of Newbury', was a clothier of great wealth and a munificent benefactor to Newbury church; his figure belies his distinction. Large groups of early sixteenth-century civilians may be found at Aldenham, Orford and Thame.

Civilian dress over the following thirty years differs only slightly. The gown is generally shown unbelted and with sleeves hanging below the elbow. The partlet — a neckerchief, often pleated — is usually worn. Shoes are narrower though still rounded at the toe. The quality of engraving is generally at its best on the kneeling figures, which being mural are also in better preservation. Shading is heavily applied, occasionally with a good and realistic effect. The following are among the more important examples:

Henry Hatche with wife, canopy, 1533, Faversham
Nicholas Leveson, sheriff and merchant of the Staple, with wife, kneeling, 1539, St Andrew Undershaft, London
Sir Thomas Nevell, kneeling, 1542, Mereworth (Fig. 238)
Sir George Monox, Lord Mayor of London, with wife, kneeling, 1543, Walthamstow (*The Craft,* Fig. 25)
John Newdegate, Esq., with wife, kneeling, 1545, Harefield
Robert Barfott with wife, 1546, Lambourne
Edward Myrfin, gent., kneeling, 1553, Kirtling
Edward Crane with wife, 1558, Stratford St Mary.

The majority of these brasses have the characteristics of the 'Gyfford' style, though the large and ugly Hatche brass is of the 'debased F' series, and Edward Myrfin is of the 'Fermour' group. Edward Crane is included as an example of the small 'H' series. The Mereworth and Harefield brasses are of very good quality, both set at the back of canopied tombs, which, in the latter case, is probably an appropriation. Sir Thomas Nevell, described as 'one of the moste honorabill counssell' to Henry VIII, wears a chain round his neck with a pendant jewelled cross, and a short scarf usually associated with mayors or civic dignitaries.

Sir George Monox was Lord Mayor of London and is shown in a fur-lined civic mantle wearing his chain of office. The large mantle, buttoned on the right shoulder, is shown exclusively during this period on brasses of mayors and aldermen or the legal profession. An ordinary example of London work is that of an unknown and mutilated man and his wife c.1520 at St John Baptist, Gloucester. John Cook 1529, at St Mary de Crypt, Gloucester, was four times mayor. His mantle is clasped with a brooch and thrown up over the left shoulder. Henry Dacres, a London Alderman 1530, at St Dunstan-in-the-West, London, wears both mantle and scarf. He is a singularly coarse 'debased F' figure and an inappropriate companion to his slender wife. Nicholas Leveson was sheriff in 1534, and wears the mantle over civil dress.

Lawyers

A small group of brasses commemorate judges and other lawyers in the dress of their profession, the more interesting are:

John Brook, Serjeant-at-Law with wife, 1522, St Mary Redcliffe, Bristol
John Newdegate, Serjeant-at-Law, with wife in heraldic mantle, 1528, Harefield
Sir Anthony Fitzherbert, Justice of the Common Pleas, with wife in heraldic mantle, 1538, Norbury, Derbs.

Sir Walter Luke, Justice of the Common Pleas, with wife in heraldic mantle, kneeling, 1544, Cople (Fig. 188)

Sir John Spelman, Secondary Justice of the King's Bench, with wife in heraldic mantle, kneeling, 1545, Narborough

Henry Bradschawe, Chief Baron of the Exchequer, with wife, kneeling, 1553, Halton

William Coke, Esq., Justice of the Common Pleas, with wife, 1553, Milton.

Most of these judges are shown in the established dress of supertunica, mantle, shoulder-piece, hood and coif, though Henry Bradschawe is bareheaded and the Norbury and Milton Judges wear the 'casting hood'. (By the sixteenth century it became customary to wear hoods of great and inconvenient size. A modified hood accordingly was worn for less formal use and normally thrown back over the right shoulder.) The mantle and shoulder-piece of Sir Walter Luke are cut away for inlay, and much of the red colouring is still intact. All the robes of Sir John Spelman are treated in this manner though his coif is not recessed. Both are set vertically above high tombs. These two figures, which are of the 'Gyfford' group, make a valuable comparison with those at Halton and Milton, both of which are finely executed 'Fermour' type brasses. Sir Antony Fitzherbert, though mutilated, is rather unusual, holding a rolled document in his right hand, and may possibly be of midland workmanship. His head is lost but the indent proves that he wore the 'pileus quadratus' — a square cap which was adopted by judges during the early sixteenth century.

The serjeants wear the supertunica, tabard, shoulder-piece with hood and the coif. John Brook wears a sleeved tabard in contrast to John Newdegate who wears a sleeveless tabard, the apertures of which are seen below the sleeves of the supertunica. Both these figures are of the 'F' series, the first transitional and the other typical of the best work of 'debased F'.

Only one notary is distinguished for certain by his pen-case and ink-horn, namely Robert Wymbyll 1506, shown with his wife and her second husband at St Mary Tower, Ipswich. A small, unknown and headless figure at New College, Oxford c.1510, has been described as a notary, but is certainly a member of the college. John Muscote 1512, a prothonotary of the Court of Common Pleas, is shown in ordinary civil dress with his wife at Earl's Barton.

Females

Female figures are remarkable for their relative consistency in dress, especially between the years 1500 and 1530. The kirtle is usually almost entirely obscured by a voluminous gown lined or edged with fur. The sleeves are fairly close fitting but end in wide cuffs which are turned back. On one brass at Kinver (d.1528) the sleeves are shown padded and decoratively slashed. Most women wear girdles, some of them very long, with weighted ends almost reaching the ground. Others are shorter terminating in two or three rosettes from which hangs a chain with ornamental pendant or pomander. Pomanders were often made of open metalwork, gold, silver or brass, to contain scents or aromatic spices. Haines records evidence that metal balls, presumably containing charcoal, were also suspended for warming the hands.[9] Joan Turnour 1500, Hadley, wears a short girdle fastened by a rich clasp at the back. Joan Wyddowsoun 1513, Mickleham, has a rosary. A few women wear pendant tau crosses, as at Lanteglos-by-Fowey, c.1525, and Sefton 1528.

Most women wear the kennel or pedimental headdress, consisting of a stiff cap and veil, and a long frontlet, usually recessed for colour inlay or decorated with lozenges or quatrefoils. The veil headdress is unusual unless worn by widows. Jaquette, wife of John Lord le Strange 1509, Hillingdon, is a large example, and there are others, such as at Dengie c.1520; Aldenham c.1525; and Pluckley 1526.

The following are good characteristic examples of women in normal dress from 1500 to 1530:

Dame Margery Calverley, canopy, d.1509, engr. c.1500, Ightfield
Gwen Shelford, 1504, Bramley
Dame Elizabeth Pownynges, 1528, Brabourne
Margaret Bulcley, canopy, 1528, Sefton

The first three are of the 'G' series, the last of debased 'F'.

Women of importance are often shown wearing a mantle over the gown. Occasionally this is plain, as on the figure of Margaret, wife of Sir John Brooke, Lord Cobham 1506, Cobham, but it is usual for the mantle to be embroidered with arms, as at Eastington 1518, Ewell 1579, and Stoke-by-Nayland c.1525. Outstanding among these are three of the wives of Sir Richard Fitzlewes 1528, Ingrave, who wear a short surcoat of ermine beneath, and the two wives of Sir William Gascoigne, Cardington, who wear both heraldic kirtle and mantle. As a contrast to these women, the small brass of Isabel Gifford 1523, Middle Claydon, deserves special note (*The Craft,* Fig. 218). Her figure is of indifferent quality, but she appears to be dressed in a maternity gown. No details in her inscription offer any explanation, but the wide opening with its expanded lacings would seem to have no other interpretation.

Three changes in fashion occur about 1530. The gown becomes fuller in its dimensions, with long hanging sleeves with wide fur cuffs. The frontlet is often doubled back exposing the neck. Long rosaries are frequently hung from the girdle or sash. The best example is Mary, wife of Roger Gyfford 1542, at Middle Claydon. Among other good examples are Joan Warner, 1538, Aldenham; and Margaret Bulstrode, 1540, Hedgerley.

Anne Danvers 1539, Dauntsey, is in the centre of an ornate, quadrangular plate, which is described later. Elizabeth Perepoynt 1543, West Malling (Fig. 193), in spite of the loss of the lower half, is a splendid full-face representation of this costume with remarkable sleeves.

A small but attractive and unusual figure is at Aldenham c.1535 (Fig. 191). The woman is unknown and engraved in the 'Gyfford' style, though the arrangement of her costume is comparable to contemporary East Anglian work. Her gown is held up in the front by two ties revealing fur beneath. She wears a bulbous cap on her head, similar to others later described in connection with the Cambridge and Suffolk workshops. This brass should be compared with another at Rettendon c.1535, through the latter is perhaps of local workmanship, copying a London model. Other later London style brasses have considerable resemblances to this, though less decorative in treatment, such as Malyn Harte 1557, Lydd, and Elizabeth Stokys 1560, Eton College Chapel.

Changes in fashion are noticeable about 1545. The kennel headdress with raised frontlet is still worn, as, for instance, by Jane Foxe 1554, Ludford. But an increasing number of women wear the 'Paris head', consisting of a close-fitting cap stiffened by wires and frequently depressed in the centre. An ornamental band frames the brow, often apparently enriched with jewels or with pearls as at Swallowfield 1554. A small veil falls to the shoulders. The gown takes a variety of forms. Anne Lovell 1545, Harlington, wears a gown with heavily padded shoulders, decorated with an interlaced strap pattern and an open embroidered collar. Similar gowns are found at All Hallows-by-the-Tower, London 1546, and St Mary's Islington 1546. Alternatively the gown is opened below the waist showing an undergown or petticoat. Joan Coryton 1551, St Mellion and other "Fermour" type wives illustrate this arrangement. At the close of the period a heavy style of gown is shown with padded shoulders, and long sleeves. The front is usually half closed by means of tied bows. Katherine Lytkott 1554, Swallowfield, is a good example, as is also the lesser known brass of Jane Seynt Johns 1557, Thornton. A kneeling figure of similar type c.1550 with children has been found at Willesden. A gown hatched for colour inlay is worn by a woman kneeling at a faldstool c.1550 at the Society of Antiquaries, London. Short girdles are commonly worn with a rich clasp, from which hangs a cord attached to an inscribed case, book or reliquary. Both at Ludford and Swallowfield the cases are engraved with the Sacred Wounds, an assertion of Catholic symbolism, which, to some extent, had been avoided during the previous ten years. An unusual female figure c.1560, clearly of the 'H' series, is shown at Upminster holding a book, and may be compared with the spirited representation of the wife at Margaretting c.1555 and Mary Stonnard 1558. A typical and well executed woman of the close of this period, depicted kneeling with her eleven children, is Jane, Lady Bray 1558, at Eaton Bray.

Several wives of the period 1530 to 1560 are represented as wearing the heraldic mantle and have been noted with their husbands. A few women on their own are heraldically dressed and two are of great interest:

Lady Elizabeth de Vere, Countess of Oxford, canopy, 1537, Wivenhoe
Elizabeth Goringe, husband lost, kneeling, 1558, Burton (Fig. 195)

The first is a very large monument, with triple pediment and super-canopy, and formerly with shafts and subsidiary figures. The figure is large, showing the Countess in a wide mantle with the arms of Scrope quartering Tiptoft. Her kennel headdress is surmounted by a coronet. She wears a chain round her neck and a pendant cross, supposedly representing one containing a relic of the True Cross bequeathed by her to the Earl of Oxford, her son-in-law. Though stiffly designed it is unquestionably one of the great brasses of the sixteenth century.

Elizabeth Goringe, (most important of the 'H' series) is very curious. Her brass is set at the back of an elaborate high tomb (Fig 194), and was, in effect, surrounded by five groups of children, now lost, together with her husband; the inscriptions and arms remain. The main peculiarity of her figure is that she wears a tabard of arms and not a heraldic mantle. This presentation is unique on brasses, though there was a precedent for it in painted glass.[10] No reason for this male attire is at all obvious, though plain error can be discounted.

Widows

Widows, represented in veil headdress with barbe, are uncommon, though a few are shown with their husbands, such as Dame Joan Cook 1529, St Mary de Crypt, Gloucester. The following individual figures are of considerable interest:

Katherine Scrop, kneeling, husband lost, 1500, Hambleden
Dame Anne Phelip, holding heart, canopy, 1510, Chenies
Elizabeth Porte, husband lost, 1512, Etwall
Alice Tayland, kneeling, 1513, Diddington.

The first is a small but finely engraved 'G' series brass, in which the surface of the veil, gown and mantle has been cut away for inlay, leaving the lines in relief. This treatment is highly unusual for English work.[11] Dame Anne Phelip has a large though worn memorial, showing her grasping a heart with flying scrolls. The Etwall and Diddington brasses have unusual representations set above the figures.

Some brasses to widows show the deceased in ordinary female dress, such as Agnes Johnson 1511, Chenies, and the small figure of Elizabeth Barton 1507, shown with her sister Katherine at Beddington.

Ecclesiastics

Brasses to ecclesiastics are numerous and reveal the coarseness of much Tudor technique and design with unfortunate clarity. Many figures are overwhelmed by their vestments, and the tonsure appears out of place in the midst of long straight hair. There is, however, historical interest in the change of vestments revealed by a few brasses of King Edward VI's reign, and the short return to Roman usage during that of Queen Mary.

Archbishops and bishops

No very large brasses of Bishops or Archbishops survive, though indents at Canterbury (Archbishop Henry Dean, 1503) and Lincoln cathedrals prove their former existence. The only archiepiscopal figure is small and most probably represents St Thomas of Canterbury. It was set high on the tower at Edenham with the kneeling figure of a donor below. It is a curious figure of the 'F' series verging on the 'debased' but notwithstanding its naïve treatment is a presentable representation of pontificals with the addition of the pallium and cross staff (*The Craft,* Fig. 47). The following brasses to Bishops show them in pontifical mass vestments with mitre and crozier:

James Stanley, Bishop of Ely, d.1515, Manchester cathedral
John Yo(u)ng, Titular Bishop of Callipolis, engr. c.1523, New College, Oxford
Thomas Goodryke, Bishop of Ely, canopy lost, 1554, Ely cathedral (Fig. 196)
John Bell, Bishop of Worcester, 1556, St James, Clerkenwell.

The first two bishops are both mutilated. James Stanley is a small and average 'debased F' series figure, from which the lowest quarter is now lost. John Yo(u)ng is an altogether finer figure of the 'G' series, with well engraved vestments and an inscription in raised letters. His dalmatic is richly embroidered and his chasuble has a broad central orphrey of unusual pattern and an edge of embroidered jewellery. His head and the crook of the crozier are lost.

Thomas Goodryke is large and originally lay under a gothic canopy, the latest of its style to be noted. His figure well illustrates the restoration of traditional vestments in the reign of Queen Mary. He was the Lord High Chancellor in addition to being Bishop of Ely, and holds a clasped book and the Great Seal. It would seem that the designer was influenced by the many earlier episcopal brasses in the cathedral, as this brass, except for its shading effects, is very conservative in treatment. John Bell is in contrast much more freely drawn, though not so well executed, and badly damaged by the loss of the bottom third. The vestments are represented with far less detail and care, and the brass is understandably rarely illustrated.

Canons and wardens

Ecclesiastics wearing full processional vestments are commemorated by a varied selection of brasses, a few of which are considerably larger than those to the bishops. Most unusual is the exceedingly large canopied brass to Edmund Frowsetoure, S.T.P., Dean of Hereford 1529. The figure is rather overwhelmed by the elaborate canopy and long foot inscription, but shows the Dean vested in a cope, almuce, surplice and an academic pileus. The design is very poor, in spite of the scale. Far superior in execution are two 'F' series figures — Walter Hewke, D.C.L., master d.1517 engr. c.1510, Trinity Hall Chapel, Cambridge, and John (?) Gygur, warden of Merton College, Oxford c.1510, Tattershall who both wear the pileus. Their copes are enriched with orphreys of canopied saints and the morses are engraved with representations of our Lord in Glory. Two other large coped priests are Thomas Worsley, L.L.B., Residentiary of Beverley 1501, Wimpole, and Richard Wylleys, Warden d.1523 engr. c.1510, Higham Ferrers. Both wear copes with embroidered orphreys, the latter decorated with a pattern of shells and small pearls.

Robert Langton D.C.L., c.1518, at The Queen's College, Oxford is the most ornate of this type of figure. He is depicted in a cope worked with fleurs-de-lys, with a rich orphrey and a morse showing a rose set in rays of light. The Dowdeswell priest c.1520 is of the same pattern but less well executed, a contrast between an 'F' series figure and an early 'debased F' successor. John White d.1560, engr. c.1548, Winchester College has a similarly rich cope but only a portion of the original figure remains; a complete restoration is set in the chapel floor. Adam Graffton, 1530, Withington, is of poor workmanship. Thomas Dalyson, d.1541 engr. c.1535, Clothall, is without the almuce. Thomas Magnus 1550, Sessay, is a noticeably late example to show the full processional vestments. The large morse, inscribed 'JESUS', is unique on brasses.

The sole example of the plain choir cope is a boldly engraved priest c.1505 at St Just-in-Roseland. The surface of the almuce is treated in an unusual manner, but there is little reason to doubt its London origin.

Two Canons of Windsor wear the Garter mantle instead of the cope. Roger Lupton, Provost of Eton d.1540, engr. c.1530, Eton College Chapel, is a clear representation of the mantle with its badge (Fig. 197). Arthur Cole, S.T.B., President of Magdalen College, Oxford 1558, is rather more detailed, and shows the long tasselled cord, holding the mantle at the breast. A palimpsest reverse at St Mary, Islington, (obv. 1546), reveals the greater part of a figure in choir dress with the tasselled pendant of the Order of St John of Jerusalem. Page-Phillips strongly suspects that this figure was connected with a palimpsest inscription at Harlington (obv. 1545) to George Barlee 1513, who 'whyle he lyved vowed hymself to — St John' Jer'l'm in England'.

Ecclesiastics shown in choir dress are few and mainly small. The exception is the large canopied figure of Henry Bost, provost 1503, Eton College Chapel, which has been partially restored and apparently recut. Far more interesting are the three rectangular plates — one at St George's Chapel, Windsor to Canon Robert Honywode, LLB., 1522, and two at St Patrick's cathedral, Dublin, to Deans Robert Sutton 1528 and Geoffrey Fyche 1537 (*The Craft*, Fig. 220). All are of evident London workmanship, showing the priests kneeling in semi-profile in unusual settings. The Irish examples have the almuce inlaid with engraved lead. Among the other examples of the type are the following, of which the last two are of special merit:

Thomas Parker, Prebendary of St Mary's Shrewsbury, 1501, Dean
Edmund Croston, kneeling 1507, St Mary-the-Virgin, Oxford
Robert Sheffelde, M.A., rector, 1508, Chartham
John Moore, M.A. prebendary of Osmonderley 1532, Sibson (Fig. 240)
James Coorthopp, Dean of Peterborough 1557, Christ Church, Oxford.

Two brasses, William Lawnder, kneeling c.1510, Northleach, and Richard Bethell 1518, Shorwell, commemorate priests wearing the surplice with scarf and rosette clasp attached to the left shoulder.

Parish Priests

Among a considerable number of priests in Mass vestments not one can be described as fine. Thomas Westley, chaplain to the Countess of Oxford 1535, Wivenhoe, is typical of the small and crudely engraved figures of the period (Fig. 200). The proportions of the body are peculiar, the facial expression stupid and the vestments poorly delineated. Apparels, maniples and stoles are often decorated with crossed lines or a jewel or lozenge pattern of irregular size. A central orphrey to the chasuble is commonly shown passing over the shoulders. There are no large figures and those of moderate size, such as Thomas Lawne 1518, St Cross, Winchester, and John ap Meredyth of Powys 1531, Betws Cedewain, are of no particular merit. The only canopied figure, Alexander Inglisshe 1504, Campsey Ash, is of average size and quality. The better work is found on some of the small figures, such as Richard Redberd 1521, Bradenham, and James Batersby 1522, Great Rollright. The stiffly drawn representation of William Wardysworth 1533, Betchworth, is of greater interest than most, illustrating the chasuble of heavy material and rounded form which was at this time replacing the lighter and more pointed 'Gothic' vestment. He holds an unusually large chalice with inscribed wafer. A small figure blessing the chalice and wafer c.1520, said to have come from North Weston, is preserved in the Museum of Archaeology and Ethnology, Cambridge.

An unusual brass at Northiam represents Nicholas Tufton 1538, in civilian dress with long sleeved gown, but shows his head tonsured. He presumably entered Holy Orders late in life in the manner of Sir Peter Legh at Winwick.

Regular clergy

Brasses to members of the Regular Orders are rare but form a valuable addition to earlier examples. Richard Bewfforeste, Augustinian Abbot, at Dorchester is a strongly engraved 'F' series figure of c.1510 (Fig. 198). He is represented wearing surplice and almuce and a monastic cloak and hood in place of the cope. His crozier rests against his right arm. An equally interesting figure is that of John Stodeley 1502, at Over Winchendon (Fig. 201). He was an Augustinian Canon of St Frideswide's Oxford, and vicar of Over Winchendon church. In addition to a cassock and cloak with hood he wears the white rochet of the Order. On the brass this habit is inlaid with lead and the pleats properly engraved. In contrast to Abbot Bewfforeste, the canon's tonsure is that of the secular clergy. Thomas Rutlond 1521, sub-Prior of St Albans, is depicted in the Benedictine habit. The inscription of Robert White, Augustinian Prior 1534, remains at Royston and a faint rubbing of the figure is in the Society of Antiquaries collection.

There are brasses to two abbesses and two vowesses. Dame Elizabeth Herwy, Abbess engr. c.1520, at Elstow is the best known of these (Fig. 199). She wears a habit, mantle, veil and barbe and is shown with a crozier. Dame Agnes Jordan, Abbess of Syon engr. c.1540, Denham, is a well engraved and dignified representation, omitting both mantle and crozier. Dame Joan Braham 1519, Frenze, described as 'vidua ac deo devota', is dressed in all respects as Abbess Herwy, though the sleeves of her habit are less full. Dame Susan Kyngeston, 1540, Shalston, is similar to Abbess Jordan, but is represented as a far younger looking woman. A few children shown in the habits of Regular Orders are mentioned later.

Academics

Representations of academics are generally small and of indifferent quality, though one of the 'F' series to Arthur Vernon, M.A., 1517, Tong, is conspicuously good. He is dressed in a long-sleeved tabard, with shoulder-piece and hood, and has an exceptionally fine chalice over his head. There is little innovation in dress. The more interesting examples are in fact found among provincial work ascribed in Chapter Thirteen to a Cambridge workshop. It is, however, worthy of note, as Dr Hargreaves Mawdesley has described, that during the early sixteenth century the tabard or other habit is increasingly omitted, and the supertunica worn with the shoulder-piece and hood as proper academic dress.[12] William Geddyng 1512, Wantage, Robert

Gosebourne 1523, St Alphege, Canterbury, and a Doctor of Law, Bryan Roos 1529, Childrey, are illustrations. An unusual brass shows the half effigies at All Souls College, Oxford, of David Lloyde, 'in utroque jure bacallarius', and Thomas Baker, 'juris civilis scolasticus'. The former is a tonsured ecclesiastic in sleeved tabard, with shoulder-piece and hood. The latter as a student of civil law or 'civilian' was a layman, and is shown in an open tabard and cloak opening on the left shoulder.

Shrouded and skeleton figures of civilians and clergy are fairly common, and are given separate consideration in Chapter Sixteen.

Children

Children are occasionally commemorated by individual brasses but usually appear in groups on small plates below their parents. These groups are in general repetitive and lack the precise representation of many late fifteenth-century examples. Most boys and girls are in a modified form of adult dress. Girls from 1500 to 1540 are shown with long free hair, or wearing the frontlet of the kennel headdress, with their hair flowing loose behind. From 1540-1560 they are often shown with loose hair, but wearing the ornamental stiffened front of the 'Paris head'. Though such groups, especially among the 'Gyfford' or 'Fermour' type brasses, are often carefully engraved they were apparently given little thought. A group of daughters, c.1520, has, for example, been appropriated for use on the Foxe brass 1554, at Ludford.

A few children groups deserve special note. One of the two daughters of Margaret Hyklott 1502, Althorne, is dressed as a nun. Three little girls with long hair, named Elizabeth, Joan and Joan, are arranged with care below Regenolde Tylney, gent. 1506, Leckhampstead. The eldest son of John Hampton engr. c.1510, Minchinhampton, is depicted as a monk and the eldest daughter as a nun. The sons of William Este 1534, Radnage, include a priest in a cope with an open book. The children groups at Margaretting c.1555 are unusually animated.

Children kneeling behind their parents occasionally show some unusual details. An academic and a nun are among the children of Sir Thomas Barnardiston 1503, Great Coates, and Thomas Wylloughbye 1513, shown behind his father at Wilne, wears armour and a tabard. On a few brasses each child is engraved on an individual plate. Examples are at Cley 1512, where each is named. In rare cases a child is engraved against the adult's figure. Alys Cryspe 1518, Birchington, has a daughter standing by her side, and a woman of the Collys family c.1510 at Dunton has the amusing detail of a son peeping round her gown (Fig. 192). This touch of realism recalls the will of Thomas Iden of Stoke who required in 1511 a stone 'wt the pictor of a man and a woman and the pictor of a little man child holdyng her by the beades'.[13]

Among children individually commemorated, two are of special interest. John, son of Walter Stonor, Esq. 1512, at Wraysbury, is represented in a long belted tunic with tight sleeves and a very curious cap (*The Craft*, Fig. 31). The cap takes the form of a low pileus with a brim, incised for colour inlay, and has a wide decorated chin-strap completely covering the ears and two 'streamers' flapping behind. The brass is undoubtedly a special design and some particular uniform is most probably intended. It has been said that this dress is that of an Eton scholar, but no evidence has been cited to support this interpretation.[14*] Another boy, Thomas Heron 1512, at Little Ilford, is shown in a tunic with a penner and ink-horn (*The Craft,* Fig. 219). A small headless figure at New College, Oxford c.1510, is comparable to this, and though usually described as a notary, with more probability represents a student.

Other children require little description. Edith and Elizabeth Wylde 1508, 'which died virgyns', at Barnes, are shown with long hair, and Elizabeth Broughton 1524, Chenies, is a well engraved full face figure with her hair flowing to her waist.

Amphillis Pekham 1545, Denham, and Wenefride Newport 1547, Greystoke, are dressed in a rather fanciful fashion, with long hair and wearing respectively the frontal part of the kennel and Paris Head.

Arrangement and composition: Figure arrangements

Leaving the description of figures for the overall arrangement of families and compositions, there is little evident change from the previous period. Most adults are dubiously recumbent though the application of shading and the occasional use of pavements as foot supports after 1550, give an increasingly vital impression. Hands are with few exceptions shown in an attitude of prayer, though at Stanstead Abbots c.1540 is one example of a husband and wife joining hands, and at Brown Candover, c.1510, the pair stand arm in arm, with a flower placed between their heads. The humble brass of Thomas Fytche 1514, Lindsell, has the hands in the orans position in profile. The largest canopied figures are highly traditional in arrangement. Kneeling figures are common, both with and without faldstools.

A comparison between rectangular plates of the period reveals gradual but significant changes. The earliest to Robert Honywode 1522, St George's Chapel Windsor, is entirely gothic in setting, with a canopy arch and St Margaret presenting the kneeling priest to the Blessed Virgin and Child, on a background of quatrefoils. Similarly Robert Sutton 1528, St Patrick's cathedral, Dublin, kneels to a defaced representation of the Holy Trinity, against a background of stars. The family group of John Haryson 1525, at St Mary Lowgate, Hull, kneel towards a defaced Holy Trinity, under a simple arch and against a hatched background. In none of these examples is there any attempt to define space or depth. Anne Danvers 1539, Dauntsey, kneels before the Holy Trinity in the confines of a room framed by a debased gothic arch, with a curtain background and receding tiled floor. More striking and certainly calculated are the settings of Geoffrey Fyche 1537, St Patrick's cathedral, Dublin, and Elizabeth Horne 1548, Shipton-under-Wychwood (*The Craft*, Figs. 220, 241). In these the interior of a room is depicted, the walls faced with linen-fold panels, and Fyche kneels before an altar above which a Pieta is placed. A transition to realistic pictorial treatment is evident, though such brasses are still unusual.

Supports to full-length 'recumbent' figures lack variety; most are grassy plots. There are a few animals. Lions, apparently copied from earlier 'F' patterns, are found, for example, at Mamble c.1500; Ashby St Legers, c.1506; Yealmpton 1508; and Longdon 1523. Dogs are rather more common. Hounds are shown at St Helen's Bishopsgate, London 1510; Cardington 1540; and Twyford 1550. Large round-eared and thick-coated dogs lie at the feet of women on the brasses noted at Longdon and Cardington. A curious little dog lies tied to a plant between the feet of Edward Cowrtney 1509, Landrake, Cornwall (it is very tempting to see this as an allusion to the Mandrake legend), and undoubtedly a pet dog is tied by a leash to the waist of Edmund Wayte 1518, at Renhold, Beds (*The Craft,* Fig. 217).

There are curiosities mainly of heraldic derivation. Most famous is the elephant and castle with a broomcod below the feet of William, Viscount Beaumont 1507, Wivenhoe. Less known but equally interesting is the fabulous calopus at Chesterfield 1529, granted as a cognisance in 1513 to Sir Godfrey Foljambe.[15] A magnificent male griffin lies below the feet of Sir Thomas Bullen, K.G. 1538, Hever, appropriate to him as Duke of Ormond. Sheep and woolpacks below Thomas Bushe and wife 1526, maintain the Northleach series of trade emblems. A squirrel plays on the gown of Lady Katherine Howard 1535, St Mary Lambeth, and it is not surprising that a cat lies below Sir Richard Catesby 1553, at Ashby St Legers. The introduction of tiled pavements below the feet, as on the brass of Richard Fermer, Easton Neston, indicates a further drift from traditional representation, though in this case the esquire's head rests on his helmet with cock's head crest.

Head supports are almost exclusively confined to military figures. Helmets are frequently used to support the head, occasionally bearing extravagant crests. Rafe Dellvys 1513, Wybunbury, shows a large winged crane and John Acworth 1513, Luton, a hand throttling a serpent. A very large helm with ornamental sight, supports Thomas Broke 1518, Ewelme, and Sir Thomas Bullen, rests against a helm of fine design and realistic size, with torse, crest and mantling. Many of the close-helmets shown behind the heads of 'Gyfford' and 'Fermour' figures are so small, as to appear absurd. The cushion behind the head of the Scarisbrick figure c.1500, Ormskirk, has no parallel in this period.

Canopies

Canopies are uncommon and form a miscellaneous collection in quality and design. All are oppressively heavy in treatment with wide shafts and pinnacles and bulbous crockets and finials. Canopies of coarse but conventional pattern are found with triple pediments at Winwick c.1505; with double pediments at Ardingly c.1500 and 1504; Cobham 1506; Hillingdon 1509; Nayland c.1510; and Little Wenham 1514; and with a single pediment at Ightfield c.1500; and Chenies 1510. A single Gothic style canopy enclosed Bishop Goodryke at Ely cathedral as late as 1554. The Cobham and Hillingdon canopies are the best executed though several of the others have good details especially in the oculi. Shields bearing Passion emblems and the Sacred Wounds appear at Cobham and inscribed ones at Ardingly 1504. Two curious faces, one male and the other female, stare from the oculi at Little Wenham (*The Craft,* Fig 216).[16*] The Ightfield canopy bears a figure of St John the Baptist in place ofa final, and at Cobham the Holy Trinity is imposed upon the central shaft. In three brasses, at Slaugham 1503, Ashby St Legers c.1506, and Islington 1540, canopies of an earlier date seem to have been utilised.

Three canopies belonging to brasses of the 'debased F' series are more original in style. Margaret Bulcley 1528, Sefton, has a canopy with a double pediment of peculiar pattern. Thomas Bushe and wife 1526, at Northleach, show the pediments filled with sheep standing and lying under the bushes with the arms of the Staple of Calais above, in allusion to the trade and name of the deceased. The pediments of the canopies of the Hatche brass 1535, Faversham, are filled with very large roses. A fourth canopy, but of the 'G' series, above John Cook and wife at St Mary de Crypt, Gloucester, was originally of three pediments, the central one supporting a large tabernacle (still existing) with a figure of St John the Baptist.

The most elaborate canopies emulate the earlier patterns with saint-filled side shafts and embattled super-canopies. Fragments of only four exist. Two of these are at Wivenhoe over the brasses of William Viscount Beaumont 1507, and his widow Lady Elizabeth, who later married the Earl of Oxford and died in 1537. Both brasses have been stripped of their side shafts, which undoubtedly contained figures. The pediments and super-canopies remain, decorated in the earlier example with elephants. The other two are at Hereford cathedral. Dean Frowsetoure's brass 1529, is complete, though worn and remarkably ugly. It is Gothic in design but distorted with early Renaissance ornament. The shafts contain some unusual representations, including the Hereford saint, Ethelbert, and the Holy Trinity shown as three persons. The other brass, to William Porter, S.T.B., Warden of New College, Oxford 1524, is a wreck but much of the canopy survives. This was a most interesting brass, in which Renaissance influence is strong and the detail most unusual. The central pediment consists of a canopied recess with a large scene of the Annunciation. Some of the remaining figure groups from the shafts are excellent, including St Catherine, a spirited St George and the decollation of St John the Baptist. This important and valuable brass was one of the many losses by neglect at Hereford during the eighteenth century.[18] An adaptation of such canopies in miniature is that framing the votive composition of William Taylard 1505, at Diddington, damaged but still retaining its saint filled shafts.

Additional ornament

Cross and bracket brasses disappear altogether from the products of the London workshops, though emblem crosses and other types of emblem brasses were laid and are described in Chapter Fourteen. The inlay of slabs with a background of scrolls or devices again passed out of fashion. The brass of John Symondes and wife 1512, Cley, contained nine scrolls inscribed 'now thus', but this is a solitary example. Representations of sacred subjects addressed with precatory scrolls, are numerous until 1540 and especially common among kneeling compositions. These are described in Chapter Fifteen. The Evangelists' symbols are frequently set in quadrilobe medallions or circular plates at the angles of marginal inscriptions or independently. These gradually fell into disuse by the close of the period; beasts take their place on the Coryton brass 1551, St Mellion, and floral devices on the Magnus brass 1550, Sessay. The wanton destruction of many brasses at the dissolution of the monasteries and the suppression of the chantries between 1536 and 1550, and increasing objections to popular religious symbolism on the part of small but active elements in the population, may have influenced the executors and engravers to eschew details of a possibly provocative kind.

Heraldry

Shields of arms were invariably laid where appropriate and are an important element in many brasses. It was an age of many quarterings of shields and in consequence their composition is often highly involved and the heraldry complex. Shields are perforce wider and less pointed than in earlier periods and some have a decorative shape. A large and good example, still preserving part of its inlay, is set above John Gille 1546, Wyddial. Rare 'tilting shields' are found at Fairford on the tomb of John Tame 1500. Achievements of arms are uncommon, examples being at Wilne 1513, Watton-at-Stone 1514, Winwick 1527 and Thames Ditton 1559. A row of five small shields for the daughters' marriages is set with three others on the brass of John Shelley 1550, Clapham. Arms and inscriptions are frequently found forming complete memorials, especially good examples being those of Sir William Sydney 1553 and Margaret Sydney 1558, Penshurst, and John Croke 1554, Chilton.

Arms of the London Guilds occur more frequently. The Mercers' arms are shown at Higham Ferrers, St Olave, Hart St., West Drayton and Lambourne. The arms of the Goldsmiths' Company are represented on a shield at Sandon. At Lowestoft is an interesting shield c.1540 showing the old arms of the Fishmongers of London as used before their union in 1512 with the Stockfishmongers who dealt in salt fish. The arms of the Fishmongers, as granted after the union, are found at Wooburn. The arms of the Drapers' allude to the Incarnation of Christ and to the Assumption-Coronation of His Mother and are shown at Newark and Walthamstow. The arms of the Merchant Taylors were first granted in 1481 but were altered in 1586 and the earlier arms appear on the tomb of Hugh Pemberton 1500 at St Helen's, Bishopsgate, and at Standon 1557. The arms of the Grocers' Company appear on the brass of Rauf Greneway 1558, Wiveton. However, unless it is known that people buried outside of London were members of the London companies this cannot be assumed from the appearance of the arms of their "occupation", as the coats of the companies are called in contemporary wills.

The arms of the great trading companies: the Merchant Staplers and the Adventurers, have several illustrations. The arms of the Staple are found at Wrangle, St Olave, Hart St., Wooburn, Northleach, West Drayton and Chicheley, those of the Merchant Adventurers at Tiverton, and Chacombe.

The civic arms of London and Bristol are at Walthamstow; the arms of the Cinque Ports at Canterbury Museum and Faversham; and those of the University of Cambridge, King's and Eton Colleges, with his own arms, are engraved on a plate to John Stokys 1559 at King's College.

Merchants' marks, monograms and rebuses

Merchants' or trade marks are as common as in the fifteenth century. The bold separately inlaid device of Walter Hichman 1521, Kempsford, takes the form of a double tau cross. Thomas Horton c.1520, Bradford-on-Avon, has a mark resembling a cross bow, which in Girling's view was based on an instrument used for handling wool sacks.[18] However that may be, the family arms, granted later in the century, incorporated a cross-bow — no doubt inspired by the merchant mark.

Marks with initials are preserved at Thame, 1502, and Minchinhampton, 1519. Other good marks are at Wrangle, 1503; Brightlingsea 1521; Northleach 1526; Faversham 1533; and Lambourne 1546. Shields bearing crossed arrows and a hunting horn are set above Thomas Forest, park-keeper, and wife 1511, Chaddesley Corbett.

Monograms or a rebus are occasionally introduced. An instance of the first occurs on the brass of Robert Serche 1501, Northleach. An excellent example of the latter is the cross with arms terminating in tuns for Edmund Croston 1507, St Mary-the-Virgin, Oxford. Two angels hold tuns, with the letters 'J cum' above for John Compton 1505, Beckington. A rectangular plate with a tun between the initials R and L (above and below) allude to Robert Langton c.1518, at The Queen's College, Oxford. At Redbourne a mutilated peacock gives interest to the dull brass of Richard Pecok 1512.

Inscriptions

Inscriptions of the period gradually changed in form and content, and by 1560 were significantly different from those of the first twenty years. Gothic black letter scripts were almost invariably used, but lost their uniform appearance, especially the capital letters. Small but very distinct differences can be traced, not merely among brasses of different dates, but among brasses of the same date and of apparently similar figure patterns. Slightly flamboyant detail gives character to scripts, and, as Page-Phillips has suggested, may well distinguish the engraver. The surface of inscriptions, especially in horizontal compositions, is often cut away leaving the lettering in relief. English with very free spelling gradually became the most commonly used language, though there are many inscriptions in Latin, and some, such as John Reed 1503, Wrangle, where the marginal inscription is in English and the rectangular foot plate in Latin verse. In a few cases (e.g. the macaronic verses for William Lawnder c.1510, Northleach) Latin and English are mixed.

The content of inscriptions is of considerable interest and deserving of a more detailed analysis than can be given here. Some are simple statements of fact, as that of Reginald Tylney 1506, Leckhampstead:

Hic iacet Regenoldus Tylney gentylman fili*us* secund*us* Radulfi tylney Civis et Alderman*us*

London*iensis* & un*us* heres isti*us* Maner*ij* qui obiit tercio die Maij A⁰ d*omi*ni M CCCCC VI

The majority, however, open or close with a request for prayers on behalf of the deceased. These conventions continue down to the last ten years of the period. The inscription of William Foxe and wife 1554, Ludford, with its record of previous benefactions to the church and concluding prayer, is traditional in character.

Here undernethe this Stone lyeth ye bodye of Wyllyam ffoxe of ludlowe yn
the Countye of Salop Esquyer and ffounder of this Ile adjeynyng unto this
Churche and which Wyll*iam* reedefyed the Almes Howse of Seynt Gyles beyng decayed, and
also Jane hys Wyff Doughter & heyre of Richard
Downe of ludlowe aforseyd. which Wyllyam decessyed the xxiiith daye of
Aprill Anno d*omi*ni MlCCCCC Liiii^0 + and the seyd Jane decessyd the (Blank)
day of (Blank) A^0 d*omi*ni (Blank) On Whose Soules Jh*es*u have mercy.

This is no expression of a Marian reaction to Catholic practice. There is no evidence of a general avoidance of phrases, that might provoke the resentment of Protestants, who only for a few years in the reign of King Edward VI exerted any official influence. In the first thirty years of the sixteenth century inscriptions ostentatiously express the tenets of the Catholic faith. The following inscription from Wooburn c.1520, set below shrouded figures (one now lost) and a representation of the Holy Trinity, is an excellent example both for its invocation and moral.

loke suche as we ar suche schall ye be
And suche as we were suche be [ye]
Of *that* which was unsur, now ar we steyne
O blissyd trinite save us fro*m* payne
Thought we be gone, & past out of mynde
As we wold be p*ra*yed for, pray for us
To the moost glorious trinite,
for ye be sure, when ye have all done
this paygant Schall ye play, ye ne wote how sone
Thorowe yow that we may have the mor mede
sey A pater noster, Ave and A Crede.

On the brass of Sir Thomas Barnadiston 1503, Great Coates, the requested prayers carry the promise of an indulgence.

& of yo*ur* charite say a p*ate*r noster ave & cred & ye schall have a C days of p*ar*don to yo*ur* med

It is, however, appropriate to compare this with the inscription of Anne Danvers 1539, Dauntsey, which despite the representation of the Holy Trinity above avoids specifically Catholic references.

What veyleth yt Riches or what possession
gyftes of high nature nobles in gentry
daftenes depuryd or pregnant pollycy
sith prowes sith power have their progression
ffate it is fatall on selff ssuccession
that world hath no thing *tha*t smellith not frealtie
where most assuraunce is most unsuertie
here lieth dame Anne the lady of dauntesey
to sir John danvers spowse in coniunction
To sir John dauntesey by lyne discencion
Cosyn and heire whose herytage highlye
fastely be firmed in Criste his mancion.

At the close of the period the inscription to Lady Mary Carew 1558, Kentisbeare, makes open statement of religious change referring to 'the most nobul and myghty prence Henry the VIII Kyng of England ffrance and Ireland defender of the feyth & immediately under God of the Churches of England & Ireland Supreme hede.'

The text from Job 19: 25-27, continued to be used on marginal inscriptions both in Latin and later in the English of the King's Primer of 1545. An example of the Latin text is set in chamfer on the tomb of Sir Robert Clyfford 1508, Aspenden. The English text occurs at Ossington 1551, and on the brass of Humfrey Cheynie 1557, West Hanney. The latter (from the Vulgate) is more complete and has at the corners the symbols of the Evangelists.

Many inscriptions give details of the rank and offices of the deceased. Sir John Huddilston, Sawston 1557, for instance, is described as a member of Queen Mary's 'most honorable pryvie counsell', and vice chamberlain and captain of the guard to King Philip. Others give the dates of death in detail, such as that of Christopher Bridgeman 1503, Thame, who died on 'holy rode day nexte before Mighelmas', or details of the cause of death. John and Anne Mohun, Lanteglos-by-Fowey engr. c.1525, are stated to have died within twenty-four hours of the sweating sickness.

Personal achievements, other than of a pious kind, are occasionally recorded. Sir John Clerk of North Weston 1539, Thame, is thus described: 'whyche toke Louys of Orleans duk of Longueville & Marquis of Rotuenlin prysoner at ye jorney of Bomy by Terouane'. This knight and his triumph are again mentioned in the inscription of his son Nicholas Clarke 1551, Hitcham, who 'dyed of the swett'. The date of death itself is sometimes related to the regnal, as well as, or instead of, the calendar year. An example of the former is at Clapham d.1526, and of the latter at Wyddial 1546. Changes in the content of inscriptions may be detected more in this increasing emphasis on the personal particulars of the deceased, then in slight modifications of religious expressions.

The decoration of marginal inscriptions with devices, fairly common in the fifteenth century, became rare in the early sixteenth. The inscription of Thomas Forest, park-keeper 1511, Chaddesley Corbett, is interspersed with oak leaves, arrows and horns. At Waterperry in the inscription of Walter Curson, another example of the Job text engr. c.1535, the words are separated by skulls and crossed bones.

Conclusion

Unlike the early sixteenth-century brasses of Flanders and Germany, many of which were conceived in accordance with the new ideas and objectives of the time, English brasses from London workshops adhered to well established patterns, changing only in their detailed presentation and evolving rather than breaking away from mediaeval design. Their record is of a very slow transition, impeded by smallness of scale, the insignificance of those commemorated and declining standards of execution. The wealth of examples emphasizes their repetitive character. It is therefore all the more fortunate that the craft was not exclusively confined to London. Provincial workshops flourished as in the late fifteenth century, equally conservative in their designs but very different in their artistic conventions. The achievement of these provincial centres during the century 1460 to 1560 is next examined.

13. English brasses: the provincial workshops, 1460-1560

The variety in the form and design of English brasses from 1450 to 1550 is very largely explained by the activity of engravers in the provinces, using different patterns to those of their contemporaries in London. Provincial brasses are often described as 'local', a term unobjectionable in itself but one which has acquired the connotation of unusual, peculiar and inferior. This inference is misleading. While engravers in such towns as York, Norwich, Bury St Edmunds and Cambridge were rarely favoured with orders from the eminent or very wealthy, the execution of their best work was in no way inferior to that of London, and the artistic merit of their designs was at times arguably superior. It is easy to assume that London styles are 'normal', and to regard divergent patterns as curiosities. Viewed however from the provincial centre, it is the local style which is normal, and in harmony with the art of the region. Provincial workshops may be most effectively described in their geographical context, arising in the North and North East, East Anglia, the South East, the West and the Midlands.

In writing this chapter particular acknowledgment is made to J. R. Greenwood, not only for an exchange of views over many years, but also for the benefit of his extensive current research into the East Anglian workshops.

York Workshops

It is all but certain that brass engraving was practised by northern craftsmen from the early fourteenth century, and towards the end of that century their activity is confirmed. Between 1460 and c.1485 examples are sufficiently consistent in style and conventions to form at least one recognizable series. Knowles has drawn comparison between fifteenth-century brasses in Yorkshire and the glass of the York painters, and suspected the participation of German craftsmen. Certain pecularities of costume and armour occur in both brass and glass, in particular the prominent bevors and sallets of the knights.[1] These features also occur in German drawings and monuments of the period. It is nevertheless unlikely that foreigners were involved in this work. The peculiarities are sufficiently explained by the current influence of Continental designs on the glass painters, who were perhaps involved in the brass patterns. Both this and the distribution of the brasses point to York as the main centre of engraving. York was the most prosperous city in northern England, celebrated among many crafts for its goldsmiths, bellfounders and glass painters. The bellfounders of York were particularly active, and one of the most interesting of the Minster windows represents their craft. They were possibly concerned in the engraving of memorials, though the earliest established engraver of a brass in York was a goldsmith.

The best known examples from the North are a closely associated group of armed figures, almost certainly engraved in York city. The most distinctive feature of these slim and artistically designed figures is their elongated and severe presentation. Their heads are protected by deep sallets, their faces peer over very high bevors which almost cover the mouth and their feet thrust downwards in long sabatons. The detail of the armour is unusual, especially the reinforcing plates on the pauldrons. Their wives are usually very simply represented in veil headdress, gown and mantle. The overall treatment is austere in comparison to London or East Anglian patterns. The military figures are:

Sir John Langton and wife, 1459, St Peter, Leeds
William Burgh, the Elder d.1442, and Younger 1465, Catterick[2*]
Richard Ask and wife, 1466, Aughton
Henry Rochforth 1470, Stoke Rocheford, (*The Craft*, Fig. 224)
William Fitzwilliam and wife, 1474, Sprotborough (Fig. 202).

Henry Rochforth is particularly elaborate, with decorative flutings in his armour and sallet. The Catterick figures have their sallets behind their heads, an unexpected treatment of this particular style of helmet. In spite of considerable differences in equipment and detail, these figures are clearly in the tradition of the early fifteenth-century brasses at Lowthorpe and Harpham.

Contemporary with these, and judged by its inscription from the same workshop, is the brass of Thomas Tonge, LL.B 1472, Beeford (*The Craft*, Fig. 221). He is depicted in amice, alb and a cope of Italian cut velvet or brocade with a bold pattern, holding a clasped book in front of him. A very similar brass, now lost, to John Lewelyne c.1470, existed at Romaldkirk. This arrangement, unusual in England, is commonly found on Flemish and French incised slabs.

The script on these brasses and on other inscriptions in York is distinctive of which William Hancock and wife 1485, St Michael, Spurriergate, and Isabel Stokton d.1503, engr. c.1471, All Saints, North Street, are good examples. The clean cut, bold lettering is recognisably different from London style, and its local character appears obvious in York itself where examples are grouped. Other brasses of the period presumably engraved in York, include three chalices described in the following chapter, and a chrysom plate at Sheriff Hutton (see Chapter Sixteen).

It is surprising that later provincial figure brasses in the North, at least until the middle of the sixteenth century, defy classification. They are isolated works, the individuality of which is perhaps explained by the losses involved in the suppression of the religious houses in the region. An armed figure attributed to Sir John Norton 1489, Wath, is worn, but is sufficiently distinctive in treatment to indicate York provenance. Two shrouded figures c.1500, Sedgefield, are presumably northern work; but there are insufficient reasons to attribute them to York. Similarly at Middleton, are two brasses, Edmund Assheton, priest 1522, and Alice Laurence 1531, with two of her husbands in armour, which are unusual. Edmund holds a chalice and is rather well engraved (*The Craft*, Fig. 229), having some affinities to midland style. In the absence of any conventional northern type or design at this period it is only possible to speculate on their source. A mutilated and palimpsest composition to (?) Sir Christopher Hildyard and wife 1538, Winestead, is more probably of York workmanship, but here again the attribution would be convenient rather than convincing.

The northern engravers have the longest traceable history of all the provincial craftsmen, and it is unfortunate that at no particular stage, except in the third quarter of the fifteenth century, have their works survived in substantial numbers. Unless documentary evidence is traced it will remain difficult to envisage the extent or scope of their activity.

North Eastern Workshops

Brasses of provincial origin in Lincolnshire present a confusing miscellany, compelling caution in attribution. It is known that John Hippis, marbler, maker in 1515 of the Willoughby tomb with brass inlays at Wollaton, worked at Newark-on-Trent in 1507 and Lincoln in 1515.[3*] He was undoubtedly an engraver of some standing. Concentration of examples also indicates that Stamford was for a period an engraving centre, which might be expected of such a thriving and well situated mediaeval town. The existing brasses however have little consistency in style, and some are apparent copies of London or other models. This derivative quality has already been noted in certain early fifteenth century examples, and scepticism is aroused over a few brasses which must for the present be accepted as London work.

Local Lincolnshire style, in as much as it can be established, is shown by the brasses of Nicholas Byldysdon and wife 1489 at St John, Stamford (Fig. 203) and Nicholas Robertson and two wives 1498, at Algarkirk. The latter is a plain, slightly comical but sensitive design, the artistry of which is best perceived in the half figure representation of the Blessed Virgin and Christ Child. A mutilated priest in mass vestments, Henry Sargeaunt 1497, at St John, Stamford, also appears to be by the same hand. Two female figures are at Lyddington 1486, and Holbeach 1488,[4*] The first is a well engraved semi-profile representation which is by no means conclusively 'local'. Its peculiarities only appear when compared closely with conventional London treatment of the pattern. In contrast, a brass of an unknown coped priest c.1490, at Fiskerton, is coarse in treatment, and undoubtedly provincial work.

Brasses from the first half of the sixteenth century include armed figures at Horncastle and Scrivelsby, a girl with flowing hair 1522, at Mablethorpe, and a priest 1536, at Rauceby. Sir Lionel Dymoke d.1519, at Horncastle, is depicted kneeling, with his representation in death close by. The inscription is finely executed, and its lettering and two children groups would establish the brasses as Suffolk work. In contrast the figure, engraved on thinner plate, is less sure in treatment and may have a different origin. Much of both brasses is palimpsest, and the author would prefer an engraving date of c.1530.[5*] Sir Robert Demoke 1545, at Scrivelsby is a bold and inexpert design. His figure is both martial and venerable, but the construction of his armour, sword and other equipment, reveals the poorest draughtsmanship (*The Craft*, Fig. 222). The brass of Sir William Ayscough in armour and tabard, and wife in heraldic mantle, 1509, at Stallingborough, has been influenced by Norwich, Suffolk and London conventions, and may be yet another example of enterprising imitation.

Lincolnshire remains a problem area, requiring further research into inscriptions, indents and records. It is nevertheless clear that engravers were active within the county, competing for business with buyers who purchased freely from London, York, Norwich and Suffolk.

Norwich workshops

The city of Norwich was a centre of unique importance in East Anglia situated in a populous region of great wealth. Bellfounders, glass painters, goldsmiths and craftsmen of all sorts congregated in Norwich as in York, producing works of art of a definite provincial style. The participation of many aliens, and close trading relationships between Norfolk and Flemish towns, influenced the character of this style, which is most satisfactorily studied in painted glass and the painted screen panels which survive in large numbers.

Norwich was undoubtedly the most prolific centre of brass engraving outside London, a claim supported by surviving examples and records of lost memorials. The identity of the engravers has yet to be established. Attention has long been drawn to the Brasyer or Brasier family, who were the most successful Norwich bell founders. Robert Brasyer was Mayor of Norwich in 1410 and died in 1435. His son Richard was twice Mayor, and his grandson Richard was Mayor in 1510. The elder Richard was admitted a freeman in 1424, as 'Ric*ardus* Brasyer Goldsmyth, fil*ius* Rob*er*ti Brasyer Belzet*er*.' The younger Richard died in 1513 having earlier left instructions for the laying of brasses to his father, grandfather, his wife and to himself, which still remain at St Stephen's Church. The Brasyer foundry stood near the junction of Red Lion St., Rampant Horse Lane and Little Orford St. The combination of titles, goldsmith, brazier and bellfounder applied to members of the family, increases the likelihood that they worked in a variety of media. There is nevertheless no conclusive evidence in their favour, and Richard's will, which has been cited as proof, shows no more than an interest in brasses. It states 'Item I will that my executors do bye a marble ston with a picture *ther*uppon with my Armys and ij ymages j for me and An oder for my wif. Item I will that my executors bye A marbull ston with a picture *ther*uppon with myn Armys for my faders grave. Item I will that my executors do sett ij ymages on my graunfers grave with his Armys'[6] The term 'bye' proves intended purchase from an independent source.

While some participation of the bellfounders is likely, there is evidence that marblers and latteners were active in the city, craftsmen most usually associated with brass engraving. A lattener, Thomas Gelyngham and a marbler Thomas Sheef are entered in the Freeman's List for 1454.[7] Though included in the goldsmith's section the descriptions 'Latoner' and 'marbeler' have been written in the margin. Equally interesting are references to Richard Foxe, marbler d.1497, who had relations with a Thomas Storme, notary public and Proctor of the Consistory Court, the latter bequeathing "as many two feet marbles as would pave the ground by the altar of our Lady" to St George Tombland.[8] William Thacker was another marbler, working in the first half of the sixteenth century.

Current research by Greenwood is concerned with a glazier, William Heyward, who received an order in 1504 for a marble with brass from a parson of East Harling, the indent of which still exists.[9] Heyward was most probably involved in the designing and possibly the engraving of the important third Norwich series, which has marked stylistic affinity to Norwich glass of the period.

There are no brasses of established Norwich provenance of the fourteenth century. The inscription of Richard-at-the-Gates 1427, St Laurence, Norwich, is engraved in a bold and unusual style. In the same church a fragment of a marginal inscription with a symbol of St Luke appears to be of local workmanship in imitation of foreign design. The width of the fragment, its outer border of flowers and the symbol itself reflect Flemish influence, and this may even be an unusual example of Flemish work. Identifiable series of brasses become clear after 1440, and among examples dating from then until c.1550 Greenwood has traced six substantial series, presenting different figure patterns and scripts. An apparent seventh series has been established on the basis of script but only two figure brasses seem to belong to it.

Among the earliest dated figure brasses which reveal peculiarities setting them apart from known London work, is that of Thomas Roose and family 1441, Sall, which is the precursor of the first Norwich series (Fig. 204). He bears many resemblances to London civilians of the 'D' or 'E' series. The cut of his tunic, laced shoes and short cropped hair are according to the usual pattern. But there the likeness ends. The features of Thomas' face are closely drawn, and his eyes are rather wide. His hands are broad but taper sharply to the finger tips. His visible shoe is large and his right foot protrudes as a prominent feature. The drapery folds on both adult figures are exceedingly stiff. Two large groups of children are set out in front of their parents. The family group is placed on an inscription, supported by an elaborate cusped bracket, the canopies and stem of which are now lost.

The stylistic peculiarities of these figures, the treatment of the hands, the drapery falling in close almost parallel folds, and the somewhat embarrassed expressions of the faces, are found in more pronounced forms on a considerable number of brasses between 1450 and 1480. They may be regarded as the distinguishing features of the first period of Norwich designs. Figures of this type are invariably associated with inscriptions of a recognisable style. A detail common to several of these brasses is the large flowers and ferns growing upon their grassy footrests. The following are other civilian and female examples in this group:

John Asger, d.1436 engr. c.1445, St Laurence, Norwich
Two wives of John Funteyn, 1453, Sall
Roger Felthorp and family, 1454, Blickling
Ralph Segrym, mayor and wife, d.1472 ?engr. c.1455, St John Maddermaket, Norwich
Unknown and wife c.1460, Stalham
Thomas Bokenham, 1460, St Stephen, Norwich
Lady c.1460, Frettenham
Edmund Bryghtye, half effigy, 1467, Barnham Broom
John Puttock and wife, 1469, Thwaite All Saints
Henry Barnabe, wife lost, c.1470, Cley
William Norwiche, mayor, wife and son, on bracket, 1472, St George Colegate, Norwich
John Everard, half effigy, 1476, Halesworth
William Pepyr and wife, 1476, St John Maddermarket
Anne Boleyn, 1479, Blickling
Margaret Wyllughby, d.1483, Raveningham (*The Craft,* Fig. 50).

Segrym and Norwiche as mayors are both shown wearing civic mantles. Margaret Willughby is an unusual and transitional figure. A finely represented butterfly headdress, the collar of suns and roses, large fur mittens, and a dragon at her feet as well as a dog are particularly good details.

Figures in armour of this style are easily recognized. Faces show the same peculiarities, armour is represented as ridged and articulated in the exaggerated 'Gothic' style of German origin. Pauldrons appear to rise to a point or ridge on the shoulder, couters are small, and greaves composed of several plates. Lions set at the feet have a merry look. The finest of these figures recorded was that of Sir Miles Stapleton and wives d.1466, formerly at Ingham, which is illustrated by Cotman, but only the indent and canopy fragments remain.[10] Sir John Curson and wife 1471, Bylaugh, are very similar to the lost Ingham figures (Fig. 205). In addition to shields of arms the brass is decorated with four scrolls bearing the motto 'yenk' (think). The slender and rather inadequate sword slung across the front of the body is characteristic of these brasses. Other figures in armour are:

Unknown (worn), c.1475, Swaffham
Ralph Blenerhaysett, 1475, Frenze
John Bomsted, 1479, Sotterley

The figure of Sir Henry Grey c.1470, Ketteringham, is now lost though his wife Emma survives. Henry Unton 1470, Sculthorpe, is of the same type, but kneels in semi-profile, a valuable but renewed example.[11*]

The ecclesiastics of this group are mainly small figures in mass vestments of enveloping dimensions. Their faces and hands are represented in a similar manner, though their hair is arranged in tufts above the ears. Four Norfolk examples are:

Robert Dockyng, 1465, Wood Dalling
Stephen Multon, 1477, Swanton Abbott
Ralph Fuloflove, 1479, West Harling
Edmund Kelyng, half eff., 1479, East Dereham.

Two coped figures create problems. John Norton with his mother (now lost) and father at South Creake d.1509, appear to be an appropriation, as the figures are clearly some thirty years older than the inscription. John is now headless but carries a crozier, which would indicate monastic status, if in fact his effigy was designed for his use. Secondly, at Winchester College, is the figure of Robert Thurberne, Warden d.1450, which was accurately restored after theft in 1875. The situation of the brass is far from Norwich, but the face, hands and drapery create the impression that it is of East Anglian origin, or at least strongly influenced by a Norwich pattern.[12*]

Another memorial related to these examples is a skeleton 1452, at St Laurence, Norwich. This, together with other shroud brasses and cadavers of Norwich work, are described in Chapter Sixteen.

The brasses of the Norwich engravers became very numerous between the years 1480 and 1500, and may be grouped into a second and third series. The second was seemingly influenced by that already described. The figures are usually shown full face, decoration is restrained and the presentation of human features and drapery is stiff, formal and inexpert. Fingers are shown as being of equal thickness to the observer. Noses are narrow and mouths small. Hair, whether for knight, civilian, or tonsured priest, is depicted thick and projecting around the ears. Robert Herward 1481, Aldborough, is an armed example. Elizabeth Berney d.1474, Reedham, and a civilian and wife c.1485, Euston, are good of their type. Norfolk priests at Great Ringstead 1482; St Laurence, Norwich 1483; Sparham c.1485; Sharrington 1486; and the Norwich Museums 1487;[13] all wear enveloping vestments without maniple or stole. The spirited shrouded pair at Brampton, d.1468, were probably engraved c.1483, and certainly belong to the second series (Fig. 242). William Berdewell and wife, c.1490, West Harling, is an armed representation belonging to this series, but showing transitional influences especially in his stance and long hair. A group of chalice brasses belonged to this series, and are discussed with later examples in the next chapter.

Brasses of the third series are of superior workmanship, and are collectively the finest products of the provincial engravers. Their merit does not depend on scale which is, with few exceptions, modest. The execution of the figures is confident and patterns artistic. Faces are well expressed, several having marked character, while hands are shown with fingers tapering towards the tips or, as a variation in more natural presentations, held up and apart in adoration. Costume is shown in simple forms, but enriched with areas of attractive detail. The influence of contemporary Flemish conventions is strong, and the relationship of the patterns of brass and glass are exceedingly close. The Grey figures at Merton, the Hevenynghams at Ketteringham, and a Wingfield at Letheringham, may be compared with the kneeling donors and other armed figures in the east window of East Harling.[14] The fur of civilians such as John Wellys, St Laurence, Norwich, is exactly reproduced on roundels at St George Tombland in the city.

The most ambitious brass of the third series is that of Joan, Lady Cromwell engr. c.1490, Tattershall (Fig. 207). Joan is depicted in court dress, with mantle, ermine-lined surcoat and loose hair. Among the saints in the canopy shafts are the East Anglian martyr King Edmund, and St George, whose extravagant armour has similarities with the screen panel painting of him at Filby. The inscription is in the typical script of the series, and insignificant in the grand design. A far smaller figure of a comparable pattern is at Felbrigg probably commemorating an unmarried girl c.1490.

No other brass of the series approaches this scale, but some are of intrinsically finer workmanship. Four men in armour are notable:

Edmund Clere with wife, 1488, Stokesby (*The Craft*, Fig. 225)
A Wingfield, one of three brothers, c.1490, Letheringham
William Grey with two wives, kneeling, 1495, Merton

Thomas Hevenyngham, Esq., with wife, 1499, Ketteringham
(*The Craft,* fig. 227).

The first of these is well known for its representation of the sallet and bevor, the last for its gilding and delicate execution. Four armed figures at Warham All Saints d.1474, Whissonsett d.1484 and c.1495 and Honing, are a closely related group, and apparently engraved between c.1490-1496. Only the last has a sword, which hangs directly in front between his legs, in the manner of the Letheringham figure. In all cases the armour is fluted and ridged, and at Whissonsett a bevor realistically covers the mouth.

Civilians, both male and female, are well represented. John Wellys, mayor 1495, St Laurence, Norwich, is perhaps the best (*The Craft,* Fig. 226), showing the rich fur-lined mantle thrown back on the left side. It is altogether a masterly representation. The bust of the Virgin, on the arms of the Mercers' company with him, should be compared with the figure of Joan Lady Cromwell. The widow Margaret Copuldyk engr. c.1495, Harrington, has very close similarities to Wellys in treatment. The following are other good examples:

Philip Bosard and wife, 1490, Ditchingham
Unknown and wife c.1490, Occold
Richard Richards, 1493, Aldborough
Robert Doughty and wife, three quarter effigy, 1493, Metton
John Horslee and wife, 1495, Norwich Museums, formerly St Swithin
Henry Spelman and wife, 1496, Narborough
Woman c.1498, Great Ellingham
Unknown mayor or alderman and wife c.1498, St Andrew, Norwich
Thomas Pallyng and wife, 1503, Clippesby.

Others are at Little Walsingham with wife, 1485, with wife ?c.1490 and c.1490, Bawburgh 1500 and Mattishall c.1500.

There is a wealth of attractive detail displayed by this group, especially in regard to dress. The first has his family set in front of the adults, an arrangement reflected on an important palimpsest reverse c.1495 at Snettisham. Spelman and the St Andrew's figure wear the civic mantle. Curteys shows the penner and inkhorn. Several have large bags, that at Aldborough being the most prominent. Maude Doughty at Metton has a late representation of the horned headdress. Fine pendants and ornaments are a feature of the women. The two most attractive are early examples of the series — Isabel Cheyne 1485, Blickling, and Anne Herward 1485, Aldborough. Their presentation of female dress of this period is among the best on brasses.

Two ecclesiastics belonging to this series are Adam Outlawe 1503, West Lynn, and the figure only of Thomas Capp D.C.L.1545, St Stephen, Norwich. The first is well depicted in mass vestments, but without stole and maniple, the inscription being in relief lettering. The other, represented in cope, has been identified by Greenwood as a blatant appropriation, lying close to another in the same church. A large academic c.1490, in hood and pileus, is preserved in the Cambridge Museum of Archaeology and Anthropology. Among shrouded figures of the series, discussed separately, are skeletons at Aylsham, and a woman at Great Fransham.

In the early years of the sixteenth century the important third series declines, being joined by a fourth and fifth, while running concurrently at the end of the fifteenth century with yet another, which Greenwood suggests may be the seventh. The last is unimportant is terms of surviving examples, the only established figures being those of Richard Rysle and wife, 1497, at Great Cressingham and a civilian with two wives at East Tuddenham. These appear to be attempted imitations of third series patterns, but have characteristics discernably different from those described.

The fourth and fifth series both register a marked decline in the quality of their design, and the fifth in terms of execution. Whereas the third series produced vital compositions, frequently with an element of realism, fourth series designs appear decorative and formalistic. The engraving is frequently deep, but excessive and meaningless shade effects are attempted, faces have prominent lips, and the drawing of armour and drapery is imaginative. Arrangements are introduced which influence the sixth series, namely the raising of women's dresses at the back to facilitate walking, and the placing of the hands so that only the finger tips touch. The masterpiece of the fourth series, and the most elaborate brass of the early sixteenth century in England, is the memorial of Sir Roger le Strange 1506, Hunstanton (Fig. 208). The knight wears armour and tabard, his hands raised in adoration, revealing the strapping of the gauntlets. His head rests on a cushion, and above is set a crested helm, the mantling of which obtrusively fills the space within the canopy. His legs are wide spread, the feet set on a mound covered with flowers, wavy vegetation and grass. The shafts of the heavy triple canopy enclose figures of ancestors similarly armed, perhaps in imitation of the Hastyngs brass at Elsing. A broad and rich bracket supports the main figure within the canopy. It is an ornate and remarkable conception, unsatisfactorily balanced and integrated but undeniably impressive.

Other comparable armed figures are at Frenze, 1510, and Rougham c.1510, the latter depicted with wife and children, together forming a very boldly cut group. The central placing of the sword occurs again on these examples.

Interesting civilian figures are those of Roger and William Bozard 1505, Ditchingham; Richard Brasyer, mayor d.1435, and wife engr. c.1513, and Robert and Richard Brasyer, mayor engr. c.1513, St Stephen, Norwich; and the figures in semi-profile of John Hook and wife 1513, Upper Sheringham. The orans position of the hands is adopted on both Brasyer brasses. Ecclesiastics of the series are found at Cley c.1512, and East Rainham 1522. The first, John Yslyngton, S.T.P., holds a chalice and wears a cassock with scarf and rosette, together with a pileus. The other, Robert Godfrey, L.L.B. is similarly dressed, but is a transitional example, and associated with the series by inscription rather than figure design. While there is no evidence that the scarf had academic significance, it appears from these examples that it may have had such a connotation in the eyes of the engravers.

Whereas the fourth series introduces conventions which were developed in the sixth, the fifth series appears to be an unsuccessful attempt to emulate the third. Existing examples date between 1502-1506, though in most cases inscriptions are lost or undated. Examples are civilians at East Rainham (Fig. 206), Wood Dalling 1504, Guestwick and Themelthorpe 1505, and Worstead; a worn priest in choir dress at Aylsham and a vowess at Witton (Blofield). In many respects the best is a shrouded priest 1505, at Bawburgh.[15]

The sixth series is a prolific finale to the significant output of the Norwich workshops. In addition to figure brasses large numbers of inscriptions, and inscriptions with arms and emblems, were laid, easily recognised by script, in which the capital O of Orate is particularly distinctive. Shields of arms, when associated with inscriptions alone, are frequently placed directly below and adjoining the inscription, an arrangement also found on earlier series.

The quality of draughtsmanship on these brasses is uneven, and excessive shading, coarse facial features, and a stiff arrangement of the hands, frequently lead to inartistic designs. Armed figures lie with their legs rather wide apart, the space intervening being filled with cross hatching. Armour is represented with little concern for form, and is valueless as a serious record. Wavy hair, verging on the 'frizzy', and long sea-weed like grass on the footrests compound the graceless effect.

The following are examples in armour:

Henry Palgrave and wife, 1516, Barningham Northwood
Edward Whyte and wife, 1528, Shotesham St Mary
Sir Robert Clere, 1529, Great Ormesby
John Wodehows and wife d.1465, engr. c.1530, Kimberley
John Brampton and two wives, 1535, Brampton.

Civilian brasses are remarkable for the treatment of their costume rather than the garments shown. Fur is usually expressed in long wavy lines, similar to the straggly grass on the foot rests. Most ladies wear kennel headdresses and the gown caught up at the back. Pomanders and ornaments suspended from belts are prominent. The most decorative of all civilian brasses commemorates a mayor, John Terry and family 1524, St John Maddermarket, Norwich, a highly unorthodox design punning on the name (*The Craft*, Fig. 228). The whole family is shown standing on brackets rising from a tree trunk. Between the adults are the arms of Norwich city, the Merchant Adventurers and the Mercers combined with Terri's merchant mark. This brass may be compared with inferior Flemish plates of the period, in particular Antonine Willebaert 1522, at St Jacques, Bruges (Fig. 123). The following are further interesting examples.

A wife of John Caus, d.1506, St John Maddermarket, Norwich
Nicholas Wren and wife, 1511, Worlingham
Anne Asteley with two chrysoms, 1512, Blickling
Margeret Pettwode (worn), 1514, St Clement, Norwich
Margaret Counforth, 1518, Cromer
Civilian and two wives, on bracket, c.1520, St Mary Tower, Ipswich
James at Hylle, c.1520, Guestwick
John Marsham, Mayor, and wife, on bracket, 1525, St John Maddermarket, Norwich
John Deynes and wife, 1527, Beeston Regis (Fig. 209)
A civilian, with a running sheep, c.1530, Wilby
Elizabeth Rokewode, 1533, Weston Longville
Civilian and wife, c.1545, Little Walsingham.

There is considerable variation in quality among these examples. The Guestwick figure is poorly designed and engraved, whereas those at Beeston Regis and Weston are well finished, the former displaying a seaman's whistle, the latter a pectoral cross.

Small and exceptionally inartistic Norfolk brasses are the three quarter length figures at Wood Dalling 1518; Worstead 1520; Binham c.1525; and Yelverton, a girl 1525; the near bust of Alice Swane 1540 at Halvergate, and the kneeling Thomasine Palmer 1544, at Moulton St Mary.

Three ecclesiastics illustrate the style. A priest c.1530 in the Fitzwilliam Museum, Cambridge, and John Athowe 1531, Brisley, are in mass vestments, the latter (head mutilated) holding an elaborate rayed chalice. John Abarfeld 1518, Great Cressingham, wears surplice and almuce. Among shrouded figures, those at St Michael Coslany, Norwich, of Henry Scolows and wife are the most important.

The sixth Norwich series appears to end about 1551. A substantial and isolated figure brass both in date and style commemorates Robert Rugge and wife 1558, at St John Maddermarket, Norwich. Robert was twice mayor and wears a civic mantle over a long-sleeved gown. His wife wears a gown, caught up at the back, and a pedimental headdress, though the design is in places uncertain. The inscription is supported by a curious corbel. The brass is almost entirely palimpsest, made up apparently from pieces of memorials from the abbey of St Benet's, Hulme, which fell after dissolution into the hands of Rugge's brother, who had been the last abbot and became Bishop of Norwich.[16]

Little can be stated of the architectural features of this provincial work. The Tattershall and Hunstanton canopies have smaller pediments than contemporary London designs, but are in similar heavy style. Canopy fragments at Ingham d. 1466 have distinctive crockets but are otherwise unexceptional. Good indents of canopied brasses are at St Michael Coslany, Norwich, and Gressenhall. Brackets were evidently favoured and are well illustrated, most having large cusps and elaborate tracery, but short stems. Examples are at Sall 1441; St George Colegate, Norwich 1472; Hunstanton 1506; St Mary Tower, Ipswich c.1520; St John Maddermarket, Norwich 1524 and 1525. The latest of these, to Mayor John Marsham, is shaped like a one-legged table strewn with bones.

The Norwich engravers rapidly reduced their output after 1545, presumably on account of the destruction of brasses in the wake of religious change. Their work in the latter part of the century is of little merit. The period of their significant activity was accordingly confined to the hundred years from 1450 to 1550. During this period however they supplied the heavy local demand for such monuments throughout east and central Norfolk. Brasses of London origin are of course found, such as the civilians and wives c.1480 at Little Plumstead and 1526 at Mileham. Coastal ports, such as Cley, have a number of seaborne imports. In Norwich itself the provincial engravers dominated the business. The limited distribution of their work is explained by the reputation of London work, obtainable by those with contacts in the capital, and by the competition and proximity of other provincial workshops.

Cambridge workshops

It has long been recognised that substantial numbers of brasses were engraved in more southerly centres of East Anglia. Haines identified two local groups, one apparently the product of craftsmen in Bedford or Cambridge, the other from a workshop most probably in Suffolk. A detailed study of the first series, made by Greenwood, supports the Cambridge location.[17] While he points out the favourable position of this town in relation to fenland waterways, and the acquisition of stone for monuments, his case is primarily based on the distribution of an easily identified series of brasses, which cluster in the vicinity of Cambridge, or in places accessible from the town. Evidence of existing brasses is greatly strengthened by that of indents of the series, which are numerous in Cambridge, especially in St Mary-the-Great, and are hardly found outside Cambridgeshire, north Essex, north Hertfordshire and eastern Bedfordshire. It is clear that there was a substantial civic and academic clientele in Cambridge, and among merchants in cloth towns such as Saffron Walden. Seemingly a workshop, which only flourished c.1500-40, was established to meet the demand, though documentary evidence for either it or its craftsmen has yet to be found.

The simplicity of Cambridge design is recognisable in a few brasses which appear to date from the first ten years of the sixteenth century. The earliest example by date is that of Richard Carlyll and wife 1489, Campton. This is however too similar to examples of the 1520's to be convincing, and is most probably a retrospective commemoration. The armed figure of Thomas Grey c.1507 with wife, at Cople is undoubtedly in Cambridge style, though imitating a London design. More typical early examples are Richard Quadryng 1511 in armour, Outwell, and John Hyll and wife 1506, Wilburton.

Fortunately about 1515 the emergence of closely related brasses establishes the series. Many of its characteristics may be readily appreciated from the illustrated civilian and wives at Elmdon c.1530 (*The Craft*, Fig. 230). The figures are very clearly, simply and deeply engraved. Shade lines are few and foot-rests plain, lightly covered with grass, or engraved with tiles. Faces are oval-shaped with rather small eyes, and the bridge of the nose is undefined. The hands touch at the fingertips and the fingers bend, a concession to realism rightly emphasized by Greenwood. Fur, when applied to garments, has a distinctive treatment. Inscriptions have an easily recognisable script, in particular with regard to certain capitals such as A and S.

Four closely related figures in armour are:

William Cokyn and two wives, 1527, Hatley Cockayne (*The Craft*, Fig. 13)
John Fysher and wife, 1528, Clifton (*The Craft*, Fig. 14)
An armed figure with wife, c.1530, Metropolitan Museum of Art, New York
John Borrell, Sergeant-at-Arms, wife lost, 1531, Broxbourne
(*The Craft*, Fig. 28).

The first two armed figures are almost identical. The armour is expressed in flowing curved lines with little detail. Mail is represented by a mesh of crossed lines. The pear-shaped sword pommel is placed within the bend of the left arm. Borrell is fully armed with visored helmet and gauntlets, and holds his ceremonial mace of office.

Civilian figures are more numerous. The style of male costume is less ornate than on London or Norwich style brasses but gowns are shown of a voluminous type. Female costume is especially noteworthy. Many women are shown wearing a wide mob cap similar to a 'tam o'shanter'. A sash with trifoliate clasp is more often worn at the waist than a belt. Children are noticeably less regimented than on London groups, and arranged on rectangular plates. The chief examples, including a few transitional figures, are:

Thomas Brond and wife, 1515, Newport
Richard Water and wife, 1515, Swaffham Prior
Owyn Avap Schankyn and two wives, appropriated 1534, engr. c.1515, Astwood
William Byrd and wife, 1516, Wilburton
John Peyton, head restored, c.1520, Wicken
Unknown, c.1520, Littlebury
John Samwel and two wives, 1529, Offley
Unknown and three wives, c.1530, Hitchin
Unknown and two wives, c.1530, Elmdon (*The Craft,* Fig. 230)
Unknown and wife, c.1530, Hempstead
John Watson and wife, c.1530, Leake
Unknown and three wives, c.1530, Offley
Unknown in rich fur coat with book, c.1530, Saffron Walden (Fig. 210)
Unknown, wife lost, c.1535, Higham Ferrers
Thomas Perys and wife, 1535, Little Barford.

Figures of women dating from 1524, c.1530, c.1530 and c.1535, are respectively at Great Canfield and Great Chesterford, Stoke-by-Clare, and Wimpole.

The majority of ecclesiastical figures represent academics of Cambridge University. Robert Hacombleyn, Provost 1528, King's College, is an especially good representation is cassock, surplice and almuce. A large scroll issues from his hands to a shield bearing the Sacred Wounds. He was the donor of the great latten lectern in King's College, the rests of which are engraved with the symbols of the Evangelists, though not reconcilable in treatment with those on his brass. Other academics are:

A Doctor, three quarter figure, c.1500, St Mary-the-Less, Cambridge
John Argentein, D.D. and M.D. 1507, King's College, Cambridge
William Blakwey, M.A. kneeling, 1521, Little Wilbraham
William Taylard, LLD. kneeling, c.1530, Offard Darcy
An academic, c.1530, Trinity Hall, Cambridge
An academic, c.1535, Queen's College, Cambridge
An academic, c.1535, Christ's College, Cambridge.

The first two doctors wear the cappa clausa, shoulder-piece, hood and pileus. William Taylard is an interesting example of transition in academic dress with pileus, shoulder-piece and supertunica. William Blakwey, who holds a rosary, affords a profile view of the sleeveless tabard, which is also worn by the unknown academics who were presumably masters.

Two small parish priests, Thomas Hundon 1520, Langford, and William Richardson 1527, Sawston, are in mass vestments, the latter without stole and maniple, holding a chalice.

The Cambridge workshop apparently had a short lived existence, falling perhaps within the active life span of one master. Its brasses, appear to be routine shop work, which failed to attract the orders of persons of great wealth or consequence. Its merit lay in the appropriate simplicity of its patterns, presumably made by a local draughtsman. Compared with debased London design and the complexity of later Norwich work, the better products of the Cambridge series are a refreshing element in Tudor monumental art.

Bury St Edmund's workshops

The considerable number of brasses of provincial origin in Suffolk and very large numbers of distinctive indents, which can neither be related to Cambridge or Norwich series, may only be satisfactorily explained by the activity of engravers in Bury St Edmunds or Ipswich. The distribution of examples, which are primarily found in Suffolk and west Norfolk, supports the former, Ipswich being easily reached by sea from Norwich and London.

Bury St Edmunds, a town situated on the river Lark, a tributary of the Little Ouse, was the most important centre in East Anglia after Norwich, on account of the influence of its immense abbey. Many crafts flourished in the town, among them being a variety of forms of metal work including bell-founding, of which the leading master during the latter part of the fifteenth century was Reignold Chirche. Reignold's bells are well known from their marks, as are also those of his son Thomas, and are distributed heavily in southern Suffolk, though occurring in Cambridgeshire, north Hertfordshire and even as far west as Northamptonshire, away from the competition of the celebrated Brasyers of Norwich. Reignold, in addition to being a bell-founder, was associated with braziers and latteners, and was almost certainly working in latten himself. In 1471 and 1475 he was executor of the wills of John Chernay and John Owey, braziers. His own will of 1498 required that 'My body to be buryed in Saynt Mary Chirche, in the Ele of Seeynt Pet*er*, under the marble ston thar be me laid. I will that Thomas Chirche my sone do make clene the grete lectorn that I gave to Seynt Mary Chirche quart*er*ly as long as he levyth.'[18] It is evident from this that he made advanced preparations for his memorial, probably a brass, and that he donated a latten lectern to St Mary's, which his son as a skilled metal worker was to keep clean. It is suggested that he made both brass and lectern in his own foundry, and that some of the brasses to be noted were prepared under his supervision. Thomas Chirche succeeded his father at the foundry, living until 1527, and attesting the will of John Horton, brazier, in 1523. Another bell-founder, Roger Reeve, worked in Bury in 1533.

Brasses attributed to Suffolk workshops are less easily classified than others in East Anglia, and those that exist are probably mere samples of the series which paved the churches of the Stour Valley, destruction in this area having been intense during the seventeenth century. They may be broadly grouped in three series. The first, dating from c.1470-c.1505, is best represented by kneeling civilian groups at Bury St Edmunds, Chrishall (Fig. 211) and Ampton, by William Style 1475 and wife, St

Nicholas, Ipswich, and by an armed figure and wife at Great Thurlow. The civilians are clearly of provincial workmanship. Their drapery and faces are distinctive in treatment, and their hands are held apart in ecstasy. The Bury figures c.1480 are quite large and kneel on tiled bases. Lavenham possesses a number of indents of presumably similar designs. Style at Ipswich is an excellent representation of contemporary dress, showing the chaperon clearly.

The Great Thurlow brass c.1470 (*The Craft,* Fig. 223) has many features appropriate to York work. His sallet and bevor are well represented. His wife in veil headdress and mantle has much of the simplicity of contemporary northern patterns yet is different in overall appearance. A mutilated brass of a woman c.1470, also at Great Thurlow, is of identical style. These brasses are complemented towards the close of the century in Suffolk by two women at Ampton, the peculiar academic William Goche 1499, Barningham, and slightly later by an armed figure and wife at Assington. The last, probably commemorating Robert Taylboys and wife 1506, is an attractive memorial, in some respects following the conventions of the third Norwich series. It may be Norwich work, but the shading, general execution and location, indicate a Suffolk origin, possibly of the series which follows.

The second series spans the years c.1500-1520, and examples are better integrated, though still including isolated designs. The following armed figures are characteristic:

William Berdewell with wife, 1508, West Harling
Unknown and wife, c.1510, Little Thurlow
Unknown, worn, c.1510, Gonville and Caius College, Cambridge
Francis Heht d.1479, engr. c.1515, Feltwell St Mary.

The hunched appearance of the males is particularly striking, as is also the straggly grass on the footrests. Affinities are closer to Norwich work than Cambridge. Greenwood suggests that a peculiar lost brass of a man in armour and wife from Great Livermere was made at this time, representing earlier armour and costume. Judged on the basis of inscription lettering the brasses at Horncastle should be included with these, though in this case the engraving of the mural inscription has been done with unusual care, and may be a copy . Other aspects of this brass, already discussed, suggest a date rather later than the apparent end of this series.

Civilian figures include a worn pair at March 1501, Margaret Mundford 1520, Feltwell St Mary, and an unknown woman at Ellough. The last is probably of c.1520 and, despite smallness of scale, the dress is unusually rich (Fig. 213).

Archdeacon John Fynexs 1514, St Mary, Bury St Edmunds, is of good quality, showing the deceased in choir dress, the almuce being realistically presented. The treatment of his hair, hands and the grass at his feet, together with the use of shading, make a revealing contrast with the provincial brasses of Cambridge academics. An important canopied brass, which judged by its treatment would seem to belong to this series, is at North Creake (Fig. 212). This has been said to commemorate Sir William Calthorpe d.1494, but does not appear to be earlier than c.1510. The deceased is attired as an ecclesiastic with cassock and either a hood or scarf fixed on the shoulder. He has in addition a rosary and a large purse, and bears a small representation of a church. Possibly the brass represents a church founder, who became a priest later in life. It is obviously a design on which special care was taken.[19*]

The third series from c.1520-1556 is more fully illustrated. Lettering analysis by S. Badham indicates that two series may be involved, the fourth beginning c.1535, though figure design hardly reflects a significant change. The period is accordingly treated as one. Armed figures make a particularly severe contrast with other contemporary counterparts. Their swords in most cases are slung across the front in the style of earlier London and Norwich patterns. The detail and form of the armour is wretchedly presented. The best of a poor selection is Henry Everard with wife 1524,

Denston (Fig. 214), both of whom are in heraldic dress. Others with wives are at Belstead d.1518; Little Waldingfield 1526; Great Thurlow c.1530; Euston c.1530; and Little Bradley 1530. Henry Bures, Esq., 1528 at Acton is a larger single figure.

Civilians are fairly numerous. The most elaborate, though mutilated, is to John Paycock 1533 and wife, Coggeshall. The woman exhibits a headdress of turban-like dimensions. John's feet splay outwards in a stance peculiar to this style of brass. Male gowns are of ample size, as is well illustrated by the brass of John Wyncoll, clothier 1544, at Little Waldingfield (*The Craft,* Fig. 232). A curiosity of the series is William Palmer 1520, Ingoldmells, described in his inscription as 'with ye stylt', who lies with a stilt or crutch at his right side. Other typical civilian figures are Robert Palmer 1515, Winthorpe; John Bacon 1528 and Robert Goodwyn and wife 1532, Necton; and civilians and wives c.1530, at Lakenheath; and Swaffham Prior. A worn couple 1521 are at Fordham, and two small female figures, both c.1520, are at Denston and Hawstead.

Three ecclesiastics illustrate the range of late Suffolk designs at their worst and best. A priest in mass vestments at Somersham c.1530, is a coarse representation, revealing a marked decline in skill from brasses such as that of Archdeacon Fynexs. The large canopied figure of John Laurence of Wardeboys, former Abbot of Ramsey d.1542, Burwell, is of similar style but vested in almuce, surplice and cassock. Part of his figure is palimpsest, and the canopy is probably an appropriation. The figure of Thomas Leman 1534, Southacre, kneeling to a representation of the Virgin, is a realistic and altogether more competent design, though engraved with overmuch shading.

The latest example of Suffolk figure engraving is probably the mutilated Anne Duke 1551, at Frenze. The craftsmen involved were evidently unable to maintain their business in the face of religious changes, which in their course had destroyed the abbey of Bury St Edmunds, and decreased the importance of the town itself. Judged on surviving evidence, the Bury engravers failed to make an original contribution in this medium. In spite of exceptions, especially among the earliest examples, most of their designs were influenced by Norwich work, and fell short of their models. They nevertheless have some integrity of style, most especially in their inscriptions and their striking numerals.

Before leaving the subject of the East Anglian workshops it is appropriate to mention the brass of Anthony Hansart and wife at March. This unusual memorial, showing the figures in heraldic attire, kneeling and praying towards a representation of the Annunciation, has long been described as of provincial workmanship. The figures would however seem to be of London 'F' design, the representation could be similarly described, and the only unexpected features are an elaborate shield with crests as supporters and a poorly engraved inscription. The last is in fact the only element inconsistent with a London origin. The brass may well be composite, and certainly has no place in the provincial series described.

North Essex Engravers

There is no documentary evidence to show that engravers worked in Colchester, neither is there any quantity of brasses in North Essex that may be recognised as essentially different from those of London or East Anglian workshops. There are, however, a selection of brasses, which appear to be of poor London workmanship, but may, in the author's personal view, be imitations.

The most important example is the extraordinary brass of the widow dame Alice Beriffe 1536, and her daughter Margaret at Brightlingsea (Fig. 217). This is engraved in a debased 'F' series style, and the figures are set upon a bracket of c.1400. In addition to this blatant appropriation, the figures are palimpsest, having on their reverses two monastic figures.[20*] These were originally placed upon the bracket, as the indent proves. The work of the obverse is exceptionally crude, and the surface has been inadequately planished. The entire memorial has the aspect of a hasty work, carried out with the minimum of trouble and expense. It is possible that the original brass was taken from the dissolved religious house at St Osyth nearby. While this may be a London product, it seems more likely to have been made by a local engraver, taking advantage of cheap material and imitating London style.

This impression is reinforced by the very curious brass of Anthony Darcy 1540, at Tolleshunt Darcy. Mill Stephenson queried this strange figure as a seventeenth century restoration, but its bold cutting and some of its details hardly support this conjecture. Anthony is a partial copy of a figure of c.1420, perhaps that attributed to John de Boys in the same church. His face has similarities to that of Margaret Beriffe in its eyes, mouth, nose, and shallow brow. The shading is of the very coarse variety in common use between 1530-45, and his sword belt, dog and other features are right for the period. The inscription of this brass is a London palimpsest, having a Flemish reverse, which was presumably monastic or chantry spoil.

Other figures possibly connected with these are females at Goldhanger 1531; Messing c.1535, and Tolleshunt Darcy c.1535. The last is palimpsest with a monastic fragment on the reverse. The first also appears to be reused and, judging from the remaining indents, belonged to a most curious group. Yet another example is perhaps a civilian and two wives at Rettendon c.1535. One of the wives has her skirt caught up to facilitate walking. Mill Stephenson interpreted this as being 'local', and referred to the fine 12th century slab in which it is set.

The absence of any distinctive or consistent style in the memorials makes their provincial provenance suspect. There are nonetheless sufficient grounds to question their London origin. The skill demanded by such brasses was not high, and access to cheap plate must have offered possibilities to opportunist craftsmen.

Kent

It is surprising that in Kent, where gentry and merchants had easy access to the London workshops, there should have been a market for some very inferior local efforts. There are, nonetheless, a group of Kentish brasses which may be attributed to engravers in Canterbury. It is relevant to note that when the Canterbury Corporation wished to alter the city seal in 1543 they employed a certain William Oldfeld, bellfounder, for this task. He was paid 2s. 8d. for 'putting out of Thomas Bekket in the comen seale and gravyng agayn of the same'.[21]

Existing brasses by Kent engravers all date from 1525 to 1545, though the craft may have been practised earlier, and a civilian and wife c.1500 at Rainham do not appear to belong to established London series.

A striking example of this Kentish group, both in its execution and careless lettering of the inscription, is the small rectangular plate to the mayor Raff Brown, now at St Gregory Northgate, Canterbury (*The Craft*, Fig. 234). The Mayor, wearing a scarf of civic office, kneels at a faldstool bearing the city arms. The lines have no flow but are formed by a series of connected independent cuts. Elizabeth Fyneux 1539, Herne, is another example imitating London work with little success; this brass has been wrongly associated with the Norfolk series. The most debased engraving is a weird representation of a civilian and wife c.1530 at Mersham. Other civilian male and female figures of distinctive provincial type are at Selling 1525; Ash-next Sandwich 1525; Capel-le-Ferne 1526; Ringwould 1530 (Fig. 215); Chartham 1530; St Paul,

Canterbury 1531; and Hoath 1532. The unusual figure of William Skott 1532, at West Malling, though reputedly local work, is a very doubtful case.

The small plain crosses at Hever and Penshurst (if original) may be associated with these brasses, but their local attribution is questionable. These emblems are described in the next chapter.

West Country Provincial Brasses

There is no evidence of a considerable production of locally designed brasses in the West of England. Certain brasses do, however, stand out for their unusual qualities, and require examination as being of possible provincial manufacture. By far the most important are the two rectangular plates of Philip Mede 1475, St Mary Redcliffe, Bristol (*The Craft,* Fig. 269), and Sir William Huddesfeld 1499, Shillingford (Fig. 216). These brasses are entirely different in design and execution. Mede's is well engraved, showing the figures kneeling below a representation of Christ set in rays of light. It is a fine but unconventional design, set at the back of a carved tomb of a local stone — Dundry colite. Bristol was an important city and port, and the centre of tomb sculptors.[22*] In the absence of clear alternative connections it is tempting to attribute this plate to a Bristol craftsman. The absence of other comparable brasses in the West is nevertheless an argument against this, reinforced by the apparent 'London quality' of the work, and the marginal inscription on the associated tomb of Sir Thomas Mede 1475, which is in London 'F' script. The loss of Philip's inscription contributes to the uncertainty. It is prudent, faced with the present evidence, to seek a London source without discounting the Bristol possibility. The Shillingford brass in contrast is a delicate but unsure engraving. The treatment of the kneeling figures is peculiar, especially the mail of the knight, which is represented as a series of abutting circles. The brass may be the work of an Exeter goldsmith, and the presumption of local origin is very strong.

Four other brasses are perhaps associated, though only two are in the western counties. They are remarkable for the execrable quality of their workmanship, which is only consistent with braziers or latteners of very low ability. The best are the kneeling figures at Hutton, to Thomas Payne and family 1528, though the execution is rough. William Att Wode and wife 1529, Doynton, is probably by the same hand but far inferior. The script is wretched and the figures are caricatures. A similar script is found on the inscription of William Dale and wife 1536, Tidmarsh. The figures are gone but their indents are a curious shape. A further example is an armed figure c.1530, Waterperry, which may take the distinction of being the worst designed brass before 1600 (Fig, 218).

These examples in the West are insufficient to establish the existence of any major workshop. They appear to be the occasional products of craftsmen and incompetents.

Midland Provincial Brasses

Engravers based in the Midlands used patterns readily distinguished from those of London, York or Norwich. Their work is found in considerable quantity in the counties of Warwickshire and Northamptonshire, though few of their brasses are illustrated or well-known. The location of their craft is not established. Mill Stephenson proposed Coventry as the centre on account of its mediaeval importance, and its situation in relation to the brasses concerned. Marblers certainly worked there. John Mervyn willed in 1492 to be buried in the chancel of St Peter of Lawford, 'and the gravestone that I bought at Coventry to be leide upon my Buriell'[23] An alternative possibility is Leicester. Bellfounders were active there, and the indent of Thomas

Newcombe, bellfounder, and wife 1520, All Saints, Leicester, is very clearly of the midland type.[24] The case for Burton-on-Trent, the great sixteenth century centre of midland slab engraving is not as strong as might be expected. While there are some similarities between midland brasses and incised slabs, there is certainly not the resemblance in design that would be expected if they were products of the same workshops. There is, furthermore, little association between the use of brass inlay and alabaster. The only recorded example is of 1498 at Stanford-on-Soar, where the Trinity and invocatory scrolls were so inlaid. A contract which has been quoted both by Mrs Esdaile and Dr Bouquet as proving this association is not necessarily significant. The names of Henry Harpur and William Moorecock of Burton are recorded in a contract of 1510, by the terms of which they agreed to supply an alabaster tomb with a marble cover inlaid with brasses for the sum of £10, to be set up in Chesterfield to the memory of Henry Foljambe.[25*] Unfortunately the brasses are lost, and those that now exist are restorations. The top is of Purbeck marble, presumably obtained from London, and it is likely that the entire cover with its inlays was obtained from a London marbler by sub-contract. The author is in favour of Coventry as the midland centre. Whatever the truth of this claim, the contribution of midland engravers cannot be doubted.

The earliest brasses attributed in the past to midland sources are the figures of Lettice Catesby 1467 at Newnham, and John Boville and wife 1467 at Stockerston (Fig. 220). The first is only part of a larger composition, once showing Richard Catesby, holding his wife by the hand. Its design is uncompromisingly midland, either being an early example of the first series to be described, or a rather later work than the date of death. The other is similarly arranged, but is very different in design, treatment and impact. Despite the loss of John's head it remains among the most impressive of brasses from the second half of the fifteenth century. The armour is defined with care, and much of the detail, notably the mail, is presented in an unusual fashion. The lady in horned headdress is less remarkable though also imposing. Arguments in support of a midland attribution are the divergence of the design from known London models, the Leicestershire location, the apparent similarity of the brass to another of the Hugeford family, formerly at St Mary, Warwick,[26*] and the fact that the handclasped pose was certainly used in a midland workshop.

The case is nevertheless weak, the location being circumstantial, the origin and detail of the Warwick brass being uncertain, and the design having less affinity with midland examples than with some London work. The figures recall the early 'F' design at Albury, though the lower part of John's figure has definite resemblances to that of Robert Eyr d.1463, at Hathersage. Details such as the flowers on the footrests are of London pattern. It would be premature to state a source for so unusual a memorial. Suffice it to say that London's claims remain stronger than those of any centre in the midlands.

The first series of midland figures appears in the last quarter of the fifteenth century. Thomas Andrewe, Junior, and wife 1490, Charwelton, is an excellent example of the style (Fig. 221). The strangely grinning faces, the man's curled hair and the thrust of his legs are characteristic. The wife's gown is caught up at the front, a common feature of the local design. The script is distinctive, and the children are engraved with similar cheerful expressions. The row of canopies below the inscription and the achievement supported by the angels above are unusual features. A knight of the (?)Lacon family and his wife and children c.1490, Harley, is very similar. His chain of circlets is noteworthy. A large double canopy has gone but the group is otherwise complete. Some comparisons may be drawn between these two brasses and the incised slab of William Villers and two wives 1481, Brooksby, especially in the pose and details of the armed figures[27], and also with stained glass in the nave of Long Melford where the large chains are prominent.

Several civilian and ecclesiastical brasses have similar features, in particular the facial expressions and heavy fur linings to garments. Thomas Andrewe the elder and family at Charwelton is an elaborate composition presumably engraved together with his son's memorial. The canopy with low quadruple pediment and traceried parapet above has counterparts in midland incised slabs, and is in marked contrast to the lofty if heavy canopies of London designs. The detail of the brass is rich, especially the canopies over the children's heads flanked by a dragon, and the achievement supported by angles and a dog eating from a pot. Sir Richard Byngham, Justice of the King's Bench and wife 1476, Middleton is another important example of the same style.[28*] Other figures of civilians and wives are: 1474 at Spratton, c.1480 Geddington and Lutterworth; 1480 Loughborough and of a civilian c.1490 at Hampton-in-Arden. Just as in Norwich work, so in these midland brasses the grasses and flowers on footrests are of distinct and easily recognized pattern. The unusual bag and knife worn by the Lutterworth civilian should be compared with those on the Vernam incised slab 1481 at Ashwell (*The Craft*, Fig. 235).[29]

Ecclesiastics of the same series are at Tredington 1482, Blockley 1488, and Walton-on-Trent 1492. The first two figures are kneeling, the earlier in choir dress, the later in academicals. The third is vested for mass without stole or maniple, and is depicted in the act of blessing the chalice and Host.

A second series is discernable, covering the period from 1500 to c.1515. The patterns retain some of the characteristics of the earlier work, but are less confidently engraved and forceful in design. A tiled floor is used as a footrest on several brasses. Henry Michell in armour and wife 1510, Floore, is a good example, as is also an ungainly figure in private possession, formerly at Peckleton. Civilians include William Knyght 1504, Norton, and Alice Clifton 1506, Coleshill. Of three priest brasses, William Abell 1500 at Coleshill, William Smyght 1510 at Ashby St. Legers (Fig. 219) and William Auldington 1511 at Whatcote, the second is of interest in depicting the cassock.

The third series is more significant, represented by three men in armour with their wives. The men are depicted with distinctive faces, their hair being roughly curled. The figures are on the whole stiffly portrayed, despite the opportunities created by the women's gowns which are caught up at the front. The widely disparate dates of death can hardly apply to the following similar memorials:

John Onley and family, d.1512 engr. c.1525, Withington (Fig.222)
Richard Verney and wife, 1526, Compton Verney
Thomas Shukburghe and wife, d.1549, engr. c.1525, Upper Shuckburgh.

Other examples are the well engraved Anne Odyngsale 1523, at Compton Verney, and the small Richard Bennet, priest 1531, at Whitnash.

A later group of brasses, apparently developed from these, is more important. The expression of the faces and particularly the posture of the hands is common to all, and the pose of the figures suggests a slight backward thrust at the shoulders. Large cushions support the heads of most of the adults. Francis Cockayne and wife 1538, Ashbourne, is the largest brass of this group, with canopy and parapet. Sir Edmund Knyghtleye and family d.1557, probably engr. c.1540[30], Fawsley, is an elaborate composition of similar style. Sir George Throkmerton and family, Coughton c.1540, is more peculiar (Fig. 223). Both adult figures are ungainly, and the armour entirely fanciful in conception. Laurence Saunders and family 1545, Harrington, is better drawn, showing kneeling figures. The armour is of parade style and profusely decorated. His wife wears a prominent peaked cap. Their boys appear to chat among themselves (*The Craft*, 233). Important among civilians are Thomas Holte, justice and family 1545, Aston, and William Hyll, with two wives and eighteen children, at Solihull, the former being very similar in treatment to the armed figures. The series appears to end c.1550, coinciding with the Edwardian iconoclasm.

Conclusion

All the provincial types of brasses described decline dramatically in numbers after 1545 or disappear completely. It is too sweeping a generalisation to state that the provincial workshops perished in the religious chaos of the mid-sixteenth century, but the activity of these workshops was certainly disrupted by 1550. This fact may confirm the view that the engravers in the provincial centres were not primarily professional tomb makers, but rather metal workers and glaziers, whose ecclesiastical business was undermined by the religious changes. Brasses of provincial manufacture of the latter half of the sixteenth century form an odd assortment, whereas for a century before they formed a substantial part of the English craft. 'Local' work embraces well over a third of the figure brasses from 1470 – 1540, and a far higher proportion of emblem and insertion plates. Provincial brasses effectively record in their medium particular regional stylistic conventions, forming a very important and under-rated element in the series of Yorkist and Tudor brasses.

14. English Emblem brasses

Commemoration by an inscription and an emblem of a religious or status significance became popular during the fifteenth century. Most emblem brasses are small, and were, in consequence inexpensive. They were engraved in great numbers in provincial workshops, especially in Norwich and York, and may be divided into two main classes — emblems with a religious or moral significance and emblems relating to a vocation or trade. In the first class are crosses, hearts, roses and a soul emblem; in the second, chalices, mitres, croziers and implements of trade.

Religious Emblems: Emblem crosses

The cross in a plain or decorative form has been noted as a very early type of brass design. As the supreme symbol of the Christian Faith the cross was a fitting emblem for Christian graves, and its use in this context may be traced to the early history of the Church. It is important to differentiate between the emblem cross brass and the figured cross brass, both of which have been described as cross brasses. The figured cross was almost certainly derived from the association of figures with emblem crosses. The resulting design, however, had little connection with the emblem; either the cross became a decorative though symbolic surrounding for a figure brass, which was the most essential element, or became little more than a framework for a votive composition. Such designs have been described in chronological sequence. The emblem cross has no association with figures of the deceased.

Most emblem crosses are simple Latin crosses, rising from three or four steps. Some have fleury terminals to the cross arms. The first and largest example, at Cassington, commemorates Roger Cheyne Esq., 1414 (Fig. 224). The cross is slender and gracefully formed, and the design completed by shields on either side of the stem. The cross at Broadwater to Richard Tooner 1445, is of a similar but heavier design, and the arms are inscribed 'Sanguis Christi salva me Passio *Christ*i conforta me'. A smaller cross c.1500 at Royston is engraved with the Sacred Heart and Five Wounds of the Crucifixion (Fig. 225). By far the earliest crosses are those at Westminster Abbey of 1276 and 1277 to the children of the Earl of Pembroke. Only fragments of the stems exist, and their main interest lies in a mosaic setting: (*The Craft*, Fig. 68).

Nine small crosses remain including:

Margaret Oliver, 1425, Beddington
Joan Brokes, 1487, Peper-Harrow
Thomas Burgoyn and wife, 1516, Sutton
Henry Bwllayen (Bullen), c.1520, Hever
Thomas Bwllayen, c.1520, Penshurst
Allice Wyrley, 1537, Floore.

The Floore cross is designed in perspective and bears the nails of the Crucifixion. The steps of the Sutton cross, a brass of the Cambridge series, are similarly represented in perspective. The two Kentish crosses are very crude and, if original, apparently provincial work.

Rubbings of two crosses now lost, though their inscriptions remain, are in the Society of Antiquaries' collection. These were at St Mary, Reading, and Sithney. The former, to William Baron 1416, was entwined with a scroll and lay in a slab powdered with small scrolls. The latter, to Roger Trewythynnyk c.1420 was inscribed 'Ih*es*u mercy'.

Three larger crosses are more important than the above:

Unknown, c.1380, Grainthorpe

Thomas Chichele and wife, 1400, Higham Ferrers (Fig 226)

Richard Pendilton, 1502, Eversley (*The Craft.* Fig. 238)

The Grainthorpe cross has a fine and elaborate head decorated with interlaced foliage. The stem is lost, but the base stands upon a rock round which fishes are swimming[1]. The Higham Ferrers cross is particularly interesting. A representation of the Deity is set upon the crossing of the arms, the terminals of which are formed of medallions bearing the Evangelists' symbols. The whole represents the dominion of God over all creation. The inscription at the foot is in excellent relief lettering. The Eversley cross is large and curious, engraved as if constructed by a series of chain links. There can be no doubt that these large and complex crosses are a type which has suffered very heavily from accidental damage and iconoclasm. Their separate inlay construction is delicate, while their form was offensive to extremist Protestant taste. The indents at Long Stow and Mildenhall are two from many examples of such destroyed memorials.

Heart brasses

Reference has been made to brasses in which figures are shown holding hearts. The heart appears as the main element in several compositions, being usually represented with scrolls issuing from it and sometimes clasped by hands. Its significance may be interpreted in one of several ways. In some cases the brass records a heart burial. Persons occasionally expressed a wish for parts of their remains to be buried in specified places with which they had connections, as, for example, Nicholas Longespée, Bishop of Salisbury who died in 1297; his bowels were buried at Ramsbury where he died, his body at Salisbury and his heart in the Abbey Church of Lacock.[2] So common did this custom become that Pope Boniface VIII attempted, in 1299, to abrogate it by the Bull Detesdandae feritatis abusum, which was nevertheless modified by Pope Benedict XI, and became a matter of Papal licence under John XXII.[3]

The scrolls surrounding the heart brass of Sir Robert Kervile c.1450, at Wiggenhall St Mary-the-Virgin, record 'cujus cor hic humatur' and the inscription of Anne Muston 1496, Saltwood, states 'Here lieth the bowells' of dame Anne Muston' (Fig. 227). At Arthuret is a curious small quadrangular plate, probably of the fourteenth century, engraved with two arms and hands holding a heart against a background of a cross fleury. The shape of the plate indicates that this may have formed the door of a heart shrine.[4]

Far more frequently the heart emblem, held by a figure or in isolation, represents the redeemed Heart made new in accordance with the prayer of Psalm 50: 12 (Douay version). The will of Guy Shuldham, who was buried in St Martin Vintry, directed that a half effigy should be laid in his memory holding a heart with this scripture 'Cor mundum crea in me deus & spiritum rectum innova in visceribus meis'.[5] Such a symbol reflects the confidence in redemption expressed in the Job quotation (19: 25-27) from the burial service. The heart to Thomas Smyth 1433, Margate, is a good example of what was most probably a typical arrangement. The Heart is inscribed 'Credo q*uo*d' and three flying scrolls bear the text 'Redemptor meus vivit' — 'De terra surrecturus sum' — 'in carne mea videbo d*eu*m salvator*e*m meam.' Other prayers or quotations were substituted for the Job passage. The heart of Robert Alen 1487, Martham, is itself inscribed 'post tenebras spero lucem, laus deo meo'. These designs were particularly favoured in Norfolk, and by c.1460, the engravers in Norwich were adapting London models. The worn but good example at Helhoughton, to William Stapilton and wife c.1450, showing the heart grasped by two slim hands issuing from clouds, is of uncertain origin, possibly London work. Nevertheless a comparable design, now lost, for William Cotyng engr. c.1480, at Brancaster, was evidently of Norwich origin. Other examples of hearts with flying scrolls remain for:

Unknown, c.1450, Kirby Bedon
Unknown, c.1460, Souldern[6]*
Denys Willys, 1462, Loddon
Unknown, c.1500, Elmstead
Unknown, c.1530, Trunch
Thomas Denton, 1533, Caversfield (Fig. 229).

Another heart of this type is set above the figure of Thomas Knyghtley 1516, Fawsley. Of these examples only those at Loddon, Martham and Trunch are of proven Norwich origin.

In a few instances the form suggests that the Sacred Heart of Jesus is intended. At Lillingstone Lovell the well engraved brass of John Merstun represents the heart as covered with drops of blood and inscribed '*ihc*' (*The Craft*, Fig. 237). Simpler hearts c.1500 at Higham Ferrers and Chichester cathedral are similarly inscribed. At Cheam a heart, on the reverse of a Trinity above Thomas Fromond, Esq. 1542 and family, is inscribed '*ihesus est Amor meus*' and is surrounded with rays of light (*The Craft,* Fig. 268). Devotion to the Sacred Heart was widespread by the close of the fifteenth century in northern Europe, and it is likely that the links of East Anglia with Flanders and north Germany stimulated a strong local interest in the heart form of brass.[7]

A few heart brasses seem to have held a less precise symbolic meaning. The large inscribed heart at Melton Mowbray to Christopher Gonson and wife 1543, is of no special type. The four double hearts inscribed 'Ih*es*u merci Ladi help' on a slab at Fakenham, Norf. c.1504, are of uncertain significance. The early fifteenth-century brass of Thomas Waterdeyn, Mayor, formerly at St Nicholas, King's Lynn, was a very curious design, showing a tree hung with two hearts, and the inscription ((ubi) vera sunt gaudia (ibi) nostra fixa sunt Corda' — the words in brackets being set on quatrefoils below the inscription.

In some cases hearts may have had little more than a punning significance, as the one (and another now lost) connected with the figure of James Hert, D.D. 1498, Hitchin. There can be no doubt that this emblem, having been accepted as a devotional symbol, was used in a variety of connections. Its character was nevertheless highly offensive to Protestant thought and the destruction of heart brasses was in consequence most deliberate. Inscriptions remain, for example, at Attlebridge, Brancaster, Itteringham and Merton though the heart plates relating to them have long ago been removed.

Rose brasses

The rose was a symbol of the transitory beauty of life, as was signified in the lost inscription to Canon John Marshal 1446, Lincoln cathedral, which read:

> 'Ut rosa pallescit, cum solem sentit abesse,
> Sic homo vanescit; nunc est, nunc desinit esse'.

One brass survives in which a rose appears to have been the main feature. This is at Edlesborough and is of uncertain date, but probably c.1450 from the fineness of the lines (Fig. 230). The centre is inscribed 'Ecce' and the inscription continues on the petals '+ quod Expendi habui quod Donavi habeo q*uo*d Negavi punior quod Servavi *per*didi' This rose is now placed with the inscription of John Killyngworth 1412, but the connection has been shown to be the result of inaccurate resetting.[8] Another rose, with a similar inscription, in English, once existed at St Peter's Church, St Albans. An impression of this is given in Gough's *Sepulchral Monuments*, II.i, p. cccxxxv. Two roses from a set of four are found with the inscription and shield to Lady Blanche Castell 1553, at Littleton, inscribed 'Ih*es*u m*er*cy' and they may be no more than a convenient setting for the invocation. The Evangelists' symbols are placed in roses at Ely cathedral on the brass of Bishop Goodryke 1554. Roses are used as subsidiary decoration in other contexts. Gough's illustration shows the canopy of Abbot Kirton 1460, Westminster Abbey, with a rose at the apex of the centre pediment perhaps an allusion to the Blessed Virgin.[9] The indents of roses around the brass of Thomas Roose and family 1441, Sall, are evidence of a punning play on the name. The centre of the flower was probably filled with the letter T, a decorative device used on bosses in the north transept at Sall to commemorate the deceased.

Soul emblems

The soul, depicted as a small naked figure, borne upwards in a sheet by angels, appears as a detail in several canopied compositions, especially those of fourteenth-century Flemish origin. A unique brass at Checkendon to Walter, son of Sir William Beauchamp c.1430, consists merely of this representation and an inscription plate (Fig. 228).

Evangelists' symbols, angels and birds

The symbols of the Evangelists have been touched on, but it may here be noted that some brasses consisted of these and inscription plate only, as that of Thomas Clerk and wife 1482, All Saints, North Street, York. The English engravers did not as a rule follow the Flemish practise of representing an angel as the main figure in a design. The only examples in which angels are found without accompanying a figure are at Saltwood 1496, holding the heart, and on the inscription to James Sayntleger Esq. 1509, Monkleigh, where they form little beyond decorative detail. A curious emblem of uncertain significance is that of a long-legged bird. Such a bird, described by Mill Stephenson as a stork, holds a scroll inscribed 'deo gracias' and accompanies an inscription and probably a chalice to Thomas Browne c.1510, at Old Buckenham. Two indents of such birds, of which the head of one remains, are at Upwell; they may represent bitterns, though if so their significance is obscure.

Vocational emblems: Chalices

Emblems signifying vocation or trade were fairly numerous, and by far the most common were chalices. Many brasses of priests depict the figure holding the sacramental chalice, and chalices of cheap material were commonly buried with a priest at his interment. The earliest existing chalice brass is dated 1429. Chalice brasses are particularly associated with York and East Anglian engravers; the only one of London or Home Counties origin is apparently that of Thomas Elys 1519, Shorne. Distribution was, in fact, wider than it now seems. There are a number of southern indents, as at Boughton Monchelsea, St Margaret, Rochester, Nutfield and Limpsfield. They were undoubtedly a speciality of the provincial workshops, though there are not sufficient grounds to attribute that at Shorne to a Kent engraver.

The earliest existing chalice brasses are in Yorkshire, and were presumably engraved in York. These are:

Richard Kendale, 1429, Ripley
Peter Johnson, 1460, Bishop Burton
William Langton, 1466, St Michael Spurriergate, York (Fig. 231)
Thomas Clarell, 1469, St Peter, Leeds.

All these brasses are engraved on plate cut to the shape of the chalice. The Ripley, Bishop Burton and Leeds chalices are heavy in form. In contrast, that in York is of a graceful shape and well finished. The bowl was stolen but has been accurately restored.

Most of the remaining chalice brasses are of Norwich workmanship, being later in date than those of Yorkshire and smaller in size. In several cases the Host is shown vertically within the chalice bowl. A small group of chalices have a carefully cut outline, three of the third series being:

John Smyth, 1499, St Giles, Norwich
Richard Grene, 1502, Hedenham
Henry Alikok, 1502, Colney.[10]

Two inferior sixth series examples are at Guestwick 1504, and Buxton 1508. A number of Norfolk indents record chalices of a more elaborate shape especially in the foot. The indent above the inscription to Simon Boleyn 1482, Sall, is a good example, as are others at Trunch, Mautby and Threxton. These appear to have been a second series pattern.

A more common type is shown in *The Craft,* Fig. 236. The chalice is engraved on a rectangular plate, usually against a hatched background and with the top edge curved for the Host. All are of the sixth series, excepting Old Buckenham and Taverham of the fifth. The best are:

?Thomas Browne, c.1510, Old Buckenham[11*]
William Westow, c.1520, Little Walsingham
William Richers, 1531, Bawburgh
William Cutes, 1540, South Burlingham.

The Walsingham and Bawburgh chalices are represented as held by hands issuing from clouds, though on the latter the thumbs alone appear.[12] Others are at Belaugh 1508; Bintry, Wood Dalling 1510; Surlingham 1513; Taverham 1515; Salthouse, 1519; North Walsham 1519 and c.1520; Scottow c.1520; and Attlebridge c.1525.

Two chalices in Suffolk at Rendham 1523, and Gazeley c.1530, may be products of Norwich, but were more probably engraved at Bury St Edmunds. They have similarities to the Colney chalice, but are stiffer in design. The extraordinary chalice for Robert Wodehouse, 1515. at Holwell is certainly of Cambridge manufacture, judging from the script of the inscription and other details. The form of the chalice is poorly represented and the two woodwoses who stand by are, apart from their canting significance, curious attendants (Fig. 232).

As with heart brasses, so also with chalices, inscriptions have been spared when the emblem was destroyed, as at Barton Turf 1497; Crostwight 1497; Sloley c.1500 and 1503; Colby d.1508; and Northwold 1531.[13] Chalices are occasionally set independently but in connection with a figure; the one at Tong above the head of Arthur Vernon 1517, is finer in detail than the emblem chalices described.

Mitre and crozier emblems

No brasses exist consisting primarily of a crozier, and the only mitre brasses surviving are of the seventeenth century. The splendid indent of Abbot John de Sutton 1349, Dorchester, nevertheless affords clear evidence of the first type; the despoiled slab showing an arm extended inwards from the border inscription, grasping a crozier which lay in the centre of the slab.[14] Mediaeval mitre brasses have no such proof, though a mitre set upon a shield of arms survives from the tomb of Bishop Russell 1494, Lincoln cathedral.

Emblems of trade

Emblems of trade as a main feature are very rare, but this may be a consequence of loss or destruction. The pair of gloves and inscription to Peter Denot, glover c.1440, Fletching, is a celebrated case (The *Craft*. Fig. 239). The will of John Browne of West Malling 1488, expressing his wishes as to his gravestone, directed that 'in every corner of the said stone I would have graven in laten a paire of taylours sheris'.[15*] The inscription of John Jobson 1525, fishmonger and Sheriff, St. Mary-le-Wigford, Lincoln, is engraved with a knife and cleaver. The fine hunting horn with bawdric enclosing a shield c.1450, Bexley may signify occupation, though a tenurial significance is more probable.[16*] The display of Merchants' marks with inscriptions could be regarded as falling within the category of trade emblems, though for convenience these have been described in connection with heraldry and were so regarded by their users, although not by the heralds.

15. English devotional panels, 1450-1550

Reference has been made in previous chapters to the representations of the Holy Trinity, the Blessed Virgin and Saints, set within crosses and canopies, placed upon brackets or incorporated as decoration on the orphreys of vestments. These and more complex subjects received comparable treatment until the middle of the sixteenth century. During the latter part of the fifteenth century there was a great increase in the number of these representations, many of which are found on otherwise insignificant brasses. Compositions including kneeling figures required a central feature of attention to explain the devotional attitude of those commemorated. A similar arrangement was widely used with recumbent figures, especially those facing in semi-profile. Appropriate precatory scrolls connected the figures with the plates above. Such pictorial panels were especially common in the early years of the sixteenth century, and were a usual element in brasses placed in a vertical setting; they were varied in subject, and, being more than subsidiary decoration, deserve special description. They are also appropriately to be considered at this point, as they were an important factor in stimulating religious zealots and plunderers in their work of destruction.

Devotional panels may be classified conveniently into six main groups. The largest consists of representations of the Holy Trinity, a particularly popular devotional subject in England. A second group is concerned with events from the life of Christ as recorded in the Gospels and His Last Judgement as predicted in the Apocalypse. A third group is concerned with events from the life of the Blessed Virgin, and a fourth depicts the vision of Pope Gregory, while a fifth represents the Five Wounds of Christ and the instruments of His passion. A sixth and miscellaneous group consists of figures of saints to whom the deceased, by his name, guild association, date of death or other circumstance was especially attached.

The Holy Trinity

The Holy Trinity was by far the most popular subject. In spite of large-scale destruction nearly forty examples survive and Childrey church still retains three. The conventional group consists of God the Father, enthroned, portrayed as a venerable bearded man, holding the crucifix on which the Dove of the Holy Spirit usually rests. In many cases the cross is set upon an orb, symbolic of the earth. The setting of these figures and their detail allowed the engravers considerable opportunity for display. The plates of outstanding merit are mostly of late fifteenth-century date. The Tideswell example of 1462, probably the finest of all and the chief element in the brass to Sir Sampson Meverell 1462, shows the Trinity surrounded by rays of light (Fig. 233). This makes an interesting comparison with an earlier plate now lost from Bobbing.[1] The Childrey plate of 1477 is large and exceptionally well engraved. At Staveley c.1480, Stoke Charity 1483; Great Tew 1487, and Chacombe c.1545, the throne and canopy setting are prominent. The intricate Dauntsey representation of 1539 is incorporated within the main quadrangular plate. A curiously late example of such a Trinity is found at Skipton-in-Craven apparently dated 1570. The brass may be slightly earlier, but its provincial origin makes accurate dating difficult. The verbal emblem of the Trinity is engraved on a shield at Northleach above William Lawnder, priest c.1510.

The Life of Christ

The second group is small. The nativity of Christ has one illustration only on a small plate c.1500, Cobham (Fig. 235). This interesting fragment, showing the Holy Family visited by the shepherds, is pleasing, but is unbalanced by the great size of Joseph's head. Christ the man is represented on a shield at Etwall 1512. The crucifixion of Christ, the subject of supreme solemnity, has no complete example, even when brasses earlier than this period are taken into account. Only the foot of the cross with a skull, a headless figure of the Blessed Virgin and scrolls survive at Chelsfield from the representation set on the side of the tomb of Robert de Brun 1417. At Kenton a mutilated crucifix survives on the quadrangular plate of John Garneys 1524. (*The Craft,* Fig. 98). More important are two palimpsest fragments. The illustration is of an engraving ? c.1460 discovered on the reverse of a shield of Robert Pygott 1561, Waddesdon (Fig. 236). Parts of a far larger representation c.1540 with accompanying figures, presumably of the Virgin and Saint John, has been found on the reverse of part of the brass to Richard Fermer 1552, Easton Neston.[2] In this case the wounds in the hands and head were inlaid in red colour. It is uncertain whether these fragments are part of a memorial brass or formed a small latten altarpiece. It may be presumed that representations of this sort were destroyed systematically in the sixteenth and seventeenth centuries, and that the subject was not uncommon. There is a very clear indent of 1518 at Isleham in which the rood group can be traced. Many of the oval shaped indents of uncertain character may well have contained plates of the Waddesdon type.

The Resurrection of Christ was an elaborate subject of which there are fortunately several good examples. These representations were frequently fixed at the back of high tombs used to house the Easter Sepulchre, the brass being an appropriate decoration as well as a devotional subject.[4] The figure of Christ is usually shown holding a cross staff with flag and stepping out of the tomb around which lie the stunned or sleeping guards, armed in a fanciful or outmoded style. The best of such representations occurs appropriately above Sir Hugh Johnys at Swansea engr. c.1500 who was 'made knyght at the holy sepulchre of our lord ih*es*u crist in the city of Jerusalem' (Fig. 245). The four armed guards are well shown, one holding a knotted and spiked club, another a fearsome 'morning star' and a third with a scimitar. Almost as detailed is another plate c.1500 at All Hallows-by-the-Tower, London. The quality of this brass has only been apparent since postwar cleaning. Other examples showing the guards are: 1503 at Great Coates, Cranley; c.1520 Hedgerley (palimpsest rev); c.1525 Slaugham (*The Craft,* Fig. 35); and 1545 Narborough. Above the kneeling figures of Edward Love, gent. and family, 1535, Stoke Lyne, Oxon., is a representation of Christ in an aureole rising from the tomb. His hands are raised displaying the wounds, and there are no guards. Mill Stephenson describes this as 'Our Lord in Pity', a superficially similar subject of different character. There is, however, a feeling of joy and triumph about the figure only consistent with a picture of the Risen Christ.[4]

Christ holding the regal orb is shown on the brass of Sir Thomas Nevell 1542, Mereworth (Fig. 238). His demi-figure appears in the clouds above Philip Mede and his wives 1475, St Mary Redcliffe, Bristol (*The Craft,* Fig. 269). Christ of the Last Judgement, enthroned upon a rainbow with his hands upraised, is set above John Moore, M.A. 1532, Sibson (Fig. 240). Indents of the same subject are easily recognized at Kingston-on-Thames 1489; Isleham 1507; and Rochester cathedral ?c.1535. An important palimpsest, now lost, from Shorne preserved part of a brass showing Christ seated on a rainbow with a sword pointing towards his head and engraved against a background of stars and a crescent moon. A comparable palimpsest fragment, though of shallow execution, was discovered in 1974 at Isfield (obv. 1558). In this case only a detail of the rainbow remains above fragments of a kneeling woman in shroud and her children. A figure of St John the Baptist is well preserved, together with an elaborate monogram and a prominent angel with curved horn. The background is stippled and strewn with Passion emblems. This may be dated c.1500, and was evidently a plate intended for mural display.

The life of the Virgin Mary

The third group, devoted to the life of Mary the mother of Christ, is now small, but was originally large. The Blessed Virgin was regarded as a supreme intercessor on behalf of sinners, and was appropriately addressed on behalf of the dead. The childhood of Mary is introduced in representations of her mother St Anne teaching her to read. In addition to the early representation at Deerhurst there is another of 1470, at Morley (*The Craft,* Fig. 72). The Annunciation was more common and like the Resurrection offered the designer considerable scope for decoration. By far the best representation of this subject is at Fovant 1492, which almost fills the quadrangular plate to the priest George Rede (Fig. 234). Mary kneels at a prayer desk, and is addressed by the kneeling Archangel Gabriel, as a dove descends towards her in rays of light. The symbolic lily-pot which is a common element in this scene, is set slightly behind the figures. A smaller representation, in which Mary faces the Archangel with her hands raised, is at March, Cambs., 1507. A later and more elaborate example forms part of the canopy of William Porter, S.T.B. 1524, at Hereford cathedral; the treatment of the subject here reflects unusually strong Renaissance influence for an English brass of the period, especially in the cherub-like figure of Gabriel. Fragments of this subject, two lily-pots and an angel, are also preserved at Cirencester and a kneeling figure of the Blessed Virgin with a scroll bearing the words 'Ecce an Cella d*om*ini' is in the British Museum.

There are two English representations of Our Lady in Pity, supporting the dead body of Christ, but neither is an independent panel. The earlier 1497, placed on the central finial of the canopy of Thomas Elyngbrigge, Esq., Carshalton is small and coarsely engraved. Far more elaborate is the group shown on the brass of Geoffrey Fyche 1537, St Patrick's cathedral, Dublin (*The Craft,* Fig. 220). In this the Blessed Virgin is surrounded by disciples and helpers including St Mary Magdalene, the scene appearing as a retable or picture at the back of an altar.

Figures of the Virgin with the infant Christ are more common as at Althorne 1502, Beaumaris, c.1530, and at Brampton the Virgin is depicted suckling the infant (Fig. 242).

The Vision of Pope Gregory

The fourth group consists of three brasses only, and emphasizes the confused character of many late mediaeval devotional subjects. Saint Gregory was associated, in the later Middle Ages, with a picture in Santa Croce in Gerusalemme at Rome, showing a half-length figure of the dead Christ standing in a sepulchre at the foot of the cross. It appears that this gave rise to a legend that the Pope beheld such a vision of Christ as he celebrated Mass, and so developed the popular representation of Pope Gregory's Mass and the subject of his vision, 'Our Lord in Pity'.[5] The astonishing indulgences supposedly earned by prayers made before representations of these subjects, made them attractive to the credulous and highly objectionable to critics of the Church, and it is perhaps surprising that any examples have survived. A plate showing the complete scene is fortunately preserved at Macclesfield on the brass of Roger Legh 1506 (Fig. 241). The pope, anachronistically wearing the tiara, kneels before the altar, and the vision of Christ appears before him from behind the altar. Below is an inscription offering a pardon of twenty-six thousand years and twenty-six days. An excellent representation of Our Lord in Pity is set above the head of Thomas Wayte 1482, at Stoke Charity (Fig. 239). The sombre figure of the wounded Christ rising from the tomb is in marked contrast to the triumphant resurrection panels. It is interesting that a carved image of Pope Gregory's Mass is still preserved in this church, and may have influenced the specifications of the brass. Another but inferior figure is set on the canopy of John Lawrence of Wardeboys, Abbot of Ramsey, at Burwell and formed part of his or another earlier memorial of c.1520.

The sacred wounds of Christ

Devotion to the wounds of Christ was widespread in the late Middle Ages, and was probably given special prominence after the Stigmatisation of St. Francis in 1224. The emblazoning of the Five Wounds, displaying the hands and feet of Christ arranged around His wounded heart, is well shown at Lower Halling among the shields and inscription to John Colard 1491 (Fig. 237). A large indent of 1531, incorporating this subject with a cross, is at St Andrew, Norwich. A small cross bearing the wounds is set before Robert Thornburgh and wife 1522, Kimpton, and a shield bearing them is placed above Robert Hacombleyn 1528, at Kings College, Cambridge. The wounds are noted in other connections as on the emblem cross at Royston, Herts., on a cross in the hands of Thomas Hylle at New College, Oxford 1468 (Fig. 169), and on a shield held by Richard Foxwist at Llanbeblig 1500.

Figures of saints

The sixth group, the saints, is now poorly represented. The most distinctive figures are those of St Christopher carrying the Christ Child on his shoulder at Morley 1454, 1470 (*The Craft*, Fig. 72), and c.1525; and at Weeke 1498. The last, commemorating William Complyn and wife, is, with its inscription, a complete memorial. St Michael is thrusting down the devil on the Trevnwyth brass 1462, St Ives. St John the Evangelist, holding his emblem of a chalice and serpent, is among the three representations at Beaumaris c.1530. St Catherine has been noted at St Mary-the-Virgin, Oxford 1507 and standing beside Robert Honywode 1522 at St George's chapel, Windsor. St John the Baptist is represented upon the finial of a canopy at Ightfield c.1500 and within an expanded canopy pediment at St Mary de Crypt, Gloucester 1529. This second brass commemorates John Cook, Alderman, who belonged to the fraternity of St John the Baptist, which was established in that church.

Conclusion

The precise specifications of the will of Robert Fabyan, who died in 1512 requiring that if he were buried in London 'over or above the said figurys I will be made a figure of the Fader of Heven inclosed in a sonne', or if he were buried at Theydon Gernon the substitution of 'the figure of our Lady with her Child sittyng on a sterr',[6] are indicative of the importance of these devotional panels and figures to their contemporaries. They emphasized the piety of the deceased, whose plea for prayers embraced and united both the faithful on earth and intercessors in Heaven. They also provide for the observer an interesting area of study in the closing periods of English mediaeval brass design. The very existence of these panels and the message that they bore was to endanger the memorials of which they were part. Many were to be destroyed, not by iconoclasts or thieves, but by respectful descendants seeking to protect the graves of their forbears.

16. English shroud and skeleton brasses

The portrayal of the deceased as a corpse, stripped of any token of former dignity, became common during the last quarter of the fifteenth century. Such representations, though unattractive as designs, are interesting for their peculiarity and motives.

The importance of a mediaeval brass as a means of securing the prayers of the living for the dead has been emphasized. A brass could arrest the attention of the spectator, not only by recording the status and meritorious works of the deceased, but by startling with a crude revelation of death itself. The fate of the dead would also befall the onlooker, who would in turn be in need of prayers and devotions. The inscription of John Brigge, 1454, Sall concludes:

> 'so frendis fre whatever ye be • pray for me y yow pray —
> As ye me se in soche degre • So schall ye be a northir day.'

The motive of the shroud brass was to move the spectator both through concern for his own future and pity for the commemorated. Thomas Morys, Grocer, willed in 1506 — 'I wil hafe an honyste Stone layed on me . . . a marbull Stone with an ymage of myselfe and another of my wife . . . And the ymagis that shuld be on the stone gravid lyke ij deade carkas as pitiou(s)lye made as canne be thoughte holdinge upp ower handes in ower wyndedinge sheats'.[1] In certain cases, such as that of Ralph Hamsterley engr. c.1515, Oddington, the brass was certainly laid in the lifetime of the commemorated for his own contemplation.

The fashion for such memorials in England can be traced from the half figure of Joan Mareys 1431, Sheldwich.[2*] Earlier Continental examples from Bruges have been described, and figures in sculpture are yet older. The ravages of the Black Death created an extraordinary awareness of the sudden end of life, which was reinforced by recurrent plagues and epidemics. Morbidity was not confined to monuments, but presented in hideous detail in wall paintings of 'the three living and three dead' and later in paintings and prints of the Dance or Triumph of Death. Shroud and skeleton brasses did not aim to be grand memorials, and it is not surprising, Continental examples apart, that few are of a great size. Some indents are large, especially one in the nave at Boston, in which the souls borne by angels were represented above the shrouded figures. Palimpsests at Harefield and Little Horkesley were cut from large late fifteenth-century shroud brasses. A few compositions containing shrouded figures are impressive by reason of their many component parts. John Symondes and family 1512, Cley, and the much mutilated brass of Sir William Catesby and two wives 1471, Ashby St Legers, are of this kind. Numerically this class of brass is quite large. Some sixty examples exist pre 1560 and many indents. Hitchin, still retains four.

Shroud and skeleton brasses may be classified into four groups according to the treatment of the subject. The first and most common are brasses showing a figure or figures with inscription and other details, in which the deceased are recumbent. It is of secondary importance whether the figures are apparently alive but shrouded, cadavers, skeletons or infants in chrysom bands. These brasses are a variation of the normal representation. The second are kneeling shrouded figures in votive compositions, being again a variation on a conventional arrangement. The third and more interesting are those upon which a Resurrection theme is imparted, the deceased represented as arising from tombs at the Last Judgement. Fourthly are brasses in which the dead is contrasted with the living and a double representation is involved. These brasses are the equivalent of the two-tiered sculptured tombs as those of Archbishop Chichele, Canterbury cathedral, and John Fitzalan, Arundel, in which the decaying body of the dead lies below the fully vested or armed effigy.

Most shroud and skeleton brasses are of the first type. One figure now survives of kneeling groups, that of Agnes Bulstrode 1472, Upton. She is almost completely covered by the shroud, only her hands, forearms and face appearing. The shroud is tied above the head and below the feet with cords, forming small bunches of drapery, which are a distinctive feature of shroud brasses and make their indents easily identifiable.

Resurrection compositions

The two examples of the Resurrection type are more important. Thomas Spryng and family 1486, Lavenham, is an excellent brass, certainly of London manufacture (Fig. 247). All the figures are shrouded including the children, and are depicted as emerging from two coffins. Invocatory scrolls were addressed to a representation now lost. The inscription is a good example of lettering hatched into relief. An unusual detail of the design is that the shrouds hang loose exposing the naked figures. Usually the shroud is shown as pinned over the thighs, or closed from the waist downwards. William Feteplace and wife 1516, Childrey, are smaller and of poorer quality. They are depicted as rising within coffins, the lids of which are falling to the side. A fragment of a composition with richer symbolism to John Hall and wife c.1530, showing Our Lord in Majesty seated on a rainbow with a sword pointing towards his head, has been lost from Shorne (see last chapter).

Living and dead in contrast

The grim comparison of the commemorated in life and death has only one certain English example — that of Bernard Brocas 1488, Sherborne St John (*The Craft,* Fig. 240). Bernard is shown in armour and tabard, kneeling towards a cross (now lost). Below him lies his skeleton in a shroud. The figure brasses of Sir Lionel Dymoke d.1519, Horncastle, and Anthony Cave 1558, Chicheley, are placed very close to shrouded representations of the same persons, and the intention of the arrangement was probably that described. The brasses of Richard Willoughby and wife 1469, Wollaton, are placed above a carved representation of a cadaver (Figs. 243-4) and an indent c.1500, Denston, is also similarly placed. In these only the record of status and dignity was presented in brass. A German composition on this theme is the brass of Bartolomäus Heisegger 1518, from the Marienkirche, Lübeck, where the shrouded figure lies in front of the kneeling praying figure of the deceased. These examples are few, but they represent effectively the motive underlying these memorials of death and decay.

Recumbent shrouds

The great majority of shrouded figures are recumbent effigies, which have few attributes of death other than the winding sheet itself. The Symondes at Cley are as alert and vital in pose and expression as any conventional civilian group of the period and arranged in an identical manner. Even on brasses where only one of the figures is represented as dead, as at Taplow 1455, Stone 1472; Newington-next-Hythe 1501, and Edgemond 1533, there is no effective contrast other than that of attire. The shroud is an essentially neutral garment, reflecting neither sex nor occupation.

Notwithstanding women are recognizable by their long hair and priests by the tonsure. The following are among the best examples of London work:

Joan Mareys, half eff., 1431, Sheldwich
John Manfeld, 1455, Taplow, with brother and sister, (Fig. 97)
John Leventhorpe and wife, d.1484 engr. c. 1465, Sawbridgeworth (Fig. 248)
Tomesin Tendryng, 1485, Yoxford
Elizabeth Mattock, husband last, 1485, Hitchin
Margaret Shelley, 1495, Hunsdon
John Hampton and wife, d.1556, ingr. c.1510, Minchinhampton
Woman, c.1510, Museum of Archaeology and Ethnology, Cambridge[3]
John Symondes and wife, 1512, Cley.

The Sawbridgeworth figures are the best engraved. Both hold hearts, as does Joan Mareys at Sheldwich, and a small shrouded priest c.1480, Stifford. Elizabeth Mattock, Hitchin, a striking 'F' series figure, and Tomesin Tendryng of the 'D' series at Yoxford, are quite large and awkwardly turned in pose. Tomesin is accompanied by three sons and two daughters in shrouds, and two daughters of Norwich workmanship in ordinary dress. The Symondes at Cley are an elaborate 'G' series group with eight detached children and a powdering of scrolls inscribed 'Now thus'.

The East Anglian shroud brasses are similar in form to those described, though their stylistic peculiarities are traceable to the Norwich series of patterns. Some are almost completely covered by the shroud. The best Norfolk examples are:

Robert Brampton and wife, d.1468 engr. c.1483, Brampton (Fig. 242)
Thomas Tyard, S.T.B., priest, 1505, Bawburgh
Henry Scolows and wife, 1515, St Michael Coslany, Norwich
Thomas Sampson and wife, 1546, Loddon.

The first is a very pleasing and animated pair, quite inappropriate to their shrouded state.[4] The Bawburgh and Loddon figures have their arms folded across their breasts. The latter is engraved in an earlier style than the date of the inscription. Thomas Wymer, 'worsted weaver' 1507, Aylsham, is an unusual figure, depicted as standing naked in an open shroud. His pose and expression indicate surprise and embarrassment.

The complete composition to Francis Yonge, Esq. 1533, Edgemond, is most probably Coventry work belonging to the third midland series. This is an elaborate brass, including armorial shields and a shield bearing the wounds of the Passion.

A particularly curious representation is that of Richard Foxwist, notary 1500, Llanbeblig. The deceased is depicted as if lying on his death bed with his head bandaged. He nevertheless appears alert and holds a shield bearing the Five Wounds. A penner and ink-horn record his profession *(The Craft,* Fig. 243).

Cadavers and skeletons

The corruption of the body is more gruesomely represented in a small group of brasses. The shrouded figure is shown completely devoid of life, or in an advanced state of decomposition. In a few cases the bare skeleton alone remains. Joan Strangbon 1477, Childrey, lies stretched out on the top of an inscribed tomb, a forlorn figure making a striking contrast with the splendid representation of the Holy Trinity above her. Elizabeth Horne 1548, Shipton-under-Wychwood, lies upon a shroud on the floor of a room, the walls of which are covered with linen-fold panels. This setting, appropriate to a family group, appears fantastic for its sole dead occupant *(The Craft,* Fig. 241). John Brigge 1454, Sall, and Thomas Fleming, LLB 1472, New College, Oxford, are both emaciated corpses on which the flesh clings tightly to the bones. Most macabre are a group of corpses in the last stages of decomposition. The best known of these is at Oddington to Ralph Hamsterley, rector engr. c.1515 (*The Craft*, Fig. 61). The figure is practically a skeleton. His remaining flesh is devoured by great eel-like worms, and from the skull issue the verses:

Vermib*us* hic donor
et sic ostendere conor
Q*uo*d sicut hic ponor
ponitur *omn*is honor.

The grinning, shrouded skeletons of Richard Howard and wife 1499, Aylsham, are a Norwich third series design of a similar kind. Brasses of comparable subjects are: c.1500 at Sedgefield, man and wife, Lowestoft, man and wife; c.1510 Hildersham (Fig. 249); 1518 Appleton; c.1530 Corpus Christi College, Oxford; and c.1540 Wiveton.

Richard Notfelde 1446, St John, Margate; Thomas Childes 1452, St Laurence, Norwich; and a man and two wives c.1480, Weybridge,[5] are represented as bare skeletons, held together by residual tendons. They are little more than anatomical caricatures, but may have been effective in emphasizing the end of earthly joy and honour. The first and third are of London work, the second of Norwich, with a characteristic foot rest.

It is pertinent to note a comparable gradation of horror in the examples from the rest of Europe which have been described. The shrouded figures of Copman, the Munters and the Baves at Bruges are sombre but dignified. The Palincks at Alkmaar, Holland, are gracefully portrayed. The Hutterocks at Lübeck are a sensitive representation of the dead (*The Craft*, Fig. 198). Yet these fine monuments have their counterparts in the worm infested fragments at Soignies, Belgium, and the hideous disembowelled corpse of Canon Bünau at Naumburg (Fig. 136). The motives of the engravers were the same. The Continental scale was more ambitious.

Chrysoms

In comparison with the grim, naive or grotesque qualities of the shroud or skeleton brasses, chrysom figures are pathetic. Children who died after baptism but before their mother's service of churching were buried in their chrysom or baptismal robe. Brasses of such infants are rare and very small. The figures are almost completely bound up in their robe, only the face being visible. Among eight of the period are:

Dorothy and John Dacre, 1491, Sheriff Hutton
Benedict Lee, c.1505, Chesham Bois
John Colvyle, c.1505, Ketteringham
John and Roger Yelverton, 1510, Rougham (Fig. 250)
Elyn Bray, 1516, Stoke D'Abernon (*The Craft*, Fig. 242).

Elyn Bray is by far the most detailed and well engraved. The baptismal cross is marked on the robe at her head. The Sheriff Hutton and Rougham brasses are both on small rectangular plates, and afford an interesting contrast of York and Norwich treatment. The former is austere, the latter decorative with a miniature canopy. John Colvyle is another example of Norwich work, being of the fifth series. Other chrysoms are depicted in association with their parents at Blickling 1512; Cranbrook 1520; and Birchington 1533.

Miscellaneous examples

It is appropriate to conclude this chapter by mentioning two brasses in which death symbolically takes a place within the composition. The first is the brass of John Deynes 1527, Beeston Regis. Part of this memorial, when on a high tomb, was a very large skull, a symbol of death, fixed to a side (*The Craft*, Fig. 244). This skull now lies on the floor near the figures. It is life size, heavily shaded and engraved on thin metal, and is perhaps a later addition. More important are the fragments of the brass of John Rudyng 1481, Biggleswade, on which the foot inscription is a dialogue between the writer and Death, who stands as a skeleton with darts. The inscription emphasizes Death's part in the dispute, and proclaims his power over all men, in answer to the complaint that Rudyng should have been spared.

This stern and uncompromising message is proclaimed, though less specifically, by all the shrouded and skeleton effigies.

17. Continental brasses: the decline of the craft

Throughout the latter half of the sixteenth century monumental brass engraving declined steadily on the Continent of Europe though maintained in certain cities such as Dresden through the interest of particular families. The causes of this decline may be surmised. The search for naturalistic representation favoured other treatment and media. More immediate in its effect was the widespread destruction of these memorials. Civil war, influenced by a blend of religious and political issues, created havoc in France, the Low Countries and the Empire. The Calvinist fury at Antwerpen on the 19th August, 1566, heralded a widespread iconoclasm in which brasses were ripped up wholesale, to be subsequently looted. For those seeking a permanent memorial, stone must have appeared a more favourable choice. Fine brasses were still made, but for a contracting clientele.

The Low Countries

Brasses made in the Low Countries are found in small numbers until 1620. The engravers of three of these monuments are known. The large brass of Abbot Léonard Betten 1607, formerly at St Trond and now in the Museum de Bijloke at Gent, is signed by Libert van Egheem of Mechelen. Dr Duncan Liddel's brass d.1613, at St Nicholas West Church, Aberdeen, is known from documentary sources to have been the work of Gaspard Bruydegoms of the Antwerpen Mint. The third, to Canon Roland Thienen 1616, at Sittard, is signed by Frederik Malders, goldsmith, of Maaseik. Only the first of these craftsmen was a marbler in the mediaeval tradition, the others being metalworkers who apparently turned their skill to this end as opportunity arose.

The majority of surviving brasses are of modest size, and intended as mural monuments. Four brasses of men in armour have been recorded, all depicting the deceased kneeling at prayer:

- Unknown in tabard charged with the arms of Clerc of Mechelen, quartering Fevere, c.1570, Museum of Archaeology and Ethnology, Cambridge (on reverse of inscription to Steven Copping, 1602)
- Lambert de Warluzel, 1572, Bois de Lessines
- Franchoys van Wychuus, Esq., with wife, 1599, St Bavon cathedral, Gent (Fig. 252)
- Willem de Clerck with wife, 1608, Musée des Métiers d'Art, Mechelen.

In every case the male figure is bareheaded, and wears a tabard over his armour. The palimpsest at Cambridge shows the man kneeling before the Blessed Virgin and Child, appearing as in a vision. Lambert de Warluzel kneels before a crucifix on an altar, aided by St Lambert vested as a bishop. The group is set beneath a classical arch with an achievement of arms and allegorical figures. The Gent brass is the best of the four. The family is arranged around a prie-dieu with a representation of the Crucifixion and the city of Jerusalem in the background. Four of the sons and the esquire wear tabards. Franchoys's gauntlets lie beside him, and his plumed helmet behind. His wife is dressed in a French hood, long-peaked bodice, skirt and fur-lined mantle. One of her daughters is dressed as a nun. The composition is set within a Renaissance arch, hung with shields and surmounted by an achievement. Willem de

Clerck kneels with his wife in a classical setting, decorated with shields of arms. It is probable that all but the third of these brasses were made in Antwerpen or Mechelen.

Civilian brasses are more varied in scale. The Spaniard Francisco de la Puebla and wife 1577, at St Jacques, Bruges, is commemorated on a large rectangular floor plate which is a recognisable descendant of earlier Flemish models (*The Craft*, Fig. 245). The border consists of an undulating inscription broken by two shields of arms and the Evangelists' symbols at the corners. An embroidered background curtain meets the receding pavement base. An achievement of arms is placed above the head of the man, while an angel holds a lozenge of arms above the woman. The figures of the adults, though apparently standing, rest their heads on cushions, their small daughter standing between them. There are considerable affinities in arrangement between this design and that of Jehan de Likerke 1518, and wife at Bruges cathedral, or the Cortewille brass in the Victoria and Albert Museum, London (*The Craft*, Fig. 190). The figures and detail are highly fashionable. Francisco is dressed in a short cloak with sleeves, ruff, doublet and trunk hose. His long and shapely legs give him a most elegant appearance. His wife wears the 'Paris head', a chain, and gown with puffed embroidered shoulders and tight sleeves. Her skirt is plain, but made of some rich material. Her daughter is similarly dressed but with a plain gown. This is an excellent brass, engraved most probably in Bruges itself or Antwerpen.

Another Spaniard, Pedro de Valencia, son of the Spanish Consul, is also commemorated with his wife on a brass of 1615 at St Jacques, Bruges (Fig. 253). The brass is large, and composed of a number of separate plates. The figures are well engraved but rather thick set and short. Both stand on pavements and rest their heads on cushions. Their dress is comparable with that of the Pueblas, but less elegant. Above on individual plates are an achievement of arms and an angel supporting a lozenge. A rectangular inscription with four shields of arms is set at the base. This memorial is a notable palimpsest and is now set in a large hinged frame. The reverse was almost certainly removed from the Convent of the Carmelites at Bruges, and the obverse was probably engraved by a craftsman of the city.[1]

The rectangular plate to Duncan Liddel, M.D. d.1613, engr. c.1619, Aberdeen, is of a very different character (Fig. 254). The brass is framed by a border inscription, and an epitaph fills about half the central space. The upper part is engraved with a picture of the Doctor, seated in gown and cap, writing at his desk. The desk is strewn with instruments of his work, and to his right and left are numerous books and other articles of his calling. A small curtain is stretched behind him and a shield of arms with a motto is set against the wall. The design is probably based on an artist's drawing, and one very possibly made in the Doctor's study. George Jamesone, the first great Scottish portrait painter, worked at Aberdeen and was studying at Antwerpen at the time this brass was made. Perhaps one of his early portraits was used as a model.

Six other civilian brasses are of lesser importance. All are mural compositions showing family groups in devotion to a sacred subject. All are in Belgium.

Pertsevael Pollet with wife, engr. c.1557, St Martin, Courtrai
Bartholomew Penneman with wife, 1560, Onze Lieve Vrowe Kerk, Dendermonde
Ghysellbrecht van Hoorenbeke with wife, 1571, same place.
Jean Localin with wife, 1579, St Jacques, Tournai
Marie and Jeanne de Lannoy, c.1585, same place
Jaques Pottier with wife, 1615, Templeuve.

The first is by date strictly outside this period, but its treatment and presentation are consistent with the latter rather than the earlier half of the sixteenth century. The family is grouped around a crucifix. The brass was set up by Canon Jan Pollet of Lille after the death of both his parents, and several of the figures, including Pertsevael and his wife, hold crosses, signifying death, or have crosses placed over their heads. The costume has little detail of interest, and the lettering of the inscription is of only fair quality. Bartholomew Penneman and his family kneel before the Blessed Virgin and Child aided apparently by St Bartholomew and St Bridget of Sweden, Bartholomew's wife being Brigitte Meulandts. The Hoorenbeke and Localin families kneel before a crucifix. Marie and Jeanne de Lannoy similarly kneel before a crucifix, and are appropriately aided by the Blessed Virgin and St John the Baptist. Jaques Pottier and wife kneel before a Calvary aided by St James the Great and St Agnes. This brass is of inferior workmanship, the main part of the plate being taken up by the inscription. The dimensions of the brass are unduly narrow for the height.

Ecclesiastics form a small and uneven collection. The largest example is Abbot Léonard Betten 1607, in the Museum de Bijloke at Gent (Fig. 255). This is a classical and over elaborate memorial, still retaining its multi-coloured inlays.[2] The Abbot is vested for mass, wearing a rich mitre and a chasuble with a central orphrey embroidered with figures of saints. His crozier with vexillum rests against his left arm. His head lies against a large cushion, though his feet appear to stand upon a pavement. The figure is set within a niche flanked by ornamental columns supporting a tympanum above. Two winged figures are seated on the cornice supporting a shield of arms surmounted by a mitre. The inscription is set on a tablet at the foot, and engraved in Roman capitals. In contrast to this Italianate design, Josse Lambrecht engr. c.1580, at the Hôpital Saint-Josse, Bruges, is based on mediaeval Flemish models, traceable to such fourteenth-century figures as Simon de Wenslaugh at Wensley. The priest lies in mass vestments, with richly embroidered orphreys (Fig. 256). His hands are crossed over his body, and a chalice lies on his breast. His head rests upon a large cushion. The brass, of separate inlay type, is large and of excellent workmanship. The following ecclesiastics are of a smaller scale:

A priest, with initials F.Q., 1570, Musée d'Antiquités, Douai
Thomas Buys, 1570, the Cathedral, Nijmegen
Michel de Herry, 1574, Froyennes
A Canon, c.1580, Nivelles
Canon Roland Thienen, 1616, Sittard.

The two earliest are in mass vestments with chalice, but rather dull in treatment. The Nivelles Canon, in cassock and surplice with an almuce over his left arm, kneels in adoration before the Crucified Redeemer. The perspective and general draughtsmanship of this design are unusually competent. Michel de Herry kneels on one side of a crucifix, on the other side of which is St Michael, trampling the Dragon. The brass is of poor quality, comparable to the civilian at Templeuve. The last is a delicate engraving, as might be expected from the workshop of a goldsmith. The canon, in cassock and surplice with biretta lying beside him, kneels before a Crucifix, the whole being executed in very shallow lines.

There are in addition to these figure brasses a few heraldic compositions of considerable interest. The following are important examples:

Adrien Bave d.1538, Louise Van Halewyn d.1534 and François Bave, 1555. The Cathedral, Bruges
Johan Dirick Hoenzoen van Suburich and wife, 1568, St Janskerk, Gouda
Willem van Bampoele and wife, 1569, St Blaise, Crombeke
Pierre de Mouscron (five shields, with inscription of 1829) 1571, Notre Dame, Bruges
Josse de Damhoudre and wife, 1581, Notre DAme, Bruges
Arms of van Hamel supported by two angels, c.1600, St. Sulpitiuskerk, Diest
Zeghers van Male and wives, 1601, St Jacques, Bruges

Anthoine de Nassoingne and wife, 1629, St Lambert, Bouvignes

Jan Quints and wife (inlaid letters, merchants mark, initials with charges from wife's arms). 1629, St Sulpitiuskerk, Diest

The brasses at Gouda and Notre Dame, Bruges 1581 are the most notable. The first consists of inlays to a large slab of blue marble carved with elaborate classical ornament in low relief. The inscription, a large circular achievement, two shields and a label remain. Another label and two shields are lost. The achievement, consisting of a tilting shield and a lozenge slung from a mantled helm with the crest of a tower, is especially fine. All the brass inlays are palimpsest and are (at the time of writing) preserved loose in the Kerckmeesters' meeting room. The brass of Josse de Damhoudere is a large rectangular composition, consisting of an inscription, an achievement and an angel supporting a lozenge, all set within a Corinthian portico, itself faced with classical funeral ornament and eight shields.

There are a few inscriptions of this period, as at Dendermonde 1585, Gent, Museum de Bijloke 1604, and Bruxelles, Musées Royaux d'Art et d'Histoire 1659, but none is of unusual merit. A heraldic composition as late as 1730 has been noted as Forêt near Bruxelles.

Allowing for destruction — and Gaillard records two important civilian brasses of the late sixteenth century which formerly existed at St Walburge, Bruges — there can be no doubt that brass engraving in the Low Countries declined in the face of a fast falling demand, and effectively ceased by 1630. So concluded the work of the most remarkable craftsmen in this medium, whose Europe-wide reputation had been held for three centuries, and some of whose products even at the end retained that excellence of execution on which their fame was based.

French brasses

In so far as the drawings of Gaignières provide an adequate record, the French engravers were equally affected. Gaignières illustrates several inscriptions with shields or mortality symbols of the late sixteenth century, but figures are few. The large Estiene de Brézé 1561, Abbot of Coulombs, was an exception, depicting a figure of traditional style in cope within a cartouche of classical design (Fig. 258). A small mural brass at St Vincent de Brissac commemorated Ysabeau, widow of Jaques Surguyen 1563. She knelt in widow's dress before a Pieta, assisted by a female with a halo holding three crowns — presumably St Elizabeth of Hungary. A later but important memorial lay in the Abbey of Fontevrault. It represented three Abbesses of Royal blood: Renée de Bourbon 1523, Louise de Bourbon 1575, and Eléonore de Bourbon 1611 (Fig. 259). All three clasp the crozier of the first, described as 'Première Réformatrice de Fontevraudt'.

The only large surviving French example of the period is a rectangular plate in the chapel of the Hospice de la Charité at Beaune. The brass commemorates Anthoine Rousseau 1663, and his wife. The surface is now worn, but the two figures are shown recumbent in prayer. Anthoine is bearded and wears a wide-sleeved gown, with buttoned doublet and deep collar. His wife wears a veil, a simple coat and plain skirt. Curious canopies are set over both, seemingly constructed like wooden seventeenth-century font covers. An octagon rises from a pseudo-Gothic base, supporting in turn a cupola on slim pillars. An achievement is set between the canopies and a marginal inscription in Roman capitals frames the whole. Dr Cameron refers to a brass at Meurcé to a priest Michel le Mesnaiger 1620, kneeling before a representation of the Crucifixion, and to another at Moyvillers 1604, consisting of the Crucifixion scene with additional figures of Saints John the Baptist and Anthony. The latter, according to its inscription, was made at Beauvais by Jacques de Nainville.

German brasses

Eastwards several centres had already become inactive. The sole recorded example of Rhenish work was the finely engraved brass of Abbess Katrina von Tecklenburg 1561, Münsterkirche, Essen, which was destroyed in the Second World War. This depicted the Abbess in her religious habit kneeling before a crucifix. A major part of the composition was filled by an achievement. There are no known engraved figure brasses of Nürnberg, Wroclaw or Kraków origin. The only recorded Polish figure brass is that of the Czarnkówskis at Czarnków. (*The Craft,* Fig. 40). The engraver, Walery Kuninck of Poznań, was an itinerant craftsman, and not a professional monumental artist. There are, however, a considerable number of engraved pewter plates with inscriptions, emblems of the Passion and crudely drawn figures both of the seventeenth and eighteenth centuries, which may be regarded as poor successors to the engraved brasses. In contrast the Baltic seaboard workshops, especially in Lübeck, engraved a small number of brasses of significance into the latter part of the seventeenth century, and the Hilligers of Dresden cast and engraved with distinction until the mid-seventeenth century. Both these centres' products require more detailed description.

Brasses from Lübeck and Baltic workshops

The most ambitious Lübeck brass of the period is that of the Lutheran Bishop Johann Tydeman 1561, which was made by the cannon founder Matthias Benning (Fig. 257). The specifications for this brass are given in *The Craft.* The brass is exceedingly large, and deeply engraved on thick plate. The Bishop stands within a classical portico, with a representation of God the Father in the tympanum of the pediment. A curtain hangs behind him; he is fully vested and holds his mitre, an arrangement made essential by the architrave. The bearded face is very possibly a portrait. The design is unbalanced, mainly on account of its excessive width, and shading is applied to excess. It is nevertheless a finely executed work, and one of the major brasses in Europe of the second half of the sixteenth century. The conservative character of the Lutheran reforms is revealed in the vestments, which are unchanged from those of the Catholic Church.

On other plates a simpler but comparable portico is used as a framework for inscriptions, shields, merchants' marks and allegorical devices. All these brasses are engraved on similar thick plate, and were probably made in Benning's foundry. The following is a complete list:

Hinrick Gruter 1524, and wife 1548, engr. 1557. Marienkirche, Lübeck
Karsten Middledorp 1562, Jacobikirche, Lübeck
A guild tablet with angels supporting shield, c.1565, St Annen-Museum, Lübeck
Ludolph Varendorf, 1571, Bremen cathedral.

Another such plate to Cord Wilbeking 1570, has been lost from the Marienkirche, Lübeck.

The brass at the St Annen-Museum, though small, is in the best condition. The architrave is ornamented with roses and a bull's head. A cherub fills the tympanum. Within the portico two angels support a shield, bearing the device of scales. The Bremen plate, though by far the largest, is now seriously damaged by wear.

A second major work, undoubtedly by Matthias Benning, is the large but little known memorial at Lebrade to Sir Iven Reventlow, his two wives and son Gabrigel dated 1569 (*The Craft,* Fig. 248). This is in many respects a more artistic and certainly more interesting composition than that of Bishop Tydeman. A classical arch with inscription takes the place of the portico of the Tydeman plate, though the same reclining female figures fill the vacant space above. The foreground is dominated by the figure of Iven, a large and impressive representation in armour, holding a halberd and grasping the hilt of his sword. The face is perhaps a portrait. A plumed helmet and gauntlets lie at his feet. The wives and son, rather plainly dressed, stand behind to the sides. The detail and arrangement has been designed to give Iven undisputed prominence. The background is engraved with clouds and distant hills, and includes unexpected detail, in particular a representation of a castle with swans swimming below.

Another Lübeck brass, probably from the same source, was the large composition of Gotthard von Hövelen and wife 1571, at the Marienkirche. The family knelt among the Apostles at the scene of the Ascension, the feet of Christ shown disappearing through the clouds, and footprints left behind on the soil below. This remarkable monument was destroyed in the burning of the Marienkirche in 1941, but was fortunately well illustrated by Creeny.

A few heraldic and inscription plates are of Baltic manufacture. A circular plate with inscription and achievement at St Mary's Gdańsk commemorates Sebald Schnitter and wife 1592. The sickle, both as a crest and in the arms, is a good example of canting heraldry. A large rectangular composition, designed by the Lübeck artist Joachim Sager, formerly in the Aegidienkirche and now in the St Annen-Museum, commemorates Adrian Müller 1642. Classical columns, wreathed with grapes and roses, frame twenty-one achievements of arms and the inscription in Roman capitals. A second inscription is engraved on a cartouche above, and below a fat child reclines amidst grass and flowers, resting his hands on a skull and winged hourglass. An inscription to Mattheus Rodde and two wives 1677, at the Marienkirche, Lübeck, is signed by Wolffgang Hartmann. Other seventeenth-century inscriptions are in the Marienkirche and (consisting of separate inlay letters) at the Cathedral of Oliwa.

Perhaps surprisingly there are three brasses of Norwegian manufacture, preserved in the Oslo Folk Museum. All are engraved on thin rectangular plates of brass and gilded, and were presumably the work of an Oslo goldsmith, of whom five are recorded as working at this period. Two of the plates are dated 1593. One from Sørum represents Erick Gertsøn, kneeling in armour before a Crucifix with his plumed helmet, sword and gauntlets before him, with an achievement set over his head. A second representing Eiller Brockenhus from Ønsøy is very similar, though a horse appears behind the kneeling figure, and two achievements are set above. The third plate, also from Ønsøy, commemorates Elsebe, wife of Peder Brockenhus, and consists of an inscription, two achievements, two winged cherubs and three representations of the sacred monogram. These, together with part of a seventeenth- or eighteenth-century achievement in the University Museum, Oslo, are the only brasses attributable to Norwegian engravers.

The Hilliger atelier at Dresden

Turning from the North to Dresden in Saxony, attention returns to the family of Hilliger, and their astonishing series of brasses in the Cathedral of Freiberg. These monuments are by far the most important collection of post-Reformation brasses in Europe, and several as individual engraved monuments have no peer in their time.

Martin Hilliger died in 1544 and was succeeded by Wolf, who consolidated the reputation of the Hilliger family, achieving a fame which attracted orders for cannon from all over Germany. He cast not only for Duke Heinrich of Saxony, and the Electors Moritz and August, but also among others for Duke Wilhelm the Younger of Braunschweig, the Duke of Pomerania and the Margrave of Küstrin. His bell-making was equally celebrated. He died on 30 November, 1576, and was laid to rest in the

Petrikirche, Freiberg, where a brass marked his grave, until the destruction of the church by fire in 1723.

During Wolf's administration of the Dresden foundry, brasses were apparently laid in Freiberg cathedral to two adults and eleven children. Some of these were undoubtedly made under Wolf's supervision. For part of the time, however, Wolf's eldest son and successor, Martin, was in fact in charge. According to a letter of appointment to Wolf given by the Elector August on 3rd June, 1567 — 'We have also permitted him [Wolf] to move freely about the land and to entrust the workshop here temporarily to his son, but he shall have to answer for the work'.[3]

The two brasses to adults commemorate Duchess Katharina 1561, and Duchess Sidonie 1575, widow of the Duke of Braunschweig. The first is undoubtedly the work of Wolf, and the second is doubtful, though the design of both is similar. Duchess Katharina is a large figure wearing a hat, mantle and wimple covering the mouth. She stands sideways against a classical arch of carefully engraved construction. The inscription is at the foot in Roman lettering, supported by two winged figures. The border is wide and filled with shields and a decoration of birds. The topmost shield is supported by sea monsters. This highly ornate treatment of the border is a characteristic of all the Freiberg brasses, traceable in origin to the later brasses at Meissen. Duchess Sidonie is similar though facing more to the front. She stands against a recess with a fluted ceiling.

The earliest of the children, Duke Albrecht 1546, was the son of Elector Moritz. He is depicted as standing wearing a gown of transparent material. The remaining children were from the family of Elector August: Johann Heinrich, 6 months old 1550; Leonore, 18 months old 1553; Joachim, 6 months old 1557; Hector, 17 months old 1558; Magnus, 3 years old 1558; Amalia, 5 months old 1565; Marie, 4 years old 1566; August, 3 months old 1570; Adolf, 8 months old 1572; and Friedrich, 7 months old 1576. There can be little doubt that Wolf was responsible directly or indirectly for all these brasses, though a few are supported by no documentary evidence. Several of the infant children are shown in transparent gowns. August and Adolf both hold crosses. Magnus and Marie are dressed as adults, the former in jacket, cloak and hose, the latter in a gown with puffed sleeves and a pleated underdress. All these brasses have elaborate shield-filled borders, but the settings vary. With some a room interior is indicated with circular lights, through which trumpets are being incongruously thrust. Others are simpler, but include mortality symbols — an hourglass, candle, urn etc. August and Amalia have very rich settings conveying the impression of a miniature picture set in a frame of jewels. Some of the inscriptions of these brasses are in black letter script, others in Roman capitals.

Martin Hilliger succeeded his father, and ably maintained his reputation in the Elector's armoury. Later having given complete satisfaction, he obtained leave of absence for a total of nine years to work at Graz for Archduke Karl of Styria. Shortly after his return to Dresden his appointment was renewed by the new Elector, Christian I. It is recorded that between 1593 and 1594 Martin cast five monumental brasses for Freiberg cathedral, and it is to these brasses that the report of the Treasurer Gaspar Tryller refers.[4] Members of the Saxon house had died during Martin's absence, and three of these memorials were laid over five years after their decease. The brasses commemorate Electress Anna d.1585; Elector August d.1586; Elector Christian I d.1591; and Elector Christian's two children Anna Sabina d.1586, and Elisabeth d.1589. All these brasses are of excellent quality, as might be expected from the supervision they received. Electress Anna is an imposing figure, wearing an open gown with high padded shoulders and short sleeves, a ruff and a lace cap. The inscription is in Roman lettering; the setting consisting of a classical recess and the heraldic border is enriched with masks. The figures and settings of the two Electors are very similar.

Both are attired in suits of etched armour with swords raised over the right shoulder, and with plumed helmet and gauntlets placed on the ground. The details of the equipment were most probably copied from armour in the possession of the deceased. The figures stand on tiled pavements against classical arches. Elector August's border is, like Anna's, enriched with masks; Christian's has a floral background. Elector August's plate bears two sets of initials. The first, H.R., in tall letters, is probably from Hilliger, though why these should appear on one brass only is curious. The other, a smaller E.B., is as yet unexplained. The two infants, wearing long dresses, stand on chequered pavements. The execution of these brasses is of a more refined quality than those of Wolf and, in spite of their wealth of detail, these memorials are striking compositions.

Martin Hilliger died in Dresden on 5 September 1601, and was succeeded by his second son Johannes, better known as Hans. He was appointed cannon founder to Elector Christian II in 1602, and, like his father, cast great quantities of cannon and bells. He made whole peals for St Anne's Dresden, and for churches in Silesia and Bohemia, and received many distant commissions for artillery. He succeeded in securing more favourable terms for his work from the Elector than had been enjoyed by his predecessors. When Hans married for the third time, he requested that a representative of the Elector should attend the wedding, and that in recognition of his faithful services he should be provided with a stag, two deer, a cask of salted wild boar venison, six hares, a cask of Rhenish wine and a cask of Zerbster beer to furnish the feast! It appears from bills that Hans was assisted in making models for cannon and designs for their decoration by the Court Sculptor Sebastian Walther and the Court Painter Andreas Götting. The latter certainly helped in the preparation of brasses.

It is known from a memorandum of 1624 that Hans undertook the making of brasses to Duchess Dorothea, Abbess of Quedlinburg d.1617, Electress Sophia, wife of Christian I d.1622, and to the infant Heinrich, son of Elector Johann Georg I d.1622. The cost of these was estimated at six hundred florins. At the same time Hans made an estimate for a life-size cast statue of Electress Sophie. A further brass to Duke Albrecht of Schleswig-Holstein was made in 1620 for the church of the Holy Cross in Dresden. Other brasses exist in the Freiberg series, to Duchess Sybilla Elisabeth d.1606, Elector Christian II d.1611, and Duke August d.1615, and also to two infants of Elector Johann Georg I, a stillborn son d.1608 (Fig. 251), and Christian Albrecht d.1612. No documentary proof connects these with Hans, but there is little doubt that he was also responsible for them.

The brasses ascribed to Hans and his expert collaborators are the most elaborate at Freiberg. They are in many respects over-shaded and over ornate, but they are superb presentations of costume, and the adults' faces appear to be portraits. Much of the detail is remarkable, in particular the inscribed cards held by Duchess Dorothea and Electress Sophia.

Elector Christian II and Duke August are comparable figures, based on the earlier designs of Elector August and Christian I. Their armour, however, is heavier in form, and more lavish in its intricate details. Both wear long sashes, and Duke August holds a baton in place of a sword. Their settings are formed by narrow arches, the background being speckled with a series of double strokes. Cracked pavements serve as an unusual base. The inscriptions are in black letter script. The initials A.G. are engraved on Christian's plate, and presumably stand for the painter Götting. The three women are remarkable. Duchess Sybilla Elisabeth is magnificent. Her bodice, sleeves and skirt are embroidered all over *(The Craft,* Fig. 247). with flowers. Her skirt is extended by an immense wheel farthingale, her lace edged collar is wide and starched, and a jewelled band is set upon her swept up hair. A heart-shaped locket or reliquary hangs from her heavy necklace. Duchess Dorothea is especially notable for the lace edging to her collar, the wired pearl frontal to her cap, and her slashed sleeves with lace cuffs *(The Craft,* Fig. 248). Her hands are folded over a small cross and a wreathed card or tablet. Electress Sophia is represented as an older woman. Her lace-edged jacket and skirt are enriched with embroidered flowers, and her hat decorated with lace. She also holds a card in the manner of Duchess Dorothea. The lettering of these cards is very difficult to interpret. Dr Gerlach proposes 'Chürfurstin und Herzogin zu Sachsen Wittwe' as the intention of the last line for Electress Sophia i.e. 'CUHZSW' but the meaning of the whole remains obscure.[6] Highly ornamental borders filled with arms surround each plate in whole or in part. Cracked pavements provide a base. The canopies, shaded with lines and flecked with short strokes, and with cherubs in their spandrels, are an unobtrusive element in the compositions. The inscriptions are engraved in most flamboyant black letter script.

The three infants are represented in a pathetic and sentimental manner. Both Christian Albrecht and Heinrich are dressed in long braided gowns, the former led by an angel with an apple, the latter by an angel with a palm branch. The stillborn son of Elector Johann Georg I, lies in swaddling clothes on cushions, resting upon a draped cradle or table. A youthful looking angel with a palm branch gestures to the onlooker.

Hans Hilliger died on 24 April 1640, and was succeeded at the Elector's foundry by Hans Wilhelm Hilliger, presumably his eldest son. He was in charge of the foundry for less than ten years, and most probably died in 1649, the year in which Andreas Heroldt from Nürnberg filled his post. Little is known of his activities. It is however certain that in 1643 he was instructed by the High Court Chamberlain, von Taube, to cast a brass for Sybilla Marie, daughter of Johann Georg I, who died in that year. This was the last brass to be placed in the Freiberg mausoleum. The plate appears to be unfinished, the inscription being blank. The little girl, in a richly embroidered dress and a cap decorated with pearls and lace, stands on a cushion. The caster's estimate of the cost of this brass fortunately survives. The following calculations were made:

> 'Metal required — 7 cwt 10 lbs (made up of 3 cwt 86 lbs of good malleable copper; 1 cwt 34 lbs of tin and 2 cwt of block brass). To mould the brass, to cast it, to clean it ready and polish it, to engrave the portrait, the coats of arms, the borders and the inscriptions, to inlay them in black and finish completely, would cost 21 florins for every cwt of finished casting; when fully worked the brass would weigh only 4 cwt 26 lbs and would therefore cost 88 florins, 15 groschen, 9 pfennigs'.[7]

Monumental brass engraving effectively ends in Saxony with the passing of the Hilligers from their long held position in Dresden. Their record in this work, spanning at least five generations, is unique, and affords an insight into the type of family business which must have been common in the Middle Ages. The distinction of their patrons placed unusual resources and opportunities at their disposal. Their brasses, though late in the history of the craft, display effectively the great merit and strength of German design, especially during the Renaissance and post-Rennaissance periods. The typical German composition of a large figure with wide border inscription or ornament, was able to bear the changes which naturalism demanded far more successfully than other conventions, where canopies and backgrounds took a more prominent place, and where the figures were reduced in scale and importance. In the author's opinion the most impressive brasses of the late sixteenth and seventeenth centuries are to be found at Freiberg, though including as their equals English plates from East Sutton and Chigwell, where it will be shown the same emphasis was made.

Miscellaneous memorials

The few remaining Continental brasses are isolated memorials with no clear stylistic affinity. At Braunschweig, in the Martinikirche, was an oval plate to Pastor Joachim

Jordan 1639, kneeling before a crucifix.[8] It was of very thin metal and probably engraved by a local goldsmith. Rheinau Abbey, in addition to some cast relief plates, has two engraved figure brasses to Abbots Theobald Werlin von Greiffenberg 1598, and Ebenhard von Bernhausen 1642. The former is vested in cassock, dalmatic, mitre and cope, to which the latter adds a tunicle; they hold a crozier with vexillum, and have an original treatment and expression. The canopy of the first is of remarkably light construction, an unexpected use of separate inlay. The later brass is signed by Johann Heinrich Amman, a painter. A third engraved plate, with mitre and crozier, arms and shield, represents Abbot Basillius Itten 1697. This is a rather plain and ugly design, decidedly inferior to the others. These brasses are probably of South German manufacture. Dr Cameron lists four inscription plates with arms at Zelking and a more interesting small brass in the same church to Ludwig Wilhelm 1634, depicting a contest between a knight and Death.

Lastly, and most inviting to speculation, is the large rectangular plate in the University Chapel, Sevilla, to Don Parafan de Ribera, Duke of Alcalá 1571. This is a virile representation of a Spanish aristocrat, presented in etched armour, holding his plumed helmet at his right hip and his sword with his left hand. A shield of arms is placed on both sides of his head. The execution is of good quality. The border of the plate is wide, decorated with a classical pattern, and frames a further inscription. This memorial has no feature which indicates a Flemish origin, the source of most brasses in Spain and Portugal. Affinities, such as they are, are closer with the Freiberg brasses, but there is no reason to suspect a connection. There is no documentary evidence to suggest it, and stylistic differences are substantial. It is only proper to conclude that this is a Spanish brass created as a special order by a gifted metalworker, who like others in this century successfully undertook the occasional commission.

18. English brasses, 1560-1620

Judged on the available evidence brass engraving by 1560 was a declining craft on the Continent, and markedly so in the centres east of the Rhine. In England, by contrast, the engravers' business flourished, in spite of the destruction in the mid-sixteenth century. The English craft, however, changed significantly both in its organization and products during the reign of Queen Elizabeth I. The decay of the Marblers' Company, the influence of emigré sculptors and the manufacture of a cheap English plate were the three important factors of change.

The decline of the Marblers

The decline of the Marblers is admitted in negotiations made on the 20 July 1585, between them and the Freemasons. According to the records of the Court of Aldermen, 'Item. this day John Recorde and John Thynne wardens of the companie of Marblers, Thomas Gardyner, John Bolstred, William Wilford, marblers, and William Kyrwyn and Thomas Kettle, wardens of the companie of ffremasons being present in this courte the saide wardens and others of the said Companie of marblers were humble suitors to the same Courte that as well in respect of the great decaie and disabilitie of their saide Companie as for many other respects they might be united incorporated and conioyned to the saide Companie of ffremasons...'.[1] This application was agreed and the marblers attending were promised acceptance by the Freemasons. William Bradley, marbler, was admitted a Freemason on 31 August 1585. On 28 September 1585, Cornelius Cure, Barnard Bole, George Anselowe and Alexander Blake, all marblers, were admitted Freemasons.[2]

It would appear that there were only ten members of the Marblers' guild remaining in 1585, and that their organization was no longer effective. No reasons are given for the decline but two may be suggested. Firstly the considerable destruction of brasses, especially during the reign of King Edward VI, and reuse of their old stones presumably disorganized their manufacture. There is an apparent fall in the number of surviving figure brasses of London origin between the years 1550 and 1560 when compared with the preceeding ten years. The absence of provincial work is especially striking. Furthermore, these disturbances coincided with the arrival in England of Dutch and Flemish tomb sculptors, for the most part escaping from religious persecution. Two notable examples are William Cure, who started work on Nonesuch Palace in 1541, and Gerard Johnson (born Janssen), both of whom came from Amsterdam. These foreigners established themselves at Southwark, well situated for water transport and outside the jurisdiction of the City Companies. Such craftsmen rapidly attracted important customers both by their skill and their knowledge of contemporary European patterns and decoration. Their workshops were for some fifty years pre-eminent in London, and it may be presumed that some brass engravers found it more profitable to be associated with these businesses outside the city either as direct employees or by accepting sub-contracts. Johnson engraved brasses in his workshop, and the evidence for this has already been cited in *The Craft*. William Cure's participation is less certain, though it is unlikely that his son Cornelius should appear among the marblers were this not the case. Cornelius was born in England, and it is possible that the family sought membership of the Company to obtain standing within the City. Cornelius is the only craftsman of known distinction of those recorded among the marblers, as he and his father later became joint master masons to James I, and made the tomb of Mary, Queen of Scots at Westminster. It is possible that the improvements in Tudor brasses noted about 1545 arose from the participation of the Southwark immigrants. Certainly by the close of the sixteenth century brasses were products of the sculptors workshops in and around the City, and in several cases the engraver can be identified.

The English brass industry

The establishment of an English brass industry, exploiting local sources of both copper and calamine ore, was stimulated by the demand for cannon and especially carding combs for the wool trade. The government invited leading German authorities to search for copper and calamine. Investigations for copper were carried out between 1564 and 1566 by Daniel Höchstetter, Ludwig Haug and Hans Louver, all of them prominent members of Haug and Company, Augsburg, aided by Thomas Thurland, Master of the Savoy. A rich deposit was discovered at Keswick in 1566, and the enterprise was formally incorporated in 1568 as the Mines Royal. Comparable investigations were carried out by William Humfrey, Assay Master of the Mint, and Christopher Schutz, manager of the zinc mining company of St Annenberg. Calamine ore was discovered in Somerset. The manufacture of brass was attempted at Bristol, but was moved to Tintern Abbey to exploit the coal and iron ore of the Forest of Dean. Brass was first produced in 1568, and the venture was incorporated in that year with the name of the Society of the Mineral and Battery Works. This activity was not long confined to the West, and in 1582 a brass factory was started near London at Isleworth. These developments are described by Henry Hamilton.[3] One effect of this industry was to supply the London engravers with large quantities of thin cheap plate, at a time of rising monumental costs. English brass, though subject to denting and even tearing, was well suited to the very detailed and shaded treatment of this period. As the abundant supply of reused looted metal was consumed by 1585, so English plate supported the craft successfully for over fifty years.

Brasses from London workshops

Large numbers of figure brasses were engraved throughout the period, and these may be broadly classified into two main groups: *pre* and *post* 1585. The first of these are easily recognized successors to the 'Lytkott' style of figures described in Chapter Twelve. The later group are to a greater extent treated in a realistic manner with occasional portraiture and heavy shading, and many have inscriptions engraved in Roman capitals or script. The engravers of the earlier group cannot be specified, though some were probably among the marblers of 1585. In addition it is certain that an R. Treswell was engaged in the manufacture of brasses in London. The evidence for this is interesting. A latten sundial dated 1582 and signed by R. Treswell, had on the reverse a portion of an early sixteenth-century shrouded figure lying on a mattress. Further portions of the reverse have been discovered reused for the shields of Erasmus Paston engr. c.1580, Paston, and part of the inscription of Wilmot Cary 1581, Tor Mohun, proving that all this work came from the same source[4] Treswell's role is uncertain. He may have been an engraver, designer, or both. A water colour painting of buildings in Westcheap bearing his signature is preserved in the British Museum. His identity is likewise doubtful, though he was perhaps Ralph Treswell of London and St Albans, whose son Robert, born in 1556, was appointed Somerset Herald in 1597.

An inscription and arms at Cheselborne, 1589, is signed by Thomas Wittes, but the unusual treatment of the brass indicates that he was probably a provincial engraver.

Figures in armour

Figures in armour during this earlier period show only slight variations in equipment from the years immediately preceding, though their overall appearance changes considerably. John Gyfforde with wife 1560, Northolt, and William Gardyner with wife c.1563, Chalfont St Giles, are in most aspects of their armour the same as Christopher Lytkott. Thomas Gascoign 1566, Burgh Wallis, is a good example though uncharacteristic in some details, the visored helmet and gauntlets being unusual at this date. Several alterations in pattern introduced after 1565 imparted a clumsy appearance, especially to full-face representations. Alexander Newton 1569, Braiseworth, is a typical example (Fig. 262). His fauld is short but spreads at a wide angle from the waist, making the hips very broad, Much of his mail skirt is exposed, his tassets being narrow and tapering slightly to a straight bottom edge. A large sword hangs at his left side and a dagger at his right. His legs are poorly drawn, with small ornate sabatons and ridiculous poleyns. His arms and shoulders are heavily protected, the latter with decorated pauldrons having high haute-pieces. His breastplate is reinforced with a ridged plackart, an apparent anachronism. A minute close helmet is set behind his head. The solidity of this figure is further enhanced by the failure of the engraver to cut out the spaces between the legs and other points, the unwanted metal being simply cross hatched; this treatment was common, especially when engraving fragile reused plate.

There are many examples of this decorative and rather unconvincing armour, of which the detail of Simon Malory 1580, Woodford-by-Thrapston (Fig. 262), is an illustration. Figures in semi-profile have generally better proportions and a slimmer aspect. Especially good brasses in this pose are those at St Decumans, to Sir John Wyndham with wife 1571, and at Churchill, to Raphe Jenyns with wife 1572. Some other military figures have a simpler treatment, and are probably more accurate, such as George Arundell with wife 1573, Mawgan-in-Pyder. The kneeling husbands of Anne Drewry 1572, from Depden are represented in this less ostentatious manner (*The Craft*, Fig. 34).

Further changes in detail become common after 1575. Arm and shoulder defences appear of more moderate size, though there are exceptions, as Sir Edmund Brudenell with two wives 1584, at Deene (Fig. 264). The mail skirt is no longer worn, exposing the trunk hose beneath. Tassets are enlarged, and evidently constructed less flexibly, and are attached to the bottom of the breastplate. Poleyns are shown of a more practical shape, often decorated with large petalled flowers. Frills appear at the neck and wrists. Francis Clopton 1577, Long Melford, is a typical example shown full face, and John Cosowarth with wife 1575, Colan, an unusually good semi-profile representation. Only a few military figures are clean shaven, and these mainly from the early years of this period. Beards pre-1575 are usually long and pointed, almost concealing the gorget and reaching the chest, and the moustache is heavy and drooping. After 1575 beards are full but trimmed closer to the chin, and moustaches have a spreading almost waxed appearance. Hair is worn short and no longer conceals the ears.

Although these brasses may be viewed as one connected series, there are nevertheless differences in the treatment of detail which indicate the introduction of new patterns. Whereas Alexander Newton is in the direct development of the 'Lytkott' style, others, such as the husbands of Anne Drewry, show a different treatment of detail, in many respects as significant as the changes in the form of the armour. Page-Phillips has drawn attention to different methods of representing frills and tasset hinges, and has through such revealing details identified a sub-series, which he describes as the 'Daston' style after an armed figure of that name at Broadway,

Worcs.[5] Simon Malory shows several of the Daston features, in particular the rectangular tasset fixtures, though this brass is an early transitional example towards the naturalistic representation of the Southwark sculptors. The author has described such brasses as 'post Lytkott' in view of their closely related characteristics, so embracing the many modifications of pattern which took place before the great changes of the last twenty years of the century.

Other notable examples from the years 1560-85 are:

Sir John Arundell with two wives, 1561 Stratton
Robert Cheyne with wife (of earlier date), engr. c.1565, Chesham Bois[6]*
Sir Edward Warner, 1565, Little Plumstead
Sir John Arundell, K.B., with two wives d.1545, engr. c.1565,
St Columb Major[7]*
Sir William Molineux with two wives c.1570, Sefton (*The Craft*, Fig. 101)
Sir William Harper with wife, 1573, St Paul, Bedford
Henry Fortescue, 1576, Faulkbourne
Sir William Baynton with two wives, kneeling, 1578, Bromham
Edmund Shorditche with wife, 1584, Ickenham.

Special mention has been made in *The Craft* of Sir William Molineux and his curious mail coif. This rather large composition is most probably London work. The wives are peculiar, but the inscription and Sir William's figure are conventional in execution. Sir William Harper was Lord Mayor of London and is shown with a civic mantle over his armour. Another unusual brass is that to the Disney family 1578, at Norton Disney in which William d.1540, and Richard d.1578, are shown with their families as half effigies, arranged on two tiers with shields and inscription. Both men wear visored helmets, one presented in profile.

The tabard is worn on the following armed figures, adding considerably to their interest:

Sir Arthur Eyre with wife, kneeling, c.1560, Hathersage
Sir Giles Strangewayes, 1562, Melbury Sampford
Sir John Russell with wife, kneeling, 1562, Strensham
Sir John Tregonwell, kneeling, 1565, Milton Abbey
Holt?, kneeling, c.1570, Society of Antiquaries, London.

Sir John Tregonwell at Milton Abbey is set at the back of an imposing canopied tomb and, with an achievement and two shields of arms, affords an arresting display.

The later military brasses of the period form a substantial collection, continuing the series just described but influenced by designers of greater skill and perception. The letters in the possession of Viscount Gage prove that the sculptor Gerard (Garrett) Johnson was responsible for several of the best examples, and it may be presumed that his workshops enjoyed a major part in the production of memorial brasses at this time. A good deal is known of this sculptor. He came to England in 1567, married an English wife, and was listed, together with his wife and five sons and seven employees, in the Return of Strangers from the parish of St Thomas in 1593. In addition to his work for the Gage family he was employed at a cost of £200 to carve and erect sumptuous tombs to the third and fourth Earls of Rutland, which were erected in 1591 at Bottesford. The difficulties of the journey and the sculptor's accommodation are recorded in the Belvoir Household Accounts. Mrs. Esdaile has attributed to Gerard Johnson the important tomb at Titchfield of Henry Wriothesley, second Earl of Southampton, both on stylistic and certain uncited documentary evidence. Gerard Johnson died in 1612, naming in his will two of his sons, Nicholas and Gerard. These carried on the workshop, making among other notable monuments the tomb of William Shakespeare at Stratford-on-Avon.

There are four military brasses at West Firle, all of which were evidently engraved under Johnson's supervision, and were made between c.1585 and 1595. These consist of representations in semi-profile of Sir Edward Gage d.1569, and wife (Fig. 261); Thomas Gage d.1590, and wife; and full-face representations of George Gage and John Gage with his two wives (*The Craft*, Fig. 75). All the male figures are well proportioned, with carefully drawn faces and hands, and hair falling in natural locks over the forehead and temples. Their armour is accurately defined. The gorgets, peascod breastplates, imitating the current civilian fashion, humped pauldrons and long tassets edged with pickadills correspond with existing late sixteenth-century armour. The legs are protected by greaves, poleyns, and laminated cuisses, the feet by sabatons. The buckles of the tassets and the hinges of leg and arm defences are properly represented. Starched ruffs appear at the neck. The figures are heavily shaded, but the hatching is purposeful and emphasizes the shape of the forms to which it is applied.

Other brasses of a very similar pattern, and apparently of a common origin, include:

Roland Lytton with two wives, 1582, Knebworth
John Wingfield 1584, Easton
Edmund Bockinge with two wives, 1585, Ash Bocking
Thomas Stoughton 1591, St Martin, Canterbury
Edward Bulstrode with wife, 1599, Upton.

These are no more than a selection of a group which from their style and general treatment were either made in Gerard Johnson's workshop or by Southwark craftsmen associated with him. Another figure of considerable merit commemorates the centenarian Thomas Hawkins 1587, at Boughton-under-Blean. The engraving and design is in the Johnson manner, but the armour is of a less common pattern, showing the thighs protected by extended tassets reaching to the poleyns. William Golding, Belchamp St Paul 1587, John Eyston 1589, with wife, East Hendred, and Thomas Nevynson 1590 with wife, Eastry, are similarly armed. Two contemporary figures of London origin with notable details are at Haccombe 1586, and Upminster 1591. The first is a small figure showing Thomas Carewe wearing a helmet with visor raised and placing a hand against his scabbard. The other, to Geerardt D'Ewes, is peculiar, and certainly not a Johnson work (Fig. 260). In the author's opinion it is a unique brass. showing a combed morion, a popular infantry helmet of the period. The frontal view confuses the shape, but the comb is perfectly clear and the shaded triangle is evidently the underside of the curved brim. This curious figure makes an interesting contrast with that of Sir John Gage.

Later patterns which may be attributed to the Johnsons are seen at their best in the large and excellent brasses of John Windham with wife 1596, St Decumans and Nicholas Wadham with wife 1609, Ilminster (*The Craft*, Fig. 64). In these the armour is unchanged, though the dagger is hung from a small waist belt by a sash. The figures are in semi-profile with the left leg placed well forward, standing upon a low circular plinth. The decorative strapwork bordering of the shields may be compared with those at West Firle. Other particularly good brasses of this pattern are the following:

John Killigrew with wife d.1567, engr. c.1600, Budock[8*]
Edward Leventhorpe with wife, d.1551, engr. c.1600, Sawbridgeworth
John Brudenell with wife, 1608, Deene
William Clerke with wife, 1611, Wrotham
Thomas Windham d.1599, engr. c.1612, Felbrigg.

Kneeling figures, often engraved on rectangular plates of thin English brass, are fairly common. These are usually fixed in mural marble settings in which the inscription is occasionally directly cut, as for John Shellee and wife, 1592, Clapham. A particularly notable example is the little known brass of John Cocke, gent., one of the four gentlemen servants to James I, at Stagsden (*The Craft*, Fig. 251). The armour is well represented, and the stiff collar and square-cut beard are typical of the early seventeenth century: the lock of hair raised above the forehead is emphasised. The brass has additional interest as it was clearly intended for John and his wife Anne, and was set up by her in 1617. However, according to the inscription, a daughter Elizabeth died while the brass was being prepared, and Elizabeth's figure was accordingly inset in the place reserved for Anne. This rather unbalanced composition affords further evidence of the close relationship between the patron and the engraver.

Another brass requires special mention, though not for the detail of the armed figure. This is the small rectangular plate to Edmund West 1618, who is depicted reclining on a tomb, while Death strikes at him with a dart (Fig. 265). He is surrounded by his mourning family, including two infants in a cradle. The symbolism of the subject in no way detracts from the evident grief of Edmund's wife and elder daughters. The brass is set at the north end of a high tomb which is further decorated with panels engraved in the stone. The brass bears the signature of Epiphany Evesham — 'Evesham Fecit' — and adds another distinguished sculptor to the engravers of brasses. Evesham was born in Herefordshire and after being apprenticed to the emigré Richard Stevens of Southwark, established his own workshop, his best known monuments being the tombs of Lord and Lady Teynham 1618, Lynsted, and Sir Thomas Hawkins 1618, Boughton-under-Blean. Both of these monuments are enriched with fine subsidiary figure work of a remarkable naturalism. The mourning daughters of Sir Thomas Hawkins share the mood of the Marsworth group. Evesham is known to have engraved the brass of Dr John Owen, once in Old St Pauls,[9] and most probably other still existing brasses by him remain to be identified.

Male civilians

Civilians are very numerous and tend by the character of their dress to be monotonous. Their chief garments were a square-cut, long sleeved doublet buttoned down the front, worn with trunk hose or stuffed breeches and small well shaped shoes. Frills or ruffs were worn at the neck and wrists. The capacious glove-sleeved gown was worn over all, and in most cases conceals the clothes beneath.

An important example from the beginning of the period is Edward Goodman 1560, Ruthin (Fig. 267). His gown is lined with fur, and the sleeves have triple apertures; a small purse is suspended from his waist band. Edward was a burgess, and wears not only a scarf of civic dignity but a hat of a type which is unique on English brasses. His face is clean shaven and his hair long, fashions which were rapidly changing. Edward appears again on his wife's brass of 1583 in the same church (Fig. 268). This is a kneeling family group, most probably set up by his distinguished son Gabriel Dean of Westminster, who is shown among the children wearing a scarf. The bearded sons are typical for the date and Edward himself is conventional except for his clean shaven face. This undoubtedly recalls the fashion prevailing in Edward's lifetime. Concern for such a point of accuracy is revealed in three brasses at Thames Ditton engraved between 1580 and 1587, that of John Polsted d.1540, being very similar to the later figure of Goodman. The extreme antiquarianism shown in the brass of John Saye at St Peter, Colchester, is noted in *The Craft*.[10*]

Occasionally the gown has additonal decoration, such as striping on the sleeves or thick and carefully engraved fur. Two admirable examples are the large full-length figure of John Webbe, Mayor 1570, with his wife at St Thomas, Salisbury, and William Gresham d.1579, kneeling, with wife and family at Titsey. This latter brass is reminiscent of the Fermour style of the early 1550's. Another kneeling figure, William

Strachleigh 1583, with wife and daughter at Ermington, illustrates the cut of the gown well, with its sleeves, padded shoulders and neatly edged aperture for the arms. Few of the later civilians are as interesting as these, though a very large but otherwise typical gentleman with his wife c.1600, at Harrow is notable. This brass is engraved in the Johnson manner, with feet firmly placed on shaded plinths. Its main defect arises from its battered condition. These are the largest figures engraved on thin English plate known to the author. Another decorative figure is the Venetian glass maker and engraver, Jacob Verzelini, Esq. 1607, at Downe. His gown is fairly wide open, revealing a rich striped and slashed doublet. His wife is among the most elaborate of Jacobean women.

Among the better examples of this style of dress are:

Robert Poynard with two wives, 1561, Barkway
Ralph Hawtrey with wife, 1574, Ruislip
Allaine Dister with wife, kneeling, c.1575, Lavenham, (The Craft, Fig. 249)
John Cutte with wife, kneeling, 1575, Burnett
John Yate with wife, 1578, Buckland
Thomas Inwood with three wives, kneeling, 1586, Weybridge
Nicholas Grobham with wife, kneeling, 1594, Bishop's Lydiard, (Fig. 272)
Edward Gage with wife, kneeling, 1595, Framfield
Thomas White with three wives, kneeling, 1610, Finchley.

It is noteworthy that seven of the brasses listed are engraved on rectangular sheets, a marked change from the established English preference for separate inlay compositions, but undoubtedly promoted by the fragility of English hammered plate.

A far smaller group of civilians are dressed in a short cloak, leaving doublet, breeches and hose exposed to view. A sword is occasionally shown hung on the left side, and passing below the cloak's edge. These figures are more valuable as illustrations of costume and include a few brasses of unusual quality. The finest is George Clifton with wife 1587, at Clifton, a little known brass, which, had it been laid in south east England, would have been much publicised (*The Craft,* Fig. 252). George is admirably drawn, and his face may be a genuine likeness. His great ruff, striped doublet and splendid breeches compose the most ostentatious dress on any Elizabethan brass. A plainer but nevertheless well designed memorial is that at Watford set up by Dorothy Lady Morrison to three family servants — Henry Dickson, George Miller and Anthony Cooper. The brass is dated 1613. These three trusty men show a sober Jacobean version of the Clifton dress. The brass is engraved in what may be generally described as the Johnson manner and is in no way peculiar. However, the Morrison family employed the great London sculptor Nicholas Stone to carve their tombs at Watford, a master who is known to have engraved brasses. This may therefore be an early plate from his workshop. Another figure with unusual details is Arthur Crafford, gent. 1606, at South Weald whose cloak has broad embroidered facings. A curious but sadly mutilated brass at Crowmarsh Gifford shows the trunk of William Hyldesley, gent. 1576, at whose waist is a bag of mediaeval dimensions.

In addition to the examples described and listed there are a few special civilians who demand individual description. Of such is the venerable octogenarian Thomas Noke, 'comenly called Father Noke', who was created an esquire by Henry VIII and 'for his excellencie in artilarie made Yeoman of the Crowne of Englond'. He is shown with his three wives at Shottesbrooke on his brass of 1567, wearing a long-sleeved gown with the crown badge on his left shoulder.

Yeomen of the Guard were established by King Henry VII as a personal bodyguard to the Sovereign, and were granted a special uniform consisting of a red tunic bearing a Crowned Rose badge, red breeches and stockings. Two brasses of the period illustrate this uniform, commemorating William Payn with three wives (one lost)

1568, East Wickham, and John Kent with wife 1592, Aston. The former is an unorthodox representation, in which William's hands are placed apart to display the badge. The Aston brass is worn and battered. A very good illustration of a guard was Robert Rampston 1585, stolen with his wife from Chingford, but fortunately illustrated by Haines.

Two civilians wear the mantle of their civic status. The rectangular brass of Agnes, wife of Allaine Dister and Robert Leache at St Peter's, Colchester was probably engraved c.1575, though the lady died in 1553. Her first husband, commemorated also at Lavenham, is in normal civilian dress, but the second one kneels in his civic mantle, of which the red inlay is almost intact.[11*] Richard Atkinson 1574, Alderman and five time Mayor of Oxford, at St Peter-in-the-East in that city, is shown wearing a scarf and with a heavy fur-lined mantle thrown back over the left shoulder. The fur surfaces are of engraved lead, and the brass is well finished. One of his two wives was stolen as recently as 1921.

Three huntsmen are commemorated by unusual brasses. Mention has been made in *The Craft*, Chapter Four, of John Selwyn 1587, keeper of Otelands Park (*Ibid.* Fig. 29). He stands with his wife and family, dressed in doublet, breeches and hose, with a hunting horn slung over his shoulder. The extraordinary panel above showing on both sides his feat of riding a stag in the presence of the queen is a notable curiosity. James Gray 1591, park and housekeeper at Hunsdon, is engraved on a rectangular plate at Hunsdon and is of equal interest. Dressed like Selwyn, but with a falchion as well as a horn, he shoots a stag with his cross bow. Death as a skeleton rises between them, and strikes Gray with a dart declaring 'sic Pergo'. Both these brasses seem to be by the same hand, and are probably the Johnsons. A pleasantly natural representation is that of William Breton 1595, at Annesley (Fig. 269), in hunting dress, with falchion, bow and arrows, depicted striding off across the grass with a long legged hound. His face smiles beneath a broad brimmed hat.

Lawyers

There are few brasses to lawyers in dress peculiar to their profession. The earliest, Nicholas Luke, Baron of the Exchequer, with wife 1563, Cople, kneels in supertunica, shoulder-piece, mantle and hood. Sir Anthony Browne, Justice of the Common Pleas 1567, South Weald, was apparently similar though only his lower half remains. Joan Bradschawe 1598 is commemorated by a good rectangular plate at Noke, kneeling with her two husbands and children. Her second husband was Henry Bradschawe, Chief Baron of the Exchequer, whose own brass has been noted at Halton. He is shown at Noke in supertunica, shoulder-piece and hood, with a ruff around his neck. A large and handsome brass at Isleham commemorates Richard Payton and his wife 1574. He is described as 'In Greys Inne student of the lawe, where he a Reader was'. Readers were in charge of the students' instruction and played an important part in the life of the Inns of Court. In addition to the figures, there are four shields, an achievement of arms and an inscription in fourteen English verses. The brass was evidently an expensive memorial to a man of recognized learning and status. Richard's dress is not peculiar, but his fur-lined gown is rich, with high collar and braided sleeves. It is worn wide open, revealing his doublet, hose and sash. He holds a small book in the left hand.

It would be inappropriate to leave the subject of civilians without further mention of the remarkable Beale memorial 1593, at All Saints, Maidstone. The brass commemorates members of the family beginning with John 1399. The plate (Fig. 266) is divided into six tiers above a long inscription, the kneeling adults being set apart from their children by classical columns. A total of fourteen adults are shown together with twenty-five children. Whereas some attempt has been made to differentiate the costume in the generations, the result is a varied display of mid and late Tudor dress, all of which was probably familiar to the designer. It is a valuable record of male civilian dress, and the less ornate forms of women's attire. Another remarkable genealogical commemoration is at Otley though only including the representation of one figure.

Females

Female figures may conveniently be described in the periods pre and post 1590. The earlier period shows for the most part a continuation of already established fashions. The overgown, either long or short-sleeved, is generally worn open, revealing the finely embroidered underdress and partlet. Frills are worn at the neck and wrists, and gradually gave way to the starched ruff. The Paris Head is worn with its pendent veil. Many of the wives listed are excellent examples of this costume, in particular Elizabeth Wyndham 1571, at St Decumans and Jane Jenyns 1572, at Churchill. Their sleeves, both of the upper and lower garments, are beautifully slashed and decorated. Anne Strachleigh at Ermington 1583, has large stuffed and heavily striped sleeves. The skirts of the underdress are often gorgeously embroidered with diaper or arabesques, and occasionally the pattern covers the breast also, as on Winifred Clifton 1587, Clifton (*The Craft*, Fig. 252). A particularly fine specimen is the mutilated brass of Elizabeth Hungerford 1571, Weston Underwood, whose skirt is decorated with pineapples and branches interlaced with a crown. Alice Cobham 1580, Newington-next-Sittingbourne, is an attractive figure with short pendent false sleeves falling from behind the shoulders. She affectionately pats her eldest son on the head.

Three important half figures were evidently based on one pattern. Anne Terrell 1592, Little Warley, is the latest and the smallest. The others are very large and were clearly engraved together in or about 1585. One commemorates Dame Katherine Plumbe d.1575 at Wyddial, and the other Elizabeth Eynns 1585, at York Minster. Both wear the Paris Head and large striped sleeves, and hold open books with texts from Psalm 119: 30 and 54. The engraving is excellent and a personal likeness may well be intended.

Heraldic dress fell out of use at the beginning of the period, though wives at Hathersage c.1560 and Strensham 1562, wear heraldic mantles, in keeping with their husbands who wear tabards. The small kneeling figure of Anne Heydon 1561, Baconsthorpe, is another example.

In contrast to these, many women, especially on small brasses, are simply dressed and neither gown or underdress bears ornament. Two of the wives of Thomas Noke are very plain and wear a rounded cap upon their heads. A similar cap is worn by Agnes Dister at Lavenham. Occasionally a form of four-cornered headdress, similar to the pileus quadratus, is adopted by women, and is shown on the remaining wife of Richard Atkinson d.1574, St Peter in-the-East, Oxford.

Several changes in fashion are discernible about the year 1585. The veil of the Paris Head is commonly turned back and fixed on the crown of the head, as is shown by Winifred Clifton. Alternatively a hat is worn, with a broad brim and wreathed crown. Such are worn by the three wives of Thomas Inwood 1586, Weybridge. By the close of the century the Paris Head was still used but often a large veil or hood was set over it, falling onto the shoulders. The loose gown gives place to a stiffer style of garment. The skirt falls from a close fitting bodice exposing the embroidered underdress which is distended by means of a farthingale. Ruffs are deep and starched to stand out from the neck and were occasionally supported by wires. Shoes are pointed, with thick soles.

Mary Leventhorpe c.1600, Sawbridgeworth, is an example of the most ostentatious costume of the time, matched by Anne Longe 1601, Bradford-on-Avon, and Radcliff Wingfield 1601, Easton. All these are based on a common pattern, most probably drawn by the Johnsons. Elizabeth Verzelini 1607, Downe, is less pretentious in shape but equally arresting, embroidery extending over her gown as well as the underdress. The most remarkable example of female dress of the period is undoubtedly Dame Margaret Chute 1614, Marden (Fig. 274). Her bodice is finely worked and her skirts extended by a wide farthingale. She wears a stiffened collar in place of a ruff, the surface of which is decorated with point lace. Necklaces encircle her throat, and her hair is combed up to a framework of lace and wires, creating the effect of a lofty crown. More representative of dress at the period's close is Elizabeth Crispe 1615, Wrotham. Her bodice and skirt are tied with large bows, and her headdress is partially covered by an enormous hood, approaching the dimensions of the Caroline calash.

Widows no longer wear a particular dress to signify their status. Anne, widow of John Sackville 1582, Willingale Doe, and Alice Talkarne, twice widowed 1605, Stoke-by-Clare, are in no respects different from other contemporary figures.

Ecclesiastics

In general, both ecclesiastical and academical brasses lack distinctive appearance. The Act of Uniformity of the first year of Queen Elizabeth's reign upheld the ornaments rubrick of the first Prayer Book of Edward VI, prescribing for Holy Communion a plain alb with a vestment or cope, thus reversing the prohibition of such garments in the Second Prayer book of 1552. Brasses, however, do not reflect this conservative settlement, and the majority of clergy are dressed in the long, false or glove-sleeved gown which was conventional civilion attire. Academics are often similarly dressed, as for example the Oxford medical Doctor Richard Ratcliffe 1599, kneeling with his wife at St Peter-in-the-East, Oxford.

A few Elizabethan figures are examples of post-Reformation ecclesiastical dress. Edmund Guest, Bishop of Salisbury 1578, in his cathedral, is shown in the approved white rochet (a modified form of alb) with capacious lawn sleeves, a black sleeveless chimere and a scarf. It is doubtful whether the sleeves are passed through the chimere or attached to it, as for practical reasons the sleeves, belonging originally to the rochet, were sometimes transferred to the chimere. He holds a staff in his right hand and a clasped book in his left. His face is bearded, as was common among ecclesiastics at this time. A later semi-profile representation of this dress is found on the two curious brasses of Henry Robinson S.T.D. 1616, Bishop of Carlisle (*The Craft*, Fig. 256), which are described later in this chapter.

Among parish priests is John Fenton 1566, Coleshill, wearing a loose-sleeved preaching gown or open surplice and holding a book inscribed 'Verbu*m* Dei' (*The Craft*, Fig. 253). This very Protestant figure may be compared with Leonard Hurst 1560, Denham, in open cassock and scarf, and Nicholas Asheton, S.T.B. 1582, Whichford. William Dye 1567, Westerham, in cassock, surplice and long narrow scarf, is almost identical with his modern counterpart; this brass is unfortunately of poor quality and badly worn.

In marked contrast are two adherents of the 'Old Religion', whose loyalty is shown on their memorials. Robert Pursglove, Suffragan Bishop of Hull 1579, Tideswell, refused to take the oath to Queen Elizabeth, and remained in retirement, a stubborn supporter of the Catholic tradition.[12*] His unusually good brass shows him in pontificals with crozier (Fig. 270). Care has obviously been take over the delineation of his face, and a personal likeness may be intended. The second and smaller brass at

Dingley commemorates Anne Boroeghe 1577, who was a nun at Clerkenwell before the Dissolution of the religious houses, and spent the remainder of her life in good works (*The Craft*, Fig. 254). Her death is recorded as 'to the greate losse of ye poore who dyverse wayes were by her relieved'. She kneels in her habit, in an interior setting common to rectangular plates of this period.

Three early seventeenth-century ecclesiastics, shown in gown, cap and scarf, are of particular note. The largest is Dean Umphry Tyndall, D.D. 1614, Ely cathedral, whose almost life size figure is set within a border inscription with foot inscription plate, four shields and an achievement of arms. The treatment of his bearded face has affinities with the best Caroline work. A smaller but comparable figure c.1610 is preserved in the Museum of Archaeology and Ethnology, Cambridge. The third, John Wythines D.D., Dean of Battle 1615, at Battle, was Vice-Chancellor of Oxford University, and is shown wearing the Doctor's cap, holding a book in his left hand. This brass is typical of good Jacobean work, accurately drawn if uninspired in design and shallow in execution.

Several ecclesiastics require no particular comment in respect to dress, and but for their inscriptions could be regarded as ordinary civilians. Four others at Barwell, Buntingford, Bletchley and Tingewick are curious in their arrangement, and described later.

Academics

Academic dress has been noted on the brasses of certain ecclesiastics, and there are other examples. It is however difficult to distinguish such dress in all cases. Oxford Doctors for example were authorised to wear on other than formal occasions a false-sleeved gown, similar to that in common civilian use. Walter Bailey 1592, Doctor in Medicine at New College is so represented. There are nevertheless some distinctive academics.

Dean Bill, S.T.D. 1561, is shown in full-sleeved gown and hood at Westminster Abbey. Anthony Aylworth 1619, Doctor in Medicine at New College wears a full-sleeved gown, a deep hood and a pileus quadratus. Also at New College is a Doctor in Civil Law, Hugh Lloyd 1601, kneeling and wearing a winged-sleeved gown decorated with braid. Four Masters in Arts, all of whom died young, kneel in gowns and hoods at prayer at St John's College, Oxford 1571, 1573, 1577 and 1578. Lewis and Griffin Owen 1607, are shown kneeling on a rectangular plate at St Aldate's, the former only being in gown and hood though both were Masters in Arts. Other Oxford graduates include Stephen Lence, M.A. 1587, depicted three-quarter length in cap, gown and hood at Christ Church; William Smith, M.A. 1580, shown kneeling at St Mary Magdalen; and both Thomas Morrey, M.A. 1584, and Thomas Thornton, M.A. 1613, also at Christ Church, Philip Biss, D.D. 1613, Archdeacon of Taunton, at Batcombe, and Isaiah Bures, M.A. 1610, vicar at Northolt, kneel wearing academic dress.

The best of the few brasses at Oxford showing undergraduate dress is that to Henry Dow 1578, at Christ Church, who kneels in a high-collared, bell-sleeved gown with small hood. This young man died at the age of twenty one, having obtained his B.A. degree. Dr Hargreaves —Mawdsley identifies his dress as that of a junior student (scholar) of that college, which is also worn by John Bisschop 1588, at Christ Church. More unusual in presentation are the brasses of Edward Chernock 1581, a commoner of Brasenose, at St Mary-the-Virgin, who wears ordinary civil dress but kneels within a carefully engraved interior setting, and the curious figure of John Pendarves 1617, commoner of Exeter at St Michael's, who stands within a wooden dock, reputedly disputing in the Schools.

The only figure of distinction to an academic at Cambridge is that of Robert Whalley 1591, Fellow at Queens' College. He is large and in civil dress, wearing a ruff, slashed doublet, embroidered breeches and a gown with rich facings. Thomas Prestone, L.L.D. 1598, Master at Trinity Hall, wears a normal civilian gown. Other academics are at North Crawley 1589, and Monewden 1595, both represented kneeling.

Children

Brasses commemorating children, though still uncommon, are more frequently found by the close of the sixteenth century. A pleasing memorial is that of Nathaniell, aged three, and Elizabeth, aged two, the children of Edward Bacon 1588, at Aveley, the boy is in a skirted gown, the girl wears a small hat decorated with lace, and a shield and two crests complete the composition (Fig. 275). Richard Best 1587, Merstham, is shown in a long dress tied at the waist with a sash. The figure of his brother Peter, in swaddling clothes, was stolen about 1845 but renewed in 1911. Other boys, such as William Browne, 1599, Holton, are dressed in doublet, trunk hose and a short cloak. All are small, and several have pathetic epitaphs, that at Woodham Mortimer 1584, beginning 'A little impe here buried is'. Children groups, set around or below their parents often differ from their elders in the detail of their dress. The daughters of Thomas Inwood 1587, Weybridge, wear bonnets, while their mothers have hats. There is generally no effort at individual identification, though names or initials are occasionally introduced, as at Burnett, 1575, and Cople c.1568. Gabriel Goodman, wearing his ecclesiastical scarf on his father's brass 1583 at Ruthin is exceptional.

Shroud and skeleton brasses

Shroud and skeleton brasses are rare, but continue this late mediaeval fashion. Alexander Belsyre 1567, first President of St John's College, Oxford, is represented as a macabre shrouded corpse at Handborough. The brass was laid by a relative, Thomas Nele, Professor of Hebrew at Oxford, who is also shown in a shroud at Cassington, 1590. John Maunsell 1605, at Haversham, is depicted as a skeleton in a coffin. Children in swaddling bands are occasionally shown alone as at Pinner 1580; Aveley 1583; Edgware 1599; and Upper Deal 1606. John Howard 1600, Great Chesterford, is wrapped in a loose cloth. Four infants on a tomb represent the children of John Bond 1612, at St Swithin, Winchester. Other examples of children in swaddling bands are found with adults, especially good examples being the son of Edward Greneville, Esq. 1587, at Wotton Underwood and the child of Mary West 1606, Marsworth, Bucks., and the infants held in the arms of Dorothy Parkinson 1592, Haughton-le-Skerne, and Elizabeth Marrowe, 1601, Clifford Chambers. David Birde 1606, at Boxford is depicted lying in a cot on an appropriately small plate.

Representations of death occasionally took a less direct form, providing some unusual compositions. At Sandford near Crediton Mary Dowrich 1604 lies as a recumbent effigy on a tomb, with her children praying. Four brasses to women who died in childbirth represent the deceased as alive in bed. The best is at Lower Halling to Silvester Lambarde 1587, depicting a splendid four poster bed with carved posts and a cradle with twins nearby (*The Craft*, Fig. 250). Better known and more naturalistic is Anne Savage 1605, Wormington, whose bed is less ornate but very competently drawn in fair perspective, with heavy hangings and a large window in the background. Her dead baby lies in swaddling clothes on the coverlet. Constance Bownell 1581, Heston, is curious, with an attendant angel beside her and a representation of Our Lord in Glory above. Alice Harison c.1600, Hurst, has another bedstead memorial, though of much poorer execution than the others. At Leigh is a design of uncertain significance c.1580, showing a woman kneeling by a tomb containing a shrouded figure, with an angel issuing from clouds and blowing a trumpet (Fig. 246), she declares 'Behold O lord I com willingly'. She may accordingly represent the deceased rising at the last trump, or the widow of the deceased expressing her willingness to follow her spouse. Her veil rather supports the latter interpretation. With the exception of Heston, all these brasses are engraved on single sheets of brass, which facilitate such complicated designs.

Brasses from provincial workshops

All the brasses so far described in this chapter are either evidently, or at least probably, of London origin, and the great majority are from the Southwark workshops. A small number of figures prove the continuity of provincial work.

Engravers carried on a limited business in York, their most important products being three trapezium-shaped plates, showing part effigies of the deceased. These brasses would seem to be based on paintings, an unsurprising development in view of the occasional use of painted panels as memorials, a notable example being the Cornwall triptych of 1588 at Burford. All three are in York:

James Cotrel 1595, York Minster

Robert Askwith, Lord Mayor, 1597, All Saints Pavement (formerly at St Crux), (Fig. 271)

Christopher Harington, goldsmith, 1614, St Martin Coney St.

The first of these is well-engraved, especially as regards the face, the detail of the fur-lined gown and the lettering of the inscription. It is a large plate, and though rather weak in draughtsmanship, is equal in merit to good London examples. The second is more peculiar but interesting, depicting the mayor in hat and scarf, and with signet ring and gloves. It is probable that it came from the same source as the first, the difference in quality arising from the model. The third is considerably smaller and damaged by wear. Other figures of a more conventional pattern though evidently of provincial origin are at Bishop Burton 1579, and Kirkby Malzeard 1604, and the superior group to John Darley and wife 1616, Rawmarsh, may also be of York manufacture. Inscriptions of provincial origin, in lettering very different from London patterns, are also found in small numbers.

A few brasses of indifferent quality are evidence of the near abandonment of effigies by the Norwich engravers. Henry Hobart 1561, Loddon, is a rather ridiculous figure in a tabard. He has a long beard and much of his head is restored. Another figure, in armour, evidently by the same hand, is that of Thomas de Greye 1562,Merton. The armed figure of Peter Rede 1568, St Peter Mancroft, Norwich, has been noted in *The Craft* as a copy of an earlier model by a local engraver. Two women are represented on badly designed brasses at Snettisham c.1570, and St Margaret's Norwich, 1577. Both these memorials are palimpsests, presumably re-used loot from Norwich chantries and churches. Another curious brass, also at Snettisham, is to John Cremer and wife 1610, all the figures including those of the seven children, being in separate inlay. The small inverted shield-shaped brass of Barbara Ferrer 1588, at St Michael-at-Plea, Norwich, is presumably of local execution, depicting a skeleton rising from a tomb, on which is set a merchant's mark. In some respects the most peculiar is the small figure at Ellough of Margaret Chewt 1607. She stands on grass, strewn with a skull and bones, and her headdress is exceptionally large and formless. Superior workmanship is found on a considerable number of inscriptions. William Lee, vicar 1617, at Stapleford may be a late Cambridge engraving.

There is no group of brasses than can be associated with midland engravers, though John Weston 1566, at Rugeley does not appear to be of London workmanship.

In the west of England individual plates, such as Margaret Rolle 1592, St Giles-in-the-Wood, and Edward Boscawen and wife 1619, St Michael Penkivel, indicate the participation of craftsmen possibly in Launceston, Plymouth and Exeter. In Somerset, the brasses of Edmund Windham 1616 at St Decuman's, and of Margery his wife d.1585 at Stogumber, appear to have been made c.1616 by a provincial craftsman. It is in this part of the country that the provenance of brasses is most difficult to establish, and a few of those listed as of London work may not be so. Unfortunately the consistent use of Roman capitals for inscriptions, and the mediocrity of a few of the brasses near the capital, make accurate discrimination very difficult. The poor brass of John Aubrey and wife at Burghill hardly looks of London quality, but yet may be so. Provincial engraving throughout the period adds little of significance to the English series, but at least provides a contrast to the prolific and highly competent London products.

Arrangement and composition: the figure

The most important aspects of the overall arrangement and treatment of compositions are the gradual departures from the spirit of the mediaeval brass, though much of the long established form persisted. The supposedly recumbent figure lingers on into the 1590s through conservatism in design, and some of its related details such as the helm head rest are even found on brasses ascribed to Gerard Johnson. But the intention of the pattern maker was to represent a living person, or to copy sculptured figures of similar inspiration. The plinth or pavement base are only consistent with a standing pose, often stressed by long shadows engraved upon it. The praying position of the hands is retained, but in family groups the adults face each other as if in shared devotion, and the room interiors of many rectangular plates give an appropriate background to the ensemble. The kneeling groups continue well established patterns, adhering closely to the Elizabethan wall monument in placing the figures, with the faldstools being replaced by a low cloth covered table across which they face each other. The framework equally followed the sculptured monuments, the surround to the brass of Anne Drewry and her husbands, 1572, at Depden being a typical example. Others are the classical arches decorated with flowers engraved on the plates at Cople and Fordingbridge, both probably of 1568. The battlements above are a reflection of earlier ideas.

Realism in faces, with possible instances of portraiture, is indicative of a striving for a more human and personal type of representation.[13*] The formal pose is occasionally relaxed. Alice Cobham 1580, Newington-next-Sittingbourne, pats her eldest son on the head, while John Browne ?1597, St John Sepulchre, Norwich, gently holds his sister's hand. William Breton 1595, at Annesley strides off with his dog. John Torksay, B.D. 1614, Barwell, is shown addressing his family from a pulpit, and on a finely engraved plate at Buntingford Alexander Strange, S.T.B. 1620, preaches to his congregation. This brass, similar in execution to a copper plate engraving, probably depicts the interior of Buntingford church, built by him, before the Victorians extended the chancel *(The Craft,* Fig. 255). Such concentration on the deceased's occupation, albeit on a small scale, reflects a similar development in sculptured monuments, such as the tomb of the organist Mathew Godwin in Exeter cathedral.

Foot supports have little place in a vital representation. Sir Edward Warner 1565, Little Plumstead, places his feet on a dog, and Geerardt D'Ewes 1591, Upminster, rests his on a wolf, an allusion to his crest. Philip Marner, clothier 1587, Cirencester, stands, staff in hand, with his dog at his feet and shears by his head. Anne Bartelot 1601, Stopham, has a small dog by her dress, probably a pet included by request.

Settings

The influence of classical designs, promoted by the emigré sculptors, is seen in the settings both of the figures and of the complete plates. Brasses continued to be riveted to floor slabs, to mural panels or to the backs of raised tombs, but the form of the background markedly changed. Continental style was fashionable, encouraging the importation of coloured marbles for the decoration of tombs. Dark stones were favoured for floor monuments, and a large number of Elizabethan brasses are set in imported slabs. Mural panels were invariably carved into the form of a classical arch, though some of the ornament was derived from Gothic precedents. High tombs were raised, entirely classical in style, which occasionally form impressive frames for brasses, well-balanced and with restrained detail as on the Wylmer tomb at Staverton (Fig. 276).

Upon the brasses themselves, the Gothic canopy gives place to classical ornament or the architectural background of room or hall, both of which are confined to rectangular plates, mostly set in a mural position. A good example of classical compartments, enriched with shields of arms and crests, is the brass of William Dunche c.1585, Little Wittenham.[14] More frequently an interior is represented with receding pavement, arches and leaded windows in the background, as at Filleigh 1570, and Constantine 1574; at St Peter's, Colchester, there are three such designs. Alternatively, the background is of brickwork, as at Lavenham c.1575, St Peter-in-the-East, Oxford 1572, Dingley 1577, and Otham 1590.

Shields of arms are inset as the balance of the composition required. Laurence Hyde and wife 1590, Tisbury, are arranged with their family in front of an italianate arcade suggesting the facade of a mansion, while an eagle appropriately holds a scroll, which states 'Every man lying in his best estate is altogether vanitye'. In contrast many of the backgrounds are left entirely plain as at Yate 1590, and Farnham 1594.

Emblematic brasses

The settings of figures in a few cases depart entirely from the established conventions. In this context a small group of brasses is of particular note, all engraved in a shallow and fine technique in the manner of the Buntingford memorial. Four of these are undoubtedly the work of Richard Haydocke, a physician, engraver and fellow of New College, Oxford, who died in 1641. All are filled with allegorical details and in two cases the entire design is symbolic. The following is a complete list:

Erasmus Williams, rector, kneeling, 1608, Tingewick
Henry Robinson, Bishop of Carlisle, 1616, Queen's College, Oxford
Henry Robinson, Bishop of Carlisle, 1616, Carlisle cathedral (*The Craft,* Fig. 256)
Henry Airay, S.T.D., Provost, 1616, Queen's College, Oxford
Thomas Sparke, D.D., Rector, 1616, Bletchley (Fig. 277)
Humphrey Willis, 1618, Wells cathedral
William Button, Esq., d.1590, engr. c.1520, Alton Priors
Robert Longe, 1620, Broughton Gifford
Thomas Hopper, Fellow, 1623, New College, Oxford.

Erasmus Williams kneels on a tomb between two columns linked by a rainbow arch. Suspended from the column behind him are books by Ptolemy, Livy, Pliny, Aristotle, Virgil and Cicero and bundles of instruments connected with astronomy, mathematics, music and painting. Above are the moon and sun. The inscription explains the choice of symbolism:

'His humane Artes behind his backe attende
Whereon spare howers he wisely chose to spende
And from Corinthiane Columne deck't with Artes,
Now to the Temples Pillar him converts.
Under the Rainebowes arche of Promise, where
Of hoped blisse noe deluge he need feare.'

A further line, 'Contrived by his Schollar and his frende', almost certainly alludes to Haydocke, whose signature is engraved on the plate.

The two brasses to Bishop Robinson are almost identical. The themes of the elaborate background are the Bishop's vocation as pastor and peacemaker, and his services to cathedral and college. Carlisle cathedral and Queen's College are depicted, with flocks of sheep safely penned, a wolf sitting with a lamb, discarded weapons, and a crowd of happy country folk. Below these people is the text 'Ad dirigendas pedes nostros in vian [sic] Pacis' and a child among them waves a book inscribed A.B.C. At Oxford several of the sheep bear the initials A.H., which Mrs Esdaile suggests stands for Alumni Haydocii. The connection of these plates with that of Airay, leaves no doubt that both are by Haydocke. Bishop Robinson was Provost of Queen's College and was succeeded by Airay. The latter is shown kneeling on a high tomb surrounded by representations of events in Elisha's life. The design presents the Provost as an Elisha on whom the mantle of Bishop Robinson had fallen. Elijah rides in a chariot of fire and his mantle, inscribed with the Spirits of Teaching and Examining, floats at the Provost's left arm, while below, on his right side, Elisha purifies the stream and in the water swims a fish inscribed with the engraver's initials R.H. The Bletchley brass is less elaborate showing the Rector's bust in an oval, with his three sons and two daughters and figures of Death casting ashes into an urn and Fame blowing a trumpet and rescuing some treatises by the deceased. There is no signature but again the treatment and proximity to Oxford point to Haydocke. Hopper's brass consists of an inscription, a device of circles and triangles, and figures of Aesculapius and Fortune. The inscription records that the monument was completed by R.H., Fellow.

The three West Country plates are engraved with a similar technique but are perhaps of different origin. Haydocke did however move his practice to Salisbury in 1605. Humphrey Willis died at the age of twenty-eight, and he kneels with his back to emblems of vanity and sport (including a tennis racket) and faces armour and weapons described as 'Armatura Dei'. A broken tree in the background with a fresh branch and pendant shield with arms is inscribed 'fracta non mortua'. Angels greet him from clouds offering him the victor's laurel crown. At Alton Priors the deceased is shown climbing out of a tomb in response to the summons of an angel with the 'key of David' as a trumpet. Mrs Esdaile suggests that this brass is the work of William Marshall, illustrator of Quarles *Emblems* in 1635. The design certainly has the character of a bookplate. The brass of Robert Longe is of particular interest. It is the only existing brass that includes the representation of a herald, standing behind a tomb holding a set of shields, from which Death (a skeleton) selects the arms of the deceased.[15] The inscription explains the design, punning repeatedly on Longe's name.

'The life of Mann is a trewe Lottarie,
Where venterouse Death draws forth lotts short & Longe,
Yet free from fraude, and partiall flatterie,
Hee shufl'd sheilds of several size amonge,
Drew Longe and soe drewe longer his short daies,
Th'auncient of daies beyonde all time to praise.'

This group of brasses is the most original contribution of the Elizabethan and Jacobean era to monumental brass design and technique. It was in many respects an eccentric contribution and its inspiration had little connection with monumental art. These compositions nevertheless reflect the ideas and concepts of the age with far greater clarity than the common figure brass.

These curiosities apart, there was little place for religious representations. The figure of Our Lord in Glory at Heston has been noted, and is unique. Occasionally bursts of light are introduced, inscribed with the name of Jehovah, as at Great Yeldham 1612, or with the Dove of the Holy Spirit as at Bishop's Lydiard 1594. An emblem cross, engraved on a rectangular plate with scrolls and floral emblems, commemorates Fridesmond Barnes 1581, at Auckland St Andrew. This is established in *The Craft*, Chapter Six, as the work of a York goldsmith. Emblems more often refer to the passing of time and mortality such as the skull on the Boorde brass 1567, Lindfield, and the little boy blowing bubbles on the brass of Nicholas Grobham and wife 1594, at Bishops Lydiard. Vocational emblems are also rare, two notable exceptions are the brasses of Roger Morris 1615, Margate, and Robert Masters 1619, Burghill. Morris is described as one of the six principal masters of attendance of His Majesty's Navy Royal, and a rectangular plate is engraved with a three-masted warship with guns protruding and flags flying. Masters was a successful adventurer who sailed twice with the famous navigator Thomas Cavendish. His brass consists of a shield of arms and inscription, and beside the inscription a plate showing a globe in a stand. The globe is engraved with a map including North and South America, but omitting the British Isles.

Heraldry and merchants' marks

Heraldry is prominent in many compositions. A few shields are exceptionally large, as that of Thomazin Playters 1578, Sotterley, and achievements of arms are quite common. The detail of the arms is usually well executed and occasionally much of the original painting remains. A remarkably elaborate heraldic plate engr. c.1570 commemorates Sir John Whyte, Alderman of London, at Aldershot, and may be compared in its surround with the figure plates at Cople and Fordingbridge of c.1568. Another brass of similar type, dated 1568, records the lease of Cheylesmore Park to the city of Coventry in 1549 by the Duke of Northumberland, and again in 1568 by his son, Robert Dudley, Earl of Leicester. This particularly handsome plate is in St Mary's Hall, Coventry. It displays the arms of Queen Elizabeth I, those of the Earl, and the arms of the City of Coventry. The ragged staff badge of the Earl of Warwick is engraved sixteen times in allusion to the first grantor.[16] Lady Katherine Capell 1572, is commemorated at Rayne by six shields and a lozenge of arms and two crests on lozenges. Shields and inscriptions are often found as complete memorials.

Though not of English workmanship it is appropriate to mention the inscriptions with arms by the Scottish engraver James Gray. The finer, at St Giles's Edinburgh, commemorates James Stewart, Earl of Moray, Regent of Scotland, who was assassinated in 1570 (Fig. 273). In addition to a large achievement of arms are seated figures of Religion and Justice. The second brass, to Alexander Cockburn, with inscription and two shields 1563, was in the chapel at Ormiston, but is now on permanent loan in the Scottish Museum of Antiquities, Edinburgh. It is probably also by Gray, and the inscriptions on both plates were composed by George Buchanan.

Arms of City and merchant companies are frequently displayed, including several unrecorded on earlier brasses. The Haberdashers' second (1503) coat of arms is found at Faversham c.1580, and South Mimms c.1600. Above the large figure of Roger James 1591, All Hallows-by-the-Tower, London, are the arms of the Brewers' Company, as granted in February 1544 to replace an earlier grant in which they were impaled with the arms of Canterbury and those attributed to St Thomas à Becket. The Brewers, like several other City Companies, relinquished elements that might cause religious offence. The arms of the Ironmongers' Company, granted in 1455 and confirmed 1560, are shown together with the arms of the Merchant Adventurers, and the City of London and a merchant's mark on the brass of John Carre 1570, Stondon Massey. The arms of the Carpenters' Company, granted in 1466, appear above the figure of Thomas Edmonds 1619, Horsell, and the elaborate arms of the Stationers' Company, granted in 1557, are on the brass of John Daye, printer 1584, Little Bradley. A fine shield at South Mimms c.1600 shows the arms of the Eastland Company, incorporated in the reign of Queen Elizabeth I. The inscription of William Doggett 1610, at Boxford has four shields around it including the arms of the best known of the great trading companies; the East India Company, together with the arms of the City of London, the Mercers and Merchant Adventurers companies.

Merchants' marks occur less frequently than in the early years of the sixteenth century, though an interesting example is engraved on a small woolpack on the brass of John Orgone 1584, St Olave, Hart St., London.

Rebuses seldom occur and a device showing a gloved hand holding a belled hawk c.1580 is at Faversham.

Inscriptions

Inscriptions in this period are very numerous and frequently detailed, giving valuable information about the persons commemorated and often expressing the wit and sentiments of the age. The majority of inscriptions are in English, though Latin verse is frequently found on epitaphs of scholars and clergy. Black letter script continued in use to the close of the sixteenth century, though by 1590 a 'lower case' Roman script was occasionally used by the London workshops, to be superseded by Roman capitals. Most inscriptions are recorded on rectangular plates, set below the figures, though marginal inscriptions are quite common.

The epitaph of John Lyon 1592, Harrow, is a good example of a factual record, concluding with a devout expression of a mildly Protestant tone. Its emphasis is directed entirely to the deceased and what was to prove his historic foundation.

> 'HEARE LYETH BVRYED THE BODYE OF IOHN LYON LATE OF PRESTON IN THIS P*AR*ISH YEOMAN DECEASED THE IIIth DAYE OF OCTOBER IN THE YEARE OF OVR LORD 1592. WHO HATH FOVNDED A FREE GRAMMER SCHOOLE IN THIS P*AR*ISH TO HAVE CONTINVANCE FOR EVER AND FOR MAINTENAVNCE THEREOF AND FOR RELEYFE OF THE POORE AND OF SOME POORE SCHOLLERS IN THE VNIVERSITVES, REPAYRINGE OF HIGH WAYES: AND OTHER GOOD AND CHARITABLE VSES HATH MADE CONVAYAVNCE OF LANDS OF GOOD VALUE TO A CORPORACION GRAVNTED FOR THAT PVRPOSE. PRAYSE BE TO THE AVTHOR OF AL GOODNES WHO MAKE VS MYNDEFVLL TO FOLLOWE HIS GOOD EXAMPLE.'

In contrast, the inscription in verse of John Daye 1584, Little Bradley, is openly anti-Catholic and deliberately devious in its presentation of information. Daye was the printer of Foxe's Book of Martyrs. It is conjectured that his widow later married a gentleman of the name of Stone, so explaining the final line.

> 'Heere lies the Daye that darknes could not blynd
> When popish fogges had overcast the sunne
> This Daye and cruell night did leave behynd,
> To view and shew what bloudi Actes weare donne
> He set a Fox to wright how Martyrs runne
> By death to lyfe; Fox venturd paynes & health;
> To give tham light Daye spent inprint his wealth.

But God with gayn retornd his wealth agayne
And gave to him: as he gave to the poore,
Two wyves he had pertakers of his payne
Als was the last encreaser of his stoore,
Who mourning long for being left alone
Set upp this toombe, her self turnd to a Stone.'

Many verse epitaphs are more fulsome in expression and degenerate into doggerel. The following lines in memory of William Barker 1575, Sonning, are an instance.

'Here lyeth the corps of William Barker Esquier, in bowell' of this grave.
Whose dayes by all mens Doome deserved, a longer lyfe to haue
You widowes wayle his losse, and orphanes wyshe his lyffe.
You dearly wante his wysdomes skyll, whose Causes are at stryffe.
Ne you allone lament, your fryndes untymely ffate;
His Ann doth morne amonge the most, who least maye misse her mate.
Ann spronge of Stowghtons stocke, an aunciet progeny,
She wyth her Chyldren wayle this Chaunce, and dolefull destenye,
Yet this bothe we and all, have iustlye to Reioyce,
His iustyce faithe and fraudles hart, hathe wonne the peoples voyce.
His bodie in this soile, and earthlye seat doth lye.
His ffame in ayre his gost for ay, dothe lyve a lofte the Skye.'

Another example of extravagent verse, including striking if macabre contrasts and a classical allusion, is that of Alis Walker 1584, at Barford St. Martin:

'Here lieth the body of Alis Walker, for whose memoriall
Thomas Walker her eldest sonne in token of his
love and dutye hath erected this monument.
whose soule (no doubte) hath pearsde ye cloudes & skalde thempire skies
whose deathe resoundinge ecchoes shewde wt piteous plaintes & cries
whoe lately like a fruitfull vine at table as she had beene,
like olive braunches rounde aboute her children might have seene:
she yesterdaie in goode estate these blessinges did behoulde,
to daie here couerd lieth wt earthe as with her fatall moulde,
the Lorde & giuer of these fruites, decreede yt shoulde be soe,
euen by the meanes he thus her blest, to worke her joyfull woe
soe noew ye wombe yt fruitfull was in yeeldinge fruite decaied
is made a place, & foode for wormes, loe, thus mans parte is plaied
such is the fickle state of man, th'uncertaine lott of life,
noe sooner spuene by Lachese handes, but cutte wt Atrops knife.
Departed this Life in ye Lord in ye calends of Januarie, beinge
after some computation ye first daie of ye yere of or lord one Thousande fiue hundred foure score & four, the 44 yeere of her age.'

Earlier lines at Harford to Thomas Williams 1566, Speaker of the House of Commons, are interesting on account of the closing pagan allusion.

'Here Lyeth the corps of Thomas Willms esquier
Twise reader he in Court appoynted was
Whose sacred minde to vertu did aspire
Of parlament he Speaker hence did passe
The comen peace he studied to preserve
And trew relygion ever to maynteyne
In place of Justyce where as he dyd serve
And now in heaven wth mightie Jove doth Raign.'

Another classical reference on an inscription at Taplow 1617, in the phrase 'mars fled in thee', is an anagram on the name of the deceased Hester Manfeild, and hardly suitable for one described as 'died in the Catholique Romane faith'. This is the only known anagram of the period on a brass. Acrostics, though rare, are found. At Mawgan-in-Pyder one to Jane Arrundell 1577 is now mutilated, but a record is preserved of it in almost complete condition. It is an excellent example of this form of wit.

'Interred here she lyes which...for lyfe well ledd in blisse
An Arrundell she was, alake we can not say shee is!
Nedeles it weare to blaze her birth whose name her stocke can tell,
Estemde in lyfe, bewaild in death of all she lyved so well.
A virtuous made she sw...fyve Queens with earned praise,
Right fitt for vertue fayme & worthe in court to wast her daies;
Recounting last her lyfe under and most assured death,
Unto that place she came to dye, where fust shee toke her breath.
Now lyving threscore yeres and twelve in Dame Diana's bandde,
Did use her bowe and shunne the shafte of Cupids foolish brande;
Even as shee lived, even so shee dyed, so well prepared was shee,
Long looking death as on forwarned wt tyme her death should be.
Loe thus shee Lived & dyed, then wish her soul in heaven to see.'[17*]

After such carefully calculated lines in honour of a spinster, it is a contrast to read the more homely achievements of Robert Gardnar 1571, at Leatherhead compiled by the versifier Thomas Churchyard:

'Here ffryndly Robartt Gardnar lyes, well borne of ryghtt good race
who Sarvd in cowrtt wyth credytt styll, in worthi rowlm and place
Cheeff Sargantt of the Seller longe, whear he dyd duetty shoe
wyth good regard to all degrees, as ffar as powre myghtt goe
He past hys youth in sutch good ffraem, he cam to aeged years
And thearby porchaest honest naem, as by reportt a peers
A ffrynd whear any cawse he ffownd, and cortess un to all
Off myrry moode and pleasantt spetch, howe ever happ dyd ffall
ffowr chyldern for to ffornysh fforth, the table rownd he had
wyth sober wyeff moest matren lyk, to mak a man ffull glad
Prepaerd to dye longe ear his day, whych argues greatt good mynd
And told us in the other world, whatt hoep he had to ffynd
we leave hume whear he loektt to be, owr lord receyve his spreett
wyth peace & rest in Habrams brest, whear we all leynth may meete
qd Churchyard.
He departed owte of thys transetory worlde
The Xth daye of Nouember Anno dn 1571
beyng then of the age of lxxxiij yeres.'

Frustrated romance evidently stirred the pathetic lines at Ditton to Rowland Shakerley 1576:

'This memoryall of his deathe made by a young gentlewoman as an argument of her unseperable good meaninge towards hym.'

It is appropriate to close this selection of Elizabethan verse with the epitaph at Boughton-under-Blean of a very stalwart gentleman.

'I now that lye within this marble stone
Was called Thomas Hawkins by my name
My terme of life an hundred yeares and one
King Henry theight I served which won me fame
Who was to me a gratious prince alwayes
And made me well to spend myne aged days
My stature high my bodye bigge and strong
Excelling all that lived in myne age
But nature spent, death would not tarry longe
To fetch the pledge which life had layed to gage
My fatall daye if thow deseyes to knowe
Behold the figures written here belowe
15 Martii, 1587.'

Conclusion

The Elizabethan and Jacobean period of English brasses is of importance, not only on account of its numerous examples, but in its gradual adaptation of debased formal mediaeval patterns into designs which were generally more natural, more consistent and more expertly drawn. Serious criticism may be raised on several counts. The

Elizabethan heavily shaded, naturalistic figure was unsuited to a flat toneless medium, which responded to a strong lineal treatment. The words of Dr Op de Beeck, applied to Flemish work, are here appropriate: 'Everything builds up to the attainment of the illusion fostered by painting at the easel in contempt of the resources of a proper technique. Monumental art had ceased to be linear in becoming pictorial. This spelt not merely decadence, but death.'[18] Within the following generation the English craft rapidly declined and approached extinction. Furthermore the technology of the period — the thin English battered plate — created a fragile type of monument, easily dented, broken and worn. There was much repetition and many civilians brasses in particular lack variety, and their very number emphasizes their dull similarity. Nevertheless, it is in comparison with the best mediaeval work that the Elizabethan brass is so unfavourably viewed. Such comparisons are invidious, and inappropriate when we consider the recovery it registers from the debasement of much of the early Tudor engraving. When the intrinsic defects and peculiarities of the period are accepted, there remains a wealth of interesting and competently executed memorials, created by craftsmen of high standing, which take an honourable place in the art of their time.

19. English brasses: the decline of the craft

Samuel Harsnett, Archbishop of York, directed in his will of 13 February, 1630, that there was to be 'a marble stone layde uppon my grave wth a Plate of Brasse moulten into the stone an ynche thicke haveing the effigies of a Bysshoppe stamped uppon it wth his Myter and Croziers staffe but the Brasse to be soe rivited and fastened cleare throughe the Stone as sacrilegious handes maye not rend off the one wthoute breakinge the other.'[1] Twenty-six years later the inscription of Thomas Mannock at Fornham All Saints was engraved with the lines 'Let noe man steale away this brass but he whoe knowes himselfe unworthie memorye'. In 1641 Sir Christopher Hatton sent William Dugdale and an artist Sedgewick to Lincoln cathedral and other cathedrals and churches to copy the brasses and monuments before their predictable destruction. Rising fears that a return of the Edwardian sacrilege was at hand, undoubtedly explains in part a steady decline in the demand for figure brasses. The widespread destruction of brasses during the Civil War and Commonwealth confirmed these fears.[2*] It is probable that the English craft would have gradually lost its vigour without these provocations, and given place to the incised ledger slab. In the event the decay was fast, and the industry of the London workshops, in all but the engraving of arms and inscriptions, had really ceased by 1645.

Brasses from London Workshops, 1620-1650

These closing years are of great interest. Macklin described the period as that of 'Caroline Decadence', conceding the existence of but one fine specimen, namely that of Archbishop Harsnett at Chigwell. This, in the author's view, is hardly fair to the evidence, and fails to recognize the work of distinguished sculptors who throughout the 1630's made brasses as well as effigies, as had their predecessors. Outstanding among these is the Royal Master Mason Edward Marshall, who carved a great number of effigies and wall monuments, and was employed in the construction of several of the notable buildings of the time including the Whitehall banqueting hall. Several brasses may be ascribed to him, and the splendid Filmer brass at East Sutton bears his signature. Marshall, in contrast to the earlier Southwark sculptors, owned premises within the City in Fetter Lane. James I's Royal Master Mason, Nicholas Stone, lived until 1647. It is known from his account book that he prepared the brass of Cecily Puckering 1636, at St Mary, Warwick, and it may be presumed that others unidentified are by his hand. A lesser but none the less fashionable London sculptor, Francis Grigs, signed three brasses at St Osyth 1640; Monk Hopton (from Upton Cressett) 1640; and Bradfield, nr Sheffield 1647, and others by their similarity to these are probably from his workshop. Later in the seventeenth century the sculptor's honourable place is to some extent taken by the Wrexham goldsmith, Sylvanus Crue, and the Welsh engravers Robert and William Vaughan who worked in London. The quality of all these craftsmen in some respects surpassed that of their Elizabethan predecessors.

There was, on the other hand, much engraving and design of an extremely low standard, remarkable only on account of its quaintness. Provincial engravers are again evident, not only in the well established centres of Yorkshire and Norfolk but in Derbyshire, Lancashire, Wales and the Western Counties. It is above all in the West that the old tradition of brass engraving persisted well into the nineteenth century, not in the form of figures but with decorated inscriptions of a good style. Provincial figure plates are without exception curious and some such as Seath Bushell 1623, Preston, are grotesque. The difference in standard, between the best of the period and the worst, is the most extreme in the history of the craft. Brasses which may be attributed to London sculptors form a fairly consistent series between 1620 and 1650. These may be described systematically and compared with contemporary provincial memorials.

Men in Armour

A small group of military brasses illustrates well both the complete and the more usual part-armour which was still widely used during the Civil War. The outstanding example is Marshall's splendid figure of Sir Edward Filmer 1629, engraved with his wife and family as a large rectangular composition (Fig. 278). His armour has etched borders, with picadills decorating the tassets and pauldrons. His high boots are typical of the period, and the ruff very prominent. The treatment of the figure is in many respects remarkable, in particular for its delicate and yet restrained shading. Much of the surface is left plain, and major lines are allowed to indicate shape. Certain details appear to be characteristic of Marshall's work, such as the slim hands, the eyes with their completely spherical eyeballs and the position of the feet, one shown in profile and the other in an awkward frontal view. The face may be a portrait, having at least the character consistent with one. Sir Edward's eldest son, Sir Robert, is similarly armed, but wears a cloak. This is in the author's opinion, the finest English brass of the seventeenth century and is a magnificent memorial by any standards. The following military brasses are also probably the work of Marshall:

Richard Barttelot, with two wives d.1614, engr. c.1635, Stopham
William Pen, with wife 1638, Penn
John Pen, with wife 1641, Penn (*The Craft*, Fig. 257).

Both the Penn groups, engraved in separate inlay, are worthy companions to Sir Edward Filmer. The other is of a rather coarser treatment but sufficiently similar to support the suggested connection. Richard Barttelot is shown in complete plate armour with bare hands and head, and long hair flowing behind his shoulders. Another military figure in a less conventional design, which again is probably the work of Marshall, is that of William Strode 1649, Shepton Mallet (*The Craft*, Fig. 258). He is armed in part armour with jack boots, and his streaming hair and 'imperial' type beard are typical of the period. He kneels with his family as if in a church, as Death rises with a dart and strikes his wife. The plate is large and the engraving is of the quality associated with this master.

Three other military brasses are engraved in the manner of Marshall, repeating many of his particular conventions, but are of a quality so inferior that they are better attributed to a London imitator. These brasses are to the following:

George Verney d.1574, engr. c.1630, Compton Verney
Sir John Arundell with wife, d.1590, engr. 1633, St Columb Major
John Arundell with wife, 1633, St Columb Major

A few other military brasses are evidently of London work, the most important being Sir Jarrate Harvye 1638, lying with his wife at Cardington. He is fully armed with plumed visored helmet and gauntlets, the latest brass to show such complete defences. The drawing is inferior to that on the brasses ascribed to Marshall, and the surface far more heavily shaded. Other examples are:

Sir Arthur Gorges with wife, kneeling, 1625, Chelsea
Henry Brockman with wife, 1630, Newington-next-Hythe

John Boscawen, kneeling, d.1564, engr. 1634, St Michael Penkivel

Richard Bugges with two wives, 1636, Harlow.

The Chelsea brass, engraved on a rectangular plate, has the neat regimental order and figures associated with the signed works of Francis Grigs. Both the Newington and Harlow brasses are poorly designed and indifferently executed. John Boscawen's is a rather curious composition and may be of local workmanship, though a London origin is as likely. Two greater curiosities are probably London work. The first at Sotterley commemorating Christopher Playters d.1547, was engraved c.1630, with antiquated armour, including an aventail. George Hodges c.1630, Wedmore, is a unique representation, showing the deceased in a plate gorget, buff coat, sash and high boots and armed with pike and sword (Fig. 287). This is an interesting illustration of the tendency towards the discarding of body armour during the second quarter of the seventeenth century.

Male civilians

Civilian brasses are more numerous than military. Most are dressed in gowns with long sleeves or short cloaks. Over their doublets fall collars, occasionally edged with fine lace. Gentlemen wearing cloaks are frequently shown wearing jack boots also, and armed with swords or rapiers.

Richard Gadburye 1624, depicted with his wife and family at Eyworth is a good example in the Jacobean style. His gown and sleeves are decorated with buttons; he wears ruffs at the wrists and neck and a hat bound with a twisted band. The shading is coarse and heavy and the outline of the figure unduly straight. The traveller John Eldred is commemorated by a brass laid by his son in 1632 at Great Saxham (Fig. 289). Eldred wears a long gown lined or edged with fur, but his figure is distinctly Caroline and almost certainly the work of Edward Marshall. His collar is lace-edged, and he wears a cap. The base is formed of a tiled pedestal. The treatment of the face and the delicacy of the engraving are in marked contrast to those at Eyworth. Robert Alfounder 1639, East Bergholt, is an excellent example showing the short cloak, sword and boots, with the unusual detail of breeches cut at the knees with a nebuly-shaped edge. The plate has not been engraved according to the outline of the figure, a treatment used on several comparable brasses, such as Robert Chambers 1638, Swaffham Prior, and William Palmer with wife 1639, Teynham. The latter brass is a good composition with achievement of arms and border inscription. Palmer wears the cloak but no boots. Walter Septvans alias Harflet, shown with his wife 1642 at Ash-next-Sandwich, is similar to Palmer in some respects, but creates the impression of an older man with a fuller beard, and wears a wide cloak of ample length with a deep falling collar.

The following are additional examples of merit or unusual interest:

Bernard Randolphe with wife, 1628, Biddenden

Robert Coulthirst, 1631, Kirkleatham

William Gardiner, 1632, Daylesford

John Bartellot, kneeling (Inscr. original 1493), c. 1635, Stopham

Abel Williams with wife, kneeling, 1637, Loughton

Richard Cressett with wife, kneeling, 1640, Monk Hopton, formerly Upton Cressett

George Coles with two wives, 1640, St Sepulchre, Northampton *(The Craft,* Fig. 260)

John Morewood with wife, kneeling, 1647, Bradfield.

Both the Daylesford and Kirkleatham figures are large. The Northampton brass is a remarkable composition explained by its epitaph. The Monk Hopton and Bradfield brasses are both signed by Grigs; the Loughton plate is also probably by him with another to William Bisse and wife 1625, Croscombe. Their arrangement is regimented and uninteresting in comparison to Marshall's treatment. The restored figure at Stopham is probably another of Marshall's works, and is a well executed brass in separate inlay. Bernard Randolphe and his wife are a curious pair, reclining with their heads on pillows. A brass at Winkfield, alluding to the charity of the deceased, commemorates Thomas Mountagu, yeoman of the guard, who holds a halberd in one hand and distributes bread to two poor men with the other. (Fig. 280). He died at the venerable age of ninety-one.

Females

Women are more elaborately dressed than the men, having a greater elegance, when well represented, than their Elizabethan and Jacobean predecessors. Lady Filmer and her daughters are clothed in typical Caroline fashions. The former wearing a bodice and open skirt revealing a petticoat with an embroidered and fringed edge, a gown, starched ruff, cap and wide hooped outer hood. The daughters display fine examples of striped sleeves, tied near the elbow with large bows. The hair of both mother and children escapes from under their caps in long curls. Most women wear high-heeled shoes often decorated at the front by bows or rosettes. Sarah, wife of John Pen, Penn, has a large feather fan hanging at her side. While veils and the voluminous hood usually cover the head, tall hats are fairly common as worn by the wives of George Coles 1640, St Sepulchre, Northampton. An unusual figure commemorates Anne Bedingfield 1641, aged 80 at Darsham, who is enveloped in a large and heavy greatcoat with turned-back cuffs.

The probable works of Edward Marshall stand out unmistakably. The Darsham brass is perhaps among these, but more noticeably the following single figures:

Dorothy Mannock, 1632, Stoke-by-Nayland
Elizabeth Culpeper, 1633, Ardingly
Lady Susan Drury, 1640, Penn.

These may be closely compared in the detail of their presentation with Elizabeth Filmer. Two other good figures of doubtful ascription are Jane Cradock (1626), Ightham, and Ann Kenwellmersh 1633, Henfield. The former wears a hat, the latter holds a fan and is standing with her grandson Meneleb (Fig. 283).

Ecclesiastics and academics

The outstanding ecclesiastical figure of the period is Archbishop Samuel Harsnett 1631, at Chigwell. This is a magnificent brass, depicting the Archbishop life size, wearing, in addition to the rochet and chimere, a richly embroidered and jewelled mitre (Fig 279). He holds a book in his right hand and crozier without vexillum in the left. The face with its large hooked nose can hardly be other than a portrait. The execution of the work is exceptionally fine. The quality and the details of execution suggest Edward Marshall as the engraver. The memorial is completed with a base inscription, four shields, and a marginal inscription with the Evangelists' symbols at the corners and roundels engraved with cherubs' heads. The text of the inscription is highly deprecatory, emphasizing the unworthiness of the deceased as Bishop of Chichester, Bishop of Norwich and Archbishop of York. The foot inscription, however, explains:

"QUOD IPPISSIMUM EPITAPHIUM EX ABUNDANTI HUMILITATE SIBI PONI TESTAMENTO CURAVIT REVERENDISSIMUS PRAESUL'

Harsnett lived as Archbishop for three years only, but in that period overshadowed his co-primate Archbishop Abbot of Canterbury. As Torr has noted, the representation of post-Reformation Anglican primates wearing the mitre was a fashion peculiar to York. The sculptured effigies of Archbishops Sterne 1683, Dolben 1686, Lamplugh 1691 and Sharpe 1714, in York Minster carry on the precedent created by Harsnett. This brass was set in a mural position, apparently in the eighteenth century. Local pride and interest in the founder of Chigwell School has undoubtedly led to its excellent preservation.

There are a few other brasses to clergy and academics. Andrew Willet, D. D., rector 1621, Barley, is shown in academic cap, gown and scarf. Thomas Palmer, 1521, Professor of Common Law and barrister of Lincoln's Inn, is shown in a gown at Epping Upland. William Procter 1627, Boddington, wears cap and gown. Maurice Hughes, vicar 1631, Abergavenny, is a larger and better executed figure, though unfortunately covered by the chancel floorboards. Thomas Stones 1627, in gown and cap at Acle is a half effigy and may be of provincial workmanship. Jerome Keyt 1631, Woodstock, is a small but good representation of the academical dress of a Bachelor of Civil Law. Other clergymen are depicted kneeling with their wives. Edward Nayler 1632, at Bigby is described as 'a faithfull and painefull minister of God's word', while Abraham Gates, S.T.B., at Western Colville 1636, is accompanied by an archangel with a trumpet. Nicholas Roope, B.A. 1637, kneels in gown and hood on a rectangular plate at St Aldate Oxford.

Children

There are several memorials to children. John Drake 1623, Amersham is a small kneeling figure. William Glynne 1633, aged two years, Clynnog, has long curly hair. This brass is probably from Edward Marshall's workshop, as is also the small figure of Elizabeth Culpeper 1634, aged seven, at Ardingly. She is dressed like her grandmother but in simpler style. John Byrd 1636, Headcorn, kneels above a surprising inscription, recording that he 'in the time of his sicknesse delivered many exhortations to his parents takinge his leave of them with such unexpected expressions as are not common in so younge a childe' (Fig 284). Other children at Collingbourne Ducis 1631 and West Deane 1641, may be of provincial workmanship.

Four further brasses to children are of remarkable design.[3] Dorothy 1630, and William 1633, infants of John and Marie King, are both represented at St George's Chapel, Windsor as lying in their cradles. The plates are carefully engraved, and set with verses and marginal inscriptions. At Wooburn Arthur Wharton 1642, aged nine months, lies on top of his tomb, holding a flower. It is probable that all three were engraved in the same workshop as apart from stylistic similarities the phraseology of the inscriptions is comparable. A pathetic brass at Llandinabo commemorates Thomas Tompkins 1629. This boy was drowned, and is depicted standing in a pond.

Groups of children, set below or behind their parents' figures, are varied in treatment. Those ascribed to Edward Marshall's workshop are lively and distinctive, and form most attractive groups. The East Sutton children are the best of several good collections. In addition to those on brasses listed should be noted the children of Sir Jerome Horsey 1626, Great Hampden, and several groups at Stopham, mostly set in earlier memorials to the Barttelot family. Meneleb Rainsford 1633, Henfield, is a well engraved boy with curly hair, holding a large hat and standing by his grandmother.

The convention of depicting children, who died before their parents, as holding a skull in their hands became quite common in the second quarter of the century.

Shroud and skeleton brasses

The convention of laying shroud and skeleton brasses was still maintained. Mary Howard 1638, West Firle, lies in death with her arms crossed downwards, and is almost concealed by her shroud (Fig 286). Henry Millner 1635, Wickenby, is entirely covered by the shroud and lies on a tomb surmounted by a shield of arms, and two urns with wreathed skulls and bones. John Eager 1641, Crondall, is commemorated by a skeleton lying on a pallet. At Lavenham 1631, and Odiham, 1636, are children in swaddling bands, and at Stowmarket an eight-year-old child, Anne Tyrell 1638, is shown as shrouded.

Brasses by provincial engravers

Some figure brasses by provincial engravers are easily recognized, though several in the North and West Country are of sufficiently orthodox style to be doubtful.

Northern engravers' work is found in both Yorkshire and Lancashire. The two most important brasses are those of Ralph Assheton and wife 1650, at Middleton, and his son-in-law Adam Beaumont and wife 1655, Kirkheaton. Both are evidently by the same hand. Assheton was a Parliamentary commander, and is represented in a vigorous pose, holding out a baton in his right hand, with his left placed on his thigh (Fig. 285). He wears cavalry armour, with long tassets and boots. Beaumont is very similar though less bold. The wives are inferior in design. The brass of Thomas Atkinson, tanner 1642, at All Saints North Street, York, is a late example of the large partial effigies, of which earlier York examples have been cited. The recumbent figures of Anne Shuttleworth 1637, Forcett, lying beneath an arch with figures of Labour and Rest, and Elizabeth Popeley 1632, Birstall, shrouded between the two kneeling figures of her daughters, are both peculiar rectangular compositions, though of less certain local provenance.

The incompetence of the East Anglian engravers is revealed in two Norfolk brasses. Thomas Holl 1630, formerly at Heigham and now preserved in the Norwich Museums, is an interesting but wretchedly drawn figure (Fig. 282). He is dressed in an ornate fashion with short cloak, sash, boots and rapier and his hair is long and crimped. The workmanship is so poor that the plate is only a curiosity. Likewise at Dunston are three figures ascribed to Clere Talbot, L.L.D. 1649, and his two wives. The engraving is slightly better than that of Holl, the man appearing in a long-sleeved gown, and the wives draped in shrouds. There can be little doubt that the females were based on the brass of Dame Katherine Sampson at Loddon. It is probable that the derivative brass at Ringsfield to the Garneys family (*The Craft,* Fig. 99) is also of local origin, and if so is of somewhat better execution.

A small brass of apparently midland origin commemorates Sir Clement Edmonds kneeling in armour and wife 1622, at Preston Deanery. In Derbyshire a minute civilian figure is included on the inscription to Latham Woodroofe, 1648, at Bakewell, and a curious infant in swaddling bands commemorates Ephraim Shelmerdine 1637, at Crich. The kneeling figures of G. and M. Box c.1650 at St Peter-le-Bailey, Oxford, are certainly not of a London type, and may be the work of an Oxford sculptor such as William Byrd.

Other peculiar brasses are found in the Western Counties. A lady c.1630, Launceston, and Richard Chiverton with his wife 1631, Quethioc, are both designed in the manner of Cornish slate memorials. Both brasses are quite carefully engraved, but the drawing verges on the ridiculous. The Quethioc children have no feet, and their father is comical (Fig. 290). Francis Hayes 1623, kneeling at St Cuthbert's Wells, is a roughly executed plate. Of superior workmanship are the brasses at Bath Abbey to Sir George Ivy in armour, and wife 1639, and at Otterton, 1641, showing the children of Richard Duke and Robert Duke. On all three plates the figures are small and arranged around the border of the inscriptions. The brass of Margaret Robertes 1637, with her child in swaddling clothes, recently stolen from Abergavenny, is a crude design apparently by an unskilled local engraver.

A singular brass requiring special mention is the latest of the 'bedstead' compositions, to Eliza Franklin 1622, St Cross, Oxford, 'Who dangerously escaping death at 3 severall travells in childebed, died together with the fourth.' Three of her children are shown in shrouds, and one in swaddling clothes lies on the coverlet. The plate is executed in the manner of Haydocke, being very lightly engraved, and is quite possibly another of his works. The affinities of the design are more with the Willis brass 1618, at Wells cathedral, than with Haydocke's known brasses in Oxford. Another brass of similar execution using another design is that of Margaret Bury d.1633, Queeniborough, set up and designed by relatives in 1634.

Figure brasses, 1650-1700

This varied assortment of figure brasses, dating to the middle of the seventeenth century is followed within the next hundred years by a further small selection, which with a few exceptions are no more than isolated memorials. These are, to all appearance, the occasional work of engravers whose energy in this field was all but entirely devoted to the making of inscriptions and arms. The great exceptions are the brasses made by Robert and William Vaughan, and to a lesser extent those of the goldsmith Sylvanus Crue of Wrexham. The Vaughans lived near Fetter Lane, London, and were almost certainly related. Robert engraved portraits of King James I, Lancelot Andrewes and other notables, and made maps for Dugdale's *Warwickshire*. He is known to have died in 1668. William executed a set of plates for *'A Book of such Beasts as are most useful for drawing, graving etc'*, by F. Barlow, in 1664. All the important brasses of these craftsmen are at Llanrwst, forming an excellent collection:

Sir John Wynn, bust, in lozenge d.1626
Lady Sydney Wynn, bust in lozenge, d.1632 (Fig. 281)
Lady Mary Mostyn, bust within inscribed oval on lozenge, 1658
Sir Owen Wynne, bust in lozenge, 1660 (*The Craft,* Fig. 76)
Katherine Lewis, half effigy in tomb in lozenge, 1669
Dame Sarah Wynne, three-quarter figure in frame, 1671 (*The Craft,* Fig. 262).

The brass of Sir Owen Wynne has been shown on the conclusive evidence of the Wynn papers to have been engraved in 1661 by Robert Vaughan (*The Craft,* chapter eight). In 1650 (letter no. 1933) Vaughan was already working for the Wynn family, and was engaged in engraving a copper plate with a family pedigree, together with portraits and arms. Many of the faces were apparently imaginary — 'for the faces I am at my owne fancy till I come to Sr John Wyn your Father' — though a few were real likenesses. The Wynn papers are far from complete and no other brasses are mentioned, but there can hardly be any doubt that Lady Sydney's brass, showing her in a magnificent ruff, lace cap and hood, was engraved much later than 1632, and was made by Robert Vaughan shortly before that of her husband Sir Owen. The lozenge to Sir John Wynn is also suspect. The treatment of the long-bearded bust is far less accomplished than that of Sir Owen, but it gives the impression of contrived antiquity.[4*] The author is of the opinion that all these three brasses were engraved by

Robert Vaughan between 1645 and 1661. The bust of Lady Mary Mostyn is different in character, and is close to being a profile representation. It is signed by Sylvanus Crue. The inscription, unlike the others at Llanrwst, is in Latin. Lady Mary was of very High Church persuasions, and may have specially requested it. Katherine Lewis appears to be by a different hand, being a restrained engraving, and lacking the confidence of Sir Owen Wynne and his wife. This may be the work of William Vaughan. The plate of Dame Sarah Wynne is signed 'Guil Vaughan sculpsit' and is a superb engraving. Photographic representation can alone do justice to the fineness of the execution. It is a most beautiful representation of a lady of Charles II's reign, in a setting wholly appropriate to the period.

There are no other known figure brasses by the Vaughan brothers. A delicate engraved skeleton under an arch, commemorating Humphrey Lloyd, Esq. 1673, at Wrexham is signed by Crue, as is also the comparable but more decorative plate at Holt in memory of Thomas Crue 1666. Inscriptions signed by this engraver are at Llangollen, 1663, Wrexham 1674, and Llandysilio 1674.

The only brass that may be compared in competence to this choice group, is the curious plate of Mrs Dorothy Williams 1694 at Pimperne. The lady, fully dressed, is represented as rising from a skeleton. The lettering of the inscription is good, and the border is carefully engraved with emblems of mortality. It is signed by Edmund Colepeper, a craftsman about whom no other details have been established.

While the remaining figure brasses of the seventeenth century are not without interest, few have merit, whether of design or craftsmanship. There are two men in armour. Thomas Carew with his wife and family 1656, Haccombe, is commemorated on a rectangular plate, engraved with exceptional quaintness, apparently by some Devonshire craftsman, possibly in Exeter. The two adults kneel before a book rest raised on a column and decorated with a skull. Their hands are disproportionately large, and their faces turned towards the spectator. The children are set behind, mounted on a peculiar pavement. A large winged cherub flies above, two other winged figures lean on a skull and an hour glass and more emblems of mortality are worked into the sides. Nicholas Toke 1680, Great Chart, kneels holding an open book. He appears in every respect to be based on an earlier pattern of c. 1640, yet his three daughters, holding a rose, a lily and a palm branch, are dressed in late seventeenth-century style. A marginal inscription and arms are incised in the stone. There can be little doubt that this is London work.

There are a few civilians. Bonham Faunce and his two wives 1652, Cliffe-at-Hoo, are a rather wild and dishevelled group, the man in cloak and gown, the wives in loose gowns, one wearing a cap the other a hood. The rectangular plate to Richard Breton and wife 1659, Barwell. is more satisfactory (*The Craft,* Fig. 259). The drapery is feebly represented, but the two figure groups are neatly arranged, the heads presentably engraved, and the achievement of arms in the centre delicately worked. Alice Breton and her four daughters with their capes and bonnets are rare examples of Commonwealth dress. John Davies is depicted kneeling on a brass of 1654 at Haverfordwest. Thomas Lawe, Mayor of Boston 1659, is commemorated there by a lightly engraved bust. The kneeling group of John Bosworth and two wives 1674, Long Itchington, is more conventional. Edward Turpin, and wife, 1683, Bassingbourne, are an extraordinary pair, evidently the work of an inexperienced provincial engraver, and, judging from their outline, cut out to fit the indent of a civilian and wife c.1520. Henry Balgay 1685, Hope, is a small figure with hat, pen and book, and long ornate breeches. He is engraved beside his inscription in the manner of the earlier plate at Bakewell. These oddities however compare favourably with the barely recognisable figures of John Harris and children 1660, at Milton.

The only brass to a lawyer, Robert Shiers 1668, Great Bookham, is good work for its period. He was a barrister of the Inner Temple and is shown bareheaded, dressed in a loose open gown with glove sleeves, and a buttoned doublet. He holds an open book, and gestures as if arguing a case.

Three female figures commemorate Katherine Morley 1652, North Petherton, an attractive kneeling figure, Mary Hall 1657, Sheriff Hutton, holding an infant, and Mary Thorne 1663, kneeling with her children at St Mary's Bedford. There are no figures of clergy, other than two shroud brasses. The earlier is to Philip Tenison, S.T.P., Archdeacon of Norfolk 1660, at Bawburgh. His face alone peeps from the shroud which with its many pleats looks like an elongated onion. The other to George Ferrars 1669, in the churchyard of Thornton Watlass shows a shrouded figure on a tomb between two cypresses. A child, Anne Dunch 1683, Little Wittenham, died at the age of nine months, and is dressed in a jacket, skirt and apron.

Figure brasses, 1700-1800

Eight figure brasses continue this type of memorial through the eighteenth century. They are exceptional among the still numerous inscriptions and heraldic plates. At Bibury, are two small rectangular compositions with skeletons and emblems of mortality, commemorating John Matthews 1707, and Mary Benning an infant, 1717. These are deeply engraved, and, in spite of their grisly character, competently executed. In contrast the children of William Massie, Mayor of Leeds 1709, St Peter's Leeds, are miserably drawn. A recumbent shroud commemorates John Calvert gent. 1710, at Beeley. A remarkable brass to Bishop Ralph Walpole is now in private possession.[5] This was engraved c.1755 by a Swiss artist Johann Heinrich Müntz and was placed in the cloister at Strawberry Hill, the home of Horace Walpole. The bishop is depicted under a canopy, the whole design being based on the brass of Archbishop Waldeby at Westminster Abbey. It is an interesting reflection of the fashion for Gothic which had its devotees in eighteenth-century England. Many references have been made to the two brasses at St Mary Cray, to Philadelphia Greenwood 1747 and her husband Benjamin 1773 (*The Craft,* Figs 264-5). They have been regarded, quite justifiably, as the last expression in the form of figures of a craft which was to be revitalised in the nineteenth century. A scholarly investigation by Torr has cleared away some misconceptions about them. Macklin, Stephenson and Griffin were all convinced, with every apparent justification, that both these brasses were made and laid down on Benjamin's death in 1773. Torr has, however, proved from Thorpe's *Registrum Roffense,* 1769, that Philadelphia's brass was in place by the mid-eighteenth century, and that a 'mark' had been made in the stone for the insertion of a later memorial to her husband.[6] The dates of engraving would seem to approximate to their dates of death. Neither brass is 'feebly scratched', as stated by Macklin and repeated by several subsequent writers. Philadelphia is a poor figure in veil, bodice and gown. Benjamin is altogether better. He stands clean-shaven, wearing a wig, coat, embroidered waistcoat and knee breeches, and points with his right hand towards a ship and with his left to a skull. The last recorded example of the century is at Northchurch, a delicately engraved bust in a medallion to Peter the Wild Boy, who died in 1785. The plate is signed 'W. Cole, sculp. Newgate Street, London, and was based on a portrait engraved by Bartolozzi (Figs. 291-2).

Arrangement and composition: The figure

Throughout the period, even into the eighteenth century, the arrangement of figure brasses differed little from that of the late Elizabethan and Jacobean years. Vitality is conveyed in a kneeling or standing pose, and prayer indicated by folded hands.

Bernard Randolphe and wife 1628, at Biddenden are exceptions, being recumbent effigies. Other arrangements are occasionally used, most striking being that of George Coles with his two wives 1640, St Sepulchre's Northampton. Both wives hold hands with their husband, and below is an emblem of two hands clasped. The theme of the memorial is the everlasting affection of the commemorated, and this message is further explained in the epitaph.

> 'Farewell true frind, Reader Understand
> By this Mysterious knott of hand in hand;
> This Emblem doth (what friends must fayle to doe)
> Relate our Friendshipp, and its firmnes too
> Such was our love, not time, but death doth sever
> Our Mortall parts but our Immortall never
> All things doe vanish here belowe above
> Such as our life is there, such is our love.'

Richard Glanfield and wife 1637, Hadleigh, hold hands in a similarly affectionate manner.[7*] Ralph Assheton 1650, Middleton, has a swaggering stance. The porter Thomas Cotes 1648, Wing, kneels with hands upraised in prayer, while his hat and key float behind him. The use of busts, such as the four at Llanrwst, and that at Biddenham is proof of an increased interest in the features of the deceased, even though, as the Wynn correspondence shows, accuracy was at times subordinated to fashion.

The setting

Architectural framework, even on rectangular plates, is rarely introduced and then little more than indicated. Grigs in particular chose to work against almost plain backgrounds. Marginal inscriptions are used on several of the larger compositions to provide a well defined border. A cartouche, with flanking columns and drawn curtains, frames the bust of Helen Boteler 1639, Biddenham (*The Craft,* Fig. 261), comparable to the design of sculptured wall monuments such as Mrs Mary Brocas 1651, at St Margaret's Westminster, made by Joshua Marshall. The cartouche is again used effectively, with accompanying cherubs, at Llanrwst, 1671.

A few brasses were evidently influenced by earlier Tudor rather than Jacobean models, most notable being the memorials of the Laudian Archbishop Harsnett at Chigwell, and the recusant Rowland Eyre 1624, at Great Longstone. The former includes the Four Evangelists' symbols at the corners of the marginal inscription, though presented in a contemporary fashion. The other, depicting the figures kneeling in prayer before a central crucifix — though now much defaced — is a rendering of a type of design which was in use over a century earlier. The Catholic emphasis is very marked, both Rowland and his wife holding rosaries (Fig. 288).

Note has been taken of peculiar compositions such as the 'Bedstead' brass at Oxford, and Death striking Joan Strode at Shepton Mallet. The former is properly associated with the Jacobean "copper plate" memorials, the latter is a fine Caroline example. It would appear, however, that unorthodox designs of this kind were very rare, and that figure brasses, in conception if not in treatment, were presented in well established forms.

Emblem brasses

Emblem brasses came back into limited use after nearly a century of neglect. Heart shaped brasses engraved with inscriptions are at Ludham 1633, Stoke-in-Teignhead 1641 (in French), and Eton College 1657. Captain Thomas Hodges, slain at Antwerpen, is commemorated at Wedmore by a brass which records his heart burial.

The plate was engraved c.1630 and shows the heart and two ensigns which he won from the enemy. A brass at Culross Abbey records the heart burial of Edward Bruce, 2nd Baron Kinloss, who was slain in a duel at Bergen-op-Zoom in 1613. The heart, bearing his arms, is engraved below the inscription, the whole plate having been remade in 1808 to replace the lost original.

Three brasses depicting mitres commemorate the following bishops:

Arthur Lake, D.D., of Wells 1626, Wells cathedral
John Prideaux, of Worcester 1650, Bredon
Henry Ferne, S.T.D., of Chester 1661, Westminster Abbey.

The Bredon mitre is the best in form and presentation, and together with four shields and an inscription constitutes a simple but impressive composition.

Symbols and devices

The Great Longstone crucifix is the only example in the period known to the author of a sacred representation, though a spirited classical St George is engraved above the inscription to John Parker 1672, at St Thomas's Brentwood. In contrast, symbols and devices depicting Time and mortality are frequently engraved on rectangular plates, in particular around or above inscriptions. Angels, winged cherubs or putti are also introduced as decoration. The full range of late seventeenth-and eighteenth-century symbolic ornament will only be appreciated when the brasses themselves are fully listed. A. B. Connor has illustrated several excellent examples in Somerset, and this county has no monopoly. Angels leaning on an hour glass and a skull, skulls and crossed bones, hourglasses with pickaxes and shovels are all introduced on the brass of Thomas Carew 1656, Haccombe. Figures of Time and Death are included on the inscription of Dan Evance 1652, Calbourne. At Kingston St Mary a skull and scroll take a prominent place on the inscription of Thomas Dyke and wife 1672. The finely engraved inscription to William Sandys 1679, South Petherton, is enriched with sarcophagus, curtains and cherubs with discarded musical instruments. The little-known Irish survival at Santry consists of an inscription to Henry Brereton 1680, with a pictorial section above, showing an achievement of arms, a clasped book with a skull upon it, an hourglass and a candle or lighthouse. Emblems of Time and Death are contrasted with those of Faith and Hope. A mourning figure, cherubs and Death are engraved on the excellent plate of Alexander Popham 1717, Wellington. An angel blowing a trumpet and cherubs accompanying three flying children, one carrying a wreath, one a palm branch and another flowers are at Pershore Abbey (*The Craft,* Fig. 266). This brass primarily commemorates the small children of Richard Roberts, but was subsequently used for the whole family. The engraving was apparently done on several occasions between 1743 and 1777. This is illustrated as typical of eighteenth-century design and execution. A striking memorial, unusual in its arrangement, is that of the Walsh family at Curry Rivel. It is good of the period exhibiting a winged infant with torch, a skeleton, a discarded crown, an urn, and a surprising back view of Time running with scythe and hourglass (*The Craft,* Fig. 263).

Heraldry

The period is rich in heraldic plates. Achievements, engraved together with the inscription, are common. Occasionally complex and ambitious heraldic designs were attempted. Of particular note are the brasses over the vaults of the Earl of Carlisle 1684, and of the Earl of Strafforde 1687 at York Minster, and of Edward Littleton 1664, at the Temple Church, London. The last is an exceedingly elaborate composition, consisting of inscriptions on scrolls, an achievement and twenty-eight shields. Excellent achievements, very different in execution, commemorate Sir Hugh Stewkeley 1642, Hinton Ampner, and Sir Robert Howard, K.B. 1653, Clun. The first is signed by Thomas Brome. The second is a rich and delicate engraving, depicting four achievements, an hourglass, a skull, crossed bones and a skeleton with a dart, all set against a flowing pattern of flowers and leaves. A ram's head crest with inscription commemorates Sir Peter Legh 1635 at Winwick. Notably large collections of late seventeenth- and eighteenth-century inscription plates, many having shields of arms, are at Kirkby Knowle and St Peter's Leeds, Malpas, and Wrexham.

Arms of the City and merchant companies appear infrequently, though the arms of the Merchant Taylors' Company are found repeated four times on brasses at Kirkleatham 1631, and Dunstable 1640. A memorial of exceptional interest is that of John Eldred 1632, Great Saxham who was an Alderman of London and a great traveller. His inscription records his visits to Babylon, Egypt, Arabia and the Holy Land. His Suffolk home, on account of his business, was locally known as "Nutmeg Hall".[8] His brass, attributed to Edward Marshall, is set in a dark marble slab with two achievements and six shields. These include the Cloth Workers' and the East India Companies, Russia and Turkey Merchants, together with the City of London. An example of a merchant's mark is found at Steeple Ashton for Peter Crooke 1633.

Inscriptions

Inscriptions are very numerous, the majority of those of the seventeenth century being engraved in Roman capitals. Towards the close of the century cursive scripts became common, some of great elegance, which remain a feature of eighteenth century plates. The investigator is referred to the excellent selection at Wrexham. In contrast much provincial lettering is of very poor quality, such as that on the inscription of John Seaman, B.A. 1664, Shillingford. The style of presentation at the close of the century is well illustrated by the combined inscription at St Mary, Taunton, to Bernard Smith d.1696, his wife d.1716, and daughter d.1714. The plate was originally engraved c.1696 and received subsequent additions as that illustrated from Pershore (*The Craft,* Fig. 266).

Many of these brasses are of considerable interest on account of their signatures, their historical references and their naïve or fulsome verses, a proper record of which would easily fill a book. Many plates during the latter part of the seventeenth century are signed by engravers additional to those already noted. In Yorkshire several bear the signatures of Thomas and Joshua Mann. Thomas was an architect of some standing, as the market cross at York was built according to his design. Examples by Thomas are at Lowthorpe 1665, Normanton 1668, Bessingby 1668, Ingleby-Arncliffe 1674 and Rudstone 1677. Thomas's signature also occurs at Colne 1670 and Whalley 1671. Joshua signed plates of 1680 at St Michael-Le-Belfrey and 1681 St Michael Spurriergate and Bedale. Other York engravers were Phineas Briggs, whose signed works at Barton 1675, Thornton-le-Street and Barton near Croft 1680; Zachariah Cooke, who signed a cursive inscription 1695 at Burneston; Richard Crosse, whose sole work is at Bedale 1694; Gabriel Hornbie, whose signature is found at Nunkeeling, 1629; Edward Giles, who engraved the record of benefactions of Lady Elizabeth Haystyngs 1739, at Ledsham; John Plumer, who signed a plate at Felixkirk 1673; and Martin Raynold, whose signature is found at Darrington 1670. A Lancashire engraver, Thomas Ainsworth, signed brasses at St Mary, Lancaster 1684, Whalley 1693, Altham 1695 and two at Prestwich, one being of 1704. Richard Mosock of Aughton, signed inscriptions at Ormskirk 1661, Aughton 1686; and at Newchurch is an inscription of 1646 signed by John Sale. The inscription of Thomas Musgrave c.1650 at Carlisle Cathedral is signed by R. Preston.

Three signed plates have been noted in East Anglia. One at Bocking 1731, is signed by Joseph Fordham of Braintree. Another at Halstead 1718, is signed by James Nutting. The third and most interesting in the Dutch church, Norwich, commemorates John Elison 1639, and was placed by his eldest son John, an Amsterdam merchant. The inscription is signed by Francis de Bruynne as the maker. This may be of Dutch workmanship, or equally probably engraved by a Dutchman resident in Norwich. At St Paul, Bedford, on the Waller inscription of 1636 is an engraver's monogram, interpreted as Matthews.

Further engravers' names have been noted on brasses in eastern Wales and the Midlands. William Antrobus signed one of a group of four inscriptions at Ince all dating from the turn of the eighteenth century. The signed plate is of 1701. George Baldwin signed a most unusual plate of 1689 to Richard Baldwin at Munslow enriched with Rosicrucian symbols. Richard Bullock of Oswestry signed an inscription of 1742 at Aston. Edmund Chambers set his initials on a plate of 1650 at Tamworth. Devereux Parry signed an inscription of 1729 at Llanvertherine. At Hayley inscriptions of 1656 are signed by Samuel Penny. A palimpsest eighteenth-century plate signed by Edward Pugh of Oswestry is lost from Llanfair Caereinion. The name Wilding is found 1714 at St Alkmund, Shrewsbury and William Wright of Northampton on a brass of 1705 at Thorpe Malsor.

Four signatures of seventeenth-century engravers have been recorded in the west of England. Thomas Boddely of Bath signed a plate of 1704 in the Abbey. Mordecai Cockey, a bellfounder of Totnes, signed the brass of John Flavell 1691, now in the Congregational church at Dartmouth. William Cockey of Wincanton, another bellfounder probably related to Mordecai, signed an inscription of 1691 at South Brewham. A lost inscription at Yeovil 1662 was signed by George Genge. Others of the eighteenth century have been noted by A. B. Connor[9]

The names of eighteenth-century London engravers will perhaps be better known as inscriptions of the period are more fully recorded, but the interest in the provinces to add signatures to such work does not seem to have been common in the capital. An engraving discloses that Thomas Oughtibridge, 'At ye Sign of ye Sun in Brooks Market near Holborn, London, engraves Armes, Crests, or Cyphers on Gold or Silver plate . . . Inscriptions in Brass, Stone or Marble, for Monuments . . .'[10] This craftsman worked in the first half of the century. An inscription at Abbotsbury to the Rev. J. Harris 1773, is signed C. Sherborn, Gutter Lane, London.

Many inscriptions contain personal particulars, which are a record of contemporary events. Sir John Burgh is described on his father's brass 1632, at Stow as 'of his Mats. forces in ye Isle of Rhe in France where he was slain in 1627'. The Civil War has several references, most remarkable being the inscription of Richard Boles 1641 in error for 1642 'Who for his Gratious king Charles ye First did Wounders att the Battells of Edge Hill'. He was subsequently surprised at Alton by five or six thousand rebels, and, fleeing to the church, defended himself for six or seven hours with eighty companions. The inscription was set up in 1689 and drafted by Richard Boles, M.A., in Winchester cathedral. At St John's College, Oxford, is an inscription with arms in memory of Archbishop Laud, executed in 1644, which was set up by his servant William Dell. Resistance to the Commonwealth is declared at St Sidwell's, Exeter, in the inscription of Hugh Grove, who 'in restituendo ecclesiam, in asserendo regem, in propugnando legem et libertatem Anglicanum, captus et decollatus'. The date recorded is 1655, but the plate was renewed in 1788 by J. Eustace. The Earl of Arlington, a member of the so-called 'Cabal' ministry of Charles II, is himself commemorated by an inscription of 1685 at Euston. The ill-fated Monmouth Rebellion of 1685 is mentioned at Bridport. Edward Coker was slain at the Bull Inn by one Venner, an officer under the Duke. Religious dissension at the close of the century is reflected both in the person of John Flavell and the history of his brass in the Congregational Church, Dartmouth. Flavell was a distinguished Puritan preacher and writer and for a while lecturer at St Saviour's Dartmouth. He died in 1691 at a meeting of Ministers. His brass was laid at his former church, but was removed in 1709 by a Sacheverell minded Council, and transferred to the Meeting House, and has remained in non-conformist hands ever since.[11] A collection of inscriptions to non-conformists is preserved at St Saviour's, Shrewsbury. The earliest is dated 1729. These were saved from the Presbyterian Chapel at Dodington.

Other inscriptions record curious details of a personal character. John Palmer 1661 and his wife Mary at Nately Scures seem to have been a loyal but restless pair — 'twice in sixteen years we lived together in sunshine and in stormy weather and ten times changed our habitation'. Robert Thompson, at Lenham, was a a grandchild of Mary Honywood, 'who had at her decease lawfully descended 367 children, 16 of her own body, 114 grandchildren, 228 in the third generation and 9 in the fourth'. At Edwardstone it is proudly recorded of Elizabeth wife of Benjamin Brand 1636, that she had six sons and six daughters 'all nursed with her unborrowed milk'. Theodoro Paleologus 1636, at Landulph, presents a remarkable line of descent 'from ye Imperyall lyne of y last Christian Emperors of Greece being the eonne of Camilio ye sone of Prosper the sonne of theodoro the sonne of John ye sonne of Thomas second brother to Constantine Paleologus the 8th of that name and last of ye lyne yt raygned in Constantinople untill subdewed by the Turkes'. Peculiar in both content and form are the inscription and verses to Sarah Scargill 1680, Mulbarton. The brass consists of two hinged plates, in the manner of an open book, resting on a painted iron shelf the form of a bible.[12] These are but examples of a large selection of curiosities.

Verses are commonly introduced, forming a complete epitaph, or as an addition to the factual record. The verses of Richard Chiverton and wife 1631, at Quethioc are a good example of a West Country composition. The verses at Henfield for Ann Kenwellmersh and her grandson, are more polished with their classical allusions. Thomas Cotes 1648, at Wing is commemorated by the following simple lines:

'Honest old Thomas Cotes, that somtime was
porter at Ascott-Hall, hath now (alas)
left his key, lodg, fyre, friends and all to have
A roome in heaven this is that good mans grave
Reader, prepare for thine, for none can tell
but that you two may meete to night, farewell.'

John Boscawen d.1564 engr. 1634 at St Michael, Penkivel is commemorated by a less direct message.

'Here Lyes John Boscawen deceased
Ere the Earths love him released
Thinke you Death did make him pay
Heavens debt before his day
Noe, he was th'Almighties treasure
Who cald for him at his pleasure
Yeat in truth it may be said
Th'Earth had loss when heaven was paid.'

The inscriptions on the 'cradle' brass to Dorothy King 1630, at St George's Chapel, Windsor, give another aspect of Caroline sentiment, and an appropriate concluding example. The marginal inscription states:

DOROTHE KING LENT TO HER PARENTS JOHN KING Dr OF DIVINITIE PRÆBENDARIE OF THIS CHAPPELL & MARIE HIS WIFE BUT SPEEDILE REQUIR'D AGAINE OCTOBR 18. 1630.

The verses below the cradle read:

'HERE LYES A MODELL OF FRAIL MAN
A TENDER INFANT BUT A SPAN
IN AGE OR STATURE HERE SHEE MUST
LENGTHEN OUT BOTH: BEDDED IN DUST
NINE MONETHS IMPRISON'D IN Y WOMBE;
EIGHT ON EARTHS SURFACE FREE Y TOMBE;
MUST MAKE COMPLEAT HIR DIARIE.
SO LEAVE HIR TO ÆTERNITIE.

The long tradition of engraving figure brasses, to which our subject owes most of its interest and importance, declined rapidly and in effect ceased in England during the eighteenth century. The isolated examples described are insufficient to constitute a survival of the mediaeval and post-Reformation series, notwithstanding the engraving of inscriptions, arms etc., that continued with vigour, especially in the West. It accordingly remains an appropriate century in which to conclude the study of monumental brasses, at least from the standpoint of an antiquary. It is nevertheless necessary to draw attention to the considerable number of brasses of the nineteenth and twentieth centuries, which will in the foreseeable future deservedly attract increasing study.

Brasses post 1800

Brass engraving in the nineteenth century owed much of its importance to the renewed interest in the mediaeval, associated with the Gothic Revival. As such, many Victorian products are essentially derivative and often reproduce the worst aspects of their models. Leading nineteenth-century engravers were J.W. Archer and T.J. Gawthorp of London, J. Hardman of Birmingham associated with A.W.N. Pugin, F. Skidmore of Coventry and J.G. and L.A.B. Waller of London. More recent work has tended to be simpler in treatment, but still adheres to traditional patterns. The small figure of William Fletcher, Alderman of Oxford 1826, at Yarnton is an exact copy of Richard Atkinson, Alderman and Mayor 1574, at St Peter-in-the-East, Oxford. Sir Robert T. Wilson 1849 and wife, under canopies, at Westminster Abbey, engraved by J. Hardman, are represented in the costume of c.1400, the knight wearing a bascinet and aventail. Clergy, such as Bishop Monk of Gloucester 1856 at Westminster, appear less incongruous. Victorian dress is blended happily with mediaeval ornament and treatment in the brass of the Rev. C. Parkins and wife 1843, Gresford, an excellent work by J.G. and L.A.B. Waller, bearing their mark on a canopy shaft. More ostentatiously Victorian, and impressive if over-ornate, is the brass to the Right Hon. George S. Nottage 1885, in the Crypt of St Paul's cathedral. He appears in half effigy, attired in his official robes and hat as Lord Mayor of London. The face is a portrait.[13] Even this is surpassed by the brass of Sara Hornby and others, made by J.G. Waller for the Great Exhibition of 1851.[14]

Small but good examples of twentieth-century engraving are in the churches of Greenford and Kingsbury (Modern Church), at Tansor, and Cheriton the last being a kneeling figure in miliatry uniform of the 1914-1918 war. W. E. Gawthrop, whose services for the preservation of monumental brasses were outstanding, was a leading engraver of this later period.

Figural compositions form only a small portion of the brasses engraved within the last century. Many take the form of elaborate crosses while others consist of inscriptions framed in heavy canopies, often of a debased style. Angels appear frequently, holding inscriptions or devices, as on the brass of John Britton 1857, Salisbury cathedral, and form the central feature of the composition. Most Victorian brasses are enriched with a variety of coloured inlays, which lie flush with the lines. Their effect is very often gaudy, and serves to confuse rather than emphasize the design. The tendency since 1900 has been to eschew this type of ornament, either inlaying with black colour only, or leaving the lines clear.

Eighteenth-century brasses have only recently received serious attention from antiquaries, and their Victorian successors have not as yet been systematically listed, illustrated or seriously discussed.[15*] They form a potential field for extensive research, especially as details of the engravers could be obtained, and signed memorials are common. It would be folly to attempt a description here, as the necessary material is not as yet available. This chapter is titled 'The decline of the craft' and is correctly described. Its revival, present activities and prospects are subjects for another study.

20. The destruction of brasses

In the course of the preceding chapters repeated reference has been made to brasses mutilated and destroyed, even to whole series of memorials of which now only an isolated example survives. The destruction of brasses is a subject of importance, both to set the number of existing monuments in perspective, and to disclose the gradual process of loss through theft and neglect, accelerated by short periods of deliberate defacement and removal. It is a process which has decimated these treasures in the past, and continues to take its toll. Since 1965 one of the oldest figures in England, and one of only three surviving brasses of friars, have been stolen though the first has fortunately been recovered. Of the figure brasses known to have existed in Poland in 1939, half had been destroyed or mutilated by 1947.

The fourteenth and fifteenth centuries

There can be little doubt that brasses began their return to the melting pot in the Middle Ages. In Chapter Twenty-one the evidence of palimpsests is cited proving that in the fifteenth-century brasses were being cut up and reused and that these could not have been workshop waste. Furthermore, loose pieces of brasses at Tournai were melted down for candelabra. There were many vagabonds and wastrels and wars were not infrequently fought with senseless ferocity and widespread plunder. Incised slabs were cut up in large numbers and reused in mediaeval buildings and there is no reason to believe brasses were sacrosanct. Under the care of local families or a religious fraternity brasses were presumably safe, but in the churches of deserted villages or the over numerous churches of the towns such monuments were vulnerable. In England 'alien' Religious houses were suppressed during the late fourteenth century and in the course of the fifteenth century, and churchmen of the distinction of Waynflete of Winchester and Alcock of Ely acquired decayed religious houses for the benefit of their foundations at Oxford and Cambridge. In most cases these properties were reused for appropriate purposes, but often long periods elapsed before the new administration took charge. It was, for example, thirty years before New College obtained use of Newington Longeville, after its suppression.[1]

The Sixteenth and early seventeenth centuries

It was, however, in the sixteenth century that destruction assumed devastating proportions. In England the main causes were the dissolution of the monasteries, the suppression of the chantries, and the spate of iconoclasm and theft by less reputable elements that followed in their train. In Flanders and France, especially in the former, religious strife caused widespread devastation. The toll further east must also have been substantial. According to Haines 'demolition of brasses at this period seems to have been trifling compared with that by the rebellious sectaries of the following century'.[2] In the author's opinion the sixteenth-century destruction in England has been much underestimated. The dissolution of the monasteries led in most cases to all but total loss of their monuments. It began with Wolsey's suppression of small houses in 1523, and the general suppression of minor houses in 1536; the forced surrender of the major houses between 1537 and 1539 was completed by the second Act of Dissolution in the latter year. Certain of the monastic churches were turned over to secular use, but only a small minority. Some, such as St Pancras, Lewes, were totally razed, others, such as Fountains Abbey, were stripped of their roofs and all their valuables, and left to stand or fall through exposure. The sale of furnishings took place on the site. Lead and copper were in high demand, especially the latter for the casting of cannon, and many bells and probably brasses were melted down in hastily constructed furnaces. In some places the furnishings etc. were sold to individuals. At Merevale, Warwick six gravestones with brasses on them were sold for five shillings, and at Dieulacres the paving of the church, with aisles, gravestones, roof etc., for a mere £13.6.8.[3] At other places odd plates were probably looted. As was reported at Reading 'as soon as I hadde taken the Fryers surrendre the multitude of the poverty of the tone resortyd thedyer, and all things that might be hadde they stole away, insomyche that they hadde convayd the very clapers of the bellys'.[4] Evidence of this destruction remains in the form of fragments of monastic plates on the reverses of Tudor brasses and of splendid indents such as those at Byland and Fountains abbeys. But the loss from immense and rich houses in the east of England, such as Bury St Edmunds, can only be imagined.

Some interested parties succeeded in saving the memorials of their relatives or connections. The brass of Judge Billyng and wife 1479, now at Wappenham, is said to have been brought from Biddlesden Abbey. Prior Langeley's brass 1437, for long at St Laurence, Norwich, though recently placed in the parish church of Horsham St Faith, was undoubtedly brought from the Priory there, and Walter Curson's c.1533, at Waterperry from the Augustine Friars at Oxford.[5*] A few of the brasses at Little Walsingham may have been moved to the parish church at the dissolution of the religious houses there. These survivals, however, can only be a proportion of the total.

Destruction was not confined to monastic property. An Act of 1545 transferred to the Crown the property of collegiate churches, free chapels, chantries, hospitals, fraternities and guilds. This was not immediately implemented on account of Henry VIII's death, but was renewed under the direction of Protector Somerset on the accession of Edward VI. Authority was furthermore given to officers in each county to remove images which had been put to superstitious uses. The suppression of the chantries, and what in effect was an open invitation to strip the churches of valuables, led to a widespread desecration of memorials within the parish churches. It is here especially that the losses were apparently more substantial than has been hitherto suggested. The Commission sent to establish what had become of church property between the years 1547 and 1552 received reports of sales and other disposal by the church wardens.[6] At All Hallows, London Wall, for instance, it is recorded: 'Item sold to Xpofer Stubbes xxxlb weight of metell which was taken upon the grave stones and other molumentes at iijd the lb'.[7] Two hundred and two pounds weight were taken from St Alphage, London Wall.[8] Symonde Ponder received two hundred and three quarters twenty four pounds of latten and candlesticks from St Dunstan in the West.[9] Other named purchasers of latten were Richard Thornwood, Wyllys Pewtere and Robert Robynson. Such transactions were not confined to London. In the Church Warden's accounts of St Martin's Leicester, for 1547 is the following remark: 'by the commaundement of Mr. Mayr and his brethern, accordyng to the King's In juncyons, they yer of our Lord (1546) . . . solde to Mr Newcome iiij hundrith and a q(uarte)r of brass for 19s per cwt three hundred weight and three quarters was sold to another at the same price; and 'a hundrith' to William Taylor.[10] At Wells cathedral between 1549 and 1550 two brass images of bishops in the choir, weighing three hundred and ten pounds, were sold to Cuthbert Bulman for £3.12.1.[11] In 1551 the Corporation of Yarmouth ordered all brasses to be torn from their stones and sent to London to be cast into weights for the use of the town. The record is similar all over the country.

The notable proclamation of the second year of Queen Elizabeth's reign was issued specifically to end the plundering of monuments by 'sundrie people, partly ignorant partly malicious or covetous'.[12] It is certain that it brought the worst of the thievery to an end, otherwise the popularity of brasses in her reign is incomprehensible. There were nevertheless further losses. According to Stowe's description of St Leonard's Shoreditch, 'of late on Vicker there, for covetousnes of the brasse which he converted into coyned silver, plucking up many plates fixed on the graves, left no memory of such as had been buried under them: A greate iniurie both to the living and the dead, forbidden by publicke proclamation, in the raigne of our soueraigne Lady Queen Elizabeth, but not forborn by many, that eyther of a preposterous zeale or of a greedy minde spare not to satisfie themselves by so wicked a meanes.[13] Misappropriation and theft continued into the seventeenth century. On 20 February 1617, Edward Davys was brought before the Justices of the Peace at Hereford and examined 'where he had the brasse w'ch was the brasse of certaine monuments of toombes w'thin the Cathedrall church', and again in 1636 John Sylvester, one of the sextons gave evidence 'that the peace of brasse now shewed and offered to be sould by Thomas Evans unto Abraham Lightfoote is some of the brasse lately lost out of the Cathedrall church'.[14] Over-zealous or disgraceful dealings took place even in collegiate buildings, where it might be expected the dead would be respected. At St George's Chapel, Windsor a visitation was made in 1556 to enquire into Canon Robinson's transactions with the Windsor goldsmiths, among many items so disposed being 'the plates of copper upon the graves'.[15] Similarly at Eton several brasses in the chapel were 'purged' by Provost Day.[16]

Destruction in Scotland and on the Continent was substantial, and in some places exceeded that in England. Churches in southern Scotland were deliberately ransacked by English troops and mercenaries under the Earl of Hertford during the invasion of 1544 — Henry VIII's 'rough wooing'. The stripping of such ornaments and brasses as remained was completed by the Calvinist's in 1559-60. In France certain places suffered from the Calvinists. In Rouen cathedral, 'aprés avoir brisé les statues des tombeaux et les tombeaux eux-mêmes, ils levèrent toutes les tombes de cuivre et autres monuments qui étoient dant l'église pour y trouver des tresors'.[17] In Flanders iconoclasm was taken to extreme lengths. The outrageous events at Antwerpen on the 18th and 19th August 1566, were a signal for frenzied destruction.[18] The public procession of the Statue of the Virgin — the procession of the Ommegang — was greeted with ribaldry and burlesque by the populace on the 18th, and the magistracy failed to take any action. The following morning a similar disorderly anti-clerical assembly entered the cathedral, and on a preconceived signal ravaged all destructible memorials, fittings and ornaments. Within weeks over four hundred churches in Flanders and Brabant had been so treated, including the cathedrals of Mechelen and Tournai. Many brasses were not immediately stolen. They were torn up and left in pieces among the debris, but soon fell prey to looters as the war of Philip of Spain's repression spread over the Low Countries. The 'Beggars' had no scruples, and the looting of church treasure was promoted by desperation, greed, and a hatred for all the churches represented.

It may be surmised with every probability that, by the early years of the seventeenth century, many churches in Western Europe had been stripped entirely of their brasses, and more had suffered substantial losses, not so much through any thought out plan of destruction as by chance iconoclasm and theft. Those churches, especially in England, which had fortunately escaped the first chaos, were exposed again within less than a century to further deliberate damage.

The English Civil War

The destruction of brasses in England during the Civil War and the Commonwealth is notorious. The statement in the preface to Ryves's *Mercurius Rusticus:*[19] 'In all places they left some infamous memorial of their frenzie and hatred of the beauty and magnificence of God's houses; and therefore in every place made it their first business to rob and deface churches, and violate the sepulchres and monuments of the dead, so they have expressed their greatest hatred against the Mother Churches', is the assessment of a prejudiced witness. But the actual damage, especially in the cathedral churches, was very extensive. Furthermore much looting was carried out for baser reasons. Writing of York Minster, James Torre stated, 'It was more the poore Lucre of the Brass than Zeal which tempted these miscreants'. Certain Parliamentary commanders, such as Waller, actually encouraged their soldiers in the havoc. The cathedrals of Canterbury, Chichester, Ely, Lichfield, Lincoln, Norwich, Peterborough, Rochester, Winchester, Worcester, York, and to some extent Westminster Abbey, were stripped of their brasses. A few brasses escaped either through oversight or protection by some local interest. Lincoln perhaps suffered the greatest losses. John Evelyn wrote in 1654, 'The soldiers had lately knocked off most of the brasses from the gravestones . . . these men went in with axes and hammers, and shut themselves in till they had rent and torne off some barge loads of mettal'.[20] Browne Willis in 1718 counted 207 despoiled slabs in this cathedral, many of which still exist today.[21] Irish cathedrals, such as Waterford, were similarly plundered in the course of Ireton's campaign.[22] Other Civil war damage was incidental. Scottish soldiers, both as raiders and later as prisoners, stole brasses from Durham cathedral, though many had already been disposed of by the iconoclastic Dean Whittingham (1563-1579). Excluding St Pauls cathedral, London, the state of which by 1660 is difficult to assess, it is probably true to say that by the restoration of Charles II, Durham, Hereford, St Albans, and Westminster Abbey alone of the English cathedrals and former monastic churches, retained a modest selection of their brasses, though these were but a poor remnant of those originally laid (Fig. 295). Spoliation had been deliberate and systematic.

Parish and other churches suffered severe loss, but rather in the haphazard fashion of the Edwardian years. In 1641 the Commons published an order for the removal of 'scandalous pictures' out of churches, an order which was liberally interpreted. County Committees were formed which appointed Parliamentary visitors to execute the order. The records of one of these officers, William Dowsing, have been preserved and published, and give an insight into his activities in Suffolk.[23] Dowsing was appointed in 1642 by the Earl of Manchester, General in charge of the Associated Counties of Essex, Norfolk, Suffolk, Lincolnshire, Cambridgeshire, Huntingdonshire and Hertfordshire, an exceedingly rich area in monumental brasses. His Commission reads:

> 'Whereas by an ordinance of the Lords and Comons assembled in Parliament bearinge date the 28th day of August last, if it is amongs other thinges ordained yt all Crucifixes, Crosses & all Images of any one or more p*er*sons of the Trinity, or of the Virgin Marye, & all other Images & pictures of Saints & superstitious inscriptions in or upon all and every ye sd Churches or Cappeles or other places of publique praier. Churchyards or other places of publique praier belonginge, or in any other open place shalbe before November last be taken away & defaced, as by the sd Ordinance more at large appeareth. And whereas many such Crosses, Crucifixes other superstitious images and pictures are still continued within ye Associated Counties in manifest contempt of the sd Ordinance, these are therefore to will and require you forthwith to make your repaier to the several Associated Counties, & put the sd Ordinance in execution in every particular, hereby requiring all Mayors, Sheriffs, Bayliffs, Constables, head boroughs & all other his Ma ties. Officers & loveinge subjects to be ayding & assisting unto you, whereof they may not fail at their perill. Given under my hand & seale this 19th of December, 1643.
>
> (Signed) Manchester.

This Commission was given to William Dowsing and 'to such as hee shall appoint'.

Dowsing has gained the reputation of a thorough and pitiless iconoclast, apparently justified if measured by the damage to church property for which he accounted. The detail of his accounts, however, give a different impression of the man. On occasions he seems to have interpreted his commission narrowly and at times overlooked items he was authorised to destroy. At Orford for instance, he recorded 'took up 11 Popish Inscriptions in Brass' (p. 17). All the mediaeval and early Tudor brasses in this church have lost their inscription plates, though most are otherwise undamaged. One even retains a representation of the Holy Trinity. In this case only recognised offensive elements in the memorials were removed. At All Hallows, Sudbury, where he took up thirty 'brazen superstitious Inscriptions, ora pro nobis, and pray for the soul &c.' (p. 15), he may well have done the same. He similarly showed remarkable restraint at Ufford, where the superb font canopy was spared for purely aesthetic reasons. At times he carried out practical destruction in abysmal ignorance of the matter he was dealing with. The representation, scroll and inscription of Dr. Billingford, at St Benet's, Cambridge, was for example removed as, 'An inscription of a mayd praying to the Sonn and Virgin Mary, 'twas in Lating, Me tibi — Virgo Pia Gentier commendo Maria; "a Mayd was born from me which I commend to the oh Mary" (1432) Richard Billingford did commend thus his daughter's soule'. (p. 8). Total destruction without his direction occurred at Walberswick, where according to the church wardens' accounts, 'Paid that day to others for taking up the brasses of gravestones before the Officer Dowson came £0.1.0."[24] Forty pounds weight of brass is stated as having been removed and sold on this occasion. Once destruction of monuments was authorised it was easy to justify or unintentionally secure complete removal.

The havoc (Fig. 293), appalling as it was, increased as powers were delegated. Francis Jessup of Beccles, one of Dowsing's appointees, was clearly worse than his master. The Rev. James Rowse described him as 'A wretched commissioner, not able to read or find out that which his commission injoined him to remove; he took up in our church (Lowestoft) soe much brasses, as hee sould to Mr. Josiah Wild for five shillings, which was afterwards, contrary to my knowledge, runn into the little bell that hangs in the town house" (p. 10). The puritanical Commission simply became an excuse for plunder. At St Margaret's Westminster, the brasses seem to have been stripped off and sold en masse. At St George's Chapel, Windsor, Captain Fogg in 1642 and Colonel Venn in 1643 carried off a number of brass valuables, probably including some memorial plates, and in 1645 Parliament decided to sett "to the best advantage of the State", the brass statue of St George and other "Broken pieces of brass". The consequences of this atrocity were widespread — destruction and mutilation of brasses in the parish churches, the severity of which was dictated as much by chance as design. Where churches were remote or local families influential, there was a fair prospect of immunity.

A curious aspect of the attack on "popery" is the mutilation of details on brasses. There are many instances in London and the Home Counties where the offending portions of inscriptions have been cut out or obliterated.[25] At All Hallows-by-the-Tower a man named Shurban was ordered by the Vestry "to erase the superstitious letters from brasses." Several inscriptions both at All Hallows and St Helen's Bishopsgate, London, have had the opening and closing phrases hatched out. Sacred representations or ornaments of a Catholic significance, inscribed morses, crosses, etc., were also subject to defacement. The Holy Trinity above John Haryson and wives 1525, St Mary Lowgate Hull, has been most carefully erased, as also the Holy Trinity on the plate of Dean Sutton 1528, St Patrick's Cathedral Dublin. In some cases the action appears to have been taken by descendants, Company members or other well-wishers, seeking to protect the memorials. The destruction of the saint-filled canopy shafts and tabernacles at Spilsby was probably so motivated. The inscription of John Berners and wife 1523, Finchingfield, has been marked for mutilation which, for reasons unknown, was never carried out.

Occasionally damage was done to brasses out of sport. the best evidence of this is afforded by the conventional Elizabethan brass of Lettice Barnarde 1593 at Newnham Murren, where the brass has been struck and dented by a musket ball. A soldier pausing by the door perhaps used it as a target.[26]

The ravages of the twenty years 1640-1660 were further extended by the Great Fire of London in 1666. It is difficult to assess the losses involved in this conflagration. Judged by the collections of some existing pre-Fire churches, many series survi ved the Commonwealth, and it must be presumed that huge numbers perished.[27]*

There has been, to date, no analysis of damage done to memorials on the Continent, though it can only be presumed that it was severe during the Thirty Years War. The Imperial generals, such as Tilly, were totally ruthless, and the Swedish armies on the Protestant side strongly anti-Catholic. Army discipline was often poor and looting uncontrolled.

Late seventeenth to the nineteenth centuries

The two centuries from 1660 to 1860 may certainly be described in England as a period of gross neglect of antiquities of most sorts. Very little value was placed upon memorials of the distant past, and, as alterations and reflooring were carried out in churches, so much of what had been spared in the Civil War was thrown away. The cathedrals of Hereford and Durham have been mentioned among the few which retained a selection of their brasses. A comparison between the drawings made at Hereford by Dingley and the brasses now remaining reveal a great discrepancy, among the most severe losses being the figure and much of the canopy of William Porter, S.T.B. Many of the plates were lost shortly after 1786, when extensive repairs were necessitated after the fall of the West Tower and "no less than two tons weight was sold to a brazier".[28] In Durham the story was even more dismal. The Chapter House was demolished in 1799 and its floor, still containing several important brasses, was destroyed by the falling roof.[29] No figure brass of any antiquity now remains. The collections at St Albans and Westminster were further depleted, though in a piecemeal manner, the most serious loss being the remarkable monument of Thomas of Woodstock 1397 (*The Craft,* Fig. 20), and Abbot Edmund Kirton 1466 at Westminster.

Chapels in famous buildings and parish churches fared no better. When Ashmole visited St George's Chapel, Windsor, in 1660 he copied inscriptions of thirty brasses. Gough noted the memorials in 1784, by which time their number was reduced, but eight brasses of canons in their mantles remained. Shortly afterwards the chapel was refloored, and the canons vanished with the old floor stones. Alterations to the chapel at Eton led to serious losses in 1699. The scandalous loss of brasses at King's Lynn and Ingham are well documented. Eleven figure brasses were noted by Mackerell at St Margaret's, King's Lynn, when he wrote his *History of Lynn* published in 1738. In 1746 there was serious damage to the nave and "It was ordered that the old brass and old iron be immediately sold by the churchwardens." In 1800 the great brass of Walter Coney 1479, was stolen by a sexton who later hanged himself, and about the same time the superb Flemish brass of Robert Attelath and wife 1376, was sold by the churchwardens for five shillings. Other important brasses were lost to St Nicholas Church. The Flemish brass of William de Bittering and wife was sold by the Chapel Reeves for the benefit of a certain Maxey Allen, and the brass of Thomas Watyrdeyn and wife "was sold for the interment of Captn John Goodwyn by the Chapel Wardens." Of Ingham (Fig. 296) it is recorded 'In 1800 the chancel at Ingham was completely swept of all its beautiful memorials of the Stapleton family. They were sold as old metal and it was commonly reported by whom they were sold and bought: but nobody sought to recover them: neither minister nor churchwarden cared for any of those things."[30] Elsewhere, as at Meopham and Luton, churchwardens and others used brasses to cast bells or make chandeliers. Where churches were demolished there was rarely anyone to care for the monuments. The valuable brasses of St Alkmund, Shrewsbury, were mostly lost in the destruction of this church. At Letheringham the demolition of the chancel completed the loss and dispersal of the fine collection of military figures to the Wingfield family.[31] Where fire necessitated major repairs, the brasses were often lost or became perquisites of the builders. Those at Gillingham to the Bamme and Beaufitz families were lost under such conditions. Comparison between the drawings by Cotman and Fisher, the early rubbings of Craven Ord and others in the possession of the Society of Antiquaries with brasses as they are today, give some indication of the losses at the turn of the nineteenth century. The record here given could be greatly multiplied, and in many cases it would appear that the church authorities were either directly responsible, or guilty of the most culpable negligence. Occasionally damage was done with good intent. According to the Astronomer Royal, Sir George Bidell Cury, in 1837 the vicar and curate of Playford, Suffolk 'Went to the church with tools, and with their own hands ripped off the canopy which covered the figure, and the whole of the inscription which surrounded it".[32] Their motive apparently was to sell the metal for the better preservation of the remains!

Irrespective of the negligence of the church authorities there was a great deal of theft, sometimes of a "polite" character. The theft of the Bacon and Fastolfe brasses at Oulton, in February 1857 was among the most serious losses of the nineteenth century. It is fortunate that several rubbings of Adam de Bacon c.1320 still exist. The fine brass of Sir Adam de Clyfton 1367, Methwold, was stolen by a tinker and smashed into small pieces, but most of it was recovered and has been skilfully reassembled. Such recoveries were, however, rare. Certain aristocrats emulated the tinkers, to add to their collections of curiosities. According to the Torrington diaries: 'Returning to Cople Church we stopp'd for the inspection, in which are . . . some brasses — but none that would travell"! [33] Other inspections, as shown in Chapter Twenty-two were more fruitful.

The period of neglect closed with the widespread restoration of churches undertaken in the nineteenth century. In the long term the growing pride in the church fabric and the interest in the mediaeval, stimulated by the Gothic Revival, were to increase care and respect for monuments. The immediate effect was nevertheless injurious. Brasses received little attention from the authorities and were left to the mercy of the workmen. Repaving the churches with coloured tiles or the laying of heating systems often led to the careless fixing of the brasses to walls, to a heedless assignment of loose plates to church chests or to a total rejection of these relics which did not fit in with the new design. The disgraceful treatment of the brasses at Warkworth during the restoration of 1841, is well known, whereat, "All the brasses of this church, excepting two were thrown away unheeded, and might have been purchased of the workmen for a pot of beer."[34] Three were later recovered from under a ledger stone. Even at Winchester College most of the figure brasses mysteriously disappeared during the restoration of 1875. Where they were preserved intact, their parts were often jumbled in their new settings, and their slabs were totally destroyed. Many brasses were fixed in ridiculous positions, mounted on furniture, set behind organs and even on ceilings.[35*] Many collections were broken up, and valuable parts needlessly lost, the remnants being reset in total confusion. The brasses at Mawgan-in-Pyder and Crowan for example, have suffered very severely through such treatment. Many brasses lay loose in church chests, only to be eventually lost. It is a sad fact that most nineteenth-century restorations took a toll of the floor monuments, in which incised slabs probably suffered as much as or more severely than the brasses. Haine's list was compiled during this period and he makes numerous references to loose, lost or missing plates.

Details of losses in Continental churches are not available to a comparable extent, but everywhere except in France a similar gradual and piecemeal destruction may be suspected.[36] Large numbers of superb brasses apparently perished at the destruction of St Walburge, Bruges.[37] The derelict state of others in that city has been described by the antiquary James Weale, and one major Flemish brass to the Cortscoef family was lost after 1840. Several memorials came into private possession and are in national museums today. The splendid Flemish brass at Altenberg to Bishop Wicbold von Kulm, disappeared in the nineteenth century. Many brasses must have been looted during the repeated wars in central Europe, especially the Napoleonic invasions. In France itself the French let loose a destruction of unique thoroughness. On 31 July 1793 it was proposed by Barère in the National Convention that the storming of the Tuilleries in 1792 should be commemorated by the destruction of the Royal Monuments in the Abbey Church of St Denis outside Paris, removing for ever these "effrayants souvenirs des ci-devant rois". In August of the same year fifty-one tombs were demolished and forty-seven sepulchral statues removed, many of which were fortunately saved by the energy of Alexandre Lenoir for the Musée des Monuments Français. The same desire to break all links with a hated past extended to the mutilation of aristocratic monuments, especially in the defacement of shields of arms, and to the removal of monuments of material value. The brasses drawn some ninety years before by Gaignières were totally destroyed. (Fig. 297) The metal itself was the chief element in stimulating the action, as incised slabs were rarely touched save for frequent defacements of the arms shown on them. So perished the superb achievement of the French engravers, and other brasses brought to France.

The twentieth century

Brasses surviving into the twentieth century are accordingly but a remnant of those laid down. But even this treasure continues to be depleted, in part by war but also by neglect and theft.

In the monstrous destruction of the two world wars it is only surprising that more has not been lost. The Belgian series suffered between 1914 and 1918, though by an astonishing chance the brasses at Ypres somehow survived. The greatest losses were at Nieuport at the burning of the church in 1914, when three brasses of importance were totally destroyed and another seriously damaged. Other brasses at Dixmude were broken into fragments. Parts of the brasses at Crombeke were stolen, it is alleged, by soldiers.

The toll of the Second World War was far more extensive. In Belgium the brasses at Nivelles were damaged. Reference has been made in the text to the numerous German and Polish losses, but a consolidated list is appropriate here. The air-raid on Lübeck in 1941 destroyed the two splendid Flemish brasses of Johann Clingenberg 1356 and Tydeman Berck and wife 1521, and the German plate of Gotthard von Hövelen and wife 1571, depicting the Ascension. The brass of Hermann Blanfort 1554, at St Columba, Köln, perished. Two sixteenth-century brasses, one bearing achievements of arms, the other to Abbess Katrina von Tecklenburg 1561, were destroyed or lost from the Münsterkirche, Essen. Similarly at Hamm the important brass of Count Gerhard von Marck 1461, was consumed in the fire, and at Emden a heraldic plate of 1500 to Duke Albrecht of Saxony disappeared. A small but fine brass at the Kupferstich Kabinett, Berlin, to Abbot Ludwig of Churwalden 1477, is confirmed as destroyed. The antiquary can only be thankful that brasses survived in such ravaged cathedrals as Halberstadt, Hildesheim, Lübeck and Xanten, and also at badly damaged churches such as the Petrikirche Braunschweig, the Stiftskirche, Kleve, St Maria im Kapitol, Köln and Linnich. Polish losses were greater, and were brought about not only by the havoc of war, but by the systematic looting by the Nazi administration of works of art attributed to German masters. With the exception of those in Kraków, all the engraved brasses made by the Vischer family have disappeared, namely those at Poznań cathedral, to Lukasz (*The Craft*, Fig. 80) and Uriel Górka 1498 (Fig. 298), together with the Flemish brass of Bishop Andrzej 1479 (*The Craft,* Fig. 81), at the Dominican Church, Poznań to Feliks Padniewski 1488, and at Samotuly to Andrzej Samotulski 1511 (*The Craft,* Fig. 197). The last was looted by the authorities as the church was not otherwise damaged. All the four early brasses at Lubiaz were mutilated, as also the plates of Bishops Peter Novak and Rudolf von Rüdesheim at the cathedral, Wroclaw, and of Duke Wenczeslaus at the Muzeum Ślaskie, Wroclaw. There is still a faint hope that the lost Vischer brasses may some day be recovered from a secret and forgotten place of security.

Destruction in England was astonishingly light. The brasses survived in gutted London churches such as All Hallows-by-the-Tower and St Olave, Hart St. In spite of heavy bombing not one Norwich figure brass was lost. Damage was sustained by the important brasses at Little Horkesley and Swansea. Others of lesser distinction at Bromley and Heigham were split or affected by fire. The following is to the author's knowledge a complete list in date order of figure brasses destroyed or stolen immediately following the destruction of the church.

Robert Lond with chalice, priest, 1461, St Peter's, Bristol
Mary Hinton, kneeling with four infants, 1594, Coventry cathedral
Roger Bishop in civil dress, kneeling, 1597, The Temple Church, London
Clement Stuppeny, civilian, 1608, Lydd
Ann Sewell, kneeling, 1609, Coventry cathedral
Vincent Huffam, M.A., Minister, and wife, 1613, St James, Dover.

Of these figures the Bristol priest was an unusually good example and the Dover group was an attractive brass. Among a few inscriptions also destroyed was the curious plate at Austin Friars, London, to the Rev. Johannes van Rooyen (1687).

Unfortunately this short list has been considerably increased by losses caused by theft. Even since 1945 the following brasses have gone, and form a more serious loss to the English series than the toll of the war.

A friar c.1440, Great Amwell (Fig. 299)
The sons of William Lucas, one an abbot, c.1460, Wenden Lofts
A lady c.1480, Greenford
A priest c.1530, Packington

Others have been stolen after churches have been closed:

Dame Anne Tyrrell 1476, East Horndon
Man in armour, kneeling with eight sons, c.1520, same place;

and others disappeared after fires:

John Welbeck, 1478, Putney
John Lymsey d.1545 engr. c.1505, Hackney
Margaret Dely, nun 1561, Isleworth
Lady c.1585, Putney
Hugh Johnson, vicar in pulpit 1618, Hackney.

In addition to these a shield and achievement 1552, have been stolen from Wing, and shields and an achievement 1567 from Gosfield.

The loss of the Great Amwell, Wenden Lofts and Isleworth brasses is serious as all were part of the small remnant of brasses to members of the religious orders. It can only be hoped that they will eventually be recovered.

It is beyond the means of authorities to make theft by unscrupulous persons impossible, but most activity of this sort can be prevented by proper care. Too often no action is taken to protect or remove brasses when conditions expose them to grave risk. At the time of the theft, Wenden Lofts church was unused and the whole brass was loose. The remains of the brass have now been refixed and moved to Elmdon but too late to save the most valuable feature. Certainly it is most fortunate that the precious Pownder brass from St Mary Quay church, Ipswich, still survives. All the brasses lay untended in the derelict war-damaged church, before complaints stirred public interest. Attempts had apparently been made to steal the plates. St Swithin's Church, Norwich, was turned over for use as a warehouse with all its brasses left in situ. The author was party to the removal of one loose inscription to the St Peter Hungate Museum, Norwich, and the well engraved figures of John Horslee and wife 1495, were subsequently moved to the same security by that tireless Norfolk antiquary, the late Revd J. F. Williams. This is but one example of the risks incurred by church redundancy. Unless brasses are removed to safe custody, well in advance of disuse let alone alternative use of the church, they are exposed to easy theft.[38] The impression is in fact given that they are no longer valued. There is an urgent need for greater awareness of this growing problem, and for procedures to facilitate prompt action. Under normal conditions many brasses are left loose in their indents for long periods — an invitation to the dishonest — while others are kept in cupboards or chests, or held in the private custody of churchwardens or the clergy. All is well until the custodian dies or hurriedly moves.[39] The chances of accidental loss are then considerable.

This chapter is a deplorable record of destruction and loss, but it also has a meaning for the future. The iconoclasm of the past is irredeemable, but the losses through heedlessness, inexcusable neglect and theft still continue to deplete the memorials that remain. It is a warning to those who value these treasures, their custodians and the public who enjoy them, that the surviving remnant is still very vulnerable. Losses will no doubt continue, but their measure is in our own hands.

21. Palimpsest brasses

Palimpsest or reused brasses have proved a major source of fresh information on the engraver's work and reference has been made to them throughout the text. Mediaeval latten plate was fairly thick, and discarded pieces could be re-engraved on the reverse without disfigurement. Palimpsest brasses by general definition are looted or rejected brasses, subsequently engraved on the reverse or altered on the obverse to serve as new memorials. As has been explained the period of most intensive spoliation of monuments, during which the material could be so reused, was the mid-sixteenth century. The suppression of the monasteries and of the chantries in England, and the Calvinist fury of 1566 in Flanders, followed by the depredations of the 'Beggars', made vast quantities of brasses available for cheap purchase. It is, however, unfortunate that this period has become associated almost exclusively with palimpsests, which have a very much longer history.

Brasses became waste for a variety of reasons. Faults of engraving could lead to the rejection of the plate by the maker or the purchaser. The brass would then be available for reuse in the workshop. Palimpsests apparently created under such circumstances are known as 'wasters'. Secondly, brasses became detached from their stones and were lost through neglect. Such brasses or their fragments were reused either for other brasses, or melted down for a different use. Thirdly, brasses were stolen by petty thieves and eventually reached the engravers. Fourthly, brasses were looted, as in the case of the religious upheavals of the sixteenth and seventeenth centuries, and sold to local engravers, or exported as scrap metal to some other country where purchasers were available. This fourth category of palimpsest is undoubtedly the largest and its products were not always reversed. Some figure brasses were appropriated and given different inscriptions, or only slightly altered to make them more fashionable. In some cases the obverse was itself re-engraved. All types of reused brasses preserve some record of destroyed monuments, or reveal aspects of the workshop practice of the engravers.

Wasters

'Wasters' were the unavoidable product of a craft in which errors were difficult to correct, and in which standards were generally high. The brasses of Isabel Hay 1455, Luton, and a wife of Sir Laurence Pabenham c.1440, Offard Darcy, have on the reverse unfinished pieces of canopies of the same period. These were evidently discarded work. At Ampton, a lady c.1490 is engraved upon another female figure a few years earlier. A similarly short period separates the obverse of a priest c.1460 at St Mary Redcliffe, Bristol, and part of a lady on the reverse.[1] Wastage which may be presumed in these cases, is convincingly revealed in others. The half effigy of Thomas Cod, vicar 1465, St Margaret, Rochester, is engraved on the reverse of a very similar figure, the main difference lying in the vestments worn. The obverse shows Cod in processional vestments but wearing the amice. On the reverse the figure is shown in the usual combination of surplice, cope and almuce. The treatment of both sides is identical. The discarded but apparently satisfactory design must have been rejected through the whim of the purchaser. The palimpsest inscription of Walter Pope 1502, Cowley, has been described in *The Craft* Chapter Seven. In this case the inscription on the reverse to Robert Symson d.1497, was undoubtedly rejected as 'Northampton' had been engraved instead of 'Northallerton'. Two later examples are equally definite. The children of William Browne engr. 1595, Cookley, are engraved on the reverse of a large part of the inscription to John Scrogs, son of Frances Scrogs. The brass of John Scrogs 1592, exists at Albury, and a comparison between the inscription and the Cookley fragments reveals a mis-spelling in the latter of the name Edward. The celebrated representation of John Selwyn 1587, riding upon a stag at Walton-on-Thames (*The Craft*, Fig. 29) is palimpsest. On the reverse Selwyn is shown in the same dramatic act, but he is hatless and the presentation is less vigorous.

Reversed palimpsests arising from loss or occasional theft

The reusing of brasses under these normal circumstances evidently occurred from the earliest years of the craft. Though the time interval is considerable, it is just possible that a palimpsest at Clifton Campville, is a workshop reject. The obverse of a lady c.1350 has on the reverse part of a knight c.1320. Similarly the Flemish brass at Topcliffe 1391, is composed of earlier fourteenth-century pieces which presumably collected in the workshop. In contrast the inscription of Edmund Rede 1435, at Checkendon is engraved on the reverse of a graceful figure of St Margaret c.1350, or perhaps later, so introducing a number of early palimpsests which can hardly have been waste, and can only be attributed to rebuilding, accident or occasional theft. It is easy to exaggerate the respect accorded to monuments in the Middle Ages. Greenhill quotes several cases of incised slabs being broken up and incorporated in mediaeval church construction.[2] An unknown writer using the name of 'Piers Plowman' wrote scathingly of the custom of the friars to clear their church floors in order to accommodate fresh and remunerative memorials.[3] Most significant is a record from Tournai. According to the Communal archives, Jehan de Jumont made two candlesticks for the church of St Piat in 1424. The source of his metal were a considerable number of pieces of canopies and inscriptions in latten, 'venant de plusiers anchiennes lames de ladite église, lesquelles avoient esté de longtemps en le Trésorerie de le dicte église'. As no steps had been taken to repair the monuments, the loose portions were used to benefit the church.[4] Furthermore, insecure brasses, especially in remote or semi-derelict churches, must have been tempting and easy profit for the petty thief.

The inscription of William Wolstanton 1403, Great Bowden, has on the reverse a Flemish canopied figure of c.1365. This pleasant little composition could not possibly be waste from an English workshop. Similarly the inscription of Henry Lee 1494, Ewelme, has been cut from a Flemish canopy c.1370 and shows on the reverse an angel playing a musical instrument within a setting of tabernacle work. Several palimpsests in Norfolk are too early to have any likely connection with monastic suppressions, yet can hardly be wasters. The following list is revealing:

Obv. canopy, Ingham d.1466. Rev. fragment of Abbot or Bishop, c.1330
Obv. inscription, formerly Trunch 1473. Rev. part of inscription, Flemish c.1400
Obv. inscription, St Swithin, Norwich, 1514 (now in Norwich Museums). Rev. part of inscription c.1470.

These examples and others are indicative of a supply of discarded or stolen brasses to the engravers of Norwich during the fifteenth and early sixteenth centuries. Similar examples are found in London work, as for instance a group of children c.1470 in the British Museum, having on reverse a fragment of a female c.1340. A large fifteenth-century palimpsest fragment at Luppitt having on both sides portions of female figures separated in date by nearly a century, is another interesting case. At St Albans cathedral a large fragment of an abbot c.1470 has on the reverse the lower part of a lady c.1390. Most remarkable is the discovery in 1970 of earlier work on the reverse of John Launcelyn 1435, and wife, at Cople. This consists of portions of two brasses. The figures on the reverse join to form the central part of a fine cross-legged man in armour c.1320, with hanging mufflers, belt and sword. The reverse of the inscription consists of another almost complete to John Veal 1375, a rather crude example of 'A' pattern work. The fact that two different brasses were used, and the range of dates involved, excludes the interpretation of wastage. The earlier monuments were presumably alien priory spoil or stolen metal. Furthermore at All Hallows-by-the-Tower, London, the heart and scroll plate of the Bacon brass 1437, has been found to be reused, its reverse depicting the face of a lady not later than 1320. It may be concluded that the engravers were prepared to use whatever suitable metal came their way, and the re-engraving of brasses was an acceptable if unusual practice. The comparative rarity of early examples may in part derive from a failure to investigate the pre-sixteenth century plates.

Reversed palimpsests arising from the Dissolution of the Monasteries and suppression of Chantries

The systematic dissolution of the English religious houses followed by the suppression of chantries and guild chapels, and the seizure of church valuables, a process traceable from 1523 to 1553, increased the quantity of discarded plate available to enormous quantities. It is a fair prediction that the majority of brasses engraved between 1545 and 1575 are palimpsests, and it is especially between 1545 and 1565 that English monastic and chantry spoil supplied the needs of the London workshops. The engravers of Norwich appear to have been amply provided by 1535. A number of reverses have been successfully traced to their place of origin and are as a consequence of special interest.

One of the most celebrated of all reused brasses, appropriated, altered and in part reversed, is that of Walter Curson and family at Waterperry. This extraordinary brass was originally laid c.1442 in the Priory Church of Holy Trinity, London, in memory of Simon Kamp and his wife Margaret. This priory went into liquidation through bankruptcy in 1532 and came into the possession of the Crown. It was then granted to Lord Audley who broke it up and sold the contents. It seems the Kamp brass was among the items sold, and was bought by the executors of Walter Curson, who died in 1527. The inscription to Kamp is on the reverse to that of Curson.[5*] The figures are described later in connection with appropriated brasses.

The reverse of the brass to Walter Barton 1538, St. Laurence, Reading, is of similar interest. It consists of three fragments one of which is part of the feet of a knight c.1390. The others are an inscription and part of the tabard of Sir John Popham, Speaker elect of the House of Commons, who died in 1463 and was buried in the London Charterhouse of the Salutation. The Carthusian monks of the Charterhouse were expelled in 1537 and the contents, including "gravestones, tombs and pavinge stones", were disposed of by the Crown the following year. Presumably Popham's tomb was sold at this time, and the stone, together with parts of the brass were reused for Walter Barton.[6]

The original location of some other reverses has been discovered with equal certainty. An inscription in French relating to the foundation of Bisham Abbey in 1333, is on the reverse of the inscription to William Hyde 1562, with wife and family, Denchworth. The inscription of Dom John Ingylby d.1499 Prior to the Charterhouse of Jesus of Bethlehem at Sheen and Bishop of Llandaff (obv. inscription of John Rufford and wives 1540, Edlesborough) was reaved from Sheen.[7] The inscription of Thomas Totyngton d.1312, engr. c.1490, Abbot of Bury St Edmunds (obv. inscription of Margaret Bulstrode, 1540, Hedgerley) was presumably taken from that Abbey. The inscription of John Reynald d.1506 (obv. inscription of William Robenson 1562, Ilkley) was originally in York Minster. The inscription of John Lovekyn d.1370, Walkern (obv. inscription of Richard Humberstone 1581) may be ascribed to St Michael's

Crooked Lane, London, where Lovekyn was buried. The inscription of John Randolf and wife, 1469 (obv. inscription of Henry Bradschawe 1553, Halton) was taken from St Margaret's Westminster[8] A shield bearing the arms of Sir John Tate d.1514, who willed to be buried in St Anthony's , Threadneedle Street, has been discovered at Great Hampden (obv. Sir John Hampden and wives 1553).[9] Margery Chamberleyn, whose inscription is on the reverse of that of Arthur Cole 1558, Magdalen College chapel, Oxford, was buried in the chapel of the Greyfriars, London, in 1431. Lastly the brass of Robert Elsmer 1512, rector of Watton-at-Stone who willed to be buried in the hospital of St Thomas at Acres, London, is on the reverse of shields to Sir Thomas Parry 1560, at Westminster Abbey.

Miscellaneous pieces from wrecked tombs were bought and sold in London and used very extensively. Odd plates were joined together, and it is not unusual to find brasses composed of fragments of half a dozen separate memorials. Robert Barfott and family 1546, Lambourne, are engraved on the reverse of the following: a civilian c.1380, probably a half figure; priest c.1440, probably a half figure; merchant c.1440, standing on a linen roll; nun or vowess c.1465, her hands raised; large ecclesiastic c.1440, a broad strip from a very large figure known from other connected fragments to be of the order of St John of Jerusalem; Evangelist symbol of St Luke c.1520; a shield of arms c.1520.[10]

An equally remarkable medley is on the reverse of Thomas Fromond, 1542, with wife and family at Cheam (*The Craft,* Fig. 268). This consists of the major part of a shrouded figure c.1510; the arms of the see of Lincoln c.1420; an inscribed heart held by hands c.1500; part of a canopy with figure of St John c.1510; part of a kneeling lady c.1520; part of a kneeling figure with surplice-like sleeves and rosary c.1500; and most curious, part of a head in bascinet, turned in half profile. This last is of poor workmanship, yet can hardly be later that c.1400.

The obverses of such brasses appear to be composed of a number of plates of curious sizes, and this patchwork impression is a significant guide to the existence of a palimpsest. Even more certain is the appearance of rivet holes from the earlier brass, plugged with lead or part of the original rivet. Nevertheless, the joins were usually made with care, and must have been barely discernible when the brass was laid.

As a consequence of this indiscriminate use of miscellaneous pieces, it is quite common for fragments on the reverse of particular brasses to be traced on the reverse of several others. Much research in these connections has been carried out by the late R. H. Pearson and by J. C. Page-Phillips, who has made a unique collection of rubbings of these pieces. The results have been valuable, not only giving a clearer picture of the original brasses destroyed, but also in dating the obverses and relating them to particular workshops. Associations based on common raw material are of course beyond question.

The number of fragments of English brasses discovered as palimpsests is now exceedingly large and growing rapidly, and it would be pointless to list them here. Their value can only be appreciated with comprehensive illustration, and analysis of related details. It is hoped that Page-Phillips will shortly publish his research on this subject which has suffered in the past from partial and piece-meal description. In the meantime by far the best sources of reference are the numerous articles in the Transactions of the Monumental Brass Society, many by Mill Stephenson having been reprinted.

Reference to four further examples will be sufficient to emphasise the unusual character of some of these survivals. At Holy Trinity Chester (obv. 1545) portions of armed legs are preserved, displaying the garter and part of the mantle of the Garter Order from a brass of c.1510. Important fragments of regular clergy have been discovered at Norwich. At St John Maddermarket (obv. 1558) is a large part of a superb figure of c.1320, most probably an abbot, holding a book and crozier, and resting his feet on a lion. It is very likely that this came from the Abbey of St Benet at Hulme[11]. At St John de Sepulchre a monk is depicted praying behind a grille, framed by a shafted canopy. The design is unique, and presumably commemorated an anchorite (Fig. 305). Lastly at Great Berkhamsted, the reverse of an inscription of 1558 shows part of another to Thomas Humfre, Goldsmith of London, and his wife c.1500. This is engraved in fine lettering, with the figure of St Jerome in the initial capital letter. Enough of the pictorial panel above survives to show the legs of kneeling figures and part of St Michael weighing souls (Fig. 300).

It has been shown in earlier chapters that a considerable number of brasses were imported into England, mainly from Flemish but also from French workshops. Some of these also became spoil. They may only be differentiated from looted plate imported from the Continent by the date of the obverses. Fragments of foreign workmanship, reused before 1565, are in some cases found in conjunction with English pieces, and it may be confidently presumed that they were obtained from English sources. Especially valuable examples of this type are the remains of French brasses at St Mary, Islington, (obv. 1540), Little Walsingham (obv. c.1545), and Norbury (obv. 1538). Among a number of Flemish pieces the most notable survivals are at Fivehead (obv. c.1565), with related pieces at Chalfont St Giles, Dinton and, Pottesgrove, and at Winestead, Yorks., (obv. ? 1538). Both the original brasses were of the finest fourteenth-century workmanship. The Scottish goldsmith James Gray appears to have used spoil locally obtained for the brass of the Regent Moray 1570, at St Giles Cathedral, Edinburgh. Sufficient wording remains of the early sixteenth-century Flemish reverse to indicate that it was prepared for a Scottish merchant.[12]

Reversed palimpsests arising from Continental spoil

As the stock of English loot became low so the spoliations on the Continent replenished the supply. A large number of brasses, dating from c.1570 to c.1585, have been revealed as palimpsests, almost all having reverses of Flemish workmanship. Some of the places of origin of these fragments have been traced, either through their own record or other circumstances. A long inscription, recording the foundation of a mass in 1518 by Adriaen Adriaenzoen and Paesschine van den Steyne in the church of Westmonstre (in the city of Middelburg) has been discovered on the reverses of brasses at West Lavington 1559, and Norton Disney c.1560. On the reverse of the inscription to Dorothy Taylare 1577, Ewell, is another to Pieter Snouc, bailiff of Vinderhoute and his wife d.1554, who were known to have been buried in Sint Michiel, Gent. Part of the reverse of Cyselle Arundell 1578 at Mawgan-in-Pyder, concerns a Gerard van der Hoyen, the performance of masses and devotions to Our Lady, with reference also to a crypt. Gerard van der Hoyen was Alderman of Gent in 1489, was buried in St Bavon, Gent, after his death in 1517. The reference to the crypt and a shrine of Our Lady, are both appropriate to this cathedral.[13] An equally certain case concerns Canon Richard Visch van der Capelle d.1511, who was buried in St Donatian's Church, Bruges. A portion of his figure in mass vestments, showing his arms embroidered on the apparel at his feet, has been discovered at Thorpe the obverse being the brass of John Bonde and wife 1578.[14] Fig. 301 shows the greater part of a brass of Jacob Wegheschede of Bergues Abbey, composed of reverses from Denham d.1574, Cheam 1579, and Yealmpton 1580. This brass presumably came from the church at the place named, and is a good example of mid fifteenth-century Flemish workmanship.[15] There was no difficulty in transporting such loot into England. The "Beggars" of the sea were extremely active and ruthless in their own depredations, and offered a ready source for the disposal of such stolen property. It is recorded in

Camden's *Annals* for 1580 that following the raid on Mechelen, "we saw . . . many tombstones sent over from thence into England and openly set to sale as arguments of their impiety". Dover was one of the beggars' chief bases conveniently placed for transport to the London workshops.

Though very numerous, the majority of Flemish reverses consist of pieces of canopy and portions of marginal inscriptions, many of which remain unconnected to any known fragments. Occasionally several pieces of one brass are cut out of a single plate, and a substantial part of the original can be reassembled. Four parts of the reverse of Sir Robert Nedeham and wife engr. c.1580, Adderley, almost join to show a fine tabernacle with a standing figure of Christ, angels, etc, of c.1380. Similarly far scattered fragments have been linked. No less than eight pieces from Lee (obv. 1582), Marsworth (obv. 1583), Walkern (obv. 1583), and Whichford (obv. 1582), are demonstrably parts of an elaborate marginal inscription with shields and Evangelists' symbols to Cornelia . . . 1474.[16] As with the fragments of English workmanship, the mere listing of examples is inappropriate. Suffice it to say that notable discoveries have been made at Burnham, Hadleigh, Harrow, Constantine and Mawgan-in-Pyder (an extensive and well published collection) and Thorpe.

Loot from churches in the Low Countries was not exclusively re-used in England Examples of palimpsests have been noted among the few late sixteenth-century brasses existing. Most of the reverses have been noted in the text but a list is given:

Head of a lady c.1350, obv. Museum de Bijloke, Gent (shield 1589)
Civilian and priest in Mass vestments under canopies, small, 1368; obv. Museum de Bijloke, 1604
Gilles van Namain, civilian under rich canopy, large c.1370, obv. St Jacques, Bruges, 1615
Fragment of canopy work c.1370, obv. Town Museum, Sluis, 1548
Fragment of canopy with saint c.1370 obv. St Annen-Museum, Lübeck c.1560
Lisbeth van den Dylis, wife of Sir Gillis Zutter, and his son 1417, obv. Museum de Bijloke, c.1450
Wife of Jan de Cuenic c.1500, obv. Bruges cathedral, 1518
Two ladies under canopy, arms etc. d.1510, obv. St Janskerk, Gouda, 1568

Reversed palimpsests post 1590

English palimpsests, other than 'wasters', later than 1590 are rare. A notable example is the inscription at Little Missenden to Francis Style, 1646, which has on the reverse an inscription to William Chapman 1446, who was buried in St Dunstan's-in-the-West. Changes to the floor in this church were made in 1630 to introduce "more commodious seating", and Chapman's brass was probably removed at that time.[18] The inscription of Peter Dolman 1621, Howden, has part of an early sixteenth-century civilian on the reverse. The entire composition of Richard Fynche 1640, with his parents, Dunstable, is engraved on the reverse of a civilian and probably his two wives of c.1600. The inscription of James Dering 1532, has been re-used for Philemon Powndall 1660, at Shepherdswell. The earlier plate was a seventeenth-century restoration or fake, originally laid in the castle church, Dover (see the next chapter). More important is the fine plate with the upper halves of a civilian and wife holding hands under a double arched canopy with a winged cherub and text on the cornice c.1630, at Hawarden. This is on the reverse of the inscription to John Price 1683, and links with further fragments at St George, Doncaster, on the reverse on an inscription of the same date. A very late and unexpected palimpsest is the brass of Deborah Marks 1730, at Steeple Ashton which is engraved on the reverse of a satirical copper plate, relating to the Church of England, used for printing in Bristol in or about 1713.

Appropriated brasses

As stated in the introduction of this chapter, brasses were not always reversed before reuse. Occasionally figures and their accessories would be associated with new inscriptions and arms to serve as fresh memorials. Innovations of costume and style were apparently of no importance. The most celebrated example of such economy is the brass to John Wybarne and his two wives, the second of whom named Agnes died in 1503. The brass was made in accordance with the will of Agnes (*The Craft,* Chapter eight), though the executors took liberties with the instructions. A figure of c.1380 armed in bascinet and aventail, was used for John Wybarne which dwarfs his two spouses, who are conventional early Tudor engravings (Fig 294). Elsewhere adult figures have been appropriated without such absurd contrasts, or entire compositions have been altered by the addition of an inscription. A particularly fine memorial, misused in the sixteenth century, is that at Bromham bearing an inscription to Sir John Dyve 1535, with his wife and mother. The original brass commemorated Thomas Widville of Grafton 1435, with his two wives (Fig. 96) as is proved by two original shields left in place. The sole alterations made were the replacement of the inscription and three shields of arms. The brasses which follow are all appropriations on which little alteration has been made other than to assert the new identity.

Joan Fenner 1516, Horley — The inscription to Joan has been added to the large figure of a lady c.1420 with single canopy. A figure of a son against her dress and two shields are lost or were removed at the appropriation.

Edward Scott 1538, St Giles, Camberwell — A fresh inscription has been added to an armed figure of c.1465. The inscription is palimpsest, on the reverse being another to John Ratford, citizen and glover. c.1480.

Thomas Andrewes and wife 1541, Charwelton — Only the male figure is an appropriation, the remainder being engraved on the reverse of earlier plates. The armed figure is of c.1510.

John Leigh and wife 1544, Addington — This is a doubtful case. The two adult figures appear to be c.1520 and the inscription, children, achievement, arms etc., to be of 1544. A use of 'old stock' may be involved, but an appropriation is far more probable. It is likely that the other pieces are engraved on earlier plate.

Sir George Cotton 1545, Nettleden — This is also a doubtful case. The knight's figure can hardly be later than 1530 and the shields of arms have been altered on the front face. An examination of the reverse side of the inscription plate would probably confirm the appropriation.

John Gille and wife 1546, Wyddial — The entire brass is engraved on the back of earlier work except for the wife, who can be no later than c.1515.

Ele Buttry 1546, last prioress of Campsey — The figure of a woman c.1410 has been used without alteration, though Mill Stephenson records two bedesmen at her feet as being later additions. They appear also to be original, and are quite unlike the sixteenth-century Norwich workmanship of the inscription. It is an amusing circumstance that, during a visitation of the Norwich Diocese in 1532, this prioress was much criticised by her nuns for her extreme parsimony, and it would seem that her economies extended to her grave.

William Dalyson and his son George, 1549, Laughton — The brass of an armed figure c.1400 under a triple canopy has been appropriated by the insertion of an inscription. The stone has been resurfaced and placed upon a high tomb, with an inscription incised on the side. Some of the canopy details were restored at the time of the appropriation, further discussed in *The Craft.*

Sir Thomas Massyngberde and wife 1552, Gunby St Peter — This is a most interesting example. The inscription of 1552 surrounds large figures under canopies of a knight and his lady, both wearing SS collars, and dating c.1405. The remaining shields are proper for the family but of uncertain date, and Sir Thomas perhaps appropriated the monument of an ancestor, possibly Sir William Massyngberde 1405. The inscription is itself palimpsest, and of a remarkable kind. The obverse has been twice engraved, firstly in incised, then in raised lettering. The earlier letters are in part still legible. On the reverse is a further inscription of the fifteenth century, with an amphisbaena. The reverse, which is evidently later than the first quarter of the century, proves that neither of the lines of the obverse relate to the earlier figures, unless the memorial was twice appropriated.

Robert Batyll and wife, 1557, Digswell — Figures of c.1530 are combined with inscriptions and children groups of 1557. An appropriation is almost certain. Another brass of this kind, now completely lost, was that of John Lymsey and wife 1545 at Hackney. An armed figure of c.1505, purporting to be John, was associated with a wife, who was in part of 1545 and in part an appropriation, and palimpsest shields.

A few Tudor brasses have details taken from earlier memorials. Children groups at Harefield c.1537, and Ludford 1554, are undoubtedly appropriated, as are probably those at Atherington 1539. A bracket c.1400 has been used to support the figures of Dame Alice Beriffe and daughter 1536, at Brightlingsea, and a fifteenth-century canopy is placed over Robert Fowler and wife 1540, at St Mary, Islington.

There are difficulties in appropriations, arising both from the possible use of old stock or the adoption of an outmoded pattern. The canopy at Slaugham 1503, is evidently of the fifteenth century, but may not have belonged to another completed monument. Similarly the figure at Blockley, and the surviving figure of John Norton and his father d.1509, at South Creake (see Chapter Thirteen), may be old plates advantageously used by the engravers. When, however, these inappropriate figures or features are found in conjunction with brasses engraved on spoil, there can be little serious doubt of their character.

A most interesting example of alteration, which can only loosely be described as appropriation, is the brass of John Laurence of Wardeboys, Abbot of Ramsey, who died in 1542. The remains of his memorial lie at Burwell consisting of the central pediment of a triple canopy, bearing in place of a finial a representation of Our Lord in Pity, and the figure of the former Abbot, vested in almuce, surplice and cassock. The canopy is of a style which may be dated c.1510, and is palimpsest. On the reverse is part of the head and dalmatic of a deacon c.1320. This was a large figure, and the features of the face are in recessed relief, indicating foreign, possibly French, workmanship. The Abbot's figure is also in part palimpsest, the lower half being engraved on the reverse of an abbot in full mass vestments. The matrix of the mitre of such a figure appears above the head of Abbot John, and it is possible from the style of workmanship that the re-used figure belonged to the canopy. Macklin offers an attractive and possibly correct explanation: 'Lawrence, the Benedictine Abbot of Ramsey, was originally represented in full eucharistic vestments, but, surviving the dissolution of the monastery, his brass was altered and he appears in cassock, surplice and almuce'.[19] The figure on the obverse is in the rather coarse style, associated with a Suffolk workshop (see Chapter Thirteen). On the presumption that the brass was prepared in the Abbot's lifetime, it is reasonable that it should have been altered by the most readily available engravers. Yet it is alternatively possible, and indeed more probable, that a despoiled memorial which proved convenient for the purpose, from Bury St Edmunds or some other house, was used for the former Abbot's brass, and that there is no connection between the earlier and later work.

Palimpsests by appropriation and alteration

Mention of re-engraved obverses at Nettleden and Gunby St Peter introduces the small but highly curious group of brasses in which extensive alteration of the original surface has taken place. The most important examples are at Waterperry and Okeover. The brass of Walter Curson and wife c.1533, has been described as made from the earlier memorial of Simon Kamp. The original inscription was reversed and re-engraved, as was the upper half of the lady. The lower part of the lady and the whole of Walter Curson's figure apart from the head are those of the Kamp brass, altered with additional detail, shading and some concealing of the earlier lines. Close examination reveals the earlier work, such as the besagews at the armpits, and the pointed sabatons (Fig. 302-3). The lion is typical of c.1440 as is the dog on the wife's folds. The head of Kamp's wife showed her in a plain horned headdress. The engraver of the brass of Humphrey Oker and wife 1538, at Okeover, was faced with greater problems of adaptation. The brass of William, fifth Lord Zouch of Harringworth, and two wives 1447, was appropriated. This was a large and elaborate monument with a fine triple canopy and embattled base below the figures, and probably lay at some monastic house. The figure of Lord Zouch was altered by the engraving of a tabard, and the replacement of his own crest with that of Oker. His first wife Alice was left untouched, but his second, Elizabeth St John, was superfluous. She was accordingly reversed and engraved with the Oker children in tiers with an oak tree, (the Oker crest) above. Elizabeth was depicted with long hair, and the shape of the plate was not altered. The shields and inscription were reversed and re-engraved. This handsome brass was stolen in about 1857, and though much of it was recovered, the male figure is almost completely lost. Waller's excellent drawing shows the whole before this damage.

Three smaller brasses reveal comparable treatment. A priest c.1440 has been altered, mainly with shading, and used with a fresh inscription for Robert Hanson 1545 at Chalfont St Peter. The half effigy of a lady holding a heart c.1440, at Great Ormesby has been given additional shading. The inscription and shields are now lost, but the later commemoration was to Alice Clere 1538. At Brightling the small figure of a civilian c.1480 has been altered to suit better a wife of c.1510. His pointed shoes have been rounded and the original lines confused with leaves. A shield on the brass of Thomas Hawtrey and wife 1544, Ellesborough, has been re-used and altered, and another on the brass of Thomas Seintaubyn and wife c.1550, Crowan, bears unexplained lines on its border edge. There are two instances where the later engraving has been applied in total disregard of the earlier design. At Hampsthwaite the figure of a civilian c.1360 has been used as the base for a crude inscription to Ad Dyxon c.1570. Similarly at Brisley the inscription of Edmund Gogney 1544 is engraved on a fragment of drapery, possibly Flemish, using the plain area of the surface only.

Other uses of despoiled brasses

Despoiled brasses were occasionally turned to peculiar uses. At St Jacques, Bruges, a large sixteenth-century civilian and wife have been cut up to form part of a tabernacle. Two civilian brasses in the British Museum collection were re-engraved with a mathematical instrument and a pair of compasses. A sundial signed by R. Treswell in 1582, was made from part of the Flemish shrouded figure which was also used for brasses at Tor Mohun and Paston. A set square, cut from an inscription, is preserved in the collection of the Society of Antiquaries, London. The fine rectangular plate to the Compton family, now in the possession of the Surrey Archaeological Society, Guildford, was for a time used as a fire-back (*The Craft*, Fig. 205). Strips of small brasses were used to make rivets for the brass of Sir Humfrey Stafford 1548 at Blatherwyck. Most dramatic is the weathercock preserved in York Minster, made up from an inscription to John Moore 1597 (Fig. 304).

Practice work

It is appropriate to note in conclusion that some engraving on the reverse of brasses is no more than the craftsman's practice work. Several Elizabethan brasses are engraved on the reverse with 'doodles', as at St John's College, Oxford 1571 and 1577; Ewell 1577; and Pinner, 1580. The palimpsest reverses at Thorpe are much decorated with this type of work. An earlier example, showing practice inscription work by a Norwich engraver, is at Colby on the back of a scroll c.1520. The very cramped letters are attempts at the opening of an inscription to a member of the Dade family.

Conclusion

Re-used brasses, in all their variations, are precious survivals of the destruction which brought them into being. Systematic examination of reverses will undoubtedly provide a most rewarding source of new material for the researcher, and cast further light on the relationship of one brass to another and other aspects of workshop practice. It is important that all loose brasses should be expertly examined before refixing, and that information on them should be passed to the Secretary of the Monumental Brass Society. An individual piece is rarely of special value, but it may well take its place in the assembly of discovered parts. It is unfortunate for the serious student of brasses that the reverses of few palimpsests are visible. The old method of mounting them in swivelled frames is no longer recommended now that the common character of palimpsests is known, and damage to such exposed plates has been sustained. Yet rubbings of reverses are now often displayed in the church and electrotypes or casts are occasionally made. A large collection of rubbings of palimpsests is maintained in the Victoria and Albert Museum, London, and an almost complete record in the Society of Antiquaries, and the researcher should be able to obtain essential information from these sources.

22. The restoration of brasses

The dismal record of destruction and neglect is in a small part relieved by acts of restoration and repair. Many brasses have been carefully moved in the course of alterations or the destruction of churches, either by descendants or the church authorities. This chapter, however, is primarily concerned with examples of renovation to brasses actually mutilated or lost. The character and motive of such work is of considerable interest, though by no means deserving unqualified praise.

Pre-sixteenth-century restorations

There is no conclusive proof that damaged brasses were restored before the sixteenth century. There is, nevertheless, evidence which indicates such care. At Tournai in 1350 the Camphin family employed Jehan d'Escamaing to recut an incised slab.[1] The stone effigy at Nysa to Bishop Wenzel d.1417 is surrounded by a variety of brass inlays, some of which are of later date. One scroll records the transfer of the monument from Otmuchaw. The brass at Naumburg to Dietrich von Buckenstorf 1466, is particularly interesting. The entire upper half of the border inscription, including two Evangelists' symbols, is engraved in an apparently later and inferior style to the rest of the composition. The Bishop's figure and canopy and the lower part of the border are entirely consistent in treatment. There are grounds for suspecting a repair of c.1500. Parts of the inscription might have been left incomplete in 1466 but hardly the symbols.

Sixteenth century restorations

An early and proven case of restoration in England, is at Minster-in-Sheppey. The legs of the knight of the Northwood family (upper part of figure engr. c.1330) have been the subject of much discussion (Fig. 306). They are obviously a later addition, and are in fact palimpsest, with part of a lady c.1330-1340 on the reverse. The style of the engraving and the design of the lion beneath the feet have counterparts in late fifteenth and early sixteenth century work. A comparison with appropriate details on brasses at Lullingstone d.1487 (Fig. 156), Winwick d.1492, Lillingstone Dayrell 1491 and St Michael Penkivel 1497, is revealing. The Lullingstone knight is particularly valuable as the form and treatment of the lion, the rough grass and the cross on the chape of the scabbard are all comparable with these details at Minster. Also important is the similarity of the Minster lion to that of William Catisby (d.1485 but engraved c.1506) at Ashby St Ledgers (Fig. 180). In this brass the lion pattern is reproduced, like that at Minster, in a debased form. The actual execution of detail at Minster, such as the mail and spurs, is most closely resembled at St Michael Penkivel. The connection of stylistic similarities turns attention to the Register of Archbishop Warham at Lambeth. The churchwardens of Minster made a presentation at a visitation held at Sittingbourne on 1 October 1511: 'That where, of long tyme agoo, in the said chapell, a knight and his wife buried, and their pictures upon theym very sore worne and brokene, that they may take away the pictures, and lay in the place a playn stone, with an epitaphy who is there buried, that the people may make setts and pewys, where they may more quietly serve God, and that it may less cowmber the rowme'.

J. G. Waller's[2] acceptance of the 1511 date as that of the restoration has been severely criticised by Ralph Griffin, and his view was accepted as conclusive by Mill

Stephenson. Griffin regarded the restoration as being of the seventeenth century and denied any connection with the Lambeth reference. Yet his argument is surprisingly confused, and is based on a connection between the existing knight and lady at Minster which he himself denied in the same paper.[3] His interpretation has now in effect been refuted by evidence traced by Goodall, which confines the date of restoration to the sixteenth century.[4]

Goodall is sceptical of the Lambeth reference, considering that it more probably referred to part incised part relief stone figures, which could equally have been described as "pictures", and would have afforded a physical obstruction to the laying of the pews. He has conclusively shown that monuments were moved at Minster following the sale of the Cheyne Chapel, for which a licence was issued in 1581/2,[5] and that the brasses of the Minster knight and lady were seen lying together as a pair at a Herald's Visitation in 1619. At that time there was an inscription with them attributing them to the founder of the church and his wife, and dating them "ante Conquestum". This inscription was also noted by Weever, who was rightly sceptical of its information.[6] There would accordingly be little reason to doubt that two independent brasses were brought together by the changes made in 1581/2, and that the opportunity was taken to present them as the benefactors, Sir Roger de Northwood d.1286 and his wife, at a time when great emphasis was placed on lineage and succession. The union of the figures required the removal of a strip to decrease the length of the man, and this was done at the only convenient point, though one effectively defacing the Northwood arms on the shield.

It might be concluded that the problem is resolved, and that the legs are an Elizabethan restoration, influenced by a model of c.1505. Objections can nevertheless be raised to this interpretation. First the workmanship of the legs appears to be inconsistent with that of most Elizabethan brasses. Secondly, had the legs gone by 1581, it is not clear why the further strip should have been cut from the centre of the figure. The design would have been renewed from the hips down. These points suggest the alternative of a restoration of the figure around 1505, unconnected with the later rearrangement. Yet there are three arguments against this second solution. Firstly there are no good precedents to suggest how late sixteenth century craftsmen would have handled such a situation, and stylistic impressions in such a case are unreliable. Secondly, the centre strip may have been removed for the very reason that the restoration prevented a matching of the pair, a factor not taken into account when the legs were engraved, presumably in London. Thirdly, the motivation for such an early Tudor restoration is very difficult to establish. In summary, the Minster restoration is an exceedingly interesting case, and certainly of the sixteenth century. The weight of probability is in favour of the early 1580's, but the author would not as yet dismiss the earlier alternative.

Whatever the facts of the Minster case, the stimulus for restoration came from the families whose ancestors were represented. The looting of the mid-sixteenth century has been described. Royal directions given in the third year of the reign of Queen Elizabeth I threatened fine and imprisonment for persons 'Breaking or defacing any parcel of any monument, or tomb, or grave, or other inscription and memory of any person deceased, being in any manner of place". The clergy were instructed to carry out a survey of despoiled monuments and to take action to secure their repair by the offenders. In the absence of any source of compensation the church authorities were authorised to use money which might be spared, 'upon the speedy repair or re-edification of any such monuments so defaced or spoiled, as agreeable to the original, as the same conveniently may be".[7] The royal order was not only prompted by respect for the church. The objection to the chaos was 'not only the churches remain at the present day spoiled, broken and ruinated, to the offence of all noble and gentle hearts, and the extinguishing of the honourable and good memory of sundry vertuous and noble families deceased, but also the true understanding of divers families in this Realme is thereby so darkened as the true course of their inheritance may be hereafter interrupted." The gentry recognised the danger, and some families took steps to remedy the matter. Others used the occasion to fabricate their pedigree. Furthermore, there was a genuine if limited revival of interest in antique works of art and memorials, stimulated by the current destruction.

A possible example of Elizabethan restoration, dated 1572, existed until the last century at Aldenham. Here a civilian of c.1530 had both head and inscription replaced, but only the earlier work still survives. A rubbing of the brass before its second mutilation is preserved by the Society of Antiquaries (Fig. 309). Unfortunately nearly all the inscription had gone, and the case may be one of appropriation.

Seventeenth-century restorations

Several brasses show obvious signs of seventeenth-century restoration. The large family series to the Bartelots at Stopham seem to have undergone a double restoration. The first was apparently carried out by a very competent London engraver about 1635, at the time when the brass of Richard Barttelot was laid. Groups of children in Carolean dress and shields of arms were added to the fifteenth-century brasses of the two John Bartelots and Richard Bertlot. A kneeling figure was added to the inscription of John Bartellot 1493, but he is also shown in seventeenth-century dress. A further but less happy restoration was carried out, probably at the same time but on the brasses in situ.[8*] The engraver employed was clearly the worst kind of amateur. New heads were added to the John Bartelots, and much of the existing engraving was apparently recut. The restoration of Anne, wife of William Bartelot, of 1601, is particularly poor. The Stopham brasses are now a complete but confusing collection.

Between the kneeling figures of Sir William Fitzwilliams and wife 1534, at Marholm, is the inscription stating, 'these monuments were repaired and beautified by ye Rt. Honble William, Lord Fitzwilliams Anno 1674'. The existing memorial is a perplexing jumble of work, though most is of 1534. A shield from another brass has been incorporated.[9*]

Among other seventeenth-century restorations may be noted the inscription and shield to King Ethelred at Wimborne Minster and the inscription to Peter Dormer d.1555, at Newbottle. The figures on the latter are evidently no later than c.1545, indicating a Tudor of later appropriation. The curious figure of Christopher Playters d.1547, at Sotterley is possibly an attempt to replace a lost figure or to complete a family series. The engraving is consistent with c.1630 and yet depicts the figure in armour with bascinet and aventail. An inscription to Matthew Parker, Archbishop of Canterbury 1559-75, was placed at the Chapel of Lambeth Palace, London, on a tomb erected by Archbishop Sancroft, to replace the original destroyed in 1648.

The most provocative restorations of this period were those carried out by Sir Edward Dering of Surrenden in Pluckley.[10*] The work might more appropriately be described as fabrication. Dering's chief interest was to justify a pedigree and arms which he adopted, and in his enthusiasm he resorted to all manner of forgery. In 1628 a vault was constructed beneath the chapel in Pluckley church where the Dering monuments lay. According to Dering's own record the monuments were rearranged at that time and the stones reduced in thickness to lessen the weight above the vault. They were clearly given additional attention. Dering was concerned that the brasses repeated his bogus pedigree in their arms, and that his adopted crest — a horse sable on a mount vert —should appear throughout the series. All the family brasses were refashioned; the brass of John Dering d.1425, showing him in bascinet and aventail, his feet resting on a horse, is completely bogus. An artificial indent, purporting to indicate a missing helmet with horse crest, was cut behind the head (Fig. 307). The brass of Nicholas Dering d.1517 has been drastically altered. The armed figure, resting his feet on a horse, is in marked contrast to the lady beside him which is original. The kneeling figure of John Dering d.1550, is an addition, though the inscription is genuine. The plate of Richard Dering and wife d.1610 was another set up in the general rearrangement. The figures of John Dering d.1517, Richard Dering d.1545, and the shield of Marie Dering 1607, are all interpolations. Other brasses treated in the same manner have been lost. Dering's meddling was not confined to Pluckley. It seems from his drawings that he altered brasses at Sevington and Dover Castle church. These are now all lost, except for the Dover inscription which survives as a palimpsest at Shepherdswell. The overall accuracy of the equipment of the military figures indicates research by the engraver, or the existence of the original figures at the time of the restoration.

The occasional repair of brasses in the seventeenth century was not confined to England. Three of the early Lubiaź brasses in Silesia bear signs of such alteration, especially in the canopy shafts. The most important replacement was the head of Duke Boleslaus, a curiosity described in Chapter One.

Eighteenth-century restorations

Eighteenth-century restorations are less significant. An inscription added to the brass of Nicholas Leveson 1539, at St Andrew Undershaft, London, states that the monument was repaired in 1764 at the expense of the parish. The inscription of Bishop Pursglove 1579, at Tideswell, was renewed in 1705, though part of an earlier attempted restoration seems to have been re-used for the inscription of Laurence Brierly, vicar in 1680. The head of Sir John Ratcliffe 1527, and four shields were restored at Crosthwaite. It is probable that the figure of Isabel, wife of John Barstaple, at the Trinity Almshouse Chapel, Bristol, was replaced at this period when the chapel was reconstructed. Thomas Lovett d.1491, Soulbury, is depicted on a thinly engraved eighteenth-century plate.

On the whole this century is remarkable for the great neglect and lack of interest in memorials, other than as curiosities for private collections. An extract from the Torrington diary, Vol. IV, concerned with a visit to Chicksands Priory in 1789, states, 'On the Cloister Walls are some Painted Glass, Monumental Stones, Brasses etc., to which Sir G(eorge Osborne) politely says I have been an ample contributor. One Brass I brought from Wrotham Church, and as I believe from a Grave Stone of The Byng Family; when in my possession They were call'd The 4 Brazen Byngs!!' Nevertheless, some collecting aided preservation. Private initiative saved the brass of Sir John Wyngefeld 1389, at Letheringham, from certain destruction.

The record of restoration is very slight in comparison to that of destruction, neglect and theft. Only in the latter part of the nineteenth century was serious interest taken in the subject. Certain families and institutions replaced lost brasses associated with them, and repaired those that were damaged. The Gothic Revival, and the widespread restoration of churches during the nineteenth century, reflected a renewed interest in mediaeval art and respect for the church fabric. Misguided enthusiasm and ignorance combined to cause much loss but this interest was more favourable in the long term to preservation than the apathy which preceded. Above all there were writers such as Haines and Boutell who effectively described the importance of brasses, and ruthlessly exposed the prevailing neglect. The founding of the Cambridge University Association of Brass Collectors and the Oxford University Brass-Rubbing Society were proof of real concern and appreciation.

Nineteenth- and twentieth-century restorations

The quite considerable amount of restoration begun in the nineteenth century and carried on to the present cannot fairly be judged as a whole. A different standard of criticism must be applied to restorations which are conjectural, those which are based on some record, and those which complete the missing portions of mutilated monuments. From the point of view of an antiquary or student conjectural restorations of lost brasses are comparatively unimportant. They have no historical value. On the other hand they may have considerable significance for the families concerned, add to the beauty of the church, and certainly offer a finer tribute to the dead than despoiled stones. The brasses at Ely cathedral to Prior Crauden d.1341, restored in 1871; Islip to John Nicoll and wife d.1467, restored in 1911; Maids' Moreton to the Peover sisters c.1450, restored 1886; St David's cathedral to Edmund Tudor, Earl of Richmond d.1456, restored c.1870; Tideswell to John Foljambe d.1358; restored in 1875; and at Worcester cathedral to Sir Griffith Ryce and wife d.1522, restored c.1860; are typical examples of their kind. Some of the detail on all is improbable. The Maids' Moreton and Worcester figures would hardly pass as originals, even to an inexperienced eye. On the other hand that at St David's is a clever adaptation of an 'F' pattern of c.1485, and makes with its heraldry a handsome memorial. In contrast, the figure of Bishop Mayo d.1516, kneeling before a Pieta, at Hereford cathedral, is a peculiar engraving done in 1857, depending overmuch on Dingley's sketch of the original.

Stricter criticism must be applied to restorations carried out, when the original design is known from drawings and other records. Among lost brasses completely replaced are the following:

Beddington, Sir Richard Carew and wife, d.1520, restored late 19th century
Chesterfield, Henry Foljambe and wife, d.1519, restored 1879.
St Patrick's cathedral, Dublin; Archbishop Talbot (d.1449), restored 1919
Durham cathedral, figure of Bishop Lewis de Beaumont, d.1333, restored 1951
St Albans cathedral, Robert Fairfax and wife, d.1521, restored 1921
Skipton-in-Craven, Sir Henry Clifford, K.G. and wife, d.1542, restored 1867; also
Sir Henry Clifford and family, d.1570, restored 1867
Winchester College, nine brasses mostly to ecclesiastics in the chapel, restored 1882.

Most of these restorations are satisfactory, in particular those at Winchester College, which are based on actual rubbings of the originals. The Beddington and St Albans brasses err on the side of 'prettiness'. The Durham restoration is based only on a sixteenth-century description in *The Rites of Durham*.

By far the most important restorations are those involving the integration of new with original work. The standard of accuracy must be exceptionally high if the repair is to serve any good purpose. W.E. Gawthorp and the Waller brothers were responsible for much careful reconstruction. The detailed research behind the restoration of the legs and inscription of John Touchet, Lord Audley at Shere is described in some detail by J. S. M. Ward[12] and is typical of Gawthorp's care. Nevertheless, many replacements have been most unsatisfactory, often without any reasonable excuse.

It is seldom appreciated that the brasses at Cobham are among the most heavily restored brasses in England. Two restorations were carried out, the first in 1839 and the second in 1865-6. Although the latter was well done under the direction of J. G. Waller, several inaccuracies were allowed. The head of Sir John de Cobham 1354, is inaccurate in detail and quite unnecessarily so as similar brasses exist in the same church.[13*] More seriously some of the restored heraldry is misleading, notably on the brass of Dame Maude de Cobeham.[14] Nevertheless, the splendid array now presented is preferable to the broken collection noted by Gough. Many of the canopies have been partly or completely restored. Nearly a third of the figure of Sir Reginald Braybrok has been replaced.

Further extensive restorations to brasses of the Cobham family were made by J. G. Waller in 1865-6 at Lingfield. These appear to be superior to those at Cobham. The heads of Lady Elizabeth Cobham 1375, and of Dame Eleanor Cobham 1420, are especially appropriate; the second of these brasses was a complete wreck before repair. Elsewhere several heads have been restored to very good effect through careful study of originals. Noteworthy examples are at Albury 1440; Audley 1385; Ightfield d.1497; St Giles-in-the-Wood, upper half of figure restored, and Trinity Hall, Cambridge c.1510. The figure of Peter Best at Merstham was accurately restored in 1911 from a rubbing. Many canopies and border inscriptions have been discretely repaired and the brasses of Sir Giles Daubeney and wife 1430, at South Petherton; Bishop John Trilleck 1360, at Hereford cathedral; and William Chichele and wife 1425, at Higham Ferrers, are examples. In Denmark the superb brass to King Eric Menved and his queen at Ringsted was carefully restored in 1883. The brass fragments replaced were accurately engraved, though the king's face in white marble is not quite consistent with the stylised Flemish tradition.

In comparison to the work just described much repair undertaken less skilfully is of a low and even lamentable quality. The figures of John Bennett c.1470 and wife at Norton Bavant have been restored in a manner far too free to replace satisfactorily the lost originals. Yet certain genuine portions have been integrated with the new, such as the daughters, part of the inscription, the merchant's mark, and a shield with shears, so as to obscure their antiquity.[15] The canopies of John Huntingdon 1458, Manchester cathedral, and John Barstaple 1411, at the Trinity Almshouse Chapel, Bristol, are in several respects inappropriate. The recutting and engraving of a civilian and wife c.1420, at Dunton is crude. The restoration and recutting of the large brass to Henry Bost at Eton College has confused the original. The figures of Sir Thomas Brooke and wife 1437, at Thorncombe were perniciously decorated with shade lines and additional folds at the time the brasses were relaid. A curious face has been added to the worn figure of St Michael on the Trevnwyth brass 1462, at St Ives. The original head of the figure was shown in profile with a large halo, but the restorer has engraved both face and halo with a gross caricature. Strange little figures on a rectangular plate have been set to replace those of Robert Harding 1503, and wife at Cranley. At Upper Shuckburgh portions of lost brasses have been cut into slate. This engraving has been well executed, but the designs are copied from other brasses in the church, different in style, date and pose. At Cirencester a head has been set on the waist of a woman of c.1490 (Fig. 308). Most wretched of all are the efforts at Fowey. Dunkin illustrates two brasses of civilians, probably of the Treffry family, dating from c.1450 and c.1465 respectively.[16] The earlier is shown full face with his wife, but the head of the man is lost. The later figure is represented in semi profile, and the wife facing him is completely missing. The indent indicated she was wearing a butterfly headdress. Since Dunkin's time these brasses have been moved to the wall and 'repaired'. The figure of the earlier wife has been duplicated to accompany the later man. The head of the later man has been copied and placed on the neck of the other who now looks curiously sideways. Not satisfied with this, the engraver has decorated the new work with all manner of inappropriate shading, which has also been applied to the original brasses!

It is a sad truth of restoration that good intentions have not been matched with equal care, research and skill. As a result the merit of the whole operation has been brought into question if not disrepute. Yet the achievement at Lingfield and

Winchester College, for example, gives ample grounds for perseverance. A shattered monument is not a pleasing spectacle. It is hardly complimentary to the persons commemorated. There would seem to be a very good case for restoration in circumstances where the original design is exactly known, and where replacement would add greatly to the beauty of the church. The fine but despoiled church of Ingham, is a striking example. The chancel floor is inlaid with great indents still containing large portions of brass canopies. Rubbings of the brasses when almost complete are preserved in the Society of Antiquaries. A replacement would have both historical and aesthetic value. Past success has demonstrated the beauty of such work; failures are a guide to the mistakes. The need for accuracy is important. Above all the employment of skilled craftsmen is absolutely essential if the work is to be truly satisfactory.

23. Epilogue

This survey of European brasses has been presented as a vantage point from which those interested may appraise, criticise and further advance our knowledge. It is accordingly right in conclusion to consider further research, indicating those areas in which present understanding could be greatly extended.

In the past brasses have especially attracted the antiquary and the enthusiastic 'brass rubber', both on account of the intrinsic interest and beauty of these memorials and the sheer pleasure of seeking and recording them. Far from being an exhausted subject the scope for the investigator is still exceedingly wide, and there remains a valuable role for the devoted student. In spite of a century of study, many brasses of great merit have not yet been illustrated, even more have not been properly described, and whole county series have received very limited attention. Of the richest English counties Kent alone has been reasonably well covered. Norfolk, Suffolk and Essex have by no means been given comprehensive or adequate treatment, though the first is now receiving appropriate analysis. Oxfordshire, Hertfordshire and Buckinghamshire have secured inadequate study, the last named being conspicuously neglected. There has until very recently been little systematic listing and examination of indents. The full record of these remains, now undertaken by the Monumental Brass Society, should undoubtedly add a major dimension to present knowledge, possibly leading to the modification of some well established views and interpretations. Indents, moreover, are frequently destroyed, or deteriorate in condition to become valueless, and their record is not advisedly delayed. There are many brasses on the Continent of Europe which have not been illustrated, and probably many that remain without serious notice. Indents on the Continent have hardly been touched upon.

Passing from basic recording, much work has yet to be done in the correlation and analysis of pattern series and provincial types, both in the examination of the brasses themselves and relating these to indent evidence. Well illustrated studies of such groups would add greatly to knowledge, especially of the sixteenth, seventeenth and eighteenth centuries, in addition to bringing to notice many little known memorials. The work of Dr Kent, which has greatly influenced the author, needs extending and consolidating, with a greater emphasis on adequate illustration, without which much of the impact of such analysis is lost. In this range of work the thorough and accurate student or collector is sufficiently equipped to make a valuable contribution.

It is nevertheless true that there is a great need for an increased interest in this subject on the part of historians, archivists and other professionals. The study of brasses has too long been the preserve of a few specialist scholars, and the great majority of students have been persons with only a very general historical interest, who have neither the wide knowledge nor the opportunity to acquire the skills for the deep analysis that is now required. While there is a great scope for general record and correlation of examples, there is an equal necessity for investigation in depth. Research into particular memorials or groups of memorials through the medium of wills, documents related to the lives of the commemorated and other original sources, is of the greatest importance. The studies, for example, by A. Colin Cole, now Windsor Herald, into the heraldy of the brass at Wytham, Berks. (*MBST*, 9 (1952-62), 172-83), and by Dr Ward into the life of Sir Robert de Bures depicted at Acton (*MBST*, 10 (1963-8), 144-50), have created a new and fuller understanding of these monuments, unobtainable from their surface evidence. Similarly records such as the Halyburton Ledger, analysed in this connection by Greenhill, have provided facts in subjects hitherto interpreted by speculation. Examination of the choice and significance of patterns has yet to be systematically undertaken, and the comparison of brasses to other art forms requires expert attention. Major advances in our knowledge will most probably be achieved by skilled investigation of the particular, as much as by consolidation at a more superficial level.

The value of scientific research would be substantial in the consistency of metal used, the nature of colour inlays and above all in the field of petrology, which may confirm or challenge views based on the evidence of the brasses alone. In this context also the author is concerned for the greater use of direct photography in reproduction. There is a considerable amount of controversy about the merits of positive as against negative rubbings, but neither of these processes gives a full or exact record of the memorial, either with regard to the engraved plate or its setting. It is hoped that some of the illustrations included here have proved the value of photographic presentation.

Mention of brass rubbing raises a topic of importance. Brass rubbers are now very numerous. The interest of the majority is only moderately concerned with historical matters, and many are solely involved in securing an article for personal pleasure. It is not unusual to meet people rubbing in a variety of bright colours. Some scholars are offended, and more serious some clergy, in the face of frivolous interest, carelessness or irreverent behaviour, have withdrawn their customary co-operation. Notwithstanding it is the author's conviction that the present level of interest in these memorials, albeit at times and in places eccentric or too intense, is in general an asset both for their future study and preservation. The market for good publications is substantial, many old books are being reprinted in the absence of more modern descriptions, and there is a stimulating challenge to meet the demand for information. Furthermore, in spite of exceptional cases of damage, the prevailing attention is more conducive to positive care than the widespread lack of interest of the past, which permitted massive losses through neglect and heedlessness. It is essential that brass rubbing should be controlled, but this may be done with discrimination. It would for example be wise to prohibit the rubbing of several of the earliest English brasses, which are being rubbed to excess, and to provide exact casts as a substitute. A casual interest may not be a far step from a real and lasting appreciation and respect for these treasures and the history they record.

The preservation of brasses must remain a supreme interest and responsibility for those who admire them. The Monumental Brass Society, as well as being a centre of knowledge, provides resources in technical skill for the repair, cleaning and refixing of brasses in need. But in many cases the necessity is prompt action, and a readiness to meet modest expense. Far too often custodians are given advice, when an appropriate donation would resolve the problem. If a fraction of the money spent and received for brass rubbing was used for preservation the state of these monuments would be incomparably better.

Finally interest in brasses must in future gain from a greater understanding of monumental art, in particular the workshops responsible for incised slabs, sculptured effigies and memorial stained glass. The regrettable ignorance of incised slabs in England and on the Continent will be greatly reduced, now that the research of Greenhill and Beetlestone is published. Yet a great deal of basic listing and recording remains to be done in England, and the work to be undertaken in Europe is immeasurable.

It is very positive progress that the Monumental Brass Society now includes the subject of incised slabs within its direct terms of reference. If the study of monumental brasses is to remain valuable, it should take a proper place in the study of antiquities as a whole, increasing its richness from other fields of research, and thereby increasing its own value to scholars in related matter. Brasses have tended to become a great but self-contained interest, ultimately in danger of becoming an antiquarian cul-de-sac.

The author has accordingly attempted to bring the craft and its masters into a wider focus, and to move towards a European perspective. The study of brasses is but a part of the study of memorials, and memorials of the art and history of their age.